ISBN 978-0-428-93522-1
PIBN 10804061

FB &c Ltd, Dalton House, 60 Windsor Avenue, London, SW19 2RR.
Company number 08720141. Registered in England and Wales.

For support please visit www.forgottenbooks.com

THE BOOKMAN

AN ILLUSTRATED LITERARY JOURNAL

VOLUME VI.

SEPTEMBER, 1897—FEBRUARY, 1898

"*I am a Bookman.*"—JAMES RUSSELL LOWELL

NEW YORK

DODD, MEAD AND COMPANY

FIFTH AVENUE AND 21ST STREET

INDEX TO VOLUME VI.

SEPTEMBER, '97–FEBRUARY, '98.

REVIEWS OF NEW BOOKS.

THE BOOKMAN

A LITERARY JOURNAL.

VOL. VI. SEPTEMBER, 1897. No. 1.

CHRONICLE AND COMMENT.

The Editors of THE BOOKMAN *cannot undertake to return rejected manuscripts, whether stamps are enclosed or not; and to this rule no exception will be made.*

George Meredith has written a long poem on the French Revolution, which will probably be published very soon in a volume by itself.

Mr. Le Gallienne's rendering of the *Rubáiyát*, some stanzas of which appeared in the July *Cosmopolitan*, will be published by Mr. John Lane in October. The edition will be handsomely printed on hand-made, deckel-edged paper, and only 1250 copies will be issued. The price is $2.50, and each copy will be signed by Mr. Le Gallienne.

Mr. Lane has just published a *Jubilee Greeting at Spithead to the Men of Greater Britain*, by Theodore Watts-Dunton, with a dedication "to our great contemporary writer of patriotic poetry, Algernon Charles Swinburne."

Mr. Lane has issued three extra numbers of the *International Studio*, containing full-page reproductions, without letterpress, of the pictures in the 1897 exhibitions at the New Gallery, the Royal Academy, and the Paris salons. In *The New Gallery* number there is a reproduction of "The Vampire," by Philip Burne-Jones, which provoked Rudyard Kipling's recent poem with the same title. These extra numbers can be had at thirty-five cents each for the English numbers, and fifty cents for *The Paris Salons*.

Messrs. Houghton, Mifflin and Company have in press a new volume of poems by Mr. Edmund Clarence Stedman. As a long interval has elapsed since Mr. Stedman's last volume of verse was published, this event will be looked for with special interest, and a warm welcome is sure to await the "late lark singing in the Western sky."

On another page will be found a criticism of Mr. W. E. Henley's treatment of Burns in the Centenary edition, the third volume of which has just been issued in this country by Messrs. Houghton, Mifflin and Company. Mr. William Wallace, the writer of the review, ranks among the foremost Burns specialists, and whatever he has to say on the subject commands respect. Recently we called attention to the masterly edition of the works and biography of Burns, edited by Dr. Robert Chambers, and revised and practically rewritten by Mr. Wallace, and published by Messrs. Longmans, Green and Company. We learn from Messrs. Houghton, Mifflin and Company that the next volume in the Cambridge edition of the poets is to comprise Burns, and will contain Mr. Henley's essay and nearly all the notes of the Centenary edition. So that the lover of Burns who may not care to avail himself of the more expensive work will welcome this one-volume edition, which will practically include all that is valuable in the edition edited and annotated by Messrs. Henley and Henderson. The volume is expected to be ready about the end of October.

We notice that Mr. Thomas Whittaker has just added *The Poetical Works of*

Robert Burns to the Apollo Poets Series. This contains a chronology of Burns's life and works, which is admirable in its brevity and completeness for reference, and is supplemented by an appendix containing memoranda, an index, and, of course, a glossary. The same firm publishes a cheap popular edition of Shakespeare, unburdened with notes or memoranda of any kind.

❀

Mr. Whittaker will issue early in September a popular edition of Boswell's *Life of Johnson*, edited by Mr. Percy Fitzgerald. It will be published complete in one volume, and will also include the *Tour to the Hebrides*. A unique feature in the editing will be a biographical dictionary of every person mentioned in the book. It will be seen at a glance that this will commend the new edition even to those lovers of Johnson who have already other editions of the incomparable *Life* on their shelves.

❀

Early in the year 1891 Messrs. Roberts Brothers had written to Philip Gilbert Hamerton inquiring whether he had decided to write a new book, and upon receiving an answer in the affirmative they wrote to him :

"Yes, we think *The Quest of Happiness* an admirable title for a book destined for the popular heart—so happy that it will of itself sell it. Don't meditate about doing it too long."

We gather from the lately published *Memoir* that the book was expected to be ready for publication in the autumn of 1893, but that it had to be laid aside for more pressing work, and was not resumed until the beginning of the year following. Two hours before his death, on November 4th, 1894, Mr. Hamerton had written these words for *The Quest of Happiness :*

"If I indulge my imagination in dreaming about a country where justice and right would always surely prevail, where the weak would never be oppressed, nor an honest man incur any penalty for his honesty—a country where no animal would ever be ill treated or killed, otherwise than in mercy—that is truly ideal dreaming, because, however far I travel, I shall not find such a country in the world, and there is not any record of such a country in the authentic history of mankind."

Messrs. Roberts Brothers now announce that this work is in press and will be ready in October. *The Quest of Happiness* will make its appeal to the class of readers with whom *The Intellectual Life* has gained so large and permanent a popularity, and a well-known critic who has read the manuscript pronounces it to be the best work Mr. Hamerton ever wrote. Its appearance will in consequence be awaited with keen interest and eagerness.

❀

Professor Edwin A. Grosvenor, the author of *Constantinople*, has just finished the translation of a Greek historical romance entitled *Andronike, the Heroine of the Greek Revolution*, by Stephanos Theodore Xenos. "Modern Greece," says Professor Grosvenor, "may be proud of having given the world a historical romance like this. Viewed merely as a story, it is a work of absorbing interest in its plot and execution. At the same time, no other book, whether of description, travel or pure romance, offers so faithful and complete a picture of Greek life to-day." Markos Botsaris, Byron, the native and foreign leaders and the common people of resurrected Greece live again in its pages. It will be published shortly by Messrs. Roberts Brothers.

❀

Jean Ingelow, who died a few weeks ago in London, became famous with her first book of verses almost at a bound. In 1863 Messrs. Roberts Brothers issued a first edition of 25,000 copies, and altogether they have sold since then upward of 150,000 copies of her books in this country. This does not include the numerous editions published at various times by other American firms. Her songs became familiar in every household ; lyrical and dramatic, graceful and fluent, she possessed that happy combination of the domestic and religious qualities which carried her popularity beyond the critics' ban into the heart of that enigmatical person, the general reader. Her high-water mark was reached in "High Tide on the Coast of Lincolnshire," which of all her poems will perhaps be longest remembered. Born in the Boston of old England, she lived all her days in quietness and seclusion, welcoming a few literary friends during her recent years at her little house and garden in Kensington. She was old-fashioned and prim in her ways, as in her dress, and although the singer of "Wedlock," she died in her seventy-seventh year, unmarried. She always wrote with a high purpose, and never had any care or thought for fame.

❀

The redoubtable Major Pond has just returned from a visit to England after "seeing everybody worth seeing"—he was even within a few feet of the Queen at the Jubilee celebration in St. Paul's Cathedral. Mr. Anthony Hope will be here to give fifty readings from his own writings in the autumn. Mr. F. Marion Crawford is to deliver a series of lectures upon Italian Art, as well as to read from his novels. The major paid a flying visit to the Isle of Man on his way home, and made a vain attempt to induce Hall Caine to deliver a series of one hundred lectures in America this autumn. Mr. Caine fears the physical fatigue of the undertaking; but Major Pond assured him that "it would make a new man of him," and pointed triumphantly to Ian Maclaren. It is possible that, under certain conditions, Mr. Hall Caine may be prevailed upon to assent to the proposition. Major Pond is naturally flushed with the success he attained with Dr. Watson, whose tour, next to Stanley's, is the most successful he has ever engineered. The clear profits, after defraying all expenses, amounted to $40,000 less fifty cents. There is a strong probability, by the way, of Mrs. Amelia E. Barr becoming Major Pond's latest candidate for platform honours. We should be inclined to think that Mrs. Barr would prove successful as a reader, for her great popularity with the people continues undiminished, and her life is rich in stores of reminiscence and literary associations.

❀

As we announced two months ago, the forthcoming biography of the late Poet Laureate will be published by the Macmillan Company, and not by the Messrs. Harper, as generally stated in the press. It is entitled *Alfred, Lord Tennyson: a Memoir*, "by his son," and will appear in October. The work will be in two volumes, and will contain numerous illustrations, portraits, and fac-similes of the poet's manuscript. It will doubtless be the biography of the year.

Tennyson, in a conversation with Professor William Knight in 1890 (*vide Blackwood's* for August), characterised Sir Walter Scott as the greatest novelist of all time. He said, "What a gift it was that Scotland gave to the world in him. And your Burns! he is supreme among your poets." He praised Lockhart's *Life of Scott* as one of the finest of biographies; and Professor Knight's quoting an anecdote of Scott from that book led to Tennyson's telling with arch humour and simplicity some anecdotes of a visit to Scotland. After he had left an inn in the island of Skye, the landlord was asked, "Did he know who had been staying in his house? It was the poet Tennyson." He replied, "Lor'—to think o' that! and sure I thoucht he was a shentleman!" Near Stirling the same remark was made to the keeper of the hotel where he had stayed. "Do you ken who you had wi' you t'other night?" "Na; but he was a pleesant shentleman." "It was Tennyson, the poet." "An' wha' may *he* be?" "Oh, he is a writer o' verses, sich as ye see i' the papers." "Noo, to think o' that! jeest a pooblic writer, an' I gied him ma best bedroom!" Of Mrs. Tennyson, however, the landlord remarked, "Oh, but *she* was an angel!"

❀

A tale of life in old New York in the first decade of the eighteenth century, by Miss E. Rayner, entitled *Free to Serve*, will be published in a few weeks by Messrs. Copeland and Day. The story starts out from England, whence the heroine is brought to America, where she plays an important part under circumstances which bring life in Puritan New England into contrast with that of Dutch New York. The life, manners and customs of the period have been elaborated with a careful and vivid pen, and the story itself is said to be one of exciting interest.

❀

Despite the keen competition—becoming keener every year—in the publishing business, another band of young men have combined to form a new publishing house in Boston, whose imprint will appear as Messrs. Small, Maynard and Company. The members composing this firm are Mr. Herbert Small, Mr. Laurens Maynard, and Mr. Bliss Carman. Mr. Carman's new volume of poetry, *Ballads of a Lost Haven*, has just been published by Messrs. Lamson, Wolffe and Company, but we presume he will be his own publisher in future. In view of the interest aroused by the discussion of Whitman in several quarters lately, it is interesting to learn that the first work to bear the imprint of this firm will be a new edition of the works of Walt Whitman, of which they have acquired the full rights from the poet's literary executors. The publication of Whitman's writings was so irregular and eccentric that the bibliographical account, given on another page, gains a certain value and importance from this fact.

❀

A correspondent calls attention to an omission in Dr. Nicoll's account of Mrs. Oliphant's work in our last number—namely, *The Wizard's Son.* She says that as a psychological study (we have not read it) it is equal if not superior to *Dr. Jekyll and Mr. Hyde.* It did not make the same sensation when published because the element of heredity, the force of inherited traditions and predispositions, do not impress the general public as that dualism of which we are always conscious, and which forms the *motif* of Stevenson's masterpiece.

❀

Nothing could show more clearly the low estate of criticism at the present day than some of the comments which have appeared on Mrs. Oliphant. The *Athenæum*, for example, which professes to be the leading critical journal in England, actually says that *Mrs. Margaret Maitland* is much superior to any production of the newer Scottish novelists, Mr. Barrie included. It may be safe for the moment to make such assertions, because a great many literary people are bitterly jealous of the success of the Scottish school, and because no human being, except a few old fogeys like ourselves, has ever read *Mrs. Margaret Maitland.* But a comparison between that dead book and *A Window in Thrums*, for instance, cannot decently be made. Mrs. Oliphant herself was far too wise not to know this. Her story, *The Marriage of Elinor*, and Mr. Barrie's story, *The Little Minister*, appeared in *Good Words* at the same time. Mrs. Oliphant's, of course, was a bit of decent craftsmanship, and in respect of plot and arrangement it might have excelled Mr. Barrie's, just as he might be excelled in that matter by some contributors to the *New York Ledger.* The difference, however, between the two was that one was a work of genius, and the other a good decent pot-boiler. Who buys *The Marriage of Ellinor* now? Who will ever buy it or read it again? Mrs. Oliphant was a supremely able woman, and she knew more than the writer in the *Athenæum* gives her credit for, but she was not a genius, and therefore all her books were mortal. Most of them are dead, and the rest are dying. We wish we had the right to quote Mrs. Oliphant's own expressions on this subject. It is not necessary, however; "the great soul of the world is just," after all.

❀

We give verbatim the contents of a postal card which hails from Messina, and which affords us a novel view of English as she is misunderstood by an Italian professor:

> Messina, (Dated as the post-timbre)
>
> After the death of Mr. Filippo Serafini, I have undertaken the Direction of the "Archivio giuridico", the most ancient italian Review, which I have intitulated by the name of its illustrious Founder.
>
> The scientific way shall remain unalterated; I only will task to give a larger developpment to the bibliographic party.
>
> I therefore address myself to Mrs. the authors and editors, who may send to me their works and inform me of the lately published.
>
> Each work diretly sent to the Direction shall be mentionnèd in the party of the Review to which it is due (*Bibliographic Bulletin*, *Annonces of latest publications*, *Notices*, *Varietes*). In proportion to the price of several works, a particular *annonce-reclame* shall be made of it.
>
> Works edited by delivery shall be mentionned on the coverture, with indication of the last numero and of relative price.
>
> ENRICO SERAFINI
> Prof. ord. di diritto nella R. Università

❀

We learn from a correspondent in London that two Chicagoan writers, Mr. Opie Read and Mr. Stanley Waterloo, are very much liked in London, and that the former's *Bolanyo* which has just been published in this country by Messrs. Way and Williams, is selling very well there. Mr. Waterloo has written an interesting introduction to a new English edition of his first novel, *A Man and a Woman*, in which he has something to say about the "'school of traced. Altogether the quest seems hopeless, although the greatest of living poets has expressed his keen desire to see what Emily Brontë was really like; and that wish finds response in the heart of every one who has come under the magic sway of her brave soul.

And so perhaps we shall never know more concerning this weird, eccentric girl, who has enchained the hearts of so many of the best men and women who have followed her. We see her arm-in-arm with her slighter, smaller sister in the garden of the Pensionnat Heger. She was thin, pale-looking, but happy. She wore old-fashioned clothes, while Charlotte tried her utmost to keep modern and trim. That is the description of a fellow-pupil. Mr. Nicholls again can add but little more. He frequently took tea at the Haworth parsonage. Tea was served in Mr. Brontë's study, a little room on the right-hand side of the entrance-hall. Charlotte and Anne were always present, Emily but rarely. She preferred to have her tea alone in the dining-room, or parlour, as it was called. She avoided strangers rigorously, as we have said.

This, in brief, is all we know and shall probably ever know of one of the greatest women in our literature. It is because she was so great that I need scarcely apologise for threading together these scanty memorials of her strange, uneventful life.

AN INTERESTING FIND; OR, THACKERAY AND CHARLOTTE BRONTË.

"There is a man in our own days whose words are not framed to tickle delicate ears; who, to my thinking, comes before the great ones of society much as the son of Imlah came before the throned kings of Judah and Israel, and who speaks truth as deep, with a power as prophet-like and as vital—a mien as dauntless and as daring. Is the satirist of *Vanity Fair* admired in high places? I cannot tell; but I think if some of those among whom he flashes the levin-brand of his denunciation were to take his warnings in time, they or their seed might yet escape a fatal Ramoth-Gilead.

"Why have I alluded to this man? I have alluded to him, reader, because I think I see in him an intellect profounder and more unique than his contemporaries have yet recognised; because I regard him as the first social regenerator of the day—as the very master of that working corps who would restore to rectitude the warped system of things; because I think no commentator on his writings has yet found the comparison that suits him, the terms which rightly characterise his talent. They say he is like Fielding; they talk of his wit, humour, comic powers. He resembles Fielding as an eagle does a vulture. Fielding could stoop on carrion, but Thackeray never does. His wit is bright, his humour attractive; but both bear the same relation to his serious genius that the mere lambent sheet-lightning playing under the edge of the summer cloud does to the electric death-spark hid in its womb. Finally, I have alluded to Mr. Thackeray because to him, if he will accept the tribute of a total stranger, I have dedicated this second edition of *Jane Eyre*.

"CURRER BELL.

"December 21, 1847."

In these burning words Charlotte Brontë dedicated the second edition of *Jane Eyre*. From that day until now much interest has been manifested in the relations between these two giants of literature and their opinions of each other. Thanks to Mr. Shorter, to whom we are indebted for some new letters, we have fresh evidence of what Charlotte Brontë thought of Thackeray. To Mr. W. S. Williams (of Messrs. Smith, Elder and Company) she writes in March, 1848:

"You mention Thackeray and the last number of *Vanity Fair*. The more I read Thackeray's works the more certain I am that he stands alone—alone in sagacity, alone in his truth, alone in his feelings (his feeling, though he makes no noise about it, is about the most genuine that ever lived on a printed page), alone in his power, alone in his simplicity, alone in his self-control. Thackeray is a Titan, so strong that he can afford to perform with calm the most herculean feats; there is the charm and majesty of repose in his greatest efforts; *he* borrows nothing from fever; his is never the energy of delirium; his energy is sane energy, deliberate energy, thoughtful energy. The last number of *Vanity Fair* proves this peculiarly. Forcible, exciting in its force, still more impressive than exciting, carrying on the interest of the narrative in a flow, deep, full, resistless, it is still quiet—as quiet as reflection, as quiet as memory; and to me there are parts of it that sound as solemn as an oracle. Thackeray is never borne away by his own ardour; he has it under control. His genius obeys him—it is his servant; it works no fantastic changes at its own wild will; it must still achieve the task which reason and sense assign it, and none

THE

POLICY

OF THE

CLERGY of *FRANCE*,

TO

Deſtroy the Proteſtants

OF THAT

KINGDOM.

Wherein is ſet down the Ways and Means that have been made uſe of for theſe twenty Years laſt paſt, to root out the Proteſtant Religion.

In a Dialogue between two Papiſts.

Humbly offered to the Conſideration of all ſincere Proteſtants; but principally of his Moſt Sacred Majeſty and the Parliament at *Oxford*.

London, Printed for *R. Bentley*, and *M. Magnes*, in *Ruſſel*-ſtreet *Covent-Garden*, near the *Piazza*. MDCLXXXI.

c

FAC-SIMILE OF TITLE-PAGE OF A BOOK IN WHICH CHARLOTTE BRONTË INSCRIBED A LETTER TO THACKERAY.

other. Thackeray is unique. I *can* say no more, I *will* say no less.

"B."

In view of these letters and the unusual intellectual sympathy between Thackeray and Charlotte Brontë, the story of the following "find" seems to me of more than usual interest and importance.

I believe it was Balzac who said the successful book-hunter should have "the patience of a Jew, the legs of a deer, and the purse of a Rothschild;" but, like many another smart saying, it is not so true as it sounds—particularly the last clause—for since the days of Richard de Bury there have been successful book-hunters as well as book-lovers who have had neither the purse of a Rothschild nor the legs of a deer. If I were to choose the most important of these three qualities mentioned by M. Balzac, I should choose the first, for patience is essential to the successful book-hunter; but I should add to the three one more—namely, instinct. Many a choice volume has been overlooked by the careless book-hunter, to be secured by the born one. A Chicago gentleman of my acquaintance bought in a New York bookshop within the year *Poems, 1830*, by Alfred Tennyson, for fifty cents which is surely worth as many dollars. It is told of the late George Brinley that he used to travel through various sections of the South in a buggy, stopping at farmhouses and out-of-the-way places, and, asking for a drink of water or milk, would say incidentally to his temporary host, "Have you any old books?" The usual answer would be, "No, no!—none of any value." Mr. Brinley would then quietly ask to look over them, and many a treasure he thus picked up. Perhaps next to instinct one might add knowledge, for without the latter little of importance can be secured. Of what avail is it to find a nugget of gold if one is colour-blind, or an autograph copy of some precious volume if one cannot tell an original from a facsimile?

The incident which I am about to relate occurred to a friend of mine who had had little experience in book-hunting, but who had an instinct strongly developed, and a knowledge ripened by years of study and interest in books and men.

One bright day last August she was in London, and espied a little book and print shop in one of the less frequented streets. Entering the shop, she asked the owner if she might look around. The request was reluctantly granted, as in London the general attitude of the old bookseller is that all people who enter their shops are thieves until they prove themselves not to be.

Rummaging among the shelves, her eyes lighted upon a duodecimo volume in brown calf with no title on the back. Now, it is one of the unwritten laws of the successful book-hunter always to examine a volume which has no title, or which is marked "Pamphlets," "Tracts," or "Miscellanies."

The first thing that attracted her eyes was the stamped coat-of-arms on the side. My friend immediately wondered whose it was. Upon opening the volume, she saw it was a book on the *Policy of the Clergy of France to Destroy the Protestants of that Kingdom*, London, 1681 (see fac-simile).

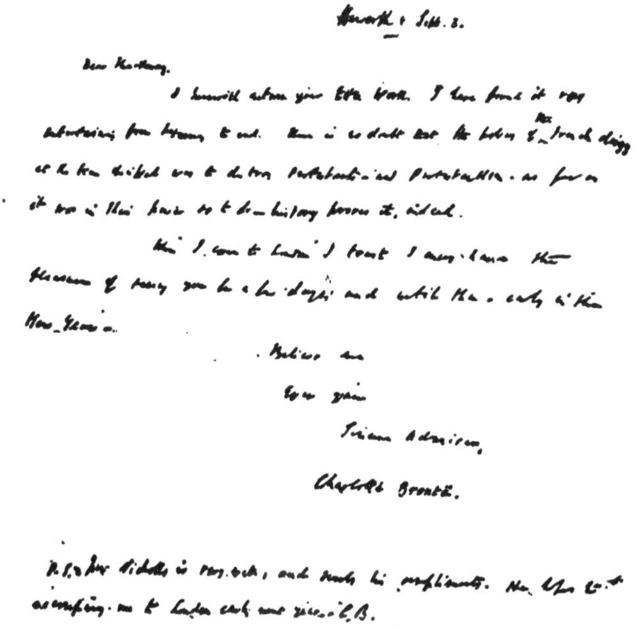

FAC-SIMILE OF LETTER INSCRIBED BY CHARLOTTE BRONTË TO THACKERAY IN A BOOK LOANED BY HIM TO HER, AND NOW PUBLISHED FOR THE FIRST TIME.

Noticing that there was a fine handwriting inside the front cover, what was my friend's delight to find that it was a letter from Charlotte Brontë to Thackeray, and was as follows (see fac-simile):

HAWORTH, September 3.

DEAR THACKERAY: I herewith return your little work. I have found it very entertaining from beginning to end. There is no doubt that the policy of the French clergy at the time specified was to destroy Protestants and Protestantism as far as it was in their power so to do—history proves it indeed.

When I come to London I trust I may have the pleasure of seeing you for a few days, and until then, early in the new year,

Believe me
Ever your
Sincere Admirer,
CHARLOTTE BRONTË.

P.S.—Mr. Nicholls is very well, and sends his compliments. He hopes to accompany me to London early next year.

C. B.

This note was written in Miss Brontë's well-known fine hand. My friend's first thought was, "Oh, this is some fabulous price! A book loaned by Thackeray to Charlotte Brontë and returned to him enriched with her own comment—surely this is beyond the means of an idler?" Walking with some excitement up to the bookseller, she said, in rather a hoarse whisper, "What is the price of this?" The bookseller, looking at the mark, answered, "Oh, three shillings, mum." "But," said my conscientious friend, "did you know it contained Charlotte Brontë's handwriting in it?" "It's only a facsimile," said the bookseller. "At any rate, it's three shillings." Imagine the joy with which the three shillings were produced and the prize secured and carried away in triumph.

The book is a dialogue between two Papists, a Parisian, and a provincial. The latter, visiting Paris, as he says, "with the design of diverting myself, of seeing my friends, of learning what passes in the world, and of losing some of the rest of the province." It was written by Pierre Jurieu, a well-known French Protestant writer, and this is a translation of the first edition. Who made the translation I do not know; but the book is well known in France, as the author wrote several others, notably *Les Derniers Efforts de l'Innocence Affigee* and also *La Politique de France*.

Where did Thackeray find the quaint little volume, and why did he lend it to Charlotte Brontë?

Thackeray first met her in London, at the house of Mr. Smith, of the well-known firm of Smith, Elder and Company. This was on December 7th, 1849. *Pendennis* was still unfinished. We have just shown what she expected to find in Thackeray. *Vanity Fair* was issued in numbers during 1847–48.

A writer of the time suggested that Charlotte had been governess to Thackeray's children, and that she was Becky Sharp of *Vanity Fair* and he Rochester of *Jane Eyre*. We all know this was not so; but it seems strange that it should have been suggested by a critic of the time; and who can say there were not suggestions in both novels to lead to such a supposition?

It had, moreover, been rumoured that Miss Brontë was so sensitive about the charge of her having satirised Thackeray and obtruded on the sorrows of his private life that she came up to London on purpose to reveal her real name to her publisher and deny the charge. Was this the time of her first meeting with Thackeray?

Miss Brontë was married June 29th, 1853, so that some time between December, 1849, and June, 1853, this volume passed between her and Thackeray. Much might be written about their intellectual intercourse—but it never has been—and what Thackeray thought of her remains to this day a comparative secret. Does not the little volume with its "Dear Thackeray" throw some light upon it? and may we not hope that something else may be found to throw more light upon their relation?

Ernest Dressel North.

TO A FLIRT.

'Twas just a glance when first we met—
  Our insincerity began;
To play at loving, and forget,
    Was then our plan.

We'd often played the game before—
  The game To Love and then Forget—
Perhaps we thought, "'Tis one fool more
    Within the net!"

And we were artists in our way,
  We knew the moves and made the signs,
Without the hurry or delay
    Of other times;

Without the tears, with hearts unfired
  By fierce delight and jealous pain.
We both loved love, but were too tired
    To love again.

So by the shore, or at the play,
  Or when the sun was in the west,
We knew the proper thing to say,
    And stood the test.

To-night, upon the moonlit hill,
  I held you softly on my arm,
And there you lay, demure and still,
    Nor thought of harm ;

And there I smoothed your hair away,
  And while you watched the stars above,
I kissed you, and forgot to play,
    And spoke of love.

But you were wise enough for two,
  And laughed that I should lose so soon ;
You found a kindly thing to do,
    And blamed the Moon.

'Twas more than folly, less than sin,
  And I've forgotten to forget :
I will not be what I have been,
    Since first we met !

So when I come to you again,
  I pray that you will be less wise,
And let me read an answer plain,
    Within your eyes.

If I be more to you to-night
  Than when, at first, I played a part,
I'll know the message, mirrored bright,
    Of heart to heart.

Or if you will that I be less
  Than I have been to you before,
You need not speak, for I can guess,
    And come no more.

Herbert Müller Hopkins.

AMERICAN BOOKMEN.

VII.—Some Humourists.

Frontispiece from *The Life and Writings of Major Jack Downing.* Boston, 1833.

There are few writings concerned with wit and humour which do not begin with elaborate definitions of these almost indefinable qualities. The present paper will increase the number of exceptions to this rule by one. If there be readers who cannot satisfy themselves with their own definitions, they need not look far to find the whole matter—even to the recognition of that third quality, a *sense of humour*—set forth in a score of different ways. The lecturer to a college class who quoted the definition of humour as "wit plus sympathy" provided at least one of his hearers, some years ago, with a practical working distinction for every-day use. But there are many others, often subtler, to be picked up in places where more potent appeals to the memory are made than in college class-rooms. Whether we consciously divide the things that amuse us into the witty and the humorous sallies of mankind, we are grateful for the provocations to mirth, and entertain toward the man who makes us merrier a feeling which separates him from the common throng.

The attempts to formulate the distinctions between American humour and that of other lands are almost as frequent as the definitions of humour itself. Again, it seems unnecessary here to repeat or add one to these attempts. We all know reasonably well how composite and yet how definite are the qualities which render most Americans recognisable wherever they may be found; and like them, to a degree equally exclusive of doubt, is the quality of humour which the world knows as American. Mr. T. W. Higginson has said "that the whole department of American humour was created, so to speak, by the amazed curiosity of Englishmen." It would be unfair to take this opinion entirely apart from its context, and adorn a tale of confusion between cause and effect by means of it. Yet whatever one may think of the origin and virtue of American humour, it would be foolish to forget that in the department of letters to which it belongs, our fellow-countrymen have done that which gives them their clearest title to a place of their own as writers.

Much of the best achievement in this direction has obviously been wrought by men whose fame is secured by other gifts than those of mere humour. It is necessary only to recall such names as Franklin, Irving, Lowell, Holmes, Warner, Curtis, Mitchell, and Bret Harte, and we remember how much besides being humourists some of our best humourists have been and are. It is noteworthy also that the names of women occupy a scanty place in the annals of our humourists. In other fields they may be counted now by hundreds, but excepting some short stories here and there, and the work of a few women like "Josiah Allen's Wife" and the

"Widow Bedott," our humorous writing has been done almost entirely by men. To be sure, there is an American volume, *The Wit of Women*, compiled by one of their sisters, who with a feminine argument of her own brings it to an end with these lines:

"If you pronounce this book not funny
And wish you hadn't spent your money,
There soon will be a general rumour
That you're no judge of Wit and Humour."

But even this *argumentum ad hominem* fails to convince. Mark Twain, happily still the living exponent of American humour in its essence, addressed the readers of his *Library of Humour*, published more than ten years ago, in a different fashion. Nothing could have been more characteristic than his "Compiler's Apology," printed in fac-simile from his handwriting: "Those selections in this book which are from my own works were made by my two assistant compilers, not by me. This is why there are not more."

ARTEMUS WARD AT 20.

From the *Century Magazine*, by permission.

But living writers are not the present theme, nor those whose names derive a lustre from more serious work. Still less is it intended to attempt a discussion of the broad theme of American humour in its ethnic and philosophic bearing. Perhaps the reader will not unwillingly join in the preference to look at a few of the typical creators and creations of our native humour. Two facts he will recognise at once: First, that the newspapers have been an important medium of humorous expression—in part because our humourists have dealt frequently with public affairs, and in part because the newspapers have mirrored nearly everything, good and bad, that is representative of American life; and, second, that an amusing, fictitious personality, something more than a mere name, has frequently been created as the mouthpiece of a humorous writer. When Lowell began writing his most effective political satires, he sent them to the editors of the Boston *Courier* and the *Anti-Slavery Standard*, and a flesh-and-blood Hosea Biglow loomed large behind the utterances. Herein Lowell, with his own skill and power, was merely elaborating, in the forties, a device which in the thirties had made the name of Major Jack Downing a household word. In the same decade, but a few years after the appearance of Major Downing, the first lines in the typical Yankee figure of Sam Slick had been drawn by the Canadian pen of Judge Haliburton; but the down-East Major was the first conspicuous figure in this field of New-World letters, and as the prototype of later creations deserves more than a passing glance.

One is confused at first by finding the origin of the collected Downing letters attributed to two persons, Seba Smith, a Maine journalist, and Charles Augustus Davis (1795–1867), a New York shipping merchant. The truth appears to be that Smith created the Downingville major, and Davis adopted him as his own offspring. In neither of the volumes in which the letters of Major Jack Downing were first collected does the

name of their real author appear, but the evidence from various sources goes to show that the Boston volume of 1833, made up of letters to the Portland *Courier*, was wholly the work of Smith, and the New York volume of 1834, made up of letters to the New York *Daily Advertiser*, wholly that of Davis. Before the first collection was printed, some of the New York letters had appeared, for an appendix to the Boston volume, declaring that "the *real* Major has never sent any letter to any other paper than the Portland *Courier*," proceeds to print "some of Major Jack Downing's letters, that he never wrote," and these are identical with letters addressed to the New York *Daily Advertiser*, and collected in the volume attributed to Davis. Any doubt that Seba Smith was the author of the first volume is removed by the book *My Thirty Years Out of the Senate* (New York, 1859), appearing over his own name, and republishing the letters contained in the Boston volume of 1833. It is not unnatural to resent in some measure the credit which Davis won for himself, abroad and among his friends, of whom Halleck was one, by the cleverness of his letters, and their superiority, according to some opinions, to those of Smith ; for in spite of it all he was clearly a trespasser on another man's ground. If he had confined himself to newspapers he would have been merely one of many imitators. Even the father of Motley, the historian, as Dr. Holmes tells us, was "the author of one or more of the well-remembered 'Jack Downing' letters."

The ethics and bibliography of the letters, however, are less important than the Major and the letters themselves. In his volume of 1859 Seba Smith tells how they first came to be written. From other sources we learn that Smith was born in Bucksfield, Me., on September 14th, 1792, was graduated from Bowdoin College in 1818, and in 1820 was in Portland as the editor of the *Eastern Argus*. From 1830 until 1837 he conducted the Portland *Courier*, and it was in 1830, according to his own story, that he began writing for its columns the Downing letters. The Maine Legislature, evenly balanced in politics, afforded a good target for ridicule, and it seemed possible by the exercise of it to profit the young and struggling *Courier*. Accordingly Seba Smith

"bethought himself of the plan to bring a green, unsophisticated lad from the country into town with a load of axe-handles, hoop-poles, and other notions for sale, and while waiting the movement of a dull market, let him, blunder into the halls of the legislature, and after witnessing for some days their strange doings, sit down and write an account of them to his friends at home in his own plain language."

From the beginning the letters were a success, not only with Maine readers, but in Boston and other places where the newspapers copied them freely. With their progress the Yankee correspondent advanced in importance. From his native town of Downingville, "three miles from the main road as you go back into the country, and . . . *jest about in the middle of down East*," he proceeded to Washington, where he soon became an intimate friend and confidential adviser of President Jackson. He represents himself even as "the Gineral's" bedfellow, and none of "Old Hickory's" actions is too important or too trivial for Major Downing to have a hand in it. The possibilities of giving the ways of the Administration a ridiculous aspect by this method need merely to be suggested. From Seba Smith's book it is worth while to transcribe some words about the memorable visit to Cambridge, when the degree of LL.D. was conferred upon Jackson, for they represent with sufficient clearness the vein of humour that was characteristic both of the original Jack Downing, who is reported to have known himself only by the scar on his left arm, and of his principal rival.

ARTEMUS WARD AS A LECTURER. SKETCHED BY BIRCH.

From *Scribner's Monthly*, now the *Century Magazine*, by permission.

"Ye see when we were at Boston they sent word to us to come out to Cambridge, for they wanted to make the President a doctor of laws. What upon airth a doctor of laws was, or why they wanted to make the President one, I couldn't think. So when we come to go up to bed I asked the Gineral about it. And says I, 'Gineral, what is it they want to do to you out to Cambridge?' Says he, 'They want to make a doctor of laws of me.' 'Well,' says I, 'but what good will that do?' 'Why,' says he, 'you know, Major Downing, there's a pesky many of them are laws passed by Congress that are rickety things. Some of 'em have very poor constitutions, and some of 'em haven't no constitution at all. So that it is necessary to have somebody there to doctor 'em up a little, and not let 'em go out into the world, where they would stand a chance to catch cold and be sick, without they had good constitutions to bear it. You know,' says he, 'I've had to doctor the laws considerable ever since I've been at Washington, although I wasn't a regular bred doctor. And I made out so well about it, that these Cambridge folks think I better be made into a regular doctor at once, and then there'll be no grumbling and disputing about my practice.' Says he, 'Major, what do you think of it?' I told him I thought it an excellent plan; and asked him if he didn't think they would be willing, bein' I'd been round in

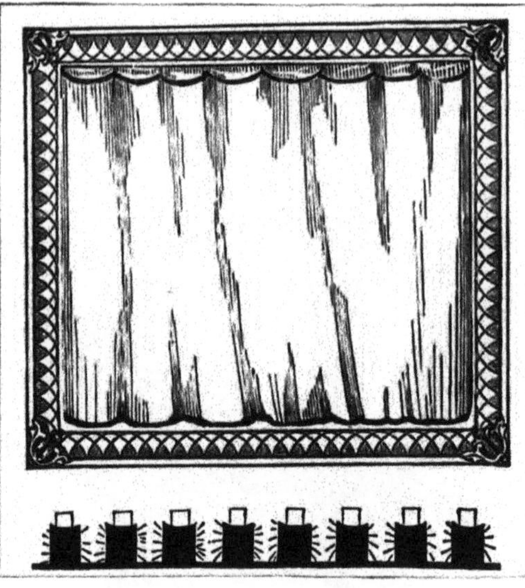

THE PROSCENIUM OF ARTEMUS WARD'S PANORAMA BEFORE THE CURTAIN WAS RAISED, AS EXHIBITED AT THE EGYPTIAN HALL, LONDON.

the military business considerable for a year or two past, to make me a doctor of war. He said he didn't know, but he thought it would be no harm to try 'em."

There are passages, both in Smith's letters and in Davis's, more broadly humorous and more conspicuously Yankee; yet it is evident that to the first Jack Downing, as the principal pioneer in a territory that has since been widely cultivated, all credit is due. In 1837, Seba Smith sold the *Courier*, and moved soon afterward to New York, where for many years he went on with the exercise of his pen, not only in Downing letters, but in producing *Powhatan: a Metrical Historical Romance*, a treatise on geometry and other labours more strictly journalistic. Of his wife, Elizabeth Oakes Smith, the author of *The Sinless Child*, a poem which, in spite of its length, called forth praise from Poe, Griswold records that "from her earliest years she has delighted in the study of philosophy, in abstruse speculations, and curious science." The Downing letters and a treatise on geometry—*The Sinless Child* and "abstruse speculations"—surely the mental range of Seba Smith and his wife was not confined within narrow bounds. He died in Patchogue, L. I., on July 29th, 1868.

According to a reported declaration of Artemus Ward, Major Jack Downing was his pattern. It is not difficult of belief, for in the use to which they put the Yankee vernacular, in their assumed familiarity with conspicuous persons, and in the "free-born-American-citizen" attitude of each writer there is much that suggests a family relationship. Artemus Ward—as the man whose real name was Charles

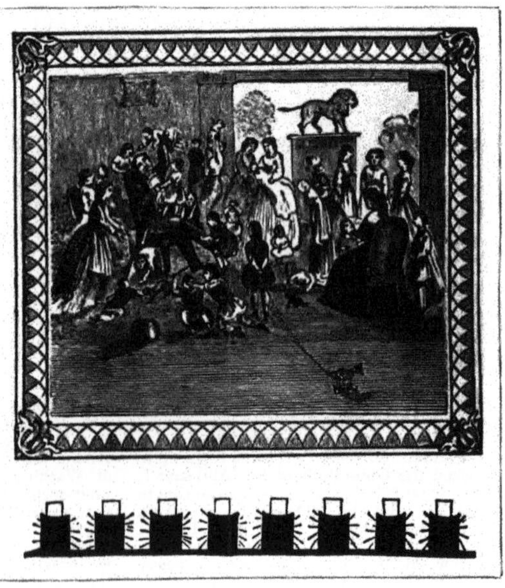

BRIGHAM YOUNG AT HOME. SCENE IN THE PANORAMA AS EXHIBITED AT THE EGYPTIAN HALL, LONDON

B. P. Shillaber

From a daguerreotype.

Farrar Browne is more familiarly called —may be regarded as a highly developed type of the humorous journalist and speaker. Certainly he has not been denied the homage of imitation, and certainly the writings he has left behind him are enough more than mere "comic copy" to give him a place of his own as a representative figure. Lowell told the truth about one of the humorous methods in which Artemus Ward excelled when he said: "There is no fun in bad spelling of itself, but only where the misspelling suggests something else that is droll *per se.*" It is the merit of Artemus Ward's verbal vagaries—for example, when a friend sends him a copy of "Chawcer's poems," and he says "Mr. C. had talent, but he couldn't spel"—that the droll personality of Charles Farrar Browne's creation is always realised more clearly by means of what may be called his mental dialect.

If Artemus Ward's descent as a humourist is to be traced from Major Jack Downing, it is thus that he accounts from the Browns, as the family name was written before he himself adopted the final *e*: "I should think we came from Jerusalem, for my father's name was Levi, and we had a Nathan and a Moses in the family. But my poor brother's name was Cyrus, so perhaps that makes us Persians." As a matter of fact, the Browns came to Maine from Massachusetts in 1783, and on April 26th, 1834, the humourist was born in the village of Waterford. He was one of four children, and, unlike many men who have made a mark in the world, could not have regarded his mother as the source of his later distinction. She is described as the fondest of parents, but a person entirely lacking in humour. It is related that when she first heard her son lecture in Boston, she was startled and irritated exceedingly by hearing him vouch for one of his statements by the use of a real name and a real formula which had frequently fallen from her own lips, and was introduced into the lecture entirely for her benefit: "I know it's true, for my Uncle Ransford Bates said so." The youthful antics ascribed to her son must have been equally trying to the good woman, and yet the devotion which he cherished for her through life helps one to realise what it must have meant to her to let the boy, only thirteen years old when his father died, go out into the world almost immediately to make his living in printing-offices. He was but fifteen when, after four experiments under country

B. P. SHILLABER ("MRS. PARTINGTON").

From an old *carte-de-visite*.

Chelsea, May 23, 1878

My dear Markle — I received yours of several days ago in bed, where I have been ever since, with my old trouble, and have been quite unable to reply to you till now. I have nothing on hand of the sort you intimate — having used up all as I went along — but I assure you I shall be pleased to help you out if I can, and if an idea comes I shall impale it for you. A sick bed, and the chafing of mustard plaster, is not conducive to humorous fancies, and alkaline draughts and liniments would bear no similitude to attic salt, therefore I must wait the return of perfect health in order to do anything in the agreeable, or properly disagreeable, way to please you. I appreciate your struggle and wonder how you can do so much, and should think that every one with a good thing to say would send it to the Porcupine.

Yours horizontally B. P. S.

FAC-SIMILE OF LETTER WRITTEN IN PENCIL BY B. P. SHILLABER.

editors in New Hampshire and Maine, he found himself in the Boston printing house from which B. P. Shillaber's (Mrs. Partington's) comic paper, *The Carpet Bag*, was issued. Setting up the type of Mrs. Partington's paragraphs and J. G. Saxe's witty verses, he ventured to write jokes himself, and had the felicity of seeing them printed.

A roving disposition carried him, soon after this humble beginning of a journalistic career, to Tiffin, Ohio. This was in 1856, and before 1860 he had won his spurs in Toledo and Cleveland, where the editor of the *Plaindealer*, hearing the fame of his wit, secured him as local editor at the salary of twelve, afterward advanced to fifteen dollars a week. At this post he remained three years. His Cleveland associates have since recalled him as a youth of surpassing awkwardness and rusticity at first, but developing by degrees a regard for his personal appearance which brought him later to an ill-advised fondness for diamonds and curled hair. But there is ample evidence in this period also of his more essential graces and virtues. Generous, companionable, and trusting, laughing over his work, serious withal, sometimes to the degree of mental suffering, given to ways eccentric and unconventional, he seems to have fallen in with the mode of journalistic life which needs but does not always receive the help of native qualities like Browne's to make it alluring. There are innumerable stories of his practical jokes, but one will suffice to indicate their audacity. One night with a fellow wag in journalism known as "the Fat Contributor," he went to the hotel where a dramatic reader, who was to give his first entertainment in the place the next day, was stopping. They called him from his bed, told him they were newspaper men, and would ruin his prospects unless he would come with them as he was to the hall near by, and show what he could do as a reader. The poor man protested, but their threats were too much for his courage, and shivering with cold, he went with them to the dreary, unheated hall, and, if the story be true, entertained them for several hours with his selections. "They had always thirsted to hear a dramatic reader in night dress," they told him; and if they did not commend his more decorous performance in public, their rather heartless idea of humour must have profited the unhappy reader but little.

It was in Cleveland that Browne began signing the name of Artemus Ward to his productions. The most credible theory of the source of this *nom de plume* is that the veritable *nom de guerre* of General Artemas Ward of the Revolutionary army appealed to the humourist, who adopted it with the change of a single letter. By degrees the new Artemus Ward became a definite character, a showman who could write of his equipment:

> "My show at present consists of three moral bares, a Kangaroo (a amoozin little Raskal—'twould make you larf yerself to deth to see the little cuss jump up and squeal), wax figgers of G. Washington, Gen. Tayler, John Bunyan, Capt. Kidd and Dr. Webster in the act of killin Dr. Parkman, besides several miscellanyus moral wax statoots of celebrated piruts & murderers, &c., ekalled by few & exceld by none."

From a photograph taken by George M. Baker in Boston, 1870.

It was in Cleveland, too, that Browne first conceived the idea of becoming a public lecturer. But that was not to be until after he went, in 1860, to live in New York, as editor of the promising comic journal, *Vanity Fair*, and one of the Bohemian set which frequented Pfaff's, and presented to Mr. Howells, picking up his first impressions of Eastern writers, an inexpensive contrast to the group of men he had just left in Boston.

On a desperately stormy night, near the end of 1861, Browne first faced a New York audience as a public speaker, and suffered a loss of thirty dollars. He had already tried his lecture, on "The Babes in the Wood," however, in Norwich, Conn., and other towns. It was a peculiarity of Ward's lectures that they had little or nothing to do with the subject announced. He would begin with a mention of it, then ask the audience to let him tell them a little story, which would wander on into irrelevant witticisms, occupying about an hour and a half, when he would take out his watch, appear to be overcome with shame and confusion, and bring his talk to a hurried, apologetic end. In Norwich the good people, who had laughed immoderately at his jokes, crowded around him when the lecture was finished to express sympathy for the nervousness through which, as they supposed, he had failed to say anything at all about the Babes in the Wood. It was a different story that he himself modestly told, at the breakfast table of James T. Fields, when he said of his first audiences: "I was prepared for a good deal of gloom, but I had no idea they would be *so much* depressed." "Artemus Ward will

Yours Cordially,
John G. Saxe

Speak a Piece" was the sum and substance of the advertising placard which announced his appearance in various places. Even the tickets were whimsical and characteristic. For one of his most popular lectures the card of admission read: "Artemus Ward Among the Mormons. Admit the Bearer and One Wife." The programmes were not without their individuality. In London they were enriched with the note, "Mr. ARTEMUS WARD will call on the citizens of London at their residences, and explain any jokes in his narrative which they may not understand." There may have been reason enough in such an offer if John Bright was reported with even an approach to truth in saying: "I must say I can't see what people find to enjoy in this lecture. The information is meagre and is presented in a desultory, disconnected manner. In fact, I can't help seriously questioning some of the statements."

Probably enough has been said to show that Artemus Ward stood entirely alone among the lecturers who galled one another's kibes on the lyceum platforms of his day. Of these sober discourses Ward said: "The men go becauz its poplar and the wimin folks to see what other wimin folks have on." To his lectures they went solely to be amused, and as their success became rapidly known, he soon found that he had done well to abandon journalism. East and West his "show" was in demand. A San Francisco manager telegraphed him, "What will you take for forty nights in California?" and his immediate response, "Brandy and water," so tickled the Western humour that when he came to Virginia City the miners took charge of the entertainment, would have no tickets sold, but invited everybody, and collected sixteen hundred dollars in gold for the lecturer by passing round hats, one of which broke with the weight of its contents. Brigham Young received him

JOHN G. SAXE.

cordially in Salt Lake City, in spite of the jests he had made and was still to make about the sect of men whose "religion is singular, but their wives are plural." There was little of appreciation left for him to win from his own countrymen, at least of those who "liked that sort of thing," when in 1866 he determined to try the fortunes of his wit in London.

Mr. Higginson's phrase, "the amazed curiosity of Englishmen," well describes the state of mind which Artemus Ward excited in the mother country. There could not have been many John Brights in the audiences which thronged Egyptian Hall for the six weeks before his failing health made the seventh his last week of public appearance. The abashed manner of the lecturer, the personal peculiarities of which he himself made fun, the difficulties with his panorama, which in general was painted as badly as possible, because excellence was expensive, the difficulties with the moon and the prairie fires, which would shoot up and flare out at the wrong moments, to the apparent consternation of the lecturer—all these, to say nothing of the humour of his talks, are reported to have kept his hearers in a frenzy of laughter. Who can wonder that they were quite overcome by the gravity with which he would point to dark regions in his canvas and say: "These are intended for horses; I know they are, because the artist told me so. After two years he came to me one morning and said, 'Mr. Ward, I cannot conceal it from you any longer; they are horses.'" It was in the full tide of success, achieved simply by the exercise of natural gifts, that his career of unique popularity was cut short. His contributions to *Punch* had won him a place on the staff of the paper, and all things indicated the continuance of success. But the cough which had made nearly all his lecturing in London difficult soon stopped it entirely. His friends took him to the island of Jersey, in the hope that its milder air might restore him. Then they tried to bring him back to London, but he could not bear the journey beyond Southampton, where he died on the 6th of March, 1867, not quite thirty-three years old.

Burlington, Vt.
Sept. 30. '71

Dear Sir:-
I very cheerfully comply with your request, and am
Yours truly
Jno. G. Saxe

FAC-SIMILE OF A LETTER FROM JOHN G. SAXE REPLYING TO A REQUEST FOR AN AUTOGRAPH.

It may be thought that an inordinate portion of this paper has been devoted to a person who stood related to literature as *bouffe* to grand opera. Yet he represented conspicuously a class of writers which it would be quite unfair to overlook in any general survey of American letters. Indeed, it would not be unprofitable to scrutinise the career and work of other men who stood less upon the dignity than the drollery of their productions; for if their appeal has not always been to the most fastidious, they have often meant more to "the great body of the plain people" than graver bookmen who escape the humourist's penalty of writing, as a rule, for one generation or decade. The mere names of these men, dead and living, would make a catalogue of no scanty length. "John Phœnix," "Orpheus C. Kerr" (Office Seeker), "Petroleum V. Nasby" would stand among the better known. B. P. Shillaber (1814–90), a Boston journalist—who took his cue from Sydney Smith's reference in a political speech to a certain Mrs. Partington's vain endeavour to mop up the Atlantic Ocean, and made a new Mrs. Malaprop of his talkative old heroine—would claim 'especial attention. So, too, would Henry W. Shaw (1818–85), who, after encountering every experience as a Western pioneer, began writing at forty-five, and over the name of "Josh Billings" put forth many witty, homely maxims, of which, perhaps, none is more memorable than that "it is better to kno less than to kno so mutch that aint so."

Somewhat apart from these newspaper celebrities stands one of whom Mr. Stedman has written: "For the most part he was a popular specimen of the college-society, lecture-room, dinner-table rhymster that may be set down as a peculiarly American type and of a generation now almost passed away." John Godfrey Saxe dealt less in humour than in clear-cut wit. The mastery of words in rhymes that Richard H. Barham or Tom Hood might at times have been glad to own gave him his distinction. Like many of those who have incited our countrymen most successfully to mirth, he was of New England origin and training. Born in Highgate, Vt., on June 2d, 1816, he spent his boyhood on a farm, was graduated at Middlebury College in 1839, and began the practise of law. Until he was twenty-five he wrote little or nothing, and then his ballad of "The Briefless Barrister" appeared in the *Knickerbocker Magazine*:

"Unfortunate man that I am!
I've never a client but grief;
The case is, I've no case at all,
And in brief, I've ne'er had a brief."

Yet with a mingling of law, journalism, and politics he went on with his Vermont life in St. Albans and Burlington, until twice defeated as a candidate for governor in his native State, he moved to New York.

"Now I am a man, you must learn,
Less famous for beauty than strength,
And for aught I could ever discern,
Of rather superfluous length.
In truth, 'tis but seldom one meets
Such a Titan in human abodes,
And when I walk over the streets,
I'm a perfect Colossus of roads."

Thus he described his personal appearance, which was in reality most attractive, and, with his skill in speaking, won him great popularity as a lecturer and reader of his own verses. In 1872 he became associated with the Albany *Evening Journal*, and in Albany he died on March 31st, 1887. The last portion of his life affords another story of the sorrow that seems especially to beset the sons of laughter. In 1874 he narrowly escaped death in a railroad accident in Virginia. This shock was soon followed by the death, in rapid succession, of his wife, three daughters and a son; and the result of his overwhelming distress was that he became the victim of attacks of melancholy which caused his complete retirement from the world. It was indeed a tragic ending for the life of the light-hearted singer of "The Proud Miss MacBride," "The New Rape of the Lock," "Riding on the Rail," and scores of other skilful rhymes and *vers de société*, which were the delight of his generation.

Of men about whom so much might be said it is a hardship to say so little. The limitations of space preclude also and entirely the consideration of that vast anonymous expression of American humour which confronts us every day and every week in the periodical press. The composite person who produces it has no dates of birth and death to record, no incidents of struggle and success to relate; yet as unmistakably as Bret Harte, Mark Twain, and the many others, living and dead, who have been mentioned or more closely regarded, he is a product of our curious civilisation, and, so far as one can see, will continue to help us in realising, still without definitions, the distinctive qualities of our national humour.

M. A. De Wolfe Howe.

The subject of the next paper in this series, to appear in the October BOOKMAN, *will be "Emerson and his Concord Companions."*

IN KEDAR'S TENTS.*

By Henry Seton Merriman, Author of "The Sowers."

CHAPTER XIX.

CONCEPCION TAKES THE ROAD.

"Who knows? The man is proven by the hour."

After the great storm came a calm almost as startling. It seemed, indeed, as if Nature stood abashed and silent before the results of her sudden rage. Day after day the sun glared down from a cloudless sky, and all Castile was burnt brown as a desert. In the streets of Madrid there arose a hot dust, and that subtle odour of warm earth that rarely meets the nostrils in England. It savoured of India and other sun-steeped lands, where water is too precious to throw upon the roads.

Those who could remained indoors or in their shady *patios* until the heat of the day was past, and such as worked in the open lay unchallenged in the shade from midday till three o'clock. During those days military operations were almost suspended, although the heads of departments were busy enough in their offices. The confusion of war, it seemed, was past, and the sore-needed peace was immediately turned to good account. The army of the Queen Regent was, indeed, in an almost wrecked condition, and among the field officers jealousy and backbiting, which had smouldered through the war-time, broke out openly. General Vincente was rarely at home, and Estella passed this time in quiet seclusion. Coming as she did from Andalusia, she was accustomed to an even greater heat, and knew how to avoid the discomfort of it.

She was sitting one afternoon with open windows and closed jalousies, during the time of the siesta, when the servant announced Father Concha.

The old priest came into the room wiping his brow with simple ill-manners.

"You have been hurrying, and have no regard for the sun," said Estella.

"You need not find shelter for an old ox," replied Concha, seating himself. "It is the young ones that expose themselves unnecessarily."

Estella glanced at him sharply, but said nothing. He sat, handkerchief in hand, and stared at a shaft of sunlight that lay across the floor from a gap in the jalousies. From the street under the windows came the distant sounds of traffic and the cries of the vendors of water, fruit, and newspapers.

Father Concha looked puzzled, and seemed to be seeking his way out of a difficulty. Estella sat back in her chair, half hidden by her slow-waving black fan. There is no pride so difficult as that which is unconscious of its own existence, no heart so hard to touch as that which throws its stake and asks neither sympathy nor admiration from the outside world. Concha glanced at Estella, and wondered if he had been mistaken. There was in the old man's heart, as, indeed, there is in nearly all human hearts, a thwarted instinct. How many are there with paternal instincts who have no children, how many a poet has been lost by the crying needs of hungry mouths. It was a thwarted instinct that made the old priest busy himself with the affairs of other people, and always of young people.

"I came hoping to see your father," he said at length, blandly untruthful. "I have just seen Conyngham, in whom we are all interested, I think. His lack of caution is singular. I have been trying to persuade him not to do something most rash and imprudent. You remember the incident in your garden at Ronda—a letter which he gave to Julia?"

"Yes," answered Estella quietly; "I remember."

"For some reason, which he did not explain, I understand that he is desirous of regaining possession of that letter, and now Julia, writing from Toledo, tells him that she will give it to him if he will go there and fetch it. The Toledo road, as you will remember, is hardly to be recommended to Mr. Conyngham."

"But Julia wishes him no harm," said Estella.

"My child, rarely trust a political man and never a political woman. If Julia wished him to have the letter, she could have sent it to him by post. But Conyngham, who is all eagerness, must needs refuse to listen to my argument, and starts this afternoon for Toledo—alone. He has not even his servant, Concepcion Vara, who has suddenly disappeared, and a woman, who claims to be the scoundrel's wife, from Algeciras, has been making inquiries at Conyngham's lodging. A hen's eyes are where her eggs lie. I offered to go to Toledo with Conyngham, but he laughed at me for a useless old priest, and said that the saddle would gall me."

He paused, looking at her beneath his shaggy brows, knowing, as he had always known, that this was a woman beyond his reach—cleverer, braver, of a higher mind than her sisters—one to whom he might perchance tender some small assistance, but nothing better; for women are wiser in their generation than men, and usually know better what is for their own happiness. Estella returned his glance with steady eyes.

"He has gone," said Concha. "I have not been sent to tell you that he is going."

"I did not think that you had," she answered.

"Conyngham has enemies in this country," continued the priest, "and despises them, a mistake to which his countrymen are singularly liable. He has gone off on this foolish quest without preparation or precaution. Toledo is, as you know, a hotbed of intrigue and dissatisfaction. All the malcontents in Spain congregate there, and Conyngham would do well to avoid their company. Who lies down with dogs gets up with fleas."

He paused, tapping his snuff-box, and at that moment the door opened to admit General Vincente.

"Oh, the padre!" cried that cheerful soldier. "But what a sun—eh? It is cool here, however, and Estella's room is always a quiet one."

He touched her cheek affectionately, and drew forward a low chair, wherein he sat, carefully disposing of the sword that always seemed too large for him.

"And what news has the padre?" he asked, daintily touching his brow with his folded pocket-handkerchief.

"Bad!" growled Concha, and then told his tale over again in a briefer, blunter manner. "It all arises," he concluded, "from my pestilential habit of interfering in the affairs of other people."

"No," said General Vincente; "it arises from Conyngham's pestilential habit of acquiring friends wherever he goes."

The door was opened again and a servant entered.

"Excellency," he said, "a man called Concepcion Vara, who desires a moment."

"What did I tell you?" said the general to Concha. "Another of Conyngham's friends. Spain is full of them. Let Concepcion Vara come to this room."

The servant looked slightly surprised and retired. If, however, this manner of reception was unusual, Concepcion was too finished a man of the world to betray either surprise or embarrassment. By good fortune he happened to be wearing a coat. His flowing, unstarched shirt was, as usual, spotless; he wore a flower in the ribbon of the hat carried jauntily in his hand, and about his person, in the form of handkerchief and *faja*, were those touches of bright colour, by means of which he so irresistibly attracted the eye of the fair.

"Excellency!" he murmured, bowing on the threshold. "Reverendo!" with one step forward and a respectful semi-religious inclination of the head toward Concha. "Señorita!" The ceremony here concluded with a profound obeisance to Estella, full of gallantry and grave admiration. Then he stood upright, and indicated by a pleasant smile that no one need feel embarrassed—that, in fact, this meeting was most opportune.

"A matter of urgency, excellency," he said confidentially to Vincente. "I have reason to suspect that one of my friends—in fact, the Señor Conyngham, with whom I am at the moment in service, happens to be in danger."

"Ah! What makes you suspect that, my friend?"

Concepcion waved his hand airily, as if indicating that the news had been brought to him by the birds of the air.

"When one goes into the café," he

said, "one is not always so particular, one associates with those who happen to be there—muleteers, diligencia-drivers, bull-fighters, all and sundry, even *contrabandistas.*"

He made this last admission with a face full of pious toleration, and Father Concha laughed grimly.

"That is true, my friend," said the general, hastening to cover the priest's little lapse of good manners. "And from these gentlemen, honest enough in their way, no doubt, you have learnt—"

"That the Señor Conyngham has enemies in Spain."

"So I understand; but he has also friends."

"He has one," said Vara, taking up a fine picturesque attitude, with his left hand at his waist, where the deadly knife was concealed in the rolls of his *faja.*

"Then he is fortunate," said the general, with his most winning smile. "Why do you come to me, my friend?"

"I require two men," answered Concepcion airily. "That is all."

"Ah! What sort of men—*guardia civile?*"

"The holy saints forbid! Honest soldiers, if it please your excellency. The *guardia civile*, see you, excellency"—

He paused, shaking his outspread hand from side to side, palm downward, fingers apart, as if describing a low level of humanity.

"A brutal set of men," he continued, "with the finger ever on the trigger and the rifle ever loaded. Pam! and a life is taken—many of my friends—at least, many persons I have met . . . in the café."

"It is better to give him his two men," put in Father Concha, in his atrocious English, speaking to the general. "The man is honest in his love of Conyngham if in nothing else."

"And if I accord you these two men, my friend," said the general, from whose face Estella's eyes had never moved, "will you undertake that Mr. Conyngham comes to no harm?"

"I will arrange it," replied Concepcion, with an easy shrug of the shoulders—"I will arrange it, never fear."

"You shall have two men," said General Vincente, drawing a writing case toward himself and proceeding to write the necessary order—"men who are known to me personally. You can rely upon them at all times"—

"Since they are friends of his excellency's," interrupted Concepcion, with much condescension, "that suffices."

"He will require money," said Estella in English, her eyes bright and her cheeks flushed; for she came of a fighting race, and her repose of manner, the dignity which sat rather strangely on her slim young shoulders, were only signs of that self-control which had been handed down to her through the ages.

The general nodded as he wrote.

"Take that to headquarters," he said, handing the papers to Concepcion, "and in less than half an hour your men will be ready. Mr. Conyngham is a friend of mine, as you know, and any expenses incurred on his behalf will be defrayed by myself."

Concepcion held up his hand.

"It is unnecessary, excellency," he said. "At present Mr. Conyngham has funds. Only yesterday he gave me money. He liquidated my little account. It has always been a jest between us, that little account."

He laughed pleasantly and moved toward the door.

"Vara," said Father Concha.

"Yes, reverendo."

"If I meet your wife in Madrid, what shall I say to her?"

Concepcion turned and looked into the smiling face of the old priest.

"In Madrid, reverendo? How can you think of such a thing? My wife lives in Algeciras, and at times, see you . . ." he stopped, casting his eyes up to the ceiling and fetching an exaggerated sigh—"at times my heart aches. But now I must get to the saddle. What a thing is duty, reverendo—duty! God be with your excellencies."

And he hurried out of the room.

"If you would make a thief honest trust him," said Concha when the door was closed.

In less than an hour Concepcion was on the road, accompanied by two troopers, who were ready enough to travel in company with a man of his reputation, for in Spain, if one cannot be a bull-fighter, it is good to be a smuggler. At sunset the great heat culminated in a thunderstorm, which drew a veil of heavy cloud across the sky, and night fell before its time.

The horsemen had covered two thirds

of their journey, when he whom they followed came in sight of the lights of Toledo, set upon a rock, like the jewels in a lady's cluster ring, and almost surrounded by the swift Tagus. Conyngham's horse was tired, and stumbled more than once on the hill by which the traveller descends to the great bridge and the gate that Wamba built thirteen hundred years ago.

Through this gate he passed into the city, which was a city of the dead, with its hundred ruined churches, its empty palaces, and silent streets. Ichabod is written large over all these tokens of a bygone glory—where the Jews, flying from Jerusalem, first set foot; where the Moor reigned unmolested for nearly four hundred years; where the Goth and the Roman and the great Spaniard of the middle ages have trod on each other's heels. Truly, these worn stones have seen the greatness of the greatest nations of the world.

A single lamp hung slowly swinging in the arch of Wamba's Gate, and the streets were but ill-lighted with an oil lantern at an occasional corner. Conygnham had been in Toledo before, and knew his way to the inn under the shadow of the great Alcazar, now burnt and ruined. Here he left his horse, for the streets of Toledo are so narrow and tortuous, so ill-paven and steep, that wheel traffic is almost unknown, while a horse can with difficulty keep his feet on the rounded cobble-stones. In this city men go about their business on foot, which makes the streets as silent as the deserted houses.

Julia had selected a spot which was easy enough to find, and Conyngham, having supped, made his way thither without asking for directions.

"It is, at all events, worth trying," he said to himself; "and she can scarcely have forgotten that I saved her life on the Garonne, as well as at Ronda."

But there is often in a woman's life one man who can make her forget all. The streets were deserted, for it was a cold night, and the cafés were carefully closed against the damp air. No one stirred in the Calle Pedro Martir, and Conyngham peered into the shadow of the high wall of the Church of San Tome in vain. Then he heard the soft tread of muffled feet, and turning on his heel charged to meet the charge of his two assailants. Two of them went down like felled trees, but there were others—four others—who fell on him silently, like hounds upon a fox, and in a few moments all was quiet again in the Calle Pedro Martir.

CHAPTER XX.

ON THE TALAVERA ROAD.

"Les barrières servant à indiquer où il faut passer."

An hour's ride to the west of Toledo, on the road to Torrijos and Talavera, and in the immediate neighbourhood of the villages of Galvez, two men sat in the shadow of a great rock and played cards. They played quietly and without vociferation, illustrating the advantages of a minute coinage. They had gambled with varying fortune since the hour of the siesta, and a sprinkling of cigarette ends on the bare rocks around them testified to the indulgence of a kindred vice.

The elder of the two men glanced from time to time over his shoulder, and down toward the dusty high road, which lay across the arid plain beneath them like a tape. The country here is barren and stone-ridden, but to the west, where Torrijos gleamed on the plain, the earth was green with the bush corn and heavy blades of the maize now springing into ear. Where these two soldiers sat the herbage was scant and of an aromatic scent, as it mostly is in hot countries and in rocky places. That these men belonged to a mounted branch of the service was evident from their equipment, and notably from the great rusty spurs at their heels. They were clad in cotton—dusty white breeches, dusty blue tunics—a sort of undress tempered by the vicissitudes of a long war and the laxity of discipline engendered by political trouble at home.

They had left their horses in the stable of a *venta*, hidden among ilex-trees by the roadside, and had clambered to this point of vantage above the highway to pass the afternoon after the manner of their race, for the Spaniard will be found playing cards amid the wreck of the world and in the intervals between the stupendous events of the last day.

"He comes," said the older man at length, as he leisurely shuffled the greasy cards; "I hear his horse's feet."

And, indeed, the great silence which seems to brood over the uplands of Spain—the silence, as it were, of an historic past and a dead present—was broken by the distant regular beat of hoofs.

The trooper who had spoken was a bullet-headed Castilian, with square jaws and close-set eyes. His companion, a younger man, merely nodded his head, and studied the cards which had just been dealt to him. The game progressed, and Concepcion Vara, on the Toledo road, approached at a steady trot. This man showed to greater advantage on horseback and beneath God's open sky than in the streets of a city. Here, on the open and among the mountains, he held his head erect and faced the world, ready to hold his own against it. In the streets he wore a furtive air, and glanced from left to right, fearing recognition.

He now took his tired horse to the stable of the little *venta*, where, with his usual gallantry, he assisted a hideous old hag to find a place in the stalls. While uttering a gay compliment he deftly secured for his mount a feed of corn which was much in excess of that usually provided for the money.

"Ah!" he said, as he tipped the measure, "I can always tell when a woman has been pretty; but with you, señora, no such knowledge is required. You will have your beauty for many years yet."

Thus Vara and his horse fared ever well upon the road. He lingered at the stable-door, knowing that corn poured into the manger may yet find its way back to the bin, and then turned his steps toward the mountain.

The cards were still falling with a whispering sound upon the rock selected as a table, and with the spirit of a true sportsman Concepcion waited until the hand was played out before imparting his news.

"It is well," he said at length. "A carriage has been ordered from a friend of mine in Toledo to take the road tonight to Talavera, and Talavera is on the way to Lisbon. What did I tell you?"

The two soldiers nodded. One was counting his gains, which amounted to almost threepence. The loser wore a brave air of indifference, as behooved a reckless soldier, taking loss or gain in a Spartan spirit.

"There will be six men," continued Concepcion—"two on horseback, two on the box, two inside the carriage with their prisoner, my friend."

"Ah!" said the younger soldier thoughtfully.

Concepcion looked at him.

"What have you in your mind?" he asked.

"I was wondering how three men could best kill six."

"Out of six," said the older man, "there is always one who runs away. I have found it so in my experience."

"And of five there is always one who cannot use his knife," added Concepcion.

Still the younger soldier, who had medals all across his chest, shook his head.

"I am afraid," he said—"I am always afraid before I fight."

Concepcion looked at the man whom General Vincente had selected from a brigade of tried soldiers, and gave a little upward jerk of the head.

"With me," he said, "it is afterward, when all is over. Then my hand shakes and the wet trickles down my face."

He laughed and spread out his hands.

"And yet," he said gaily, "it is the best game of all; is it not so?"

The troopers shrugged their shoulders. One may have too much of even the best game.

"The carriage is ordered for eight o'clock," continued the practical Concepcion, rolling a cigarette, which he placed behind his ear, where a clerk would carry his pen. "Those who take the road when the night birds come abroad have something to hide. We will see what they have in their carriage—eh? The horses are tired for the journey to Galvez, where a relay is doubtless ordered. It will be a fine night for a journey. There is a half moon, which is better than the full for those who use the knife; but the Galvez horses will not be required, I think."

The younger soldier, upon whose shoulder gleamed the stars of a rapid promotion, looked up to the sky, where a few fleecy clouds were beginning to gather above the setting sun, like sheep about a gate.

"A half moon for the knife and a full moon for firearms," he said.

"Yes; and they will shoot quick enough if we give them the chance," said Concepcion. "They are Carlists! There is a river between this and Galvez, a little stream, such as we have in Andalusia, so small that there is only a ford and no bridge. The bed of the river is soft. The horses will stop, or, at all events, must go at the walking pace. Across the stream are a few trees . . ." he paused, illustrating his description with rapid gestures and an imaginary diagram drawn upon the rock with the forefinger . . . "ilex, and here, to the left, some pines. The stream runs thus from northeast to southwest. This bank is high, and over here are low-lying meadows, where pigs feed."

He looked up, and the two soldiers nodded. The position lay before them like a bird's-eye view, and Concepcion, in whom Spain had perhaps lost a guerilla general, had only set eyes on the spot once as he rode past it.

"This matter is best settled on foot; is it not so? We cross the stream and tie our horses to the pine-trees. I will recross the water, and come back to meet the carriage at the top of the hill—here. The horsemen will be in advance. We will allow them to cross the stream. The horses will come out of the water slowly, or I know nothing of horses. As they step up the incline you take them, and remember to give them the chance of running away. In midstream I will attack the two on the box, pulling him who is not driving into the water by his legs, and giving him the blade in the right shoulder above the lung. He will think himself dead, but should recover. Then you must join me. We shall be three to three, unless the Englishman's hands are loose, then we shall be four to three, and need do no man any injury. The Englishman is as strong as two, and quick with it as big men rarely are."

"Do you take a hand?" asked the Castilian, fingering the cards.

"No; I have affairs. Continue your game."

So the sun went down, and the two soldiers continued their game, while Concepcion sat beside them and slowly, lovingly sharpened his knife on a piece of slate, which he carried in his pocket for the purpose.

After sunset there usually arises a cold breeze, which blows across the tablelands of Castile quite gently and unobtrusively. A local proverb says of this wind that it will extinguish a man, but not a candle. When this arose the three men descended the mountain-side, and sat down to a simple, if highly flavoured meal, provided by the ancient mistress of the *venta*. At half-past eight, when there remained nothing of the day but a faint, greenish light in the western sky, the little party mounted their horses and rode away toward Galvez.

"It's better," said Concepcion, with a meaning and gallant bow to the hostess—"it's for my peace of mind. I am but a man."

Then he haggled over the price of the supper.

They rode forward to the ford described by Concepcion, and there made their preparations carefully and coolly, as men recognising the odds against them. The half moon was just rising as the soldiers plashed through the water, leading Concepcion's horse, he remaining on the Toledo side of the river.

"The saints protect us!" said the nervous soldier, and his hand shook on the bridle. His companion smiled at the recollection of former fights passed through together. It is well, in love and war, to beware of him who is afraid.

Shortly after nine o'clock the silence of that deserted plain was broken by a distant murmur, which presently shaped itself into the beat of horses' feet. To this was added soon the rumble of wheels. The elder soldier put a whole cigarette into his mouth and chewed it; the younger man made no movement now. They crouched low at their posts, one on each side of the ford. Concepcion was across the river, but they could not see him. In Andalusia they say that a contrabandist can conceal himself behind half a brick.

The two riders were well in front of the carriage, and, as had been foreseen, the horses lingered on the rise of the bank, as if reluctant to leave the water without having tasted it. In a moment the younger soldier had his man out of the saddle, raising his own knee sharply as the man fell, so that the falling head and the lifted knee came into deadly contact. It was a trick well known to the trooper, who let the insensible form

"Depends!" said Chuffey. "I want to do what pays me best."

"You won't get another penny out of me, you villain."

"Vurry well, Keptin. We'll try another way." The bell rang for dinner, and the deck cleared as if by magic. It was becoming dusk, and our two quondam friends were alone in the dim light. "After dinner this evening I shall tike the opportunity to offer a few remarks in public concerning you and your past, and I shall tike care that Mrs. Vanderboodle, the rich American widow——"

"You devil!" screams Captain Crawleigh furiously. "Take that!"

Chuffey Small dodges the blow adroitly, and Crawleigh, staggering, is at his mercy. With an impetuous movement Chuffey throws himself upon Crawleigh, and a terrific struggle ensues. Slowly they approach (in their excitement) the side of the good ship *City of Paris*. A twist of Chuffey's leg, a sudden lurch of the vessel, and Captain Crawleigh goes overboard, never to rise again.

And then Mr. Chuffey Small strolls below and makes an excellent dinner.

(CONCLUDED.)

* * * * *

No. IV.

And the happy marriage bells rang out a merry peal, signalling to all and sundry the wedding of Gerald and Lady Beatrice, together, after all their troubles, in unending happiness till death should part them.

There are little children now at the Hall, numbering altogether fifteen, and Lady Beatrice, their proud mother, is no longer the slight lissom creature whom we encountered for the first time in the hunting field. Her figure has become more rounded, her face has more repose, but she has still her happy girlish laugh, and her love of practical jokes has not been diminished by time. A hair-brush in a visitor's bed, the sudden withdrawing of a chair, the filling of silk hats with lard; these and other pleasantries of our now happy heroine make the Hall ring with jovial mirth.

Lord Rooke went abroad and married an elderly actress, and thinks no doubt sometimes of his mis-spent life. Trotter, the faithful trainer, is also married and happy. The Dean of Wilborough unfortunately lost his amiable wife a few years since, but he instantly married again, and this union has been blest by a numerous progeny. Charlie Hinde of the Tenth (Gerald's old friend) is wooing Gerald's sister, and if one may peep into the future, one may premise for him the success he deserves. Mrs. Hards, the housekeeper at the Hall, is about to accept the hand and heart of Farmer Kite, who still prides himself on his "vamous brew of zider." Phyllis, the under-housemaid, has made a railway porter happy, and the curate is supposed by the gossips to have designs on the heart of the eldest Miss Streake.

Here we may well leave our friends. Here too, reader, you and I must part. We have been companions for a long journey; now we have come to the parting of the ways. Maybe in this busy world's stress and conflict you and I may meet again. Who knows?

THE END.

* * * * *

It is only necessary to add that no charge of plagiarism will be brought by the present writer against those who avail themselves of the foregoing conclusions.

W. Pett Ridge.

FINIS.

O Earth! our lives are but a day;
  About thy mother-feet we creep,
Till tired at last of all our play,
  We nestle in thy breast and sleep.

Benjamin F. Leggett.

LONDON LETTER.

Trade is slowly reviving after the Jubilee, and is perhaps better at present than it is in an average August. It is expected to receive a fillip from the production of Mr. Hall Caine's book, which runs to 160,000 words, and 50,000 copies of which have been printed as a first edition, exclusive of American and colonial editions. This will bring the number fully up to 100,000. Messrs. Ballantyne and Company have had seven machines working on the book, and have beaten the record of the trade in the matter of rapid production. Mr. Hall Caine receives between £6000 and £7000 before publication. He has taken immense pains in the revision of the book, having had authorities of various kinds reading it carefully and giving him their suggestions. It is now three years since *The Manxman* was published.

The talk is still about the coercion of the booksellers by the publishers—I mean the proposal that no books should be supplied except to those who will pledge themselves to give only twopence discount in the shilling. The great discount booksellers who give threepence in the shilling seem inclined to fight the proposal. It has also important bearings upon authors, and the Authors' Society committee is considering it. I have no doubt at all that the result would be to bring the price of six-shilling novels down to five shillings. As a rule the public does not get much for six shillings, but it pays the present price, four shillings and sixpence, cheerfully enough. I predict that if the change is carried out novels will have to be published at five shillings. The result will be that the public will get them at four shillings and twopence. This will mean a great loss alike to publishers and authors. I am told that the apparent unanimity of the publishing trade is not real; that many of the leading members have the greatest misgivings as to the step proposed to be taken, and that it is quite on the cards that the previous decision will be reversed and the old discount kept up. It is doubtless a misfortune that the discount is so large, but it is not easy to redress steps of this kind.

Mr. Kipling has acquired great credit by his Jubilee verses printed in the *Times*. They have presented a new side of that versatile mind to many. Their high religious tone is in strange contrast with much of Mr. Kipling's patriotic poetry, and many have felt as if they had witnessed a conversion more complete and more sudden than has ever been accomplished in the annals of the Salvation Army. Still it remains true that Mr. Kipling's are the only verses on the subject that have touched the popular heart; and if he continues in this strain he will rapidly find a new public still larger and more influential than the public he has already gained.

There is a movement going on among authors which, if it comes to anything, will diminish the gains of the literary agent. Most of the novelists of our country are in the hands of two or three literary agents. These agents have done very well for them. They have increased their profits largely, and have kept strict account of their business. The agents of late have been competing with one another in raising the price of work. They have given another turn to the screw, and through the competition of new firms they have been able to get immense royalties even for authors who have no very great public. But the authors are beginning to complain that if the agents can accomplish their purpose they will receive one tenth of the whole literary income of the country. They argue that this is unfair; that the service of an agent should be remunerated according to a fixed scale, just as the services of a lawyer are. If a lawyer is successful in gaining a suit for a client he does not receive forever ten per cent. of the net income that follows. He is paid his fees and the matter is done with. Authors, or at least many of them, think that it should be so with their agents. They should be paid for their trouble and then the matter should take end. This change cannot come at once, but it is certain to arrive, as the competition between agents, which is now comparatively very little, increases. That it will increase seems likely enough when it is considered that the agent almost alone among business men requires no capital, can incur no risks, has no losses, and gains by every item of work he is able to transact. For a long time the agents were careful to be on good terms with publishers and to give publishers a fair chance, and it will be regrettable if this policy is departed from. For if an exorbitant royalty is put upon a book, it is certain that the publisher will not and cannot advertise and push the book as he would on a lower price. Therefore such exorbitant royalties lead to the grinding down of every one concerned, printers and bookbinders especially being included. It is no secret that both these trades in London have been much less profitable lately than they used to be. The bookbinding trade in particular has suffered. More business has been done and less profit has been made. The consequence is that many girls are employed in the trade at starvation wages, which virtually force many of them upon the street.

Some changes have taken place or are likely to take place in our magazine world. Mr. Pearson, of *Pearson's Weekly* and *Pearson's Magazine*, has been considering the purchase of the *Idler*. The *Idler* was started by Mr. Jerome and Mr. Barr at sixpence, and obtained a large circulation. Ultimately Mr. Barr received payment for his share, and quitted the periodical, which since then has been in the hands of Mr. Jerome. Mr. Jerome raised the price from sixpence to a shilling, and has put a good deal of his own work into it. It is, however, more difficult to sell a shilling magazine than a sixpenny, and Mr. Jerome seems to be willing to concentrate his energies upon *To-day*, which he has made successful after the expenditure of a comparatively large capital. Mr. Strachey, it is said, is to quit the editorship of the *Cornhill Magazine*, which he has held for rather more than a year. The *Cornhill* was edited as a sixpenny magazine by Mr. James Payn. When Mr. Payn withdrew it was raised to a shilling, and Mr. Strachey has done his best to revive it at that price. His successor, it is said, will be Mr. Graves, the clever author of *The Hawarden Horace*. I do not believe that there is any future for shilling magazines in this country. One can imagine a shilling magazine of sport conducted on very different lines from the *Badminton*, which might attain great popularity.

Mr. Barrie and his wife went to the Engadine after the copyright performance of Mr. Barrie's new play, *The Little Minister*. Readers of *The Little Minister* will find enormous changes made in the plot. The whole conclusion is different, and has been made bright, light, and pleasant. The play will be produced in the early weeks of October, and all concerned are very sanguine that a great success will be achieved both here and in America. Mr. and Mrs. Cyril Maude, who are to take the chief parts, were to go to Thrums to learn the dialect, but have changed their minds, and are taking a rest in rural England.

The beautiful new edition of Scott, which Messrs. Dent are producing, will be prefaced by Mr. Clement Shorter, who will be able to throw much new light upon Scott.

The title of Mr. Barrie's conclusion of *Sentimental Tommy* will probably be *The Celebrated Tommy*.

Many of your readers will hear with sympathy of the death of Mr. Samuel Harraden, the father of the gifted novelist, Miss Beatrice Harraden. Mr. Harraden's illness has not been of long duration, and it was only at the last that he became aware of its very serious nature. He suffered much, but was happily tranquil at the last. He was carefully nursed by his devoted daughters, who idolised his fine, chivalrous character, his great abilities, and his wonderful versatility. Miss Beatrice Harraden, who is bearing up wonderfully, testifies that she owes all her success in literature to her father.

We have to lament the death of Sir John Skelton, known as a writer by his pseudonym "Shirley." He was another prop of *Blackwood's Magazine*, which has suffered much in his death and in that of Mrs. Oliphant. Sir John Skelton, who enjoyed his knighthood, if he can be said to have enjoyed it at all, only for a fortnight or so, was an accomplished man, a good critic, a careful writer with a touch of poetry, and an ardent champion of Mary, Queen of Scots. His books on Mary, however, are not to be trusted. They are characterised by Mr. D. Hay Fleming, the first volume of whose great work on Mary will be published in October, as "most unscrupulous." Personally Sir John Skelton was a man of most amiable and delightful character.

W. Robertson Nicoll.

LONDON, July 31, 1897.

PARIS LETTER.

If Henri Meilhac's death had occurred a few years ago people would have wondered how Ludovic Halévy could remain alive. The union of the two writers was almost as complete as that of Erckmann and Chatrian, and they might have been called the Siamese twins of the stage. But the partnership came one day to an end, and now Meilhac has left us and we still possess his quondam literary associate. The question that naturally arises in literary partnership is, How much was the work of one of the partners and how much of the other? We now know that when Meilhac was one of the partners the other one wrote nothing. It is a fact that not a line was ever allowed by Meilhac to be written by one of his associates; but he corrected, revised, erased a great deal when advised by them to do so; never, though, without a struggle. Criticism always made him jump to his feet; he protested against it; he was sure he was right; he never would do what was asked of him, etc. The next day the thing was done, and done with remarkable skill and cheerfulness. And note that in about two thirds of one hundred plays or so that he wrote Meilhac had partners! With Halévy he wrote about one third of the total number, including the best known of them, *La Belle Hélène*, *La Grande Duchesse de Gérolstein*, *Les Brigands*, *La Périchole*, and last, but certainly not least, *Froufrou*. He continued to write charming things for the stage after severing his literary connection with Halévy, and the latter devoted himself to novel-writing. Without Meilhac's help he dared not appear on the boards, for *L'Abbé Constantin* is a dramatised novel and not really a play.

Meilhac's will caused quite a sensation. He had no near relatives, and all his estate goes to his young friend Louis Ganderax, one of the two editors of the *Revue de Paris*. The estate consists of a fine library, a clear two hundred thousand francs, and an income from copyrights of from fifty to one hundred thousand francs, all this due to honest and sturdy literary labour! Everybody is glad of Ganderax's good fortune, and the will will not be contested. So this man of letters' savings will go where he wanted them to go. Will it be the same with Goncourt's?

Causidici (!) certant et adhuc sub iudice lis est.

The *causidici* have had their say; they were Maître Chenu for the contestants, and Maître Raymond Poincarré, the brilliant young politician, for the executors. The Ministère Public who, in this case, is M. Edmond Seligman, will speak next week, and it is now greatly feared that he will reluctantly advise the judges to set the will aside. There can be no doubt about Goncourt's intentions and about his mental sanity; but unfortunately he managed to heap irregularities upon irregularities. The most curious and, if the will does not stand, the most fatal, was his copying an old will made in 1884, introducing into it new clauses, one of which referred to Maupassant's insanity which began in 1892, and preserving the old date of 1884! So you see that the prospects of the Goncourt Academy are not exactly bright at the present writing. But *all* hope is not yet lost that the bench of judges may disregard technical irregularities and pay attention only to the question of the testator's intention and ability to decide for himself.

Among the literary events of the month I must mention (*une fois n'est pas coutume*) a debate which took place in the session of the Chamber of Deputies which has just been closed. The subject of the debate was an interpellation of Professor Jean Jaurès, the Socialist leader, on the causes of the present agricultural distress in France. The debate took place on three successive Saturdays, the first two of which were filled by Jaurès's speech and the last one by an answer by Paul Deschanel, the gifted son of the old professor and literary critic, Émile Deschanel. He admitted that no such treat has been offered for years in the French Parliament to lovers of fine oratory. Jaurès was at his best, and when at his best he is as good as he is bad when at his worst, which is saying a good deal; and Deschanel's finished speech carried the House by storm, and was ordered to be placarded as an official document in every city, town and village of France. His concluding sentences are among the most melodious that ever came from the lips of any French public speaker, and their delivery was as effective as could be. All this is said by me without entering at all into the merits of the controversy.

I may mention here a pleasing incident of the debate. Deschanel had just said that he was afraid that he and his colleague were wasting the time of the House. "You slander yourself!" Jaurès broke in. "Thanks for the compliment," Deschanel rejoined. "Coming from so accomplished a judge as you it cannot but flatter me!" It is the more pleasing that the two men are comparatively young, only forty or forty-two years old.

Not so young as these political athletes are the two men whose letters, now for the first time published in the *Revue de Paris*, are being read, or rather devoured by every thoughtful reader in Europe. One, Renan, is dead; the other, Berthelot, is past seventy. The great chemist prefaces the letters with an introduction which is a delight to every lover of terse and clear-cut French. The two great men's lifelong friendship, though, does not make one forget the inscription which Renan once jocosely proposed for his friend's still unopened grave: "Here lies Berthelot, who occupies here the only situation that was not coveted by him!" But great men's vices and foibles pass and their best work endures.

The name of Ganderax's co-editor on the *Revue de Paris*, Professor Lavisse, will soon appear on the title-page of a work of commanding importance, a *History of France*, which will be published by Hachette. It will fill no less than eight stout volumes. They will not be all Professor Lavisse's work, but he is himself to write a part, and to edit carefully every line. His associates will be Professor Marcel Dubois, for the geographical introduction; Professor Gustave Block for the Roman period; Professor Luchaire for the Middle Ages; Professor Mariejol for the sixteenth century; and Professor Lemonnier for the earlier part of the seventeenth. Lavisse's own share will consist of the reigns of Louis XIV. and Louis XV. The narrative will not go farther than the year 1789.

Strange to say, there is now no standard history of France; Henri Martin's is too bulky and ponderous, Michelet's lacks proportion, Guizot's is marred by the author's too systematic way of looking at history, and also by being originally intended for children. So Professor Lavisse's work is sure to be welcomed, and the names of the writers give every promise of success.

I have not many new books to report this month. The warm season is also the *morte saison* for literature. Abel Hermant, whose clever play, *La Carrière*, I mentioned in one of my last letters, publishes a rather exasperating volume, *Transatlantiques*. It is a series of conversations, in which most of the characters claim to be Americans. But what strange Americans these are! I do not say that Hermant never met them, but if he did it reminds me of a story that is told of Max O'Rell, who having heard an American clergyman just back from France inveigh against the wicked, immoral way in which the French spend their Sundays, answered, "I do not say the gentleman did not see these things, but, then, where did he spend his Sundays when in France?" Still there is wit in *Transatlantiques*, as in everything that comes from the same pen, though a somewhat hysterical kind of wit.

But the book which is in everybody's hands now, and the praises of which are on everybody's lips, is not a French book. It is a translation; and it is as wholesome a book as can be read. It is Nansen's account of his last voyage, *Vers le Pôle*. The French translation, the author of which, Charles Rabot, is himself an explorer of considerable energy, is an admirable piece of work. The book reads as though it had been written in French. I doubt whether Nansen will find a better interpreter in any language. No one will say here, "*Traduttore, traditore!*"

The stage, of course, is rather barren at this time of the year, but the actors of the Théâtre Français are about to start on a kind of literary pilgrimage. In the old restored Roman theatre at Orange they are to play Leconte de Lisle's *Erinnyes* and Jules Lacroix's version of Sophocles's *Antigone*, and in Valence they will assist in the fêtes organised for the inauguration of Émile Augier's statue. Yet while honouring the dead they are not neglecting the living. It is rumoured that next year, or the year after at the latest, they will give one of Ibsen's plays. At any rate, it is known to be the desire of the manager, Jules Claretie. He will meet opposition, no doubt. Will he bear it down? *Qui vivra verra.*

Alfred Manière.

NEW BOOKS.

HALL CAINE AS A DECADENT.*

When, some months ago, we read that Mr. Hall Caine had stated or allowed it to be stated, that the plots of his novels were drawn conjointly from the Bible and the New York *Herald*—that one was the story of Jacob and Esau, another of David and Bathsheba, not forgetting Uriah the Hittite—when we read this we were very sorry. Not that we are squeamish about the dignity of Scripture, or that a great deal of truth as well as of human nature may not be found in the New York *Herald;* but that it seemed to us distinctly a pose, and that a poseur is too self-conscious for great achievements in literary art. But let us be perfectly understood. *The Manxman* is a great book; if the *motif* were taken from that immortal story of Uriah, the Hittite gentleman, we have only to say that the Manx fisherman Pete is not unworthy of his prototype, though Philip is scarcely a King David. Nevertheless, there is a certain scene in *The Manxman* which, in its realistic effect upon the imagination, is distinctly immoral; and when we find the worst features of this scene dragged, by the head and shoulders, with no justification whatever, into *The Christian*, we feel by no means disposed to submit without a protest.

If Mr. Caine had dared, he would have called his new novel *The Christ*, so hard does he labour to convince us of the Christ-like character of "the Hon. and Rev. John Storm." And, indeed, as first presented to us, there seems very little harm in the young man; he is deeply, darkly and desperately in love with Glory Quayle, and a trifle fanatical in his proposed methods of accomplishing certain reforms, glaringly necessary, and which, despite the modern date of the story, no one but John Storm has apparently ever thought of attempting. But all young reformers are, to their own selves, first in their particular field, and invariably just a little fanatical; we could easily pardon these things. Glory, who has come up from the Isle of Man to serve as nurse in a hospital, we are required, at the expense of as great a tax upon our credulity as in the case of Mr. Hardy's Tess, to accept as a pure, innocent, and unsophisticated maiden; but although there are girls who, out of sheer innocence, do things quite as *risqué*, and associate with people quite as questionable as does Glory, they are not altogether of the same brand; Glory is not for a moment innocent at heart; and the sequel proves it.

Other characters of the story, together with the entire stage setting, impress us as if seen reflected in a convex mirror; there is a "Canon Wealthy," who (though wealthy and worldly clergymen abound never so unhappily) strikes us as an impossible sort of type; there is a monastery of the Anglican brand, stricter than any La Trappe, except in regard to the facility with which John Storm enters and leaves it; there are bad, bold, and fashionable men folks, and a herd of theatrical and other sinners, for whom Storm has a marked repulsion and Glory an equally marked affinity. Finally, having taken his "life-vows," John Storm goes utterly and totally insane; prophesies the judgment of God as about to fall on the modern Sodom, *à la* Savonarola, is arrested on the charge of inciting a breach of the peace, and thereby causing a murder; and the charge being fully sustained, he is married to Glory—for reason good and sufficient—and dies in the odour of sanctity, after refusing to give the names of the men who caused his death, murmuring, "Father, forgive them, for they know not what they do."

Now we submit, with all deference, that while a conjunction of Old Testament characters and the New York *Herald* may not be out of reason, the conjunction of the life of Christ and the *Police News* is a great deal too strong; and in the second place that if Mr. Caine wishes to draw such a character as a would-be religious fanatic, insane for love of a woman, and such a woman as Glory Quayle, it is an insult to all Christendom to speak of him as a "Christ-like person," and to indicate by certain pseudo-resemblances, such as that above cited, an analogy which of a

* The Christian. A Novel. By Hall Caine. New York: D. Appleton & Co. $1.50.

surety we should never have discovered for ourselves.

Undoubtedly Mr. Caine wrote his story with a moral purpose ; nor does the present writer belong to that school which would consider such a purpose as vitiating its claim to rank as a work of art. On the contrary, we consider that art without a moral purpose is no art at all, or at the best is of the grade of blue jars, tomatoes and carving knives—all very good things in their way no doubt. But to serve any purpose, moral or otherwise, art must be true ; the representation, even of a blue jar, must be correct. Mr. Hall Caine's drawing, however, is such as might be accomplished by a pocket kodak, held just a little off line ; his colouring reminds us of the toy books of our childhood, in which the red of the Princess Badroulboudour's dress was washed over Aladdin's nose, and Cinderella's slipper, by a halo of weaker blue, was enlarged to fit a Chicago girl. But these reflections are frivolous, while it is very serious indeed to have such a book to reckon with as *The Christian*, which, when all is said, has a sort of insane intensity and power that holds the reader's interest from first to last—and a very long last is more than five hundred pages !

Is it possible to show just where and how the book itself, not merely any or all of the characters, is insane ? Any reader will detect that John Storm is perfectly futile, that he takes up orphanages, working girls' clubs, and what not, and lays them down at Glory's bidding with as much readiness as the fellow in *Venice Preserved* plays dog and barks at his mistress's command. Is this the typical reformer ? Are such institutions managed by such men ? If so, then, indeed, good Lord deliver us ! As a matter of fact, however, despite the popular superstition that all reformers are cranks, the reverse is the truth ; and no reformer can hope to accomplish anything at all worth while until, as was said by somebody, his sympathy has ceased to be an emotion and become a motive. The very sanest and jolliest people whom the present writer knows are reformers ; the next jolliest are both reformers and monks.

But "The Society of the Holy Gethsemane" presents about the most flagrant instance in the story of what we mean by insanity. It is supposed to be under the Benedictine rule, and in the communion of the Church of England ; the "bishop" is the ecclesiastical visitor, and conducts himself in that capacity as surely no bishop ever did, whether in heaven, on the earth, or in places under the earth ; inasmuch as he says : "Whether I approve of your rule or not is a matter with which we have no concern at present ; my sole duty is to see that it is lawfully administered."

The strictness of this "rule" would be burdensome to a Trappist, for the members of the order are not only required to renounce all communication with those whom they loved "in the world," but are even forbidden to pray for them—a refinement of cruelty and a self-defeating ordinance impossible to a Torquemada. Furthermore, having no fear of the Kilkenny cats before his eyes, our author, after many other evidences of inveterate confusion of thought between the Churches of England and of Rome, actually represents the Honourable and Reverend John Storm as on the point, following what he supposed to be Glory's desire, of going out to take the place of Father Damien, taking Glory with him ; the mere idea of which, even minus the wife, would surely have caused that hero, saint and martyr to turn in his grave ! However, when the papers had all announced his departure Glory refused to go. And so did John !

Still, it is very difficult to prove a negative ; and, doubtless, the rules of our modern monasteries being entirely eclectic, it would be a possible thing for any community to elect to live under one such as is described in the text ; but even in Bunyan's time asceticism had had its teeth drawn and its nails pared ; and it would have no chance of survival at all at the present time in the Anglican Communion, except, as we find it, very decidedly modified by modern ideas.

It is a pity that Mr. Caine should have stultified by inaccuracy—which has the effect of ignorance—what should have been a great book ; but it is a greater pity to attempt to destroy vice by familiarising innocent readers with its features, or to present to them, as a champion of woman, and the modern equivalent of Christ, such a weak, futile, hysterical victim of Masochism as "the Hon. and Rev. John Storm."

Katharine Pearson Woods.

A NEW CROP OF DIALECT.*

We have long been resignedly aware that wickedness outvies goodness as literary material. We have had it dinned into our ears, too, that nothing is so lacking in picturesqueness as spick-span cleanliness. Zola's Clorinde was "dirty and untidy," we read, "but nevertheless she looked very beautiful, like some antique statue which is soiled by the dust of a broker's shop, but whose beauty is beyond the power of dirt to conceal." It now remains for some good American to prove that dialect, so far from being a blemish in a novel, is *per se* a thing of beauty, and better than the literary language cultivated by the masters, in that it puts a premium on ignorance and illiteracy, and extols the man o' the people to a pinnacle where he may exert his just influence.

Just what kind of influence this is, it would not be gracious precisely to state. Perhaps those who are stationed in the "central office," where, as over converging wires, the discordant messages of the dialect hunters die in the large and charitable air of no Volapük, are in a position best to know. I well remember the case of a certain reviewer, who, when a Scots tidal wave threatened to inundate our literature and even our stage, now lifting high on its plaid-flecked crest Julia Marlowe and anon splashing the green-and-gold portals of Daly's, gradually lost command of the mother tongue and adopted the lachrymose, skirling *patois* of Ian Maclaren's and Mr. Crockett's stories. To this day his friends believe that he was born in Scotland, and his kailyardish, thistle-downy proclivities give indelible colour to this misapprehension. If it were only Scotch, the dialect which the genius of Burns immortalised, one might consume his own smoke like a good engine; but Scotch is the least part of it. For many years now with what varying delight have we not been obliged to listen to Bret Harte's miners, Mr. Cable's Creoles, Mr. Riley's Hoosiers, Miss Murfree's Tennessee mountain folk, Mr. Garland's Wisconsin farmers, Miss Wilkins's "rural maids in the North," and Mr. Joel Chandler Harris's plantation fables. And latterly there have been Yiddish and Chimmie Fadden and Pink Marsh; and he who readeth the *Sun* finds that there is simply no limit to the elasticity of his dialectic horizòn. On one wire Sheriff Tamsen enriches our literature thus: "Who say dot ding? Der wass no exgayib at all. He wass dischairgdt from der chail." On another wire some one expatiates: "What is ut keeps the childer home from th' parochial school wid their toes shtickin' outen th' holes in their little shoes? Whusky." Then Li Sing of Mott Street pipes up: "No sabe—you talkee flee slilvah. Too much dam bly-and-bly," in marked contrast with which is the leisurely communication of Ole Oleson from the far northwest: "I tell you hay bin vork hard vit skupe schkovel a schkovelin schmoke." From beneath this avalanche of consonants, one attunes his ear to the plaintive contribution of Ambrose Bierce's Little Johnny, who says: "Ime a Repubcan, and my father he is another one, jest like me, but Uncle Ned he is a Demcrat, cos the hethens in their blindnesses bows down to wooden stone, but Mister Pritchell he is a good man and preeches hel fier." Of course the chatter of these types is nothing now to what it will be—when they all begin to intermarry and produce other types. If Johnny or Chimmie should be spared to wed an Hungarian lady, or Ole should become enamoured of Miss Li Sing, or one of Mr. Cahan's Poles should seek the hand of a Bowery "loidy," will any one vouch for the consequences? Surely the American novelist has taken on himself a tremendous linguistic burden.

It is with no small degree of sympathy and self-commiseration, then, that amid this Babel of discord we turn our attention to a new voice from Hell-fer-Sartain (which "empties, as it oughter, of co'se, into Kingdom-Come") in the Cumberland mountains. The sketch which plays the title rôle in this volume is barely five pages long, and consists entirely of dialect. So do five of the sketches which follow. The remaining four are done in plain, direct English. Now it so happens that the ones that possess either a picturesque or a sufficiently subtle tragic interest are clothed in dialect, while all but one of the English sketches ("Through the Gap," a tense, suggestive piece of work) deal with individuals rather than types, and are painfully sad either in theme or in the

* Hell-fer-Sartain. By John Fox, Jr. New York: Harper & Brothers. $1.00.

glimpses they afford of grim, sordid humanity. Hence it is doubly difficult to determine how largely Mr. Fox depends upon dialect for creating his effects—to what extent, in other words, his dialect is vitalising.

A writer in *Macmillan's*, in discussing the abuse of dialect, has observed that Burns's power lay in his clear vision and genial sympathy, not in the use of a particular vocabulary. Scott's elisions and contractions are either melodious (*na* for *not*, and *pu'd* for *pulled*) or as normal as in Latin verse. Wordsworth did not speak the language of the Cumbrian folk; and Charles Lamb confided to John Clare that he was sometimes startled by the provincial phrases in some of the latter's story-telling ballads. "I think you are too profuse with them," he said. From the citation of many examples it is intimated that a genius here and there has been smothered under the speech he used; and one or two principles are enunciated which may be profitably applied to such a writer as Mr. Fox:

> "A dialect literature cultivated for its own sake inevitably tends downward to the utterly provincial or parochial."

And again, granting that we "think in words,"

> "When a thought has been born in dialect, dialect is appropriate for its expression. . . . But as no true artist paints everything he sees, no discriminating writer repeats literally everything he hears."

Mr. Fox has shown that he is capable of avoiding the pitfalls here mentioned. While "A Cumberland Vendetta" is blindingly illiterate, "A Mountain Europa," truly the best thing he has written, is not. Even the sketches of the present volume are so far toned down from their native ruggedness as to be gratefully intelligible. It is probable that the Cumberland mountaineer would ask: "Got ary merlasses?" To which the storekeeper would reply: "Yes, thur's a bar'l out yan in th' back room. Hit taken me a week ter make." Suffice it to say that this is not the manner in which Mr. Fox's characters converse. He does not "repeat everything he hears," nor cultivate dialect literature primarily for its own sake. Nevertheless, a long novel bristling even with the chastened dialect of Mr. Fox, in which the hero and heroine should flounder through successive swirls of their own obscurity, speaking a language we have never heard and, for the time being, throwing into disuse our noble English, would have the specific gravity of Mark Twain's jumping frog—the one that was incommoded in its movements by having swallowed a handful of quail shot. Happily, *The Kentuckians*, now running in *Harper's*, appears to be modelled after "A Mountain Europa" rather than "A Cumberland Vendetta."

Beneath the rough exterior of Mr. Fox's tales there is much penetration and a strong sense of reality. His mountaineers have something elemental in them which makes them interesting despite their strangeness. This, it seems to me, is the true test. When curiosity is sated, we want to feel the impact of a common humanity. There are only a few motives that can appeal to the universal heart. Omar listed them—Fate, Doubt, Roses, Love, Wine. Where Mr. Fox grapples with any of these, though his wine should be "moonshine," he has no infirm touch. With each new story from the hills the question arises, how much pulsating life is there enswathed in the local colour? Is there a clam in the fritter? It is easily possible for the fritter to predominate to the entire exclusion of the clam

George Merriam Hyde.

THE FRENCH REVOLUTION AND ENGLISH LITERATURE.*

It is a sad thing that the critic cannot sometimes strip his mind of things unconsciously borrowed—peel off some of the vestural tissue that Herr Teufelsdröckh talks so much about—and lay bare his literary infidelities. In religious and political matters, this peeling process is too much to expect, for who shall say how much another man's soul needs to keep it warm, or blame him for snatching the first decent covering he can get? If he waited for a perfect spiritual or political fit, the poor creature might never be dressed at all—or at best stalk about in outlandish homespun creeds—mere variations of aborig-

* The French Revolution and English Literature. By Edward Dowden, LL.D. New York: Charles Scribner's Sons. $1.25, net.

inal fetichism. But in matters of taste, in the licensed anarchy of literature, where no man is persecuted for his preferences, where, in fact, individualism is at a premium, there is something pathetic in the way this imitativeness dominates us. It is humiliating to think we take even our tastes at second hand, and that when once told by one having authority that a given author should produce certain effects upon us, we develop all the predicted literary symptoms as faithfully as a hysterical patient who has taken a bread pill.

Crabbe, Coleridge, Wordsworth, Southey, Byron, and Burns are among the authors discussed in Professor Dowden's *French Revolution and English Literature*, and about whom (Heaven help him!) he tries to say something new. It is a heroic attempt, and the spirit of it is fine, if somewhat over-confident, for of these poets, Wordsworth, Shelley, and Burns at least are mere idols, before whom we bow and cross ourselves and mutter literary formulas. The others are classified, stuck through with pins, scientifically named, and that is the end of them. The language we use about them all has long since crystallised into set phrases, and criticism has become an involuntary liturgy. With heads benumbed by the din of imitative praise, we read things into them, but never read them.

When some one comes along and unties those neatly labelled little packages in which industrious classifiers have done up our "standard" writers, we are a trifle annoyed by the disturbance. Professor Dowden, however, does them no harm. He leaves them just as they were, a little the better, perhaps, for that kind of praise which does not cheapen, because it is genuine. Moreover, his object is neither to rhapsodise nor to classify, but to show the effects of French revolutionary thought on contemporary English writers. The antics of reformers who believe in social regeneration by means of phrases, and who monotonously repeat the word "simplification" as a sort of incantation against every kind of evil, are described in an amusing way. Across the Channel the quick translation of metaphysical theorems into practice was tragic enough, but in England, where there was sufficient good, hard sense to prevent such wholesale experiments, the incipient Robespierres are more diverting than deadly. A good specimen of these comical British Jacobins was Mr. Thomas Day, "a worthy eighteenth-century Briton, essentially prosaic, though much out of the common in the degree of his benevolence and generosity; and the burning rays from Rousseau's *Nouvelle Héloise*, *Contrat Social*, and *Émile* fell direct upon his British brain." Professor Dowden goes on to summarise the results very delightfully. Resolving to cultivate the life of simplicity, he began by discarding the use of the comb and brush. Next he sought a wife, but in this his views about hair were an obstacle, although he himself was very moderate in his requirements, placing no value on feminine accomplishments or good looks, and owning but one weakness—namely, a liking for large, white arms. Having broken with one lady on the comb question, he adopted a very safe and logical plan. He took two girls from a foundling asylum and brought them up himself, with a view to choosing as his wife that one of them who showed herself the more thoroughly versed in the knowledge of Nature and Rousseau. But one turned out dull and the other unworthy of his teaching, having shown agitation when to give her hardihood he fired pistols at her petticoats or dropped melted sealing-wax on her arms. Nevertheless he remained true to Rousseau, and in the end gave his life for a principle. "He observed that horses suffer much in the breaking, and decided for himself to apply the pedagogic principles of Rousseau to equine training; the author of *Sandford and Merton* was thrown on his head and received a fatal concussion of the brain."

A better analysis of Godwin's work and influence than that given in Professor Dowden's chapter on the "Theorists of Revolution" would be hard to find. He is a disagreeable old person, this frigid philosopher, and it is pleasant to have him dragged from his grave and put on trial again. And the study of Godwin is the study of the time itself. "The fallacies as well as the truths of *Political Justice* belong less to the individual writer than to the extraordinary epoch in the world's history in which he lived and moved." His view of mankind as "a mass of incarnate syllogisms" contrasts well in the author's hands with Burke's healthy recognition of the intricacy of life as it really is. To Burke Professor Dowden offers up a chapter packed solid with praises, but his admiration is not of the hypnotised sort. It is spontaneous, and hence contagious.

As this book of Profesor Dowden's is limited to the specific object of showing the effects of the revolutionary philosophy on English literature, and as these effects are more or less clear to every one who has read the works of the writers he discusses, it is perhaps unfair to complain of a lack of novelty in his chapters on the old familiar writers. It is no reflection on a man's sincerity that he happens to take the obvious and usual views, and to fall into the obvious and usual manner of expression. Only there are so many books just exactly like other books, and of all people on the face of the earth, the adult American is the least blameworthy for being a bit *blasé*. Our adaptive fellow-countrymen are always interesting except when they write. Then they go off like so many hand-organs reiterating the well-known. Books and reviews give the impression of a patchwork of unconscious quotations. Here and there an American writer gives us his own impressions in his own way, but we could count these on our fingers and possibly on our thumbs. An admired poet of the Connecticut Valley, singing somewhat neurotically, declares that she likes a look of agony because she knows it is real. It is a bloodthirsty sentiment, but excusable. She had tried to see things through the medium of American literary description. It is the same spirit of weariness that drives us to the pages of the "degenerates," for which we are unjustly abused, because apparently the only active brains are those which are diseased. We feel that any actual sensation is better than none, and prefer to shudder through disagreeable pages than stare at blank ones. Such, for instance, is the secret of our interest in a play like Ibsen's *Ghosts*, probably the most unpleasant composition ever written. It is the study of a gradually developing inherited brain disease, but the genius of the author holds you fast, and you read every line of the revolting drama down to the last yell of the full-fledged maniac on the final page. Neurotic prose and paranoiac poetry and the minute scrutiny of the disagreeable are merely the resort of a pardonable ennui, a callousness from contact with the commonplace. Of course it would be pleasanter if talent chose more cheerful paths. We do not really prefer to linger in gutters or hospitals or traverse ten chapters in company with a drunken heroine, but a real writer somehow gets a grip on us, and we cannot leave him. Genuine art has its fascination, even if its origin is pathological and its subject-matter repulsive, not altogether an evil fascination either, for there is a morality in mere good workmanship, while the most virtuous botchwork makes no proselytes to goodness. So we go on reading the works of our decadents up to the last moment when the doors of the sanitarium close behind them, and we would urge that it is not our native depravity that makes us do it, but the unfortunate fact that these men have a certain monopoly of power.

All this is digressive except as an apology for a lack of interest in a new and very praiseworthy book on a praiseworthy topic. It all resolves itself into a feeling of disappointment in its contents, because they do not happen to show the stamp of genius. One little drop of originality undefiled by unwholesomeness would trickle so gratefully down our parched throats. And what a kingdom some unborn critic has waiting for him! Let some real interpreter of literary art come along in this day of critical log-rolling, and he will find the world at his feet, but he will be a real critic, not a Baedeker of classic beauties, telling us to mark the pathos of this phrase, or the genius that animated the poet's mind in the selection of that particular order of words. He will not, for instance, be like our modern contributors to "Shakespeariana," cheapening what is most dear, trampling down the grass in pleasant places; for we are growing tired of taking a cicerone with us when we go for a stroll in our own pastures. When a man throws himself in between us and the books we like, analyses and describes them, tells us what emotions we should have, and ascertains the literary paternity of our author's phrases, we have a right to feel a grudge against him if he is not a genius. Even so modest a book as Professor Dowden's, and one so limited in scope, arouses a little of this antagonism. He has saturated himself with the works of his authors. He proves what he sets out to prove, and he writes agreeably enough. But he is not a great critic, and till the great critic comes, we are better occupied, after all, in reading real books instead of books about books. So the author of *The French Revolution and English Literature* should forgive an American reviewer who ventures mildly to complain that the estimates of Shelley, Byron, Burns, Wordsworth, and Coleridge do not give him the thrill of novelty. It is a gentle impeachment, and merely implies that Professor Dowden's writing has neither the charm of genius nor the fascination of an unsound mind, and that one or the other of these qualities (which he is much happier for being without) is wickedly demanded in these days of voluminous commonplace, especially if one starts to say anything about Shelley, Byron, Burns, *et al.* Yet the complaint seems unfair, when it is remembered that the book is a collection of lectures, delivered originally for pedagogic purposes, and repeated on the occasion of the Princeton Sesqui-centennial. As a series of little studies they are agreeable and instructive, especially for rather young people. It is ill-tempered to find fault with them because they do not happen to meet fantastic requirements. The excuse for this ill temper is, as has been urged before, that these are the days of literary inflation, the era of identical literature as posterity will term it, and the American muse, like the American factory, is remarkable for its enormous output and the uniformity of its products.

Frank Moore Colby.

BURNS'S DEBT TO HIS POETIC FORBEARS.*

What did Burns really owe to the predecessors from whom he openly borrowed much, at whose "flame" (mentioning specifically Ramsay and Fergusson) he acknowledged frankly that he "kindled"? The question is one that should hardly need to be put at this time of day, when criticism has reached a fairly sane estimate of the value —intellectual and ethical—of "loans" in literature, whether of matter or of form. But it has been seriously raised in the Centenary Burns, and as the editors' defective answer to it, announced in their first volume as a "theory" which it was their object to "emphasise," has been reiterated with a trifle of violence in the third volume recently issued, it is well to thresh the subject out at once. The main interest of this third volume, indeed, lies in the restatement of the theory, and in the efforts made in the annotations to supplement the insufficient proof of its validity offered in volumes I. and II. Messrs. Henley and Henderson, then, repeat their argument that, "genius apart," Burns was "*ultimus Scotorum*, the last expression of the old Scots world;" and declare that if it erred, it was not by excess. They proceed to amplify their theory (Vol. I.) that he was "the heir to a flourishing tradition," "the outcome of an environment;" that he "derives from a numerous ancestry," and "is partly an effect of local and peculiar conditions, and partly the product of immediate and remote forbears." These phrases are of course innocent enough in themselves; what they predicate might be predicated of any poet; only, few professional critics would condescend so to hammer the obvious. They are objectionable, in this instance, because they are applied to Burns for a purpose aforethought. In the first volume of the Centenary edition, the theory of Burns's indebtedness to his "ancestry" was propounded as an avowed and deliberate assault on a counter-theory that Burns was "the founder of a dynasty," and also upon another theory of straw, namely that he was an "unnatural birth of poesy and time." It has been said that the theory is reiterated here with violence. It is really only the language that is violent, although in its expanded form the depreciation of Burns which the theory aims at is aggravated; but the attack on the counter-theory is dropped. Messrs. Henley and Henderson do not repeat in set terms their denial that Burns was "the founder of a dynasty." On the other hand, stricken apparently by the obloquy which their affected gibes against the poet's parochialisms had drawn

* The Centenary Burns. Edited by W. E. Henley and T. F. Henderson. Vol. III. Boston: Houghton, Mifflin & Co.

down upon them, they hasten to atone for their fault by elevating Burns to the pedestal of "sole great poet of the old Scots world," although a strict regard for—shall we say justice?—compels them to qualify the eulogy with "those forbears aiding," and a regard for—shall we say consistency?—prompted them still to limit Burns's pre-eminence to "the *old Scots* world."

What is the true theory of Burns's relation to his predecessors and of his place in the poetic hierarchy? He did undoubtedly "derive from a numerous ancestry." He was undoubtedly "partly an effect of local and peculiar conditions, and partly the product of immediate and remote forbears." These are trite and otiose sayings. They are of no value unless as against the theory of straw which makes him "the unnatural birth of poesy and time." Burns borrowed manner, metre, and matter from his Scotch predecessors. The facts, properly stated, without bias, are admitted by everybody everywhere. Much of his song-writing was emendation and reconstruction of familiar Scottish songs; he himself gloried in the fact, and considered it not the least of his services to his race. He purified his country's treasury of song, and made polished jewels out of the rough stones quarried by the hundred forgotten singers who, as Messrs. Henley and Henderson put it, "went to the making of his achievement and himself." Granted that he was not an inventor of new metres; that the four-accent couplet of "The Twa Dogs" and "Tam o' Shanter" had been employed by the Scottish school, and borrowed by it possibly from the "Romaunt of the Rose;" that Fergusson supplied Burns with the stanza of the "Holy Fair" as well as furnishing him with actual models of substance and form in his "Hallow Fair" and "Leith Races." Granted that Burns's realism was a legacy to him from the Scottish school, that, apart from the native bent, he was stimulated to write of that which he saw in the little world about him by the example of his Scottish forbears, from the author of "The King's Quair" downward. Granted that he was the "last of the Scots" in this sense that he crowned the achievements of the Scottish school, beat all the scholars at their own game, and is rightly classed among them, albeit he is the sole occupant of the sixth form and none of his mates rise above the fourth. Yet it is more true to say of him that he was a pioneer, and that by genius and craftsmanship alike he is more closely related to those who came after him than to any of his forbears. Let us look at the point of his taking off from the family-tree of the Scottish school. Compare his "Hallowe'en" and "Holy Fair" with Fergusson's "Hallow Fair" and "Leith Races." The imitation is fully admitted. But what a gulf between the purely "external," aloof, descriptive, unimpassioned comedy of Fergusson's "Leith Races" and Burns's powerful satire, in "Holy Fair," upon the falsehood in religious thought and action that insults reason and corrupts conduct. "Hallow Fair," compared with "Hallowe'en," is as unsympathetic as a photograph. Burns has brought a new thing into the Scottish school, namely, heart, sympathy, humanity—the contribution of an artist and a great man. Burns saw the universal in the particular. That faculty ranks him with the greatest writers of the world; it differentiates him from his forbears of the Scottish school. Take his supreme original creation, "The Jolly Beggars," in connection with which Messrs. Henley and Henderson have made their chief failure to square facts with their hypothesis, interesting as the result of their grubbing for "origins" is. Take their own collation of it with the scene in "Auerbach's Cellar":—"With a superb intelligence the Scot created his people from within, while the German's apprehension of his company is merely intellectual and pedantic." Was it worth while, in face of the convincing genius of Burns, of his admitted influence in the poetic revival of the nineteenth century, of the strong bias he gave to Wordsworth and Byron by his force, fire and truly classic form, and by the example of his success in dealing with the materials he found in himself and the actual life around him—was it worth while to attempt to ventilate Burns's derivation from his "forbears"? Surely not; much less was it worth while to insist, with a show of authority, that he was "not the founder of a dynasty," but "the last expression of the old Scots world." The theory seems, indeed, merely absurd to such as know what Dunbar, the Semples, Hamilton, Ramsay, and Fergusson were capable of, and who know the real value of the Scottish *corpus poeticum*. Its iteration depreciates the work of Messrs. Henley and Henderson considerably in the estimation of serious Burns students. Yet their pursuit of the "origins" of Burns has resulted in the collation and discovery of a number of interesting facts, which in themselves are invaluable aids to criticism. In the third volume of the Centenary edition they present, along with some things that are irrelevant, a good deal of evidence, not hitherto available to the general reader, throwing light upon Burns's process of song manufacture. But a candid reader of their body of annotations cannot but rise from the perusal with the conviction not only that Messrs. Henley and Henderson have failed to prove that "much of the thought, the romance, and the sentiment for which we read and love him [in his songs] were included in the estate which he inherited from his nameless forbears," but that they would have made out a better case on behalf of exactly the opposite contention.

William Wallace.

PROFESSOR RAMSAY'S "IMPRESSIONS OF TURKEY."*

The study of politics was no part of Professor Ramsay's purpose during his wanderings in Turkey and Asia Minor. He is an archæologist with one strong ambition, "to understand the old history of the country which has always been the battle-field between the Oriental and the Western spirit." His first object was to find unknown monuments; but, as he says, "the practical problem of discovery in Asia Minor always presents itself as a study in human nature." To find the monuments you must gain the good-will of the people; to gain their good-will you must deal intelligently with them. The intelligence does not come without watchful observation; and you cannot treat them by invariable rule, for the races and race characteristics are many and diverse. A successful archæologist in Turkish lands, then, is learned in Turkish human nature and in racial and local divergencies; and his observations on the modern condition of the country where he has travelled are worth listening to by politicians. We are the more willing to accept Professor Ramsay's impressions as the truth, because of his excellent candour. He refers you, in most respectful terms, to the evidence of such as think differently both on archæological questions and on politics; he holds his own opinions strongly, but insists on the complexity of the problems, and the limitations of a sojourner's opportunities.

The most fascinating portion of his book, the history of the continuous struggle in Asiatic Turkey between East and West, has of necessity to be brief. This struggle is seen in the Trojan war, in the strife of Xerxes with the Greeks, Europe triumphing splendidly under Alexander the Great, organising its triumphs under the Roman Empire, and spreading them subtly by the Christian religion. Meanwhile the Oriental spirit did not die, but influenced its conquerors, revived under the Byzantine Empire, and steadily grew in power, till at last the Turk reigned in the city of Constantine. Then for centuries it was supreme; but the old enmity has been surging up, and everywhere the Greek element is strengthening. "The Asiatic Greeks have the future in their hands," says this observer, and he adds that the Turks acquiesce. As to the recent revival of Mohammedan feeling, he believes it to be artificial and almost wholly engineered from the palace, and by "that remarkable man, the present Sultan," the Mithridates of the century. It is one of the many independent observations of the book, inviting useful controversy, that the "Turks are not a deeply religious race," and that the fanatical crusade against Christians is mainly artificial—that the Sultan alone is sincere. The conduct of the Powers, and the zealous help of Germany, have aided him magnificently; but Professor Ramsay's experience leads him to believe that there are irresistible forces waging against him in the west and centre of Asia Minor, and that even in the east the Oriental spirit is doomed. "The tide of Western ideas and Western thoughts is flowing and strong; eight

* Impressions of Turkey during Twelve Years' Wanderings. New York: G. P. Putnam's Sons. $1.75.

centuries of strict and stern repression are behind it and drive it onward." The victory is not for the immediate future ; the Oriental revival is directed, he considers, not impartially, but against the intelligent, the orderly, the moderate in Western civilisation. These elements, at least among the Armenians, are being exterminated, with the help of Europe.

His brief survey of the long struggle opens up a vast field for investigation and thought ; but perhaps his notes on the different races in Asia Minor are more useful, and newer to many of us. "The interlacing and alternation of separate and unblending races" is the feature he most insists on. "Christian and Moslem" is a crude, misleading distinction. The Turk hates the Mohammedan Circassian more than he does the Greek. It is not mere information Professor Ramsay gives ; he asks questions, too : whether the Turks are not merely settled Turkomans, those spirited, hospitable nomads, those utter barbarians, to whom must be given the chief credit for the destruction of Roman civilisation ; and whether the fierce Kurd is not merely the Mohammedan Armenian. The unpopular, mean-spirited, crafty, inhospitable Armenian is, he believes, only the product of a persecution which is very, very old ; the free Armenians cling desperately to their freedom, are haughty and spirited, as the story of the Zeitunli proves. And though a wanderer in Turkey will prefer, as a rule, to deal with Turks, Professor Ramsay puts a limit to this preference. The Turk is a good fellow, but stupid according to every Western test. Educated he becomes unpleasant. The moral discipline of intellect is always a possibility to the Armenian, the finer specimens of whom rise immeasurably higher. He is probably more in general agreement in his judgments on the Armenians than on the Greeks ; but here, as in every judgment on human nature, Professor Ramsay convinces us by his unexaggerated recitals of experiences, by his admissions, that his opinions are both first-hand and trustworthy.

"The instinct to trade and to haggle and to extort is just as real in the Turk as in the Greek ; but in the former it is often dormant, owing quite as much to pure ignorance as to real generosity. I have experienced, proportionately, at least as much kindness and generosity and hospitality among Greek villages as among Turks ; but, as it happens, I have stayed at a hundred times as many Turkish villages as at Greek."

The cultivated Greeks, too, he has found lavishly generous and helpful to any archæologist who takes the trouble to be genial. But neither Greeks nor Turks have the making of a strong nation by themselves. "In union and amalgamation of the races lie the hope of Asia Minor." There is the "bar of religion ;" but the "example of the third century shows that the bar is not indestructible."

It is impossible even to suggest all the interesting points of Professor Ramsay's travel experiences, or the new questions suggested in archæology, ethnology, history and politics. One of these, perhaps, he will investigate and develop at some later day—the question of the possible existence of a Jewish aristocracy in the Eastern Roman Empire. We can only assure readers that no more attractive and no more independent book has been written about the troubled Turkish countries. We should also like to mention a little detail of arrangement in which the writer ought to find many imitators : his systematic references to the pages of his book where kindred subjects are dealt with.

A SON OF THE OLD DOMINION.*

A Son of the Old Dominion is a blend of an old-fashioned love-story and an historical study. And when it has been said that the history sometimes gets the better of the romance, the work has received as harsh a criticism as it merits.

There have been several ambitious attempts of late to write the great American novel. But the great American novel is like the sea-serpent, an unrealised monster which is discovered about once every six months, and is never seen by more than three people at a time. Those who are enamoured of New England local history professed to find it in *King Noanett*, Mr. Stimson's laborious compilation ; but I fear we can hardly award so great an honour to that monument of diligence. Perfection in art is

* A Son of the Old Dominion. By Mrs. Burton Harrison. Boston : Lamson, Wolffe & Co. $1.50.

so difficult, and success so delicate a matter, that the least unhappy touch or trend, the least fault in aim, may mar a noble undertaking. Even a too great care, a too strenuous endeavour may spoil everything, by giving us a sense of strain, rather than of strength ; the artist may be warped by the very force of his determination to accomplish great things ; and his own air of set purpose steals into the work under his hand, and all unknown to him robs it of that fine flavour of inevitable and unconscious charm.

Both *King Noanett* and *A Son of the Old Dominion* show the loving and scrupulous pains that have been lavished upon them. As pictures of colonial times, they are not easily to be surpassed ; as pieces of fiction they would have gained in freedom, in effectiveness, in beauty if their authors had been a little less familiar with their subject, and a little less impressed with the importance of endeavour. In affairs, to try hard enough is to succeed ; but in art, to try too hard is certainly to fail. Both these recent historical novels are examples of the danger I mean. So bulky a work as *King Noanett* may very well seem to its author his most considerable contribution to the difficult art of story-telling, yet a cool judgment can hardly give it a place beside *Guerndale* or Mr. Stimson's short stories ; nor will *A Son of the Old Dominion* bear comparison, as an artistic achievement, with Mrs. Burton Harrison's slighter society sketches.

Our conscientious school of realism has taught us, by dint of much example, the importance of details and the value of common life ; but as we recede from contemporary subjects, the details become of less and less importance, the every-day life becomes more and more tedious ; the human action alone holds the place of exclusive interest. Shakespeare is full of glaring historical inaccuracies, absurd anachronisms, and ridiculous local colour ; and it does not matter in the least that he is so.

So that while the highest praise is due Mr. Stimson and Mrs. Harrison for their last books, that recognition is due to their labour in the field of historical research rather than in the realm of original creation.

A Son of the Old Dominion is well constructed, well written, simple and straightforward in sentiment ; it has love, romance, war, intrigue, politics, patriotism, two heroes, two heroines, a heavy villain, a leading old lady, a leading old gentleman, a changeling heir to an English title, a naughty but penitent old nurse, Indian massacres, a crazy old woman who lives all alone in the wilderness, a desperate fight in a stockade, stolen papers, a foot-race, riding to hounds, daring feat of a young girl under the eyes of painted savages, General George Washington — in short, everything that a good, stirring, married-and-were-happy-ever-after-with-destruction-to-the-villain romance should possess.

It has only one fault : there are too many words in it. It is too accurate in its atmosphere ; the tedious elaboration of the eighteenth century has been reproduced for us too faithfully. At least this will be so for the average reader, who desires rapidity in his tales before all else. To the more careful and deliberate student of letters and times the book will appeal as an interesting experiment in the manner of a hundred years ago, reviving for us the very life of those colonial days, which were at once so exciting to the senses, so soporific to the mind. Both these qualities of a bygone age Mrs. Harrison has reproduced with a charming faithfulness, so that, turning its leisurely pages of a summer afternoon, one hardly knows whether to be aroused by its adventurous plot and stirring incidents, or to fall asleep over the interminable prolixities of its style.

Bliss Carman.

SCHOPENHAUER ON HUMAN NATURE.*

Schopenhauer was nearly always dealing with human nature, and as a living, suffering organism, too, not merely as a subject for anatomical study. That has given him his philosophical influence, and not feats in logic or intellectual subtlety. The essays translated here are no rigid summary of his views ; they only contain scraps of them. On the whole they seem more insubstantial,

* On Human Nature. Essays (partly posthumous) on Ethics and Politics. By Arthur Schopenhauer. Selected and translated by T. Bailey Saunders. New York : The Macmillan Co. 90 cts.

as was Uncle Jack that "this here thing people calls love it takes holt of people in differ'nt and war'ous ways." But it is perhaps a cause for gratitude that Colonel Johnston has attempted to delineate so small a segment of Georgia life, he does it so feelingly and entertainingly. The characterisation is vital so far as it goes. Eben Bull with his slow wink, contemplative manner, and asthmatic utterance, is a type of man with which the plays have made us tolerably familiar; and Mr. Pate, who in Georgian parlance "had heard it thunder too often" to distinguish one morning the clarion notes of his pet rooster, tells the story of his deafness with a sorrowful air which is very humanising. Taken as a whole, the book is emotional rather than intellectual, and lacks the sedulous minuteness and breadth of realistic treatment inhering in the earlier work, while it gains immensely in refinement and chivalrous regard for woman.

G. M. H.

A BUNDLE OF STRANGE TALES.*

There is a wide difference between the "Jules Verne of England" and the "Bret Harte of the Pacific," as Messrs. Wells and Becke have been respectively dubbed—a difference made plain to the reader by the distinct classification into which they have fallen in the public estimation. Like Jules Verne, Mr. Wells, in these thirty strange stories of his, entertains and delights with his inexhaustible power of invention, his quick, dexterous legerdemain, and startling ingenuity. It is like watching a conjuror to read these stories, and each story, like a new trick, but increases your wonder and piques your curiosity to see what the performer will make of the next venture. And like a trick that, once seen, is apt to be forgotten and can be enjoyed again, so we have read with fresh zest a number of these stories which originally appeared in an English magazine. They make no appeal to the emotions, their aim is simple entertainment, and we should say that few books published this summer for light reading afford the amount of pleasure to be derived from these five hundred pages. "The Strange Orchid,' for example, relates the strange adventure of an orchid-hunter, who almost became the victim of a strange specimen, which he exultantly carried from the auction room to his hothouse, and which used its tentacle-like, aërial rootlets one day as leech-like suckers upon its owner. Fortunately he was extricated from its tenacious grasp just in time to save his life, as he was being bled to death by the horrible plant. "Æpyornis Island" tells a wonderful tale of the discovery of an Æpyornis egg, "Sindbad's roc was just a legend of 'em," and of its hatching on a small island where its finder had been cast adrift, with only this monstrous bird for company. "The Plattner Story" is of a man who got blown out of space into the Fourth Dimension, and who, after an absence of ten days, was again accidentally blown back again. But the funny part of it is that somehow before Plattner returned to space an inversion of his right and left sides had taken place, just as if his reflected body had walked out of a mirror. "The Story of the Late Mr. Elvesham" is a sort of Faust-up-to-date, with Marguerite left out; and so on with the whole thirty stories; each turns on some fresh and ingenious idea, which is worked out with a mathematical nicety that for the time being gives realism to the story and makes it appear very probable and perhaps possible. Mr. Wells has a quiet, sly sort of humour, too, that keeps his stories within the domain of comedy, and few of them end so tragically as "The Argonauts of the Air," those daring pioneers of the flying machine. A better book of short stories for the idle hour or for that tired feeling it would be hard to find.

Pacific Tales is of another sort. Here, as in Bret Harte, we are brought into contact with rough, uncivilised forms of life and with exhibitions of untamed, savage aspects in nature and in human nature. The luxurious colour and riotous vegetation of the tropics form the background of these tales; life throbs behind the pages; and as onlookers, the artist in the author has the power to make us quicken with sympathy or sicken with disgust, as he unveils the wickedness, the weakness, the crime existing alongside of the loveliness, the

* Thirty Strange Stories. By H. G. Wells. New York: Edward Arnold. $1.50.
Pacific Tales. By Louis Becke. New York: New Amsterdam Book Co. $1.50.

pathos, the strange, wild beauty of life in the islands afar off in the South Seas. A weird spell falls upon the reader when he comes under Mr. Becke's sway—a spell that seems of the land, the atmosphere, the clime. There is a grim tenacity about the way in which his work fastens upon the imagination and haunts the memory, as if for the nonce you had passed with him into that strange land and had lived through the sights and scenes painted before your eyes with magic writing, not with a descriptive pen. In the search for local colour it is to Mr. Becke the student or the reader or the romancer must go for a true picture of the native life and customs in the South Sea Islands. Mr. Becke knows the Pacific as few men have ever known it, as few men with the experience of a lifetime since boyhood could know it. He is also one of the rare men who have been talented enough to combine roaming and writing to a degree that has commanded interest and respect for their work. Those who have visited the South Seas testify to the accuracy of detail and the fidelity to truth which stamp all his work. But something more than mere observation and knowledge is needed to impart the thrill of pleasure and touch of potency that give force to these stories and invest them with their supreme attraction, and this is the endowment of the artist. Mr. Becke has this power to vitalise the raw material which he has come by so richly, and with it he has also the power to enthrall, to fascinate, but as frequently with repulsion as with attraction.

James MacArthur.

THE GREATER NORTHWEST.*

Of the three handsome volumes just issued by Mr. Francis P. Harper, entitled *New Light on the Early History of the Greater Northwest*, the first two contain the diary of Alexander Henry, a fur-trader in the service of the Northwest Company, together with a digest of the manuscripts of David Thompson, astronomer, geographer, explorer, and discoverer, whose work was done first for the Hudson Bay Company and afterward for its energetic and hated younger rival. The third volume, thinner than its predecessors, is filled up with maps, and an index of most scholarly and minute comprehensiveness. The material is edited by Dr. Elliott Coues, with a critical and explanatory commentary, so copious and so painstaking that the whole work, as it stands, is a monument to the editor no less than to the author. It is issued in a limited edition of eleven hundred numbered copies.

As a contribution to the history of the Northwest Henry's journal is invaluable. Other explorers in the same field have left more or less complete records of their achievements. The work before us does not cause any great reversal of accepted conclusions, but corroborates and immensely enlarges our store of knowledge on the subject. The journal covers the years from 1799 to 1814, and a tract of country extending from Lake Superior to the Pacific, from the southern borders of Wisconsin and Oregon to the northern limits of Saskatchewan and Alberta. It is written with all the freshness and veracity of immediate observation, the author's custom having obviously been to post up his diary at the end of each day's travelling or trafficking. It is written also with the bold fidelity to fact of the unimaginative man who sees no further than before his feet, and is not concerned to make deductions. For the annalist this is the ideal temper; and the historian who has to draw upon these pages for material will gratefully recognise their simplicity.

It is at first a matter of wonder that the author of such an important work as this should have so long remained unknown. The reason is found in the fact that Henry was by no means versed in the arts of composition, and left his manuscripts in such a shape that no publisher could undertake to print them as they stood. The source of the volumes before us is a manuscript copy made by one George Coventry, about 1824, and now lying in the library of Parliament at Ottawa. It consists of more than sixteen hundred pages of legal cap, and bears every evidence of being a faithful transcript of Henry's

* New Light on the Early History of the Greater Northwest. The Manuscript Journals of Alexander Henry, Fur Trader of the Northwest Company, and of David Thompson, Official Geographer and Explorer of the same Company, 1799–1814. Exploration and Adventure among the Indians on the Red, Saskatchewan, Missouri, and Columbia Rivers. Edited with Copious Critical Commentary by Elliott Coues. New York: Francis P. Harper.

own note-books. The style is so stilted, cumbersome, weighted with circumlocution and repetition that readers would have been hopelessly repelled by it. This mine of information, therefore, had to wait for an editor with the requisite patience and requisite knowledge for its development, as well as for a publisher ready to take the risk of so costly a venture. In Dr. Coues the old fur-trading diarist has found at last the editor whom he needed for the establishment of his fame. His writings, under tactful revision and condensation, have been made extremely readable, without sacrifice of the author's personality; and Dr. Coues, from the fulness of his scholarship in this field, has brought out the full value of Henry's material by presenting it in its relation to the works of other authorities, such as McKenzie, Franchin, Ross, and Samuel Hearne.

It is not for his contributions to our geographical knowledge that Henry is significant. He followed, for the most part, beaten trails. But none of the chroniclers of his time could rival his knowledge of the Northwest Indian tribes. He knew their habits, customs, and points of view; and his unshrinking pen describes them with a merciless lack of extenuation. The picture is not generally a romantic or attractive one, but it bears the stamp of truth; and the editor has done wisely to remember that in a book of this sort, which makes its appeal to the student rather than to the family circle, expurgation would have been an impertinence. It would have seriously impaired the accuracy of a picture which perpetuates vanished conditions.

The whole of Volume I. is taken up with the Red River region, which includes a strikingly picturesque account of a tour among the Mandans, in 1806. The force and directness of the narrative are at times startling in their effect. The incidents stand out in unforgettable relief. The second volume contains Part II., dealing with the Saskatchewan country, and Part III., describing the Columbia. Both accounts are of the highest ethnographical value, and should be studied by all who are concerned in those Indian problems for whose solution our race is unquestionably responsible. Henry shows a remarkable skill, throughout the whole work, in differentiating the numerous tribes that came under his observation. It was late in 1813 that he arrived at the mouth of the Columbia, at the Astoria settlement, which Irving's work of that name has immortalised. Had Irving been fortunate enough to have access to Henry's papers his romance, without sacrifice of literary quality, might have been made more like history and less like fiction. Here, on May 22d, 1814, Henry was drowned in the waters of the Columbia while on a canoe expedition from Fort George.

The contributions of David Thompson to this work are of great extent and value, but not incorporated with the main text. Embodied in the foot-notes they serve the purposes of comparison and elucidation. The manuscripts of Thompson's notes, covering the whole of his active career, are preserved in the archives of the Crown Lands Department of Ontario, at Toronto. Only those documents, however, which cover approximately the period treated in Henry's diaries are made use of by Dr. Coues. Consisting as they do of tables, reports, bare scientific data, astronomical calculations and meteorological records, they could have no interest to the reading public and no place in book-form except when presented as Dr. Coues has presented them. In this connection their value and significance are made to appear. The journeyings of the two men often coincided both in time and place. They were continually coming at least within rumour of each other. But they betrayed so little affection for each other's companionship that it seems the very irony of fate that their names and their work should at last come to be so inextricably bound up together as they are in the present volumes.

Charles G. D. Roberts.

A DOG'S VIEW OF THINGS.*

In painting, notably in the work of Sir Edwin Landseer and his followers, animals are almost invariably endowed with human characteristics and attributes; in literature, embracing all the folk-lore concerning animals from *Æsop's*

* Diomed: The Life, Travels, and Observations of a Dog. By John Sargeant Wise. Boston: Lamson, Wolffe & Co. $2.00.

Fables to Joel Chandler Harris's *Uncle Remus*, and Kipling's *Jungle Books*, this is also true. Indeed, until the appearance of *Diomed* there has been no literature from the point of view of animals. It is the distinction of *Diomed* that this canine narrative carries conviction with it as being decidedly the dog's view of things. *Diomed*, in short, is a unique achievement in the realism of animal literature.

Hunting and travelling in reminiscence with men and dogs of all sorts and conditions, "Di" ranges the country from New York to Texas, from Florida to Minnesota, making philosophical reflections and comparisons, finding the best and healthiest in every one and in everything with the same infallible instinct that guided him in finding birds.

Diomed is a setter of the old Virginia stock, proud of his pedigree and of his master's family, with an aristocrat's indulgent contempt for the *parvenus* who come from nowhere or anywhere, and are anybody or nobody, but who just happen somehow to get hold of or live upon a James River plantation, and before five years have gone by begin posing and talking about the olden times and the genuine representatives of the old Virginia stock. "James River water," he reflects, "must put such notions in men and dogs."

On the other hand, in the chapter called "High-Toned Shooting," Di expresses his opinion of one Dash, a huge, heavy-looking liver-and-white setter, which an English gentleman brings with him on a memorable hunt. Dash is undoubtedly of the highest breeding; but Diomed is more impressed by his appetite for Devonshire hams than by the report of his work in "the turnips." Indeed, what "the turnips" are Di does not even know until Dash—whom the hams have made thirsty—exhausts his capacity as a reservoir and comes lumbering up, looking over the beautiful brown stubble, which to an energetic American dog promises unlimited sport, and says: "Where are the turnip fields?" "The what?" says Di. "The turnip fields, where the birds are," says Dash. "See here, Dash," Di remonstrates, "you cannot expect ham and turnips both. What do you want—the earth?" "Well, you know," the English dog protests as they gallop along, "one cawn't be expected to scour a beastly wilderness like this for birds. How shall we ever think where to look for them, seeing there are no turnip fields?"

With its quietly sustained humour the narrative rambles along over a half score years or more—the long life of a dog who knows, sees, and feels no more than we have known a dog to do if he has come into our life and shared our good and ill fortune in comradeship. Mr. Wise, in his preface, holds himself responsible for Diomed, however, and invites the reader to put down to the author's score whatever Di thinks or says that he believes a dog could not think or say. But there is nothing undoglike in the pure fun Di has with all the world. The narrative is told in retrospect, and once in a while a rheumatic twinge arrests the old dog's thoughts, causing him to reflect sadly on the vanities of life. The sincerity, the optimism, the keen yet kindly analysis of life under many aspects, among men who are known in the world and men who are known in the army, in the rugged distances of Texas, or the decay of Williamsburg, that "Diogenes of corporations which, having nothing, wants nothing, asks nothing save that the sunlight, in which its burghers bask in idleness, be not obstructed by intruders"—these, with its wealth of cheer and unfailing humour, are the characteristics which will distinguish *Diomed* from all other books of the day, and which will place what purports to be the autobiography of a dog beside the great human autobiographies and similar literary achievements that reach out beyond their special audience to one of universal interest.

The author thoughtfully suggests in his preface that "it is all so arranged that it may be taken in broken doses. Every chapter is independent of the other save that all are bound together by the thread of a dog's life—and who minds clipping that?"

But we do mind; and as we lay down the story of Diomed we place it beside those few fortunate books that are not of fad or day, but which are read and reread even as Di and his master return again and again to the scenes that they cherish. We are richer for the memory, which this book has brought us, of some true friends.

Marguerite Tracy.

BOOKS AND THEIR MAKERS.*

Mr. Putnam has brought his noble task to a worthy conclusion. His first volume dealt mainly with the monasteries and their *scriptoria*, and brought us down to the beginning of the sixteenth century and the early printer-publishers of France. As Mr. Putnam points out, any account of the production and distribution of books during the two centuries immediately succeeding the invention of printing "must, of necessity, be chiefly devoted to the operations of the printer-publishers of the period." Thus it happens that this present volume deals with the Estiennes of France, Caxton of England, the Kobergers of Nuremberg, Froben of Basel, Plantin of Antwerp, and the Elzevirs of Leyden and Amsterdam. As it happened, a few great scholars of the time had also special influence on the development of the new art, and Mr. Putnam devotes three chapters to Isaac Casaubon, Erasmus, and Luther.

The printing offices of the middle ages were mainly busied with the production of editions of the Bible, the Greek and Roman classics, the works of the Fathers, and a few philosophical and legal treatises. With the Reformation a new impetus was given; a new reading public arose, and to meet their demands for cheap literature the pamphlet and the *Flugschriften*, or fly-leaf literature, came into existence. These brought about the censorship (ecclesiastical and civil) of the press, with its consequent *Indices Expurgatorii*. As the influence of the Reformation became more marked, and the effects of the Renaissance extended and deepened, and finally gave birth to a contemporary literature, the printers forsook the older works, and took to printing the new literature of the enlightenment. Whereas before, printers themselves selected what the public was to read, the time had now come when they were compelled to produce what the people wanted, and what the people wanted was quickly made known by the poets, historians, theologians, and philosophers who came after the great revivals in religion and learning.

Mr. Putnam, with a care truly astonishing, traces the growth of this story in all its details. He is so anxious to omit nothing that he often repeats himself; but in a work which will not be read consecutively, but used for reference largely, such repetition is perhaps a gain.

We have little to say for Mr. Putnam's volume that is not in its praise. An exhaustive treatment of it would, we are convinced, but make more evident its many good qualities. We have tested it in several instances, only to find it admirable alike in its presentation of facts and in the faithfulness of the record of the facts themselves.

Temple Scott.

* Books and their Makers during the Middle Ages. By G. H. Putnam. Vol. II., 1500–1709. G. P. Putnam's Sons. $2.50.

NOVEL NOTES.

LEONORA OF THE YAWMISH. By Francis Dana. New York: Harper & Brothers. $1.25.

The would-be hero of this tale descended somewhat abruptly and mysteriously upon Leonora's premises. As nearly as we can gather he had been following a watercourse up among the Olympics in the far Northwest and fell over a precipice, not all at once, but from tree to tree, till he was gently deposited, with his clothing considerably torn, on a bed of deep, rich moss. Two faces were soon bending over him, one pale and fair, the other that of Leonora's butler, who inquired: "Am you broke at all, sah? May I take the liberty of feeling for shattered bones, sah?" With careful nursing the adventurous wayfarer was soon in a condition to be teased by his captor, who, despite her gold-mounted revolver and other up-to-date trappings, posed with some effect as the ignorant girl of the forests, and drew from him much trite information about the "outside world." However, his inability to take a joke did not deter him from asking her hand before his departure for Boston. There, after a couple of years, a Mrs. Merivale, who "needed him"—that is, his money—inveigled him into another engagement, and the remainder of the tale is occupied with the tactful execution of her plans respecting the disposal of Leonora, which were nothing less Shakespearian than to palm off upon the latter a younger brother of her *fiancé*, who looked for all the world like him. Tom was at that moment "keeping death off at the pen's point," and had first to be reinstated in a competence. After much coaching he crossed the continent and essayed his merry task; but neither by athletic prowess nor by the telling of an unconscionable number of lies did he succeed in convincing Leonora that he was not an impostor. Ever fond of laying "springes to catch woodcock," she entrapped him into the admission that he "remembered" what never had occurred. His identity known, he made love on his own account, and won her, remaining in the West to "live down" the impression made by his duplicity. Having declined his brother's bribe, he was again cast upon his own resources, and went to Seattle, where the only employment offered him was that of a hearse driver, which he refused. His cedar stick, however, attracted the attention of a lumberman, and these twain soon had hewn a fortune out of the forests surrounding Leonora's Olympic home. So that the grumpy old father who had followed a wounded bear up the Yawmish and "located" far from human strife builded better than he supposed.

Not less clever than the plot which we have outlined is Mr. Dana's manipulation of incidents. These are not only closely interwoven with the story, but in themselves are amusing, and at times even startling. His natural description is like a tin cup of water from one of the cold eddies of a mountain stream—unadorned but refreshing. He is conventional, and in that degree disillusionising, only in the love scenes, which are by far the weakest part of a rugged and not altogether polished but very fascinating story.

PINK MARSH. By George Ade. Chicago: H. S. Stone & Co. $1.25.

Why should there not be pink marshes as well as red scaurs or yellow pines? A volume put forth by a Chicago journalist and bearing the title *Pink Marsh* should not only be tinged with local colour but smack delicately of the soil. One bethinks oneself not unnaturally of the berouged historic soil of Clark Street, and wonders if the post-office is by this time sufficiently unbuilt to have permitted Mr. Ade to consult the displaced river slime upon which it rested for some years. Imagine our surprise, then (in confessing which we betray, perhaps, an unpardonable ignorance of Chicago newspapers), on glancing at the numerous drawings which Mr. Ade's sketches illustrate and discovering that Pink Marsh is William Pinckney Marsh, bootblack and "brush" in one of the subterranean barber shops indigenous to the Windy City, and that the "collah" that pervades the little volume is racial rather than local. This young Afro-American speaks a *patois* that differs phonetically both from that invented by Mr. Joel Chandler Harris, and that which, thanks to the *Sun*, obtains in New York City. It may be questioned whether one would wish to recognise such linguistic eccentricities as "disohdehly" and "p'opehty" outside of their context. In the main, however, Pink's characteristics are convincingly truthful, and as picturesque as is compatible with his tonsorial environment. He appeals widely to the great workaday heart, where he is represented as suffering from too much domination: "Misteh Cliffo'd, he's boss; Misteh Adams, he's sup'ntenden'; Misteh Bahclay, he's manageh, and 'at new bahbeh, he's fo'man. Yes, seh; I'm wuhkin' faw fo' men heah." Many of his ideas are so original that one could wish his interlocutor used less hackneyed means of eliciting them. Such cues as "Be virtuous and you will be happy" and "Procrastination is the thief of time" are fatiguing and jar on the humour or pathos of the situations in which they occur. And the parade of long words which left Pink open-mouthed and staring into vacancy produces a sense of shame even in the reader. Here was a chance, incidentally and by way of contrast, to sketch a gentleman, who should impress Pink by his freedom from priggishness and braggadocio and the other spurious qualities with which his understudy may be inoculated locally. Next time we wish Mr. Ade would bestow more attention on his lay figures.

CONSTANTINE. By George Horton. Chicago: Way & Williams. $1.25.

This is a very informing tale, by which epithet we mean that the author has smothered a tender little love-story, capable of being as simple and impressive as Mr. Jorge Isaacs's *Maria*, under a detailed account of Grecian social and domestic customs. Two men are like brothers, and one dies. This is an opportunity for divers information respecting rites of burial, a mœrologist being called in to sing a mœrologian, or death song, which Mr. Hudson "actually heard." Then the orphan Constantine is baptised at great length, and through a professional match-maker, who affords a text for another excursus, a wife of Xanthippe extraction is secured for his godfather. They beget a daughter, whom on page 126 Constantine discovers that he loves. Meanwhile, the children play *mora* together, and with religious pomp christen a cat Cinnamon String Bean, availing themselves of the shreds of ceremonial left over from Constantine's own baptism. They also look forward to Easter Day, when Christian brothers and sisters may exchange the kiss of holy love, which is the author's excuse for introducing an elaborate description of a church service. So, throughout the story, there is always something to divert the reader's interest from the main affair. One could wish that the superfluous explanatory matter, however timely it may be, had been embodied in a separate volume. Constantine displays all the impetuousness and loyalty a Greek lover should, and comes to the lovelorn, bedraggled state in which, at the Poros monastery, the sea captain who tells the story of his life finds him, through no fault of his own, but, we are asked to believe, by one of those ironical twists of fate whereby "the best laid plans o' mice and men gang aft agley." His godfather, who sympathised with his love affair, dying inopportunely, the treasure-trove which he rightfully inherited was withheld from him through the perfidy of a friend until Aneza, whom he loved, yielded to circumstances and her mother's stronger will and became the bride of another. Henceforth we read of Constantine as the "crazy man" presenting the pitiable spectacle, with which novelists have familiarised us, of a human mind in ruins. Nothing is more unique or touching than the love letter wherein he writes to Aneza: "You are sweeter than cold water, . . . my little bird, my orange." The simplicity of the author's style is marred by an occasional choice of the wrong word, as where the raindrops are said to have "pimpled" the harbour. "Frenchy" and "Greeky," too, are more colloquial than exact. Thrice does "bah, bah, bah" occur as a Greek exclamation of surprise, and we are at a loss to

last is dim, for in the story, as in real life, the shadow lingers till the end. The author does not convince the reader of what he himself apparently believes—that the man and the woman who have suffered most win the long denied happiness at last. It is true that they are married, but from the wedding day "years of struggle and ostracism lay before them," and the husband says to the wife at the close of the story:

"Nothing that a man or a woman alone can do can restore lost honour or self-reverence. No fasting or penance or sacrifice is of any use."

DEAR FAUSTINA. By Rhoda Broughton. New York: D. Appleton & Co. $1.00.

Other times, other manners, guises and conversation Miss Broughton gives us in her very clever novel, *Dear Faustina*, the adventuress up to date. She is not so bewitching as in the days of Becky Sharp, but what she lacks in charm she makes up for in energy. With her quick intelligence she knows this is not the day of individual power, but of associated effort; and her greatest harvest is reaped not in the exploitation of persons, but of causes—persons, of course, are convenient tools, to be used with skill and flung aside when done with. To Althea Faustina is apostle and saint, for whom she is called to give up kith and kin and comfort Following her into the wilderness—that is, the slums and the working-places of the world, she finds her sainthood the worse for wear, her apostleship a sham; while from the disciple, in the name of a cause, are expected dishonour and vulgarity. Miss Broughton resists the temptation of sending Althea permanently back to domesticity when her disillusionment takes place. She makes satire effective by keeping it within bounds, and saving a few public-spirited persons and the general philanthropic idea from its lash. Miss Broughton's humour plays around and tests all, but only the humbugs are mercilessly flayed.

THE MASSARENES. By Ouida. New York: R. F. Fenno & Co. $1.25.

"Ouida" here lashes the sins and follies of Society—very high society, of course; the chief lady-villain is accustomed to walk about in Homburg with the King of Greece on one side of her and the Duc d'Orleans on the other. She lives in an exceedingly corrupt world in London, has a disreputable noble husband, and is noble and gracefully disreputable herself. All the vices that extravagant habits and constant impecuniosity can breed are hers. When in desperate straits she hangs on to the impossible new millionaires from Kerosene City, N. D.; and for very substantial wages she agrees to convince the finest society that these dreadful people are not only possible, but absolutely must be swallowed. But Massarene, the millionaire, was never robbed or humbugged in his life, and he makes her pay in more than society favour. The story is a very ugly one; and her career is studded with others as bad. One stumbling-block in her path is Massarene's daughter. In spite of her birth the girl might have been the daughter of kings—Ouida knows how to make them such—but she has no vulgar ambitions. This singular and meritorious young woman "preferred to be alone in the music-room, with her violin and harmonium, or in the library comparing Jowett's *Dialogues* with the original." Needless to say, the lady-villain's plans are a good deal upset by the heiress's charitable disposal of the wealth so soon as it comes into her keeping, and, of course, virtue is rewarded by marriage with a high-minded nobleman. It is a pitiful confession to make; but at no point are we deeply indignant at the condition of things Ouida exposes. Perhaps never are we quite convinced that they just happened so. Yet in a rough-and-ready, exaggerated fashion she lashes sins that do exist, and we can only hope that her satire may accomplish some of the good it evidently intends to do. It is not going out of the way to remark that though Ouida's popularity may have been lessened by the tremendous success of Marie Corelli, in intellectual merits, in imaginative and structural faculties, as well as in versatility, she still keeps far ahead of that beloved-of-the-nations disciple and rival. But the book provokes one protest from even an easy-going reader. Let her lash "Society" if she likes. Let her slander it, if she will only leave children alone. There may be detestable little atoms among them; but she has invented the cynical, evil-minded worldling of four. Happily it is not in her power to make the little monster live.

THE STEPMOTHER. A tale of Modern Athens. By Gregory Xenopoulos. Done into English by Mrs. Edmonds. New York: John Lane.

That a delicate subject is handled in a delicate manner in this Greek story of to-day is what had best be kept prominent in a judgment of the book. A father and son are rivals for the love of a beautiful young woman. The father, a gay, good-natured, charming, not very observant person, marries her, and never discovers his son's misery. The son, in the end, behaves like an honourable man. Mrs. Edmonds, by writing a preface in which she seems to treat this very slight story as capable of vividly presenting domestic life in Athens among the comfortable classes, has attached to it too much responsibility. But so, too, does its author, whose chief purpose was to show the evils of early marriage. That a grown-up son may fall in love with his stepmother is a possible consequence of his father marrying, for the first time, too young; but the evil might be attacked on several stronger grounds.

THE FOLLY OF PEN HARRINGTON. By Julian Sturgis. New York: D. Appleton & Co. $1.00.

Pen, a very fortunate young woman, with health and wealth, beauty and audacity, queen in her own London set, went out to remotest Africa. To tell how this came about is the purpose of Mr. Sturgis's story. The reader is left to determine for himself to what portion of her career Pen's "Folly" belongs; but few will place it at the end. She is a masterful, generous, and harum-scarum young woman, whose popularity we believe in; and that is a great admission concerning a mere book-heroine. At the same time we think even obstinacy does not altogether explain her temporary consent to the overtures of Pharamont, so obviously detestable even before his wickedness was discovered. There is an unusual amount of bright and capable character-drawing in the book; and if the Bobbys, those pathetic and most obliging adventurers, seem to have jumped straight out of the pages of Mr. Henry James, we are bound to say they are Mr. Sturgis's own—only conceived in a Jamesian mood. Perhaps the old-fashioned machinery that brought Pen and Pharamont and Blake together in their relations to Kitty Trevor is a little out of place in a book so up-to-date, so lightly, so pleasingly modern. But the answer of most would be that the coincidence makes so much more of a story.

THE DEVIL TREE OF ELDORADO. By Frank Aubrey. New York: New Amsterdam Company. $1.50.

Here is an adventure story, which, so far as we know, is written around an absolutely new monster. In the traditional city of Manoa—the veritable Eldorado which sprang into being around the camp-fires of Cortez and Pizarro—Mr. Aubrey writes of a gigantic and blood-thirsty tree, which is alive with coiling, writhing branches, and has a man for breakfast every morning. This vegetable horror grows in the middle of a sort of amphitheatre, and is worked as a religious spectacle, and for the private ends of one Coryon, a treacherous but imposing high-priest. Readers of sentiment will find a relief from the performances of the "Devil Tree" in a well-sustained love story, for there is a beautiful princess and more than one plucky young Englishman. The book is strikingly original in its central idea, is undeniably gruesome, and frequently exciting. Mr. Aubrey, however, is too lengthy, and his style is by no means a thing of beauty. It is a great pity that writers of books like this are not content to say less and to say it better. But, in spite of such drawbacks, we must acknowledge that Mr. Aubrey has really given us a capital tale.

THE BOOKMAN'S TABLE.

EYE SPY. Afield with Nature among Flowers and Animate Things. By William Hamilton Gibson. New York: Harper & Brothers. $2.50.

"From my baby days," Mr. Gibson once told the writer of "A Naturalist's Boyhood," the chapter which introduces us to *Eye Spy*, "I was curious about flowers and insects. The two were always united in my mind. What could not have been more than a childish guess was confirmed in my later years." This chapter derives a special value from its autobiographical interest; in a series of conversations which the writer, Mr. Barnet Phillips, had with the late Mr. Gibson, he has pieced together the naturalist's recollections of his boyhood, which tell in his own words the story of his first impressions of nature, his early observations, his studies and favourite books, his first experiments at collecting, and the beginning of his career not only as the most observant and sympathetic of naturalists, but as a distinguished artist and author. The chapters which compose the book are intended primarily for young people, to give them an impulse to observe and to study nature for themselves. But *Eye Spy* is a book that will engross readers of all ages; it makes its appeal to old as well as young. Few of us use our eyes as we might, and thus rob ourselves of much of the beauty of nature—the nature that lies at our feet. For instance, how many of us would ever look for "Fox-fire" around our refrigerators, or think of associating it with a piece of bread? how many of us can account for the appearance of spiders at sea, or for the fact that certain spiders are argonauts and sail through the air when they feel like leaving *terra firma* for a change? Some of us have crowed over finding a four-leaved clover; but who can boast of having seen a nine-leaved clover, as Mr. Gibson did? This chapter on "Luck in Clovers" is an example of the amount of interest that can be worked out of the simplest and most familiar flower of the field. Mr. Gibson's sharp eyes went so far as to note that "the clover says its prayers and goes to sleep, with its two side leaflets folded together like reverent palms, and the terminal leaflet bowed above them. So the normal leaf spends the night in the dews." There are chapters on beetles, the housefly, wasps, spiders, snakes, grasshoppers, pansies, cocoons, clovers, mushrooms, primroses, and other insects and flowers. There are also over a hundred of Mr. Gibson's illustrations, and a fine frontispiece portrait of him which is very characteristic. It is a book that ought to be in the hands of every boy and girl; and it will make many older readers lament that their eyes are no longer sharp nor their observing faculties acute with the fine perceptiveness of fresh young life.

CITIZEN BIRD. Scenes from Bird-life in plain English for beginners. By Mabel Osgood Wright and Elliott Coues. New York: The Macmillan Co. $1.50.

This is another book of natural history which makes the older reader envious of the younger when he looks back with melancholy regret on the days of his own youth, barren of such rare delights. Those who have made the acquaintance of Mrs. Wright's *Birdcraft*, but especially her *Tommy-Anne and the Three Hearts*, published last Christmas, will be prepared for the charming narrative which she has spun around the story of the birds, their classification, habits, songs, and so forth. Sympathy with all living things through greater knowledge of them is Mrs. Wright's aim, and she has the inborn gift of telling a story so as to move the reader; and in the case of boys and girls, she knows just how to tap their primary emotions and how to call forth their kindlier instincts and to shame them out of their savage estate. For an explanation of the title, in which lies the central motive of the work, we quote the words of Dr. Roy Hunter, a naturalist, to his small and much-interested audience, Olive, Dodo, Nat, and Rap :

"I told you the other day how the body of a bird was planned and built to fil! a place no other animal could take. Thus by his habits and character every bird fills a place as a citizen of our Republic, keeping the laws and doing work for the land that House People, with all their wisdom, cannot do. Every such fellow-animal of ours, besides having eyes to see with, and a brain which, if it does not tell him as many things as our brains tell us, yet teaches him all that he need know to follow the laws that Heart of Nature has set for him, has the same feelings and affections as ourselves. Parent birds love each other and their little ones, and often lose their lives in trying to protect them. They build their homes with as much care and skill as House People use in making theirs. Then they work hard, very hard indeed, to collect food to feed their children. . . . So you can see for yourselves that we may well call the bird a fellow-being."

As Andrew Lang has put it for the birds :

"We would have you to wit, that on eggs though we sit,
And are spiked on the spit, and are baked in a pan ;
Birds are older by far than your ancestors are,
And made love and made war, ere the making of man"

The birds that sing their songs and build their nests and nestle their young around Orchard Farm contrive with the aid of Dr. Hunter to convince the children, known to the birds as "House People," that there "are no such things as common birds, for every one of them has something very uncommon about it." And this is certainly the impression which has been left upon our minds after going through with the keenest interest and pleasure Mrs. Wright's pages, teeming with the colour and romance and wonderland of bird life. The hundred odd illustrations by Louis Agassiz Fuertes, which enrich the text, and are drawn to help the eye to identify the birds, are excellent in execution and design. We are certain that no better book than this has ever been written upon ornithology for the young reader ; the skill and care with which the authors have retained the facts of science and yet have made them attractive to the youthful imagination by their romantic treatment is a rare achievement, and one that calls for the gratitude of the reader, old as well as young. For. as nearly always happens when a scientific subject is treated with authority and lucidity, with freshness and poetic feeling, the readers of *Citizen Bird* will know no limit of age.

THE PRIVATE LIFE OF THE QUEEN. By a Member of the Royal Household. Illustrated. New York : D. Appleton & Co. $1.50.

The Private Life of the Queen, by one of Her Majesty's servants, is a readable and apparently trustworthy chronicle of gossip. How far one of Her Majesty's servants is justified in writing such a book is a question which one is not called upon to decide. It abounds in facts like these : "The Queen has a sweet tooth, and receives three or four times a week a packet containing one box of biscuits, one box of drop tablets, sixteen chocolate sponges, twelve plain sponges, one sponge cake, one princess cake, one rice cake, one box of wafers" and some other things. More interesting is the account of the Queen's reading. She is, it seems, a great reader, and among her favourites are Scott, Jane Austen, Mrs. Oliphant, and others less creditable. We miss, however, the magic name of Marie Corelli. How is this? The writer, who has evidently no sense of humour, tells a perfectly ridiculous story about Dickens falling in love with the Queen, with "the girlish beauty which she retained unimpaired for very many years after her marriage." The origin of this is an amusing letter of Dickens. There are plenty of people, alas ! who never can be made to understand a joke. Those who want to know how many strawberries and gooseberries are consumed in the royal household in the course of a year, what spoons and plate the Queen uses, what Her Majesty's opinion of orchids is, and similar facts, will find them here.

THE VICTORIAN ERA. By P. Anderson Graham. With 75 illustrations and two maps. New York : Longmans, Green & Co.

The Victorian Era is a fair specimen of Jubilee literature. The subjects are necessarily treated in a very superficial way, and many of the portraits are dreadful. Writing of literature, Mr. Graham mentions Dickens and Thackeray, and goes on : "Of those that come later I shall mention only two--Robert Louis Stevenson, who died in his prime at Samoa after writing a number of stories that deserve reading for the English in which they are written, and the veteran Mr. Meredith, whose difficult style has prevented him from being read as much as he deserves." The "veteran Mr. Meredith" is distinctly good. Of course every one knows that Mr. Graham can write much better than this, but he is here accomplishing a bit of task work, and on the whole he has done it well.

THE LAND OF THE DOLLAR. By G. W. Steevens. New York : Dodd, Mead & Co. $1.50.

These journals of an English newspaper correspondent in America last year, during the Free Silver clamour and contest, were well worth reprinting. They have no pretensions to solidity or to permanent value. Mr. Steevens is not a philosophic watcher of the whole of American social life like Bourget, nor does he, in the wake of Mr. Bryce, try to account for the political conditions of the States. He writes of the day and for the day. It is all pure journalism, and light journalism at that, but every line is lively, common-sensible, quick-witted, and unprejudiced. He sometimes flashes an observation in a word or two which Bourget would have taken a chapter to elaborate. And what a Presidential election is really like to the onlooker—quite apart from its moral and material significance—has never been half so well described before. East and west, north and south, he cast a shrewd and good-natured eye over American politics and labour, over national and local traits ; and we take his report none the less seriously that there is not a heavy paragraph in his book from first to last.

BOOKMAN BREVITIES.

The Story of the Atmosphere is the title of the latest volume issued in the Messrs. Appleton's admirable little Library of Useful Stories. The author, Mr. Douglas Archibald, is associated with the Royal Meteorological Society, London, and in producing a popular statement of our knowledge of the conditions of our atmosphere as interpreted through the science of to-day, he has, as he admits, levied largely upon the original works of the modern school of meteorologists so ably represented in America, India, and Germany. The author has borne well in mind that he is writing not for a minority of students, but for a numerous section of seekers after information without technical training in the laws of physics. (With 44 illustrations. Price, 40 cents.) The same firm has added another out-of-doors book to the valuable list of such works already published by them. *Insect Life*, by Professor John Henry Comstock, introduces us to the study of a fruitful field for intellectual growth. The subject is so treated that it can be applied to Nature study in schools or taken up as a recreation when tired of the daily occupation. Its chief object is "to serve as a guide for those who wish to acquire a knowledge of insects from a study of the insects themselves; it is intended to lie open before the observer while the subject of study is examined." The needs of the beginner in the study of insects, be he old or young, are constantly kept in mind; facts are not only treated in a scientific manner, but with an imaginative mind also, and the result is such as to conduce to a closer sympathy with the teeming world of life around us. Everything in the way of drawings and diagrams that really help to illustrate the meaning of the text has been provided, and the book most admirably supplies a vacant place in the literature of the subject. (Price, $1.75.)

Messrs. Harper and Brothers have put together in a volume a collection of eighteen short stories by Mr. Edward Everett Hale. *Susan's Escort and Others* will bring a good deal of entertainment, food for thought, moral and psychological, and what Mr. Poor called "litrary fooling" to the reader; some of the stories he may have already read in the periodicals; but what matter? Mr. Hale's quaint fancy and delightful humour blending with a deep serious vein of moral earnestness always invest his stories with a charm which wears well. (Price, $1.50)——The Messrs. Harper have also published in book form four chapters of studies on *The People for whom Shakespeare Wrote*, by Charles Dudley Warner. "It is impossible for us," Mr. Warner writes in his opening chapter, "to enter into a full, sympathetic enjoyment of Shakespeare's plays unless we can in some measure recreate for ourselves the atmosphere in which they were written." Mr. Warner has sought to do this for us, and has endeavoured to carry us in imagination back among the people—their daily life, customs, costumes, manners, habitat—of the Elizabethan age. How well he has realised this can only be learned fully and profitably after a careful reading of a very pleasant and delightful volume. (Price, $1.25.)——Another volume on Shakespeare which deserves to find interested readers has just been published by Messrs. Lee and Shepard—namely, *The Genesis of Shakespeare's Art*, by Edwin James Dunning. It is an original and capable study of the sonnets and poems. Mr. Dunning believes that the Youth of the sonnets is a purely imaginary character, like as Beatrice was to Dante, "the inspiration of his genius and the soul of his poetic life." The treatment of the whole subject is not only ingenious and commanding, it is serious, oftentimes profound, and always suggestive. It is really a book to be reckoned with in the study of Shakespeare's life and art, and whatsoever theory we may hold regarding the sonnets, it is clear that the beauty and significance of the poet's lines are ably and felicitously interpreted, and that it would be impossible to peruse the book without having gained a fresh and suggestive view of the sonnets and poems and a nobler conception of Shakespeare's genius. The book is the outcome of a long and reverent study of the Bard of Avon, during years in which the author has brooded over the development of his thought and purpose in that darkness made visible which sightless eyes cast upon the mind. This fact lends a pathos to the work so patiently and lovingly pursued—work that must leave a deep impression on the mind of the reader who approaches it in a like spirit. (Price, $2.00.)

The Macmillan Company have issued Balzac's *A Distinguished Provincial at Paris* in the Dent Edition, for which Professor Saintsbury writes a preface. There are three etchings by W. Boucher. (Price, $1.50.)

THE BOOK MART.

For Bookreaders, Bookbuyers, and Booksellers.

AMERICAN AUTHORS: A BIBLIOGRAPHY.*

That interest in the first editions of the great American authors is still keen among collectors is shown by the high prices brought at the Bierstadt and Roos sales in April. But only the works of about a dozen of the great writers are all that collectors care for apparently, or that bring high prices These are Hawthorne, Longfellow, Lowell, Whittier, Holmes, Emerson, and Poe, with perhaps as many more in slightly less degree.

There is need of a good bibliography of American authors, but the one which will satisfy a collector has not yet been written. Mr. Bierstadt, before his death, published in the *Book Buyer* an admirable bibliography of the writings of Whittier; and Mr. Chew, some years ago, published his *Longfellow's Collector's Hand-Book*. A satisfactory bibliography of

* American Authors, 1795–1895. A Bibliography of First and Notable Editions, Chronologically Arranged, with Notes. By P. K. Foley. With an Introduction by Walter Leon Sawyer. Boston: Printed for Subscribers. 1897.

American first editions should give a full transcript of the title-page, the date of copyright, an accurate collation of the book, a description of the form in which it was published, whether in paper, boards, or cloth, whether with edges cut or uncut, and, if possible, the approximate market price from auctioneers' or booksellers' catalogues. Collectors of this class of books, more perhaps than of any other, demand that the books shall be in the original binding and in good, clean condition. Many books were issued in pamphlet form, with the title on the cover, and it is of the highest importance that these covers be preserved.

When we saw the announcement oi Mr. Foley's book we hoped that it would supply these particulars, but on examination we are disappointed with it. It is called a "bibliography," but is, in fact, little more than a list of books. The titles are abbreviated, the names of publishers are not given, nor the dates of copyright. There are no collations and no descriptions of the original bindings, with a few rare exceptions. It can, therefore, do little more than serve the purpose of a check-list.

The compiler, in the preface, states that "in most cases the titles have been copied from the title-pages." It is indeed a pity that, when the books were before him, he did not note down further particulars—at least the publisher, the date of copyright, the number of pages, and the form in which it was originally issued. If he had confined the book to one fourth or one half the number of authors, and had given fuller particulars regarding their works, it would have been more serviceable to the collector, book-seller, or librarian seeking information from it.

Though only a check-list, it is by far the most accurate and complete work of its kind thus far published. The first work of this class was the catalogue of Leon and Brother, published in 1885. This was a bookseller's priced catalogue, and an admirable one of its kind, and was for many years the best book of reference on the subject. Following this was the hastily and carelessly compiled *First Editions of American Authors* of Herbert Stuart Stone, published in 1893. Mr. Stone gave lists, often faulty and imperfect, of books by two hundred and thirty-nine authors, including many early writers. Mr. Foley, in the book under review, excludes those authors whose works were published before 1795, and those whose works were for the most part juvenile, technical, religious, or historical rather than literary. He has, for these reasons, discarded sixty authors from Mr. Stone's list, but, on the other hand, he has added one hundred and thirty, not included by Mr. Stone, making the total number of authors whose works are enumerated three hundred and eleven.

In looking over the host of minor authors whose works are included, it seems strange that such names as Henry Ward Beecher, Edward Everett Hale, and James Freeman Clarke should have been discarded, even though their writings were largely religious. Nor do we quite understand why the names of Horace Greeley, George Cary Eggleston, John Habberton, Albion W. Tourgee, Henry Cabot Lodge, and a few others are omitted. The above were all included in Mr. Stone's book.

Collectors nowadays like to get everything containing the first appearance of any work by their favourites. Thus oftentimes biographies, reports of celebrations, etc., of little interest in themselves, have great interest and bring a high price because they include a poem or essay by Holmes, Whittier or Lowell. Mr. Foley has incorporated these in his lists, and has usually added notes stating the points of interest in the several items. Largely on account of the insertion of these items, Mr. Foley's lists of the works of the more important authors are much larger than those of Mr. Stone. Thus, Holmes has one hundred and thirty-four titles, while Stone gave only sixty-seven ; Longfellow has seventy-six, while Stone gave only forty-six ; Whittier has one hundred and ten, while Stone gave only sixty ; Lowell has seventy-six, while Stone gave only thirty-seven, and so on.

There are interesting notes appended to many titles, giving points of interest about the books, a few records of sales of the most important items, and occasionally "points" by which the true and genuine "first" may be distinguished from a later issue of the same date. These notes are, however, often indefinite. For example, from the description it would be impossible to distinguish the first and second issue of Hawthorne's *True Stories from History and Biography* without having both before the eye, to note that one contained additional matter. Nor would it be possible to distinguish a copy of the second edition of *A Fable for Critics*, having the additional leaves of Preface removed from a genuine copy of the first edition, though there are several points of difference on the title pages, the most noticeable being the introduction, in the second edition, of an entire new line : "A vocal and musical medley."

The book is printed from type, in an edition limited to five hundred copies in 8vo, and fifty copies on large paper in 4to. The paper used is too soft and weak for a reference book whose margins may be used for notes, but otherwise the volume is a very presentable piece of book-making notwithstanding some slips in the reading of the proof.

L. S. L.

A BIBLIOGRAPHY OF WALT WHITMAN.

The first edition of *Leaves of Grass*, published in Brooklyn, N. Y., in 1855, is one of the most curious-looking books in American bibliography. It is a thin quarto containing only 95 pages, the size of the page ($7\frac{1}{4} \times 10\frac{1}{4}$ inches) allowing all except the longest of the irregular verses to be printed as one line. There was no publisher, the book being printed by Mr. A. H. Rome, of Brooklyn. Whitman set most of the type himself. No author's name appeared on the title-page, but a steel-engraving from a daguerreotype by the famous "Gabe" Harrison was used as a frontispiece, and has been retained in almost all later editions. This edition contained twelve poems and a prose preface. The latter has never been reprinted since as a part of *Leaves of Grass*, but portions of it were afterward incorporated into poems.

Although the first edition had practically no

sale, the following year (1856) brought forth the second edition, a small sixteenmo of 384 pages, containing thirty-two poems, including all in the first edition. It was on the back of this volume that Whitman printed the commendatory line from Emerson, "I greet you at the beginning of a great career." This edition was published by Messrs. Fowler and Wells, New York, but their name did not appear on the title-page.

The first edition to appear through regular publishers was issued by Messrs. Thayer and Eldridge, in Boston (1860–61), and was said at the time to have been one of the finest specimens of typography which had appeared from an American press. It was a bulky volume, very curiously bound, and is quite familiar in the shape of spurious reprints surreptitiously put forth by a New York publisher who purchased the plates at a sheriff's sale, Messrs. Thayer and Eldridge having failed at the outbreak of the war.

The fourth edition in 1867 (New York, no publisher's name) is chiefly interesting from the fact that in this volume the poems commenced to assume the general arrangement of the final editions.

The war poems were published originally in a small volume, *Drum Taps*, in 1865, and afterward included as a part of the 1867 edition.

The fifth edition (Washington, 1872) was a well-printed volume containing considerable new matter, and was published and handled by Whitman himself. Some portions of this edition had been originally published in three small brochures entitled *Passage to India*, *After All Not to Create Only*, and *As a Strong Bird on Pinions Free*.

One of the most interesting editions was the sixth (published by Whitman at Camden, N. J., in 1876), which was issued in two volumes entitled *Leaves of Grass* and *Two Rivulets*, the latter containing prose and poetry. They were bound in half leather, and each volume was autographed as sold. The prompt pecuniary response (especially from England) which this edition received was undoubtedly the means of prolonging the life of the poet, whose courage, purse, and health were then at the lowest ebb.

In 1881–82 the poet again found a regular publisher, the firm of James R. Osgood and Company publishing the seventh edition of *Leaves of Grass*. It is a curious fact that in the first twenty-six years of its history the only two publishers whose imprint appeared upon this work were Boston houses. Unfortunately, owing to a threat of prosecution arising from an imperfect knowledge of the nature of the book, Messrs. Osgood and Company abandoned the publication and turned the plates over to Whitman, who at once brought out another edition through Messrs. Rees, Welch and Company (Philadelphia, 1882). Mr. David McKay, then manager of this firm, succeeded to their general publishing business about 1884, and since that time has published all of Whitman's works.

The final edition issued during Whitman's life appeared while he was on his deathbed, in the winter of 1891–92. Since his death a paper edition (1896) has been issued by Mr. McKay, with a special view toward supplying a book within the means of the working people of England, where Whitman has so many ardent admirers.

EASTERN LETTER.

New York, August 1, 1897.

Again, by the sales of the past month, the fact that most of the reading done during the summer is of fiction has been very decidedly demonstrated. While there has been an undercurrent of miscellaneous literature sold, the demand has been overwhelmingly for fiction and confined largely to a limited number of titles. *The Choir Invisible* has led in point of sale, closely followed by *Quo Vadis*, which has almost been equalled by *Soldiers of Fortune*. The sales of these books have simply been tremendous for this time of year. *Equality* has improved in sale, and may be said to lead the second class, with *The Pursuit of the House-Boat*, *The House-Boat on the Styx* (which has picked up materially since the publication of the sequel), and *The Martian*, which has hardly come up to expectations. In addition to the above, *Uncle Bernac*, *The Honourable Peter Sterling*, *The Triumph of Death*, *The Massarenes*, *An Old Gentleman of the Black Stock*, and *Many Cargoes* are selling readily.

The month's publications have been comparatively light. They include, however, in fiction, *Mrs. Creighton's Creditor*, by Mrs. Alexander; *Wolfville*, by Alfred Henry Lewis, illustrated by Frederic Remington; and *A Colonial Free-Lance* and *The Folly of Pen Harrington* in Appleton's Town and Country Library. In miscellaneous subjects we have had *Peter the Great*, by K. Waliszewski; *The People for whom Shakespeare Wrote*, by Charles Dudley Warner, and *Montaigne and Other Essays*, by Thomas Carlyle.

The outdoor department in literature still shows some activity, *Citizen Bird*, by Mabel Osgood Wright, and *Familiar Features of the Roadside*, by F. Schuyler Mathews, being in good demand.

The interest in the Klondike gold region has occasioned considerable call for guide-books and works on Alaska at present. Among those obtainable are *Alaska*, by Miner W. Bruce, and Ballou's *Alaska*, while others are announced for early publication.

The publishers are now showing their lines for the fall trade. They consist as usual of the various editions of sixteenmo and twelvemo sets, illustrated works, booklets, calendars, and board and cloth-bound juveniles. These all bid fair to be as numerous and attractive as in former years. The juveniles are perhaps to the fore more than any other class, and there are now published new books by such well-known juvenile writers as Hezekiah Butterworth, Orison Sevett Marden, and Kirk Munroe. *Phronsie Pepper*, by Margaret Sidney, is likely to be one of the leaders during the season.

Trade in general has naturally been rather quiet during the month. Library business has been moving, and advance orders for text-books have been noticeable. The travellers from the West report comparatively good sales and a more hopeful feeling, so that the outlook seems to be good for an increased business during the coming months.

The leading books of the month, as indicated by their sales, were:

The Choir Invisible. By James Lane Allen. $1.50.

Quo Vadis. By Henryk Sienkiewicz. $2.00.
Soldiers of Fortune. By Richard Harding Davis. $1.50.
Equality. By Edward Bellamy. $1.50.
The Martian. By George Du Maurier. $1.75.
The House-Boat on the Styx. By John Kendrick Bangs. $1.25.
The Pursuit of the House-Boat. By John Kendrick Bangs. $1.25.
Uncle Bernac. By A. Conan Doyle. $1.50.
The Honourable Peter Sterling. By P. L. Ford. $1.50.
The Triumph of Death. By Gabriele D'Annunzio. $1.50.
The Massarenes. By Ouida. $1.25.
An Old Gentleman of the Black Stock. By Thomas Nelson Page. 75 cents.
On the Face of the Waters. By Annie Flora Steel. $1.50.
The Sowers. By Henry Seton Merriman. $1.50.
Phroso. By Anthony Hope. $1.50.
Many Cargoes. By W. W. Jacobs. $1.00.

WESTERN LETTER.

CHICAGO, August 1, 1897.

Trade is always very sluggish in July, and the bookseller who makes more than his expenses during this, the dullest of the dull months, is the exception rather than the rule. Customers are out of town, schools and other institutions of learning are closed, and what reading is done is usually of the lightest kind. In fact, the dog days have come to be regarded as a kind of vacation term for literary people, and no one reads much.

In accordance with expectations, therefore, the demand last month was confined for the most part to fiction, and books in other classes went, with a few exceptions, very slowly. On every hand one hears the complaint that there is very little doing, but from a comparative standpoint the month's business was, on the whole, fair—relatively, of course, as the sum total of July trade never amounts to much.

Dulness prevailed also in publishing circles, and the output was very small, only one book, *The Martian*, being produced entitled to rank among the best selling books of the month. *Phronsie Pepper*, by Margaret Sidney, deserves mention, as it will probably be one of the best selling juvenile books of the coming season, and *Citizen Bird* is a work of more than average merit, even for a season so rich in ornithological literature.

The Klondike craze has been responsible for an increased demand for books on mining and kindred subjects, and during the first week or so of the gold fever many calls were received for pocket maps of Alaska. Customers could not at first be satisfactorily accommodated, but with ready enterprise the publishers soon met this defect, and now there are a dozen or more of desirable maps in the market.

Chicago was the rendezvous of nearly all the travelling bookmen in the country last month, and local booksellers were busy buying their fall bills. Samples of current books and forthcoming new publications which will appear later were shown, and orders secured for the same. It would, perhaps, be conducive to larger orders if an effort were made to provide for the July trade more adequate samples of the new books than those usually shown. Each year less attention seems to be paid to this important particular, and in many cases a doubtful-looking cover or a rough proof or two of the illustrations are all that the salesman has to show. Most people nowadays, from the wholesale to the retail buyer, wish to see the complete article or an approximation to it.

Among the new books are some which will be heavy sellers. Publishers are striving to make the books as attractive as possible, and the standard of excellence promises to be advanced materially. Trade was good, so the salesmen report, during the whole of the "Fair," as it is now called, and it is a long time since so much confidence in regard to a good fall business was to be seen on every hand. The outlook is decidedly a bright one.

The Choir Invisible and *Soldiers of Fortune* were again the best selling books of the month. *Equality* sold very largely for a book that is not considered exactly summer reading, while *Quo Vadis* still keeps up its extraordinary sale. *The Honourable Peter Sterling* continues to gain in popularity, and J. K. Bangs's latest effort, *The Pursuit of the House-Boat*, went very well. Generally speaking, sales of popular fiction were above the average of the previous month.

The following books were most prominent in last month's demand:

The Choir Invisible. By James Lane Allen. $1.50.
Soldiers of Fortune. By Richard Harding Davis. $1.50.
Equality. By Edward Bellamy. $1.25.
Quo Vadis. By H. Sienkiewicz. $2.00.
The Martian. By G. Du Maurier. $1.75.
The Hon. Peter Sterling. By P. L. Ford. $1.50.
The Pursuit of the House-Boat. By J. K. Bangs. $1.25.
A Rose of Yesterday. By F. Marion Crawford. $1.25.
Menticulture. By Horace Fletcher. $1.00.
After Her Death. By Lilian Whiting. $1.00.
The Law of Psychic Phenomena. By Thomson J. Hudson. $1.50.
Phroso. By Anthony Hope. $1.75.
On the Face of the Waters. By Mrs. F. A. Steel. $1.50.
Miss Archer Archer. By C. L. Burnham. $1.25.
Arnaud's Masterpiece. By W. C. Larned. $1.25.

ENGLISH LETTER.

LONDON, June 21 to July 24, 1897.

With the Diamond Jubilee celebrations completed, trade has again resumed its normal condition. So many counter-attractions out of doors obviously cause the present season to be a quiet one for the sale of general literature. On the whole booksellers may be congratulated on the fact that it is no worse, for a considerable reaction was anticipated. Trade with the colonies and abroad generally pursues the even tenor of its way, and orders are received, satisfactory both in volume and number, but an increase is always welcomed.

The decease of Mrs. Oliphant has stimulated the demand for her works, and a 2s. 6d. issue of her works, which has just been brought out, is deservedly popular.

It is hardly the time of the year for a very brisk trade in 6s. novels. Nevertheless, a considerable amount of business is being done in this class of work, and the principal book is *Soldiers of Fortune*, by R. H. Davis. *On the Face of the Waters* and *Flames* come next in favour, the popularity of the former being remarkable for its continuance.

A pamphlet on the ΛΟΓΙΑ ΙΗΣΟΥ, the recently discovered biblical manuscript, has attracted much attention, in short (to quote Micawber) has sold well. Books dealing with Butterflies and Moths, Birds and Flowers, with beautifully coloured plates, are in the height of their season. Gordon's series seem to be the favourites.

The interest evinced in works dealing with the life and times of St. Augustine is very marked.

Publications obviously issued for the Jubilee season are enquired for in a moderate way. *The Queen's Resolve* and *The Private Life of the Queen* still find buyers.

The forthcoming issue of the *Life of Queen Victoria* by the librarian of Windsor Castle is anxiously awaited. It is announced that, among other reasons, the publication has been postponed in order that an account of the recent celebrations may be embodied. Dickens is decidedly reviving in popularity, and the work by his daughter entitled *My Father as I Recall Him* is a distinct success.

There is still a considerable issue of new books and new editions, some hundreds having been published during the present month—some, valuable treatises and publications of a class that will be in demand for years to come, and others, probably the larger number, that, after the lapse of a few weeks, will never again be mentioned. Has the proportion of the latter to the former ever been ascertained?

The list of favourite books which follows is based upon actual business done in the works mentioned, and may make a fair claim to being a reliable index of the popular fancy.

Soldiers of Fortune. By R. H. Davis. 6s.
On the Face of the Waters. By F. A. Steel. 6s.
Flames. By R. Hichens. 6s.
A Rose of Yesterday. By F. M. Crawford. 6s.
My Run Home. By R. Boldrewood. 6s.
Dracula. By B. Stoker. 6s.
Dear Faustina. By R Broughton. 6s.
Uncle Bernac. By C. Doyle. 6s.
Patience Sparhawk. By G. Atherton. 4s. 6d. net.
Quo Vadis. By Sienkiewicz. 4s. 6d. net.
The Quest of the Golden Girl. By R. Le Gallienne. 5s. net.
The Indiscretion of the Duchess. By A. Hope. 3s. 6d.
Many Cargoes. By W. W. Jacobs. 3s. 6d.
The Rejuvenation of Miss Semaphore. By H. Godfrey. 3s. 6d.
My Father as I Recall Him. By M. Dickens. 3s. 6d.

SALES OF BOOKS DURING THE MONTH.

New books in order of demand, as sold between July 1, 1897, and August 1, 1897.

We guarantee the authenticity of the following lists as supplied to us, each by leading booksellers in the towns named.

NEW YORK, UPTOWN.

1. Farthest North. By Nansen. $10.00. (Harper.)
2. The Choir Invisible. By Allen. $1.50. (Macmillan.)
3. Pursuit of the House-Boat. By Bangs. $1.25. (Harper.)
4. Soldiers of Fortune. By Davis. $1.50. (Scribner.)
5. The Martian. By Du Maurier. $1.75. (Harper.)
6. Letters to an Unknown. By Merimée; trans. by Du Bois. $1.25. (Brentano.)

NEW YORK, DOWNTOWN.

1. The Choir Invisible. By Allen. $1.50. (Macmillan.)
2. Soldiers of Fortune. By Davis. $1.50. (Scribner.)
3. Quo Vadis. By Sienkiewicz. $2.00. (Little, Brown & Co.)
4. On the Face of the Waters. By Steel. $1.50. (Macmillan.)
5. Pursuit of the House-Boat. By Bangs. $1.25. (Harper.)
6. Uncle Bernac. By Doyle. $1.50. (Appleton.)

ALBANY, N. Y.

1. The Choir Invisible. By Allen. $1.50. (Macmillan.)
2. Soldiers of Fortune. By Davis. $1.50. (Scribner.)
3. The Martian. By Du Maurier. $1.75. (Harper.)
4. The Hon. Peter Stirling. By Ford. $1.50. (Holt.)
5. The Sowers. By Merriman. $1.25. (Harper.)
6. Phroso. By Hope. $1.75. (Stokes.)

ATLANTA, GA.

1. The Choir Invisible. By Allen. $1.50. (Macmillan.)
2. Soldiers of Fortune. By Davis. $1.50. (Scribner.)
3. A Rose of Yesterday. By Crawford. $1.25. (Macmillan.)
4. Old Gentleman of the Black Stock. By Page. 75 cts. (Scribner.)
5. Pursuit of the House-Boat. By Bangs. $1.25. (Harper.)
6. House-Boat on the Styx. By Bangs. $1 25. (Harper.)

BOSTON, MASS.

1. The Choir Invisible. By Allen. $1.50. (Macmillan.)
2. Soldiers of Fortune. By Davis. $1.50. (Scribner.)
3. Quo Vadis. By Sienkiewicz. $2.00. (Little, Brown & Co.)
4. Pursuit of the House-Boat. By Bangs. $1.25. (Harper.)
5. The Martian. By Du Maurier. $1.75. (Harper.)
6. Farthest North. 2 vols. By Nansen. $10.00. (Harper.)

BUFFALO, N. Y.

1. Soldiers of Fortune. By Davis. $1.50. (Scribner.)
2. Quo Vadis. By Sienkiewicz. $2.00. (Little, Brown & Co.)
3. Equality. By Bellamy. $1.25. (Appleton.)
4. The Choir Invisible. By Allen. $1.50. (Macmillan.)
5. Great K. & A. Train Robbery. By Ford. $1.25. (Dodd, Mead & Co.)
6. The Martian. By Du Maurier. $1.75. (Harper.)

CHICAGO, ILL.

1. The Choir Invisible. By Allen. $1.50. (Macmillan.)
2. Soldiers of Fortune. By Davis. $1.50. (Scribner.)
3. Equality. By Bellamy. $1.25. (Appleton.)
4. Quo Vadis. By Sienkiewicz. $2.00. (Little, Brown & Co.)
5. The Martian. By Du Maurier. $1.75. (Harper.)
6. Menticulture. By Fletcher. $1.00. (McClurg & Co.)

CINCINNATI, O.

1. The Choir Invisible. By Allen. $1.50. (Macmillan.)
2. Soldiers of Fortune. By Davis. $1.25. (Scribner.)
3. Quo Vadis. By Sienkiewicz. $2.00. (Little, Brown & Co.)
4. Equality. By Bellamy. $1.25. (Appleton.)
5. Pursuit of the House-Boat. By Bangs. $1.25. (Harper.)
6. Pink Marsh. By Ade. $1.25. (Stone.)

CLEVELAND, O.

1. Soldiers of Fortune. By Davis. $1.50. (Scribner.)
2. The Choir Invisible. By Allen. $1.50. (Macmillan.)
3. Pursuit of the House-Boat. By Bangs. $1.25. (Harper.)
4. Equality. By Bellamy. $1.25. (Appleton.)
5. A Rose of Yesterday. By Crawford. $1.25. (Macmillan.)
6. A Story-Teller's Pack. By Stockton. $1.50. (Scribner.)

INDIANAPOLIS, IND.

1. Soldiers of Fortune. By Davis. $1.50. (Scribner.)
2. The Choir Invisible. By Allen. $1.50. (Macmillan.)
3. Pursuit of the House-Boat. By Bangs. $1.25. (Harper.)
4. Quo Vadis. By Sienkiewicz. $2.00. (Little, Brown & Co.)
5. Hon. Peter Stirling. By Ford. $1.50. (Holt.)
6. A Story-Teller's Pack. By Stockton. $1.25. (Scribner.)

KANSAS CITY, MO.

1. Quo Vadis. By Sienkiewicz. $2.00. (Little, Brown & Co.)
2. Soldiers of Fortune. By Davis. $1.50. (Scribner.)
3. The Choir Invisible. By Allen. $1.50. (Macmillan.)
4. The Sowers. By Merriman. $1.25. (Harper.)
5. King Noanett. By Stimson. $2.00. (Lamson, Wolffe & Co.)
6. Pursuit of the House-Boat. By Bangs. $1.25. (Harper.)

LOS ANGELES, CAL.

1. Quo Vadis. By Sienkiewicz. $2.00. (Little, Brown & Co.)
2. The Martian. By Du Maurier. $1.75. (Harper.)
3. Soldiers of Fortune. By Davis. $1.50. (Scribner.)
4. Equality. By Bellamy. $1.25. (Appleton.)
5. The Choir Invisible. By Allen. $1.50. (Macmillan.)
6. Pursuit of the House-Boat. By Bangs. $1.25. (Harper.)

LOUISVILLE, KY.

1. The Choir Invisible. By Allen. $1.50. (Macmillan.)
2. Great K. & A. Train Robbery. By Ford. $1.25. (Dodd, Mead & Co.)
3. Soldiers of Fortune. By Davis. $1.50. (Scribner.)
4. Pursuit of the House-Boat. By Bangs. $1.25. (Harper.)
5. The Triumph of Death. By D'Annunzio. $1.50. (Richmond & Co.)
6. Checkers. By Blossom. $1.25. (Stone.)

MONTREAL, CANADA.

1. The Martian. By Du Maurier. $1.75. (Harper.)
2. Soldiers of Fortune. By Davis. $1.50. (Scribner.)
3. Equality. By Bellamy $1.25. (Appleton.)
4. Pursuit of the House Boat. By Bangs. $1.25. (Harper.)
5. The Well Beloved. By Hardy. $1.50. (Harper.)
6. The Landlord at Lion's Head. By Howells. $1.75. (Harper.)

NEW HAVEN, CONN.

1. Soldiers of Fortune. By Davis. $1.50. (Scribner.)
2. The Choir Invisible. By Allen. $1.50. (Macmillan.)
3. The Martian. By Du Maurier. $1.75. (Harper.)
4. Equality. By Bellamy. $1.25. (Appleton.)
5. On the Face of the Waters. By Steel. $1.50. (Macmillan.)
6. Kites, How to Make and How to Fly Them. By Varney. 15 cts. (Walker & Co.)

PHILADELPHIA, PA.

1. Soldiers of Fortune. By Davis. $1.50. (Scribner.)
2. Quo Vadis. By Sienkiewicz. $2.00. (Little, Brown & Co.)
3. Uncle Bernac. By Doyle. $1.50. (Appleton.)
4. A Rose of Yesterday. By Crawford $1.25. (Macmillan.)
5. Equality. By Bellamy. $1.25. (Appleton.)
6. The Martian. By Du Maurier. $1.75. (Harper.)

PITTSBURG, PA.

1. Soldiers of Fortune. By Davis. $1.50. (Scribner.)
2. Quo Vadis. By Sienkiewicz. $2.00. (Little, Brown & Co.)
3. The Choir Invisible. By Allen. $1.50. (Macmillan.)
4. Pursuit of the House-Boat. By Bangs. $1.25. (Harper.)
5. The Hon. Peter Stirling. By Ford. $1.50. (Holt.)
6. The Master Beggars. By Cornford. $1.50. (Lippincott.)

PROVIDENCE, R. I.

1. Soldiers of Fortune. By Davis. $1.50. (Scribner.)
2. Equality. By Bellamy. $1.50. (Appleton.)
3. Captain Shays. By Rivers. $1.25. (Little, Brown & Co.)
4. The Martian. By Du Maurier. $1.75. (Harper.)
5. Quo Vadis. By Sienkiewicz. $2.00. (Little, Brown & Co.)
6. In Simpkinsville. By Stuart. $1.25. (Harper.)

ROCHESTER, N. Y.

1. The Choir Invisible. By Allen. $1.50. (Macmillan.)
2. Quo Vadis. By Sienkiewicz. $2.00. (Little, Brown & Co.)
3. Soldiers of Fortune. By Davis. $1.50. (Scribner.)
4. Pursuit of the House-Boat. By Bangs. $1.00. (Harper.)
5. Equality. By Bellamy. $1.25. (Appleton.)
6. The Martian. By Du Maurier. $1.75. (Harper.)

SALT LAKE CITY, UTAH.

1. The Choir Invisible. By Allen. $1.50. (Macmillan.)
2. Soldiers of Fortune. By Davis. $1.50. (Scribner.)
3. A Kentucky Cardinal. By Allen. $1.00. (Harper.)
4. Pursuit of the House-Boat. By Bangs. $1.25. (Harper.)
5. House-Boat on the Styx. By Bangs. $1.25. (Harper.)
6. Pomp of the Lavilettes. By Parker. $1.25. (Lamson, Wolffe & Co.)

SAN FRANCISCO, CAL.

1. Soldiers of Fortune. By Davis. $1.50. (Scribner.)
2. Quo Vadis. By Sienkiewicz. $2.00. (Little, Brown & Co.)
3. The Choir Invisible. By Allen. $1.50. (Macmillan.)
4. Seven Seas. By Kipling. $1.50. (Century.)
5. Phroso. By Hope. $1.75. (Stokes.)
6. Mutable Many. By Barr. $1.50. (Stokes.)

ST. PAUL, MINN.

1. Soldiers of Fortune. By Davis. $1.50. (Scribner.)
2. The Choir Invisible. By Allen. $1.50. (Macmillan.)
3. Miss Sheriff. By Thanet. $1.25. (Harper.)
4. Seats of the Mighty. By Parker. $1.50. (Appleton.)
5. Equality. By Bellamy. $1.25. (Appleton.)
6. That Affair Next Door. By Green. $1.00. (Putnam.)

TOLEDO, O.

1. Soldiers of Fortune. By Davis. $1.50. (Scribner.)
2. The Choir Invisible. By Allen. $1.50. (Macmillan.)
3. A Rose of Yesterday. By Crawford. $1.25. (Macmillan.)
4. Equality. By Bellamy. $1.25. (Appleton.)
5. Pursuit of the House-Boat. By Bangs, $1.25. (Harper.)
6. Landlord Lion's Head. By Howells. $1.75. (Harper.)

WORCESTER, MASS.

1. The Choir Invisible. By Allen. $1.50. (Macmillan.)
2. Soldiers of Fortune. By Davis. $1.50. (Scribner.)
3. The Martian. By Du Maurier. $1.75. (Harper.)
4. Private Life of the Queen. By a member of royal household. $1.50. (Appleton.)
5. Quo Vadis. By Sienkiewicz. $2.00. (Little, Brown & Co.)
6. Equality. By Bellamy. $1.25. (Appleton.)

FAC-SIMILE OF A LETTER FROM LORD LYTTON.

favour, perhaps more generally in favour with all classes of readers than those of any other novelist. The New Amsterdam Book Company has had a new edition of his novels, to be issued in twenty-eight volumes, under preparation for some time, and has now ready *The Last of the Barons* in two volumes, *Rienzi*, and *The Caxtons*, each in one volume, and each with a photogravure frontispiece from a painting by J. Steeple Davis, made especially for this edition. Binding, type, and paper are excellent, and the price ($1.25 per volume) is cheap enough to make the edition popular and acceptable.

❧

The first Lord Lytton has been more universally known as Sir Edward Bulwer, or Sir Edward Bulwer Lytton, under which names many of his most famous novels appeared. One of the earliest of his novels to arouse attention was *Eugene Aram*, a subject which was, it is said, suggested to him by the fact that the wretched murderer had been a tutor in the family of his grandfather. His fame was established by *The Last Days of Pompeii* and *Rienzi, the Last of the Tribunes*, in 1835. The custodian at Pompeii told Dean Farrar very recently that in the ruins of the old city no name is more frequently mentioned than that of Bulwer, and at Rome those who look with interest at the spot where Rienzi fell constantly refer to Lord Lytton's novel. Dean Farrar was several times the guest of Lord Lytton at Knebworth. In noting various objects of art scattered over the delightful old house he mentions a skull of remarkable formation—

evidently the skull of some man of marked genius—which reposed on a side table under a glass case in the drawing-room. This skull had been found at Pompeii, and had suggested to Lord Lytton the character of Arbaces, the Egyptian priest of the Temple of Isis. One part of the grounds around the house was known as the "Horace Garden." Horace was Lord Lytton's favourite author, and this secluded walk was surrounded by busts of Augustus, Mæcenas, Horace, and many of the friends mentioned in the *Odes* with the relevant passages carved beneath. The letter which we reproduce from the September number of the *Temple Magazine*, containing further reminiscences by Dean Farrar, has reference to the translation of the *Odes and Epodes of Horace*, upon which he was engaged at the time of writing, and which, published in 1872, was very favourably received. As Lord Lytton was not in the technical sense a classical scholar, he had requested Dean Farrar to subject the translation to a close scrutiny and to make whatever criticisms or suggestions occurred to him. "There were *some* actual mistakes," the Dean remarks, "but not many. One lesson the pleasant task brought home to my mind very vividly; it was the immense labour which Lord Lytton brought to bear on all his works. Buffon says somewhere, '*La Génie c'est la patience.*'" Dean Farrar adds the weight of his personal testimony against the attacks often made upon Lord Lytton both in public and private. "All that I saw of him made me regard him as kind, high-minded, and sincere, unprejudiced in his sympathies and anxious to make those about him happy."

❀

Among books of the first importance to be published in the spring of next year we may mention a new volume of stories by Mr. Rudyard Kipling. Mr. J. Lockwood Kipling has, we hear, now completed the whole of the decorations which the Messrs. Scribner commissioned him to model for illustrations in the Outward Bound edition of Mr. Kipling's works. Eight out of the twelve volumes in this edition have now been published.

❀

The Scribners have just added four very popular books to their attractive Cameo Edition—namely, Mr. Barrie's *Auld Licht Idylls* and *A Window in Thrums*, and Dr. Van Dyke's *Little Rivers* and *The Poetry of Tennyson*. They will publish shortly the new edition of George Meredith's poems under the title *Selected Poems*, uniform with Bunner's *Poems* and Stevenson's *Poems and Ballads*. Stevenson's *St. Ives*, now being completed by Mr. Quiller-Couch, will issue before the end of the year from the same house; also a new volume of short stories by Mr. F. J. Stimson, whose *King Noanett* is now in its twentieth thousand. We hope this will have the effect of drawing attention to previous stories published by Mr. Stimson as "J. S. of Dale" through the same firm. A new generation of readers has sprung up since they were written, and yet we have few stories to-day to match that fascinating tale, *The Residuary Legatee* with its inimitable sequel, *Guerndale*.

❀

Benjamin Swift's new novel, *The Tormentor*, to be published this autumn by the Messrs. Scribner, is now ready for the press. A friend of the author, who has been spending some weeks with him in Normandy, writes us that he has read the manuscript, and describes it as "a book of great passion, originality and power, and should make a stir." His first novel, *Nancy Noon*, published about a year ago, is now in its fifth edition. If it be true, as Hall Caine says, that the genius of a novelist is shown in his power to break away from the conventional novel, then Benjamin Swift is a most striking exemplar of the fact. The motive of *The Tormentor* is so fresh and bizarre as to be startling. Strength of passion and originality of invention, those essentials of imaginative art, enter into this work even more than in its predecessor with dramatic intensity and emotiveness. Mr. Paterson, as "Benjamin Swift" is known to his friends, has almost completely recovered from the severe accident which sent him abroad last autumn, and has just returned to his native city of Glasgow.

❀

Messrs. Houghton, Mifflin and Company will publish shortly a novel which in all probability will achieve as great a popularity as *The Honourable Peter Stirling*. Like that story, *The Federal Judge* depicts certain phases of our public life, commercial and political, using in the development of its plot and in the portrayal of character those subtle and characteristic influences of our current social and business activities which fasten so readily on the imagination of the American people. Stories there may be with the same elements at work, but *The Federal Judge* has a distinct originality and power which take it quite out of the course of the average novel. A railway magnate, whose road is exposed to attack, secures the appointment of an upright man to the office of federal judge. This judge has gained a reputation as a friend of the people and a rigid opposer of great corporations, and the story consists mainly in the dramatic portrayal of the relations which these two men bear to each other—the honest judge under the influence of a great business manager, and the manager astutely seeking to shield and strengthen his vast corporation with the judge's authority and honourable prestige. It will be seen, at a glance, that the situation offers great dramatic possibilities, and has required extraordinary skill and power to handle it with success. The author, Mr. Charles K. Lush, is a well-known journalist in Milwaukee, and this is his first book.

❀

Mrs. James T. Fields has written a *Life of Harriet Beecher Stowe*, which will be published this autumn by Messrs. Houghton, Mifflin and Company. Mrs. Fields's article in the *Atlantic*, on "Days with Mrs. Stowe," which appeared a year ago, at the time of Mrs. Stowe's death, indicated very clearly that she possessed the intimate knowledge and sympathy and insight necessary to the performance of such a task. Besides availing herself of the *Life of Mrs. Stowe*, written by the Rev. Charles E. Stowe, she has had access to much material not contained in that work or available at the time of its publication. This material comprises many letters by Mrs. Stowe, personal recollections and characteristic anecdotes of the author of *Uncle Tom's Cabin*.

❀

We are to have another fragment of Hawthorne in the shape of *Hawthorne's First Diary*, with an account of its discovery and loss, by Mr. Samuel T. Pickard, the author of the *Life of Whittier*. That this diary, written by Hawthorne when a boy, possesses more than an autograph interest or gives any indication of the bent of his genius in after years is very doubtful, but curiosity will lead many to peruse its contents. In his preface Mr. Pickard gives this interesting account of the *Diary*:

> "A Diary kept by Nathaniel Hawthorne during his residence at Raymond, Maine, came to light in Virginia during the late civil war, and fell into the hands of a coloured man named William Symmes, who by a curious chance was a companion of Hawthorne in his fishing and gunning sports on the shores of Lake Sebago. Symmes said he had the book from a Maine soldier whom he found in a hospital. Because of his boyish friendship for Hawthorne, he so prized the Diary that he could not be induced to part with it. After holding it several years, he sent extracts from it to a Maine newspaper."

These extracts Mr. Pickard reprints in this little book, preceding them with an account of Hawthorne's home in Raymond and the story of William Symmes.

❀

Mrs. Maud Wilder Goodwin, author of the successful colonial romance *White Aprons*, has turned her pen to the writing of a modern story whose scenes are laid in a New England seashore resort and in New York. It is entitled *Flint: His Faults, his Friendships and his Fortunes*, and will be published this autumn by Messrs. Little, Brown and Company. An illustrated holiday edition of *Quo Vadis* in two volumes is also announced by the same firm. The artists at work on the pictures are Howard Pyle, Evert Van Muyden and Edmund H. Garrett. There will also be a new portrait of Sienkiewicz. A new volume of stories by the author of *Quo Vadis* is also under way.

❀

A book of stories for children by the late Professor Drummond, with illustrations by Louis Wain, is in preparation.

❀

Mr. Anthony Hope has, we understand, signed a contract with Major Pond to lecture in America during the months of October, November, and December. Mr. Hope expects to be back in England toward the end of January next, when it is probable that his new story, *Simon Dale*, will be published in book form.

Two important translations have just been completed, and will be published shortly by Messrs. Roberts Brothers. *Antichrist*, by Ernest Renan, has been translated and edited by Mr. Joseph Henry Allen, late Lecturer of Ecclesiastical History in Harvard University. Following the author's *History of the People of Israel* and his *Life of Jesus*, this volume continues the history of the Hebrew people, and covers the period from the arrival of the Apostle Paul at Rome to the end of the Jewish Revolution, A.D. 61–73, including the persecution under Nero. The other work is the third volume of Dr. Adolph Harnack's *History of Dogma*, the translation of which has been made by Mr. Neil Buchanan from the third German edition.

❀

A reviewer of *The Christian* in the *British Weekly* claims that Glory Quayle is herself in that supreme hour when with much giggling she proposes to marry John Storm on his deathbed. It needs no prescience, he says, to see that within a few weeks after John Storm is laid in his grave we shall be able to read on a music hall bill:

MISS GLORY QUAYLE,
(WIDOW OF THE REV. FATHER STORM),
WILL APPEAR IN HER FAVOURITE TURN, ETC.

"Appraise me the price of a pang made perfect."

❀

Ten miles east of Mentone the coast runs out into a picturesque headland which claims to have more hours of winter sunshine than any other spot on the Riviera. Tall gray and white houses nestling up under its fine campanile form the old Italian fishing town of Bordighera. Below, toward the shore and the station, among groves of olives and lemon trees, and great gardens of palms, lie the red-tiled villas of the foreign colony, largely English, and in creasing year by year. Dr. George Macdonald, who has just added another novel, *Salted with Fire*, to his packed repertory, must be one of its oldest permanent members, for it is more than twenty years since he settled there. The house stands aloof from the main road, with the pretty little English Church just beyond and behind it. Passing inside and up two flights of marble staircase you will probably find Dr. Macdonald sitting alone in his study—a lofty, spacious chamber entirely lined with books, which include many rare volumes. A typewriter stands upon one table, and long sheets of carefully corrected proofs hang from a bookcase. The windows look westward across fields and orchards bathed in golden afternoon sunshine, toward the steep blue hills and shining expanse of sea beyond. The veteran novelist has aged perceptibly during the last few years, and his eyes have lost a little of their gleam and fire, but something venerable seems added to that personal grace and distinction which have always been characteristic of George Macdonald.

❀

A visitor to Dr. Macdonald's sanctuary last winter says that it was reassuring to hear his voice still full and sonorous declaring that he felt well—well for an old man. "I shall be seventy-two before the year ends, and that's far on; it's about time to be going Home." Younger men often come, he said, to see him, that they might tell him how much they had learned from making acquaintance with Robert Falconer and Alec Forbes. On Wednesday afternoons he is still at home to many strangers and friends, and after tea he will often read from some favourite poet like Browning, with added comments and elucidations in that style of which he is a master. For it must not be imagined that Dr. Macdonald is decrepit. Most fine days see him on his tricycle on the Bordighera roads. He talked very freely and cordially to his visitor of the new Scottish novelists. It was refreshing to hear his genuine and generous appreciation of their work. Mr. Barrie he considered the foremost of them all. He had been especially delighted with *The Little Minister*, and also expressed his admiration for parts of *Margaret Ogilvy*, which was "somewhat in the nature of an elegy." He spoke warmly of Ian Maclaren, and recalled how he had himself lectured and preached in Sefton Park Church. He recognised Dr. Watson's great power of humour and also of pathos, "for these two are near akin; the springs of laughter and tears lie close together." He noted that Dr. Watson has brought the Highlander down into the Lowlands, and depicted him in that setting—"a thing which seems new at least to me. I myself," he added, "am a pure Highlander on both sides, though I have no Gaelic." Speaking of Mr. Crockett, Dr. Macdonald recognised very readily the verve and vigour of his narrative and how it carries you irresistibly along. He had been impressed with *The Gray Man*, and referred to the much-discussed episode of the cannibalism among the cave-dwellers. "Terrible, but quite true; it is on record. I remember it was once pointed out to me in an old volume, and only yesterday I was trying to search out and verify the reference."

GEORGE MACDONALD.

From his latest photograph by Elliott and Fry.

With reference to the title of Mr. Le Gallienne's new book, which was recently announced—namely, *If I Were God*—we have authority for stating that his title is an adapted quotation from Dr. Macdonald's *David Elginbrod*. The lines in question, which are familiar to all readers of Dr. Macdonald's famous story, are:

> "Here lie I, Martin Elginbrodde;
> Hae mercy o' my soul, Lord God,
> As I wad do, *were I Lord God*
> And ye were Martin Elginbrodde."

The first three numbers of the English translation of *The Polychrome Bible* will be published by Messrs. Dodd, Mead and Company in October. These are *The Book of Judges*, *The Prophecies of Isaiah*, and *The Book of Psalms*. This work, which has been in preparation for a long time, has aroused a great deal of interest, and the scheme has been already widely discussed in several magazines and periodicals. The major part of *The Polychrome Bible* (so called because of a novel use of colour printing to indicate the composite origin of the various books) has already been published in the original Hebrew text, but it has been thought that an English translation would receive a very hearty welcome at the hands of the reading public. *The Polychrome Bible* is under the general editorship of Professor Paul Haupt, of the Johns Hopkins University, with Dr. Horace Howard Furniss, the famous Shakespearian scholar, as associate editor. Under their editorship the work of translation has been prepared by eminent biblical scholars of America and Europe. Dr. Haupt puts the case for a new edition of the Bible in this wise:

"A translation in modern English, it seems to me, is the best commentary on the Old Version. I do not approve of a revision of the Authorised Version. Our beautiful old English Bible should not be tampered with. There *is* a general consensus of opinion among the best scholars regarding the principal results of modern biblical criticism, so that the attempt to make these scholarly labours accessible to the general public is certainly not premature. I think our new version will help to arouse a new enthusiasm for the Bible, which, as the late James Darmesteter not unjustly remarked, 'is more celebrated than known.' Our new Bible aims to give the actual results of modern biblical scholarship in a popular and attractive form, leaving it to the faith and common sense of the reader to draw his own conclusions. Nor do I think that an acquaintance with the results of modern criticism will impair our reverence for the Scriptures as the Word of God. Honest truth cannot affect the cause of true religion. Criticism is but systematised common sense, and it is a pity to think that Faith and Reason should be incompatible. I believe with the late W. Robertson Smith, than whom England never had a more brilliant biblical scholar, that the Bible does speak to the heart of man in words that can only come from God. Modern criticism may throw a new light on the circumstances in which they were first heard or written, but no amount of change in the background of a picture can make white black or black white. . . . Our new Bible will certainly not be a *fin-de-siècle* Bible, but, God willing, I trust it will become the Bible of the twentieth century."

PROFESSOR PAUL HAUPT.

Editor of "The Polychrome Bible."

Canon T. K. Cheyne, who contributes *The Book of Isaiah* to the Polychrome edition of the Bible, is accepted as the most eminent living authority upon Isaiah. The version which is now to be given to the public is the result of more than thirty years' unceasing devotion and labour. In 1870 he published a first venture, which took the shape of a new translation in chronological order. Later he issued a revised translation and an exhaustive commentary in two volumes, and only two years ago he finished his *Introduction to Isaiah*. Canon Cheyne has divided *Isaiah* into five books, and backgrounds of different colours are used to indicate the various authors. Canon Cheyne, by the way, will visit this country in November to deliver a series of lectures.

CANON T. K. CHEYNE.

❀

The Century Company will publish at once Dr. S. Weir Mitchell's story of the American Revolution which has been appearing serially in the *Century Magazine* during the past year. *Hugh Wynne*, "Free Quaker, sometime Brevet Lieutenant-Colonel on the Staff of His

Excellency General Washington," to give the book its full title, came very near being published last autumn. The book had been prepared and printed, and was ready to be issued in October, 1896. It was practically complete in two volumes, in the shape in which it is now published, and orders had been solicited from the booksellers and were awaiting shipment. But the editor of the *Century* saw in it a fine opportunity for publishing a stirring serial in the magazine, and ere it was too late the advance orders for the book were recalled and arrangements were made for its serial use in the *Century*. The publication of *Hugh Wynne* in book form was therefore deferred until this autumn. This is the authorised version of a story which has already been in circulation in a more or less garbled and apocryphal form.

Yours very truly
S. Weir Mitchell

Mr. Stanley J. Weyman's new novel will not be published until the early spring of next year. This will be the novel entitled *Shrewsbury*, now running serially in the *Idler*, and not a volume of stories, as was announced some little time ago.

Mr. Henry Seton Merriman's next novel is to be entitled *Roden's Corner*, and as at present arranged will be published serially both here and in England in *Harper's Magazine*.

"The other day," writes a correspondent to the Glasgow *Evening News*, "I paid a visit to the old Dumfriesshire farmhouse of Craigenputtock, where Carlyle wrote his *Sartor Resartus*. The farm is still in the hands of the Carlyle family, the present occupant being a grandnephew of the sage. This gentleman—who, by the way, in features as well as in manner, suggests a striking likeness to his illustrious relative—speaks not too cordially of the way in which his farm and steading are overrun at this season by 'pilgrims.' In the neighbouring village of Dunscore there still survive a few of the Carlyle contemporaries. These aged worthies think little of 'Tam,' as they call him. They remember him only as a 'soor-tempered body' who did not get on too well with his brother, at that time the farmer of Craigenputtock, and they are fond of illustrating the 'cussedness' of the sage

THOMAS CARLYLE BETWEEN HIS BROTHER AND NIECE.

by telling of an occasion when, having quarrelled with everybody about the place, he drove off one night in a 'huff' to Dumfries and refused to come back again. Few Scotch people think of visiting the place; all the 'pilgrims' are English, American, or foreign." The above group is from an interesting old photograph, in which "Tam" is seen fondly indulging in his customary clay pipe of "infinite black tobacco." The Centenary edition of Carlyle's works being imported by the Scribners now numbers eleven volumes. *Past and Present* and *The Life of John Sterling* have just been added to this handsome library edition.

"DAN QUIN" (ALFRED H. LEWIS).

Mr. Alfred Henry Lewis, the author of *Wolfville*, recently published by the Frederick A. Stokes Company, had already won a wide reputation among Western readers before his introduction to the East. Himself a Westerner, born in Cleveland, and a cattleman for some five years on the plains of Texas, New Mexico, and Arizona, he is well equipped to describe the life treated in his humorous and entertaining stories. He began by sending fugitive sketches of the picturesque life of the cattlemen to the San Francisco *Examiner*, the St. Louis *Republic*, the Cincinnati *Enquirer*, and other Western papers under the pseudonym of "Dan Quin;" and it is a selection of these tales which is now presented to the suffrage of a wider reading public and built under Sir Walter's own eye, and the grounds laid out after his own ideas. There is an utter absence of stiffness and formality; vegetables and strawberries thrive on sunny banks sloping down from the lawn, and are not relegated to an ugly kitchen garden. Flowers, fruit, and vegetables live amicably together in a setting of lawns and grassy slopes and under the protecting care of fine old trees which Sir Walter did not plant. Possibly the favourite child in the garden is a young quince-tree, looking as promising as its owner could desire. As you enter the house from the side porch, covered with greenery and flowers, it seems that the brightness and sunshine from without accompany you into Sir Walter Besant's study. It looks literally like a room set in a garden. From his writing-table in the centre of the room Sir Walter looks from the large open window upon a secluded piece of lawn covered with trees and shrubs which shut out from his gaze every other object save the sky and the thrushes, starlings, and blackbirds who peck in the grass, and are his particular friends and companions.

Of Sir Walter's genial personality one need not speak, nor of his command of language and flow of ideas which render him an ideal "interviewee." He loves to talk pacing the room to and fro, to and fro, staying by the window now and again to take note of a starling, or varying the exercise with a rest on the arm of his study chair. It is indeed difficult to fix upon one special topic for conversation with Sir Walter Besant, for he is ever evolving some new scheme. We all know of "The People's Palace," the splendid outcome of the ideas set forth in his story, *All Sorts and Conditions of Men*, and of that great and ever-increasing literary organisation the Authors' Society, whose excellent aims and objects are recognised alike by author and publisher, and I found Sir Walter full of a new scheme which applies very particularly to women.

One may at the outset say that Sir Walter Besant is partial to the feminine type known as the "womanly woman," and that he especially admires a woman at home. In that sad and pathetic story of struggling girl-life in London, *Katharine Regina*, Sir Walter writes that "the joy, the crown of love is to sit down and let a man work for them [women] and pour into their ample laps the harvest of his labours."

Now this is all very chivalrous and delightful; indeed, so chivalrous is Sir Walter Besant that, like another Sir Walter, he would lay down his cloak to save any woman's feet from the mud, even though she were not a queen. Although he has voted against opening the degrees of Cambridge University to women, a curious anomaly, he is quick to recognise the absolute futility of telling all women to confine themselves to domestic duties, and wishful to safeguard those who enter professional life against injustice. Indeed, Sir Walter Besant's attitude to women, though not so much in keeping with the spirit of the time as one could wish, has a tendency to disarm criticism. We know that he places woman on a pedestal and worships at her shrine.

The idea of establishing a Working Women's Bureau has been in his mind for some time, and during the last few months has begun to take shape. When I asked him how he proposed to start and carry on this much-needed institution, he replied:

"I have for many years had in my mind an idea of starting an association which should be of assistance and guidance to women in the various branches of professional work into which they are now so rapidly coming forward, and in which unfortunately they are often extremely ill-paid. Though I speak of an association as for working women, I do not include factory girls or servants; it is for the benefit of a class who need it even more—the educated woman who has to earn her own living. It would be of the greatest advantage to ladies engaged in literary and journalistic work, and one may also add that it would indirectly benefit men, by keeping up the price of such work. Women who enter fields of labour in competition with men should demand a fair price for what they do, but my experience leads me to the conclusion that the entrance of women into journalism at the present time depreciates prices, and should this continue, journalism will come to the same sad condition here as it is in America."

"One would have supposed that in a country where newspapers are so much in demand journalism was an excellent profession—and you think, Sir Walter, that its decadence has begun in America?"

"There can be no doubt about it. I will tell you an incident which occurred when I was leaving America after my recent visit. I was in the midst of packing my portmanteau before leaving the hotel in New York for the steamer, when some journalists came and asked for a parting interview. I replied that I had talked myself out in about fifty interviews and had nothing further to say. One man pushed forward and said, 'I have an important question to ask, and I beg that you will give me a few minutes.' I agreed, and he said, 'I want to ask you when you get back home to write something in the English newspapers that will draw attention to the terrible state to which journalism has come in this country.' Then he related a distressing story of how he had been cut down and cut down in price until he now found it almost impossible to make a decent living, work as hard as he might. I told him that if he would write out the story and sign it with his name, I would undertake to get it printed in an English newspaper. Possibly he was afraid of bringing worse consequences upon himself if he published his name, for he did not comply with my suggestion. I had my doubts about the truth of his statements at the time, but now I believe that every word which he said was true. Well, such is the sad state of journalism in America, and to prevent a similar depreciation in this country, it is to the interest of men and women alike that the work of women should be protected by organisation. We hope that the establishment of a Women's Labour Bureau will afford the needed protection, and prevent women from working either in literature, journalism, or any other profession under a standard price."

"And do you think, Sir Walter, that it is only women who work under price? Are there not plenty of men ready to write for just what they can get?"

"Certainly; my experience in connection with the Authors' Society has shown me that there is an appalling number of both sexes who desire to get published at any price, or at no price at all. They come to us with their manuscripts and say, 'We do not mind about payment, but we want to get our matter into print.' There is far too much of this idea of getting published without the work offered being able to secure proper remuneration. If a thing is worth publishing, it is worth paying for."

"And what are your plans for organising the Women's Labour Bureau?"

"There would be a head office in London and branch societies throughout the country, and we should require a very able secretary with the gift of organisation, and I may add," continued Sir Walter, "that I consider that women have superior administrative gifts to men; they know how to organise. We should have honorary secretaries in the villages and smaller towns, but in big cities like Liverpool, Manchester, and Birmingham, where the work would be very heavy, we should require paid secretaries, who would devote the whole of their time to the work. All branches would be in communication with the head office, where a complete registry would be kept of women seeking employment in the various professions. Any one requiring a secretary, governess, journalist, and so forth would apply to the head office, and we should send them exactly the person to suit their requirements, and make it our business to see that proper remuneration was given. Our Society would itself be a guarantee as to the character and ability of any one entered on its books. Women wanting appointments would in like manner apply to us, and we should introduce them to employers."

"The scheme sounds very delightful, Sir Walter, and could not fail to be of immense help to professional women, but how do you propose to make it pay?"

"There need be no difficulty about that," was Sir Walter's cheery rejoinder; "we should need a paper as an organ for the Association, and naturally each member would be a subscriber. In large centres, like London and Manchester, we should probably dispose of ten thousand copies per week, so you see at once that the paper would alone give us a substantial revenue. I have also an idea that each member of the Association should pay a small yearly subscription —say half-a-crown, which would be cheaper for those benefiting by our introductions than agents' fees. Then we should certainly have a colonial edition of the paper, and probably a continental one, too, as we wish the scheme to be as far-reaching as possible, and it would be part of our work to introduce English ladies to appointments in the colonies and abroad.'

"Do you intend to appeal to the public for subscriptions to assist in the founding of the Women's Labour Bureau?"

"No, I should not like to have it regarded from a charitable or philanthropic standpoint; it should be self-supporting, like the Authors' Society; my idea is simply to form an association for guarding the work of women on exactly the same principles as in the Authors' Society we protect the interests of members engaged in literary and journalistic pursuits. A part of my scheme is to provide technical instruction for women. Another important point is that we should have our own firm of solicitors to advise the members gratis on legal matters, such as wrongful dismissal, obtaining money owing from insolvent debtors, in the same way in which the Authors' Society assists its members. Here is an example. A paper lately gone bankrupt is in debt to members of the Society to the extent of hundreds of pounds. Our solicitors will recover as much of this as is possible, and what they obtain will be handed to those entitled to it *without any deduction for legal expenses*. If they had not been members of our Society, they must have lost their money or have consulted a private solicitor, and expended the greater portion of the money which he succeeded in obtaining in fees. Upon this principle we mean to work in the Women's Bureau."

SIR WALTER BESANT.

From his latest photograph.

This is the scheme which Sir Walter Besant's fertile mind has formulated, and in order to bring it before those interested in the work of women, he read a paper before the National Union of Women Workers. Mrs. Creighton, the wife of the Bishop of London, presided, and at the close of the address she suggested to Sir Walter that he should formally propose that the Women's Labour Bureau should be started as a branch of the National Union of Women Workers, which he accordingly did. He feels that it is a fitting thing for women to push forward a scheme to help their sister women in the struggle of earning a livelihood. There is, however, always a fear that when a scheme becomes a mere branch of another association it will dwindle into a secondary kind of thing and partake a little of the form of charitable philanthropy, which would be fatal to the success of a Women's Bureau if it is to be of use to the professional class of women, "working ladies," as Sir Walter prefers to call them. It is time that they were lifted out of that kind of thing and organised, if they be organised at all, on self-supporting and strict business principles. Should the Bureau not attain the far-reaching aims which have been laid down, Sir Walter will, we believe, in the future be willing to float it as the large, comprehensive, and independent association which all professional women who value their own dignity and desire to compete in the various avocations of life on equal terms with men, and ask for no favour, would desire to see the Women's Labour Bureau made, and there could be no better model than the Authors' Society. The present year is rich in schemes for the advancement of women, and scarcely had the formation of the Bureau been taken up by the National Union of Women Workers when Mrs. Wynford Philipps came forward as the reorganiser of the Pioneer Club and the founder of a Women's Institute, which is to include in its scope a Labour Bureau, and to which will be affiliated most of the existing societies for women. It has been arranged that Sir Walter Besant's scheme adopted by the National Union of Women Workers shall practically be worked through the Women's Institute to be founded at Grosvenor Crescent.

It is nearly ten years ago since Sir Walter Besant wrote in his story, *Katharine Regina*:

> "Among the many useful and beneficial inventions which wait for Man—I am sure that the Woman will never bring any of them along—is an Institute or Home for Working Ladies which they will love. It is very much wanted, because in these latter days there are so many ladies who have to work, and the number is daily increasing, so that it will be wanted very much more. In fact, we seem to be getting so poor that in all probability the next generation will know of no ladies except those who work."

Rapid strides have been made, and by women, too, in spite of Sir Walter's prophecy to the contrary, in the direction of forming Homes and Clubs for women which shall be free of the absurd restrictions and prim, soul-killing proprieties which rendered the Harley Street Home of Sir Walter Besant's story little better than a prison. When reference was made to this subject, Sir Walter took from his drawer a newspaper cutting which described a Woman's Hotel shortly to be opened in America, where it is proposed to provide accommodation for some two thousand women, each having a separate room and living *en famille*. "Now does not that strike you with horror?" he inquired; "do you think two thousand women shut up in an hotel to themselves are likely to be happy?" I was weak enough to confess that the idea was not exhilarating, and that a judicious modicum of male society would be an improvement.

"That is just what I think," replied Sir Walter; "women are not happy shut up in these residential houses by themselves, even on the small scale in which they exist in London. It may be cheap and helpful to single women working professionally, that I do not deny, but after the first novelty has worn off it becomes dreary and monotonous. I am convinced that, to be happy, a woman must have the semblance of a home about her. She does not take naturally to the more public kind of living, neither is it good for colonies of women to be shut up to themselves; neither men nor women are helped by living apart, and these residential schemes should try and include provision for social intercourse between the sexes. When the Women's Labour Bureau is sufficiently advanced, I hope to see in connection with it a club for women made as homelike as it is possible for it to be made, where they will have recreation rooms, evenings for social gatherings, and reference libraries."

It was useless to point out to Sir Walter that there is an increasing number of social clubs for women in London of an unrestricted character where man is welcomed, and where he "many a time and oft" doth venture; Sir Walter is fully persuaded that the right sort of thing has not been arrived at yet. If he is able in the future to formulate a scheme for a residential club which will render single women happy, he will have earned the thanks of all women.

As the former Chairman of the Authors' Society, Sir Walter Besant has been brought into con tact with great numbers of struggling women and of girls seeking an outlet in life. Letters from such pour in upon him in great numbers, and it occurred to me to ask him whether he did not find among his correspondents a growing dislike to the teaching profession, a tendency among girls to "strike" against being governesses.

"FROGNAL END," SIR WALTER BESANT'S HOUSE.

"Yes," he replied, "I find that spirit of distaste growing, and small wonder at it when you consider the revelations made by my friend Miss Low on how poor ladies live. The thought of devoting the best years of your life to the arduous work of teaching upon a salary which does not permit saving for old age, is enough to make girls shrink from being governesses and to turn to other means of earning a livelihood in preference."

"Do you think, Sir Walter, that there should be any restriction regarding the work which women undertake in competition with men?"

"I think that it is a pity for them to force themselves into positions which they are not able adequately to fill, and so depreciate the pay, because it is not easy to raise it again when men follow them. The whole field of literature and journalism should be freely opened to women, for they have very decided abilities for that class of work and are succeeding all along the line, but I think it is a pity for a girl to take the place of a clerk in a business house in the city at half-pay. A man is turned out of the position to make way for her, and is frequently unable to secure as good a berth in its place. He has to live on some small pittance, and is unable to marry, and the girl who has taken his place has a meagre salary which does not make it possible for her to support herself comfortably in a home. I think everything is bad, in an economic sense, which tends to prevent marriage, it being the great safeguard of our national life. Speaking of women's capacity," he continued, "I do not think that they have shown themselves equal to men in intellectual achievements."

"But what chance have they had, Sir Walter? They have for centuries had next to no education, or at best a superficial and ornamental one."

"True; I am not prophesying about the future. Improved education will show great development in the capacity of women, but I say that up to the present they have not shown themselves equal to men—where is your great woman dramatist, where your musical composer, and where your great woman poet?"

"When you come to fiction," continued Sir Walter, "women excel. Now

SIR WALTER BESANT'S STUDY.

it is in the world of fiction that women have made, and will, I venture to predict, make their greatest mark."

"Whom do you consider our greatest woman novelist?"

But Sir Walter evaded committing himself to criticism upon the women who to-day are taking a leading place among novelists, and cautiously expressed his admiration for Jane Austen and Maria Edgeworth. "No one can deny," he said, "the great intellectual power and wonderful gifts of a novelist like George Eliot, but I must confess that I have not that unbounded admiration for George Eliot which many people have. Mrs. Gaskell is a more charming and delightful novelist, so beautiful and womanly in all her instincts, as well as being a most accomplished writer."

"What about the proposed school of fiction, Sir Walter? Are they going to manufacture novelists?"

"A great deal of nonsense has been written about this. I am not engaged in starting any such school. But I quite approve of a College of Literature. Of course no one expects to make novelists simply by educating people in the mere technique of the art. I remember some time ago when I was about to give a lecture on the 'Art of Fiction,' my old friend James Payn looked at me in consternation and said, 'For God's sake don't tell them how to do it.' Well," continued Sir Walter, with a laugh at this reminiscence, "I am not advocating a scheme to flood the world with novelists; but I should like to see established a college which would be devoted entirely to the cultivation of literature in all branches, and it should be opened equally to girls and youths. There might be courses of lectures on Literature, Criticism, Style, Rhetoric, on the Drama, on Construction. There would be a school for English composition, including fiction. I am perfectly certain that a college for literature is needed. I should like to say to some of the promising young novelists of the day, 'How much better you would have written if your natural abilities had had specific training.' No amount of education can supply the writer's faculty, which is inborn, but a college would train those who have it to use it in the very highest way. We do not suppose that we are going to make geniuses. People complain of the Art Schools that they have not produced great artists, but I would say that if they have not made artists, they have at least cultivated the taste for art, and raised its standard. Look into old volumes and see what an advance has been made in the matter of illustration in present-day literature. Think of the illustrations of such artists as Leech, and how greatly we have improved upon them."

I had further proof of Sir Walter Besant's versatility and antiquarian lore as I said good-bye under the sunny porch. It was a history of my own name, derived, I was assured, from St. Olaf, the patron saint of Scandinavia, and I quitted Frognal End with the astonishing information that my husband's ancestors must have been Vikings, that they probably destroyed old London Bridge, built the church of St. Olaf to appease the unfortunate Saxon, and that Tooley Street grew up hard by, and is the rightful possession of the family. Let all people who wish to trace their ancestry repair to Sir Walter Besant, and he may, as the newspaper advertisements have it, be able to tell them of "something to their benefit."

Sarah A. Tooley.

THE PHOTOGRAPH.

See dis pictyah in my han'?
Dat's my gal;
Ain't she purty? goodness lan'!
Huh name Sal.
Dat's de very way she be—
Kin' o' tickles me to see
Huh a-smilin' back at me.

She sont me dis photygraph
Jes' las' week;
An' aldough hit made me laugh—
My black cheek
Felt somethin' a-runnin' queer;
Bless yo' soul, it was a tear
Jes' f'om wishin' she was here.

Often when I's all alone
Layin' here,
I git t'inkin' 'bout my own
Sallie dear:
How she say dat I's huh beau,
An' hit tickles me to know
Dat de gal do love me so.

Some bright day I's goin' back,
Fo' de la!
An' ez sho' 'z my face is black,
Ax huh pa
Fu' de blessed little Miss
Who 's a smilin' out o' dis
Pictyah, lak she wan'ed a kiss!

Paul Laurence Dunbar.

The main distinction of Nottingham journalism lies in the fact that it is associated with the name of Mr. J. M. Barrie. But to-day the famous author is only a tradition in this pretty Midland town. His press days take us back to a past era of local journalism, and save for the old files of the *Nottingham Journal* and his own novel, *When a Man's Single*, there is little or no evidence of his sojourn in Laceland. There are one or two men still engaged on the *Nottingham Press*, who were so employed during Mr. Barrie's brief connection with the *Journal*, but they never met him, never even heard of him while he was a fellow-labourer in the same field, and only know him by his subsequent fame. This is readily accounted for, as he led a very retired and secluded life, meeting nobody outside his own office and familiarising with few within. Writing on this point to the Rev. A. H. Watts, of Nottingham, who was lecturing on his works recently, Mr. Barrie says :

"I thank you for your letter, and wish you had a better subject for your lecture. I don't know of any personal article about myself that is not imaginary and largely erroneous. But there is really nothing to tell that would interest any one. Yes, I was in Nottingham for a year, and liked it well, though I was known to scarce any one. If you ever met an uncouth stranger wandering in the dark round the castle, ten or twelve years ago, his appearance unimpressive, a book in each pocket, and his thoughts three hundred miles due north, it might have been the subject of your lecture."

The newspaper on which Mr. Barrie was engaged was discontinued and incorporated with a more successful rival shortly after he went to London to enter that larger field of literature in which he has achieved such a brilliant and lasting success. So that his old colleagues have been scattered far and wide, Mr. Gilmour, now a successful barrister-at-law and private secretary to Lord Rosebery, and formerly a reporter on the *Journal*, being the only one with whom the old friendship seems to have been maintained. Thus it is that you may ask in vain of any on the local Press for a souvenir of the distinguished author whom Nottingham once entertained unawares.

Mr. Barrie had graduated in 1882, and was in Edinburgh for several months waiting, like Micawber, for something to turn up. The something did turn up in the shape of an offer of the post of leader-writer on the *Nottingham Journal*, this resulting from an application which Mr. Barrie had made in reply to an advertisement. The salary offered was not princely : three guineas a week, in fact. But it was a splendid opportunity for putting his journalistic ability to the test, and in February of 1883 he commenced his brief career as a journalist in Nottingham. In some respects Nottingham is an ideal town for a literary man ; it presents so many interesting phases of life that one who is a student of character cannot fail to profit by a stay in it. Neither an important city nor yet a sleepy town, it is something of both. The bustle of commerce and money-making is seen in its busy streets and its frequent factories; but it retains much of the old-fashioned village or parochial spirit. The city and the village seem to be mixed up in Nottingham, and though the village predominates, it is slowly succumbing. The town is really a congeries of large villages which have put their arms round each other's necks and made the modern Nottingham. The new and the gaudy mingle with the old and the historic, the rude rustic lingers beside the smart "city" man, the factory and the warehouse fight an unequal battle with the orchard and the garden even to the very heart of the town. Here, in a place of many-beauties and not a few blemishes, in a town with some intellectual aspirations and with tendencies in other directions, there is much food for the mind of the novelist, and it is evident that Nottingham has left its impress on Mr. Barrie.

THE OLD OFFICE OF THE "NOTTINGHAM JOURNAL."

The newspaper with which Mr. Barrie had become attached in 1883 was a very old-fashioned specimen of journalism, yet it was conducted during its long career as an independent publication with considerable ability, and would compare not unfavourably with many existing dailies of the same class. Mr. Barrie was not editor-in-chief, but he was editor *de facto*; for he was allowed to write as much as he liked and whatever he liked, his safety valve being the foreman compositor, whose setting power—that is, the capacity of his men for putting into type the matter produced by the literary staff—seems to have dictated the contents of the paper. But the young leader-writer, or editor, or whatever we may term him, must have had a prodigious capacity for work, as the columns of the *Journal* in 1883 and 1884 bear witness. In addition to writing his daily editorial contributions, which often panned out to two or three columns, he also contributed every Monday a special article signed "Hippomenes," and every Thursday the same signature was appended to a column of sparkling notes headed "The Modern Peripatetic." Of these various writings the most interesting to-day are, of course, the special articles, many of which would bear republication. The range of topics to which the young author turned his pen seems to have been without limit; he was equally at home discussing "The Marriage Knot," or "The Midnight Oil," "An Old Morality Play," or "Tom, Dick, and Harry." These articles have all a rich literary flavour, and prove their author a man of wide reading. The notes of "The Modern Peripatetic" are of unequal merit. Taken in the bulk they are excellent journalism, and occasionally they rise to the height of literature. Such little reflective passages as this are above the usual newspaper standard:

MR. BARRIE IN 1883.

From a photograph taken in Glasgow.

"The glue that keeps the world together is self-esteem. It is terrible to think of what might happen did Smith some time take it into his head that it was not worth his while to try to out-do Robinson, or Brown that life would still be worth living though his income was fifty pounds per annum short of Jones's. Self-esteem takes the form of a vehement desire to rise superior to our neighbours, and in all Great Britain there is not in all probability a single street which does not contain at least one superior family. A superior family is one that esteems itself so very much that it cannot avoid looking down on its surroundings, and it is perfectly happy in the knowledge that its drawing-room is one foot by one and a half larger than any other in the vicinity."

Or this:

"The candid critic is a gentleman of whom all authors approve when he praises their last volume. 'What I wanted,' they explain, 'is no gush of praise, as from a friend, but simply a calm, just review, slating my work if it deserves slating, commending it if it deserves commendation.' Noble fellows! Then when the critic, who is very young in this case, observes that the work bears distinct traces of genius, is Shakespearian without Shakespeare's coarseness, reminds one of Milton in his best moments, and suggests Tennyson before the Poet Laureate's hand lost its cunning, the author smiles gently to himself, and repeats that what he wanted was an honest criticism, and he thinks he has got it."

The Nottingham Journal

REDUCED FAC-SIMILE OF THE "JOURNAL" PAGE.

There is subtle humour in the following:

"A great deal of nonsense will be talked over the Queen's book for the next nine days. It is said that too many benefits were showered upon John Brown, but that is nonsense. In the new book the Queen tells how she presented her attendant on one occasion with an oxidised silver biscuit box, which drew tears from his eyes and the exclamation that this was too much. 'God knows it is not,' is Her Majesty's remark, and I cannot see that it was."

This is also a good specimen of Mr. Barrie's capacity for delicately exaggerating a story in a semi Yankee fashion, and yet without the boisterousness of the American humourist. His effects, though striking and laughter-compelling, are always attained with a delicacy of touch which no trans-Atlantic "funny man" can ever hope to equal:

"A public meeting friend of my acquaintance used to attend every meeting in his neighbourhood for the purpose of calling out 'Here, here,' 'Question,' 'Order,' and 'No, no,' and always turned to the newspapers of the next day with anxiety to see if his share in the proceedings had been reported. Where they were attended to he carefully preserved copies of the newspapers, and there can be little doubt that this is the most singular case of literary vanity known since the introduction of printing."

One more extract from these early writings of our distinguished author is worth quoting:

"The scene was a law court in Paris, and an eloquent young advocate was pleading the cause of his client in a way that brought tears to the eyes of many of his hearers. The speech was recited from memory, and the pleader had taken the precaution of distributing printed copies among the reporters, so that his speech should read properly in the morning's newspapers. 'And now,' he exclaimed, 'I feel myself wholly unworthy to occupy the proud position I hold this day. The onerous nature of the task makes me tremble lest I should not do my unhappy client justice, and I would to God that an abler advocate would take my place.' Here he faltered, put his handkerchief to his eyes, and seemed overcome with emotion. Unfortunately one of the reporters did not understand, and fearing that the lawyer had forgotten what came next, he hurriedly looked up the place in his copy of the speech to prompt him. 'But the tears I see now,' he exclaimed in a loud whisper, 'in the eyes of my unhappy client, nerve me to the task.' Of course, the tables were dissolved in laughter, and the eloquent pleader found that untimely interruption had been sufficient to rob him of a reputation."

In these columns of *obiter dicta*, Mr. Barrie occasionally attempted verse, and even endeavoured to give renderings of Horace; but it would be wrong to say that he wooed the tuneful Nine with any measure of success. Although these early efforts would make excellent "copy" if reproduced to-day, we shall not seek to disturb their repose in the forgotten files of the old *Journal*.

I cannot agree with Dr. Robertson Nicoll that Mr. Barrie's hand is not traceable in the "leaders" which he wrote for the *Journal*. One could scarcely fail to recognise it in such a passage as this, which I take from the "first leader" in the *Journal* of January 12th, 1884:

"There are optimists and pessimists all over this miserable world. The optimists believe that everything is on the road to being better, and take a cheerful view of civilised society. They know that men have made serious mistakes in the past, and will continue to make them to the end of the chapter, but, taking one thing with another, they are firmly convinced that mankind is advancing, and that this wretched world is not a bad place to live in—especially after dinner. The pessimists take the gloomiest view of matters. Everything is awry and out of joint. Property is not diffused as it ought to be, nor is wealth. Providence will persist in ramming round men into square holes and square men into round holes. The rich have it all their own way, the poor are nowhere. [I have always understood they were everywhere!] Society is sitting on a powder magazine which some fine morning will go off with a crash and wreck the work of ages. Nothing is as it ought to be. Men are not fed as they should be, nor housed, nor taught. The earth is an antechamber to hell, and the sons of man are whirled through space at the rate of 60,000 miles an hour, with their God's face averted from them."

Mr. Barrie seems to have had two pet subjects for editorial treatment: Mr. Chamberlain and Mr. Henry George. Russell of the *Scotsman* (Edinburgh) told a lady once that when he was hard up for a topic he just had another "dirl at Dr. Chalmers." Mr. Barrie returns again and again to the consideration of various phases of the political protagonist, and he is never tired of denouncing Mr. George's Single Tax. They seem to have been as useful to him as Dr. Chalmers was to Russell.

It is well known of course that *When a Man's Single* is the result of Mr. Barrie's stay in Nottingham. With the merits of the book as a novel I do not purpose dealing, and will only say that it strikes me as rather juvenile, the character of Rob Angus quite failing to convince. Its real value lies in the more or less accurate glimpses it affords behind the scenes of literary life; for, though Mr. Barrie's journalistic experience at the time he wrote the book was inconsiderable and very circumscribed, he has the true novelist's genius for typifying, and, if we exclude Rob Angus, the literary characters of the story may be described as studies from life. One might say this were like criticising *Hamlet* with the Prince left out; but I believe that what I state will be endorsed by those who are familiar with literary life behind the scenes. The Silchester of the book is Nottingham, and the *Daily Mirror* is the old *Nottingham Journal*; but beyond the incidents relating to the experiences of Rob Angus on the *Mirror* staff, there is practically no attempt at "local colour." The description of the *Mirror* headquarters is very much in keeping with the reality.

"The *Mirror's* offices," writes the author, "are nearly crushed out of sight in a block of buildings left in the middle of a street for town councils to pull down gradually. This island of houses, against which a sea of humanity beats daily, is cut in two by a narrow passage, off which several doors open. One of these leads up a dirty stair to the editorial and composing rooms of the *Daily Mirror*, and down a dirty stair to its printing rooms It is the door at which you may hammer for an hour without any one's paying the least attention."

The block of buildings still remains, and there is no reason to suppose that the Corporation will seek to pull it down any time within the life of the present generation; for it is an exaggeration to say that it stands in the middle of a street, and the ocean bed which carries the "sea of humanity" on either side is wide enough for all practical purposes. The "dirty stair" is still there, though a recent coat of paint has temporarily falsified the adjective, and the narrow passage where Rob Angus lingered so long still cuts the island of houses in two.

The interior of the old office is more interesting, if less imposing than its elevation. All the fittings and appliances used in the production of the *Mirror* have vanished long since, but in Mr. Barrie's pages these have found something like immortality.

"The editor's room had a carpet, and was chiefly furnished with books sent in for review. It was more comfortable, but more gloomy-looking than the reporters' room, which had a long desk running along one side of it, and a bunk for holding coals and old newspapers on the other side. The floor was so littered with newspapers, many of them still in their wrappers, that, on his way between his seat and the door, the reporter generally kicked one or more into the bunk. It was in this way, unless an apprentice happened to be otherwise disengaged, that the floor was swept.

"In this room were a reference library and an old coat. The library was within reach of the sub-editor's hand, and contained some fifty books which the literary staff could consult, with the conviction that they would find the page they wanted missing. The coat had hung unbrushed on a nail for many years, and was so thick with dust that John Milton (the junior reporter) could draw pictures on it with his finger. According to legend, it was the coat of a distinguished novelist, who had once been a reporter on the *Mirror*, and had left Silchester unostentatiously by his window."

The slight touch of obvious caricature in this description does not interfere with its truth; for any one who has had experience of journalistic life in the office of a newspaper of the standing of the *Mirror*, will immediately recognise the fidelity of the picture. That reporters' room, with the long desk running along one side of it, its old newspapers, and the economical method of sweeping its floor, are all familiar to the scribe who has toiled on provincial newspapers, and on the London press for that matter. And

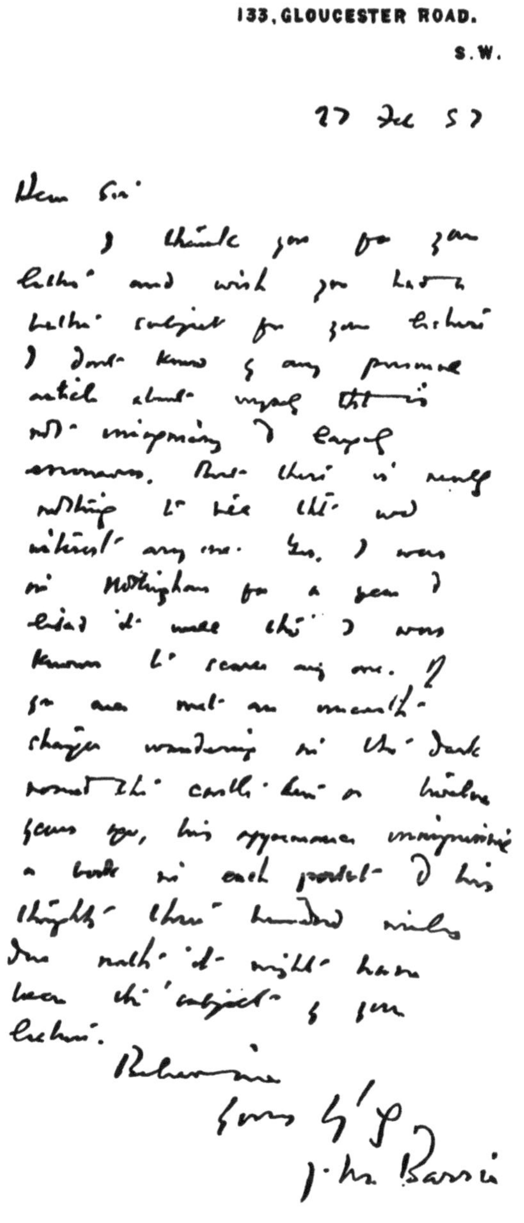

133, GLOUCESTER ROAD.
S.W.

27 Dec 97

Dear Sir

I thank you for your letter and wish you had a better subject for your lecture. I don't know of any personal article about myself that is not [illegible] & [illegible]. But there is really nothing to tell that would interest any one. Yes, I was in Nottingham for a year. I lived there quietly and was known to scarcely any one. If you [illegible] met an [illegible] stranger wandering in the dark round the castle hill [illegible] years ago, his appearance [illegible], a book in each pocket & his thoughts three hundred miles due north, it might have been the subject of your lecture.

Believe me
yours v t
J. M. Barrie

FAC-SIMILE OF MR. BARRIE'S LETTER TO THE REV. A. H. WATTS (SEE PAGE 116).

where is the journalist who has not experienced over and over again the delight of turning to the scanty reference library, to find that the page he requires in one or other of its books has been destroyed, to light a pipe, perhaps, or through a mishap to the junior reporter when he has been trying how many volumes he could balance on his nose? The coat, too: where is there a reporters' room without that coat, and its tradition?

The charm of the *Mirror* staff, who, for the most part, belong to a bygone Bohemian era, is only heightened by the artistic touch of caricature with which the author rivets them in our memory. Chief among them stands Penny, the foreman compositor. He was the most important man in the office, not excepting Mr. Licquorish, the editor (an entirely fictitious character), and Barrie depicts him as "a lank, loosely jointed man of forty, who shuffled about the office in slippers, ruled the compositors with a loud voice and a blustering manner, and was believed to be in Mr. Licquorish's confidence. His politics were respect for the House of Lords, because it rose early, enabling him to have it set before supper time." Penny is a wonderfully typical character, he might serve for any foreman compositor; and his scenes with Protheroe, the sub-editor, are pictures of events which are happening in hundreds of newspaper offices every day and every night. For your true foreman believes he is autocrat of the press, and will not alter the time of getting his stereo plates ready for the machines though the heavens should fall. I know of one of the fraternity who actually refused to correct the proof of his editor's leader because it had not been returned in time—and that editor was the proprietor of the paper, a baronet and a member of parliament to boot!

Penny not only ruled the *Mirror* compositors, he domineered the sub-editor, and, if the truth must be told, Mr. Barrie, the nominal editor of the paper, was at the mercy of this picturesque tyrant. There were occasions, however, when Penny's nature underwent a change.

"Sometimes about two o'clock in the morning Penny would get sociable, and the sub-editor was always glad to respond. On these occasions they talked with bated breath about the amount of copy that would come in should anything happen to Mr. Gladstone; and the sub-editor, if he was in a despondent mood, predicted it would occur at midnight. Thinking of this had made him a conservative."

Mr. Gladstone still holds on with remarkable tenacity to the silver thread of life, while the *Journal* disappeared many years ago.

The original of Penny, who, in person, is not to be recognised in Mr. Barrie's fancy portrait, is still alive; but he gave up the struggle with editors, sub-editors and smaller newspaper fry, long ago, and is now spending an age of ease as the proprietor of a neat little hotel in one of the suburbs of Nottingham. He is about the only one in Nottingham who remembers anything of Barrie, and in the course of a chat with him the other day he told me that in those far-off days Barrie gave him the impression of one who, behind a shyness of manner, had the capacity for winning success. Though others, who might have been expected to appreciate the literary talent of which Barrie gave unmistakable evidence during his connection with the *Journal*, were blind to his qualities, or not sufficiently interested in his work to recognise its promise, the living representative of Penny will assure you that he always felt Barrie would make his mark. Depend upon an old comp for nosing out literary talent—especially after it has been discovered. But Penny can claim some slight share in Barrie's early literary labours; for one of the first articles which our novelist managed to "place" in London was the description of a descent of a coal mine in the neighbourhood of Clifton Grove, which Kirk White's muse has rendered famous, and on this expedition Penny acted as guide, philosopher and friend to the young journalist. Penny's devotion to literature, however, had not, at a very recent date, extended so far as *When a Man's Single*, which he confessed he had not read! But he means to read it some day—when he gets time—and he would like to see Barrie again, "before I peg out;" for the snows of many winters are gathering on the old compositor's head.

Billy Kirker, the chief reporter of the *Mirror*, represents a journalistic type which is not yet extinct. He was a thorough Bohemian, "his ring, it was noticed, generally disappeared about the middle of the month, and his scarf-pin followed it by the twenty-first. With the beginning of the month they reappeared together. The literary staff was paid monthly." And, oh! how many Billy Kirkers I have known; always "talking shop," drawing lurid pictures of the inadequacy of their own staffs as compared with their rivals', in order to show how much more and how much better work they can produce with their limited resources. "Enterprise without outlay is the motto of this office," were among the first words of Billy's greeting to Rob Angus when he had summoned the courage to mount that dirty stair and face his fate inside the *Mirror* office. Here Barrie is absolutely faithful to fact; for these words might well have been substituted for the legend "*Pro Rege, Lege, Grege,*" which adorned the editorial page of the old *Journal.* But Billy Kirker had no ill-will to his deadly rival on the opposition paper, as he explained with charming naïveté to Rob. "Oh, no," said Kirker, "we help each other. For instance, if Daddy Walsh, the *Argus* chief, is drunk, I help him, and if I am drunk he helps me. I am going down to the 'Frying Pan' to see him now."

Before going to the "Frying Pan" he borrowed five shillings from the new recruit from Thrums. The "Frying Pan" is the fictitious name for a small public-house of very uninviting aspect, which still stands near to the *Daily Express* office; but it is frequented by a class to whom Barrie's is a closed book. Time was when a convivial crew, known as the Kettle Club, whose chief delights were spinning yarns and hard drinking, had their headquarters there. Rumour says that Barrie was once induced to visit this home of intellectual refinement; but rumour could have given even the members of the Kettle Club points and a beating. To-day, the so-called "Press House" is a tavern a few yards removed from the "Frying Pan," and there penny-a-liners and half-fledged reporters drink beer and fancy themselves full-blown journalists, carrying down tradition of Billy Kirker and that bright Bohemian band. But there are no Barries among them.

J. A. Hammerton.

TWO APOSTLES OF SIMPLICITY.

"Art for art's sake" in France refuses to give place to the utilitarian formula "art for life's sake," so dear to sundry "neo-Christians" and writers with a purpose. Indirectly, however, recent French fiction is often almost as didactic as the Philistine could desire; for many a writer, disgusted with perverse rationalism, seeks some high compulsion to idealistic conceptions and more decent living, and having found his satisfaction depicts the manner of its attainment. Huysmans, for instance, in his recent novel, *En Route*, described an act of faith, the perfectly unreasoning process by which he jumped out of dirty scepticism into a morbid and somewhat heathen catholicism. But even before this and long before "the bankruptcy of science" became a Parisian byword, Maeterlinck had turned from reason to mysticism. In gruesome plays he had expressed the mysterious terror of death. In essays on Novalis, Emerson, and the unknown but "admirable" Ruysbroeck he then meditated the vague beauty of sundry metaphysical intuitions. And at last, fascinated by the spiritual life and disgusted with stage conditions, he devoted himself to "pale ideals of silence and of darkness." But the dramatist in him was not quite dead. His old art still tempted him. He has yielded, and in *Aglavaine et Sélysette** has come from his dreams almost a didactic dramatist.

This is a new rôle for our caricaturists' favourite butt. Will he be safe now? Probably, for he has changed his odd technique. Renouncing his Ollendorff method of question and answer, he has turned to harping on single words, to a musical alternation of names, and to the lull of balanced sentences. His greatest foible is gone, but so is much of his force. His picturesqueness, too, his power to suggest

* See review by Mr. W. B. Yeats on page 151.

charmingly to the eye's imagination comes seldom to him now. Yet he has gained in this; his temper is less afraid, more loving; and he recognises the power of naturalness in life.

Indeed, the dramatic motive of *Aglavaine et Sélysette* is the destruction of an unnatural though aspiring ideal by spontaneous sweetness. In less abstract terms what Maeterlinck shows us is the attempt of a somewhat nebulous Méléandre to carry on a beautifully exalted *ménage à trois*. There is to be no selfishness, no sorrow. He loves Aglavaine, the beautiful propounder of theories; but he also loves his exquisitely childlike wife Sélysette. Aglavaine in turn loves Sélysette and also, of course, Méléandre. And Sélysette, by her help, passing through jealousy, attains a pathetically joyful sympathy that seems to make the triple household lovingly possible. But love cannot safely be coerced; it is wild.

"We watch it in our depths like a vulture or a strange eagle in a cage. The cage belongs to us, but the bird belongs to no one. We watch it, we warm it, we feed it, but we do not know what it is going to do, whether it will fly, or wound itself against its bars, or sing."

In Sélysette it can now only wound itself. She pines in the bliss of her self-sacrifice, which, shy as it is, proves to her rival that the three "cannot live happily, for the time has not yet come when human beings can so unite together." Therefore Aglavaine would willingly leave them. Sélysette, however, has a better plan for the general happiness—a plan that she cannot yet explain, she says. And she wanders off to an old tower by the sea, there to catch a rare "green-winged bird." But when from the top she sees the shining ocean and the sunny castle-garden she falters, goes to kiss her old grandmother once more, then, at cold twilight, after the glory of the day, quickly, before the stars can pierce the sky and hold her in the world, she leans over the crumbling wall and, clutching for the "green-winged bird," falls to the beach. Thus by death the unreasoning impulse and devotion of Sélysette conquer. For even Méléandre, the theorist of reasoned ideals of beautiful living, is now filled with disgust for the beauty that brings sorrow and for reason that aspires falsely.

Is this Maeterlinck's feeling? Perhaps, on the contrary, he deems the impossibility of unnatural but "beautiful" ideals the most tragic fact in his play. Most readers, however, will probably agree with Aglavaine where this personification of what Maeterlinck might call superhuman beauty affirms:

"When I watch Sélysette I ask myself each moment whether all that she does as she gropes in her childlike heart is not greater and a thousand, thousand times purer than all that I could have done. She is unspeakably beautiful. She needs only to stoop to find unheard of treasures in her heart, and she comes and tremblingly offers them like a blind child that does not know that both its hands are full of jewels and pearls."

Now whether in his play Maeterlinck preaches such ignorant impulse or not, that spirit brings him rest from the problem which has troubled his mind. So, too much French thought, after tortured reasoning, has turned to the opposite, the intuitive extreme. A vague desire for simple faith hovers in the air. And though faith alone cannot give the balanced strength and higher wisdom which the decadent race must gain if it is to be saved, the tender beauty and high pathos of devoted simplicity have endeared it to many men of sensitive perceptions.

Marcel Schwob, especially, has warmly recognised that simplicity induces delicate moods—moods for the artist to caress and to render. He has felt them sympathetically, and with the seemingly guileless skill of a cunning artisan has expressed them in his *Croisade des Enfants*. This fragile little book is not what one might hastily dub it, the pretty babble of a sentimental youngling. Schwob has conned Plato and Aristotle, dusty mediæval parchments, French literature, German metaphysics, the Elizabethan dramatists, Defoe, Stevenson, George Meredith; he has commented on them in essays now thorough, now slight, always keen for the artist's methods; and he has applied his acquirements in half a dozen volumes of tales, largely horrible, ironical, or sad, but vividly visualised and compact, and sometimes told with rhythmic sonorousness skilfully adapted to the mood expressed. Thoroughly equipped, then, and, despite his sophistication, in artistic sympathy with childlike faith he has studied perhaps its most touching manifestation, the Children's Crusade in the thirteenth century; and putting himself imaginatively in that time he has given tongue to the experience of a leper, of a child, of a pope, or again of a merchant. Thus he has at once depicted the successive events of the Crusade and brought out various ways of regarding the faith which underlay it. By judiciously varying his manner he has suggested the mood and the personality of each speaker; yet he has kept a certain unity of style corresponding to the single underlying motive. In brief, he has written a symphonic movement in the form of variations on the theme of ignorant faith.

To realise this technical feat or the curious charm of the book one must read the whole series of monologues. For a mere hint of the author's novel power, however, it is enough, after learning that the inspired horde of children had overrun the province of the Loire, to turn to this bit of horror and pathos. The leper speaks:

"If you would understand what I am going to tell you, know that my head is covered with a white cowl, and that I shake a clapper of hard wood. I no longer know how my face looks, but I am afraid of my hands. They run before me like livid and scaly beasts. I would gladly cut them off. Whatever they touch fills me with shame. They seem to make the red fruits that I pick decay, and the poor roots that I tear up seem to wither beneath them. *Domine ceterorum libera me!* The Saviour has not atoned for my pallid sin. I am forgotten until the resurrection. Like the toad sealed by cold moonlight in a dark stone I shall remain enclosed in my hideous gangue when others rise again with their bodies bright. *Domine ceterorum, fac me liberum: leprosus sum.* I am alone and full of horror. Only my teeth have kept their natural whiteness. Beasts are afraid, and my soul longs to flee. The light turns from me.

"Twelve hundred and twelve years ago their Saviour saved them, and He did not have pity on me. I was not touched by the bloody lance that pierced His side. Perhaps the blood of the Saviour of others would have cured me. I often dream of blood: I might bite with my teeth; they are clean. Since He did not deign to give it to me, I am greedy for blood that belongs to Him. That is why I lay in wait for the children who came down from the land of Vendôme toward this part of the Loire. They had crosses, and they were subject to Him. Their bodies were His body, and He did not grant His body to me. I am encompassed on earth with pale damnation. I spied about to suck innocent blood from the neck of one of His children. *Et caro nova fiet in die iræ.* On the day of judgment my flesh shall be made new. And behind the others walked a fair, red-haired child. I marked him; I bounded suddenly; I seized his mouth with my dreadful hands. He wore only a rough shirt; his feet were bare and his eyes remained placid. And he looked at me without surprise. So, knowing that he would not cry out, I longed to hear a human voice once more, and I took my hands from his mouth, and he did not wipe his mouth. And his eyes seemed far off.

"'Who are you?' I said to him.

"'Johannes the Teuton,' he answered. And his words were limpid and healing.

"'Where are you going?' I said further.

"And he answered: 'To Jerusalem, to conquer the Holy Land.'

"Then I began to laugh, and I asked him: 'Where is Jerusalem?'

"And he answered: 'I do not know.'

"And I said further: 'How will you be able to get there?'

"And he said to me: 'I do not know.'

"And I said further: 'What is Jerusalem?'

"And he answered: 'It is Our Lord.'

"Then I began to laugh again, and I asked: 'What is your Lord?'

"And he said to me: 'I do not know; He is white.'

"And that saying threw me into fury, and I bared my teeth under my cowl and leaned toward his pure neck, and he did not draw back at all, and I said to him: 'Why are you not afraid of me?'

"And he said: 'Why should I be afraid of you, white wayfarer?'

"Then I was shaken with great sobs, and I stretched myself on the ground, and I kissed the earth with my horrible lips, and I cried out: 'Because I am a leper!'

"And the Teuton child considered me, and said limpidly: 'I do not know. . . .'

"He was not afraid of me! My monstrous whiteness seems to him like the whiteness of his Lord. And I took a handful of grass and I wiped his mouth and his hands. And I said to him: 'Go in peace to your white Lord, and say to Him that He has forgotten me.'

"And the child looked at me without speaking. And I went with him out of the blackness of the forest. He walked without trembling. I saw his red hair vanish at a distance in the sun. *Domine infantium, libera me.* May the sound of my wooden clapper come to you like the pure sound of bells. Master of those who do not know, deliver me!"

With this helpless appeal from the mysterious injustice of his suffering the leper leaves us. The child whose trust has subdued him is lost among the seven thousand little crusaders as they wander toward slavery and death. Pathetic tragedy is proved to be the only possible result of their impossible ideals. Yet when we lay down the book in which Schwob has shown us this, his pope's words, "Let us return to ignorance and simplicity," persist in our ears and fix in our mind the pseudo-Franciscan, child-like feeling of the whole.

Thus Schwob, like Maeterlinck and many another, has found in the most primitive qualities rest from problems and from intellectual wanderings. The spirit that they turn to will please and perhaps even influence. But it cannot prevail, for it is not fully natural and not quite sane. Indeed, these young writers are not robust enough to move France; they live their imaginative lives not in the healthful heat of the sun, but by moonlight. Yet even if they were lunatics—which is not the same thing—their skill, their delicacy, and their individual charm would give them a noteworthy place in contemporary art.

Henry Copley Greene.

PARIS LETTER.

The most important piece of information for bookmen here this month is that the Goncourt Academy will live. The fears I expressed to you in my last letter in regard to Edmond de Goncourt's will have proved groundless. The court, by the mouth of its presiding judge, M. Bacedouin, has declared that the will shall stand, and the facts that were revealed during the trial can leave no doubt that the decision is a good one, at least from a French jurist's standpoint. You remember the principal argument of the opponents of the will. The deed was dated 1884, yet contained references to facts that did not take place until several years later. The general opinion was that this was due to Goncourt's own carelessness. It was shown that the truth was exactly the reverse. In 1892 Goncourt, wishing to introduce changes in the will, sent it, with a note specifying the changes to be made, to his family's notary. You know that a French notary is an important man, usually entrusted with the care of estates, the making of wills, etc., and that the same firm, or *étude*, will often transact a family's business for generation after generation. French notaries are notoriously accurate and even punctilious. Goncourt therefore thought that the safest thing for him to do, after receiving the corrected will, was to copy it with his own hand, exactly as it was; and as it happened that the notary had omitted to change the original date, the new will was dated 1884, just as the old one was. The court therefore determined to overlook what was nothing more than a *lapsus calami*, and to allow Goncourt's executors, Daudet and Hennique, to carry out their friend's clearly expressed intentions.

The executors do not seem to fear the results of any appeal, and will soon be at work perfecting the plans for the establishment of the "Academy." The funds at hand are almost sufficient. They already amount to one million and a half of francs. Daudet wishes the Academicians very soon to fill the two vacancies now existing in the membership, and then to select the young *littérateur* who is to be the first recipient of the Goncourt prize of five thousand francs. Several candidacies are already mentioned for the two vacancies, chief among them being those of Léon Alphonse Daudet, Paul Alexis, George Rodenbach, and Lucien Descaves. The last three are men of decided talent; as for Léon Daudet, he is . . . *le fils de son père.*

There is one thing, however, which Daudet wants the Goncourt academicians to do, even before they organize: it is to commence their series of monthly dinners. So a Parisian wit quickly improvised the following, which has received great applause:

> " A date fixe ils se réuniront,
> Fourchette en main, les dix chers maitres,
> Et les Goncourt mériteront
> D'être appelés ' Restaurateurs des Lettres.' "

The impending foundation of the new Academy does not seem greatly to impair the prestige of the old one. Although no election is to take place for quite a while, already three writers of note have announced their candidacies for the chair vacated by Henri Meilhac. They are Henri Becque, a dramatist; Ferdinand Fabre, a novelist; and Émile Faguet, a critic. Ferdinand Fabre came so near succeeding in his last candidacy that he is generally expected to be elected this time. This will be gall for Henri Becque, for in his characteristically imperious manner the author of *Les Corbeaux* and *La Parisienne* announces that this will be his first and last candidacy. Either now or never!

One writer of importance has disappered during the month; but he was hardly known by the present generation. Few men, however, were ever more popular with the *élite* of the Paris *jeunesse* than Étienne Vacherot was in the neighbourhood of 1861. He was then the victim of a double persecution. He had been a few years before deprived of his position as professor of philosophy in the École Normale, through the influence of Abbé Gratry, because of his anti-Catholic views, and he had just been prosecuted before the courts and sentenced to a fine because of the republican ideas expressed in his beautiful work *La Démocratie*. No less popular than Vacherot was the brilliant lawyer who had assisted him before the courts, Émile Ollivier. Curiously enough, both men afterward left the republican camp—Émile Ollivier to become a minister of Napoleon III., Vacherot considerably later and for much more disinterested motives. His greatest work is his three-volume philosophical disquisition, *La Métaphysique et la Science*, which is not only one of the most strongly thought out, but one of the most beautifully written French philosophical works of this century. He was of course a member of the Academy of Moral and Political Sciences in the Institute of France. He was one of the oldest members of the Institute, having just passed his eighty-eighth birthday when he died.

I have mentioned Émile Ollivier. He has been a good deal before the public of late, as a reference to some of my later letters may show. He is now about to publish in *Cosmopolis* a series of letters which were years ago addressed to him by Richard Wagner. They are said to be very interesting, and will undoubtedly be received with a good deal of eagerness, not as much, though, I suppose, as the two volumes of unpublished letters of Napoleon I. which have just appeared.

A good deal of fun is often indulged in in regard to President Faure. His love for military display causes a good many good naturedly to accuse him of wishing to play *son petit Napoléon*. It turns out now that, like Napoleon, he is also a little of a bookman. I give you herewith the full title of a volume which has just been discovered, and which was published in 1869, when its author certainly did not dream that he could be one day President of the French Republic : "Le Havre, son Commerce, son Industrie, sa Navigation. Renseignements réunis et annotés par Félix Faure, Consul au Havre de sa Majesté le Roi des Hellènes."

Although this was the only time that M. Faure submitted any production of his to the public, we doubt whether he once alluded to it during the trip he has just taken in the south of France with a crowd of men of letters, prior to his departure for Russia. The object of the trip was to glorify a number of men of letters, and it was managed by the "Félibres" with all the skill in organising public rejoicings which is so characteristic of the French southerners. There were no less than four statues to be unveiled ; two in Valence—those of Émile Augier, the illustrious author of *Le Gendre de M. Poirier*, and of Baucel, a political orator who died in 1870, and who was a good deal of a literary scholar ; one in the little Alpine town of Sisteron—that of Paul Arène, the author of the charming story *Domnine* and of a number of pretty poems, which are just about to be collected in book form ; and finally, in Pézenas, a new statue of Molière, who had acted there several times during the period of his provincial wanderings. The trip included a stop at Orange, where performances were given in the superbly restored Roman theatre. Sophocles' *Antigone* and Leconte de Lisle's *Erinnyes* were played ; and I am compelled to say that the French poet's production entirely failed to win in those imposing surroundings the success it had had in its Paris performances. Both plays, of course, were acted by the members of the Comédie Française.

The same company are soon to perform for the first time Murger's *La Vie de Bohème*, a play of genuine literary merit, which has time and again won a good deal of success on other stages.

I cannot say that all the incidents in Murger's play deserve to be called strictly moral. But they would seem to be almost so by the side of so many productions which for a few years past have disgraced some of the Parisian show-houses and show-windows. In regard to the show-houses to which this applies, and which are nearly all situated on the celebrated Butte Montmartre, just under the shadow of the church of the Sacré Cœur, the Paris police has begun, though timidly as yet, a house-cleaning campaign, which has the support of every lover of art and decency. In fact, the police have done little more than, if even as much as, Francisque Sarcey has declared necessary for quite a while. Obscenity without wit was the rule of some of these houses, and they have been warned that unless they reform considerably they will be closed and their keepers prosecuted for offences against public morals. The warning has had some effect. At the same time an effort is made to make the law against such offences a good deal more effective and stringent than it was in the past. You certainly have heard of Senator Bérenger, whom the Parisians have good-naturedly dubbed *le Père la Pudeur*. In consequence of his efforts in this direction the Government, on May 18th of this year, introduced a bill intended to make more effective the law voted in 1882 for the protection of public morals. The bill was quickly referred to a committee, of which Senator Bérenger was made chairman; and he soon reported it favourably to the Senate, with amendments which made it still more stringent. The bill was, after full discussion, adopted by the Senate on June 18th; it now awaits favourable action by the Deputies. It will very likely be made a law early in the extra session, which is to open in October. Its text is as follows:

"ARTICLE I.

"Article I. of the law of August 2d, 1882, is modified as follows:

"There shall be punished by imprisonment of not less than one month and not more than two years, and a fine of not less than one hundred nor more than five thousand francs whosoever shall have committed an offence or outrage against public morals, either by selling or offering for sale, writings or printed matter other than a book, prospectuses, drawings, engravings, pictures, emblems, images, or articles, that are obscene or such as incite to vice;

"Or by the distribution of the same, even free, by the mailing thereof or the handing of them to any agency for distribution or transportation;

"Or by exposing or posting them on a public thoroughfare or in any public place;

"Or by uttering or delivering in public discourses and speeches, songs or cries of the same nature;

"Or by advertisements or published correspondence of a licentious character or such as incite to vice.

"The writings, drawings, posters, etc., upon which the prosecution is based, and any article that has been used in committing the offence shall be seized or torn from the walls. The destruction thereof will be ordered by the judgment of the Court.

"The Court shall have the right to double the penalty if the offence shall have been committed against minors.

"ARTICLE II.

"The statute of limitation for offences against public morals committed through the book shall take effect one year from the date of publication or introduction upon French territory.

"The sale, or offering for sale, or advertising of condemned books will be punished by the penalties described in Article I. of this law."

It is thought that every loophole through which the offenders have hitherto managed to creep will now be closed. But if it should not be so, Parliament is ready to resort to even more stringent measures. You will observe the regulation relating to the introduction into France of obscene books. It is a new one, and was made necessary by the enormous number of such books smuggled into this country from Belgium and Germany.

Alfred Manière.

EXPERIENCE.

Nay, when upon thy lashes lie the tears,
Seek not to weigh the lesson dearly learned:
Truth's face in weakness may not be discerned
But in the strength of wisdom brought by years.

Robert Adger Bowen.

IN KEDAR'S TENTS.*

By Henry Seton Merriman, Author of "The Sowers."

CHAPTER XXII.

REPARATION.

"Il s'en faut bien que l'innocence trouvé autant de protection que le crime."

For those minded to leave Spain at this time there was but one route—namely, the south, for the northern exits were closed by the Carlists, still in power there, though waning fast. Indeed, Don Carlos was now illustrating the fact, which any may learn by the study of the world's history, that it is not the great causes, but the great men who have made and destroyed nations. Nearly half of Spain was for Don Carlos. The Church sided with him, and the best soldiers were those who, unpaid, unfed, and half clad, fought on the southern slopes of the Pyrenees for a man who dared not lead them.

Sir John Pleydell had intended crossing the frontier into Portugal, following the carriage conveying his prisoner to the seaport of Lisbon, where he anticipated no difficulty in finding a ship captain who would be willing to convey Conyngham to England. All this, however, had been frustrated by so unimportant a person as Concepcion Vara, and the carriage ordered for nine o'clock to proceed to Talavera now stood in the courtyard of the hotel, while the baronet in his lonely apartment sat and wondered what he should do next. He had dealt with justice all his life, and had ensured it not from love, but as a matter of conscience and a means of livelihood. From the mere habit, he now desired to do justice to Conyngham.

"See if you can find out for me the whereabouts of General Vincente at the moment, and let the carriage wait," he said to his servant, a valet-courier of taciturn habit.

The man was about half an hour, and returned with a face that promised little.

"There is a man in the hotel, sir," he said, "the servant of Mr. Conyngham, who knows, but will not tell me. I am told, however, that a lady living in Toledo, a Contessa Barenna, will undoubtedly have the information. General Vincente was lately in Madrid, but his movements are so rapid and uncertain that he has become a by-word in Spain."

"So I understand. I will call on this contessa this afternoon, unless you can get the information elsewhere during the morning. I shall not want the carriage."

Sir John walked slowly to the window, deep in thought. He was interested in Conyngham despite himself. It is possible that he had not hitherto met a man capable of so far forgetting his own interests as to undertake a foolish and dangerous escapade, without anything in the nature of gain or advantage to recommend it. The windows of the hotel of the Red Hat, in Toledo, look out upon the market-place, and Sir John, who was an indoor man, and mentally active enough to be intensely bored at times, frequently used this opportunity of studying Spanish life.

He was looking idly through the vile panes when an old priest passed by and glanced up beneath shaggy brows.

"Seen that man before," said Sir John.

"Ah!" muttered Father Concha, as he hurried on toward the Palazzo Barenna. "So far, so good. Where the fox is will be found the stolen fowl."

Concepcion Vara, who was saddling his horse in the stable-yard of the inn, saw the padre pass.

"Ah, clever one!" he muttered; "with your jokes about my wife. Now you may make a false journey for all the help you receive from me."

And a few minutes later Concepcion rode across the ridge of Alcantara, some paces behind Conyngham, who deemed it wise to return to his duties at Madrid without delay.

Despite the great heat on the plains, which, indeed, made it almost dangerous to travel at midday, the streets of

Toledo were cool and shady enough as Sir John Pleydell traversed them in search of the Palazzo Barenna. The contessa was in, and the Englishman was ushered into a vast room, which even the taste of the day could not entirely deprive of its mediæval grandeur. Sir John explained, in halting Spanish, that his name was unknown to the Contessa Barenna, but that, a stranger in some slight difficulty, he had been recommended to seek her assistance.

Sir John was an imposing-looking man, with that grand air which enables some men not only to look, but to get over a wall while an insignificant wight may not so much as approach the gate. The señora's curiosity did the rest. In a few minutes the rustle of silk made Sir John turn from the contemplation of a suit of armour.

"Madame speaks French?"

"But yes, señor."

Madame Barenna glanced toward a chair, which Sir John hastened to bring forward. He despised her already, and she admired his manner vastly.

"I have taken the immense liberty of intruding myself upon your notice, madame—"

"Not to sell me a Bible?" exclaimed Señora Barenna, with her fan upheld in warning.

"A Bible! I believe I have one at home, in England, madame, but—"

"It is well," said madame, sinking back and fanning herself rather faintly. "Excuse my fears, but there is an Englishman—what is his name, I forget—"

"Borrow."

"Yes, that is it—Borrow. And he sells Bibles, and Father Concha, my confessor—a bear, but a holy man, a holy bear, as one might say—has forbidden me to buy one. I am so afraid of disobeying him, by heedlessness or fear or forgetfulness. There are, it appears, some things in the Bible which one ought not to read, and one naturally—"

She finished the sentence with a shrug and an expressive gesture of the fan.

"One naturally desires to read them," suggested Sir John; "the privilege of all Eve's daughters, madame."

Señora Barenna treated the flatterer to what the French call a *fine sourire*, and wondered how long Julia would stay away. This man would pay her another compliment in a moment.

"I merely called on the excuse of a common friendship, to ask if you can tell me the whereabouts of General Vincente," said Sir John, stating his business in haste and when the opportunity presented itself.

"Is it politics?" asked the lady, with a hasty glance round the room.

"No; it is scarcely politics; but why do you ask? You are surely too wise, madame, to take part in such. It is a woman's mission to please, and when it is so easy!"

He waved his thin white hand in completion of a suggestion which made his hearer bridle her stout person.

"No, no," she whispered, glancing over her shoulder at the door—"no; it is my daughter. Ah, señor, you can scarce imagine what it is to live upon a volcano!"

And she pointed to the oak floor with her fan. Sir John deemed it wise to confine his display of sympathy to a glance of the deepest concern.

"No," he said; "it is merely a personal matter. I have a communication to make to my friend, General Vincente, or to his daughter."

"To Estella?"

"To the Señorita Estella."

"Do you think her beautiful? Some do, you know. Eyes, I admit—yes, lovely."

"I admire the señorita exceedingly.

"Ah, yes—yes! You have not seen my daughter, have you, señor? Julia. She rather resembles Estella."

The contessa paused and examined her fan with a careless air.

"Some say," she went on, apparently with reluctance, "that Julia is—well—has some advantages of Estella. But *I* do not, of course. I admire Estella excessively—oh, yes—yes."

And the señora's dark eyes searched Sir John's face. They might have found more in sculptured marble.

"Do you know where she is?" asked Sir John, almost bluntly. Like a workman who has mistaken his material, he was laying aside his finer conversational tools.

"Well, I believe they arrive in Toledo this evening. I cannot think why. But with General Vincente one never knows. He is so pleasant, so playful, such a smile; but you know him. Well, they say in Spain, that he is always where he is wanted. Ah—" madame paused and cast her eyes up to the ceiling—"what it is to be wanted somewhere, señor!"

And she gave him the benefit of one of her deepest sighs. Sir John mentally followed the direction of her glance, and wondered what the late count thought about it.

"Yes, I am deeply interested in Estella, as, indeed, is natural, for she is my niece. She has no mother, and the general has such absurd ideas. He thinks that a girl is capable of choosing a husband for herself; but to you, an Englishman, such an idea is naturally not astonishing. I am told that in your country it is the girls who actually propose marriage."

"Not in words, madame; not more in England than elsewhere."

"Ah!" said madame, looking at him doubtfully, and thinking despite herself of Father Concha.

Sir John rose from the chair he had taken at the señora's silent invitation.

"Then I may expect the general to arrive at my hotel this evening?" he said. "I am staying at the Red Hat, the only hotel, as I understand, in Toledo."

"Yes; he will doubtless descend there. Do you know Frederick Conyngham, señor?"

"Yes."

"But every one knows him!" exclaimed the lady vivaciously. "Tell me how it is. A most pleasant young man, I allow you, but without introductions, and quite unconnected. Yet he has friends everywhere—"

The contessa paused, and closing her fan leant forward in an attitude of intense confidence and secrecy.

"And how about his little affair?" she whispered.

"His little affair, madame?"

"*De cœur*," explained the lady, tapping her own breast with an eloquent fan.

"Estella," she whispered, after a pause.

"Ah!" said Sir John, as if he knew too much about it to give an opinion. And he took his leave.

"That is the sort of woman to break one's heart in the witness-box," he said, as he passed out into the deserted street; and Señora Barenna, in the great room with the armour, reflected complacently that the English lord had been visibly impressed.

General Vincente and Estella arrived at the hotel of the Red Hat in the evening, but did not, of course, appear in the public rooms. His dusty old travelling carriage was placed in a quiet corner of the courtyard of the hotel, and the general appeared on this, as on all occasions, to court retirement and oblivion. Unlike many of his brothers in arms, he had no desire to catch the public eye.

"There is doubtless something astir," said the waiter who, in the intervals of a casual attendance on Sir John, spoke of these things, cigarette in mouth—"there is doubtless something astir, since General Vincente is on the road. They call him the Stormy Petrel, for when he appears abroad there usually follows a disturbance."

Sir John sent his servant to the general's apartment about eight o'clock in the evening, asking permission to present himself. In reply the general himself came to Sir John's room.

"My dear sir," he cried, taking both the Englishman's hands in an affectionate grasp, "to think that you were in the hotel, and that we did not dine together. Come—yes, come to our poor apartment, where Estella awaits the pleasure of renewing your acquaintance."

"Then the señorita," said Sir John, following his companion along the dimly lighted passage, "has her father's pleasant faculty of forgetting any little *contretemps* of the past?"

"Ask her," exclaimed the general, in his cheery way—"ask her."

And he threw open the door of the dingy salon they occupied.

Estella was standing with her back to the window, and her attitude suggested that she had not sat down since she had heard of Sir John's presence in the hotel.

"Señorita," said the Englishman, with that perfect knowledge of the world which usually has its firmest basis upon contempt and indifference to criticism—"señorita, I have come to avow a mistake, and to make my excuses."

"It is surely unnecessary," said Estella rather coldly.

"Say rather," broke in the general, in his smoothest way, "that you have come to take a cup of coffee with us, and to tell us your news."

Sir John took the chair which the general brought forward.

"At all events," he said, addressing Estella, "it is probably a matter of indifference to you, as it is merely an opinion expressed by myself which I wish to retract. When I first had the pleasure of meeting you, I took it upon myself to speak of a guest in your father's house, fortunately in the presence of that guest himself, and I now wish to tell you that what I said does not apply to Frederick Conyngham himself, but to another whom Conyngham is screening. He has not confessed so much to me, but I have satisfied myself that he is not the man I seek. You, general, who know more of the world than the señorita, and have been in it almost as long as I have, can bear me out in the statement that the motives of men are not so easy to discern as younger folks imagine. I do not know what induced Conyngham to undertake this thing, probably he entered into it in a spirit of impetuous and reckless generosity, which would only be in keeping with his character. I only know that he has carried it out with a thoroughness and daring worthy of all praise. If such a tie were possible between an old man and a young, I should like to be able to claim Mr. Conyngham as a friend. There, señorita, thank you ; I will take coffee. I made the accusation in your presence, I retract it before you. It is, as you see, a small matter."

"But it is of small matters that life is made up," put in the general, in his deferential way. "Our friend," he went on after a pause, "is unfortunate in misrepresenting himself. We also have a little grudge against him, a little matter of a letter which has not been explained. I admit that I should like to see that letter."

"And where is it ?" asked Sir John.

"Ah !" replied Vincente, with a shrug of the shoulders and a gay little laugh, "who can tell ? Perhaps in Toledo, my dear sir—perhaps in Toledo."

CHAPTER XXIII.

LARRALDE'S PRICE.

"It is as difficult to be entirely bad as it is to be entirely good."

To those who say that there is no faith, Spain is in itself a palpable answer. No country in the world can show such cathedrals as those of Granada, Cordova, Seville, Toledo, Burgos. In any other land any one of these great structures would suffice. But in Spain these huge monuments to that faith which has held serenely through war and fashion, through thought and thoughtlessness, are to be found in all the great cities. And the queen of them all is Toledo. If the Christian faith be, as some state, a mistake, then those who built Toledo Cathedral were mistaken to good purposes, and for us, who follow and cannot do likewise in architecture, it may be wise to make, at all events, the same mistake in faith.

Father Concha, that sour-visaged philosopher, had a queer pride in his profession and in the history of that Church which is to-day seen in its purest form in the Peninsular, while it is so entangled with the national story of Spain that the two are but one tale told from a different point of view. As a private soldier may take pleasure in standing on a great battle-field, noting each spot of interest—here a valley of death, there the scene of cavalry charge, of which the thunder will echo down through all the ages—so Concha, a mere country priest, liked to pace the aisles of a great cathedral, indulging the while in a half-cynical pride. He was no great general, no leader, of no smallest importance in the ranks ; but he was of the army, and partook in a minute degree of those victories that belonged to the past. It was his habit thus to pay a visit to Toledo Cathedral whensoever his journeys led him to Castile. It was, moreover, his simple custom to attend the early mass, which is here historical ; and, indeed, to walk through the church, gray and cool, with the hush that seems to belong only to buildings of a stupendous age, is in itself a religious service.

Concha was passing across the nave, hat in hand, a gaunt, ill-clad, and somewhat pathetic figure, when he caught sight of Sir John Pleydell. The tall Englishman paused involuntarily and looked at the lean Spaniard. Concha bowed.

"We met," he said, "for a moment in the garden of General Vincente's house at Ronda."

"True," answered Sir John ; "are you leaving the cathedral ? We might walk a little way together. One cannot talk idly . . . here."

He paused and looked up at the great oak screen, at the towering masonry.

"No," answered Concha gravely ; "one cannot talk idly here."

Concha held back the great leathern *portière*, and the Englishman passed out.

"This is a queer country, and you are a queer people," he said presently. "When I was at Ronda I met a certain number of persons—I can count them on my fingers—General Vincente, his daughter, Señora Barenna, Señorita Barenna, the Englishman, Conyngham, yourself, Señor Concha. I arrived in Toledo yesterday morning. In twenty-four hours I have caught sight of all the persons mentioned here in Toledo."

"And here in Toledo is another of whom you have not caught sight," said Concha.

"Ah!"

"Yes; Señor Larralde."

"Is he here?"

"Yes," said Concha.

They walked on in silence for some minutes.

"What are we all doing here, padre?" inquired Sir John, with his cold laugh.

"What are you doing here, señor?"

Sir John did not answer at once. They were walking leisurely. The streets were deserted, as, indeed, the streets of Toledo usually are.

"I am putting two and two together," the great lawyer answered at length. "I began doing to in idleness, and now I have become interested."

"Ah!"

"Yes, I have become interested. They say, padre, that a pebble set in motion at the summit of a mountain may gather other pebbles and increase in bulk and spread, until in the form of an avalanche it overwhelms a city in the valley."

"Yes, señor."

"And I have conceived the strange fancy that Frederick Conyngham, when he first came to this country, set such a pebble in motion at the summit of a very high mountain. It has been falling and falling silently ever since, and it is gaining in bulk. And you and General Vincente, and Estella Vincente, and Señorita Barenna, and Frederick Conyngham, and, in a minor degree, myself are on the slope, in the track of the avalanche, and are sliding down behind it. And the general and Estella, and yourself and Conyngham are trying to overtake it and stop it; and, reverendo, in the valley below is the monarchy of Spain and the Bourbon cause."

Father Concha, remembering his favourite maxim, that no flies enter a shut mouth, was silent.

"The pebble was a letter," said Sir John.

"And Larralde has it," he added after a pause; "and that is why you are all in Toledo, why the air is thick with apprehension, and why all Spain seems to pause and wait breathlessly."

"Will the avalanche be stopped, or will it not? Will the Bourbons, than whom history has known no more interesting and more satisfactory race, except our own Stuarts—will the Bourbons fall, Señor Padre?"

"Ah!" said Concha, whose furrowed face and pessimistic glance betrayed nothing—"ah!"

"You will not tell me, of course. You know much that you will not tell me, and I merely ask from curiosity. You, perhaps, know one thing, and that I wish to learn from you not out of curiosity, but because I, too, would fain overtake the avalanche and stop it. I am no politician, señor, though, of course, I have my views. When a man has reached my age he knows assuredly that politics merely mean self-aggrandisement and nothing else. No, the Bourbons may fall, Spain may follow the lead of France, and make an exhibition of herself before the world as a republic. I am indifferent to these events. But I wish to do Frederick Conyngham a good turn, and I ask you to tell me where I shall find Larralde, you who know everything, Señor Padre."

Concha reflected while they walked along on the shady side of the narrow street. It happened to be the street where the saddlers live, and the sharp sound of their little hammers on the leather and wood came from almost every darkened doorway. The padre had a wholesome fear of Esteban Larralde and an exaggerated estimation of that schemer's ability. He was a humble-minded old man, and ever hesitated to put his own brain against that of another. He knew that Sir John was a cleverer man than Larralde, deeper versed in that side of human nature where the seams are and the knots and the unsightly stitches, older, more experienced, and probably no more scrupulous.

"Yes," said the priest, "I can tell you that. Larralde lodges in the house of a malcontent, one Lamberto, a scribbling journalist, who is hurt because the world takes him at its own valuation and not his. The house is next to the little synagogue in the Calle de Madrid, a small stationer's shop, where one may buy the curse of this generation, pens and paper."

"Thank you," said Sir John, civilly and simply. This man has, no doubt, been ill painted, but some may have seen that with different companions he wore a different manner. He was, as all successful men are, an unconscious actor, and in entering into the personality of the companion of the moment he completely sank his own. He never sought to be all things to all men, and yet he came near to the accomplishment of that hard task. Sir John was not a sympathetic man, he merely mistook life for a court of justice, and arraigned all human nature in the witness-box, with the inward conviction that this should by rights be exchanged for the felon's dock.

With Concha he was as simple, as direct, and as unsophisticated as the old priest himself, and now took his leave without attempting to disguise the fact that he had accomplished a fore-set purpose.

Without difficulty he found the small stationer's shop next the synagogue in the Calle de Madrid, and bade the stationer, a spectacled individual with upright hair and the air of seeking something in the world which is not usually behind a counter, take his card to Señor Larralde. At first the stationer pretended ignorance of the name, but on discovering that Sir John had not sufficient Spanish to conduct a conversation of intrigue, disappeared into a back room, whence emanated a villainous smell of cooking.

While Sir John waited in the little shop Father Concha walked to the Plazuela de l'Iglesia Vieja, which small square, overhanging the Tagus and within reach of its murmuring voice, is deserted, except at midday, when the boys play at bull fighting and a few workmen engage in a grave game of bowls. Concha sat, book in hand, opened honestly at the office of the day and hour, and read no word. Instead, he stared across the gorge at the brown bank of land which commands the city, and renders it useless as a fortress in the days of modern artillery. He sat and stared grimly, and thought perhaps of those secret springs within the human heart that make one man successful and unhappy, while another who, possessing brains and ability and energy, yet fails in life, and is perhaps none the less the happier of the two, for it had happened to Father Concha, as it may happen to writer and reader at any moment, to meet one who in individuality bears a resemblance to that self which we never know and yet are ever conscious of.

Sir John Pleydell, a few hundred yards away, obeyed the shopman's invitation to step upstairs with something approaching alacrity, so easily is the interest of a lonely man aroused.

Larralde was seated at a table strewn with newspapers and soiled by cigarette ash. He had the unkempt and pallid look of one who has not seen the sun or breathed air for days, for, as Concepcion had said, this was a conspirator who preferred to lurk in friendly shelter while others played the bolder game at the front. Larralde had, in fact, not stirred abroad for nearly a week.

"Well, señor," he said, with a false air of bravado, "how fares it with your little undertaking?"

"That," replied Sir John, "is past and paid for, and I have another matter for your consideration."

Sir John's manner had changed. He spoke as one having authority, and Larralde shrugged his shoulders, remembering a past payment.

"Ah!" he said, rolling a cigarette with a fine air of indifference.

"On the one hand," continued Sir John judicially, "I come to make you an offer which can only be beneficial to you; on the other hand, Señor Larralde, I know enough to make things particularly unpleasant for you."

Larralde raised his eyebrows and sought the match-box. His thoughts seemed to amuse him.

"I have reason to assume that a certain letter is now in your possession again. I do not know the contents of this letter, and I cannot say that I am at all interested in it, but a friend of mine is particularly anxious to have possession of it for a short space of time. I have, unasked, taken upon myself the office of intermediary."

Larralde's eyes flashed through the smoke.

"You are about to offer me money; be careful, señor," he said hotly; and the lawyer smiled.

"Be careful that it is enough," he suggested. "Keep your grand airs for your fellows, Señor Larralde. Yes, I am about to offer you two hundred pounds—say three thousand pesetas—for the loan of that letter for a few hours only. I will guarantee that it is read by one person only, and that a lady. This lady will probably glance at the first lines, merely to satisfy herself as to the nature of its contents. Three thousand pesetas will enable you to escape to Cuba if your schemes fail. If you succeed, three thousand pesetas will always be of use, even to a member of a republican government."

Larralde had ceased smiling. There is a time in the schemes of men, and it usually comes just before the crisis, when the stoutest heart hesitates and the most reckless conspirator thinks of his retreat. Esteban Larralde had begun to think of Cuba during the last few days, and the mention of that haven for Spanish failures almost unnerved him.

"In a week," suggested Sir John again, "it may be . . . well . . . settled one way or the other."

Larralde glanced at him sharply. This Englishman was either well informed or very cunning. He seemed to have read the thought in Larralde's mind.

"No doubt," went on the Englishman, "you have divined for whom I want the letter, and who will read it. We both owe Conyngham a good turn—I in reparation, you in gratitude, for he undoubtedly saved the Señorita Barenna from imprisonment for life."

Larralde shrugged his shoulders.

"Each man," he said, "must fight for himself."

"And the majority of us for a woman as well," amended Sir John. "At least, in Spain, chivalry is not yet dead."

Larralde laughed. He was vain, and Sir John knew it. He had a keen sight for the breach in his opponent's armour.

"You have put your case well," said the Spaniard patronisingly, "and I do not see why, at the end of a week, I should not agree to your proposal. It is, as you say, for the sake of a woman."

"Precisely."

Larralde leant back in his chair, remembering the legendary gallantry of his race, and wearing an appropriate expression.

"For a woman," he repeated, with an eloquent gesture.

"Precisely."

"Then I will do it, señor—I will do it."

"For two hundred pounds?" inquired Sir John coldly.

"As you will," answered the Spaniard, with a noble indifference to such sordid matters.

CHAPTER XXIV.

PRIESTCRAFT.

"No man, I fear, can effect great benefits for his country without some sacrifice of the minor virtues."

The Señora Barenna was a leading social light in Toledo, insomuch as she never refused an invitation.

"One has one's duties toward society," she would say, with a sigh, "though the saints know that I take no pleasure in these affairs."

Then she put on her best Seville mantilla and bustled off to some function or another, where she talked volubly and without discretion.

Julia had of late withdrawn more and more from that life of continued and mild festivity, of which, it is to be feared, the existence of many women is composed. This afternoon she sat alone in the great, gloomy house in Toledo, waiting for Larralde; for she, like thousands of her sisters, loved an unworthy object—*faute de mieux*—with open eyes and a queer philosophy that bade her love Larralde rather than love none. She had lately spent a great part of her existence in waiting for Larralde, who, indeed, was busy enough at this time, and rarely stirred abroad while the sun was up.

"Julia," said Señora Barenna to Concha, "is no longer a companion to me. She does not even attempt to understand my sensitive organisation. She is a mere statue, and thinks of nothing but politics."

"For her, madame, as for all women, there would be no politics if there were no politicians," the priest replied.

This afternoon Julia was more restless than ever. Larralde had not been to see her for many days, and had only written a hurried note from time to time, in answer to her urgent request, telling her that he was well and in no danger.

She now no longer knew whether he was in Toledo or not, but had sufficient knowledge of the schemes in which he was engaged to be aware of the fact that these were coming to a crisis. Esteban Larralde had, indeed, told her more than was either necessary or discreet, and it was his vanity that led him into this imprudence. We are all ready enough to impart information which will show our neighbours that we are more important than we appear.

After a broiling day the sun was now beginning to lose a little of his terrific power, and in the shade of the *patio*, upon which the windows of Julia's room opened, the air was quite cool and pleasant. A fountain plashed continuously in a little basin that had been white six centuries ago, when the Moors had brought the marble across the Gulf of Lyons to build it. The very sound of the water was a relief to overstrained nerves, and seemed to diminish the tension of the shimmering atmosphere.

Julia was alone, and barely made pretence to read the book she held in her hand. From her seat she could see the bell suspended on the opposite wall of the courtyard, of which the deep voice at any time of day or night had the power of stirring her heart in a sudden joy. At last the desired sound broke the silence of the great house, and Julia stood breathless at the window, while the servant leisurely crossed the *patio* and threw open the great door, large enough to admit a carriage and pair. It was not Larralde, but Father Concha, brought hither by a note he had received from Sir John Pleydell earlier in the afternoon.

"I shall have the letter in a week from now," the Englishman had written.

"Which will be too late," commented Concha pessimistically.

The señora was out, they told him, but the señorita had remained at home.

"It is the señorita I desire to see."

And Julia, at the window above, heard the remark with a sinking heart. The air seemed to be weighted with the suggestion of calamity. Concha had the manner of one bringing bad news. She forgot that this was his usual mien.

"Ah, my child!" he said, coming into the room a minute later and sitting down rather wearily.

"What?" she asked, her two hands at her breast.

He glanced at her beneath his brows. The wind was in the northeast, dry and tingling. The sun had worn a coppery hue all day. Such matters affect women and those who are in mental distress. After such a day as had at last worn to evening the mind is at a great tension, the nerves are strained. It is at such times that men fly into sudden anger and whip out the knife. At such times women are reckless, and the stories of human lives take sudden turns.

Concha knew that he had this woman at a disadvantage.

"What?" he echoed; "I wish I knew. I wish at times I was no priest."

"Why?"

"Because I could help you better. Sometimes it is the man and not the priest who is the truest friend."

"Why do you speak like this?" she cried. "Is there danger? What has happened?"

"You know best, my child, if there is danger; you know what is likely to happen."

Julia stood looking at him with hard eyes, the eyes of one in mortal fear.

"You have always been my friend," she said slowly—"my best friend."

"Yes; a woman's lover is never her best friend."

"Has anything happened to Esteban?"

The priest did not answer at once, but paused, reflecting, and dusting his sleeve, where there was always some snuff requiring attention at such moments.

"I know so little," he said. "I am no politician. What can I say? What can I advise you when I am in the dark? And the time is slipping by—slipping by."

"I cannot tell you," she answered, turning away and looking out of the window.

"You cannot tell the priest; tell the man."

Then suddenly she reached the end of her endurance. Standing with her back toward him she told her story, and Concha listened with a still, breathless avidity, as one who, having long sought knowledge, finds it at last when it seemed out of reach. The little fountain plashed in the courtyard below, a frog in the basin among the water-lilies croaked sociably, while the priest and the beautiful woman in the room above made history, for it is not always in kings' palaces nor yet in parliaments that the story of the world is shaped.

Concha spoke no word, and Julia, having begun, left nothing unsaid, but told him every detail in a slow, mechanical voice, as if bidden thereto by a stronger will than her own.

"He is all the world to me," she said simply in conclusion.

"Yes; and the happiest women are those who live in a small world."

A silence fell upon them. The old priest surreptitiously looked at his watch. He was essentially a man of action.

"My child," he said, rising, "when you are an old woman with children to harass you and make your life worth living, you will probably look back with thankfulness to this moment, for you have done that which was your only chance of happiness."

"Why do you always help me?" she asked, as she had asked a hundred times.

"Because happiness is so rare, that I hate to see it wasted," he answered, going toward the door with a grim laugh.

He passed out of the room and crossed the *patio* slowly. Then, when the great door had closed behind him, he gathered up the skirts of his cassock and hurried down the narrow street. In such thoroughfares as were deserted he ran with the speed and endurance of a spare, hard-living man. Woman-like, Julia had, after all, done things by half. She had timed her confession, as it seemed, too late.

At the hotel they told the padre that General Vincente was at dinner and could not be disturbed.

"He sees no one," the servant said.

"You do not know who I am," said Concha, in an irony which under the circumstances he alone could enjoy. Then he passed up the stairs and bade the waiter begone.

"But I carry the general's dessert," protested the man.

"No," said Concha, half to himself; "I have that."

Vincente was, indeed, at the table with Estella. He looked up as the priest entered, fingering a cigarette delicately.

"How soon can you take the road?" asked Concha abruptly.

"Ten minutes, the time for a cup of coffee," was the answer, given with a pleasant laugh.

"Then order your carriage."

Vincente looked at his old friend, and the smile never left his lips, though his eyes were grave enough. It was hard to say whether aught on earth could disturb this man's equanimity. Then the general rose and went to the window, which opened upon the courtyard. In the quiet corner, near the rain-tank, where a vine grows upon trellis-work, the dusty travelling-carriage stood, and upon the step of it, eating a simple meal of bread and dried figs, sat the man who had the reputation of being the fastest driver in Spain.

"In ten minutes, my good Manuel," said the general.

"*Bueno!*" grumbled the driver with his mouth full, a man of few words.

"Is it to go far?" asked the general, turning on his heel and addressing Concha.

"A long journey."

"To take the road, Manuel!" cried Vincente, leaning out. He closed the window before resuming his seat.

"And now, have you any more orders?" he asked, with a gay carelessness. "I counted on sleeping in a bed to-night."

"You will not do that," replied Concha, "when you hear my news."

"Ah!"

"But first you must promise me not to make use of the information I give you against any suspected persons; to take, in fact, only preventive measures."

"You have only to name it, my friend. Proceed."

The old priest paused and passed his hand across his brow. He was breathless still and looked worn.

"It is," he said, "a very grave matter. I have not had much experience in such things, for my path has always lain in small parochial affairs, dealings with children and women."

Estella was already pouring some wine into a glass. With a woman's instinct she saw that the old man was overwrought and faint. It was a Friday, and in his simple way there was no more austere abstinent than Father Concha, who had probably touched little food throughout the long, hot day.

"Take your time, my friend, take your time," said the general, who never hurried, and was never too late. "A pinch of snuff now, it stimulates the nerves."

"It is," said Concha, at length breaking a biscuit in his long, bony fingers, and speaking unembarrassedly with his mouth full—"it is that I have by the merest accident lighted upon a matter of political importance."

The general nodded, and held his wine up to the light.

"There are matters of much political importance," he said, "in the air just now."

"A plot," continued Concha, "spreading over all Spain. The devil is surely in it, and I know the Carlists are. A plot, believe me, to assassinate and rob and kidnap."

"Yes," said the general, with his tolerant little smile—"yes, my dear padre, some men are so bloodthirsty; is it not so?"

"This plot is directed against the little Queen, against the Queen Regent, against many who are notable Royalists, occupying high posts in the government or the army."

He glanced at Estella, and then looked meaningly at the general, who could scarcely fail to comprehend.

"Let us deal with the Queen and the Queen Regent," said Vincente; "the others are probably able to take care of themselves."

"None can guard himself against assassination."

The general seemed for a moment inclined to dispute this statement, but shrugged his shoulders and finally passed it by.

"The Queen," he said; "what of her?"

In response Concha took a newspaper from his pocket and spread it out on the table. After a brief search up and down the ill printed columns he found the desired paragraph and read aloud:

"The Queen is in Madrid. The Queen Regent journeys from Seville to rejoin her daughter in the capital, prosecuting her journey by easy stages and accompanied by a small guard. Her Majesty sleeps at Ciudad Real to-night, and at Toledo to-morrow night."

"This," said Concha, folding the newspaper, "is a Carlist and revolutionary rag, whose readers are scarcely likely to be interested for a good motive in the movements of the Queen Regent."

"True, my dear padre—true," admitted Vincente, half reluctantly.

"Many kiss hands they would fain see chopped off. In the streets and on the plaza I have seen many reading this newspaper and talking over it with unusual interest. Like a bad lawyer, I am giving the confirmation of the argument before the argument itself."

"No matter, no matter."

"Ah! but we have no time to do things ill or carelessly," said the priest. "My story is a long one, but I will tell it as quickly as I can."

"Take your time," urged the general soothingly. "This great plot, you say, which is to spread over all Spain . . ."

"Is for to-morrow night, my friend."

(*To be continued.*)

UNDERTOW.

In boreal calm the spirit feels
  A far-off thunder-roll,
And through each tropic passion steals
  A current from the pole.

John B. Tabb.

NEW BOOKS.

A GREAT AMERICAN NOVEL.*

It is a good custom, and not without justification in human nature, when you come to think of it, that makes the devout Catholic resort to the confessional before entering upon some arduous enterprise or grave undertaking. Confession once made, he goes about his business presumably with a clear conscience in his breast, and a new hope and purpose inspiring him. The present writer has a confession to make before venturing on a review of the book now under consideration, and hopes thereby to gain peace with himself and the author. A year ago it began to be bruited that Dr. Mitchell had written a great novel, the press took up the cry and cackled over this prodigious piece of hatching as it appeared in the magazine, then later came a circular with the gratuitous information that the Great American Novel had arrived, and here it was! All this to one who comes of a stubborn, stiff necked race had the effect of antagonising him, and his persistence in having nothing to do with the story lasted throughout its serial appearance. Indeed, he would not have read it now even in book form had it not been that he was afraid to trust it to some other reviewer who, under the weight of pressure from every side, would be sure to praise it without stint, which would be gall and wormwood. Taking up the book himself, therefore, he started with fierce joy to look out for those false notes and discords which he was sure the critics had sworn in secret to cover with a loud voice. He began making notes, with not much satisfaction, but before he had got half way into the first volume he had forgotten all about his quest. He has since carefully erased these trifling criticisms, lest in appearing to seek for peccadilloes, he meet with the condemnation of the man with the muck rake.

Hugh Wynne has the distinction of belonging with the few great historical novels of American life produced by American writers. It is a novel of the Revolution, with its interest concentred in Philadelphia. Taking the Quaker city as its base of operations, it combines the peculiar and conflicting social forces of the time, and follows the ramifications of the martial struggle in the North and in the South with a fidelity to history that has a singular charm for the reader, and a positive value for the student familiar with the historic characters and their setting. The coign of vantage thus afforded the author in distributing the interest over the movements of the army, and in preserving a just perspective to the procession of history during the uprising of the nation, is evident, when one reflects upon the concatenation of events that forms the history of this period, which events are skilfully threaded in the story. We have had stories that have given us a partial picture of this period, centred in New England, in New York and Virginia, but in no other do we remember having had passed in review so complete and comprehensive a panorama of this stirring crisis in American history. To have accomplished this is in itself a great feat. Coming fresh to the reading of *Hugh Wynne* after a recent perusal of Fiske's *American Revolution*, it surprised and delighted us to see with what ease and mastery the prominent characteristics of the war were brought before the mind's eye. Needless to say, that all that transpired during that time is by no means chronicled in these pages—that were to give us history and not romance—but the salient features and critical points are fastened on and depicted in the foreground of the picture, while in the background the less important features are lightly sketched in, so that the effect is one of harmony and unity of design. The conception of the whole picture is unique and satisfying, the point of view is novel and excites fresh interest in a familiar subject, the scenes are drawn with vividness of detail and picturesqueness of treatment that prove the possession in the artist of the historical imagination in a rare degree. No finer and more highly executed presentation of the War of the

* Hugh Wynne: Free Quaker. Sometime Brevet Lieutenant-Colonel on the Staff of His Excellency General Washington. By Dr. S. Weir Mitchell. New York: The Century Co. 2 vols. $2.00.

Revolution has ever been focussed in fiction.

But to award to the author this high rôle in historical romance is not the highest virtue nor the most commendable in this book. *Hugh Wynne* is a story of strong human interest and vigour; it is a drama of compelling attraction and power. It is alive with the comedy and tragedy of human life. There are situations of thrilling intensity and climax in it which with an artist of less reserve and delicacy would have shrunk to mere melodrama. The only weak character in the book, to our thinking, is Captain Wynne; Dr. Mitchell is not at home with villainy. We feel that less unsophisticated creatures than Hugh Wynne, Jack Warder, or Darthea even, would have suspected and found means of denouncing him long before they did. But he is a very plausible villain, though just a trifle stagy, and we can put up with him for the sake of the noble and gallant company among whom this wolf in sheep's clothing stalks. Even him Dr. Mitchell could not portray without imparting a creative touch to his character which will always haunt our memory. Like Carker's grinning teeth in *Dombey and Son*, Captain Wynne's trick of half shutting his eyes and dropping his lower jaw in moments of craft or excitement will ever identify him. By the way, it is curious that another recent historical novel of this period, *A Son of the Old Dominion*, has for its villain an English lord bent on the same mischief of seeking and purloining an old title deed to an ancient seat in England.

The form of the story is autobiographical fiction. At first this seemed a serious drawback, but Hugh Wynne, who tells the story, becomes so real and holds us with so human a thrall that the illusion is soon complete, and when the reader is once fairly launched among the scenes and characters of the story the disadvantages of autobiography, if there be any in *Hugh Wynne*, are artfully concealed. Besides, the author saves his hero from seeming egotism by frequent use of excerpts from Jack Warder's diary at such junctures when the course of events requires in good taste the commentary of a disinterested person. And as happens sometimes, notably in *King Noanett*, the real hero is not he who tells the story and who figures prominently in the moving drama of these pages. To us it will be Jack Warder, Hugh Wynne's trusty and tender friend, with the heart of a woman encased in the armour of a man—the "girl-boy" of Aunt Wynne, the "Captain Blushes" of Darthea—who will have more power to draw us back to the book which contains glimpses of his life. Hugh Wynne will be the charmer for women, and rightly so; but find us the man whose heart will not beat quicker to the music of Jack's simple, noble life; as it always beats to that something noble and high, so seldom realised by men, but nevertheless so potent as an ideal. "All men can love," said George Sand, "but few have the capacity for friendship." Jack Warder was one of the favoured few, as Hugh Wynne himself once testified, and in his fidelity to Hugh Wynne and to Darthea we have another of those rare and precious tributes to the reality of friendship between men and women. David had no more faithful, true, and constant friend in Jonathan than Hugh Wynne had in Jack Warder. But surely the spell is upon us again; for it is not of living folk we speak. And yet, after all, are there not characters in fiction that are more real to us than many who are in life about us? As to that charming, delightful, most captivating of heroines, Darthea, who could resist her, and who will not bear away in his bosom some feeling of pain and pleasure that her presence has left behind? The immortality of beauty!—it is that which in Darthea, in the manly lineaments of Hugh Wynne, in the tender and finer lines of Jack Warder, in all this stately company, stamps *Hugh Wynne* with what seems to us the excellence that has the promise of permanence in it. The love of honour, the love of purity, the love of life, the love of love, these permeate the high purpose of the story, and nothing untrue, nothing ignoble, nothing unseemly sullies its pages. Albeit it is a chapter out of the book of humanity, and its handling of character, its view of life is sane and normal. Dr. Mitchell has succeeded with the character of Hugh Wynne in portraying a gentleman of the old school without an atom of priggism about him. His General Washington is the most accurate and human portrait we have yet had in fiction of that much-behaloed character, if we except Thackeray's portrait in *The Virginians.*

It would be impossible to do justice to the delightful surprise, which Dr. Mitchell has at least given one reader, within the limits of a review. It is full of characters, real and imaginative, which one and all clamour for honourable mention. There is Hugh's father, as severe and unbending in his Quaker discipline and prejudice as was ever Puritan of Plymouth, and yet he stands for us, as he did for his son, head and shoulders above the crowd ; there is Hugh's Aunt Wynne, and second mother, a host in herself ; Hugh's own mother, the fascinating little lady of the Midi in France, who bequeathed of her vivacity and affection that which broadened out and humanised the Quaker creed for her son, the "Free Quaker ;" and there are all the personages of history who cross the thread of the story and are once more resurrected and shone upon with the light of a glory at once borrowed and bestowed. The life of the old *régime* in Philadelphia is rehabilitated with all the variety and charm, the delicacy and grace, the elegance and refinement which we know belonged to it then. We step quietly into the old colonial society of that day with the ominous sounds of the oncoming storm entering as faint rumours brought from afar, to be taken seriously by a few, deemed ridiculous of belief by most. Then the narrative catches fire as circumstances begin to fan the flames of the passion of patriotism, and of the passion of love. To the end we are held absorbed by the interplay of these two great passions working in good and evil until the curtain is rung down on the happy *dénouement*, victory-crowned conquest, both in love and war.

It is outside the province of criticism in this generation to pronounce definite judgment for posterity upon contemporaneous literature ; we can only attempt to appraise it for ourselves and show why we believe certain books to contain the elements of permanence. We may not have been successful in convincing the reader that *Hugh Wynne* possesses this virtue of endurance—the book itself must do that ; but to us it seems to bear upon it the unhasting marks of work written for the future. The impression of *Hugh Wynne* on the whole is that it is a great novel of its kind—that is to say, in the field of historical and dramatic fiction. It approximates more nearly than any novel we know to what may be regarded as the only great novel of early American life and history. Strange that this should be the work of an Englishman. In *The Virginians* we have the best model of what an American novel laid on broad lines of human life and dealing with the periodic movements of its history should be. In the wide sweep of *The Virginians*, extending from Washington's enlistment before Braddock's defeat to the resignation of Washington after the seven years' war ; in its picturesque presentment of the contrasts of life in the Old World and in the New ; in its portrayal of Virginian colonial life and character ; in its subordination of the historic trend to the social aspects of life in the two countries ; still more in its faithful portraiture of the young Virginian, in whom Thackeray's sane art found a fit subject for the blending of human weakness and strength, of foibles of temperament and conduct, with nobility of character and high endeavour—in these essentials Thackeray's great novel stands unapproached by anything that has since been written. There is one great scene in the last chapter where with a few strokes Thackeray painted one of his undying pictures. It is when the general lays down his victorious sword and meets his comrades of the army in a last adieu. In Dr. Mitchell's novel this scene is also described and forms an artistic climax to the historical cast of the story, but it fails to rise to the dignity, the reserve, the completeness of Thackeray's picture. The parting as Thackeray portrayed it will remain one of the memorable scenes in historical fiction. Eye-witnesses reported it ; historians have described it ; but Thackeray immortalised it.

James MacArthur.

CICERO AND HIS FRIENDS.*

The good name of Cicero must always be dear to literature, and though he will probably never recover the unique position which the splendour of his style

* Cicero and his Friends. By Gaston Boissier, translated by A. D. Jones. New York : G. P. Putnam's Sons. $1.75.

once secured him, yet he has in recent years been the object of such virulent attacks, notably at the hands of Drumann and Mommsen, that it is pleasant to see his conduct and character discussed in a more reasonable, because a more sympathetic spirit. M. Boissier fully acknowledges that Mommsen is "the master of all who study Rome and her history," but with regard to his treatment of Cicero he strongly protests against the paradox that "this pretended statesman was only an egotist and a short-sighted politician, and this great writer only made up of a newspaper novelist and a special pleader." "Here," he writes, "we perceive the same pen that has just written down Cato a Don Quixote and Pompey a corporal;" and he claims that the correspondence of Cicero, in which he lays bare to us every passing emotion, should not be scrutinised by professors with "conscientious malevolence," but judged in a larger spirit by those who have "more acquaintance with life than one usually finds in a German university."

In this M. Boissier is undoubtedly right. An impulsive and excitable man who, during twenty years such as those which preceded the murder of Cæsar, plays a leading part in politics and is also a writer of exceptional brilliancy and power, cannot indulge in a large and intimate correspondence without revealing to the inquisitive eyes of posterity a thousand weaknesses, inconsistencies, and errors. With the letters to Atticus in his hand a schoolboy can make Cicero appear contemptible. Has he not secured for his reputation what Dogberry desired, writing himself down "a genuine ass" (*scio me asinum germanum fuisse—Ad Att.* iv. 5), and should not this be taken as a final judgment on his character, just as the equally famous remark which he makes about his philosophical writings—"they are copies; I only supply words, in which I abound" —is quoted by Mommsen as the final verdict which sober criticism should pass on works such as the *De Officiis* and the *De Natura Deorum?* These works were written, according to that great authority, "with equal peevishness and precipitation . . . in rude imitation of Aristotle" during the few months before the orator's death, and no contempt can be too great for them or for their writer. Yet, after all, the old man who, mastering at last his natural timidity, had signed his own death-warrant by publishing the *Philippics* might seem to deserve consideration rather than contumely, if, before the sword fell, he spent his latest hours in seeking to place before his fellow-countrymen some account of those philosophical speculations which then afforded the poor but only substitute for religion. "When, in studying his history," writes M. Boissier, "I am tempted to reproach him with irresolution and weakness, I think of his end; I see him as Plutarch has so well depicted him, 'his beard and hair dirty, his countenance worn, taking his chin in his left hand as his manner was, and looking steadily at his murderers,' and I no longer dare to be severe." This is the language of humanity, and it is also the language of justice.

To deride Cicero and deify Cæsar, "saluting in advance that popular despot who can alone give unity to Germany," was no doubt natural for Mommsen, but the French have learned in this century that even wise men may, as Cicero did, halt between two opinions and admire Cæsar, but love the Republic. The French temperament, too, with its love of wit, eloquence, and literary grace, its versatility and impulsiveness, is far more akin than the more phlegmatic mood of Germany to the character of Cicero, and in consequence M. Boissier writes with that sympathetic insight without which no man's life can be written well. He understands Cicero, and he makes us understand him. He does not seek to describe him as a hero, but he does show us how this man, whose rare gifts have endeared him to thousands of readers during twenty centuries, being called upon in a time of unexampled difficulty and danger to take a great place in public life, did, in spite of human infirmities, so bear himself as to deserve almost always our sympathy, and not infrequently our respect.

It only remains to add that the exceedingly complex characters of Atticus, Brutus, and Augustus are discussed with great tact and discrimination, while throughout, the work of translation is executed with taste and accuracy. The book is an excellent book, and deserves to be widely read.

T. E. Page.

JEROME, A POOR MAN.*

That which a young preacher denominated "the naked beauty of perfect holiness" does not make up well in fiction. It usually lacks the individuality or warmth to be real. John Halifax, so far from being a gentleman, was probably more a woman than a man. Romola is less rememberable than Tito, Hester Prynne than Arthur Dimmesdale, Agnes Wickfield than Becky Sharp, Miss Burney's Evelina than Richardson's Clarissa, and King Arthur of the Round Table than Eugene Aram. When in their quest of reality the novelists have not so far missed the very essence of goodness as to produce characters that are icily regular or faultlessly null, they have generally succeeded in caricaturing it; witness John Storm, who is either a melodramatic abortion or merely a bore, according to one's point of view. Miss Wilkins, with a shrewd discernment of the ethical as well as the literary bearings of her theme, has made Jerome Edwards neither vapid nor tawdry, but so excessively good that he actually sins (in a mild but reprehensible and human way) from conceit of holiness. "By the Lord Harry," said Squire Merritt, "he shall swallow his damned pride before he gives my girl an anxious hour!" But from one end of the novel to the other he didn't swallow his pride; and Lucina, who was yearning to share his much-obtruded poverty, and had every reason to be treated otherwise, suffered many an anxious hour and received rebuffs which only one who loved not the right, but his love of the right, whose conscience was surcharged with egotism—in fine, a Puritanic prig, could inflict. From the spring day when, from his sunny nook beneath the rocky ledge, he spurned Lucina's gentle proffer of gingerbread with the cry: "Ain't hungry; have all I want at home," to his impulsive acceptançe of Simon Basset's bet, in the corner grocery, that no one present would give away money if he had it, and his subsequent distribution among the poor of the village, according to his boyish promise, of the $25,000 bequeathed him, and his devoting the hard-earned savings that should have built his mill to the amelioration of his relatives and neighbours—"drivelling idiocy of benevolence" some one called it—and the destruction of the mill when it finally materialised (all of which deterred him from marriage or even sympathy with his brave, wistful Lucina), he was, as the author repeatedly intimates, the miser of a false trait in his own character, neglecting with that curious, dogmatic selfishness, which sometimes has its roots in unselfishness, to consider the effect on Lucina of the seeming repulse of her love and constancy. Of course he should have realised that without him she was poorer than he could possibly be, that birth is an accident anyway, the conditions into which we are born accidents, and that, not having earned the wealth her father lavished upon her, it was purely accidental that she was not at that moment nibbling shredded wheat and sassafras root rather than lollipops.

But to what lengths,

> "O ye douce good folk that live by rule,"

will your pig-headed rectitude carry you when you make a fetish of an idea and try to fit all the divinest impulses and emotions of your nature to its procrustean measure! "Blind as a bat," you probably flatter yourselves, is an apt comparison; but if there is a horrid, clammy, circling, clawing, blood-sucking vampire on Brooklyn heights that is half as blind as you are, it has yet to be encountered in the night-time. One who no more intended to sermonise than the present writer, and who knew the pitiable excesses of the unco guid perfectly, said that "tempers strain and recover, hearts break and heal, strength falters, fails, and comes near to giving way altogether, without being noticed by the closest lookers-on"—which is a very accurate delineation of the havoc wrought by such a person as Jerome. And yet he was a chip of the old block, for had not his father, after an ineffectual attempt to lift the mortgage, concluded that he was only a burden to his family, and secreted himself in a neighbouring town till he could make his little pile and return to find that funeral rites in his behalf had been punctiliously observed years before?

There is a great deal in the story to relieve the little tragedy which is its kernel. Besides Jerome and Lucina there are Elmira and Lawrence, who

* Jerome, a Poor Man. By Mary E. Wilkins. New York: Harper & Bros. $1.50.

progress in much the same way, the author now taking a pull at one pair of lovers and now at the other, often in the same chapter. The two plots are dovetailed together like Crandall building blocks, and perhaps could be separated without organic rupture. In the last hundred pages one feels that the wires are being laid for a happy ending. With whatever high-minded determination Miss Wilkins may have begun the story, she apparently came, in the fashion of Mrs. Oliphant, so to sympathise with her lovers as to be morally incapable of killing or parting them in deference to the rules of art. Then, too, Lucina's father is altogether a genial personage, a sort of Will Wimble and Uncle Alec (can it be that you have forgotten *Eight Cousins?*) rolled into one. There is also Aunt Camilla, with her lavender-scented garments making harp music on the rails of the banisters and delicately acquiescing with Lucina's illusions when that stately, demure little lady drank tea with her in the summer-house. She agreeably offsets the grimness of Jerome's mother, whose face, "curiously triangular in outline, like a cat's, with great hollow black eyes between thin, parted curtains of black false hair," confronts us all too often. Lucina herself, daintily prim, acquiring by degrees a knowledge of herself and the big world in which she loved and Jerome struggled, wondering in her childhood if poplars were really trees and digging cautiously around the roots of one to see if it would topple over; ever timid until she knew and then confiding, yet possessed of the quick impulse of maidenhood to flee, when unsought, is a vivid and sweet presentment of girlish development. From Jerome's sudden transition to manhood, too, one gains a rare insight into the workings of a boy's mind when responsibility hardens despair and crystallises dreams into action.

If Miss Wilkins had bestowed as much care on the form of her story as she did on its psychology and subdued picturesqueness, it would deserve to win a permanent place in our literature. To begin with, it is about two hundred pages too long. Its movement, which is necessarily no swifter than that of village life in New England or the sluggish currents of Jane Austen's and Charlotte Brontë's domestic scenes, is retarded by shoals of superfluous descriptive matter. One wearies of hearing what Lucina or her Aunt Camilla wore on this and that occasion, and conceives a positive abhorrence of the trees in Squire Merritt's front yard, lest Jerome, whose moods are incessantly reflected in nature, shall never reach the door by reason of the author's excursions among them. Thus the significant detail, which it is the high prerogative of the artist to select, and that by instinct, is too frequently lost. The dialogue, too, instead of carrying its own weight and colour, is accompanied by profuse explanations of how the speaker enunciated his words, and felt when speaking them. This running commentary of emotional analysis would manifestly be out of place in a short story; and even in a novel, where it does not imply a feeble grasp of character, it robs the reader's imagination of half its pleasure. Then the story "crawfishes" at times. Chapters VIII. and IX. belong before Chapter VII., and Chapters XVI. and XVII. before Chapter XV. As long as no serious confusion results, this may seem to be a trivial criticism; but I am persuaded that the clearest and best stories (with a few classical exceptions), whether they most resemble a straight line or a spiral, or a Hittite inscription, do not double on their tracks.

Finally, the carelessness of Miss Wilkins's writing in little affairs of diction and good taste is amazing. The story has on it the brand of forced marches for hurried serial publication. What, pray, is the meaning of the sentence "There the juvenility of comparison was hers"? Or of Lucina's turning to her father rather than her mother "to ask that she might go or have"? And why does Miss Wilkins split every infinitive that comes to hand? Why does she dilute similes to insipidity and mix metaphors and jangle sounds as in "disrespect of discomfort"? George Eliot, and even Rose Terry Cooke and Miss Alcott, thought it worth while to attend to such matters. Has Miss Wilkins reached the point where she no longer cares for the good opinion of educated persons? Is she willing ultimately to be ranked with the throng of novelists who are as incapable of turning out literary work as the majority of readers are of appreciating it? The aged woman who moved with "a stiff wobble of black bombazined hips," and the clergyman who in his prayer for relatives of the deceased "had a fine instinct for other people's corns and prejudices," in some way fail to appeal. In actual life it is entirely probable that an old lady who had driven ten miles to attend a funeral would whisper audibly in the midst of the decorous service, "I smell the tea—I do, I smell it. Yes, I do—I told ye so. I tell ye, I smell the tea;" but one rather wishes that in the story she would smell it once and be done with it. Nor is there any particular use, that I can see, in repeating *ad nauseam* such banalities as "Who's that?" "What's goin' to be done?" "Where are you, husband?" Novels should be a little less stupid than life, and, after all, in moments of excitement there are those among us New Englanders who have a really varied and entertaining assortment of interrogatives and expletives.

G. M. H.

THE LIFE OF A JOURNALIST.*

Almost twenty years ago, in March, 1879, a career of brilliant promise was cut short by the sudden death, at the early age of thirty-seven, of James Macdonell, a leader writer on the London *Times*. Dr. Robertson Nicoll's story of the strenuous effort and achievement crowded into the latter half of those thirty-seven years, introduced to the American public in Mr. George W. Smalley's *Tribune* letters when it first appeared in England, has now received the recognition of an American edition. Looked at simply as a contribution to biographical literature, it is a story of wonderful vividness and power. Told for the most part through Macdonell's own letters and the familiar sketching of his intimates (which are admirably edited), it brings the reader into close touch with the man himself, a man well worth knowing, a man of brilliancy of intellect and charm of character.

But the book is more than a picture of a full and interesting and even fascinating life. It is a picture of journalism under modern conditions. As Dr. Nicoll himself says in his opening sentence, it is "the life of a journalist—perhaps the only life of a journalist pure and simple ever written." It is the life of a man who was an enthusiastic journalist, who believed in journalism and its high and noble mission, who was devoted to it as to an art or a science, who was true to it and to his ideals of it under every stress, who abhorred what was cheap and unworthy in it, and who proved its satisfactory possibilities for the man with a genius for it, although holding unflinchingly in the service of others to the demands of his own self-respect. Perhaps by way of contrast it may be permitted to quote from a private letter received recently by an American friend from a London journalist in a position to-day very similar to that which was occupied by Macdonell:

> "The daily paper is becoming more and more contemptible. It is a mere vulgar, catch-penny, sensational production, in which men of a low, vulpine order of talent succeed best."

That kind of pessimistic treason would have been impossible to James Macdonell. Living, it would have stirred loyal wrath. Dead, it finds in his career, brief as it was, stout protest and refutation.

The story of James Macdonell begins among those picturesque Scottish scenes, made so familiar of late. He was born at Dyce, "a bleak little village some six miles from Aberdeen," of a curiously contrasted parentage. His father was a Highlander and a Roman Catholic. His mother was an Aberdeenshire woman and a Protestant. From the one he inherited "the dreamy, passionate, chivalrous nature of the Celt;" from the other "the industry, tenacity, and shrewdness" of the Saxon. To the father was appointed that commonest of unlucky dispensations, a large family and narrow means—he was an excise officer in a district where smuggling, especially of whiskey, was held to be legitimate. Yet he got much out of life, for he was refined in his tastes, enjoying books, music, and the society of his intimate friends. Three dominating influences determined the boy's career. The first was that of a stimulating teacher of the type of Ian Maclaren's Domsie; the second, that of a notable provincial editor—a sort of Scotch Sam Bowles of the Springfield *Republican*—William McCombie of the Aberdeen *Free Press*, whose warm friendship

* James Macdonell, Journalist. By W. Robertson Nicoll, M.A., LL.D. New York: Dodd, Mead & Co. $2.75.

turned the bent of young Macdonell's mind from business to journalism ; the third, that of an atmosphere charged with an intensity of theological difference of every kind and degree. This was accentuated in Macdonell's case by his own peculiar inheritance—the Roman Catholic creed in a Scotch Presbyterian environment. He emerged from it, after a severe struggle, a liberal Protestant, but never so liberal as to lose his grip on the basal realities of religion. The training thus received so young kept him to the end an expert theological controversialist.

Macdonell's career as a professional journalist began at twenty, as sub-editor of the Edinburgh *Daily Review* under Henry Kingsley—a brother of Charles, and author of the Australian stories (recently reissued)—who, however, was not successful as an editor. Next Macdonell became editor of the *Northern Daily Express* of Newcastle, at a salary of $750 a year, a position of no small responsibility, where he bade fair to spend the rest of his days as a provincial editor. But a kindly fate intervened in the person of a London purchaser of the property, a sort of "syndicate" man. This typically modern newspaper proprietor had his news, and even his editorials, prepared and stereotyped in London, shipping them the same day to the various provincial papers he controlled, and leaving for the nominal editor latitude only in the matter of local news—exactly the principle of production of the numerous "plate" papers which to-day fill every small city and town all over the United States. This curtailment of position piqued Macdonell's professional pride. Through the influence of friends, and a rising reputation for exceptional ability, he obtained the place of assistant editor, when just turned twenty-three, in the office of the London *Daily Telegraph*, barely missing a similar berth on the Edinburgh *Scotsman*, the great journal across the border, to his then great regret. Thus was launched his metropolitan career. On the *Telegraph* he remained ten years, representing his journal in Paris after the German war and contributing occasional articles to *Fraser's*, the *Spectator*, or some other periodical of equal standing. Later he joined the staff of the London *Times* as a leader writer.

This is the skeleton of Macdonell's career. Its osseous details are only clothed in the living flesh of interest and significance as we see the man himself always absorbed in his work, even in moments of apparent rest. A leading New York journalist once said that every newspaper proprietor should make it compulsory for his editorial writers to spend at least two nights a week at some leading club, so that the men who speak for the press might keep in closest contact with the men who make news and opinions about it. In Macdonell's case such a rule would have been superfluous. Much of the secret of his journalistic success lay in the magnetic charm of a personality that made many acquaintances and turned them into friends. Their respect for his high ideals became first respect for himself, and then respect for the journalism he represented. They turned their best side to him, they opened up to him, by the simplest natural law of human intercourse, the attraction of a bright and sympathetic personality. In Paris he was on terms of more or less intimacy with such widely separated men as Lord Lyons, the English ambassador, the Comte de Paris, Louis Blanc, M. Guizot, and M. Taine, who gave him his close personal friendship. In England he numbered among his friends James Anthony Froude, Mr. Delane, the great editor of the London *Times*; Alfred Austin, Sir D. Mackenzie Wallace, Richard H. Hutton, the editor of the *Spectator*; J. R. Seeley, William Black, and George W. Smalley. From all he drew that stimulus to freshness of view which made him on the journalistic side so effective a commentator on any subject that he touched. But he bestowed as well as received. He was a deep and hard thinker, with an exceptional capacity for the acquisition of facts—he made himself especially an authority on French politics—and thus what he said or wrote carried weight. He had the gift of versatility too, as when in a single week he contributed leaders to the *Times* on Burmah, Spanish affairs, Russia in Central Asia, Canadian affairs, and ironclads. In short, he had that all-roundness which is the true test of journalistic genius.

In having to say so much about the man and his career in order to explain what he was and why—owing to the anonymous character of journalistic work, which Macdonell himself rejoiced in, calling his leader writing on the *Times* "having the use of the most powerful speaking trumpet in the world"—one is left almost no space for the series of charming pictures which begin with his London career. Now it is a glimpse of Holman Hunt in his studio; now he is with Ruskin at a garden party given by Miss Jean Ingelow; again it may be a call on Carlyle, a meeting with Renan, or perhaps an afternoon at M. Guizot's or M. Taine's. Once more the scene changes, and we see the journalist creating a mild theological sensation by "writing up" the Archbishop of York as he officiated "on the quiet" in a dissenting Presbyterian church in a little Scotch town where he was visiting; or perhaps we see him as he went with sickened heart to witness the execution of a condemned Paris communist, a brave young fellow who refused to have his eyes bandaged, but faced the murderous fire of the soldiers. Kaleidoscopic is the effect of the constant shifting, yet never so quickly done as to slight successive pictures of a beautiful and tender home life, into which entered so many distinguished social and intellectual relationships, and out of which radiated so much to so wide a circle. That, after all, is the side of a many-sided life on which one lingers the longest.

Arthur Reed Kimball.

BALLADS OF LOST HAVEN.*

A new volume of poems by Mr. Bliss Carman is a literary event which appeals not only to the love of beauty but to the love of novelty as well. Each of Mr. Carman's books has a note of its own, which differentiates it sharply from its fellows. These differences do not represent stages of development, but merely Mr. Carman's devotion to unity of effect. They are due to the system on which he makes up his collections. In love with simplicity, he sacrifices not only the cheap charm of variety, but sometimes even the richness of the full harmonic chord, in order to secure his music from confusion and the jarring of unrelated themes. He published no book until he had a quantity of mature and perfected verse on hand. From this he selected, without reference to the dates of their composition, a number of poems bearing an obvious relationship to each other in mood and key, and thus made up his first volume. Successive volumes have been made up on the same system; and each, therefore, whatever the charge of monotony now and then urged by the captious, has made its distinctive impression, and lives by virtue of its own personality. The system is not only admirable for the moderation which it expresses and the reserve force which it implies, but is likely to justify itself on the purely practical side. While each volume stands absolutely on its own merits, it plays its part, at the same time, as a single member of a collective edition, and suggests the need of its companion volumes, past or to come.

Mr. Carman's first volume, *Low Tide on Grand Pré*, was pitched in a poignant minor key. Lyric emotion in this volume takes precedence of lyric thought, though this latter factor is in no degree lacking. The two *Vagabondia* volumes, made up of poems by Mr. Carman and Mr. Hovey, sound a joyous and virile note. Their voice is that of the lover of life and love, of freedom and sane mirth. *Behind the Arras* is well characterised as "a book of the unseen." It is in a major key throughout, pervaded by a largeness of utterance and a vibrant depth of tone. Generally mystical, sometimes obscure through over-persistent pursuit of curious thought, often harsh in phrase and wording, it yet must stand as one of the most significant and enduring works in pure poetry that this century's end can show. Lyric thought, in this case, dominates lyric emotion; but the latter factor is nowhere insufficient.

Mr. Carman's latest volume, *Ballads of Lost Haven*, just issued in beautiful and dignified dress, carries the obvious sub-title of "A Book of the Sea." Its prevailing note is one of a large sadness and overbrooding mystery. It is the most elemental, massive, unhasting of Mr. Carman's books. There is little of the plangency of *Low Tide on Grand Pré*—the mood is too grave for complaint. There is none of the curious thought that piques the reader in *Behind the Arras*. But there is the pathos of human

* Ballads of Lost Haven. A Book of the Sea. By Bliss Carman. Boston: Lamson, Wolffe & Co. $1.00.

life at issue or at truce with unsolved mysteries. The vast force of external nature fills all the lines.

Most of the poems in the collection are true ballads—lyric narratives of human action or human passion, such as "The Yule Guest," "The King of Ys," and "The Marring of Malyn." This predominantly human character of the collection should win it a circle of readers not quite reached by the preceding volumes. The appeal here is to all who love the sea and are concerned to ask how it touches the heart of man.

In spite of its unity of theme and sentiment the volume affords a comparatively wide range. At one limit stands the splendidly masculine song of "The Gravedigger," which belongs to the big-limbed company of the "Spring Song" and "Gamelbar." The following extracts from this poem can give but a partial idea of its quality :

"Oh, the shambling sea is a sexton old,
  And well his work is done.
With an equal grave for lord and knave,
  He buries them every one.

"Then hoy and rip, with a rolling hip,
  He makes for the nearest shore ;
And God, who sent him a thousand ship,
  Will send him a thousand more ;
But some he'll save for a bleaching grave,
  And shoulder them in to shore—
Shoulder them in, shoulder them in,
  Shoulder them in to shore.

* * * * *

"Oh, he works with a rollicking stave at lip,
  And loud is the chorus skirled ;
With the burly rote of his rumbling throat
  He batters it down the world.

"He learned it once in his father's house,
  Where the ballads of eld were sung ;
And merry enough is the burden rough,
  But no man knows the tongue.

"Then hoy and rip, with a rolling hip, etc."

At the opposite boundary are the poignant cadences of "The Yule Guest," one of the most rememberable and genuine of all modern ballads. The structural looseness so frequent in Mr. Carman's longer poems is not noticeable in this ballad, as it is in the suggestive but rather chaotic and inexplicable "Kelpie Riders." This latter poem leads one to wonder if Mr. Carman does not once in a great while let himself write something designed exclusively for the innermost circle of his disciples. He can be, and generally is, quite clear in his thought as in his music. But each volume contains at least one poem, such as "The Kelpie Riders" in this collection, "The Silent Lodger" in *Behind the Arras*, and "The House of Idiedaily" in *Songs from Vagabondia*, which the illuminated may love, indeed, but which surely no one, not even Mr. Carman himself, can wholly understand.

As a whole, this volume contains much of Mr. Carman's most mature and perfect work, with his faults so far subdued as not at all to mar the general effect. The critic may, for purposes of light and shade, call attention to a diffuseness here or a pet mannerism there in certain of the poems. But the reader reading for delight will be conscious only of the fulness of colour, imagination, and mystery, of the close approach to nature, of the unforgettable lines and phrases that crowd the pages of this volume.

The following poem, "A Son of the Sea," which occupies the first page of the book, in a sense epitomises the whole collection :

"I was born for deep-sea faring ;
  I was bred to put to sea ;
Stories of my father's daring
  Filled me at my mother's knee.

"I was sired among the surges ;
  I was cubbed beside the foam ;
All my heart is in its verges,
  And the sea wind is my home.

"All my boyhood, from far vernal
  Bourns of being, came to me
Dream-like, plangent, and eternal
  Memories of the plunging sea."

Charles G. D. Roberts.

THE BRONTËS: FACT AND FICTION.*

Mr. Mackay's little book about the Brontës is mainly concerned with two questions. First, did Charlotte Brontë lose her heart to a Belgian dominie at Brussels? Next, what is the historical value of Dr. Wright's entertaining book about the Brontë family in Ireland? There can be only one reason for discussing the former problem. Perhaps a critic may ask himself, Are Miss Brontë's pictures of unhappy passion suggested merely by fancy and observa-

* The Brontës : Fact and Fiction. By Angus Mackay, B.A. New York : Dodd, Mead & Co. $1 50.

tion of other distressed ladies, or are they coloured by her own experience "of love that never found his earthly close"? The enigma has a certain curious interest, as a question concerned with "the mechanism of genius." But I confess that I do not care to pry into the most sacred intimacy of a lady whose husband is still alive, and whose surviving friends have feelings to be considered. The curious may turn to Mr. Mackay's pages for themselves. They are well reasoned. As to Dr. Wright's book, Mr. Mackay blames the critics for universally accepting its narrative. But I remember that, for one, I myself urged a number of difficulties, geographical, genealogical, historical, and ethical. Dr. Wright replied. There was a correspondence, in what periodical I cannot recollect.

Mr. Mackay very judiciously prints a genealogical chart of the ancestral Brontës, as he gathers their dates and affinities from Dr. Wright. I quote the Family Tree.

The wild improbabilities of the relations of Hugh II. and Welsh are merely accounted for by the oddity of all Brontës. Then Welsh only becomes a father about thirty years after his marriage. So Mr. Mackay goes on, and Dr. Wright's reply will be awaited with interest. Mr. Mackay decides that "the stories are not true, and it seems now equally certain that it was not Hugh II. who propagated them." The ghost stories of Hugh III. suffer terribly from Mr. Mackay, and certainly will not satisfy the S.P.R. The legend of the celebrated Avenger, Hugh III., who wanted to destroy the *Quarterly* reviewer of *Jane Eyre*, is said not to contain "a word of truth." Mr. Murray never heard of it, there is no record of it; I can vouch for a total dearth of allusions to it in Lockhart's letters to his daughter; but I have not seen his letters to Mr. Murray. Mr. George Smith knows nothing of it; Hugh's visits to the Museum reading-room are not in the Museum record. *Jane Eyre* was reviewed,

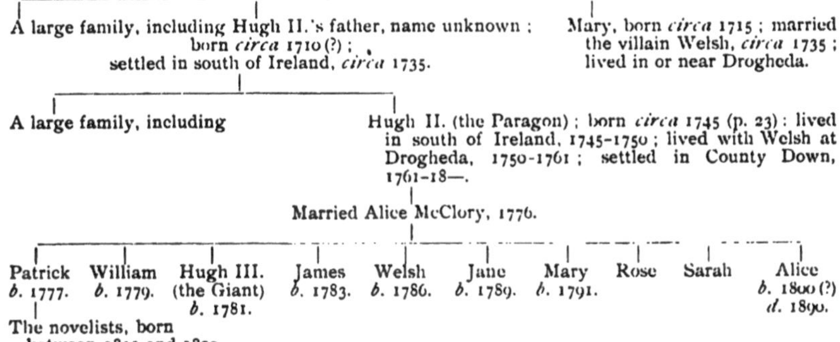

Dr. Wright urges that his dates are but vaguely approximate. Mr. Mackay does not believe in most of the *facts*, but the facts demand these dates, these, or nearly these. The facts, as given by Dr. Wright, are now as well known as romantic, and are said to have suggested *Wuthering Heights*. The story comes, it seems, from Hugh II., and Mr. Mackay points out that, if Hugh II. is right, Hugh I. must have begun to beget his large family when he was about eighty.

in the *Quarterly*, in December, 1848. "Shortly after February, 1849, Charlotte knew that Miss Rigby was the reviewer." But Dr. Wright argues that Hugh III. arrived at Haworth, with his club, before Christmas, 1848, and left England, *brédouille*, before the end of January, 1849. Now Emily died December 19th, 1848, Anne was very ill, Hugh says nothing of this, his nieces say nothing about his inopportune visit. Mr. Mackay does not think that Anne really encouraged Hugh in his purpose of slaying the reviewer. Perhaps Anne did not expect Hugh to go so far, but it is a very improbable story, at the least. Old Mr. Brontë sent to Hugh a copy of a *cheap Jane Eyre* in January, 1853, saying, "This is the first work published by my daughter under the fictitious name of Currer Bell," and added explanations quite needless, being already well known to the Avenger, if the Avenger story is true. Old Mr. Brontë (*teste* Charlotte) did not even know of the *Quarterly* review, ten months after date. Yet how could he avoid knowing of it, if the Avenger came over to Haworth as soon as the review appeared? Then we are told that the old parson took Hugh to a prize-fight, "almost before his daughter Emily was cold in her grave." The niece and grand-niece of the Avenger never heard the tale, "nor do we believe it." Dr. Wright may be able to explain these circumstances; we can only wait. As to my own old opinion that the editor of the *Quarterly* had inserted the offensive passages in the review of *Jane Eyre*, my discovery of Lockhart's letter on the subject of course altered my view. The real wonder is that Lockhart allowed the article to appear as Miss Rigby wrote it, so enthusiastic—too enthusiastic—was his admiration of the novel.

Mr. Mackay's book confirms the doubts which I expressed when Dr. Wright's book first appeared. We cannot, of course, expect history from the lips of mere tradition, but the origin of these legends seems to need exploration. Dr. Wright is obviously sincere in his beliefs; *he* did not invent the stories, and the exact history of their growth in the popular fancy would be of curious interest. When Hugh III. is made to say that his grandfather, Hugh I., suffered, somehow, under George III., we may suspect a misprint. George I. must be intended, if any George, and, if so, some anachronisms will disappear, and some miracles with them. The Avenger story, being modern, is the most difficult to explain, and even the oddity of the Brontës hardly makes the contradictory circumstances intelligible. No letters from Mr. Murray to Lockhart on the subject exist at Abbotsford.

Andrew Lang.

A STORY OF MODERN AMERICA.*

The author of *The Federal Judge* has made a bold stroke at the outset for public suffrage. The life which he depicts is the life of to-day, the life that is reflected in the newspapers everywhere in America, and with which every citizen of the United States is more or less familiar. The colossal financial fraud engineered by the railway magnate and his fellow-conspirators is a modern story, and the "judge" as well as the "magnate" are both products of our civilisation. The story in all its details is not only convincing because of its strong realism, but because we are familiar with the facts upon which it is based. We breathe the very atmosphere which makes it live before our eyes; the conditions of life which hem and press us in on every side have begotten it; it is a piece of our American life incarnated and realised in fiction, so that few readers will be able to lay down the book without recognising the likeness.

The Federal Judge bears witness in a striking manner to the power of unconscious influence. Judge Tracy Dunn had laid the beams of his life on the pillars of justice and rectitude. He began his career as a strenuous opponent of corporations and trusts, and gained a reputation as a friend of the labouring class. We see the country judge plucked from his quiet home and dropped into a new world "at a time of his life when he had formed all the habits of the old one, in which he had lived for more than half a century. And never did the vivid imagination of an Arabian story-teller conceive a fable in which the mortal was more helpless or less able to direct the course of events which governed him." In the whirlpool of circumstance, which nearly ends in a fatal maelström for him, the judge is doggedly convinced that he is steering intelligently and conscientiously, and never doubts but that he is launched on a voyage that will make the office he fills shine with a new lustre, and that his judgments will put on record a wise and far-seeing precedent for future administrators in the federal court. The subtle and determining influences which undermine the judge's prejudices against corporations; the pathetic falling-in of all his hopes

* The Federal Judge. By Charles K. Lush. Boston: Houghton, Mifflin & Co. $1.25.

and strong convictions when he is left stranded by those whom he helped in blindness to frustrate the very ends he had sought all his life to serve ; the unflinching integrity and sterling honesty of the man all through the duplicity which befooled him ; the simplicity and sincerity, the fidelity and truthfulness of his character sharply visualised by the contrast of his surroundings—nothing exists in the picture here drawn which it might not be possible to duplicate somewhere in the life about us.

But if the judge appeals to our sympathies by reason of his uprightness and simplicity and rugged traits of character, the railway magnate moves us to admiration by his intellectual supremacy over men, his daring invention, his splendid audacity and dexterity in playing with men and money on the great chess-board of life. His insight into human nature, his knowledge of men and women, his adroit and unscrupulous machinery in handling and moulding them to his will excites our wonder. He saw the weak side of Judge Dunn—"A fine gentleman, an honest man, an upright judge, but—human." Well, that is the vulnerable spot in all of us ; and Elliott Gardwell himself was not exempt from it. Had it been so he would not have fallen in love with the judge's daughter Harriet, nor would he have overreached himself and miscalculated events at the eleventh hour, and this story would not have been written. The *dénouement* is as startling as it is unexpected, and is one of the strong climaxes in fiction. It is dramatic, for it is inevitable ; we see that Nemesis has all along had a strand in the web which Gardwell has been spinning with the cool assurance of the self-deceived, and the self-deceived are the damned. Yet is there something in Gardwell that arouses awe as well as pity—the awe which we feel in the presence of a magnificent human ruin.

These are but the two poles of contrast by which the various characters in the story are repulsed or attracted to work out their purpose. The book is strong in characterisation and incident and the excitements that fire the imagination. It has humour and the sentiment of fine feeling ; it aims more at broad, effective strokes than at refined analysis or description. There is no literary quality to speak of ; the captious may find structural faults and inartistic flaws not a few—and welcome. All we claim for it is that it is successful in achieving the end at which it aims—it is a capital story of the hour, and for the hour. As we have said, the types of character are familiar to us and the movements traced are current in our history ; but the setting of these characters, the motives which empower them to act, the clash of principle and interest, the graphic picture of prominent features in American life are endowed with originality ; and the moral force of the book as well as the great attraction of the story is undeniably felt. By no preaching or array of platitudes are the social and commercial evils of our life arraigned, but by the concrete presentment of their disintegrating influence in human action. *The Federal Judge* is a book that every American who reads will be thoroughly interested in, and it is a book that ought to be read by every American. No more thrilling tale of the American life of to-day in the arena of commerce and politics has yet been published.

J. M.

AGLAVAINE AND SÉLYSETTE.*

The literary movement of our time has been a movement against the external and heterogeneous, and like all literary movements, its French expression is more intelligible and obvious than its English expression, because more extreme. When one compares *La Tentation de Saint Antone* of Flaubert, the last great work of the old romantic movement, with the *Axël* of Villiers de l'Isle Adam, the first great work of the new romantic movement, one understands the completeness of the change. A movement which never mentions an external thing except to express a state of the soul has taken the place of a movement which delighted in picturesque and bizarre things, for their own sakes. M. Maeterlinck has called himself a disciple of Villiers de l'Isle Adam, who, in the words of a recent French critic, "opened the doors of the beyond with a crash that our generation might pass through them"—I quote from memory

* Aglavaine and Sélysette. By Maurice Maeterlinck. Translated by Alfred Sutro. London : Grant Richards.

—but he has carried his master's revolt farther than his master, and made his persons cries and shadows. We do not know in what country they were born, or in what period they were born, or how old they are, or what they look like, and we do not always know whether they are brother and sister, or lover and lover, or husband and wife. They go hither and thither by well-sides, and by crumbling towns, and among woods, which are repeated again and again, and are as unemphatic as a faded tapestry; and they speak with low voices which one has to hold one's breath to hear. The old movement was full of the pride of the world, and called to us through a brazen trumpet: and the persons of *Axël* were lifted above the pride of the world, of the pride of hidden and august destinies, the pride of the Magi following the star over many mountains; but their souls are naked, and can only tremble and lament. Until this last play they have not needed to do more, for they were created to prolong the sense of terror Shakespeare put into the line, "the bay trees in my country are all withered," the terror at we do not know what, mixed with a pity for we do not know what, that we come to in contemplation when all reasons, all hopes, all memories have passed away, and the Divine ecstasy has not found us.

M. Maeterlinck has, however, created the persons of Aglavaine and Sélysette with a partly different purpose, for he has found a philosophy in his search for the quintessence, the philosophy of his beautiful *Trésor des Humbles*, and he would have his persons speak out of its wisdom. It will make his plays more beautiful in time, for the serious fault of his best plays, even of *Les Aveugles* and *L'Intruse*, is that they have not the crowning glory of great plays, that continual raving about destiny that is, as it were, the raiment of beautiful emotions. Its immediate effect is mischievous, for Meleander and Aglavaine, his most prominent persons, continually say things which they would say differently or not at all if their creator were only thinking of them as persons in the play. The first act and part of the second act are a little absurd even, because Meleander and Aglavaine explain when they should desire and regret; and because their overmastering sense of certain spiritual realities has blinded them to lesser realities, to which natures of so high a wisdom could not have been blind; and because the art, which should be of a cold wisdom, has shared in their delusions and become a little sentimental. One is not indeed moved until the play begins to eddy about Melegrane, an old grandmother, Yesalene, a child, and Sélysette, a childlike woman, persons whose natures are so narrowed because of forgotten and unknown things, that M. Maeterlinck cannot speak through their lips, but must let them speak as their destinies would have them speak. They speak more movingly than the persons of *Les Aveugles* or *L'Intruse*, for though still shadows and cries, they have each, as the persons in Shakespeare have, her portion of wisdom, and all they say is beautiful with the pathos of little interests and extreme weakness. I do not think M. Maeterlinck has indeed written anything as beautiful as one thing that is said by old Melegrane to her granddaughter, Sélysette.

"So do I often think of those days, Sélysette. I was not ill, then, and I was able to carry you in my arms or run after you. . . . You wandered to and fro, and your laughter rang through the house; then suddenly you would fling open the door and shriek in terror, 'She is coming, she is coming, she is here!' And no one knew whom you meant, or what it was that frightened you; you did not know yourself; but I would pretend to be frightened too, and would go through the long corridors with you till we reached the garden. And it all went for so little, and served no purpose, my child; but we understood each other, you and I, and smiled at each other, night and morning. . . . And thus, thanks to you, have I been a mother a second time, long after my beauty had left me; and some day you will know that women never weary of motherhood, that they would cherish death itself, did it fall asleep on their knees."

W. B. Yeats.

THE SECRET ROSE.*

"Although I wrote these stories at different times and in different manners, and without any definite plan, they have but one subject, the war of spiritual with natural order," says Mr. Yeats. So, at the very outset, he points dull readers to their inner meaning. This is a pity, just because the allegory is so

* The Secret Rose. By W. B. Yeats. With Illustrations by J. B. Yeats. New York: Dodd, Mead & Co. $2.00.

little obvious. One can think of the stories delighting yet giving no hint of a moral, for which the "different times," the "different manners," are to be thanked, and, most of all, Mr. Yeats's artistic sense. But as there is a well-founded prejudice against allegories, it should be insisted on, in any recommendation of these, that they bear excellently the test of all good symbolism—namely, that the qualities of its outer garment shall sufficiently justify its existence. The underlying truth is there, because it lies always at the base of Mr. Yeats's House of Life, and whenever he builds, of whatever stuff and pattern, he must build on that.

If the sap of your life be drained by spiritual and visionary demands, it is a poor chance you have of prospering, or even of living meritoriously in the world of common men. In a more arrogant form Villiers de l'Isle Adam puts the converse, and it is one of the mottoes of the book—"As for living, our servants will do that for us." There is the theme, then, the recognition of an allegiance to something other than the worldly and moral powers and principalities that ordain and rule and reward in accordance with the tried experience of men. "O Aodh, promise me to sing the song out before the morning, whether we overcome them or they overcome us," says the young Queen to the bard, amid the havoc of war and slaughter. The far vision was nearer than the horrors encompassing her body. She is of the kin of this people, this sparse and scattered people, "who have come but seldom into the world, and always for its trouble, and to bind the hearts of men with a leash of mystery; the dreamers who must do what they dream, the doers who must dream what they do." "Men of verse," says the wise King who had discovered his lonely greatness, "why did you make me sin against the secrecy of wisdom, for law was made by man for the welfare of man, but wisdom the gods have made, and no man shall live by its light, for it and the hail and the rain and the thunder follow a way that is deadly to mortal things." Then he set out to find his kindred.

It would be easy to classify the stories in accordance with their artistic merits, which are so various that one might reach with grumbling to a third-best section. But, save to mention that the moods are almost as varied as in *The Celtic Twilight*, a comparison between the stories or between them and their predecessors is not the most profitable work of a reviewer. Mr. Yeats's abundant humour is not wanting in the tales of Hanrahan the Red, and we find it softened to a gentle irony in "Out of the Rose," which might be a page out of *Don Quixote*, and in "The Heart of the Spring." That is no unexpected quality, though his reputation rests rather on his visionary suggestions. One has noted before, too, but the power of it is growing in him, the frequent association of spiritual truth with familiar circumstance. This is the sign of the effective poet, of the poet with vigour in his imaginings. The great secret was whispered to the old magician in "The Heart of the Spring," by "one who wore a red cap, and whose lips were white with the froth of the new milk."

To me the best tales are the six that tell the story of Hanrahan the Red. Hanrahan is a very distinct and special human being, a hedge-schoolmaster, a poet and a ne'er-do-well, too much himself to be just like any other hedge-schoolmaster, poet, or ne'er-do-well. But I doubt if ever the poet's history has been set forth with such proud truth before, without fear of the world for his shortcomings, without seeking its favour for this "ruler of the dreams of men." Hanrahan is very vain, and he loves notoriety; he is of evil repute, yet an excellent fellow withal in his convenient moods. He is drunken very often with the Brew of the Little Pot, and sometimes with dreams. He sells the Book of Wisdom for a pig, the pig for whiskey, and after being disgracefully intoxicated has a night of splendid ecstasy. The Powers "passed through his dreams crowned with rubies, and having roses in their hands; and in the morning he awoke, a rough-clad peasant, shivering on the earthen floor." This episode is followed by his making unscrupulous love—and being ignominiously defeated by her careful elders—to a young girl. He is the king of lovers, if constancy be not asked for. In truth, Cluna of the Wave, an immortal, sought him, but she was repulsed, for the earthly temper was on him then. A vagabond, with a "devil in the soles of his feet," a humorous rascal, who teaches English out of *The Lives of Celebrated Rogues and Rapparees*, he uses his school-children as mediums by which to widen the sound and the fame of his terrible satires, yet is he beloved of women young and old, and much dependent in his tamer moods on human shelter and sympathy. No one can curse more bitterly his enemies, yet while lamenting his own insults, as in the songs he made out of the grotesque story of "The Twisting of the Rope," his mind reaches beyond himself: "as he made them his dreams deepened and changed until he was singing about the twisting of the Rope of Human Sorrows." His last days were black misery pierced by visions of eternal beauty. But by degrees the body made fewer demands on him, and "it was as though he became incorporate with some more poignant and fragile world, whose march-lands are the intense colours and silences of this world." He died a sordid outcast, ministered to by a mad vagrant. When his body was found it was given a great burying. And so let us all be grateful for the limitation of our gifts that keeps us in safe paths. And, likewise, may all poets find some time an interpreter of such brave sympathy as this initiate of *The Secret Rose*.

The tales are clear and simple on the outside, as if for children's eyes, wise and beautiful on the inner side, with a dangerous wisdom and beauty; for their sweet and bitter secrets do not feed this world's strength. But they will only call fatally to a few. The rest of us, if we linger and wonder as at an entertainment, will then go our cheerful, prudent ways, with apologies to the world for an hour of idle, alien dreaming.

Annie Macdonell.

BRICHANTEAU: ACTOR.*

"I am a Bohemian, a free lance of art, but I have had my hour!—my hours!" These are the words of an optimistic failure, a type of actor which M. Sarcey shrewdly surmises is probably unknown to us in America. Certain it is that only a man of stout heart could talk habitually in this strain—when, with gaping holes in his gloves and no perceptible crease in his trousers, a back number, an old-fashioned boulevard actor, he very likely does not know where he will sleep the next night—without betraying either a wounded pride or an affected bravado. Vanity is common enough, but pride, carrying its banner to the last, never once admitting defeat, peopling many a dream with phantoms of glory, is as rare as it is exhilarating, and makes a prince, unworthy of this mercenary world, out of the starveling who wears it.

Brichanteau's life was keyed high from the beginning. His parents permitted him to go upon the stage only on condition that he would be a Talma. He first made up with his father's face as the *Vicaire de Wakefield*. He had a voice like a peal of thunder, like a howitzer. His instructor at the Conservatory was maliciously jealous: *hinc illæ lacrimæ!* After a bawling contest with M. Beauvallet, in which he did not win a single prize, there was friction, and, unwilling to be shunted off from tragedy to comedy, he swore he would never again set foot in that hole. He went upon the road—even sought the bread of renown in foreign lands. He was imprudent. But he had his hours.

He gravitated from the rôle of Louis XI., which he essayed one night at Compiègne "without preparation," when M. Talbot refused to act because the Comédie Française costumes had not arrived, to a starter of bicycle races, standing erect in his pride every inch of the way. He held the world a stage, where every man must play a part, and his no sad one. When he wished to crush a dramatic critic, he assumed the pose of Don César staring Don Salluste out of countenance. When his voice wore out poor Jenny's lungs and she must needs choose between life and her place as *jeune première*, taking her in his arms and kissing her forehead, he plunged instinctively into that tearful scene from *Le Cid*, she giving him his cues. It required a Frenchman from Buenos Ayres, who proclaimed his intention of defying the Germans in the costume of D'Artagnan, to fire Brichanteau's patriotism; and when himself caught spying upon their fortifications, he acted the Norman peasant—"That's the good God's true truth!" he said—supremely glad of an opportunity to

* Brichanteau: Actor. By Jules Claretie. Boston: Little, Brown & Co. $1.50.

show those swashbucklers what a dramatic artist's soul really was. In the face of a threatened shooting, his first thought was of the Porte Saint Martin, the Gaiété, the Châtelet, and the Comédie Française, where he ought to have been engaged. As to dungeons, he knew all about them—he had played Buridan and Latude. While he was in the clutches of the enemy, his easily inflammable brain conceived the idea of kidnapping the King of Prussia; for did not D'Artagnan, with his three friends, Athos, Porthos, and Aramis, all but rescue the King of England? When the siege was raised, he rushed to his lodgings and opened his Corneille. That comforted him. It is small wonder that he sometimes spoke of the bicycle race as a rehearsal, and, when he had given the signal in that grand voice which M. Beauvallet envied, imagined with closed eyes that it was the signal for a duel rather, and listened breathlessly for the clash of swords and the roar of applause.

But had Brichanteau no humiliations, no vices, no colossal bump of personal vanity, to make him an object of pity? Ah, yes, an elegant sufficiency of them all. Was he not pelted with green apples at Lille, and lampooned at Compiègne? When the gas threatened to fail them in Pau, did not the manager order him to gain time by undressing on the stage while, with his back to the audience, he cut down a large cedar, a button with each blow? Was there not the woman that wrote comedies in her leisure and had engaged apartments opposite the house where Bernadotte was born—who asked him for his photograph, that, forsooth, her husband, who had killed his eleventh tiger, might have a fetich and come with a devilish, vitreous stare to pay his respects? And was it not a great disappointment to learn that Virginie, for whom, in her distress, he was trying desperately hard to arrange a benefit—Virginie, who long ago had sworn by her father's head that she loved but one being in this world, him—really had not gone to the dentist's those long afternoons when they were parted, but to M. Lanteclave, who was now only too glad to contribute his pension to the receipts of the performance? Yes, that last little rosy dream was a soap-bubble like the rest. But he had the brave discretion to be quiet respecting these matters. There were other things to talk about, cheerfuller things. There was the wreath that he had carried in his trunk, the presentation of which on his tours had always deeply moved him. Then, there was "The Roman Soldier Humiliated Under the Gallic Yoke," for which he had posed to Montescure. How he lingered over the molten bronze, saying to himself: "That blazing stream is perhaps your forehead; those bursts of flame are from your eyes!" And how willingly he used to carry, in a basket or in his pockets, the coke that warmed the miserable little studio! To the artist's despairing question, "How can I pay you for your sittings?" he had replied (and he recalled it with pride), "Was it not understood that this was not to be spoken of between us?"

It is probable that if a noble-hearted Brichanteau should appear on upper Broadway, he would be eyed with the same sullen suspicion with which honest bourgeois, on both sides of the Atlantic, regard other theatrical folk. Truth would compel a great many people to remark that no turkey-cock ever gave itself such airs. And yet, whether an actor or a model or a velodromist, Brichanteau's devotion to art was the same. As M. Sarcey says, there are very few such optimistic failures in America. The majority cease to be interesting when they cease to be of public interest. They are down in spirit when they are down at the heel. Being a good fellow with them means hanging around the bar and treating everybody within sight, or ostentatiously giving the dollar which they owe to their landlady to a beggar. They are inveterate gossips, but their gossip is keyed considerably lower than Brichanteau's. Art, which in all probability has never seriously affected them, is not a source of enduring delight to those who mistrust their own sprightliness if their trousers bag at the knees. They are in bondage, generally, to no fine distinctions. They would consent to appear at a café concert for considerably less than "an empire," and would infinitely prefer the doldrumiest vaudeville to starting bicycles. As to passing whole nights on a little balcony, repeating Shakespeare, with New York at their feet . . . !

George Merriam Hyde.

THE STORY OF THE WEST.*

Three books of uncommon interest have lately come from the press. The first volumes of a series known as the Story of the West, they are intended, in the words of the editor, "to present peculiar and characteristic phases of earlier development in that portion of our country which lies beyond the Missouri River." In other words, they are to tell, in popular form, the story of those typical figures—the Indian, the miner, the cowboy, the soldier, the trapper, and the railroad builder—which have made the West what it is to-day. Mr. Grinnell—one of the foremost living authorities on Indian life—tells, in the first volume, *The Story of the Indian*, and he does it extremely well. The Indian has always been a picturesque and romantic figure in our history; hence he has fallen an easy prey to unveracious authors, who are responsible for many popular misconceptions as to his character and habits. Mr. Grinnell sweeps these aside and shows us the Red man as he really is—not a grave, taciturn, and sullen man, but a man like ourselves, fond of society, gossipy, a great talker, with a keen sense of humour and quick at repartee. The popular notion that his women are little better than slaves, that they are merely beasts of burden, is corrected by Mr. Grinnell, who asserts that the labours of savage life are equally divided. In short, the writer takes us with him into the wigwam and council, and shows us how the Indian woos and fights, how he hunts and prays, how he eats and sleeps, and how he amuses himself. *The Story of the Indian* is full of human interest, and contains more information about the Indian, set forth in readable form, than any book we have seen on the subject.

The second volume of the series is written by Charles Howard Shinn, who relates *The Story of the Mine*, as illustrated by the great Comstock Lode of Nevada. Mr. Shinn has a thorough grasp of his subject, and describes, from the point of view of an eye witness, the thrilling and romantic discovery of the world-famous Comstock Lode. In vivid and picturesque language, bristling with characteristic anecdotes, he paints the mad rush across the Sierras, old times in Virginia City, days of the great bonanza, the dramatic rise to vast wealth of the great bonanza kings; and he winds up his stirring narrative with a description of the Comstock as it is to-day—a brilliant and fascinating account of one of the most colossal enterprises of the century.

Mr. Shinn, by the way, relates an anecdote anent Mark Twain:

> "The *Territorial Enterprise*, the pioneer newspaper of the region, had five men on the editorial staff and twenty-two compositors. Five hundred dollars a month was the salary of the managing editor. Mark Twain and Dan Quille were reporters. About this time Tom Fitch, of the *Union*, challenged Joe Goodman, of the *Enterprise*, to a duel in Six-Mile Cañon. Mark Twain recorded his disappointment in the next issue: 'Young Wilson and ourselves at once mounted a couple of fast horses and followed in their wake at the rate of a mile a minute; since when, being neither iron-clad nor half-soled, we enjoy more real comfort in standing up than in sitting down. But we lost our bloody item, for Marshal Perry arrived early with a detachment of constables, and Deputy Sheriff Blodgett came with a lot of blarsted sub-sheriffs, and these miserable, meddling whelps arrested the whole party and marched them back to town.'"

But the palmy days of the Comstock have vanished, and the dominant note of the scene to-day is one of wreck, abandonment, and decay. Pathetic is the description of the optimistic spirit which still pervades the almost deserted camp:

> "The catastrophe . . . does not attract serious attention. One is told elsewhere that 'times are dull on the Comstock.' One hears on the Comstock itself that 'after a little things will pick up;' that there is plenty of good rock down in the mines. . . . Nor is this merely the despairing cry of unacknowledged defeat. . . . It is neither more nor less in its higher manifestations than the sublime spirit of patriotism, defending to the last the lonely mountain fortress of the miner State of the Comstock."

Mr. Shinn is to be congratulated on the admirable way in which he has handled his theme. His volume abounds in just the sort of information one wants to know, and it reads like romance. Few who pick it up will lay it aside before finishing it.

Among the swiftly vanishing heroic figures whose iron nerve and indomitable

* The Story of the Indian. By George Bird Grinnell.

The Story of the Mine. By Charles Howard Shinn.

The Story of the Cowboy. By E. Hough. Story of the West Series. New York: D. Appleton & Co. $1.50 per volume.

energy have subdued to our uses the most splendid domain the world has ever seen—that of the cowboy, will, through the coming years, probably stand out with most distinctness. Mr. Hough, in a volume just come from the press, takes up this unique figure, and out of his thorough and intimate acquaintance with the subject spins *The Story of the Cowboy*—a story, it is needless to say, of surpassing interest. Mr. Hough does not endow the cowboy, as some writers have too often done, with superhuman powers, nor depict him as a devil-may-care, roistering fellow, "full of strange oaths." He paints him as he really is—a "steady, hard-working, methodical man, able in his calling, faithful in his duties, and prompt in their fulfilment." The cowboy's outfit, his horse, the stirring scenes of the "round-up," branding, the "rustler," society in the cow country—in fact, everything pertaining to the cowboy and his manner of life is fully and picturesquely set forth by Mr. Hough. His description of "broncho busting" —the breaking-in of wild range horses—is wonderfully vivid, and I wish I could quote the whole of it. I must content myself, however, with a very brief excerpt. The cowboy has just succeeded in mounting the broncho, when

"down goes the pony's head and into the air he goes in a wild, serio-comic series of spectacular stiff-legged antics. His nose between his knees, he bounds from the ground with all four feet, and comes down again with all legs set and braced. . . . He 'pitches a-plungin''—that is, jumping forward as he bucks . . . or he may stand his ground and pitch. He may go up and down, fore and aft, in turn . . . or he may spring clear up into the air and come down headed in the direction opposite to that he originally occupied, or he may pitch 'fence-cornered,' or in a zigzag line . . . bounding like a great ball from corner to corner of his rail-fence course of flight. . . . The pony soon exhausts himself in his rage. . . . At last he begins to realise that he is a captive. . . . The cow-puncher urges him gently with his knees, talking to him softly. 'Come, bronch,' he says. 'It's 'bout dinner time. Let's go back to the ranch.' And the broncho . . . turns and goes back to the ranch, his head hanging down."

Mr. Hough has given us a remarkably entertaining book, and all who have lived in the West and are familiar with life on the "range" cannot fail to recognise the fidelity to truth of his narrative.

In the limited space at their command —for it would require an *Iliad* to tell the whole story of the West—these writers have performed their tasks with great care and skill; and if the forthcoming volumes are as interesting as those already published, the series ought to be in every way successful. The value of the volumes are enhanced by being provided with indices and numerous illustrations—which are excellent—drawn from life.

A. E. Keet.

A SURVEY OF GREEK CIVILISATION.*

Professor Mahaffy has done such good work and has such a pleasant pen that his publication of the present volume is to be regretted. In the first place, judging from internal evidence, it is not strictly a book at all, but a reprint of certain lectures delivered in America, and when we read that "to start from the knowledge and love of God as a great first principle and pass from it into the broadest and most various survey of human knowledge" is not only "the true method of general education," but may also "be called the Chautauqua idea," the only explanation of so strange a statement seems to be that the lecturer is desirous of propitiating a "Chautauquan" audience. In the second place, the title of the book is a misnomer, for about the civilisation of the Greeks—about their farms and houses, their industries and commerce, their social and civil institutions—there is hardly anything said, and the book really deals only with Greek art and literature—that is, with much the same matter as the writer has discussed in previous volumes, to which in consequence he makes frequent reference, in one instance quoting from them no less than fifteen consecutive pages.

As lectures, Professor Mahaffy's remarks must have been very bright and interesting to listen to, and he is often really instructive, but, on the whole, when read in the study, what he has to say seems somewhat thin and unsubstantial, while little tricks of style, such as "I gladly repeat in this place an ode translated for me by Robert Browning," by which a lecturer gives personal inter-

* A Survey of Greek Civilisation. By J. P. Mahaffy. Meadville, Pa.: Flood & Vincent. $1.00.

est to his words, somehow fall flat in print, and might have been removed. Showy phrases, too, which when spoken give a certain pleasant shock of surprise, appear less satisfactory when considered calmly, and probably few readers will think that they know Pindar, Plato, and Horace better by seeing them described as "the Gray of Greek Poetry," "the Attic Moses," and "the Roman Tom Moore." Above all, however, the fatal temptation to be attractive which besets a lecturer is most strikingly exhibited in the number of startling paradoxes with which these pages are filled. "The Spartans," we are told, "had better food, better climate, and hence more luxury than their neighbours;" "the pastoral charms of Arcadia" are "a fable;" the "so-called tyrants" were "materially speaking the benefactors of Hellenedom" and the protectors "of many a humble home" from "aristocratic outrages;" the Bœotians were no more stupid than "the ass and the goose, which are among the most intelligent of domesticated creatures;" Marathon was "an unimportant skirmish;" Thucydides has no deep meaning, but in his "contorted and obscure periods . . . the same idea, often in itself obvious enough, is taken up and tossed about like a shuttlecock between the battledores of antithesis;" Demosthenes is "overrated as a politician," and cannot be called "a gentleman;" of Brutus finally, whose name is almost synonymous with inflexible philosophy and patriotism, it is recorded that "there has seldom been a worse criminal."

It is not necessary to discuss these amusing platform paradoxes, all of which contain—as a good paradox must—a certain interesting element of truth, but there is one statement of Professor Mahaffy's which is so positively stupendous that it deserves special note. On page 182 this sentence occurs:

> "The most perfect master of prose as prose had arisen, the master whom our Milton in vain attempted to rival in his ponderous and clumsy Areopagitica."

The "perfect master" is Isocrates, and of Isocrates it may fairly be said that he never wrote a sentence which deserves to be remembered, and that no one can read six pages of him without yawning. He has had an immense reputation, because he was the first to examine and apply the rules for building up an artistic period in prose. His clauses balance one another with perfect accuracy; no final vowel in one word runs rudely into an initial vowel in the next; each concluding cadence has its proper measure of adjusted syllables. In the history of the evolution of prose style he has a distinguished place, for students of rhetoric he has even still some value, but of the splendid genius which illuminates the writings of Milton he has not a spark. In technical excellence he may be compared with Milton, who, however, in numberless passages wholly excels him, but in no other way can any comparison be drawn between the two. Of that quickening spirit, which alone can make even rhythmic sentences worth reading, in Isocrates there is none, while Milton's periods live and breathe with heaven-sent inspiration, immortal "as that soul was whose progeny they are." But why add more? The words I quote recall to every reader that famous passage on "books" which is without a rival in all literature, both for the nobility of its thought and for the majestic splendour of its language. There is no need to print it, for it has stamped itself on the memory of every man who loves either liberty or literature, and to speak of it as "ponderous and clumsy" is not merely a paradox, but a crime.

T. E. P.

PETER THE GREAT.*

There is something in Waliszewski's analysis of Peter's character that suggests the modern novel. This would be enough to condemn the book in the opinion of at least one American historical scholar, who said with great emphasis that the reading of fiction was a bad thing for a historian because it "dissipated the mind." This latter view, however, is not likely to carry much weight. It makes truth a mere matter of blue books and state papers, exalts the copyist of records above genius and confounds the historian with the fact-gatherer. Those who hold it might perhaps take refuge in the phrase "historical imagination," urging that it is this power combined with ability as an investigator that enables a man to reproduce a historical character to the

* Peter the Great. By K. Waliszewski. Translated from the French by Lady Mary Loyd. New York: D. Appleton & Co. $2.00.

life. But wherein does the historical imagination differ from any other kind? The historian constructs his picture from limited materials, while the novelist has the whole world present as well as past to choose from for his; but the power of construction is the same in each, and the one is as much an artist as the other.

At all events, any amount of the training that schools of political science afford would not have enabled the author of the present volume on Peter the Great to have done what he has. Whether or not history is a science, the writing of it is an art and must be judged as literature, not as laboratory material. Judged from this point of view, M. Waliszewski's Peter is a fine bit of realism. The description is so very realistic in fact as to be almost painful. The reader gets somewhat too near a view of this dirty, perspiring, Russian giant, with his twitching head and contorted features, his darned stockings and cobbled shoes, and his perpetual reek of brandy and vodka. For the Peter of this volume is not an attractive character; and if, as the author states, he sums up in himself the attributes of his people, it is a severe indictment to bring against a nation. He is a brutal savage, without human affections or moral sense, subject to fits of uncontrollable rage, obscene and cruel. He has a trick of losing his temper at trifles and thrusting about with his sword, of insulting women, beating his friends, and slapping the faces of foreign ambassadors. He kills a servant with his own hand for some slight negligence. He and some of his officers run amuck in a monastery and murder several of its inmates for using the word "schismatics." He complains because a German prince in a town he is visiting will not break some one on the wheel so that he can see how the machine works. "What a fuss about the life of a man! Why not take a member of his own suite?" He has a morbid interest in surgical operations and dissecting-rooms, dabbles in surgery of the simpler sort himself, pulls any number of teeth (often sound ones) and taps a woman for dropsy. In the last case, however, he has the grace to attend the funeral. In his lighter moments he drinks huge bumpers of brandy, fraternises with scullions, falls in love with servant girls, and plays practical jokes of the kind that leave scars for life. Wherever he goes he surrounds himself with an atmosphere of bestiality and bad smells.

If this were all—and it is to these matters that the reviewers have given their chief attention—the author would have to be set down as a Zola in history, merely one of the shrewd delineators of the disgusting. But along with this clear perception of the unpleasant side of Peter's life, he gives you an equally strong impression of his greatness. The task that Peter had before him would have been impossible to a man of finer fibre. Without coarseness, callousness, and a brutal egotism he would have sickened of it before it was half done—for a whole race had to be kicked and beaten into submission before reforms were possible.

"This entire absence of scruple, this disdain for the usual rules of conduct and scorn of propriety were accompanied by a very deep feeling, and absolute respect for law, for duty and for discipline. Why and how did this come to pass? Doubtless because in this case we have something beyond a mere unthinking negation of the indispensable foundations of any social edifice; in spite of a large amount of caprice and whimsicality, which gave birth to many inconsistencies, a more worthy motive did exist in Peter's mind. He had undertaken to reform the existence of a whole people, whose scruples and prejudices make up a good half of their religion and morality. He regarded these, with a good deal of correctness, as the principal obstacle to any progress, and, therefore, very logically, he never lost an opportunity of warring against them. . . . Peter felt himself called to clear the national conscience of the dross left by centuries of barbarous ignorance. But he was too impetuous, too rough and coarse, and above all too passionately eager, to perform this work with real discernment. He hit out wildly in all directions. Thus even while he corrected, he depraved. The mighty teacher was one of the greatest demoralisers of the human species. Modern Russia, which owes him all its greatness, owes him most of its vices also."

This is a hard saying to those who insist on finding virtue triumphant in the pages of history. Not to imply that the author denies Peter all virtues. He had some amiable qualities, but they had little to do with his success. This was a product of genius and brute force. Not long ago, when one of our leading publicists ventured to say that a people had no moral right to savagery, that the higher civilisation was in duty bound to impose itself upon the lower, and that dominion belonged to those who were fit to exercise it, he was damned as a preacher of spoliation, of the doctrine that might makes right. Peter's success must seem strange to these critics. It was as complete as the methods by which it was achieved were revolting; and the great author of it all lived his life out in the happy assurance that his work was good and would endure. It is a strange story, with a plot like some of Balzac's novels, in which the wrong people get all the good things. It is a very hard tale to fit a moral to.

But in the telling the author shows unusual skill. He is always interesting—a fact due in part, no doubt, to the liberal sprinkling of anecdotes. Perhaps he has been too liberal in this respect and included some with too little scrutiny of their trustworthiness. Critics of the microscopic kind have already picked him up in regard to several of them, as, for instance, whether or not the Czar was really scared in the presence of the Emperor Leopold; whether Sophia, Peter's sister, wrote any plays, and so on, in the style of a recent review of a volume on American history in which the critic gives half his space to discussing the question whether one of the springs at Saratoga was surrounded by barrel staves at the time of Washington's journey into the interior of New York. It is doubtful, however, whether this faculty for minute criticism can coexist with a power to appreciate an historical work as a whole—whether it is not like a hen's sharp eye for little bugs and seeds, coupled with her general indifference to the landscape. Nor is testimony to the general accuracy of Waliszewski's statements lacking. Certainly he bestowed enough pains on the verification of comparatively unimportant data, as in the case of Peter's visit to Zaandam, citing authorities freely in support of his view. In fact, he is quite conscientious enough in minor details, and further quibbling about them would be tiresome.

It is a more serious question whether his Polish sympathies do not betray him into an occasional error of historical interpretation, as when he speaks of the provinces which the leadership of Poland "had carried over five centuries before to European civilisation." And again it is at least doubtful if he has not exaggerated the magnitude of Peter's work in attributing all of Russia's greatness to it. Did not Russia in fact lose something by being brought too early into European politics? The author freely admits the moral drawbacks of Peter's reforms. He admits, too, from the political point of view that "the sudden introduction of a foreign form of government may have prevented the organisation thus imposed on the country from harmonising with the natural tendencies and aspirations of the nation." But he holds these tendencies and aspirations of comparatively small account. The "seeds of original culture" were destroyed, not by Peter, but by the Tartar domination. He quotes with sympathy the Latin epitaph:

> "Let the ancient heroes hold their peace; let Alexander and Cæsar bow before him. Victory was easy to men who led heroes and commanded invincible troops; but he, who never rested till his death, had subjects who were not men, greedy of glory, skilful in the arts of war, and fearless of death, but brutes scarce worthy of the name of man. He made them civilised beings, though they had been like the bears of their own country, and though they refused to be taught and governed by him."

Frank Moore Colby.

GEORGE MACDONALD'S NEW NOVEL.*

Long ago Dr. Macdonald established his claim to rank as an artist, and in now considering any work of his, the judicious critic will turn his attention rather backward than forward, since that which is to-day chiefly important for the student of this author is an understanding of the broad general principles upon which all his work is based; after which we may consider the value of the present book in relation to all that has gone before.

There is, after all, something real and sincere beneath the various phases of our *fin-de-siècle* literature—its mysticism, its realism, even its decadence—a struggle of the *Welt-Seele* to express that of which it has gained a dim perception—that naked Truth is not less modest than were Adam and Eve within their garden; that to us, who are men, nothing human can be uninteresting; that the present relation of the sexes is far from the ideal, and in need of readjustment. Nevertheless, it has oftentimes seemed to the present writer that the final word regarding the decadent novel, the novel

* Salted with Fire: The Story of a Minister. New York: Dodd, Mead & Co. $1.50.

of realism as regards the passion of love, has not yet been spoken. It is, moreover, a difficult word to utter, with due regard to the very principle involved, and likewise to the fact that the matter has never received, perhaps from the nature of things never can receive, the exhaustive scientific treatment which alone entitles one to speak with authority. Nevertheless, science has already gone far enough to allow us to assert that a certain section of the brain, to which this literature of a single passion more particularly appeals, is one which author or reader will allow to be over-excited at his own proper peril. For, as we have already seen in the work of many, who at the beginning were without doubt entitled to rank as sane men and also as artists—our subject forbids any citing of names—the apparent result is a loss of the sense of proportion, so that the question of sexual relation becomes more and more the one absorbing topic. With any other consequences, whether ethical or psychopathological, we have naturally, at this moment, nothing to do; our only point of inquiry is whether art which permits itself this sort of realism can remain, for any length of time, either sane or authentic?

The subject of Dr. Macdonald's present work is one which, in the hands of some writers whose works are by no means yet banished from the popular magazine or the table of the family sitting-room, would have proved very possibly deleterious to the family morals. By our present author it is treated with a dispassionate freedom of analysis, which, while it may remind some readers rather of the surgeon's scalpel than of the chisel of the artist, is assuredly in accordance with the principle which we have endeavoured to establish. James Blatherwick, a young student of divinity, having, in a moment of weakness, wronged a girl with whom he has been thrown (through the fault of a social system fundamentally unsound) into very intimate daily relations, attempts to conceal his sin by ignoring it, thereby throwing all the consequences of the same upon the weaker vessel, whose sex, as well as her spirit, forbids her to follow the same selfish policy. Through no influence save that of "Don Worm," his conscience, the man is brought to repentance, gives up his pulpit, confessing his sin, and marries his victim, whom, until that moment, we are inclined to consider as far too good for him; but our author provides for his spiritual growth, and we attain to a real interest in him before the story closes. This is all that can be called plot; but the phenomena of what is called "conversion" are very carefully worked out, and in the case of the "soutar," or shoemaker, MacLear, one of those super-spiritual characters whom Dr. Macdonald delights in drawing, certain psychological processes are laid open in which some of us will find it difficult to believe. But with this difficulty on the part of his readers Dr. Macdonald has had always to reckon; it is, however, a tribute to the reality of what he has striven to incarnate in his life work, that while in the present volume the art is less finished, his vision of the eternal verities is perhaps yet clearer than when his strength was in its prime. The essential of art which seeks to present ethical or religious truth is that the truth should be perfectly incarnated, leaving no residuum to be administered in the form of homily. The neglect of this precept by writers who feel that what they have to teach far outweighs in importance any consideration of literary merit, explains the genesis of the Sunday-school story. With its due observance we cannot properly consider even the dryest and most abstruse theological proposition as an improper subject for the art of the novelist, though it may, very possibly, be so destitute of life-blood as to be an impossible subject for such incarnation. And yet, in carefully recalling our author's various writings, we fail to convince ourselves that the principle here enunciated has ever met with his formal acceptance; that he has ever distinctly told himself that as life in the actual world must embody religion, so, in the world of art, characterisation and the story must incarnate doctrine.

However, in the greatest of his writings instinct has served Dr. Macdonald as well as theory; and in this matter of incarnation, *Sir Gibbie Malcolm* and its compeers leave little to be desired. Even the soliloquies of Donal Grant and the sermons of Thomas Wingfold may be defended as tending to elucidate the characters of their eponymous heroes; while the fairy-tales, whether for children or older people, contain absolutely no residuum of homily—that is to say, of artistic self-consciousness, while in many respects autobiographic; and they should, therefore, upon this principle of criticism rank as the very best work that our author has produced.

August Max.

TALES BY AN OLD CATTLEMAN.*

Under the name of "Dan Quin" Mr. Alfred Henry Lewis has been known for some years to readers of Western papers as the author of many humorous and entertaining stories of life on the plains. These stories have now been gathered together and printed in book form with a score of illustrations by Mr. Frederic Remington. The pictures will undoubtedly serve to commend *Wolfville* to that large part of the reading public which cherishes a fondness for the literature of the plains. But once introduced, the letter-press will tell its own stories, and it will be found that the utterances of the philosophic old cattleman will need no further bush. I believe that this is Mr. Lewis's first appearance between covers, although he has been for several years a writer not only of humorous stories, but of political essays as well.

Mr. Lewis has one peculiarity which I commend with all due respect to our brothers and sisters in letters. He seldom writes on any subject with which he is not familiar. He understands national politics and the men who find themselves bedfellows in that great game, and he writes of them in a manner that betrays the keenest sort of insight and a broad knowledge of American statesmanship of the past and present. I have long regarded him as the one man in this country who possessed the art of making American politics interesting.

He knows the plains as well as he knows Washington, and in *Wolfville* he gives us the cream of many years' experience in the Far West and Southwest. All that he has to say comes from the lips of a typical old cattleman, whose face, with its mingled shrewdness, determination, and straightforward kindliness, Mr. Remington has admirably portrayed in a frontispiece. The stories that he has to tell are of the inhabitants of that tough living, quick dying, hard drinking, high playing Southwestern town of Wolfville. He deals with such folks as Tucson Jennie, Cherokee Hall, Faro Nell, Doc Peets, and others calculated to awaken memories of Bret Harte. But the characters are not those of Bret Harte, nor is the book in any way an imitation of the half dozen idealised mining stories that made the California story-teller's fame a quarter of a century ago. Mr. Lewis has not fallen into that too common error of monkey-like imitation. He knows the life and characters that he describes, and he tells his stories in his own way.

There are two dozen of these tales in *Wolfville*, and I find it no easy matter to say of any one of them that it is the best. The first of them is called "Wolfville's First Funeral," and it tells of the burying of one Jack King, who is, according to the narrator,

> "corpse eemergin' outen a game of poker as sech. Which prior tharto, Jack's been peevish, an' pesterin' an' pervadin' 'round for several days. The camp stands a heap o' trouble with him an' tries to smooth it along by givin' him his whiskey an' his way about as he wants 'em hopin' for a change. But man is only human, an' when Jack starts in one night to make a flush beat a tray full for seven hundred dollars, he asks too much."

It is the first chance that the town has had for a funeral of its own, and the citizens resolve to take the best possible advantage of it. Doc Peets, a gentleman in whose higher culture and sound horse sense the town has unlimited faith, is appointed to "deal the game," and instantly gives orders to have the grave dug at least one mile from the camp, saying:

> "In order to make a funeral a success you needs distance. That's where deceased gets action. It gives the procession a chance to spread an' show up. You can't make no funeral imposin' unless you're plumb liberal on distances."

Doc Peets preaches the funeral discourse, referring to the departed as

> "a very headstrong person, who persists yesterday in entertainin' views touchin' a club flush, queen at the head, which results in life everlastin'."

At the conclusion of his remarks

> "the little girl from Flagstaff cl'ars her valves with a drink, an' gives 'The Dyin' Ranger;' an' when the entire congregation draws kyards on the last verse it does everybody good."

* Wolfville. By Dan Quin. New York: F. A. Stokes Co. $1.50.

The grave is marked with a headboard bearing this epitaph :

> "Jack King. Life ain't in holding a good hand, but in playing a poor hand well."

Another story, called "Tucson Jennie's Heart," affords the cattleman a chance to moralise as follows :

> "You've got to ketch folks young to marry 'em. After they gets to be thirty years they goes slowly to the altar. If you aims to marry a gent after he's thirty you has to blindfold him an' back him in. Females, of course, ain't so obdurate."

Tucson Jennie comes to the local restaurant under contract to its proprietor to fry flapjacks, and proves such an attraction that Mr. Jim Baxter sets out in dead earnest to win her. The camp takes an interest in the affair, and finally decides to bring matters to a head by pretending to shoot Baxter in order to force the coy maiden's hand and make her show her real feelings. It is arranged also to give a touch of reality to the scheme by pretending to lynch Dave Tutt, the murderer. The game is well carried out, and although Baxter is laid out in such a way that Jennie can "swarm in at him" and embrace him, that young woman upsets all previous calculations by rushing into the Red Light saloon, where the vigilance committee is in session, and falling upon the neck of Dave Tutt.

> "'You-alls should have asked me,' says Faro Nell, who comes in right then an' rounds up close to Cherokee. 'I could tell you two weeks ago Jennie's in love with Tutt. Anybody could see it. Why she's been feedin' of him twice as good grub as she does anybody else.'"

James L. Ford.

THE CONFESSIONS OF A COLLECTOR *

Why is it that Mr. Hazlitt fails to enlist our sympathies? How is it that his self-assertions and self-justifications arouse in others a conviction that his detractors have not been altogether in the wrong? Is it that Mr. Hazlitt is not able to state his case with judicial simplicity? Or is it that he lacks the saving sense of humour? We fear that we must lay on him the negative qualities which both these alternatives imply. And yet here is a book brightly written, crammed full of interesting information, detailing a series of experiences which come to but few men. More than half of it, dealing as it does with rare books, is certain to be read by book lovers and book collectors with keen appreciation. His relations with Mr. Huth, Mr. Ellis the bookseller, Mr. Quaritch, and the "knowing ones" of the auction-room and "the trade," have a side to them which, apart from the objectionable personal one Mr. Hazlitt always emphasizes, have an educating value.

We confess to a feeling of envy in reading of the many bargains Mr. Hazlitt made, and of the many occasions on which he was able to profit by an experience and knowledge which included more than was in the ken of the great rulers of the "book mart." Mr. Jeffreys, of Bristol, sold him a copy of Caxton's *Golden Legend* for £85, which Mr. B. M. Pickering took away for £150. From Mr. John Pearson he bought two folio volumes of "old newspapers" for twelve guineas, a portion of which he retailed to Mr. Miller for £42, and the residue," a collection of penny *Garlands*, went to the British Museum." A manuscript bought by Mr. Ellis at the Corser sale for £70, was "sold by him to me for £105, and by me to Cosens for £157 10*s*., fell to me at £24. It has found its probably final resting-place in the Bodleian." "But the most signal acquisition on my part was the series of the Somers Tracts in thirty folio volumes . . . I forget what I left with the auctioneers ; but the price at which the hammer fell was £61. A single item was worth double that sum ; and there were hundreds and hundreds."

Is not this a sufficient excuse for our envy? What book collector *could* read this without dissolving in tears? Happy Mr. Hazlitt! And yet—and yet—why all these pages of triumphant complacency? We have a faint suspicion that now Mr. Hazlitt is revenging himself on those "professional gentlemen" who scorned and gibed at the "amateur."

We can pardon Mr. Hazlitt's fairly numerous references to his many literary achievements, even though they have nothing to do with "collecting;" but his jaundiced criticisms of Mr.

* The Confessions of a Collector. By W. Carew Hazlitt. New York: Dodd, Mead & Co. $2.00.

Locker's *Confidences*, Mr. Locker's Rowfant Library, and Mr. Daniel's books are not in the finest taste. It seems, also, now almost impossible for Mr. Hazlitt to write at all without a gingerly sniff at Canon Ainger. These are blemishes which somewhat mar what is, otherwise, a very readable narrative of "booky" and other experiences. Did he but allow himself to bask, for a while, in the sunny light of humour, we are convinced that Mr. Hazlitt would yet achieve distinction.

Temple Scott.

NOVEL NOTES.

IN SIMPKINSVILLE. By Ruth McEnery Stuart. New York: Harper & Bros. $1.25.

The publishers' slip accompanying this volume, which is "intended as an aid" rather than an obfuscation "to editors," states that "the strong feature" of Mrs. Stuart's writing is dialect. This ought to mean, if anything, that Mrs. Stuart not only finds dialect a convenient vehicle for her characterisation, but that the latter has its point and validity in the former. This we deny. Her strength lies in her truthful and kindly discernment of the foibles and inconsistencies of human nature and in her shrewd perception of the picturesque possibilities of details which have been generally overlooked. We live in the hope that she will some day fling dialect to the winds and fearlessly construct enough stories of unobscured humour and pathos to disprove the theory of her dependence on anything but literary skill and a vivid sense of neighbourhood to produce her effects.

The "strong feature" of her work appears nowhere more obviously than in the story entitled "Weeds." Elijah Tomkins had promised his dying wife to lay a rosebud on her grave every day—a sufficiently hackneyed situation. In the performance of this vow he would sometimes sit under a weeping-willow with the widow Christian, who atoned for her past severity with her husband's one failing by arranging bottles about the bed of pansies on his grave.

"There be 'weeping-willows' that truly weep, while some, with all the outward semblance of sorrow, do seem only to whine and whimper, so sparse and attenuated are their dripping fringes—fringes capable even of flippancy if the wind be of a flirtatious mind."

It is needless to say that a deep mutual respect ensued. The widow consoled Elijah by alluding to the "big freeze" prophesied for the coming winter. "An' ef buds give out, ez they're more'n likely to," she said, "it won't be your fault." What was even more encouraging was the widow's discovery that one of her pansies opened with a "sassy little pink face" and "quizzical eyebrows." From this moment a significance attached to Elijah's neighbourliness in going into the widow's lot to "give way." They soon reached the "Good-bye" stage, and the tale closes with Elijah extracting infinite comfort from a rusty hairpin. By way of postscript, the writer wishes to say that "the report which went abroad at the time of their marriage, some months later, to the effect that they had begun their courting in the graveyard, is utterly without foundation." Is anything more *cute?* Again, the sequel of "The Dividing Fence" is implicit in Widow Carroll's remark: "If he [Elder Billins] jest wouldn't slit his boots over his bunions! . . . . An' then, somehow, I don't know ez I care for a prayer-meetin' voice for all purposes." How many times Deacon Hatfield and Miss Euphemia Twiggs had changed hymn-books was satisfactorily answered by the Simpkinsville gossips when they said: "Th' ain't no fun in havin' your whole livelong life overshaddered by a man with no earthly intentions." The sad story of May Day's infatuation for a bigamous land-agent is epitomised in these words:

"A red-cheeked peach thet don't know nothin' but the dew and the sun, and to grow sweet and purty—it goes wrong when it's wrenched off the stem and et by a hog. That's one way o' goin' wrong."

"The Unlived Life of Little Mary Ellen" is startlingly original in conception. Here, as elsewhere, Mrs. Stuart wavers formally between a sketch and a short story, the result being a composite structure with a disproportionately spacious vestibule. Her village loafers are considerably more than gentlemen, and possess an imagination that is truly wonderful.

BOLANYO. By Opie Read. Chicago: Way & Williams. $1.25.

Whether Mr. Read has stuffed this story "like a sausage with his own garrulity," as the Bolanyo senator threatened to stuff one of his fellow-townsmen, is a delicate question, involving personal acquaintance with Mr. Read. It is so "crazy" a patchwork that we would gladly believe it the clever affectation of a very young man to be in his anecdotage. To say that the story lacks organic unity would imply, perhaps unwarrantably, that it was not purposely constructed on that "hit-er-miss" plan which, according to Helen Hunt Jackson's Aunt Ri, controls all our lives, but which, nevertheless is notoriously inadmissible in anything that deserves the name of fiction. Mr Maurice Belford, the leading man of the National Dramatic Company, was blown into space from the deck of a Mississippi steamboat. He found himself, naturally enough, convalescing in Bolanyo. He also "tried to find his legs"—and found them. The other members of the company were no less lucky, being "all right—the most of them." It was the "biggest send-off" they had ever had. As the manager of an opera-house and a man of quick endearments, in a southern town where it was a crime even to be a stranger, Belford was soon in a position to contribute actively to his manufacturer's plot. This he steadily refuses to do till the very end, the bulk of the story consisting of the irrelevancies of other puppets who are introduced at the rate of, perhaps, one a chapter. Washington Smith, an educated negro with a hand "like the wing of a buzzard," when he is not parading his favourite tense, the future-perfect, is prying into the aqueously Platonic love of Belford for the married daughter of the senator. Bugg Peters and Joe Vark (names perhaps "aptly fitted," but we prefer the Smith) look in upon us often with their slouching figures. Unhappily for the stagnation which followed the explosion, the hero does not forget for a single moment to lock the door of his heart—nay, obedient to the dictates of hospitality, he bars even its windows. In the absence of any genuine sentiment, there remains little to delectate us but what the humourist of Belford's profession would call the "property laugh," evoked from the shattered company by time-worn jests in which the reader cannot join. The story concludes, however, with a dash—a dash along a squirrel track which ultimately runs up a tree. A newspaper scandal, a rush to pistols, a murder, a lynching interrupted by the woman in the case, an unaccompanied flight to Chicago, and an engagement there as cab-driver, are all compressed into the last fifty pages. Such congestion of the brain belies the summery, decorative dress in which Mr. Read's story is covered.

"BOBBO" AND OTHER FANCIES. By Thomas Wharton. New York: Harper & Bros. $1.50.

This slender volume contains the last and best literary work of a young man who left the law for journalism and died but a few months ago, at the age of thirty-seven, when a long-deferred and well-deserved success was almost within his grasp. In a prefatory memorial of his lamented friend, Mr. Owen Wister belabours Philadelphia for its "civic instinct of disparagement," and attributes Mr. Wharton's "isolation from his kind" in part to the local chill which his budding talent experienced. Why, pray, should not a Philadelphian be "torpid in approval"? Is not Boston, even, far more interested in prize fights than in tempering the wind to the shorn lambs of an inchoate literary genius? It seems to us that a man with so rare a touch of fantasy and so exquisite a capacity for absorbing the thought and sentiment of another age could have cared very little what Philadelphia, or any other city, thought of him, and that the few preliminary years of tentative effort and comparative failure in which he submitted his spirit to the influence of this or that master were the best possible preparation for achieving what he might have achieved had he lived. As it is, "Bobbo," than which, perhaps, M. Coppée has written no *conte* more polished, nor Mr. Lang *Ballades in Blue China* more delicately fragile, places the author well within that small circle of American writers who merit the name of artist. Droll and sprightly, it is yet suffused with a warmth which does not leave unsubstantial the stuff whereof such dreams are made. It partakes of the comedy favoured by Mr. Meredith, a comedy which reveals the weakness and lovableness of human nature even beneath the carnival paint of a Pierrot or a Punchinello. "The Last Sonnet of Prinzivalle di Cembino" is a clever little Italian romance in which Madonna Ghita is petulant and dreamily ecstatic by turns, and withal affords an abundance of tropical comfort to her gallant knight. In "Ratu Tanito's Wooing" the Princess Ekesa is obliged to submit to no test more searching than the question, when a woman should disobey her husband. She won the day by replying, "Never, O my father, save when he bids her leave him." "Old and New" deals facetiously with the stalking-horse of the new womanhood. The verses with which the volume closes, several of them translations of Villon, are restrained and suggestive. One can only regret that their author was not spared to cultivate his pretty talent for *fabliaux*.

CAPTAIN SHAYS, A POPULIST. By George R. R. Rivers. Boston: Little, Brown & Co. $1.25.

"My name is Shays,
In former days
In Pelham I did dwell, sir;
I was obliged to quit that place
Because I did rebel, sir."

While the Captain Shays of Mr. Rivers's documentation is not quite the comic-operatic figure suggested by these premonitory lines, he is altogether insignificant, fond of skulking about and picking quarrels, and doomed to the pose of a captured criminal rather than of a war prisoner when his awkward squad of several hundred rowdies and disgruntled farmers were compelled, "in the name of the commonwealth of Massachusetts," to lay down their arms. While the rebellion lasted there was much ill feeling against the rich merchants of Boston and Salem, the courts were closed, and business blocked. "God knows we ain't got freedom yet," said Deacon Smith to his daughter; "we are more slaves than before the war, and I sometimes wish we'd never gone through it." It is such a state of discontent and political hesitancy which Mr. Rivers has chosen as the frame of an old-fashioned love story, with the purpose of showing that the disposition of demagogues to array the masses against the classes is deep-rooted in American history. His portraiture of a young Boston lawyer who flashed his silver knee-buckles upon the gaze of the impoverished farmers and, despite the advice of his friends, fell in love with a dairymaid whose father, a red-haired, vituperative fellow, wondered why he didn't "take to some honest calling," is sufficiently good to detract from the interest of the historical background. The only flaw in his character is his fatalistic optimism on the occasion of the foreclosure of the mortgage on the farm owned by Ruth's father. Notwithstanding the fact that the sheriff had carried the belligerent tenant away in irons, the all but immaculate young lawyer consoled Ruth, who had just consented to be his wife, thus: "I don't think you need worry about him -that is, I don't think he'll be maltreated." Mr. Rivers has invented one truly novel situation. Out of the stimulated consciousness induced by a day of fellow-suffering and a night of dreams, in which each seemed to hear the other speaking, these two young people discovered the reality of their love. What with such a climax and its accessories, no particular piquancy attaches to the continuance, through fifty pages, of the populistic rebellion. The kite has too long a tail.

THE KING OF THE MOUNTAINS. By Edmond About. New York: Rand, McNally & Co. $1.00.

The author of *The Man with the Broken Ear* is one of the French writers of several decades ago who, even since their demise, have received scant recognition in English reading lands, because of the inadequacy or paucity of translations. Mrs. C. A. Kingsbury's version of *Le roi des Montaghes* is marred by many typographical inaccuracies, for which we suppose she was not responsible. "Voracity" is printed "veracity;" such un-Anglicised expressions as *table d'hôte* appear without italics (a font of type which can scarcely be dispensed with in a translation from the French), and usually without accents; and errors of punctuation and capitalisation are numerous. The translation itself is passably good, but would be improved, in our opinion, if the French names *Taygète*, *Erechthée*, *Locuste*, etc., were returned to their Latin or Greek forms, and if greater care were taken, as, for instance, in the appellation "Society for the Moralisation of Malefactors" in preserving the English idiom. Despite these trifling matters, the sum total of which is calculated to induce a *crise de nerfs* in the reader of ordinarily refined sensibilities, it is possible for an imagination attuned to the droll potentialities of opéra bouffe to enjoy the adventures of Hermann Schultz, the Hamburg botanist, among the brigands and fleas and garlic-scented maids of modern Greece. That he should have travelled so far to fall in love with Mary Ann, an English girl with eyes of the colour of Siberian garnets, a dimple in her left cheek, and skin (what French author ever omitted to describe a woman's skin?) of the finest texture and transparency, and have been assisted in his schemes for a rich marriage by Hadgi-Stavros, the King of the Mountains, to whom brigandage was both a speculation and a philanthropy, is, of course, not a whit more improbable than his rescue by one Harris, an American, who had been teacher, lawyer, journalist, miner, clerk, and was now commander of a despatch boat carrying sixty men and four cannon.

THE TOUCHSTONE OF LIFE. By Ella MacMahon. New York: Frederick A. Stokes Co. 75 cents.

This is a pleasant little story of a bastard son who refused to abrogate his feelings of honour at the price of three thousand a year, and within fifty pages of his emancipation from the disgrace of inheriting what he called the price of his mother's shame returned from the colony of New Britain a self-made millionaire, qualified to oppose the political ambitions of Lord Sithrington, the legitimate son, and to win from him the young woman who was going to marry him for the pleasure of having a coronet worked on the corner of her handkerchiefs. As Governor of New Britain Lord Sithrington was a target for the attacks of his brother's newspaper, and on the platform cut a sorry figure. Susan, who was of the opinion that the woman who jilted a man was no worthier than the man who jilted a woman, contented herself with modelling Clay, and contracting a union of souls with Clay, and bicycling a long distance in the dark to save Clay's life—until circumstances induced Clay to inform her *fiancé* of a plot to blow up Government House, whereupon Sitherington "went one better" and made over Susan to his rival. Despite the author's amateurish disposition to ruminate by the way and avail herself of old-time jests, she has written a readable, optimistic tale, placing her lovers on a reasonable basis of congeniality and showing well the invigoration of character which results from an act of self-sacrifice. Lady Honoria is better ticketed by the "wicked little wrinkles round the corners of her mouth" than by the constant mention of her Rabelaisian humour; and the journalist Arkwright is somewhat of a monstrosity, however faithfully he may have been drawn from life. The illustrations are in exceptional harmony with the text.

THE BOOKMAN'S TABLE.

CROMWELL'S PLACE IN HISTORY: FOUNDED ON SIX LECTURES DELIVERED IN THE UNIVERSITY OF OXFORD. By S. R. Gardiner, D.C. London and New York: Longmans, Green & Co. $1.00.

Without being eloquent, or picturesque, or epigrammatic, or paradoxical, Professor Gardiner holds your interest by the singular fairness which he displays on every page of this little book. To him Cromwell is something of a hero, but a hero who, as he tells you, failed in every great permanent result that he aimed to bring about as completely as he succeeded in attaining immediate and temporary ends. Such a very subdued form of hero-worship as is discernible in this careful, pondering analysis of the Protector's work is not likely to mislead any one. In fact, so much emphasis is laid on Cromwell's limitations and failures that he seems rather a sorry figure for a demigod when the author is done with him. With no gift whatever for constructive statesmanship, he accomplished only negative results.

"Hostile armies were not allowed to be victorious; kings were not to be allowed to wield absolute power in disregard of the condition of the time or the wishes of their subjects; Parliaments were not allowed to disregard public opinion; Irishmen were not allowed to establish a government hostile to England; foreign powers were not allowed to disregard the force of England."

In this destructive rôle he showed great qualities; but of his positive work very little survived him. No one has made a more careful study of this period, and no one has a better title to respect for fair dealing and accuracy in treating it than the author of *England During the Civil War*; but in his final estimate of Cromwell, Professor Gardiner does not seem consistent with himself. Being a good deal of a historian and nothing of a special pleader, he comes to a conclusion hardly justified by the moderate, balancing, conscientious spirit of what precedes. "It is time for us to regard him as he really was," he says at the end of the essay,

"with all his physical and moral audacity, with all his

tenderness and spiritual yearnings, in the world of action what Shakespeare was in the world of thought, the greatest because the most typical Englishman of all time. This in the most enduring sense is Cromwell's place in history."

As there is no infallible dynamometer for measuring the strength of heroes, we ought not to quarrel with each other's superlatives. It is only in graduating essays that we find perfect certainty in the grading of geniuses. Among adults a dispute over the comparative greatness of men is more or less a dispute *de gustibus*. It is not, therefore, with the truth or falsity of Professor Gardiner's conclusion that our objection is concerned, but merely with its inconsistency with the idea which he himself gives us of the man.

The fairness and truthfulness of this essay appeal to us most strongly and a good deal is done in it to correct misapprehensions. For instance, the popular view of Cromwell as a harsh, tyrannical man employing radical measures by preference can hardly survive the reading of this book. If ever there was a man who suffered fools gladly, who sought to influence and persuade, and who was ready to get something tolerable done by consent rather than get something better done by forcing it on unwilling minds, that man was Cromwell.

To those, however, who with more reason accuse Cromwell of hypocrisy—of trying to conceal from others and possibly from himself the real nature of his very secular statecraft by the free use of sanctimonious phrases—the author gives no answer. This perhaps is the weakest point in the little volume.

HALLUCINATIONS AND ILLUSIONS. A Study of the Fallacies of Perception. By Edmund Parish. Contemporary Science Series. New York: Charles Scribner's Sons. $1.25.

A fairly complete review of the work of eminent scientists in this field of inquiry up till now can be obtained from this book, which, in its English form, is a considerable improvement on the German original, published three years ago. But Mr. Parish is not merely, and not very successfully, a populariser. His copious references to the principal works on the subject are of great use; but he is too much of a combatant to be the best exponent of other men's views. Indeed, it is for its own methods and its own propositions that the book is mainly valuable. The subject is of widespread interest, but we can promise the lover of eerie sensations no satisfaction from the treatment allotted to it here, which is on strictly scientific lines, and sometimes needlessly obscured by cumbrous and difficult terms. The matter, too, might be dealt with in a more orderly form. But the chief faults all regard the form. The writer has done more than any other on this subject to simplify the question by rasing to the ground clumsy barriers which marked no real distinctions. First of all, he does away with the old division between the illusions and hallucinations of the diseased and of the sane. He holds that "fallacious perception has nothing morbid in itself. The state that occasions it is not morbid. Of course, the underlying cause which induces the psychological state may be, and frequently is, pathological." The false perceptions of the sane and the insane follow the same laws. Likewise, though he still uses the terms "illusion" and "hallucination," it is not in the old sense, which regarded the things so named as different in origin and quality, but in a new one, which refers to the psychological character of the phenomena, and implies only a difference of systematic order.

He has arrived at his conclusions by what is popularly called materialistic methods, that is by physiology, and his success is a guarantee that physiology is a good guide along some part of the way. But the way traversed is as yet very short; and an attentive student of the results so far obtained, who is not a fanatic about physical science, must wonder if the scientists will not have to be helped out at some part of their career by others whom they now despise. At least, the weakest part of Mr. Parish's book is his criticism of the critics of the physiological method. Regarding the illusions of the sane, which, after all, are of the greatest interest to the most of us, touching, as they do, on the states of exaltation in which poets and prophets find inspiration, and more ordinary mortals, at least, vivid suggestions, the greatest lack is reliable evidence. The madman is truthful; but the sane man lies. Inventions and after-additions are constant in his record of illusory experience; and perhaps we shall never know very much of the strange workings of the mind till we force the lips to reveal the picture episodes of dreams, before the dreamer has the chance of forgetting or inventing. Yet even then the lips would lie with the clumsiness of all words. It may be mentioned that the question of dreams, a far too little considered one in science, is but slightly touched on here.

He is no toyer with the ideas of phantasms and portents. The evidence collected by the English Society for Psychical Research and the Munich Psychologische Gesellschaft has been carefully considered by Mr. Parish, and even respectfully; but his conclusion is always Not Proven. This amusing instance out of the Munich Collection is only, according to him, an exaggeration of the usual desperate attempts to connect striking events with each other: "I hereby certify that in May, 1888, my wife and I were awakened simultaneously by a loud noise, which sounded like the breaking of a glass door and the falling of the splinters. There was no such door in our house. I went to see what was amiss, but found everything as usual. Three weeks after my father-in-law died." All telepathic hallucinations he regards with distrust; those of clairvoyance he will not even examine. His attitude is that of the extreme scientific sceptic, who rejects and rejects evidence that does not respond to an almost ideal amount of certainty—a wholesome attitude of warning to persons who are only too easy to convince by statements if they happen to be put forward in scientific form or language. He touches probably on the right source of willing belief in phantasms when he speaks of the satisfaction of the dramatic sense It is not evidence of immortality the popular mind demands in ghosts; a belief in them is only the sign of the love for a good story. But Mr. Parish, calling from his cold heights for absolute proof, is unconvinceable. And if his methods are right, he will remain so. This, the most popular part of his book, is useful in a negative way; but where he renders most service is in his clearing the whole subject of many unnatural and hindering distinctions, a process which always stimulates to fresh and freer investigation.

HANNIBAL. By W[illegible] Morris. New York: G. P. Putnam's Sons. $[illegible]

In writing the life of Hannibal for the series of "Heroes of the Nations," Mr. Morris has had a difficult task. Practically we are wholly dependent for our information on Polybius and Livy, and their narratives have been reproduced, commented on, and criticised in so many histories that little which is new can be said upon the subject. Every schoolboy, even though the knowledge of the average schoolboy is hardly what Macaulay supposes, knows the main outlines of the second Punic war, and they are on the whole definitely settled, while, on the other hand, as a biography, any account of Hannibal must suffer from the fact that "scarcely a phrase of his nor a line of correspondence" is in existence. No one accepts as truth the prejudiced rhetoric of Livy—*inhumana crudelitas, perfidia plus quam Punica, nihil veri, nihil sancti, nullus Deum metus*—but the materials for forming a real estimate of his character are wanting. Mr. Morris, on his title-page, boldly describes him as "soldier, statesman, and patriot." The justice of the first epithet is beyond dispute; whether, however, the other two are equally deserved must always remain uncertain. Judged by the standard of success, his gigantic plans, in spite of his military achievements, proved a splendid failure and precipitated the ruin of his country, while in his estimate of the resisting power of Rome, of the value of his Macedonian alliance, and of the reinforcements he might look for from Carthage, he seems to have erred largely. As to his patriotism, Mr. Morris quotes Thiers, who describes him as offering "*le plus noble spectacle que puissent donner les hommes—celui du génie exempt de tout égoisme, et n'ayant qu'une passion, le patriotisme, dont il est le glorieux martyr,*" but to determine the motives of great military leaders, to distinguish between personal ambition and the sense of public duty, is never an easy task, and in the case of Hannibal we possess no evidence at all sufficient for arriving at a decision.

It is as a master of the art of war that his name lives. "War was Hannibal's sphere; his exploits have, in all ages, claimed the attention of competent judges of the military art." His extraordinary power of moulding into a great army "a motley array of Phœnicians, Africans, Spaniards, and Gauls," and his surpassing strategic skill are exceedingly well exhibited in this book, the writer of which, so far as a layman can judge, seems to possess considerable technical knowledge of his subject, while in some cases, as in the remarks which he borrows from Captain Mahan's *Sea Power*, on the loss which Hannibal suffered from being unsupported by a fleet, he admirably supplements, though he cannot be said to supersede, the able narratives of Arnold and Mommsen. He has made excellent use, too, of the remarks on Hannibal which are to be found in the writings of Napoleon. That masterly intellect fully grasped the greatness of Hannibal and ranks him among the seven strategists whose campaigns ought to be carefully examined by all students of tactics.

OCCASIONAL PAPERS. Selected from the *Guardian*, the *Times*, and the *Saturday Review*, 1846-90. By the late R. W. Church, M.A., D.C.L. 2 vols. New York: The Macmillan Co. $3.00.

Lord Blachford has connected the name of Dean Church with the origin of the *Guardian*. When Newman joined Rome, and left those who had adhered to him, "headless, unorganised, suspected by others, and suspecting each other, it occurred to them that a newspaper might give them coherence and a medium of influence. James Mozley, Thomas Haddan, Church, Bernard, and Lord Blachford himself formed the original promoters and staff. Dean Church continued to be a regular weekly contributor both of reviews and articles until 1871. Between the years 1874 and 1880 he was not in sympathy with the line of policy taken by the *Guardian* in ecclesiastical affairs, and accordingly during that period he contributed only an occasional review; but subsequently he resumed his more constant support. The papers are not long, but they are quite worth exhuming from the files of inaccessible journals. Together they form a fairly complete survey of the literature of the past generation, passing in review Carlyle's *Cromwell*, Newman's *Apologia* and *Sermons*, Frederick Robertson's *Sermons*, *Ecce Homo*, Renan's various writings, Mark Pattison's *Essays*, Lecky's *History of European Morals*, Ranke's *History of the Popes*, and other books of mark. The judgments pronounced in these volumes cannot be said to be absolutely unbiassed. Dean Church was a man of ripe culture, but that he felt intensely appears in both his antipathies and his predilections. The note of partisanship which characterises so much of the writing of his school is probably due to the circumstances which brought its members together. But the same charm attaches to these papers as to all that the late Dean Church wrote. Of crudeness in form, of hastiness in expression, of carelessness in style, there is not a trace. Frequently there occur passages of remarkable grace and elevation; while the criticisms are throughout characterised by a singular particularity of analysis. Such papers should reassure the public that the reviewing of books is at least sometimes conscientiously done by competent hands. And all who have learned to recognise in Dean Church one of the masters in English style will give these fresh examples of his art a cordial welcome.

THE FIRST CROSSING OF SPITSBERGEN. By Sir W. M. Conway, F.R.G.S. With Contributions by J. W. Gregory, D.Sc., A. Trevor Battye, and E. J. Garwood. Illustrated. New York: Charles Scribner's Sons. $10.00.

This is a record of a journey that fulfilled its aim and something more. The main object of the explorers was to cross Spitsbergen and reveal the character of the interior, which was practically unknown. The island had never been crossed, though it had been described—most inaccurately, of course. The coast, which is familiar enough, was to be left alone. They carried out their plan, crossing from Advent Bay to Klok and Sassen bays, from Sassen to Agardh Bay, on the east coast, and back to Advent Bay. They surveyed nearly six hundred miles in the middle of the country, and some other strips of hilly land. They made thirteen mountain ascents; and the coast was not let alone, almost all the great fjords being entered in the "most complete voyage of reconnaissance ever accomplished in a single season." The scientific results are not yet recorded in detail. There is no question as to the geographical value of the journey. The plan of the mountain system of Spitsbergen, of its valleys, its rivers, and its glaciers, is now known, and all previous knowledge built on guess-work overturned. Succeeding travellers can only amplify, profiting by the experiments, mistakes, and experience of this expedition.

But we have been with Sir William Conway on more interesting enterprises. The island was under fog for most of the time of their visit, the summer of 1896, and some of the fog has got into the book. The ploughing through bogs and mud, the continuous, monotonous hardships, without the excitements that strike the imagination of a reader, make a rather dreary story—speaking as mere readers; and then most of us are men before we are geographers. Now and again we are made to feel a thrill and some understanding of the wonderful Arctic skies, which explorers who have had their pick of the effects of the world say are equalled nowhere else. But, on the whole, the actual information is the most entertaining thing presented to us—a sad thing to say of a book of travels. The pictures—we do not mean the coloured plates—are for the most part depressing, not at all enticing to the possible tourists that Sir William, in the interest of exploration and science, hopes will be drawn every summer to Spitsbergen by the Vesteraalen Steamship Company—general director, Captain Sverdrup. To sum up, this is an important and a dull book. But if it had been the most entertaining one imaginable, the publishers could not have done better for all its externals.

THE POETICAL WORKS OF ROBERT BURNS. New York: Thomas Whittaker. $1.75.

If the "Apollo Poets," imported by Mr. Thomas Whittaker from the new English publishing house of Bliss, Sands and Company, are continued as they have been begun, they may well be called the premier series of reprints in England. Nothing equal to them has been published at the price. They are perfect in every detail, and ought at once to sell by the thousand. We cannot doubt that they will supersede all their rivals The publishers have been particularly successful in producing books that are thoroughly tasteful and at the same time adapted to the needs of the multitude. The binding is in buckram and the decoration is both liberal and chaste in design. The printing has been done with great care, the paper is excellent, the size is convenient, and the volumes have a gilt top. In addition, the work of editing has been very conscientiously performed. We should prefer, for our part, an edition of Burns that was not complete, but those who think otherwise will find here what they want. They will also find a good chronology, a judicious selection of notes, an index, and a glossary. The highest credit should be given to the projectors of this spirited series.

THE BOOK MART.

FOR BOOKREADERS, BOOKBUYERS, AND BOOKSELLERS.

EASTERN LETTER.

NEW YORK, September 1, 1897.

August to the retail dealer in books is the dullest month in the year; at no other time is trade in general so quiet. While the past month has been no exception to this rule, sales have kept up remarkably well owing to the unusual number of popular works of fiction in large demand. These have been practically the same as during July, with the notable addition of *The Christian*, by Hall Caine; *Jerome*, by Mary E. Wilkins, and *The Chevalier d'Auriac*, by S. L. Yeats. Other publications, while fairly numerous, have reached no considerable sale.

There is no diminution in the sales of *The Choir Invisible*, *Quo Vadis*, and *Soldiers of Fortune*, and these, as enumerated last month, are still followed by *Equality*, *The Martian*, *The Honourable Peter Stirling*, and the *House-Boat* books.

The publications on the Klondike region seem to be rather in excess of the demand, for while the calls for books on Alaska are still numerous the number of new books, maps, and guides is out of all proportion to the sales, at least in the East. *The Official Guide to the Klondike* and *Gold Fields of Alaska*, *Klondike*, by L. A. Coolidge, and *Golden Alaska*, by Ernest Ingersoll, are reliable works on the subject.

The school book season may now be said to have fairly commenced. Orders at present are mostly for the lower grades, those for the higher naturally coming later with the opening of the colleges and universities.

While fiction has monopolised the sales of the summer season there has been no lack of miscellaneous works published, and prominent among them has been a considerable number of biographies, including *The True Story of U. S. Grant*, by E. S. Brooks; *Hannibal*, by W. O'C. Morris; *Lady Hamilton and Lord Nelson*, by J. C. Jeaffreson, and *The Life and Adventures of Nat Foster*, by A. L. Curtiss-Byron; it is perhaps to be regretted that they do not find a larger circulation.

The season of paper-bound books is now practically over, and as noticed in previous letters, it has been rather a light one. At present the most popular titles are *A Colonial Free Lance*, by C. C. Hotchkiss; *Mifanwy*, by A. Raine, and *Barbara Blomberg*, by G. M. Ebers.

Among the autumn announcements are some notable works of fiction, including *Captains Courageous*, by Rudyard Kipling; *Hugh Wynne*, by Dr. S. Weir Mitchell, and *In Kedar's Tents*, by Henry Seton Merriman. Religious subjects will be represented in a number of series of small books, such as "The Eternal Life Series," "The Precious Thoughts Series," and "The Perfected Life Booklets."

Illustrated editions will be numerous, such as *Quo Vadis*; *Morocco*, by De Amicis; *The Winning of the Northwest*, by Washington Irving; *Irish Idylls*, by Jane Barlow, and new drawings by Charles Dana Gibson and Frederic Remington.

The outlook for a busy season is undoubtedly good. The buyers, mostly from the South and West, already in town, speak encouragingly of the prospects in their localities.

The popular books of the month in their order of sale are as follows:

The Choir Invisible. By James Lane Allen. $1.50.
Quo Vadis. By Henryk Sienkiewicz. $2.00.
Soldiers of Fortune. By Richard Harding Davis. $1.50.
The Christian. By Hall Caine. $1.50.
Equality. By Edward Bellamy. $1.50.
The Martian. By George Du Maurier. $1.75.
Jerome. By Mary E. Wilkins. $1.50.
The House-Boat on the Styx. By John Kendrick Bangs. $1.25.
The Pursuit of the House-Boat. By John Kendrick Bangs. $1.25.
The Honourable Peter Stirling. By P. L. Ford. $1.50.
The Triumph of Death. By Gabriele D'Annunzio. $1.50.
The Sowers. By Henry Seton Merriman. $1.50.
The Chevalier d'Auriac. By S. Levett Yeats. $1.25.
The Massarenes. By Ouida. $1.25.
An Old Gentleman of the Black Stock. By Thomas Nelson Page. 75 cents.
Uncle Bernac. By A. Conan Doyle. $1.50.
Trix and Trixy. By John Habberton. 50 cents.

WESTERN LETTER.

CHICAGO, September 1, 1897.

A steady improvement in business appears to have taken place, and things are decidedly brighter than they were at this time last year. August business was as good as could reasonably be expected. Library business was brisk last month, and some good country orders were booked for autumn goods. The different series of twelvemos and sixteenmos were especially remarkable for the activity they have shown, and much interest is being manifested in forthcoming books.

Just a year ago silver was on everybody's tongue; now the pendulum has swung to the opposite side and Klondike and its gold are the current topic. Publishers of the minor rank must be realising not a little benefit from this new craze, for a vast amount of Klondike literature has sprung up and is at present occupying the most prominent place in nearly all the bookstores and bookstalls. Like most things of mushroom growth, much of this is worthless, having been gotten up simply to sell, and is for the most part a *réchauffé* of articles that have appeared in the daily press.

The Christian is having an extraordinary run, and is at present the most widely discussed book of the hour. Every one is reading it and talking about it, and for a month or two at least it will in all probability lead the van as a seller.

The Chevalier d'Auriac is a notable addition to historical fiction of the present fashionable kind. The work is enjoying a good sale, and it is interesting to notice that the demand for books of this class shows no signs of abatement. In fact, a good interesting historical novel with plenty of incident in it is about as easy to sell as anything nowadays.

The autumn announcements do not appear at first sight to be as heavy as last year, but as they are likely to be largely supplemented later on the probability is that the output will be quite up to the average. Several houses, notably Messrs. Scribner's Sons and Dodd, Mead and Company, have even larger lists than usual of valuable and interesting books, but many of the smaller houses are not doing much.

The demand for *The Choir Invisible* is keeping up well, especially in the country. It is a long time since the month of August has seen such popular books as *The Christian*, *The Choir Invisible*, *Soldiers of Fortune*, *Equality*, and *Quo Vadis*. The last named seems to be following in the wake of *Ben Hur*, having been preached about and widely recommended by the clergy. No better advertising than this can be given to a book.

Jerome, by Miss Wilkins, and *A Son of the Old Dominion*, by Mrs. Burton Harrison, were respectively the second and third best sellers among the August publications. Generally speaking, the rest of last month's books, though plentiful, were rather an indifferent lot.

The tendency with publishers this year seems to be to keep books back until late in the autumn, but it is hardly a wise one, for a book stands a much better chance if it is published early in the season, to say nothing of its being easier for the publisher to measure the probable holiday demand when the work has been out two or three months before Christmas.

The following books led the demand last month in the order named, and it may be added that the sale of each title was, for the time of the year, remarkable:

The Christian. By Hall Caine. $1.50.
The Choir Invisible. By James Lane Allen. $1.50.
Soldiers of Fortune. By R. H. Davis. $1.50.
Quo Vadis. By H. T. Sienkiewicz. $2.00.
Equality. By E. Bellamy. $1.25.
The Martian. By G. Du Maurier. $1.75.
Jerome. By Mary E. Wilkins. $1.50.
Hon. Peter Stirling. By Paul L. Ford. $1.50.
Pursuit of the House-Boat. By J. Kendrick Bangs. $1.25.

The Law of Psychic Phenomena. By Thomson J. Hudson. $1.50.
A Rose of Yesterday. By F. Marion Crawford. $1.25
The Chevalier d'Auriac. By S. L. Yeats. $1.25.
Menticulture. By Horace Fletcher. $1.00.
On the Face of the Waters. By Mrs. F. A. Steel. $1.50.
Sentimental Tommy. By J. M. Barrie. $1.50.
Uncle Bernac. By Conan Doyle. $1.50.

ENGLISH LETTER.

LONDON, July 26 to August 21, 1897.

The art and craft of the bookseller have not been in demand to a very large extent during the past month The money spent by the holiday-making public does not find its way into the coffers of the needy bookseller. Still the dull season is nearly over for another year, and the reassembling of the schools, though a trifle late this year, will be the harbinger of busier times.

Trade outside the United Kingdom seems to be going on in a satisfactory manner, although the continued issue of colonial editions of the leading new books, at a comparatively nominal price, does not tend to help matters.

As may readily be imagined, *The Christian*, by Hall Caine, is the leading six-shilling novel. It is selling in very large numbers, and it needs to do so if the publisher is to be recouped the cost of the copyright, particulars of which have appeared in the press. This is the only six-shilling novel that calls for any comment.

The demand for Prince Ranjitsinhji's *Jubilee Book of Cricket* has shown in some measure the hold that the national game still has on the heart of the people. Several editions of the work have already been sold, the publishers being at times unable to supply the orders in hand.

For some reason or other, probably on account of the holidays, enquiries for theological literature are at a considerable discount. Books of this nature have nearly dropped out of the orders received for the present.

The Publishers' Association are still busy with the question of curtailing the discount on new books. It is difficult to see how they can prevent underselling unless they limit the output of books, which is doubtful, if not impossible.

A considerable quantity of magazines are still used every month. The *Quiver*, *Cassell's Magazine*, *Pearson's Magazine*, the *Strand Magazine*, the *Woman at Home*, the *Pall Mall Magazine*, and *Chambers's Journal* are among the principal favourites. There are few new periodicals being issued at present. These are usually more abundant earlier in the year.

The report for this month is really the most difficult one of the whole year to draw up as the trade generally presents so few features

The appended list of new books gives a fair idea of the kind of literature that finds favour with the public for the moment. As usual the selections are based upon actual business done, and may be taken as correct :

The Christian. By Hall Caine. 6s.
The Jubilee Book of Cricket. By K. S. Ranjitsinhji. 6s.
Soldiers of Fortune. By R. H. Davis. 6s.
Equality. By E. Bellamy. 6s.
A Rose of Yesterday. By F. M. Crawford. 6s.
On the Face of the Waters. By F. A. Steel. 6s.
Flames. By R. Hichens. 6s.
The Massarenes. By Ouida. 6s.
Dracula. By B. Stoker. 6s.
The Fascination of the King. By G. Boothby. 6s.
Salted with Fire. By G. Macdonald. 6s.
The Rejuvenation of Miss Semaphore. By H. Godfrey. 3s. 6d.
The Indiscretion of the Duchess. By A. Hope. 3s. 6d.
While the Billy Boils. By H. Lawson. 5s.
Quo Vadis. By Sienkiewicz. 4s. 6d. net.
Many Cargoes. By W. W. Jacob. 3s. 6d.
Mrs. Oliphant's Works. 2s. 6d. edition.
How Money Makes Money. By Duncans. 2s. 6d.
Life in Early Britain. By B. C. A. Windle. 3s. 6d.
The Ascent of Man. By H. Drummond. 3s. 6d.

SALES OF BOOKS DURING THE MONTH.

New books in order of demand, as sold between August 1, 1897, and September 1, 1897.

We guarantee the authenticity of the following lists as supplied to us, each by leading booksellers in the towns named.

NEW YORK, UPTOWN.

1. Letters to an Unknown. By Mérimée. $1.25. (Brentano.)
2. Quo Vadis. By Sienkiewicz. $2.00. (Little, Brown & Co.)
3. The Choir Invisible. By Allen. $1.50. (Macmillan.)
4. The Massarenes. By Ouida. $1.25. (Fenno.)
5. Soldiers of Fortune. By Davis. $1.50. (Scribner.)
6. Chevalier d'Auriac. By Yeats. $1.25. (Longmans.)

NEW YORK, DOWNTOWN.

1. The Choir Invisible. By Allen. $1.50. (Macmillan.)
2. Quo Vadis. By Sienkiewicz. $2.00. (Little, Brown & Co.)
3. The Christian. By Caine. $1.50. (Appleton.)
4. Jerome. By Wilkins. $1.50. (Harper.)
5. Chevalier d'Auriac. By Yeats. $1.25. (Longmans.)
6. Soldiers of Fortune. By Davis. $1.50. (Scribner.)

ALBANY, N. Y.

1. The Choir Invisible. By Allen. $1.50. (Macmillan.)
2. Soldiers of Fortune. By Davis. $1.50. (Scribner.)

3. Quo Vadis. By Sienkiewicz. $2.00. (Little, Brown & Co.)
4. Quest of the Golden Girl. By Le Gallienne. $1 50. (John Lane.)
5. Jerome. By Wilkins. $1.00. (Harper.)
6. Colonial Free-Lance. By Hotchkiss. 50 cts. (Appleton.)

ATLANTA, GA.

1. The Hon. Peter Stirling. By Ford. $1.50. (Holt.)
2. Quo Vadis. By Sienkiewicz. $2.00. (Little, Brown & Co.)
3. The Choir Invisible. By Allen. $1.50. (Macmillan.)
4. Soldiers of Fortune. By Davis. $1.50. (Scribner.)
5. A Rose of Yesterday. By Crawford. $1 25. (Macmillan.)
6. Chevalier d'Auriac. By Yeats. $1.25. (Longmans.)

BALTIMORE, MD.

1. Quo Vadis. By Sienkiewicz. $2.00. (Little, Brown & Co.)
2. Soldiers of Fortune. By Davis. $1.50. (Scribner.)
3. The Choir Invisible. By Allen. $1.50. (Macmillan.)
4. Old Gentleman of the Black Stock. By Page. 75 cts. (Scribner.)
5. The Hon. Peter Stirling. By Ford. $1.50. (Holt.)
6. The Christian. By Caine. $1.50. (Appleton.)

BOSTON, MASS.

1. The Choir Invisible. By Allen. $1.50. (Macmillan.)
2. Quo Vadis. By Sienkiewicz. $2.00. (Little, Brown & Co.)
3. The Christian. By Caine. $1.50. (Appleton.)
4. Soldiers of Fortune. By Davis. $1.50. (Scribner.)
5. Jerome. By Wilkins. $1.50. (Harper.)
6. Farthest North. By Nansen. $10.00. (Harper.)

BOSTON, MASS.

1. The Christian. By Caine. $1.50. (Appleton.)
2. Soldiers of Fortune. By Davis. $1.50. (Scribner.)
3. Quo Vadis. By Sienkiewicz. $2.00. (Little, Brown & Co.)
4. Farthest North. By Nansen. $10.00. (Harper.)
5. The Choir Invisible. By Allen. $1.50. (Macmillan.)
6. History of Our Own Times. Vol. III. By McCarthy. $1.75. (Harper.)

BUFFALO, N. Y.

1. Jerome. By Wilkins. $1.50. (Harper.)
2. The Choir Invisible. By Allen. $1.50. (Macmillan.)
3. The Christian. By Caine. $1.50. (Appleton.)
4. Quo Vadis. By Sienkiewicz. $2.00. (Little, Brown & Co.)
5. Equality. By Bellamy. $1.25. (Appleton.)
6. Lyrics of Lowly Life. By Dunbar. $1.25. (Dodd, Mead & Co.)

CHICAGO, ILL.

1. The Christian. By Caine. $1.50. (Appleton.)
2. The Choir Invisible. By Allen. $1.50. (Macmillan.)
3. Soldiers of Fortune. By Davis. $1.50. (Scribner.)
4. Quo Vadis. By Sienkiewicz. $2.00. Little, Brown & Co.)
5. Equality. By Bellamy. $1.25. (Appleton.)
6. The Martian. By Du Maurier. $1.75. (Harper.)

CHICAGO, ILL.

1. Soldiers of Fortune. By Davis. $1.50. (Scribner.)
2. The Sowers. By Merriman. $1.25. (Harper.)
3. Bolanyo. By Read. $1.25. (Way & Williams.)
4. Pursuit of the House-Boat. By Bangs. $1.25. (Harper.)
5. The Choir Invisible. By Allen. $1.50. (Macmillan.)
6. Quo Vadis. By Sienkiewicz. $2.00. (Little, Brown & Co.)

CINCINNATI, O.

1. The Choir Invisible. By Allen. $1.50. (Macmillan.)
2. The Christian. By Caine. $1.50. (Appleton)
3. Soldiers of Fortune. By Davis. $1.50. (Scribner.)
4. Quo Vadis. By Sienkiewicz. $2.00. (Little, Brown & Co.)
5. Equality. By Bellamy. $1.25. (Appleton.)
6. The Hon. Peter Stirling. By Ford. $1.50. (Holt.)

CLEVELAND, O.

1. The Christian. By Caine. $1.50. (Appleton.)
2. Soldiers of Fortune. By Davis. $1.50. (Scribner.)
3. The Choir Invisible. By Allen. $1.50. (Macmillan.)
4. Equality. By Bellamy. $1.25. (Appleton.)
5. Jerome. By Wilkins. $1.50. (Harper.)
6. Trix and Trixie. By Habberton. 50 cts. (Altemus.)

DETROIT, MICH.

1. Soldiers of Fortune. By Davis. $1.50. (Scribner.)
2. Quo Vadis. By Sienkiewicz. $2.00. (Little, Brown & Co.)
3. Jerome. By Wilkins. $1.50. (Harper.)
4. The Choir Invisible. By Allen. $1.50. (Macmillan)

5. Pursuit of the House-Boat. By Bangs. $1.25. (Harper.)
6. The Martian. By Du Maurier. $1.75. (Harper.)

INDIANAPOLIS, IND.

1. Soldiers of Fortune. By Davis. $1.50. (Scribner.)
2. The Choir Invisible. By Allen. $1.50. (Macmillan.)
3. Quo Vadis. By Sienkiewicz. $2.00. (Little, Brown & Co.)
4. Lads' Love. By Crockett. $1.50. (Appleton.)
5. The Martian. By Du Maurier. $1.75. (Harper.)
6. Equality. By Bellamy. $1.25. (Appleton.)

KANSAS CITY, MO.

1. Quo Vadis. By Sienkiewicz. $2.00. (Little, Brown & Co.)
2. The Christian. By Caine. $1.50. (Appleton.)
3. The Martian. By Du Maurier. $1.75. (Harper.)
4. The Choir Invisible. By Allen. $1.50. (Macmillan.)
5. Seats of the Mighty. By Parker. $1.50. (Appleton.)
6. King Noanett. By Stimson. $2.00. (Lamson, Wolffe & Co.)

LOS ANGELES, CAL.

1. The Choir Invisible. By Allen. $1.50. (Macmillan.)
2. Quo Vadis. By Sienkiewicz. $2.00. (Little, Brown & Co.)
3. The Martian. By Du Maurier. $1.75. (Harper.)
4. Soldiers of Fortune. By Davis. $1.50. (Scribner.)
5. Pursuit of the House-Boat. By Bangs. $1.25. (Harper.)
6. The Descendant. By Glasgow. $1.25. (Harper.)

LOUISVILLE, KY.

1. Quo Vadis. By Sienkiewicz. $2.00. (Little, Brown & Co.)
2. The Choir Invisible. By Allen. $1.50. (Macmillan.)
3. Equality. By Bellamy. $1.25. (Appleton.)
4. The Martian. By Du Maurier. $1.75. (Harper.)
5. Soldiers of Fortune. By Davis. $1.50. (Scribner.)
6. The Hon. Peter Stirling. By Ford. $1.50. (Holt.)

OMAHA, NEB.

1. Soldiers of Fortune. By Davis. $1.50. (Scribner.)
2. Quo Vadis. By Sienkiewicz. $2.00. (Little, Brown & Co.)
3. The Choir Invisible. By Allen. $1.50. (Macmillan.)
4. Pursuit of the House-Boat. By Bangs. $1.25. (Harper.)
5. The Hon. Peter Stirling. By Ford. $1.50. (Holt.)
6. The Martian. By Du Maurier. $1.75. (Harper.)

PHILADELPHIA, PA.

1. Quo Vadis. By Sienkiewicz. $2.00. (Little, Brown & Co.)
2. Pursuit of the House-Boat. By Bangs. $1.25. (Harper.)
3. Martian. By Du Maurier. $1.75. (Harper.)
4. Rose of Yesterday. By Crawford. $1.25. (Macmillan.)
5. Soldiers of Fortune. By Davis. $1.50. (Scribner.)
6. The Choir Invisible. By Allen. $1.50. (Macmillan.)

PITTSBURG, PA.

1. Quo Vadis. By Sienkiewicz. $2.00. (Little, Brown & Co.)
2. The Choir Invisible. By Allen. $1.50. (Macmillan.)
3. The Martian. By Du Maurier. $1.75. (Harper.)
4. The Christian. By Caine. $1.50. (Appleton.)
5. Chevalier d'Auriac. By Yeats. $1.25. (Longmans.)
6. Soldiers of Fortune. By Davis. $1.50. (Scribner.)

PORTLAND, ORE.

1. Equality. By Bellamy. $1.25. (Appleton.)
2. The Martian. By Du Maurier. $1.75. (Harper.)
3. Land of the Snow Pearls. By Higginson. $1.50. (Macmillan.)
4. Soldiers of Fortune. By Davis. $1.50. (Scribner.)
5. Jerome. By Wilkins. $1.50. (Harper.)
6. Wolfville. By Lewis. $1.50. (Stokes.)

PROVIDENCE, R. I.

1. Jerome. By Wilkins. $1.50. (Harper.)
2. The Christian. By Caine. $1.50. (Appleton.)
3. Equality. By Bellamy. $1.25. (Appleton.)
4. The Choir Invisible. By Allen. $1.50. (Macmillan.)
5. Soldiers of Fortune. By Davis. $1.50. (Scribner.)
6. The Martian. By Du Maurier. $1.75. (Harper.)

ROCHESTER, N. Y.

1. The Choir Invisible. By Allen. $1.50. (Macmillan.)
2. The Christian. By Caine. $1.50. (Appleton.)
3. Quo Vadis. By Sienkiewicz. $2.00. (Little, Brown & Co.)
4. Jerome. By Wilkins. $1.50. (Harper.)
5. Chevalier D'Auriac. By Yeats. $1.25. (Longmans.)
6. Pursuit of the House-Boat. By Bangs. $1.25 (Harper.)

SALT LAKE CITY, UTAH.

1. The Choir Invisible. By Allen. $1.50. (Macmillan.)
2. Soldiers of Fortune. By Davis. $1.50. (Scribner)
3. A Kentucky Cardinal. By Allen. $1.00. (Harper.)
4. Checkers. By Blossom. $1.25. (Stone.)
5. Pursuit of the House-Boat. By Bangs. $1.25. (Harper.)
6. A Rose of Yesterday. By Crawford. $1.25. (Macmillan.)

SAN FRANCISCO, CAL.

1. Quo Vadis. By Sienkiewicz. $2.00. (Little, Brown & Co.)
2. Many Cargoes. By Jacobs $1.00. (Stokes.)
3. The Christian. By Caine. $1.50. (Appleton.)
4. Soldiers of Fortune. By Davis. $1.50. (Scribner.)
5. The Choir Invisible. By Allen. $1.50. (Macmillan.)
6. Wolfville. By Lewis. $1.50. (Stokes.)

ST. LOUIS, MO.

1. The Choir Invisible. By Allen. $1.50. (Macmillan.)
2. Soldiers of Fortune. By Davis. $1.50. (Scribner.)
3. The Christian. By Caine. $1.50. (Appleton.)
4. Wolfville. By Lewis. $1.50. (Stokes.)
5. Uncle Bernac. By Doyle. $1.50. (Appleton.)
6. Pursuit of the House-Boat. By Bangs. $1.25. (Harper.)

ST. PAUL, MINN.

1. The Choir Invisible. By Allen. $1.50. (Macmillan.)
2. Chevalier d'Auriac. By Yeats. $1.25. (Longmans.)
3. Soldiers of Fortune. By Davis. $1.50. (Scribner.)
4. Quo Vadis. By Sienkiewicz. $2.00. (Little, Brown & Co.)
5. The Christian. By Caine. $1.50. (Appleton.)
6. The Gray Lady. By Merriman. $1.25. (Macmillan.)

TOLEDO, O.

1. The Christian. By Caine. $1.50. (Appleton.)
2. The Choir Invisible. By Allen. $1.50. (Macmillan.)
3. Equality. By Bellamy. $1.25. (Appleton.)
4. Quo Vadis. By Sienkiewicz. $2.00. (Little, Brown & Co.)
5. Jerome. By Wilkins. $1.50. (Harper.)
6. Spanish Castles by the Rhine. By Foster. 75 cts. (Holt.)

TORONTO, CANADA.

1. * Soldiers of Fortune. By Davis. Paper, 75 cts.; cloth, $1.25. (The Copp-Clark Co., Limited.)
2. * The Martian. By Du Maurier. Paper, 75 cts.; cloth, $1.25. (The Copp-Clark Co., Limited.)
3. Chevalier d'Auriac. By Yeats. Paper, 75 cts.; cloth, $1.25. (Longman's Colonial Edition.)
4. * In Kedar's Tents. By Merriman. Paper, 75 cts.; cloth, $1.25. (The Copp-Clark Co., Limited.)
5. * Seats of the Mighty. By Parker. Paper, 75 cts.; cloth, $1.25. (The Copp-Clark Co., Limited.)
6. Uncle Bernac. By Doyle. Paper, 75 cts.; cloth, $1.25. (Bell's Colonial Edition.)

TORONTO, CANADA.

1. * The Christian. By Caine. 75 cts. and $1.50. (Morang.)
2. * In Kedar's Tents. By Merriman. 75 cts. and $1.25. (The Copp-Clark Co.)
3. † Farthest North. By Nansen. $1.50 and $2.00 per set. (Harper.)
4. * The Martian. By Du Maurier. 75 cts. and $1.25. (The Copp-Clark Co.)
5. Quo Vadis. By Sienkiewicz. $2.00. (Little, Brown & Co.)
6. * Equality. By Bellamy. 75 cts. and $1.25. (Morang.)

WACO, TEXAS.

1. The Martian. By Du Maurier. $1.75. (Harper.)
2. The Well Beloved. By Hardy. $1.50. (Harper.)
3. Soldiers of Fortune. By Davis. $1.50. (Scribner.)
4. The Choir Invisible. By Allen. $1.50. (Macmillan.)
5. Quo Vadis. By Sienkiewicz. $2.00. (Little, Brown & Co.)
6. A Rose of Yesterday. By Crawford. $1.25. (Macmillan.)

WORCESTER, MASS.

1. Soldiers of Fortune. By Davis. $1.50. (Scribner.)
2. The Choir Invisible. By Allen. $1.50. (Macmillan.)
3. Jerome. By Wilkins. $1.50. (Harper.)
4. The Christian. By Caine. $1.50. (Appleton.)
5. Quo Vadis. By Sienkiewicz. $2.00. (Little, Brown & Co.)
6. Pursuit of the House-Boat. By Bangs. $1.25. (Harper.)

* Canadian Copyright Editions.
† Colonial Libraries.

THE BOOKMAN

A LITERARY JOURNAL.

VOL. VI. NOVEMBER, 1897. No. 3.

CHRONICLE AND COMMENT.

The Editors of THE BOOKMAN *cannot undertake to return rejected manuscripts, whether stamps are enclosed or not; and to this rule no exception will be made.*

We desire to call especial attention to the very interesting article contributed to the present number of THE BOOKMAN by Professor John C. Rolfe, of the University of Michigan. So much notice has been attracted of late years to dictionary-making and lexicographical methods in general, that this paper will appeal to a circle of readers not limited to those who are classical students; and they will find its narrative giving a splendid illustration of the scientific accuracy and precision of modern classical scholarship. In some of its details the mammoth lexicon whose inception and plan are described by Dr. Rolfe will be quite unique; and it will surpass the great dictionary of our own language now preparing under the direction of the English Philological Society in at least two respects—in the eminence of its editors and contributors, and in its approximate finality.

❀

We always study with pleasure any new points in the present *régime* of the German Empire, for there is always sure to be found on every side a delightful blend of scientific thoroughness with a most fascinating lack of humour. One item of news recently wafted across the ocean has greatly tickled our fancy. It appears that the Kaiser's military establishment has for some time included a regularly organised corps of cats, whose function it is to protect the military stores from mice. Those cats are trained in their duties by the inevitable drill-sergeant; they wear badges, receive rations and medical attendance, and draw annual pay amounting to the sum of eighteen marks per cat. Now the announcement is officially made that this corps is to be disbanded, inasmuch as Professor Löffler has discovered a species of typhus-bacillus which is fatal to mice, and whose services will in consequence be substituted for those of the cats.

❀

Probably no German sees anything comical in this bulletin; but to the American mind the whole thing is simply delicious. One involuntarily finds himself dwelling upon the little incidents that are implied in it. We love to picture the military cat after passing the physical examination and being mustered in, donning his badge and reporting for duty. We joyfully imagine the same cat drawing his daily rations of milk and cat's-meat; of the cat gravely saluting the *schneidig Offizier* in the barrack-yard; of the cat lining up at the paymaster's for his quarterly wages; of the cat applying for a few hours' leave of absence and riotously squandering his pay on unlimited catnip, and then failing to return to the *caserne* at roll-call; of the cat inebriated and uttering seditious yowls opposite the officers' clubs; and of the cat bedraggled, headachy and repentant, being haled at last before a court-martial for constructive desertion and *Majestätsbeleidigung*. It is all fine, wonderfully fine. But what we really want is some official information as to how much pay the typhus-bacillus is going to draw, and whether it will also wear a badge.

❀

The removal of Columbia University to its new site has been accomplished; and leaving out of consideration the delays for which the university authorities were not responsible, it has been accomplished with remarkable celerity and smoothness. It will not be many months before this will be one of the great show places of the city, both because of the external impressiveness of the whole mass of buildings, and because of the remarkable perfection and completeness of the appliances for academic work that are to be seen even in the minutest details of the installation. While the buildings were still incomplete a good deal of criticism was bestowed on the incongruity, from an architectural point of view, that was found in the sharp contrast presented between the strictly classical style of the great library and the severely modern, not to say utilitarian, aspect of the surrounding halls. Some one epigrammatically described the whole as "four factories facing a mausoleum;" but now that the effect of the combination can be seen, one is more conscious of a happy combination of the useful with the beautiful than of their contrasts. The noble library, indeed, with its thoroughly imposing approach, so dominates the whole as to give an *ensemble* of exceeding magnificence; and when the brick halls shall have clothed themselves with ivy, there will be nothing to mar the harmonious effect of what is undoubtedly one of the most admirably housed and equipped universities of the world.

❀

Scribner's Magazine offers a tempting array of good things in its programme for 1898. A leading feature will be the appearance during the year of "The Story of the Revolution," by Mr. Henry Cabot Lodge, in which the author of *The Life of Washington* will endeavour to present the fight for American independence as a vivid picture of a vital struggle, reproducing the atmosphere and feeling of the time, and to make clear the historical significance and proportion of the events described, as they can now be discerned with the perspective of years. Interesting pictorial effects may be expected from the fact that a corps of artists started out last summer to sketch the historic scenes, which will be reproduced to accompany Mr. Lodge's work. Mr. Howard Pyle will also prepare a full-page drawing for each instalment of the story. Another feature of decided interest will be a series of articles on "The American Navy in the Revolution," by Captain A. T. Mahan, dealing largely with the romantic side of our sea fighting. These papers will be illustrated on the same plan. Mr. Walter A. Wyckoff will continue his series on "The Workers—an Experiment in Reality," which has stirred up a great deal of interest already; there will be political reminiscences by Senator Hoar, "Search-Light Letters," by Robert Grant, more about the conduct of great businesses, and life at girls' colleges. Bits of Europe in America will be described by Octave Thanet, Cornelia Atwood Pratt, and Elia W. Peattie, and short stories will be contributed by Rudyard Kipling, Kenneth Grahame, George W. Cable, and other well-known writers of the best short stories.

❀

The announcement which has especial interest for us, however, we propose to keep for a separate note. The serial in fiction for the year in *Scribner's* will be from the pen of the author of *Marse Chan* and *Meh Lady*. Thomas Nelson Page has written his first long novel, entitled *Red Rock*—"A Chronicle of Reconstruction." It is a story of the era when the Old South had been lost forever and the New South had not yet found itself. Mr. Page has devoted four years to this work, which he may be pardoned for considering his best. It has been matter of regret often that Mr. Page has remained so long silent, but the fruits of that silence are now about to be made evident.

❀

We have just read the advance sheets of a story of the old South during the war, which has made us reverse the opinion that Mr. Thomas Nelson Page had given us the last word on the subject from the "darkey's" point of view. Not since *Marse Chan* and *Meh Lady* took American readers by storm have we had in the literature of the South anything so searching, so pathetic, so picturesque, so impregnated with the homely humour and raciness of the soil. Like Mr. Page's stories, *Brokenburne* has that touch of human nature which makes the whole world kin, breaking through the barriers of dialect and going straight for the heart. In the hands of an artist dialect properly used becomes the fit vehicle of speech for the soul that seeks expression in its own way, and this is what the author of *Brokenburne* has accomplished for "Aunt Bene." Slight as it is—there are, as we reckon, about twenty thousand words—the story is a great achievement, and we predict for it a ready and enduring popularity. The book will be beautifully made with several half-tone illustrations by Mr. William Henry Walker, and a picturesque cover design by Mr. Walter C. Greenough. The author is Mrs. Virginia Frazer Boyle, of Memphis, Tenn., whose *Centennial Ode* was last year widely appreciated throughout the Southern States. *Brokenburne* will be published immediately by Messrs. E. R. Herrick and Company.

❀

The silhouette of Burns's "Clarinda," herewith reproduced, forms the frontispiece to a work published by the same firm, entitled *Burns's Clarinda: Brief Papers Concerning the Poet's Renowned Correspondent*, collected and edited by John D. Ross, LL.D., a well-known Burns scholar and enthusiast. This portrait of Mrs. McLehose, who played Clarinda to Burns's Sylvander with more tragic results to herself than befell the poet, now reposes in the National Portrait Gallery, and there is an especial interest attached to the accompanying silhouette inasmuch as it is a perfect fac-simile of the original picture drawn for Burns by the celebrated silhouettist Miers. The following are the letters which passed between Clarinda and the poet on the subject:

"*Thursday Noon, February* 7, 1788

"I shall go to-morrow forenoon to Miers alone. What size do you want it about? O Sylvander, if you wish my peace, let *friendship* be the word between us. I tremble at more."

"*Thursday Night, February* 7, 1788.

"I thank you for going to Miers. Urge him, for necessity calls, to have it done by the middle of next week. Wednesday the latest day. I want it for a breast-pin to wear next my heart. I propose to keep sacred set times to wander in the woods and wilds for meditation on you. Then, and only then, your lovely image shall be produced to the day, with a reverence akin to devotion."

The papers collected in this volume form a valuable addition to Burns lore; especially do they vindicate the unstained character of the hapless Clarinda with, as her only weakness, an acknowledged love for the poet that wrecked her life's happiness. Her life-story is subjected to a variety of treatment in these papers, beginning with a "Memoir of Mrs. McLehose," by her grandson, W. C. McLehose, and including, among other interesting chapters, "A Tribute," by the late Professor Blackie; "A Brief Sketch," by Principal Shairp; "A Visit to Clarinda;" "Clarinda and Sylvander," by Alexander Smith. The volume concludes with the cluster of poems inspired by Agnes McLehose, under the heading of "The Poet's Immortal Wreath," among which "Ae Fond Kiss" not only stands alone, but ranks with the immortal love songs of the world.

BURNS'S "CLARINDA."

❀

Tom Hall is to follow up the success of *When Hearts are Trumps* with a new collection of his humorous versicles, to be entitled *When Love Laughs*. The book will be printed on a decorated page, with the decorations in two colours, designed by Frank M. Gregory. *When Hearts are Trumps* was published by Messrs. Stone and Kimball about two years ago, and has passed through several editions. The advance orders for the new volume are so numerous as to promise to exhaust the first edition almost before the date of publication, which will take place in a few weeks. Many of the things that Tom Hall has written have made us wish sometimes that he would take himself more seriously and give us something worthy of his art. His trickles of wit and fancy, trifles light as air, have added to the mirth of the moment, and after all he is perhaps wise in his generation in playing with hearts in the present, and laughing with love while it lasts than he would be in aping the bard and baying the moon, like so many futile minor poets of the day. *When Love Laughs* will be published by Messrs. E. R. Herrick and Company.

❀

A new weekly is projected for publication in New York, the initial number to appear about November 1st. It is to be called *L'Enfant Terrible*, and will be devoted to "humour for humour's sake." The editors are Mr. Gelett Burgess, late of the *Lark*, and Mr. Oliver Herford, epigrammatist of the Players, and Mr. James Jeffrey Roche. The editorial policy of the paper, judging from the antics of the *Lark* and the "Purple Cow," will very naturally be rather eccentric. Once a week the editors are to dine together, and on this evening the matter for the next number of the publication, both text and illustrations, will be conceived and expressed on paper, the staff being pledged not to leave the room until the entire copy is ready for the printer. But oh, what a difference in the morning!

❀

We learn with regret that the Frederick Stokes Company have decided to postpone the publication of Mr. George Gissing's novel *The Whirlpool* until February next. This will cause disappointment to many of Mr. Gissing's admirers in America, who have been patiently awaiting the appearance of the book in this country. *The Whirlpool* was published in England last spring.

❀

Mr. Gissing has been engaged on the proofs of a book of short stories which will shortly appear under the title *Human Odds and Ends*. Mr. Gissing leaves shortly for Italy, where he will remain until the spring, as his health forbids his spending the winter in England.

Mr. H. G. Wells has an article on the novels of Mr. George Gissing in the August *Contemporary Review*, which contains some very acute criticism. For example, he points out that in *The Whirlpool* Mr. Gissing for the first time takes serious account of children. He sums up by saying that Mr. Gissing has written a series of extremely significant novels, perhaps the only series of novels in the last decade whose interest has been strictly contemporary. But Mr. Wells is wrong, as so many critics have been wrong, in saying that what checks Mr. Gissing's popularity is his depressing tone. It is not that; it is the fact that he seems to be without poetic imagination, and without that touch no man's work rises into real greatness. Mr. Gissing lacks that which Thomas Hardy possesses and which compels the public to read books which are more depressing in their general import than any that Mr. Gissing has written.

❀

Editors of magazines and periodicals are always on the lookout for stories that will raise the circulation of their publications. As a rule, these are very hard to find and are very uncertain. Even stories by eminent authors often fail, but in two cases at least of recent date a marked effect has been produced on sales by the serial. We refer to the two stories of Mr. H. G. Wells, which appeared during the summer months in *Pearson's Weekly* and *Pearson's Magazine*. The former of these stories, *The Invisible Man*, has just been published by Mr. Edward Arnold. One of the shrewdest literary men in London prophesies that it will be the book of the season. The story in *Pearson's Magazine* has also been appearing in the *Cosmopolitan* in this country, and is called *The War of the Worlds*. Mr. Wells is a scientific as well as a literary man, and can give a strange verisimilitude to his astounding tales. He has not until now been a really popular writer, although he has done some very fine work; but it would seem as if his hour had now come.

❀

To the uninitiated or to those puzzled by the title of Mr. Wells's new story, *The Invisible Man*, we submit the author's own explanation to a representative of the *Sketch*. "The leading idea, which has already been used by Mr.

Gilbert in one of the *Bab Ballads*, is that a man is able to make his living tissues invisible. But this invisibility, being not a magic quality, but the result, as I have shown, of certain applications of the science of optics, does not extend to his clothing, to any matter that may descend upon him, or to his food before it is assimilated. The story consists in the realistic treatment of this leading idea, the experimenter being represented as an extremely egotistical and irritable person." Asked whether he did not think of doing anything more in the vein of *The Wheels of Chance*, he replied: "I have had a novel of commonplace people in hand for some time, and I continue to work at it intermittently. It is called *Love and Mr. Lewisham*. But I shall probably not finish it for some time, as I am also working at a romance of the immediate future, somewhat on the lines of Mr. Bellamy's *Looking Backward*. But it is by no means a political Utopia; the story is rather a horoscope. I hope to finish it by the end of the year, but it has taken me from the beginning of May until now to do half. I have given my time entirely to it, but I find myself getting more and more anxious about the quality of my work, and I was never a quick worker except under pressure of stern necessity." This last is good news, as we were beginning to fear that the publishers were going to run Mr. Wells's remarkable abilities to earth.

❀

Mr. Edward Arnold is publishing some very interesting books this season, especially the *Recollections* of Aubrey de Vere, the friend of Wordsworth, Newman, Sir Henry Taylor, Sir W. Rowan Hamilton, F. D. Maurice, and many others. He will also publish the life of Miss Clough, by her niece, who was her secretary, and on terms of the closest intimacy with her. Another important biographical book published by Mr. Arnold will be *The Life and Letters of J. A. Roebuck*, the bitter and sturdy Radical. After 1832 Mr. Roebuck's career is described in the main through his own letters to his wife. Mr. Arnold also publishes a short work on *Style* by Professor Walter Raleigh, of Liverpool, who wrote the *Quarterly Review* article on Robert Louis Stevenson.

❀

We are glad to hear that the indefatigable Andrew Lang has undertaken no less an enterprise than the writing of a history of Scotland. Too much of Mr. Lang's energy has been spent in ephemeral work, and there is room for a good work on Scottish history that will fill a permanent place in literature. Mr. Lang is also engaged in writing a popular life of Napoleon.

❀

A story for boys, entitled *The Adventures of Napoleon Smith*, by Mr. S. R. Crockett, is almost ready. One prescient critic has ventured the prophecy that it will turn out to be one of his most entertaining and popular books.

❀

The announcement that Messrs. Dent and Company of London are preparing a new edition of the Waverley novels in their very attractive Temple Classics has aroused a great deal of interest. So far the rule has been in this popular series to omit prefaces, but in the case of Scott a reversion has been made to the plan adopted with the Temple Shakespeare, and a short bibliographical account will preface each novel. These brief introductions are being written by Mr. Clement K. Shorter, and they bid fair to be of exceptional value. Among other things, Mr. Shorter has at his command the unique collection of Scott materials accumulated by the late Mr. Dykes Campbell. The edition will be published in this country by Messrs. Charles Scribner's Sons, and will be complete in forty-eight volumes. Two or more volumes will appear before the end of the year.

❀

While Dr. S. Weir Mitchell has written a story of the American Revolution in *Hugh Wynne* for older readers, another well-known American author, Mr. W. O. Stoddard, has presented the younger generation with a story of the same period in *The Red Patriot*, which is about to be published by the Messrs. Appleton. Mr. Stoddard has been for the last few years a resident of Madison, N. J., in the vicinity of Morristown, and has had ample opportunities for studying the background of Washington's campaigning in New Jersey, which furnishes some of the stirring scenes and historical events of the story. The book takes its title from a leading actor, "the last of the Susquehannocks," who shares the boy hero's adventures.

famous. The origin of the Saracinesca stories, probably the best and the most popular of all his novels, was a walk he took with a tutor, when he was a boy, in the interior of Italy, the region in which he places the Saracinesca estates. When he wrote the first novel of the series he did not intend a group, but the plan grew upon him, and the first story was received so kindly that he decided to continue the history through several generations, and to make it in a sense representative of the life of the nobility of a certain class in modern Italy. Personally he does not care very much for the series; but in this his readers seem to disagree with him. The book which has the most reality for him is *Pietro Ghisleri*, and the book he enjoyed most in writing is *Mr. Isaacs*. As is well known, Mr. Crawford has produced a group of New York novels in which the fortunes of a family are elaborated after the manner of his Saracinesca tales, but in this series he has not been so successful.

❁

Mr. F. Marion Crawford is the youngest of four children, and was born at Bagni di Lucca, Italy, August 2d, 1854. His boyhood was spent in Italy, and he studied mainly under a French governess, and to this day writes French with the ease of English. When twelve years of age he was sent to America and went to St. Paul's School, Concord. Thereafter he studied in England, then at Karlsruhe and Heidelberg from 1874–76, and spent two years at the University of Rome, where he had a tutor who taught him Sanskrit. Becoming interested in the language, he went to India to gain a more profound knowledge of Sanskrit. After a series of troubles he got an engagement on the *Allahabad Indian Herald*, an afternoon daily paper of which he became the editor. He picked up a great deal about Buddhism and other Oriental lore, and at Simla he met the original of *Mr. Isaacs*, a real man, whose name was Jacobs. He says that his work on the *Herald* was the hardest he ever did. Returning to Italy in 1880, he again found himself without means or work, and so took passage in an old steamer for America in the year following. He entered Harvard as a special student, taking a course in Sanskrit. During this time he wrote numerous book reviews and articles on philosophical themes.

❁

On May 5th, 1882, his uncle, Samuel Ward, the original of Horace in *Dr. Claudius*, asked him to dinner at a New York club. In the course of conversation Mr. Crawford related with a great deal of detail his recollections of an interesting man whom he had met in Simla. When he had finished, Sam Ward said to him, "That is a good magazine story, and you must write it out immediately." That night he began *Mr. Isaacs*, and finished it on June 13th, 1882. The novel was accepted by the Messrs. Macmillan, and was followed by *Dr. Claudius*. *Mr. Isaacs* became popular immediately, and at Mr. Aldrich's request Mr. Crawford wrote *A Roman Singer* for the *Atlantic Monthly*. Since then his other stories have followed in quick succession, most of them written very rapidly. *Marzio's Crucifix* was produced in ten days, and *The Tale of a Lonely Parish* in twenty-four days, at the rate of a chapter of about five thousand words a day. He was married to a daughter of General Berdan in the year 1884 in Constantinople, and in 1885 went back to Italy, to Sorrento, where he has a villa, and where he has lived ever since, broken only by his visits to America. In these fifteen years he has produced some thirty novels, and his popularity is not only unabated, but seems to increase both in England and in America. Mr. Crawford has only turned forty, so that his best work as a novelist may still lie before him.

❁

The series of lectures which Mr. Crawford will deliver this winter in various cities of the United States and Canada comprises the following subjects: "The Early Italian Artists," "Italian Home Life in the Middle Ages," "Leo XIII. in the Vatican," and "The Italy of Horace." Mr. Crawford's lecture tour is under the direction of Major Pond.

❁

Anthony Hope will have begun his series of readings in this country, also under Major Pond's management, before this meets the eye of the reader. We understand that his first appearance in New York will be on October 24th, and that on that morning and those of the two following days Mr. Hawkins will give readings in the Lyceum. His programmes, which we have seen, consist of selections from his best-known books, and cover a wide range, from grave to gay. As an example we give one of them, taken at random :

1. "The Philosopher in the Apple Orchard."
2 From *The Prisoner of Zenda*, "If Love Were All."
3. From *The Dolly Dialogues*, "The Other Lady."
4. From *The Heart of the Princess Osra*, "The Victory of the Grand Duke."

Anthony Hope is considered one of the wittiest and most graceful of after-dinner speakers in London, and we have heard this attested by several American persons who have listened to his happy, fluent oratory. This will make his readings all the more inviting, as we understand they are to be pleasantly interspersed with notes by the way.

❀

The following letter is now being circulated by the American Committee acting in behalf of the Stevenson Memorial :

38 UNION SQUARE, NEW YORK.

It has been proposed to erect in his native city of Edinburgh a memorial to Robert Louis Stevenson, and a committee of his Scotch and English admirers and friends, headed by Lord Rosebery, and having among its number those as near to Stevenson as Mr. Sidney Colvin, Mr. George Meredith, and Mr. J. M. Barrie, has been already formed to carry out the project But Stevenson is nowhere held in greater admiration or affection than in America, and it seems certain that many of his American readers would be glad of an opportunity to take part in this tribute to his memory. Many of them have felt through his books the vital and stimulating personality that made him one of the most attractive figures in recent English literature ; and the idea of this memorial has appealed to them with an unusual force.

With the authority of the English organisation an American Committee has been formed, which asks American readers and admirers of Stevenson to contribute to the work. The memorial is to take the shape of a "statue, bust, or medallion with such architectural or sculpturesque accompaniment as may be desirable," and the character of those having the matter in charge ensures its dignity and fitness.

Subscriptions of whatever amount will be received for the American Committee by the undersigned, its chairman, and receipts returned in the name of the committee To the subscribers of sums of $10.00 and upward there will be sent by the American Committee, as a memorial of participation in the undertaking, a special edition, printed for the committee, of Stevenson's *Æs Triplex*, bearing the subscriber's name and having as its frontispiece a reproduction of the portrait by John S. Sargent. It need hardly be said that this edition will not be otherwise obtainable.

CHARLES FAIRCHILD,
Chairman.

The members of the American Committee are Messrs. Henry M. Alden, E. L. Burlingame, Beverley Chew, Charles B. Foote, Richard Watson Gilder, Clarence King, Gustav E. Kissel, John La Farge, Will H. Low, James MacArthur, S. S. McClure, Augustus St. Gaudens, Charles Scribner, J. Kennedy Tod, George E. Waring, and Miss Jeannette L. Gilder.

❀

One of the most remarkable contributions—perhaps the most remarkable—that have been made to the literature that has grown around the warrior saint of France is Mrs. Catherwood's *The Days of Jeanne d'Arc*, which is concluded in the October *Century*, and is now published by the Century Company in book form. Of all the books that we have read on the subject, this one appears to us to get nearest to an essential understanding of the character of the Maid of Domremy. The way in which the study of the subject suggested itself to Mrs. Catherwood will probably provoke a sneer from the sceptical ; but her statement is worthy of respect, and is of decided interest. "At the risk of raising a smile," she says, "I will confess that I felt—so strongly that it was like an instant's experience of a blow—that Jeanne d'Arc herself had laid upon me the task of writing her story. I was on the train going to my summer home. The feeling, without any premonition, swept through me that I would be obliged to make a careful study of her life and times, and of the present geographical aspect of France, and that I would have to give unstinted labour to the undertaking." Mrs. Catherwood may be pardoned for the seeming egotism of believing that in her *Days of Jeanne d'Arc* she has shown us the Maid as she really was, now that we are able to compare the result of her labours with the portraits existing of this wonderfully romantic figure in history. She went among the Vosges and Lorraine peasants in France and studied their characteristics. Many of the notes she had accumulated in America during a year's hard study in the best libraries she threw away, making others at first-

Mary Hartwell Catherwood.

hand from her own observations. The geography, the atmosphere, the characteristics of the people are absolutely correct; the age itself, of course, could only be studied through the best existing authorities.

❀

When the inspiration first came to her, Mrs. Catherwood wrote at once to the Century Company, and Mr. Gilder, of the *Century Magazine*, astonished her by saying that they had been thinking of that very thing. This strange coincidence greatly strengthened Mrs. Catherwood in the belief of her literary mission and stimulated her to proceed immediately with the work. An amusing incident occurred about this time relative to Mark Twain's *Personal Recollections of Joan of Arc*, purporting to be a translation from the French of the Sieur Louis de Conte, her page and secretary, which had just begun to appear serially in *Harper's Magazine*. Mrs. Catherwood pointed out an error in transcribing the name "Conte," it ought to be "Coute," she said; and Mark Twain was informed of the mis take. "Have I been studying this subject for fourteen years to be told that I could make such a mistake as that?" he replied with characteristic brusqueness. The name continued to be spelled as originally written by Mr. Clemens, and notwithstanding that proof was brought to bear on its inaccuracy, he persisted in having his own way. "Conte I have written," said he, "and Conte it will remain!" And sure enough Conte it remains in the book, which now perpetuates his hypocephalous decision.

❀

The new edition of Thackeray's novels which was announced in our London Letter just one year ago is now in active preparation. The novelist's accomplished daughter, Mrs. Richmond Ritchie, is to write a series of introductions to the new issue of her father's works, which will no doubt cause this edition to take its place as the final and standard edition of the greatest among English novelists. These introductions will be full and elaborate; they will contain much personal as well as much literary information, and Thackeray's letters and manuscripts will be freely used in their preparation. It need hardly be said that all that Mrs. Ritchie has written in various forms about her father has been done in exquisite taste in view of the injunction put upon posterity by Thackeray that no biography of him should appear after his death. She has resolutely declined hitherto to prepare a formal biography, in spite of repeated offers and suggestions, but she has now seen her way to use the material at her sole disposal in connection with Messrs. Smith, Elder and Company's important project.

❀

The copyright of *Henry Esmond* having recently expired, Messrs. Downey and Company met the opportunity with a cheap edition in England at sixpence. The Blackwoods have also published an edition of George Eliot's *Scenes of Clerical Life* at the same price, and an enormous sixpenny edition of *Lorna Doone* has just been put on the market by the English publishers. *Lorna Doone* was first published in 1860; *Dariel, a Romance of Surrey*, Mr. Blackmore's new novel, has just appeared.

❀

EARLY PORTRAIT OF MRS. RICHMOND RITCHIE.
From a photograph by Julia Margaret Cameron.

Visitors to London have probably remarked the famous photographic studio in Mortimer Street, under the auspices of Mr. Henry Hay Herschel Cameron, and those who have visited the studio have probably found there much gratification by viewing the countless examples of his mother's portraits of the great dead—Tennyson, Browning, Longfellow, Lowell, Darwin, Herschel and many others. There is also exhibited there the plain, old-fashioned camera which has reflected the images of more famous men and women than any existing lens. For not only was Mrs. Julia Margaret Cameron, the mother of the present photographer, one of the first seriously to realise all the art possibilities of photography, but she herself possessed one of those rare personalities which draw to themselves all that is greatest and best in their own generation, and her most distinguished sitters were almost without exception her own intimate friends. One of these was Mrs. Richmond Ritchie, Thackeray's daughter, an early portrait of whom, taken by Mrs. Cameron, we reproduce. It is all the more interesting because Mrs. Ritchie is one of the few literary worthies whose features have not become familiar to us through frequency of appearance in the public prints.

❀

Mr. Cameron will tell you that famous people often make the best sitters; this is of course owing to a variety of causes. Thought, learning, intellect—power of any kind—leaves its stamp on a face, and indeed on the whole individuality of a man. Tennyson, for instance, had a magnificent presence. Mr. Cameron thought he looked like a latter-day Homer, and though he always grumbled at the ordeal, he made the most admirable of sitters, and was invariably kind and patient. The photograph of the late Lord Tennyson and Lady Tennyson and their son, the present Lord Tennyson, which is reproduced on the next page, is from Mr. Cameron's collection, and has not been published before. Two of Mrs. Cameron's photographs of the poet have been published in the *Memoir* by his son, but for some reason this one has been omitted. It has a peculiar interest in view of the biography of the

THE LATE LORD TENNYSON, LADY TENNYSON, AND THEIR SON.

From a photograph by Cameron, London.

late Poet Laureate, which has just been published by the Macmillan Company.

Lord Tennyson's *Memoir* of his father appears as we go to press and too late for review in this number. Meanwhile a word may be said for the extrinsic merits of the work. It is one of the handsomest pieces of bookmaking we have seen in a long time, and everything about the book evinces the greatest care and finish The type is large and clear, the printing and paper excellent, the binding serviceable and in good taste. The illustrations—there are twenty-four of them, consisting mainly of portraits, and partly of fac-similes of poems in the poet's handwriting—are works of art, and enhance the beauty and value of the book. The work is published in two volumes, each having over two hundred pages. It was announced for publication on October 6th, the anniversary of the poet's death, but it was found impossible to fill the advance orders and publish it earlier than the 12th.

BRET HARTE.

From a photograph by Fradelle and Young, London.

The accompanying fine portrait of Bret Harte was recently photographed from a painting made about two years ago, and is now reproduced for the first time. It is considered to be a striking likeness. A review of Bret Harte's new story, *Three Partners*, published by Messrs. Houghton, Mifflin and Company, appears on another page.

❀

Our London correspondent refers in his current letter to the elaborate prepa-

MAUDE ADAMS AS "BABBIE."

From a photograph by Sarony.

rations which are being made for the production of Mr. Barrie's dramatisation of *The Little Minister* in London, where it is anticipated it will be the play of the season. Whatever the results may be in England, the success of *The Little Minister* on the boards in America seems to be an assured thing. The ovation given to the star, Miss Maude Adams, on the first night was to be expected ; but in spite of cantankerous criticisms in certain quarters concerning this warm reception accorded to the play through Miss Adams, the interest of successive audiences has been fully sustained to the first pitch, and the play is now fairly launched for the season. It must be gratifying to Mr. Barrie to learn that Miss Adams has been so successful with his creation of Babbie. When he was in this country a year ago Miss Adams was playing with John Drew in *Rosemary*, and if we remember aright, he was much pleased with her performance in this play. Miss Adams is ably supported, with the exception of Mr. Robert Edeson, whose Gavin Dishart, the Little Minister, is very inadequate and unsatisfactory. By the way, all through the play it was noticeable to the Scotch part of the audience that the pronunciation of "Dishart" was amusingly travestied. It is pronounced by the players Dīs'-hart instead of Dĭsh art. Mr. Frohman, please note. We give a portrait of Miss Adams as she appears when masquerading as the roguish gypsy.

❀

Madame Sarah Grand's new novel bears the unattractive title *The Beth Book*, "being a Study from the Life of Elizabeth Caldwell Maclure, a Woman of Genius." It will be published about the beginning of November by Messrs. D. Appleton and Company. *The Beth Book* is the book of the life history of the heroine, Beth, whose development the author traces from birth to marriage and after. The earlier scenes of the story are laid in Ireland, but the action takes place for the most part in London.

❀

The Skipper's Wooing is the longest story that Mr. W. W. Jacobs has written, but its success as a serial in England, and the warm reception given to the book, have emboldened him to try his hand at a full-length novel. He has been more or less engaged on it all summer, but he is a slow worker, and it is not likely to be finished until next year. The F. A. Stokes Company are Mr. Jacobs's publishers in America.

Copyright, 1897, by W. E. Benjamin.

CHARLES DICKENS AT HIS DESK.*

OLD LAMPS FOR NEW ONES.

Sketches and Essays by Charles Dickens, now Published in America for the First Time.

When Dickens reversed the cry of the magician in *Aladdin*, and made it "Old Lamps for New Ones," in a scathing satire on the Pre-Raphael Brotherhood nearly fifty years ago, he little dreamed that this finger-post of scorn would be used at the end of the century to wile the

* From a painting executed from life when Dickens revisited this country in 1867, by Sol Eytinge, who was then renowned as the most popular illustrator of Dickens's works in America. The picture is now in the possession of Mr. W. E. Benjamin, 10 West Twenty-second Street, New York, through whose courtesy we are permitted to reproduce it. With possibly the exception of a limited number of lithographs made in Boston some years ago, no print of this portrait has ever appeared before.

CHARLES DICKENS.

From a drawing by "Spy" in *Vanity Fair*, 1870.

reader to certain writings of his own which have only now been collected in book-form, and which have never before been published in America in any form. The title is an apt one. In the main we prefer new lamps to old ones; but when those old lamps happen to be lighted by the genius of a Dickens, we are very willing to give in exchange for them, even at a sacrifice, many of our new *fin de siècle* lamps. To Mr. Frederick G. Kitton, the well-known Dickens authority, we are indebted for the recovery of these papers from what Dickens himself designates "the Old Lamp Market!" Mr. Kitton is a thorough scholar, and he has been at great pains searching out, identifying and collecting the miscellaneous sketches, essays, letters, reviews, etc., which Dickens contributed for the most part anonymously to *Bentley's Miscellany*, *Household Words*, *All the Year Round*, the London *Daily News*, and other periodicals. The results of this industry have been gathered in a volume of no mean bulk, judging by the number of articles which have been unearthed. Mr. Kitton has written an Introduction for the book, which we have not yet seen, but we have been permitted through the courtesy of the publishers, the New Amsterdam Book Company, to examine the proofs of the Dickens material. The English edition will be entitled *To be Read at Dusk*, and will contain a paper of that name and several others published under the same title some years ago by Messrs. Houghton, Mifflin and Company. The major part by far, however, has never been collected before, and the American edition now being published consists only of matter that has not hitherto appeared in this country. The American title, as we have said, will be *Old Lamps for New Ones*.

When, like the magician, we come to rub these "old lamps," what do they evoke? Are they ineffectual and useless for entertainment or enlightenment, or do they still retain the alchemic power of summoning once more the genii of the lamp? It is often a thankless task, not to say an unworthy one, the raking together of material which a great writer has let fall by the wayside during his lifetime. The demand of posterity on the product of a writer is often beyond any just claim it has upon him, and it is bred not infrequently of an unhealthy curiosity and pragmatical instinct, which

Dickens himself has severely castigated in one of these collected papers. But so long as there is a public with an insatiate maw, and a publisher with the enterprise to conjure with a great name, we cannot expect these poor ghosts to be allowed to rest unmolested. Yet this retrogressive principle has its compensation: sometimes by its means a pearl is found in the oyster embedded in the journalism of the past, or to revert to our original figure, a light is discovered that has been hidden under a bushel. Frequently instructive facts or hints of truth are elicited that throw light upon the author's personality or explain more fully his methods of working, his development as a writer. At the least, they afford passing amusement or temporary relief from the *ennui* of the hour produced by the newest indigestibles. It may be, too, that they induce a fresh interest in an old favourite, and make us hark back to the works that fed the perennial springs of our youth.

"A TALE OF TWO CITIES"

But to our question regarding these "old things" of Dickens. The genii is never far away, without doubt, sometimes very dimly apprehended, oftentimes in all the vigour and presence of his better self. The stamp of Dickens's mind is upon them all, they bear his unmistakable imprint. The fun and frolic, the wit and humour, the satire and savagery, the advocate of reform, and the special pleader of the poor, the chivalry of literary brotherhood and the pride of letters, the prejudices, the whimsicalities, the affectation of pomposity and bombast, the intense feeling and burning sincerity—all are here, and as a flame in the midst shedding its glow and irradiating its vital spark throughout, there is the unfailing light of Dickens's imagination. To be sure, these qualities play upon subjects that belong to a day that is dead, and in so far as they are remote from our present interests in life, the sum total of their bygone attraction is diminished for us now. But to the lover of Dickens, especially to the admirer of his satire and humour, these papers will be full of delight and reminiscent pleasure when read in the light of his standard works. Many of them are the incarnation of Boz. Indeed, in reading them, we are reminded of the words of the distinguished scholar, poet, and philosopher yet among us, who, when asked what he considered "the best bits of literature," made bold answer, "The buried thoughts in anonymous journalism."

But we must hasten to give the reader a foretaste of these forthcoming sketches of Dickens. From the initial article, which gives the book its title, we cull the following *jeu d'esprit* from the writer's stream of satire :

"In literature, a very spirited effort has been made, which is no less than the formation of a P.G.A.P.C.B., or Pre-Gower and Pre-Chaucer Brotherhood, for the restoration of the ancient English style of spelling, and the weeding out from all libraries, public and private, of those and all later pretenders, particularly a person of loose character named Shakespeare. It having been suggested, however, that this happy idea could scarcely be considered complete while the art of printing was permitted to remain unmolested, another society, under the name of the Pre-Laurentius Brotherhood, has been established in connection with it, for the abolition of all but manuscript books. These Mr. Pugin has engaged to supply in characters that nobody on earth shall be able to read. And it is confidently expected by those who have seen the House of Lords, that he will faithfully redeem his pledge."

There is published the humorous announcement which appeared at the opening of the second number of *Bentley's Miscellany*, edited by Boz, in 1837, headed "Extraordinary Gazette," and containing the "speeches of His Mightiness, the Editor," who is described in his progress to New Burlington Street as

"receiving with the utmost affability the numerous petitions of the crossing-sweepers ; and being repeatedly and loudly hailed by the cabmen on the different stands in the line of road through which he passed. His Mightiness appeared in the highest possible spirits ; and immediately after his arrival at the House delivered himself of the following most gracious speech ."

Then follow several fictitious speeches to various bodies, one of them beginning :

"MY LORDS, LADIES, AND GENTLEMEN :

"I continue to receive from Foreign Powers undeniable assurances of their disinterested regard and esteem. The free and independent States of America have done me the honour to reprint my Sketches, gratuitously ; and to circulate them throughout the Possessions of the British Crown in India, without charging me anything at all. I think I shall recognise Don Carlos if I ever meet him in the street ; and I am sure I shall at once know the King of the French, for I have seen him before."

As a dramatic critic we have Dickens's criticism of "Macready as 'Benedick'" in *Much Ado About Nothing*, given at Drury Lane in the year 1843. From quite an extensive and interesting critique of the great actor, we quote this passage :

"Judging of it by analogy ; by comparison with anything we know in nature, literature, art ; by any test we can apply to it, from within us or without, we can imagine no purer or higher piece of genuine comedy than Mr. Macready's performance of the scene in the orchard after emerging from the arbour. As he sat, uneasily cross-legged, on the garden chair, with that face of grave bewilderment and puzzled contemplation, we seemed to be looking on a picture by Leslie. It was just such a figure as that excellent artist, in his fine appreciation of the finest humour, might have delighted to produce. Those who consider it broad, or farcical or overstrained cannot surely have considered all the train and course of circumstances leading up to that place. If they take them into reasonable account, and try to imagine for a moment how any master of fiction would have described 'Benedick's' behaviour at that crisis—supposing it had been impossible to contemplate the appearance of a living man in the part, and therefore necessary to describe it at all—can they arrive at any other conclusion than that such ideas as are here presented by Mr. Macready would have been written down? Refer to any passage in any play of Shakespeare's, where it has been necessary to describe, as occurring beyond the scene, the behaviour of a man in a situation of ludicrous perplexity, and by that standard alone (to say nothing of any mistaken notion of natural behaviour that may have suggested itself at any time to Goldsmith, Swift, Fielding, Smollett, Sterne, Scott, or other such unenlightened journeymen) criticise, if you please, this portion of Mr. Macready's admirable performance."

Again as a critic of art in an article on George Cruikshank's *Drunkard's Children* "in eight plates," Dickens shows an acquaintance with the technique of the subject, and an observation of the people it depicts, which illustrate the versatility of his genius. In a digression on Hogarth in this paper he touches on a phase of his art which adds to our enlightenment of the artist's method and purpose. He says :

"Hogarth avoided the Drunkard's Progress, we conceive, precisely because the causes of drunkenness among the poor were so numerous and widely spread, and lurked so sorrowfully deep and far down in all human misery, neglect, and despair, that even *his* pencil could not bring them fairly and justly into the light. That he was never contented with beginning all the effect, witness the Miser (his shoe new-soled with the binding of his Bible) dead before the Young Rake begins his career; the worldly father, listless daughter, impoverished nobleman, and crafty lawyer in the first plate of the *Mariage à la Mode;* the detestable advances in the Stages of Cruelty; and the progress downward of Thomas Idle! That he did not spare that kind of drunkenness which was of more 'respectable' engenderment, his midnight modern conversation, the election plates, and a crowd of stupid aldermen and other guzzlers amply testify. But after one immortal journey down Gin Lane he turned away in grief and sorrow--perhaps in hope of better things one day, from better laws, and schools, and poor men's homes—and went back no more. It is remarkable of that picture that, while it exhibits drunkenness in its most appalling forms, it forces on the attention of the spectator a most neglected, wretched neighbourhood (the same that is only just now cleared away for the extension of Oxford Street), and an unwholesome, indecent, abject condition of life, worthy to be a Frontispiece to the late Report of the Sanitary Commissioners, made nearly one hundred years afterward. We have always been inclined to think the purpose of this piece not adequately stated, even by Charles Lamb. 'The very houses seem absolutely reeling,' it is true; but they quite as powerfully indicate some of the more prominent causes of intoxication among the neglected orders of society, as any of its effects. There is no evidence that any of the actors in the dreary scene have ever been much better off than we find them. The best are pawning the commonest necessaries and tools of their trades, and the worst are homeless vagrants who give us no clue to their having been otherwise in by-gone days. All are living and dying miserably. Nobody is interfering for prevention or for cure in the generation going out before us or the generation coming in. The beadle (the only sober man in the composition except the pawnbroker) is mightily indifferent to the orphan child crying beside its parents' coffin. The little charity girls are not so well taught or looked after but that they can take to dram-drinking already. The church is very prominent and handsome, but coldly surveys these things in progress underneath the shadow of its tower (it was in the year of grace eighteen hundred and forty-eight that a Bishop of London first came out respecting something wrong in poor men's social accommodations), and is passive in the picture. We take all this to have a meaning, and to the best of our knowledge it has not grown obsolete in a century."

There is also an appreciation of John Leech's *Rising Generation*, a series of twelve drawings "from original designs in the Gallery of Mr. Punch." At the close of this paper, which was written in 1848, there is a fling at the Royal Academy's excluding such men as Cruikshank and Leech from its membership, and a prescient forecast which, as everybody knows, has been since verified.

"Will no Members and Associates be found upon its books, one of these days, the labours of whose oils and brushes will have sunk into the profoundest obscurity, when the many pencil marks of Mr. Cruikshank and of Mr. Leech will still be fresh in half the houses in the land?"

In such themes as "The China Junk," a floating bit of Chinatown near London; in "The American Panorama," an extraordinary exhibition of Banvard's Geographical Panorama of the Mississippi and Missouri Rivers given at the Egyptian Hall in 1848; in "An American in Europe," who

"in an evil hour committed the two volumes before us, in which—

'He talks so like a waiting gentlewoman,
Of napkins, forks, and spoons (God save the mark!)'

that the dedication of his book to Lady Byron is an obvious mistake, and an outrage on the rights of Mr. N. P. Willis!"—

in two papers on "The Amusements of the People," in which Dickens follows the ecstasies of one Joe Whelks through his favourite form of the drama —*May Morning, or the Mystery of 1715, and the Murder!* at the Victoria, for instance ——; in "Whole Hogs," which is so delightfully Bozian with its Teatotal Procession, its distinguished Vegetarians and Fleshmeatarians; its Reverend Jabez Fireworks, fond of speaking; its Mr. Gloss, the gentleman with the stand-up collar; Mr. Glib, with the massive watch chain, who smiles so sweetly on the surrounding Fair; Mr. Scradger, looking like a converted Hyæna; the dark-eyed brown gentleman, the Dove Delegate from America; in "Trading in Death," which bares the travesty of State Funerals, particularly Wellington's; in "The Other Public," which includes another facetious American "Note;" and in "The Tattlesnivel Bleater," which strikes at the subtle and malevolent influence wielded by the "London Correspondent"—in these and in others we have not enumerated, the Pickwickian wit and penetrating satire are at work; and despite the distance which separates us from the contemporaneousness of the subjects we are constantly entertained by Dickens's immortal spirit of humour, which now glances and gladdens with the harmless incandescence of summer lightning, and again flashes and strikes with the electric charge of a deadly current. The latter effect is strongly exemplified in the handling of "The Ballantyne Humbug," relative to the base charges made by the younger Ballantyne against the reputation of Sir Walter Scott, and also in the papers on "The Worthy Magistrate" and "Capital Punishment."

THE STUDY AT GADSHILL.

Americans will read with mingled feelings of amusement and mournful interest the paper entitled "The Young Man from the Country," written in 1862, twenty years subsequent to the writing of *American Notes*. The article begins:

"A song of the hour, now in course of being sung and whistled in every street, the other day reminded the writer of these words—as he chanced to pass a fag-end of the song for the twentieth time in a short London walk—that twenty years ago a little book on the United States entitled *American Notes* was published by 'A Young Man from the Country,' who had just seen and left it.

"This Young Man from the Country fell into a deal of trouble, by reason of having taken the liberty to believe that he perceived in America downward popular tendencies, for which his young enthusiasm had been anything but prepared. It was in vain for the Young Man to offer in extenuation of his belief that no stranger could have set foot on those shores with a feeling of livelier interest in the country and stronger faith in it than he. Those were the days when the Tories had made their Ashburton Treaty, and when Whigs and Radicals must have no theory disturbed. All three parties waylaid and mauled the Young Man from the Country, and showed that he knew nothing about the country.

"As the Young Man from the Country had observed in the Preface to his little book, that he 'could bide his time,' he took all this in silent part for eight years. Publishing then a cheap edition of his book, he made no stronger protest than the following:"

Then follows the preface which appeared in 1850, but of which only the first paragraph in the preface as it is now printed remains intact. The words "—but not wilfully" were added later at the end of this paragraph, and instead of the warm expression of regard for this country, which characterises the second paragraph as it now stands, the following is what was originally printed in 1850, and which was, subsequent to Dickens's second visit to America, in 1868, eliminated:

"I have nothing to defend or to explain away. The truth is the truth, and neither childish absurdities nor unscrupulous contradictions can make it otherwise. The earth would still move round the sun, though the whole Catholic Church said, No!"

But this article we must remember was written in 1862. The Young Man from the Country goes on to make large quotations from his "little book," and then concludes:

"The foregoing was written in the year eighteen hundred and forty-two. It rests with the reader to decide whether it has received any confirmation or assumed any colour of truth in or about the year eighteen hundred and sixty-two."

It is matter of history, and still within the painful remembrance of the living, that Dickens stirred up a hornet's nest when he published his *American Notes*, and that although he modified his opinions and estimate of the country and its people when he revisited it twenty-six years later, the disagreeable and unfavourable impressions created by his *Notes* have never been wholly eradicated. Only the other day the writer was talking with a highly cultivated woman of refined tastes, who recalled the disillusionment which her young girlhood's dream of Dickens encountered, and who spoke with ill-concealed contempt of the effect of his public appearance upon her mind. With the rise of a younger generation this may in time disappear.

Meanwhile to the student of modern literature in general, and of Dickens in particular—to all who would forego new lamps for old ones to illumine the dusk of a leisurely evening hour we commend this heterogeneous mosaic of Dickensiana. To the disciples of Dickens the volume will carry its own credentials without any other introduction. The Introduction which Mr. Kitton is to contribute will, we may be sure, enhance vastly the bibliographical value and interest of the collection.

James MacArthur.

FAC-SIMILE OF THE AUTOGRAPH SIGNATURE "BOZ."

WITHIN THE WALLS.

O Bertrand, I am dying, I, a nun,
But life was not in cloister walls begun,
    As life is done,
But midst the surging passions of the world,
Where life in myriad colours lies unfurled,
    All opal pearled.

My years have passed in twilight monotone
Of kindly nuns and stern, unyielding stone.
    I lived alone.
In dying, twilight comes to every soul,
All passion still, wherein God takes control.
    God will console.

And now as on dim journeying I start,
Where life begins, where life must first depart,
    Come thou, sweetheart.
Kiss the pale hands laid on my quiet breast ;
The poor clay loved thee well, thus let it rest,
    By love reblessed.

If in my face unmasked by death you see
The love that needs must live, my love to thee,
    God gave it me.
Rebuke me not. Earth's love came next to Heaven.
My life thus forced on God was truly given,
    Although heart riven.

So once again I bid my love farewell,
As long ago in sunny Rosendell,
    Now in my cell.
No tears, beloved one, as heretofore.
What God has taken He will fain restore
    For evermore.

Alice Wardwell.

THE PROGRESS OF "FONETIK REFAWRM."

There is in this city a firm of publishers whose energetic optimism and tireless activities have always found the field of their nominal occupation to be prosaic, cramping, and hopelessly commonplace. They do, indeed, occasionally publish books, or at least we have so understood; but the work which is the nearest to their hearts is the instant abolition of the traffic in strong drink, the universal reign of total abstinence, and the immediate elimination from the human breast of all desire for stimulants and nicotine. Yet, of course, a trifling task like this, so absurdly simple, and as easy as rolling off a log, has very naturally left these earnest gentlemen with a good deal of spare time upon their hands, and they have very often been in danger of becoming seriously bored; so that by way of filling in their idle moments and preventing any waste of power, they have lately taken up another bagatelle in setting modestly about the reformation of the English language, and more particularly of its orthography.

Some time ago they made a list of words of which the current spelling troubled them; and after thinking very hard indeed, and after conferring with some other very wise and thoughtful persons, they tabulated and printed all these words and spelled them in a new and better way, a way that was more pleasing both to the earnest publishers themselves and to the wise and thoughtful persons with whom they had conferred. Then they sent a copy of the list to many men throughout the length and breadth of our beloved country—to authors, to teachers, to clergymen, to editors, to statesmen; and they announced that as soon as one hundred very eminent men should agree to adopt these new and better spellings, then the publishers who had made the list would also use them in their printing office. Time passed; and now the publishers are carrying out their promise; for one hundred very eminent men *have* approved the list. And we know that these very eminent men are really very eminent, because the publishers admit it frankly. They do not even attempt to deny it. And the very eminent men themselves have never published any contradiction of their own eminence. So it is all right.

Now, this is only one of a good many attempts that have been made to knock a few foundation-stones out of the orthographic structure of the English language, to substitute for definite and accepted forms with which every one is perfectly familiar, which have a meaning and a history of their own, and which ensure a practical uniformity in our printed books, some other way of spelling. Ever since old Noah Webster, that half-baked, priggish, and conceited pedant, first produced the book which several generations of abler men, by throwing out pretty nearly everything that he had put in it, have at last made over into a work of some authority, somebody or other has always been tinkering with reformed orthography. Josh Billings tried it; some theoretical persons in the American Philological Association have taken a crack at it; and, indeed, very seldom is any notorious crank kept awake at night by the tooth-ache, without concocting before daylight a brand-new, hand-painted scheme for the reform of English spelling.

Well, this sort of thing has been going steadily on for some three-quarters of a century, and the accepted forms have not been substantially altered in the usage of educated men. Perhaps this last attempt of the earnest publishers has shown the very fewest signs of producing any tangible results. So far as our observation goes, they will not see their list in vogue until long after the arrival of the Greek Kalends on which they shall have finally dethroned the demon Rum. In fact, only once have we seen their system publicly adopted. This solitary instance was when another publisher in a reckless moment sent out an advertisement of a religious book, printed in large capitals, and with a sort of centre-piece which demanded sternly of the reader

"DOO YOO BELEEV IN HEL?"

—an entirely unnecessary question, since every one who has ever had to do with spelling reformers is absolutely obliged

THE OLD MANSE, THE FIRST CONCORD HOME OF EMERSON AND HAWTHORNE.

AMERICAN BOOKMEN.

VIII.—Emerson and Concord.

When Dr. Holmes finished his *Life of Emerson* in 1884, he wrote in a letter about it: "The truth is that Emerson's life and writings have been so *darned over* by biographers and critics that a new hand can hardly tell his own yarn from that of his predecessors, or one of theirs from another's." Three years later appeared the more complete *Memoir of Ralph Waldo Emerson*, by James Elliot Cabot, his literary executor, and almost incessantly since then the process of darning and re-darning has been kept up. It is less with the hope, therefore, of saying new things than of refreshing the memory of the old that any attempt to consider the circumstances of Emerson's life must now be made. The teachings of his philosophy may receive new illumination from its disciples. New applications of it to new problems will doubtless be possible for many years to come. The story of his living told itself, and it is enough if somebody will merely repeat it from time to time. It is its own interpretation, and needs no commentator to point out either the seeming unattainableness of some of its standards for common flesh and blood, or the lofty value of its example as a freed life of intellect and spirit, a breath as of "winds, austere and pure," in the thick air of a workaday world.

There are two ways of using a village as a place to live in. The one is to take the freedom from the engrossing concerns of city life as an excuse for falling back upon the pettinesses of a small community, and standing so close to trivial things that their size is magnified out of all proportion, and the prospect of larger things beyond is blotted out. The other way is to use one's freedom for seeing things both near and far in their true dimensions. The Massachusetts village of Concord, for a considerable part of our century, has been a place where the practice of this second method was to be found. Any village in which Emerson, Hawthorne, and Thoreau, to cite its greatest names, were living at one time must have been such a place. It is not unnatural that the villagers themselves should have magnified the importance of some of their lesser names. When the amusing writer who made it his task to describe America and the Americans from the

EMERSON'S HOUSE AT CONCORD.

French point of view, native or acquired, was taken to Concord, he had to confess that some of the names with which he was expected to be familiar—"that of a man named Alcott, for example"—were quite unknown to him. His point of view was as much that of the outside world as Alcott's own outlook seems to have been parochial. Emerson himself told the story of having asked Alcott one day what he could show for himself, what he had really done to justify his existence. "If Pythagoras came to Concord," was the triumphant reply, "whom would he ask to see?" The sage was safe in his retort, but whatever the parochial illusions may have been, any pilgrim to Concord in the days of its distinction must have recognized it as a place where the better sort of village life was eagerly lived, and have known that men and not the village had brought him on his pilgrimage.

Of all the men of thought and letters who contributed in a greater and less degree to this distinction of the town, Thoreau was the only one who was born in Concord. Yet Emerson, by every right of inheritance, was more truly its son. The town was founded by a direct ancestor, the Rev. Peter Bulkeley, who came to America in 1635. His granddaughter married an Emerson, a minister, who died in Concord in 1680; and his grandson, William Emerson, the minister of the town at the time of the Revolution and the first occupant of the "Old Manse," was the grandfather of Ralph Waldo Emerson, whose father was another Rev. William Emerson, minister of the First Church in Boston. Made up of ministers and graduates of Harvard College, the race was eminently of the sort which Dr. Holmes has defined as academic. Ralph Waldo, born in Boston on May 25th, 1803, was the fourth of eight children. Two girls and a boy died in early childhood, and of the boys that remained their remarkable aunt, Mary Moody Emerson, well said, "They were born to be educated."

This was no easy end for their mother to achieve in the straitened days that followed the death of the Rev. William Emerson in 1811. But the First Church and a few kind friends and kinsmen lent their aid, and the established training of good Bostonians, through the Latin School and Harvard College, was made possible. There were times when Ralph, as he was then called, and his brother Edward had to share the use of one overcoat, and jeering school-fellows would ask, "Whose turn is it to-day?" The boys helped in the household duties, such as driving the cow from the house where they once lived, near the present site of the Boston Athenæum, to a pasture beyond the Common, and took far less time for play than for the improvement of their minds. At school and college Emerson made himself the name which is commonly won by studious boys of slender health and means, and of talents not phenomenal. He was fourteen years old when he entered Harvard College, and became "President's freshman," a kind of errand-boy for the faculty, with the privilege *ex officio* of serving as a waiter at commons, and paying thereby for three fourths of his own board. During his course he took prizes for dissertations and declamation, and wrote the class poem after seven youths had declined the honor; but at the end his college rank was only a little above the middle of the class.

A CURIOUS EARLY PORTRAIT OF EMERSON.

From college Emerson followed the path he might have been expected to take, the path of a school-teacher. His purpose to make it the means of approach to the ministry was less definite than in many cases like his own. It seems to have been a disappointment to him that in teaching others he did not learn more himself. His scholars in various places, however, were unconscious of shortcomings One of them has recorded the efficacy of his reproof, consisting merely of the words, "Oh, sad!" soberly spoken to a youthful offender. His own youthfulness was not overlooked by the young ladies, some of them older than himself, whom he taught in Boston. On Election Day, it is told, they used to ask him for a holiday that he might vote, and would rejoice in the blushes of their master, still a minor. To Emerson the period was one of dissatisfaction and drudgery. In his journal of 1824, a week before he came of age, he made the entry: "I deliberately dedicate my time, my talents, and my hopes to the Church;" and before a year had passed—that is, in February of 1825—he found himself established in Divinity Hall at Cambridge as a student for the ministry.

The ministerial period of Emerson's life was full of struggle and perplexity. Ill health was the first obstacle he had to overcome. The weakness of his eyes interrupted his studies at once, and the weakness of his lungs made it necessary for him to spend nearly the whole winter and spring of 1827 in the South. Then there were inward questionings about the rightfulness of his place even within the flexible boundaries of Unitarianism. Whatever the younger men of his day may be writing to aunts who have their confidence, Emerson at twenty-three was not using the language of his contemporaries when he wrote to Mary Moody Emerson: "'Tis a queer life, and the only humour proper to it seems quiet astonishment." One of the maxims of his life, early inculcated by this strenuous aunt, was, "Always do what you are afraid to do." Both in the earlier and in the later days of his ministry this rule must have been in some measure his guide. He did not do the easy thing in establishing himself successfully as a minister; and when the time came to choose between the pleasant incumbency of the Second Church in Boston and an adherence to his personal opinion in a matter of worship, it would have been the course of least resistance to retain his post and modify his views. The issue between him and his parishioners was vital; he had ceased to think the regular administration of the communion essential or even desirable; naturally his people thought otherwise. He made no attempt to impose his views upon them, but when it was clear that no common ground was tenable, he set forth in a sermon his reasons for thinking as he did, and brought to an end his connection with the parish. There was the best of good feeling on each side. In many ways he had shown eminent fitness for the ministry. When a good choir sang, "its best was coarse and discordant after Emerson's voice." His sermons delighted even those who failed to understand them. The sincerity of his more personal relations and the inherent charm of the man made him abundantly beloved. In his strictly ministerial functions it appears that he was not always successful. The story is told that once when he was called to the death-bed of a Revolutionary soldier, and showed some difficulty in administering the usual consolations, the veteran summoned all his strength to exclaim: "Young man, if you don't know your business, you had better go home." But it was the inward voice and not rebuffs like this that brought him to the wise decision that his work in the world could not be that of a regular minister.

Emerson had married his first wife, Miss Ellen Louisa Tucker, in September of 1829, and early in 1831 she had died. It was in 1832 that he resigned his ministry at the Second Church. It is no wonder that the end of a period so filled with anxiety was marked by the breaking down of his own health. On Christmas Day of 1832 he sailed in a small brig for the Mediterranean, and devoted the greater part of 1833 to regaining his strength in Italy, France, and England. That he could describe Venice as "a great oddity, a city for beavers, but, to my thought, a most disagreeable residence," may suggest that the picturesque interest of foreign lands was less to him than the human. Indeed, it was the hope of searching out Carlyle, in whose contributions to the English reviews he had detected the accent of a spiritual kinsman, that hurried him from Paris to London, and from London to Craigenputtuck in Scotland, where guest and host each discovered in a day and night what was best in the other, and laid the foundations of the friendship which for nearly forty years survived the difficulties of correspondence. The basis of their sympathy has been well defined by Dr. Holmes: "The hatred of unreality was uppermost with Carlyle; the love of what is real and genuine with Emerson." It was through Emerson in the thirties that Carlyle first found an American audience, and through Emerson in 1870 Carlyle's gift of the books he had purchased and used in writing *Cromwell* and *Frederick the Great* was made to Harvard College.

I see the inundation sweet,
I hear the spending of the stream
Through years, through men, through Nature fleet,
Through passion, thought—through power and dream.

R. Waldo Emerson

Concord, Massachusetts—
December 10, 1878.

AUTOGRAPH LINES FROM EMERSON'S "TWO RIVERS."

From an engraving, by W. Wright Smith, of the crayon drawing by Rowse

It has often been questioned, however, whether the friendship could have been so well maintained if Carlyle had yielded to Emerson's constant solicitations to come to Concord.

In Concord Emerson established himself soon after his return from Europe. Before his second marriage, in 1835, to Miss Lydia Jackson, of Plymouth, he and his mother went to live in the "Old Manse" with the Rev. Dr. Ripley, who long before had become the second husband of Emerson's grandmother. Here he worked upon his essay, "Nature," which, published anonymously in 1836, was the first important statement of his philosophy; and here he bore the first weeks of grief for the death of his gifted younger "brother of the brief, but blazing star," Edward Bliss Emerson, of whom he wrote in prose, "I am bereaved of a part of myself," and in poetry the lines, "In Memoriam." Within two years died another brother, Charles Chauncy Emerson, who was soon to have married Miss Elizabeth Hoar, of Concord, and Emerson wrote to his young wife: "You must be content henceforth with only a piece of your husband; for the best of his strength lay in the soul with which he must no more on earth take counsel." It was the same sense of loss which found expression in the "Threnody" on the death of his oldest child, Waldo, in 1842:

> "The eager fate which carried thee
> Took the largest part of me:
> For this losing is true dying;
> This is lordly man's down-lying."

When Emerson "dodged the doom of building," and, in 1835, bought the Coolidge house, standing on the road over which the British fled from Concord to Lexington, he settled into the ways of life from which thenceforth he made few departures. For about three years he continued to preach in one place and another where he was wanted, and then made a complete end of his active ministry. But there were other ways of delivering to men the messages he had to impart, and the lecture took with him the place of the sermon. The growth of the lyceum system was opportune for Emerson. "His, if any one's," said Alcott, "let the institution pass into history, since his art, more than another's, has clothed it with beauty, and made it the place of popular resort." Early and late, east and

EMERSON IN 1878.

From *Scribner's Monthly*, now the *Century Magazine*, by permission. Reproduced from an engraving by T. Cole of Wyatt Eaton's drawing.

west, he went about with his lectures, bearing delight and stimulus to many minds. For the discomforts he suffered, his journal speaks :

"It was, in short—this dragging a decorous old gentleman out of home and out of position, to this juvenile career—tantamount to this : 'I'll bet you fifty dollars a day for three weeks that you will not leave your library, and wade, and freeze, and ride, and run, and suffer all manner of indignities, and stand up for an hour each night reading in a hall ;' and I answer, 'I'll bet I will.' I do it and win the nine hundred dollars."

The beginnings of this work were made nearer home, in courses of lectures in Boston, in the notable Phi Beta Kappa oration, "The American Scholar" at Harvard, in 1837, and in the address to the Senior Class of the Divinity School at Cambridge in 1838. The religious radicalism of this address caused indeed what Emerson defined in a letter to Carlyle as a "storm in our washbowl." It determined Emerson's separation from the churches, and, for many years, from his *alma mater*. The University at the close of the war made amends for its share in the estrangement by asking him to speak at the commemoration exercises ; in 1866 he was made an overseer and a Doctor of Laws ; and in 1867 he delivered for the second time a Phi Beta Kappa oration. It was after hearing this that Lowell wrote to Mr. Norton the words which described all the weaknesses of Emerson's oratory, especially in later years, and also set forth its peculiar strength :

"It began nowhere, and ended everywhere, and yet, as always with that divine man, it left you feeling that something beautiful had passed that way—something more beautiful than anything else, like the rising and setting of stars. . . . He boggled, he lost his place, he had to put on his glasses ; but it was as if a creature from some fairer world had lost his way in our fogs, and it was *our* fault, not his."

If the lecturing began near home, the source of the lectures themselves was still more intimate. Through all of Emerson's life he kept a journal, of which he wrote in 1837 :

"This book is my savings bank. I grow richer because I have somewhere to deposit my earnings, and fractions are worth more to me because corresponding fractions are waiting here that shall be made integers by their addition."

To Carlyle Emerson wrote in 1840 :

"I dot evermore in my endless journal a line on every knowable in nature ; but the arrangement loiters long, and I get a brick-kiln instead of a house."

From this store of material the builder frequently drew when the time came to write. If his writing has been found disjointed by others, and has seemed to himself a collection of "paragraphs irrepressible, each sentence an infinitely repellent particle," it is well to remember this fractional origin of it. If the form has suffered, surely the spirit has gained in the spontaneity of thoughts recorded almost at the moment of their birth. From the journal to the lecture, from the lecture to the essay, pruned of anecdote and illustration—such was the evolution of a great part of Emerson's prose. Many of the poems had a sim-

RALPH WALDO EMERSON.

From an original drawing, artist unknown, now reproduced through the courtesy of W. E. Benjamin.

ilar origin. Extracts from the journal have shown the first conceptions, for example, of his "Two Rivers" and "Sea-Shore." Of "Days" there is the remarkable record in the journal for 1852, almost as of another "Kubla Khan:"

"I find one state of mind does not remember or conceive of another state. Thus I have written within a twelvemonth verses (Days) which I do not remember the composition or correction of, and could not write the like to-day, and have only for proof of their being mine various external evidences, as the manuscripts in which I find them, and the circumstances that I have sent copies to friends, etc. Well if they had been better, if it had been a noble poem, perhaps it would have only more entirely taken up the ladder into heaven."

Deep the dusk of the darkened room,
Touched with a sombre tinge of gloom.
Curtained window and hooded wall
Prison the silence of evenfall ;
While, from the hearthstone's ample pyre,
Thin red flames of the sea-coal fire
Pierce through the wreathing rings of smoke
To gleam on the panels of polished oak.

Over the hearth, with a dreamy air,
Bends a form that is brooding there ;
One who reads in the heart of flame,
Changing ever yet still the same,
All the tale of an ended strife,
All the years of a happy life ;
Years of the past that have gone before,
Years that the future holds in store,
Blazing there in their frame of night,
Written in letters of lambent light.

First in the pictured past he sees
Plenty and peace and fruitful ease ;
Labour crowned with a swift success,
Free from the taint of bitterness ;

Friends whose truth he has learned of old,—
Faithful friends with the heart of gold ;
And men have praised and women have smiled,
He has heard the laugh of a loving child,
And never a sky is overcast
In the sunlit years of the pictured past.

Flames the fire : it glints and glows
Red as the heart of a royal rose.
There the path of the coming years
Bright in the blazing fire appears,
Still the tale of a conquered fate,
Still the promise of guerdon great :
Fortune's favour that giveth all ;
Gold that gleams at the master's call ;
Honour and health and hope unroll
Written large in the flaming scroll,
Till at the last he sees his name
Touched by the spark that men call Fame.

Just for a moment he stirs—and then,
Bending over the fire again,
Seeks and finds in the fateful coal
The hidden thought of his secret soul.
Clear and true in its subtle grace
Glows the curve of a woman's face,
Fringed with tresses in silken strands,
And lightly leant on a woman's hands.

Leaps his heart and his pulses swell
At the haunting charm that he knows so well—
Eyes that promise and then deny,
Wake desire and bid it die,
Lips whose kiss it were all to win,
Sweet as the savour of secret sin,
And hands that were made so slim and white
To beckon a lover through the night.

Long he looks on the scorching scroll,
Looks and longs with a yearning soul ;
Looks till the red pales into grey,
Looks till the picture fades away
And his aching eyes with a mist are dim,
For well does he know they are not for him.
Not for him is the sweet surprise
That lures and laughs in the slumbrous eyes,
Not for him is the loosened tress,
Not for him is the long caress,
And the warm white hands and the fingers slim
That thrill with a touch are not for him.

Thus, though the past is flushed with light,
Though the future shines with a promise bright,
His heart is stilled by a sudden pain,
Past and Present and Future wane,
And all would he give for the hope within
Of that which he sought and failed to win.

Deepens the dusk : the sea-coals burn,
Into a dull grey ash they turn.
One by one each crimson eye
Dies in the dark as passions die ;
Till, when only an after-glow,
Sombre and sullen and strange and slow,
Fades and falls to a fitful gleam,
What is left of the vanished dream ?
Only the throb of a dumb desire
And the flickering flame of the failing fire.

Harry Thurston Peck.

AN EPOCH-MAKING LEXICON.

That there is an urgent demand for a great Latin lexicon, on modern lines, is obvious to any serious student of the language. The rapid advances which have been made in all branches of classical philology, and the vast amount of new material which has come to light, particularly in the form of inscriptions, together with the progress which has marked the science of lexicography itself, have rendered the earlier works in that line antiquated. Even De Vit's revision of Forcellini's great dictionary is very far from being satisfactory, and the excellent handbook of the late Professor Georges, while admirable for the purpose for which it was designed, and in not a few respects superior to the Forcellini-De Vit, does not pretend to fill the gap.

For the carrying out of such an undertaking we naturally look to Germany ; and in fact the project has been agitated there at intervals for upward of a century. In 1858 fulfilment seemed near at hand, when Max II., King of Bavaria, guaranteed the sum of 10,000 gulden for the purpose, and Professors Ritschl, Halm, and Fleckeisen received editorial charge of the work. But just as everything seemed to be progressing favorably, certain difficulties of organisation rendered the plan abortive. This postponement of the enterprise was not in all respects an unmixed evil, for the thirty years which have elapsed have been years of great activity in classical studies, and the times are now decidedly riper for the successful carrying out of the difficult task. It is true that even now satisfactory editions of very many texts, especially in the later Latin, are not yet at hand ; but the same thing will be true a good many years from now, and there really seems to be no sound reason for further delay.

After the failure of the plan of 1858 nothing definite was done until 1883, when the single-handed enterprise and devotion of one man gave new life to the scheme. This was Professor Wölfflin, the successor of Halm in the chair of Classical Philology at Munich, who, with some support from the Bavarian Academy of Sciences, but at considerable personal expense, established the *Archiv für lateinische Lexikographie und Grammatik*, a periodical whose sole design was to prepare the way for a great thesaurus of the Latin language. The services of a large number of collaborers were secured, and a great amount of material, in the form of Archiv-slips, had been sent in, in answer to the "ques-

IN KEDAR'S TENTS.*

By Henry Seton Merriman, Author of "The Sowers."

CHAPTER XXV.

SWORDCRAFT.

"Rien n'est plus courageux qu'un cœur patient, rien n'est plus sur de soi qu'un esprit doux."

The general set down his glass, and a queer light came into his eyes, usually so smiling and pleasant.

"Ah! Then you are right, my friend. Tell us your story as quickly as possible."

"It appears," said Concha, "that there has been in progress for many months a plot to assassinate the Queen Regent and to seize the person of the little Queen, expelling her from Spain and bringing in not Don Carlos, who is a spent firework, but a republic, a more dangerous firework, that usually bursts in the hands of those that light it. This plot has been finally put into shape by a letter. . . ."

He paused, tapped on the table with his bony fingers, and glanced at Estella.

". . . A letter which has been going the round of all the malconents in the Peninsula. Each faction-leader, to show that he has read it and agrees to obey its commands, initials the letter. It has then been returned to an intermediary, who sends it to the next—never by post, unless unavoidable, because the post is watched—always by hand, and usually by the hand of a person innocent of its contents."

"Yes," murmured the general absently, and there was a queer little triumphant smile on Estella's lips.

"To think," cried Concha, with a sudden fire less surprising in Spain than in England—"to think that we have all seen it, have touched it! Name of a saint, I had it under my hand, alone and unobserved, in the hotel at Algeciras, and I left it on the table. And now it has been the round, and all the initials are placed upon it, and it is for to-morrow."

"Where have you learnt this?" asked the general, in a voice that made Estella look at him. She had never seen him as his enemies had seen him, and even they confessed that he was always visible enough in action. Perhaps there was another man behind the personality of this deprecating, pleasant-spoken, little sybarite—a man who only appeared (oh, *rara avis!*) when he was wanted.

"No matter!" replied Concha, in a voice as hard and sharp.

"No, after all, it is of no matter so long as your information is reliable."

"You may stake your life on that," said Concha, and remembered the words ever after.

"It has been decided to make this journey from Seville to Madrid the opportunity of assassinating the Queen Regent."

"It will not be the first time they have tried," put in the general.

"No; but this time they will succeed, and it is to be here to morrow night, in Toledo. After the Queen Regent's death, and in the confusion that will supervene, the little Queen will disappear, and then upon the rubbish-heap will spring up the mushrooms, as they did in France, and this rubbish-heap, like the other, will foul the air of all Europe."

He shook his head pessimistically till the long, wispy gray hair waved from side to side, and his left hand, resting on the wrist-bone on the table, made an indescribable gesture that showed a fœtid air tainted by darksome growths.

There was a silence in the room, broken by no outside sound but the clink of champed bits as the horses stood in their traces below. Indeed, the city of Toledo seemed strangely still this evening, and the very air had a sense of waiting in it. The priest sat and looked at his lifelong friend, his furrowed face the incarnation of cynical hopelessness. "What is, is worst," he seemed to say. His yellow, wise old eyes watched the quick face with the air of one who, having posed an unsolvable problem, awaits with a sarcastic humour the admission of failure.

General Vincente, who had just finished his wine, wiped his moustache delicately with his pocket-handkerchief. He was thinking quickly, systematically, as men learn to think under fire.

Perhaps, indeed, he had the thoughts half-matured in his mind, as the greatest general the world has seen confessed that he ever had, that he was never taken quite by surprise. Vincente smiled as he thought, a habit he had acquired on the field, where a staff, and perhaps a whole army, took its cue from his face and read the turn of fortune there. Then he looked up straight at Estella, who was watching him.

"Can you start on a journey now, in five minutes?" he asked.

"Yes," she answered, rising and going toward the door.

"Have you a white mantilla among your travelling things?" he asked again.

Estella turned at the doorway and nodded.

"Then take it with you and a cloak; but no heavy luggage."

Estella closed the door.

"You can come with us?" said the general to Concha, half command, half interrogation.

"If you wish it."

"You may be wanted. I have a plan—a little plan," and he gave a short laugh. "It may succeed."

He went to a side-table, where some cold meats still stood, and taking up a small chicken daintily with a fork, he folded it in a napkin.

"It will be Saturday," he said simply, "before we have reached our journey's end, and you will be hungry. Have you a pocket?"

"Has a priest a pocket?" asked Concha, with a grim humour, and he slipped the provisions into the folds of his cassock. He was still eating a biscuit hurriedly.

"I believe you have no money," said the general suddenly.

"I have only enough," admitted the old man, "to take me back to Ronda, whither, by the way, my duty calls me."

"I think not. Your Master can spare you for a while; my mistress cannot do without you."

At this moment Estella came back into the room ready for her journey. The girl had changed of late. Her face had lost a little roundness and had gained exceedingly in expression. Her eyes, too, were different. That change had come to them which comes to all women between the ages of twenty and thirty, quite irrespective of their state. A certain restlessness or a quiet content are what one usually sees in a woman's face. Estella's eyes wore that latter look, which seems to indicate a knowledge of the meaning of life and a contentment that it should be no different.

Vincente was writing at the table.

"We shall want help," he said, without looking up. "I am sending for a good man."

And he smiled as he shook the small sand-caster over the paper.

"May one ask," said Concha, "where we are going?"

"We are going to Ciudad Real, my dear padre, since you are so curious; but we shall come back—we shall come back."

He was writing another despatch as he spoke, and at a sign from him Estella went to the door and clapped her hands, the only method of summoning a servant in general use at that time in Spain. The call was answered by an orderly, who stood at attention in the doorway for a full five minutes while the general wrote further orders in his neat, small caligraphy. There were half a dozen letters in all, curt, military despatches, without preamble and without mercy, for this soldier conducted military matters in a singularly domestic way, planning his campaigns by the fireside, and bringing about the downfall of an enemy while sitting in his daughter's drawing-room. Indeed, Estella's blotting-book bore the impress of more than one death-warrant, written casually on her stationery and with her pen.

"Will you have the goodness to despatch those at once?" was the message taken by the orderly to the general's aide-de-camp, and the gallopers, who were always in readiness, smiled as they heard the modest request.

"It will be pleasant to travel in the cool of the evening, provided that one guards against a chill," said the general, making his final preparations. "I require but a moment to speak to my faithful aide-de-camp, and then we embark."

The moon was rising as the carriage rattled across the bridge of Alcantara, and Larralde, taking the air between Wamba's Gate and the little fort that guards the entrance to the city, recognised the equipage as it passed him. He saw also the outline of Concha's figure in the darkest corner of the carriage, with his back to the horses, his head bowed in meditation. Estella he saw and recognised, while two mounted attendants, clattering in the rear of the carriage, testified by their presence to the fact that the general had taken the road again.

"It is well," said Larralde to himself. "They are all going back to Ronda, and Julia will be rid of their influence. Ronda will serve as well as Toledo so far as Vincente is concerned, but I will wait, to make sure that they are not losing sight of him."

So Señor Larralde, cloaked to the eyebrows, leant gracefully against the wall, and, like many another upon the bridge after that breathless day, drank in the cool air that rose from the river. Presently, indeed before the sound of the distant wheels was quite lost, two horsemen, cloaked and provided with such light luggage as the saddle can accommodate, rode leisurely through the gateway and up the incline that makes a short cut to the great road running southward to Ciudad Real. Larralde gave a little nod of self-confidence and satisfaction, as one who, having conceived and built up a great scheme, is pleased to see each component part of it act independently and slip into its place.

The general's first thought was for Estella's comfort, and he utilised the long hill, which they had to ascend on leaving the town, to make such arrangements as space would allow for their common ease.

"You must sleep, my child," he said. "We cannot hope to reach Ciudad Real before midday to-morrow, and it is as likely as not that we shall have but a few hours' rest there."

And Estella, who had travelled vast distances over vile roads so long as her memory went back, who had never known what it is to live in a country that is at peace, leant back in her corner and closed her eyes. Had she really been disposed to sleep, however, she could scarcely have done it, for the general's solicitude manifested itself by a hundred little devices for her greater repose. For her comfort he made Concha move.

"An old traveller like you must shift for yourself," he said gaily.

"No need to seek shelter for an old ox," replied Concha, moving into the other corner, where he carefully unfolded his pocket-handkerchief, and laid it over his face, where, his long nose protruding, caused it to fall in fantastic folds. He clasped his hands upon his hat, which lay upon his knee, and, leaning back, presently began to snore gently and regularly, a peaceful, sleep-inducing sound, and an excellent example. The general, whose sword seemed to take up half the carriage, still watched Estella, and if the air made her mantilla flutter, flew to the window with the solicitude of a lover and a maternal noiselessness. Then, with one hand on hers and the other grasping his sword, leant back, but did not close his eyes.

Thus they travelled on through the luminous night. The roads were neither worse nor better than they are to-day in Spain, than they were in England in the middle ages, and their way lay over the hill ranges that lie between the watersheds of the Tagus and the Guadiana. At times they passed through well-tended valleys, where corn and olives and vines seemed to grow on the same soil, but for the greater part of the night they ascended and descended the upper slopes, where herds of goats, half awakened as they slept in a ring about their guardian, looked at them with startled eyes. The shepherds and goatherds, who, like those of old, lay cloaked upon the ground and tended their flocks by night, did not trouble to raise their heads.

Concha alone slept, for the general had a thousand thoughts that kept him awake and bright-eyed, while Estella knew, from her father's manner and restlessness, that these were no small events that now stirred Spain and seemed to close men's mouths, so that near friends distrusted one another and brother was divided against brother. Indeed, others were on the road that night, and horsemen passed the heavy carriage from time to time.

In the early morning a change of horses was effected at a large inn near the summit of a pass above Malagon, and here an orderly, who seemed to recognise the general, was climbing into the saddle as the Vincentes quitted their carriage and passed into the common room of the *venta* for a hasty cup of coffee.

"It is the Queen's courier," said the innkeeper grandly, "who takes the road before Her Majesty, in order to secure horses."

"Ah !" said the general, breaking his bread and dropping it into his cup ; "is that so ? The Queen Regent, you mean."

"Queen or Queen Regent, she requires four horses this evening, excellency ; that is all my concern."

"True, my friend—true. That is well said. And the horses will be forthcoming, no doubt ?"

"They will be forthcoming," said the man ; "and the excellency's carriage is ready."

In the early morning light they drove on, now descending toward the great valley of the Guadiana, and at midday, as Vincente had foreseen, gained a sight of the ancient city of Ciudad Real, lying amid trees below them.

Ciudad Real is less interesting than its name, and there is little that is royal about its dirty streets and ill-kept houses. No one gave great heed to the travelling carriage, for this is a great centre, where travellers journeying east or west, north or south must needs pause for a change of horses. At the inn there were vacant rooms and that hasty welcome accorded to the traveller at wayside houses, where none stay longer than they can help.

"No," said the landlord, in answer to the general's query ; "we are not busy, though we expect a lady, who will pass the hour of the siesta here and then proceed northward."

CHAPTER XXVI.

WOMANCRAFT.

"Il est rare que la tête des rois soit faite à la mesuré de leur couronné."

In the best room of the inn, where Vincente and his tired companions sought a few hours' rest, there sat alone and in thought a lady of middle age. Somewhat stout, she yet had that air which arouses the attention without being worthy of the name of beauty. This lady had, doubtless, swayed men's hearts by a word or a glance, for she still carried herself with assurance, and a hundred little details of her dress would have told another woman that she still desired to please.

The hour of the siesta was over, and after the great heat of the day a cool air was swaying down on the bosom of the river to the parched lowlands. It stirred the leaves of a climbing heliotrope, which encircled the open windows and wafted into the ill-furnished room a scent of stable-yard and dust.

The lady, sitting with her chin resting in the palm of her small, white hand, seemed to have lately roused herself from sleep, and now had the expectant air of one who awaits a carriage and is about to set out on a long journey. Her eyes were dark and tired-looking, and their expression was not that of a good woman. A sensual man is usually weak, but women are different ; and this face, with its faded complexion and tired eyes, this woman of the majestic presence and beautiful hands, was both strong and sensual. This, in a word, was a queen who never forgot that she was a woman. As it was said of the Princess Christina, so it has been spoken of the Queen, that many had killed themselves for hopeless love of her, for this was the most dangerous of the world's creatures, a royal coquette. Such would our own Queen Bess have been, had not God, for the good of England, given her a plain face and an ungainly form, for surely the devil is in it when a woman can command both love and men. Queen Christina, since the death of a husband, who was years older than herself (and, as some say, before that historic event), had played a woman's game with that skill which men only half recognise, and had played it with the additional incentive that behind her insatiable vanity lay the heavier stake of a crown.

She is not the first to turn the strong current of man's passion to her own deliberate gain ; nay, ninety-nine out of a hundred women do it. But the majority only play for a suburban villa and a few hundred pounds a year ; Queen Christina of Spain handled her cards for a throne and the countenance of an ill-starred dynasty.

As she sat in the hotel chamber in Ciudad Real, that forlornest of royal cities, her face wore the pettish look of one who, having passed through great events, having tasted of great passions, and moved amid the machinery of life and death, finds the ordinary routine of existence intolerably irksome. Many faces wear such a look in this country—every second beautiful face in London has it. And these women—Heaven help them !—find the morning hours dull because every afternoon has not its great event, and every evening the hollow excitement of a social function.

The Queen was travelling *incognita*, and that fact alone robbed her progress of a sense of excitement. She had to do without the shout of the multitude, the passing admiration of the man in the street. She knew that she was yet many hours removed from Madrid, where she had admirers and the next best possession, enemies. Ciudad Real was intolerably dull and provincial. A servant knocked at the door.

"General Vincente, your Majesty, craves the favour of a moment."

"Ah !" exclaimed the Queen, the light returning to her eyes, a faint colour flushing her cheek. "In five minutes I will receive him."

And there is no need to say how the Queen spent those minutes.

"Your Majesty," said the general, bending over her hand, which he touched with his lips, "I have news of the greatest importance."

The suggestion of a scornful smile flickered for a moment in the royal eyes. It was surely enough for any man that she was a woman, beautiful still, possessing still that intangible and fatal gift of pleasing. The woman slowly faded from her eyes as they rested on the great soldier's face, and the Queen it was who, with a gracious gesture, bade him be seated. But the general remained standing. He alone, perhaps, of all the men who had to deal with her, of all those military puppets with whom she played her royal game, had never crossed that intangible boundary which many had overstepped to their own inevitable undoing.

"It concerns your Majesty's life," said Vincente bluntly, and calm in the certainty of his own theory that good blood, whether it flow in the veins of man or woman, assuredly carries a high courage.

"Ah !" said the Queen Regent, whose humour still inclined toward those affairs which interested her before the affairs of State ; "but with men such as you about me, my dear general, what need I fear ?"

"Treachery, madam," he answered, with his sudden smile and a bow—"treachery !"

The lady frowned. When a Queen stoops to dalliance a subject must not be too practical.

"Ah ! what is it that concerns my life—another plot ?" she inquired shortly.

"Another plot, but one of greater importance than those that exist in the republican cafés of every town in your Majesty's kingdom. This is a widespread conspiracy, and I fear that many powerful persons are concerned in it ; but that, your Majesty, is not my department nor concern."

"What is your concern, general ?" she asked, looking at him over her fan.

"To save your Majesty's life to-night."

"To-night !" she echoed, her coquetry gone.

"To-night."

"But how and where ?"

"By assassination, madam, in Toledo. You are three hours late in your journey, but all Toledo will be astir, awaiting you, though it be till dawn."

The Queen Regent closed her fan slowly. She was, as the rapid events of her reign and regency proved, one of those women who rise to the occasion.

"Then one must act at once," she said.

The general bowed.

"What have you done ?" she asked.

"I have sent to Madrid for a regiment that I know. They are as my own children. I have killed so many of them that the remainder love me. I have travelled from Toledo to meet your Majesty on the road here."

"And what means have you of preventing this thing ?"

"I have brought the means with me, madam."

"Troops ?" asked the Queen doubtfully, knowing where the cankerworm lay hidden.

"A woman and a priest, madam."

"And . . . ?"

"And I propose that your Majesty journey to Madrid in my carriage, attended only by my orderlies, by way of Aranjuez. You will be safe in Madrid, where the Queen will require her mother's care."

"Yes; and the remainder of your plan?"

"I will travel back to Toledo in your Majesty's carriage, with the woman and the priest and your bodyguard, just as your Majesty is in the habit of travelling. Toledo wants a fight, nothing else will satisfy them. They shall have it before dawn—the very best I have to offer them."

And General Vincente gave a queer, cheery little laugh, as if he were arranging a practical joke.

"But the fight will be round my carriage."

"Possibly. I would rather that it took place in the Calle de la Ciudad or around the Casa del Argantamiento, where your Majesty is expected to sleep to-night."

"And these persons, this woman who risks her life to save mine, who is she?"

"My daughter," answered the general gravely.

"She is here in the hotel now?"

The general bowed.

"I have heard that she is beautiful," said the Queen, with a quick glance toward her companion. "How is it that you have never brought her to court, you who come so seldom yourself?"

Vincente made no reply.

"However, bring her to me now."

"She has travelled far, madam, and is not prepared for presentation to her Queen."

"This is no time for formalities. She is about to run a great risk for my sake, a greater risk than I could ever ask her to run. Present her as one woman to another, general."

But General Vincente bowed gravely and made no reply. The colour slowly rose to the Queen Regent's face, a dull, shamed red. She opened her fan, closed it again, and sat with furtive, downcast eyes. Suddenly she looked up and met his gaze.

"You refuse!" she said, with an insolent air of indifference. "You think that I am unworthy to . . . meet your daughter."

"I think only of the exigency of the moment," was his reply. "Every minute we lose is a gain to our enemies. If our trick is discovered Aranjuez will be no safer for your Majesty than is Toledo. You must be safely in Madrid before it is discovered in Toledo that you have taken the other route, and that the person they have mistaken for you is in reality my daughter."

"But she may be killed!" exclaimed the Queen.

"We may all be killed, madam," he replied lightly. "I beg that you will start at once in my carriage, with your chaplain and the holy lady who is doubtless travelling with you."

The Queen glanced sharply at him. It was known that, although her own life was anything but exemplary, she loved to associate with women who, under the cloak of religion and an austere virtue, intrigued with all parties and condoned the Queen's offences.

"I cannot understand you," she said, with that sudden lapse into familiarity which had led to the undoing of more than one ambitious courtier; "you seem to worship the crown and despise the head it rests on."

"So long as I serve your Majesty faithfully . . ."

"But you have no right to despise me!" she interrupted passionately.

"If I despised you should I be here now, should I be doing you this service?"

"I do not know. I tell you I do not understand you."

And the Queen looked hard at the man who for this very reason interested one who had all her life dealt and intrigued with men of obvious motive and unblushing ambition.

So strong is a ruling passion, that even in sight of death (for the Queen Regent knew that Spain was full of her enemies and rendered callous to bloodshed by a long war) vanity was alert in this woman's breast. Even while General Vincente, that unrivalled strategist, detailed his plans, she kept harking back to the question that puzzled her, and but half listened to his instructions.

Those desirous of travelling without attracting attention in Spain are wise to time their arrival and departure for the afternoon. At this time, while the sun is yet hot, all shutters are closed, and the business of life, the haggling in the market-place, the bustle of the barrack-yard, the leisurely labour of the fields are suspended. It was about four o'clock; indeed, the city clocks were striking that hour when the two carriages in the inn-yard at Ciudad Real were made ready for the road. Father

Concha, who never took an active part in passing incidents while his old friend and comrade was near, sat in a shady corner of the *patio* and smoked a cigarette. An affable ostler had, in vain, endeavoured to engage him in conversation. Two small children had begged of him, and now he was left in meditative solitude.

"In a short three minutes," said the ostler, "and the excellencies can then depart. In which direction, reverendo, if one may ask?"

"One may always ask, my friend," replied the priest. "Indeed, the holy books are of opinion that it cannot be overdone. That chin-strap is too tight."

"Ah! I see the reverendo knows a horse . . ."

"And an ass," added Concha.

At this moment the general emerged from the shadow of the staircase, which was open and of stone. He was followed by Estella, as it would appear, and they hurried across the sunlighted *patio*, the girl carrying her fan to screen her face.

"Are you rested, my child?" asked Concha, at the carriage door.

The lady lowered the fan for a moment and met his eyes. A quick look of surprise flashed across Concha's face, and he half bowed. Then he repeated his question in a louder voice.

"Are you rested, my child, after our long journey?"

"Thank you, my father, yes."

And the ostler watched with open-mouthed interest.

The other carriage had been drawn up to that side of the courtyard where the open stairway was, and here also the bustle of departure and a hurrying female form, anxious to gain the shade of the vehicle, were discernible. It was all done so quickly, with such a military completeness of detail, that the carriages had passed through the great doorway, and the troopers, merely a general's escort, had clattered after them before the few onlookers had fully realised that these were surely travellers of some note.

The ostler hurried to the street to watch them go.

"They are going to the north," he said to himself, as he saw the carriages turn in the direction of the river and the ancient Puerta de Toledo—"they go to the north, and assuredly the general has come to conduct her to Toledo."

Strange to say, although it was the hour of rest, many shutters in the narrow street were opened, and more than one peeping face was turned toward the departing carriages.

CHAPTER XXVII.

A NIGHT JOURNEY.

"Let me but bear your love, I'll bear your cares."

At the cross-roads, on the northern side of the river, the two carriages parted company, the dusty equipage of General Vincente taking the road to Aranjuez, that leads to the right and mounts steadily through olive groves. The other carriage, which, despite its plain and sombre colours, still had an air of grandeur and almost of royalty, with its great wheels and curved springs, turned to the left and headed for Toledo. Behind it clattered a dozen troopers, picked men with huge, swinging swords and travel-stained clothes. The dust rose in a cloud under the horses' feet and hovered in the sallow air. There was no breath of wind, and the sun shone through a faint haze, which seemed only to add to the heat.

Concha lowered the window and thrust forward his long, inquiring nose.

"What is it?" asked the general.

"Thunder; I smell it. We shall have a storm to-night." He looked out, mopping his nose. "Name of a saint, how thick the air is!"

"It will be clear before the morning," said Vincente, the optimist.

And the carriage rattled on toward the city of strife, where Jew, Goth and Roman, Moor and Inquisitor have all had their day. Estella was silent, drooping with fatigue. The general alone seemed unmoved and heedless of the heat, a man of steel, as bright and ready as his own sword.

There is no civilised country in the world so bare as Spain, and no part of the Peninsula so sparsely populated as the Castiles. The road ran for the most part over brown and barren uplands, with here and there a valley where wheat and olives and vineyards graced the lower slopes. The crying need of all nature was for shade, for the ilex is a small-leaved tree, giving a thin shadow, with no cool depths amid the branches. All was brown and barren and parched. The earth seemed to lie fainting and awaiting the rain. The horses trotted with extended necks and open mouths, their coats wet with sweat. The driver, an Andalusian, with a face like a Moorish pirate, kept encouraging them with word and rein, jerking and whipping only when they seemed likely to fall from sheer fatigue and sun-weariness. At last the sun set in a glow like that of a great furnace, and the reflection lay over the land in ruddy splendour.

"Ah!" said Concha, looking out; "it will be a great storm, and it will soon come."

Vast columns of cloud were climbing up from the sunset into a sullen sky, thrown up in spreading mare's-tails by a hundred contrary gusts of wind, as if there were explosive matter in the great furnace of the west.

"Nature is always on my side," said Vincente, with his chuckling laugh. He sat, watch in hand, noting the passage of the kilometres.

At last the sun went down behind a distant line of hill, the watershed of the Tagus, and immediately the air was cool. Without stopping, the driver wrapped his cloak round him, and the troopers followed his example. A few minutes later a cold breeze sprung up suddenly, coming from the north and swirling the dust high in the air.

"It is well," said Vincente, who assuredly saw good in everything; "the wind comes first, and therefore the storm will be short."

As he spoke the thunder rolled among the hills.

"It is almost like guns," he added, with a queer look in his eyes suggestive of some memory.

Then, preceded by a rushing wind, the rain came, turning to hail, and stopping suddenly in a breathless pause, only to recommence with a renewed and splashing vigour. Concha drew up the windows, and the water streamed down them in a continuous ripple. Estella, who had been sleeping, roused herself. She looked fresh, and her eyes were bright with excitement. She had brought home with her from her English school that air of freshness and a dainty vigour which makes Englishwomen different from all other women in the world, and an English schoolgirl assuredly the brightest, purest, and sweetest of God's creatures.

Concha looked at her with his grim smile, amused at a youthfulness which could enable her to fall asleep at such a time and wake up so manifestly refreshed.

A halt was made at a roadside *venta*, where the travellers partook of a hurried meal. Darkness came on before the horses were sufficiently rested, and by the light of an ill-smelling lamp the general had his inevitable cup of coffee. The rain had now ceased, but the sky remained overcast, and the night was a dark one. The travellers took their places in the carriage, and again the monopoly of the road, the steady trot of the horses, the sing-song words of encouragement of their driver monopolised the thoughts of sleepy minds. It seemed to Estella that life was all journeys, and that she had been on the road for years. The swing of the carriage, the little varieties of the road but served to add to her somnolence. She only half woke up when, about ten o'clock, a halt was made to change horses, and the general quitted the carriage for a few minutes to talk earnestly with two horsemen who were apparently awaiting their arrival. No time was lost here, and the carriage went forward with an increased escort. The two newcomers rode by the carriage, one on either side.

When Estella woke up the moon had risen, and the carriage was making slow progress up a long hill. She noticed that a horseman was on either side, close by the carriage window.

"Who is that?" she asked.

"Conyngham," replied the general.

"You sent for him?" inquired Estella, in a hard voice.

"Yes."

Estella was wakeful enough now, and sat upright, looking straight in front of her. At times she glanced toward the window, which was now open, where the head of Conyngham's charger appeared. The horse trotted steadily with a queer jerk of the head, and that willingness to do his best, which gains for horses a place in the hearts of all who have to do with them.

"Will there be fighting?" asked Estella suddenly.

The general shrugged his shoulders.

"One cannot call it fighting. There

may be a disturbance in the streets," he answered.

Concha, quiet in his corner, with his back to the horses, watched the girl, and saw that her eyes were wide with anxiety now, quite suddenly, she who had never thought of fear till this moment. She moved uneasily in her seat, fidgeting as the young ever do when troubled. It is only with the years that we learn to bear a burden quietly.

"Who is that?" she asked shortly, pointing to the other window, which was closed.

"Concepcion Vara, Conyngham's servant," replied the general, who for some reason was inclined to curtness in his speech.

They were approaching Toledo, and passed through a village from time to time, where the cafés were still lighted up, and people seemed to be astir in the shadow of the houses. At last, in the main thoroughfare of a larger village, within a stage of Toledo, a final halt was made to change horses. The street, dimly lighted by a couple of oil lamps, swinging from gibbets at the corners of a cross-road, seemed to be peopled by shadows surreptitiously lurking in doorways. There was a false air of quiet in the houses, and peeping eyes looked out from the bars that covered every window, for even modern Spanish houses are barred, as if for a siege, and in the ancient villages every man's house is, indeed, his castle.

The driver had left the box, and seemed to be having some trouble with the ostlers and stable helps, for his voice could be heard raised in anger, and urging them to greater haste.

Conyngham, motionless in the saddle, touched his horse with his heel, advancing a few paces, so as to screen the window. Concepcion, on the other side, did the same, so that the travellers in the interior of the vehicle saw but the dark shape of the horses and the long cloaks of their riders. They could perceive Conyngham quickly throw back his cape in order to have a free hand. Then there came the sound of scuffling feet, and an indefinable sense of strife in the very air.

"But we will see—we will see who is in the carriage!" cried a shrill voice, and a hoarse shout from many bibulous throats confirmed the desire.

"Quick!" said Conyngham's voice —"quick! Take your reins; never mind the lamps!"

And the carriage swayed as the man leapt to his place. Estella made a movement to look out of the window, but Concha had stood up against it, opposing his broad back alike to curious glances or a knife or a bullet. At the other window, the general, better versed in such matters, held the leather cushion upon which he had been sitting across the sash. With his left hand he restrained Estella.

"Keep still," he said. "Sit back. Conyngham can take care of himself."

The carriage swayed forward, and a volley of stones rattled on it like hail. It rose jerkily on one side and bumped over some obstacle.

"One who has his quietus," said Concha. "These royal carriages are heavy."

The horses were galloping now. Concha sat down, rubbing his back. Conyngham was galloping by the window, and they could see his spur flashing in the moonlight as he used it. The reins hung loose and both his hands were employed elsewhere, for he had a man half across the saddle in front of him, who held to him with one arm thrown round his neck, while the other was raised and a gleam of steel was at the end of it. Concepcion, from the other side, threw a knife over the roof of the carriage—he could hit a cork at twenty paces—but he missed this time.

The general from within leant across Estella, sword in hand, with gleaming eyes. But Conyngham seemed to have got the hold he desired, for his assailant came suddenly swinging over the horse's neck, and one of his flying heels crashed through the window by Concha's head, making that ecclesiastic swear like any layman. The carriage was lifted on one side again and bumped heavily.

"Another," said Concha, looking for broken glass in the folds of his cassock. "That is a pretty trick of Conyngham's."

"And the man is a horseman," added the general, sheathing his sword—"a horseman. It warms the heart to see it."

Then he leant out of the window and asked if any were hurt.

"I am afraid, excellency, that I hurt one," answered Vara—"where the neck joins the shoulder. It is a pretty spot for the knife, nothing to turn a point."

He rubbed a sulphur match on the leg of his trousers, and lighted a cigarette as he rode along.

"On our side no accidents," continued Vara, with a careless grandeur, "unless the reverendo received a kick in the face."

"The reverendo received a stone in the small of the back," growled Concha pessimistically, "where there was already a corner of lumbago."

Conyngham, standing in his stirrups, was looking back. A man lay motionless on the road, and beyond, at the cross-roads, another was riding up a hill to the right at a hard gallop.

"It is the road to Madrid," said Concepcion, noting the direction of the Englishman's glance.

The general, leaning out of the carriage window, was also looking back anxiously.

"They have sent a messenger to Madrid, excellency, with the news that the Queen is on the road to Toledo," said Concepcion.

"It is well," answered Vincente with a laugh.

As they journeyed, although it was nearly midnight, there appeared from time to time, and for the most part in the neighbourhood of a village, one who seemed to have been awaiting their passage, and immediately set out on foot or horseback by one of the shorter bridle-paths that abound in Spain. No one of these spies escaped the notice of Concepcion, whose training amid the mountains of Andalusia had sharpened his eyesight and added keenness to every sense.

"It is like a cat walking down an alley full of dogs," he muttered.

At last the lights of Toledo hove in sight, and across the river came the sound of the city clocks tolling the hour.

"Midnight," said Concha, "and all respectable folk are in their beds. At night all cats are gray."

No one heeded him. Estella was sitting upright, bright-eyed and wakeful. The general looked out of the window at every moment. Across the river they could see lights moving, and many houses that had been illuminated were suddenly dark.

"See," said the general, leaning out of the window and speaking to Conyngham; "they have heard the sound of our wheels."

At the farther end of the Bridge of Alcantara, on the road which now leads to the railway station, two horsemen were stationed, hidden in the shadow of the trees that border the pathway.

"Those should be *guardia civile*," said Concepcion, who had studied the ways of these gentry all his life, "but they are not. They have horses that have never been taught to stand still."

As he spoke the men vanished, moving noiselessly in the thick dust which lay on the Madrid road.

The general saw them go and smiled. These men carried word to their fellows in Madrid for the seizure of the little Queen. But before they could reach the capital the Queen Regent herself would be there, a woman in a thousand, of inflexible nerve, of infinite resource.

The carriage rattled over the narrow bridge, which rings hollow to the sound of wheels. It passed under the gate that Wamba built, and up the tree-girt incline to the city. The streets were deserted, and no window showed a light. A watchman in his shelter at the corner by the synagogue peered at them over the folds of his cloak, and noting the clank of scabbard against spur, paid no further heed to a traveller who took the road with such outward signs of authority.

"It is still enough and quiet," said Concha, looking out.

"As quiet as a watching cat," replied Vincente.

(*To be concluded.*)

LONDON LETTER.

The literary subject of the moment is the new literary paper which the *Times* announces. The title is to be *Literature*.* The editor is Mr. H. D. Traill, and the price is sixpence. When I started THE BOOKMAN here my friend, the late Professor Drummond, urged me to take the title *Literature*; but I have had no reason to repent my choice. *Literature* is to be devoted mainly to reviews, giving more attention to continental and American publications than other English journals. In addition some bibliography is promised us. Whether this will captivate the English public remains to be seen. Mr. Traill is an able writer, but he is not accepted, at least by the younger authors, as a guide or authority. He was for some time an associate of Mr. Frederick Greenwood in the *St. James Gazette* and the *Pall Mall*. There was a difference between him and Mr. Greenwood, and he went over to the *Daily Telegraph*, where he is one of the leader writers. His best-known book is a series of dialogues, *The New Lucian*, but I think the one that shows most power is a collection of verses entitled *Recaptured Rhymes*, published by Messrs. Blackwood a good many years ago, and very little known. It is understood that the publication is the idea of the able and masterful manager of the *Times*, Mr. Moberley Bell. Under his direction the review department of the *Times* has much improved, Mr. Lang, Mr. Anstey, and Mr. James Payn being regular contributors. The books of the week are mostly done by an accomplished Oxford scholar, Mr. J. B. Thursfield. Mr. Thursfield, it is said, took the Home Rule side when the Liberal Party split up, and prefers to write on literary rather than on political subjects. The new paper is to be independent of the *Times*, Mr. Traill having full control. I shall be very glad to see it flourish, for it is somewhat depressing that nearly all the new publications have recently been of the popular type, and indeed it has been confidently predicted that the day for sixpenny reviews is past. That the *Times* office is of an opposite opinion is a singular fact, and no doubt the new paper will have every chance.

At the same time there is no doubt that the undertaking is one of the greatest difficulty. For one thing, the price is sixpence, while the *Athenæum* and the *Academy* are sold at threepence. The *Athenæum*, though carrying much less weight than formerly, now that the daily papers do so much in reviewing, is still a considerable force. It is read by many people for its advertisements; but it is fair to say that the editor, Mr. Norman MacColl, has shown himself a strong man. The paper has not now and never had a reputation for fairness. But it has some very good men on its staff, particularly Mr. Theodore Watts, whose reviews, whether one agrees with them or not, are always worth reading for their wealth of literary knowledge; and a *protégé* of Mr. Watts, Mr. Francis Hindes Groome, one of the most accomplished men of letters in England, a man who has never come to his own. Mr. Groome is one of the leading members of the staff of Messrs. Chambers of Edinburgh, and had a good deal to do with the new edition of their excellent encyclopædia. The *Athenæum* has also in every number a certain amount of fresh news. The *Academy* under Mr. Lewis Hind no longer signs its articles. But it has good contributions from Mr. Wilfrid Meynell and his accomplished wife, as well as many others. It has not yet, however, been a very serious rival to the *Athenæum*. Enormous sums have been spent first and last in its development, and it is now understood to be a paying property. But some of us remember how it was started from the great publishing house of John Murray, and with men like Huxley and Matthew Arnold as contributors, and how it failed to succeed in spite of all these advantages, and although at that time it was published only monthly. The great difficulty with weekly literary journals is that they have practically no advertisements except those of publishers, and as everybody knows, there are dead months during which publishers advertise but little. A very strong firm of proprietors has been contemplating for some time the establishment of a penny

* An American edition will be issued by Messrs. Harper & Bros.

illustrated weekly literary journal. Here the question is whether there are a sufficient number of people interested in literature to provide at the very least 20,000 weekly subscribers. I question it. The provoking thing is that so many literary people read their literary papers at the clubs, or not at all. I remember speaking with an eminent literary man about the *Academy*, a paper to which he had been one of the most frequent contributors. He confessed that he had never purchased a single number. Nevertheless whatever our private opinion may be as to its chances, all of us wish Mr. Traill every success, and it is certain that he will to his very utmost make the paper fair and even appreciative. This would be his wise policy even from a commercial standpoint. The slashing system does not pay in England, as various costly enterprises have abundantly proved.

I am able to say that Mrs. Oliphant has left behind her materials for a biography. They are, I believe, largely autobiographical. It is not likely and it is not desirable that anybody should write the full story of the tragedies which marred so many of her years and against which she bore up with such wonderful courage. But her life should be a very interesting one, and is sure to contain much racy comment and narrative. She saw in her time much of society, and nothing escaped her eyes or her memory.

The new publishing season is now upon us, and my prediction that the number of books would not greatly exceed the average has so far been fulfilled. Publishers are more and more restricting themselves to enterprises which are fairly certain to pay. They are finding out that it is not the number of books published, but the number of books sold which tells when the accounts are made up. They are also to a large extent refusing to publish books on commission, although to this rule there are one or two very notable exceptions. So far, of course, the book of the season has been Mr. Hall Caine's *The Christian*. As your readers know, it has been criticised with extreme severity, but the circulation has been enormous. It has been largely read by clerics who have preached upon it, and this has helped to give it its immense vogue. The publisher, Mr. Heinemann, who is one of the most enterprising and successful men in London, will issue shortly Mr. Harold Frederic's new book, which is said to be even better than his last, and which is sure of a great welcome. Madame Sarah Grand's novel is also being published through Mr. Heinemann. As is well known, Madame Grand's real name is Mrs. McFall ; but she has dropped this altogether, and is now to be known alike to her friends and the public as Madame Sarah Grand. Mr. Heinemann has many other attractive books, and he makes it his boast that not one of these has been obtained through a literary agent. The work, however, which is looked forward to with most eagerness is the life of the late Lord Tennyson, of which a very large first edition has been printed notwithstanding its high price.

Few English journalists were more looked up to than Mr. R. H. Hutton, the late editor of the *Spectator*, who has passed away after a very painful illness. Mr. Hutton was the son of a Unitarian minister, and originally a candidate for the Unitarian ministry. He failed, however, to get a pulpit. He was shortsighted, and in no way fitted to be a popular orator, though later in life he acquired a considerable debating faculty. After some chequered and troubled years, during which he edited the *National Review*, he became the associate of Mr. Meredith Townsend on the *Spectator*, a paper which came to be one of the most influential organs, if not the most influential, in English journalism. Mr. Hutton's history was largely the history of his paper, to which he devoted his whole energy, contributing a minimum of two elaborate articles a week, and often more. His peculiar influence was that of a profoundly religious man who was at the same time a thoroughly able and well-equipped literary and philosophic critic. Of such there are few indeed in the ranks of journalism. By thoughtful clergymen especially Mr. Hutton's paper was very much valued, and he never felt free to withdraw from it, although he often wished to do so in order to make some independent contribution to literature. He remained at his post almost to the end, and wrote with undiminished freshness and power. Many journalists after a certain period become what is called old fogeys, and are unable to appreciate the movements that are taking place around them. Mr. Hutton was not one of these. He will be very much missed on the *Spectator*. His successor, Mr. Strachey, is a young man of considerable ability and seriousness, but in no way to be compared to his predecessor. Mr. Meredith Townsend is one of the most able journalists of the time. He does not write on religious subjects or pronouncedly from a religious point of view. The fate of the *Spectator* will be watched with great interest. It is one of those papers which cannot possibly be transformed. There is a proposal to issue a journal somewhat of the same kind, but with a news element, at a penny, and many leading men have promised both financial and literary aid, but whether it will ultimately come to anything I cannot say at present.

Mr. Barrie has commenced the second part of *Sentimental Tommy*. He has been much engrossed with preparations for his play *The Little Minister*. The most elaborate arrangements have been made, and it is expected to be the success of the winter. Mr. Crockett is more industrious, if possible, than ever; and you may hear soon of his breaking out in new directions. Americans will be interested in his picture of their countrywomen given by him in his new story, *The Woman of Fortune*, which is to run through the *Woman at Home*, commencing in January.

The prospects of the discount being reduced on books do not seem to brighten. The only way in which the plan could possibly succeed would be the securing of absolute unanimity among publishers and booksellers. Some of the leading booksellers in London decline to yield, and if the plan were carried out in defiance of them the chances are that much of the country trade would be diverted to London. Neither is it easy to see how the publishers could possibly coerce them. What is to hinder them establishing under another name book shops where books are sold at twopence off the shilling and getting unlimited supplies by that means? The same difficulties are being felt in Germany, where loud complaints are being made at the intention of the publishers, and it said that even the publishers themselves are not holding together. I am sure that if the reform could be carried out it would be ultimately for the advantage of every one, but it cannot be carried out unless all are agreed. I have spoken to a good many authors on the subject, and find them generally disinclined to do anything. They are afraid that the sales of their books may be diminished. If the Authors' Society report unfavourably the whole scheme will immediately be dropped. If not, I believe a considerable majority of publishers will be found to support it.

W. Robertson Nicoll.

LONDON, September 24, 1897.

PARIS LETTER.

The month of September is, perhaps, the poorest month of the year for literary news from Paris. Everybody who can, in France (and bookmen manage to be among those who *can*), leaves in the first week of the month *pour faire l'ouverture*, as the phrase goes—that is, to open the hunting season—and for several weeks thinks of nothing but quails and partridges. There is one form of literary activity, though, which manifests itself earlier than the other ones, and it is one of greater importance in France than anywhere else; we mean dramatic production. Leaving out the triumphal appearance of Murger's *Vie de Bohème* at the Théâtre Français early in the month, we find the living playwrights very busy at the present time. The busiest, undoubtedly, are Armand Silvestre and Paul Déroulède. The former is already superintending the rehearsals of his verse play, *Tristan de Léonois*, the first performance of which is to take place at the Théâtre Français on October 16th. I suppose I need not say to the readers of THE BOOKMAN that the side of Armand Silvestre's double nature which is to appear in this new play of his is the elegiac and not the *gaulois* side.

Paul Déroulède, undismayed by the failure of his *Duguesclin*, is almost ready with a new historical drama, *La Mort de*

Hoche ; and, undismayed, too, Coquelin is to produce it at the Porte Saint-Martin. This new drama has already been the cause of a long controversy between its author and the grandson of General Hoche, the hero of the drama. Strangely enough Paul Déroulède has chosen to present Hoche's death as having been self-inflicted, and the Marquis des Roys protests that no one can suppose for a moment that his grandfather committed suicide. Hoche's death has always seemed to have had something mysterious, but the only suppositions that had been discussed thus far had been sickness and murder by poison. Lanfrey, in his celebrated and unfinished history of Napoleon, had even more than hinted that Hoche had been put out of the way by his rival in glory and power. What remains to be seen is whether the playwright has succeeded in placing his hero in one of those pathetic positions from which there is no escape except through death.

Among the other new plays which are to be performed in the near future none is awaited with as much interest as *Les Trois Filles de M. Dupont.* The author is M. Brieux, whose *L'Evasion* scored a good deal more than a *succès d'estime* a year ago at the Théâtre Français. We are to have also *Le Nouveau Jeu*, by Henri Lavedan, and *Jalouse*, by Alexandre Bisson, the merry and lucky dramatist whose five earlier plays have had together at the Vaudeville Théâtre no less than 938 performances. Last, and perhaps not least, the author of *La Douloureuse*, Maurice Donnay, is at work on a new play which will be performed at the Renaissance by Sarah Bernhardt's company, with Sarah, of course, in the most important part. I know that all of this is not literature ; but some of it is sure to be, and that is why I mention it to the readers of THE BOOKMAN.

Among the books recently published, the only one that has created a sensation is *Sale Juif!* by M. Dollivet. All the Jew baiters at once threw themselves upon it, expecting to find it entirely in keeping with their own passions. Imagine their disgust when they discovered that the book is entirely on the other side of the question. It is even rumoured now that Dollivet is only a *nom de plume*, and that the author is himself a Hebrew.

Another *nom de plume* has just come before the public, Pierre de Coulevin, whose novel of American life, *Noblesse Américaine*, which appears now as a *feuilleton* in the *Temps*, has, I understand, been just published also on your side of the Atlantic. Pierre de Coulevin is a woman, Mademoiselle Favre, who has been teaching French for several years in Boston, and is, I think, a relative of the late French orator and statesman Jules Favre.

The most interesting of the forthcoming publications will be M. Brunetière's accounts of his American trip. It was presented to the editor of the *Revue des Deux Mondes*, who, of course, at once accepted his own production. It will form three articles : the first one on the Universities, the second on the Woman question, and the third one on Catholicism in the United States. The articles will be published also, but not in their entire text, in *McClure's Magazine.* I think I may safely say that one of the results of the celebrated critic's visit to the United States will be that American affairs will henceforth occupy much more space than before in the *Revue des Deux Mondes.*

You will be, I suppose, somewhat startled by the announcement that a new work on Balzac, *Balzac Imprimeur*, will have on the title-page the name of our present Minister of Foreign Affairs, M. Gabriel Hanotaux. But the busy statesman and academician has a *collaborateur* whose name will appear with his, M. Georges Vicaire.

Then we are to have a flood of new old books, reprints of works the copyright of which is just coming to an end. Fréderic Soulié died on September 24th, 1847 ; so all his copyrights ran out three days ago. His celebrated *Mémoires du Diable* will be reprinted before the close of the year. Stendhal and Chateaubriand both died in 1848 ; this will be quite a boon for publishers. I suppose that few copyrights will have had as long a life as Chateaubriand's *Atala*, which appeared in 1800, or his *Essai sur les Révolutions*, which was first published in 1797.

I am glad to inform you that François Coppée, whose life was almost despaired of a few weeks ago, after he had undergone a severe surgical operation, has now fully recovered. Another literary man who is open for congratulations is Henri Rochefort, who has just been married for the third time. His new wife is his niece, or rather his brother-in-law's niece. Her maiden name was Marguerite Vervoort, and she has for years been the head of the celebrated pamphleteer's establishment.

Alfred Manière.

PARIS, September 27, 1897.

THE BOOKMAN'S LETTER-BOX.

Returning from our vacation with the salty savour of the sea still lingering in our nostrils, and with a general sense of ability to cope with any editorial problems whatsoever, we nevertheless felt a certain lurking apprehension as we entered the scene of our wonted labours. It was not because THE BOOKMAN had split an infinitive or two in our absence, for we had expected that; nor was it because Miss Katharine Pearson Woods, in the August number, had used an apparent object after a verb in the passive voice; for by signing her name to her work she had sufficiently relieved us of any personal responsibility for the outrage. It was neither of these things that troubled us. But we had been absent and idle for two whole months, and we knew that all this time our readers with diabolical ingenuity had been cooking up complicated questions for us to answer. We knew that they had been laying pipe to entangle and confound us. We knew that a swarm of the subtlest kind of problems would overwhelm us, and that we should have to solve them instantly and get ourselves into the worst sort of a scrape. In fact, we knew a lot of other things that were sure to happen when we got around to the Letter-Box again. So, when the young lady who kindly preserves our editorial correspondence for us began to grope in the fateful pigeon-hole, we looked out of the window for a few moments and breathed hard. And then—then we found, apart from a number of left-overs, just a meek little package of letters, scarcely as many as we usually receive in a single fortnight, and all of them obviously innocent. For an instant we were astonished and perplexed; but as we are naturally very bright and full of intuition, the explanation flashed upon us immediately. As we had been taking our vacation, so had our esteemed critics been taking theirs. Well, we hope they all enjoyed it as much as we did ours. And now let us see what the Box contains.

I.

We understand that a good deal of private discussion has been going on in various quarters about our dictum regarding the expression "To-morrow *is* Sunday;" but no one had had the courage to tackle the subject in print up to the present moment, when we are favoured with a vivid letter from Miss Carolyn Wells, a lady who has gained for herself a roomy niche in the pronaos of Fame, as the person who first projected the Purple Cow into literature. We give that part of her letter which contains her argument, omitting for lack of space some of her appended illustrations:

"Your statement in the June Letter-Box that the sentence 'To-day is Thursday; yesterday, to-morrow was Thursday; to-day, to-morrow is Friday; and to-morrow, to-morrow will be Saturday,' is both grammatically and psychologically correct, invites the test of a further application, and out of thine own mouth will I judge thee.

"If to-morrow, as such, and in its essential to-morrowness, has no objective existence, but must always be a purely mental conception, then, logically, yesterday, as such and in its essential yesterdayness, has no objective existence, but must always be a similar and equally pure mental conception. For when the time thought of as 'yesterday' was here, it was not yet 'yesterday,' but 'to-day.'

"Hence it can exist only in the present, and one should say on Monday, 'Yesterday *is* Sunday,' and not 'yesterday *was* Sunday,' for it wasn't."

Like everything that Miss Wells writes, this is distinctly clever, and she obviously thinks that she has got us in a hole. But she hasn't. There are two answers that may be made to her argument, one of them theoretical and the other practical. A distinction is clearly to be drawn between "to-morrow" and "yesterday;" for, at the time of speaking, "to-morrow" has no objective existence, we know nothing of it save as a present mental conception. "Yesterday," however, may be held to have an objective existence in the results and experiences that came from it, and hence it may be properly thus spoken of. This is the theoretical argument. But the practical argument for "yesterday was" is better and also simpler. Universal usage has sanctioned only this one form of speaking of it; while the usage regarding "to-morrow" is still unsettled. Many persons say, "to-morrow will be;" many others say "to morrow is." Hence this question is still open, and when we are asked to decide which is the better expression, we may answer with a due regard to the psychology of it, as we did. And now, having replied to her, we salute Miss Wells respectfully as she returns once more to the mystical contemplation of her empurpled kine.

II.

A correspondent who evidently does not know that the same question has already been asked and answered once before, propounds the following:

"In the Letter-Box why do you say so much about yourselves?"

Because that is the subject which we know the most about. See also our reply to a correspondent in THE BOOKMAN of last June.

III.

A lady who resides in Binghamton, New York, compliments us by asking our advice on a serious matter.

"I always read what THE BOOKMAN has to say on educational questions with great interest, and I want to ask you to advise me. My niece, who is eighteen years of age, has finished her regular education so far as ordinary school work goes, and I want to give her a year or two more to finish her off. What is the best place for her to spend the next two years in?"

Home.

IV.

An earnest and indigenous citizen of Libertyville, Indiana, who uses, we think, a quill pen, writes us the following letter:

"Out in these parts, we are just about dead tired of the way THE BOOKMAN spells. Why do you write 'honour,' 'theorise,' 'sombre,' etc., instead of 'honor,' 'theorize,' 'somber'? The leading American dictionaries are all against you. I suppose you are trying to be very English; but who cares how the English spell? Isn't America big enough and strong enough to have her own kind of spelling without crawling in the dirt before a lot of English literary dudes? Come off, and buy a Webster's Dictionary for yourselves!"

We have never had the pleasure of spending any time in the interesting town of Libertyville, Indiana, but we entertain a well-defined suspicion that it is just the sort of place to harbour the sort of person who would write this sort of letter. If we are wrong in this, we apologise most abjectly to Libertyville, Indiana.

V.

A Boston gentleman on whose statements we can fully rely sends us the following:

"In your October number you repeat, though you do not actually vouch for it, the story that the Boston Public Library forbids anarchists to read anarchistic books. I must inform you that this report is wholly unfounded. It was denied in the *Chap Book* some time ago, and if you had read that periodical you surely would not have given currency to the statement."

Yes, we observed that the *Chap Book* denied it; but, to be frank, that was precisely our reason for thinking that there must be quite a little truth in the story.

VI.

This is a mean sort of letter:

"DEAR BOOKMAN: The appearance of your Letter-Box would indicate that you never make mistakes. Is that a fact? Or do you only print and answer letters that you *can* answer?

"A DOUBTFUL ONE."

What shall we say to this? In the first place, we assure our correspondent that every letter that has a grain of sense in it is sooner or later noticed in these pages. It sometimes happens that several letters refer to the same subject, in which case we print our reply only to the brightest and briefest of them. And, as we have often stated, we do not usually comment on letters written in criticism of signed articles in THE BOOKMAN. But if any other letter has remained unanswered, it must have been lost in the maelström of our desk; and if its writer will repeat his inquiry, we will reimburse him for his postage out of the large bin of confiscated stamps that is contiguous to our elbow. In the second place, we must ask our sceptical friend to refer to the back numbers of the Letter-Box. He will there see that again and again some keen-eyed correspondent has detected a crevice in our editorial armour and has thrust his weapon through it and twisted it in the wound. And when this has happened, we have not gone off into a corner and suffered obscurely, but have writhed as publicly as possible for the general satisfaction of our delighted readers. Come now! Be honest. Look up the record and then write us something nice by way of amends.

VII.

Here is a pert postal-card, unsigned.

"If 'stanch' (minus the *u*) is good enough for the Century, Webster, and the Standard dictionaries, why is it not good enough for THE BOOKMAN?"

Because we are more difficult to please than the persons who compiled these dictionaries, and because our taste is better.

VIII.

Another postal-card from Astoria, Oregon, asks two questions:

"1. Which is the better form: 'some one else's,' or 'some one's else'?

"2. Did Jean Ingelow die in her sixty-seventh or in her seventy-seventh year? The *Century Cyclopædia of Names* gives 1830 as the year of her birth."

We answer:

1. Either form is allowable, but "some one's else" is preferable.

2. Jean Ingelow was born in 1820.

IX.

The lady in Sierra Madre, California, who has questioned us once before, and who writes a beautiful English hand, sends us the following inquiries which we summarise:

"1. In *The Port of Missing Ships* the 'Ay, ay' (yes, yes) of the sailors is invariably spelled 'Aye, aye' (ever, ever), and I have observed this mistake in other books. Why is this?

"2. In American books one always finds 'behooves' instead of 'behoves.' Why? The word with one *o* has dignity and sonority; with two, it is elephantine.

"3. Why do educated Americans say 'There is nothing *to* a man,' for 'There is nothing *in* a man'? It is obviously an elliptical phrase. What is the word understood?"

We answer:

1. Both forms of the affirmative ("aye" and "ay") are recognised by English as well as by American lexicographers. In fact, "aye" is etymologically the more accurate of the two.

2. Both these forms are also recognised in English as well as in American usage. See, for example, Stormonth.

3. We do not consider the phrase elliptical, but idiomatic, and one that finds a perfect analogy in the German use of *an*.

This lady also sends us another letter calling our attention to some of the *Critic's* lapses from correct English usage. But we cannot give space to the enumeration of these. If THE BOOKMAN were to undertake the supervision of the *Critic's* English we should have to begin issuing monthly supplements.

This lady always signs herself "An Ardent Admirer of THE BOOKMAN," leaving her real name a mystery. We wish that she would kindly consent to reveal it for our own personal information. It would be a real pleasure to know who it is who can write with so much courtesy, good temper, and cleverness.

X.

A suspicious lady of Worcester, Massachusetts, presumably young, writes to declare that she doesn't believe the writer who criticised Mr. Richard Harding Davis in our August number had ever read *Soldiers of Fortune*. Well, if he hadn't he ought to have done so; and if he wrote any real mean things about dear Mr. Davis without having read every line of that gentleman's books, we say unhesitatingly that he is a bad man.

XI.

This is from San Juan, California, and shows a taste for false analogies:

"Is there any good reason why a verb following the pronoun 'you,' used with a singular meaning, should not have the singular form, according to the same logic that makes it right to use a singular verb after a noun plural in form, but singular in meaning, as 'United States *is*'?"

This is, of course, a concealed defence of "you was." But one says "you were" because this is the plural of courtesy (plural of excellence), and is a bit of historical politeness. Our friend in San Juan need not be polite unless he chooses to, but in that case he should say "thou wast." It will sound rather queer, but at any rate not vulgar, as "you was" will always be in spite of the heroic efforts of certain language-mongers to defend it.

XII.

"Constant Reader" in Wheeling, West Virginia, with whom we had a friendly bout in the June number, turns up again. We wish we could spare the space for his whole letter, which is most amusing.

"There you go again.

"On page 454 of the August number you say: 'In answer to a number of inquiries concerning the significance of the title, etc., of *Quo Vadis*, we give an extract, etc.:

"'St. Peter met the Master and inquired of Him, "*Dominie quo vadis?*" to which he received the reply, "*Venio iterum crucifigi*," whereupon, etc.'

"But what does it *mean?* Confound it! why don't you say what it *means?* Does it translate 'Which way,' or 'Whither goest thou?' And what does the Saviour's reply mean? In the May or June number of THE BOOKMAN you gave us half a column of French untranslated.

"Do you imagine that all your readers are French and Latin scholars? Do you think to flatter us by presuming that we are? Or are you just airing your own accomplishments? . . . I have read *Quo Vadis*—read it twice—the second time to a blind friend, aloud, and I—he—we—want to know, and from some authoritative source, whether *Quo Vadis* means 'Which way,' or 'Whither goest thou?'

"THE BOOKMAN is good enough authority for *me;* but THE BOOKMAN says *Quo Vadis* means *Quo Vadis*. Thanks! And *Venio iterum crucifigi* means *Venio iterum crucifigi*, I presume. Thanks again."

Quo Vadis means "Whither goest thou?" And *Venio iterum crucifigi* means, "I am coming to be crucified a second time." The Latinity of the latter sentence, by the way, is like that of the much-discussed *Omnia reliquit servare rem publicam*, which has so agitated Boston this year.

XIII.

From Kittery Point, Maine, comes a letter signed "N. P.," stating that an English friend claims to have heard Americans say "I did have" and "I do have" for the simple form "I had" and "I have." We think the English friend is mistaken, for we have never heard anything of the kind, except, of course, when special emphasis is intended; and this is as British as it is American. "N. P." wishes us to give her friend a lecture on Briticisms; but we can do better than that by referring her to Professor Brander Matthews's book *Americanisms and Briticisms*, where the thing has already been done far more efficiently than we could do it.

XIV.

A gentleman in Cincinnati asks the following:

"Is the following sentence correct: 'Moses was the daughter of Pharaoh's son'?"

We are not going to consider any mouldy old catch such as this. We print the inquiry only to show our readers what things an editor has to put up with.

XV.

The following note seems to require no answer. We are inclined to think it is intended to be a bright bit of sarcasm, so we print it for the gratification of its perpetrator, who signs his name and writes from Sonyea, New York—a place of which, we confess, we had never heard before.

"DEAR EDITORS: I noticed in a recent issue of THE BOOKMAN that a writer had submitted some manuscript to you after he had received many favourable notices from well known authors. Well, what I cannot understand is, why he sent the manuscript to THE BOOKMAN at all."

XVI.

Another dissatisfied soul clamours for attention.

"I notice in THE BOOKMAN'S treatment of certain very popular authors a tone of disdain that seems to me to be rebuked by the facts. The real test of literary merit is the extent of the public approval given to it. So you may sneer as much as you please, but it is a sufficient answer to your sneers to say of an author: 'His reputation is known to every intelligent man and woman in America and England.'"

And so is Jack the Ripper's.

XVII.

A purist in language stoops to aid us with his light and leading. He is not severe, only kindly and compassionate. This is what he says:

"In looking over the back numbers of THE BOOKMAN I find it said (editorially) of an English writer that 'at last she got into print.' Now, as your journal is a *literary* journal, if you had taken a little time to reflect, could you not have expressed this idea somewhat more elegantly? Could you not have said, for instance, that 'she ultimately attained the honour of publication'?"

No; we really couldn't, any more than we could go about our daily work with gilt-paper spangles on our trousers.

XVIII.

This last letter is like several others that have come to us, written by persons who complain of what they are pleased to call our "colloquial tone," our "levity," and of the general lack of solemnity in our style. We have read so many of these that we might just as well say something about them now as at any other time. We hold that a writer who has only one kind of style at his disposal is in the same case as a man who has only one suit of clothes in his wardrobe. It may be the very finest suit of evening clothes, and cut by Poole, yet its owner will surely feel rather awkward when he has to wear it on the golf links or at a bicycle breakfast. And in like manner, the possessor of a single style will cut an absurd figure when he settles down to chat in the ponderous periods of a Gibbon. We thank goodness that our stylistic wardrobe is more plentifully furnished; and that while we can treat serious things in a serious and sober manner, so can we gossip with our esteemed readers in the language of the easy-chair. We strive to avoid the fault ascribed by Goldsmith to Johnson; and we hope that we never make our little fishes talk like whales, but that we make a proper use of both the piscicular and the cetaceous manner. Sometimes, to be sure, we inject a few cetaceous words into a piscicular discussion; but this is always done when we want to get a rise out of somebody —and the device never fails. The fact is, it is we who are editing THE BOOKMAN, and we have to do it in our own way; for if we didn't do it in our own way we couldn't do it at all—and we rather enjoy doing it. When the time comes for a successor to take our place, he will doubtless have a better way, but it will also be his own way and wholly natural to him. So this is what we have to say, and we are sorry if any very, very serious readers do not see it in that light. We hate to differ from them, for they are all clear, white souls, and we have the greatest respect for them even though they do not think as we do about style.

XIX.

A highly esteemed correspondent in Quincy, Massachusetts, sends us a six-page letter, of which the first sentence is as follows:

> "You're a brick!"

We should like to print the rest of the letter, but we can't, because we are so painfully modest. Yet we feel constrained to call attention to the sentence just quoted, in spite of the ceramic compliment which it contains; for it seems to us to be in its way a perfect model of style. It is simple and direct, terse, nervous, and forcible, conveying a great truth in a compact and impressive way, stripping the thought of all superfluous verbiage, and yet obviating any possibility of baldness, by the use of a strictly classical metaphor. We commend its careful study to the Clear White Souls.

THE OAK IN AUTUMN.

The Druid monarch swings his branches low,
  His sinuous leaves aflame with Autumn dyes,
As if they reddened in the altar-glow,
  Amid the hush, around some sacrifice.

Benjamin F. Leggett.

NEW BOOKS.

AUBREY DE VERE'S "RECOLLECTIONS."*

Aubrey de Vere was born at the beginning of the century in the year 1814—at least, so we gather from the context, for nowhere is it precisely stated in these pages. There is a delightful disregard of dates outside of the chapter headings, which rids the book of the tedium of a chronicle and invests it with the panoramic picturesqueness of a series of graphic portraits and personal reminiscences. "Recollections" and "Autobiographies," as the author himself says in his preface, are very different things; and this book belongs to the former class, not to the latter. "We have seen persons and places which have amused or interested us, and it occurs to us that if accurately described they might amuse or interest others also; but this is a very different thing from writing one's biography, with which the world has little concern. Moreover," with a touch of Hibernian humour, "Self is a dangerous personage to let into one's book." So reasons the author with the maturity of wisdom and common sense which old age does not always bring to such a task, for it must be remembered that Aubrey de Vere has climbed the white summit—the "Mont Blanc of fourscore," as the Autocrat said over the teacups—and has rested there for five years. "Self" has entered into his book we must say, but not as a dangerous personage, rather as a delightful personality; and the quality of it is blended with urbanity, humour, sensibility, sapience and a gracious garrulousness unspoiled by the egotism of small minds. In the long retrospect of nearly a century the danger of massing together one's recollections, especially of such a century as the nineteenth, lies more in remembering too much than too little. But the art of forgetting the uninteresting and the remote has been wisely cultivated by Aubrey de Vere, and only those familiar scenes and events made sure to the touch of memory and quick to the awakening response of the imagination by the intimacy of association and experience are reproduced in these chapters from a life teeming with many interests, political, social, religious, and literary. Although avoiding the method of autobiography, the recollections are grouped and sorted after a chronological fashion that gives them sequence and order; they are not of the kind called "rambling." Nor do they degenerate into what the author calls "inferior matter." Indeed, whether it arise from literary parsimony or a judicious fear of boring the reader, we have been deprived of some half dozen portraits of eminent men, and a second chapter on the great Irish Famine (1846–50); "however," adds the aged but irrepressible Celt with the resiliency of his race, "another volume may remedy such deficiencies."

* Recollections of Aubrey de Vere. New York: Edward Arnold. $4.00.

Aubrey de Vere's earliest recollections are of his Irish home, Curragh Chase, standing back from the merry misery of the poor in a flood of summer sunshine. One advantage of civilisation, then, whatever its disadvantages, was that the hall door of the house could be left open all night and property run no danger of being molested. "O Ireland," he exclaims at a later date, "barbaric Ireland! How little were thy merits appreciated in the days before railways!" It was the time when England may have "expected every man to do his duty," but when Ireland expected every man to do, possibly, some other man's duty, in any case to do whatever amused him—ride well, stand by a friend, say good things and fight duels. Duels were in those days the most mirthful of pastimes.

"In Dublin there still remains a tradition of two lawyers—one the biggest, and the other the smallest man in Irish society—who met in the Phœnix Park, just after sunrise, to indulge in that amusement. As they approached each other, the big man set his glass to his eye and exclaimed: 'But where is my honourable opponent? For I really cannot see him.'

"'What's that he's saying?' demanded the little man.

"'I just remarked,' replied the big man, 'that I am so large that if you miss me, you are like the man who, when he took aim at the parish church, never succeeded in hitting the parish.'

"'What is that big Golumbus of a man babbling about?' was his small antagonist's rejoinder. 'That I can't miss him and he cannot see me? Let his second get a bit of white chalk and draw my exact size and shape on that huge carcass of his; and any bullet of mine that hits outside that white line shall not count.'"

It is recorded of Mr. de Vere's grandfather, who had no taste for duels, that at a great public dinner, when the "health" of Lord Castlereagh, to whom he had a strong aversion, was proposed, he parried the insult of refusal to drink, which could only be expiated by a duel, by lifting his glass with the others and saying: "Here's to the health of my Lord Castlereagh;" adding with a significant expression of face, "The Lord be troublesome to him!"

The earliest political event which Mr. de Vere remembers is the death of King George III. About this time the child of seven years old was taken to England. The family travelled in a very large old coach with four black horses. It took them four days to reach Dublin, and twice as many more to reach London. The compensation for slow travelling in those days was, however, the leisurely enjoyment of many fair sights and scenes which the traveller now misses. During their residence in London his father, Sir Aubrey de Vere, published his first drama, *Julian the Apostate*, and also his second, *The Duke of Mercia*, the former of which was declared—by Hartley Coleridge it is believed—to be a drama of a higher order than any which Lord Byron had written. Byron was then the popular poet, "who must have deprived the world of as much poetry as he ever produced," quaintly remarks our author. "I remember asking my father whether Byron or Scott was the greater man, and his answering, 'Scott, because he is as great, and he is a good man also.'"

Gerald Griffin, a friend of Mr. de Vere's in youth and a man of remarkable genius, whose early promise in *The Collegians* was so quickly blighted by the religious cloud which engulfed his erratic nature, was one of his first literary familiars. Griffin's novel *The Collegians*, better known by the vulgar sensationalism of its dramatic condensation, *The Colleen Bawn*, was a great and immediate success, and the author was pronounced by several critics to be the best novelist of the time next to Sir Walter Scott. We have the critical testimony of Aubrey de Vere for it, that it presents the best picture existing of Irish peasant life—at once the most vivid and the most accurate. "Its comic parts are the most comic, and its tragic the most trágic to be found in Irish literature." We submit this to the editor of the Illustrated Standard Novels Series being published by the Macmillan Company. Surely a work of fiction of this rank, which although frequently reprinted is now very rare, is worthy of being included in such a series. Griffin had a knowledge of early Irish history, and a long series of historic romances illustrating Ireland, as Scott's had illustrated Scotland, was expected of him. But the country he loved so well lost its chance of an Irish Burns or an Irish Scott; and, adds his biographer, the unfriendly critic will say, "So fares it with Irish gifts; the lower hit their mark, the highest miss it, sometimes by going to one side of it, and as often by going above it!"

Aubrey de Vere has been a warm, loyal-hearted patriot, and his love of Ireland and her people, his deep sympathy with her struggles and aspirations, his appreciation of her sterling virtues, his benign pity for her faults, and his veneration for her great sons who have toiled and sweated for her emancipation, morally, socially and politically, are sounded in fearless accents that have in them not only the Celtic fire, but the cool judgment of reflection and moderation. There are racy accounts of Daniel O'Connell, Feargus O'Connor, Shiel, and others, all of them known to the author; and he devotes a chapter to clearing up misapprehension and unjust representations regarding the Irish proprietors during the troublous years of the Irish famine. The statement of an impartial writer in the opposing political camp which he quotes sums up his own conclusions: "The bulk of the Irish landlords manfully did their best in that dread hour. . . . Cases might be named by the score in which such men scorned to avert the pressure on their suffering tenantry the fate they saw impending over themselves. They went down with the ship."

But though dear to his heart is the country of Erin, and though fruitful to the student of history these mature and sage political reflections may be, yet we find the peculiar flavour and attraction of this book to lie in the reminiscences of Wordsworth, of Sir Henry Taylor, Christopher North, Cardinal Newman, and especially of Cardinal Manning. Many of his recollections have already been embodied in letters contributed by him to the Memoirs of Lord Tennyson, Lord Houghton, and Sara Coleridge; and in his *Essays*, published in three volumes by the Macmillan Company, he has familiarised us with his pleasant personal relations with Wordsworth, Taylor, Trench, Coventry Patmore, Landor. and others. But there is much more here and more of it interesting. It was in the early forties that he visited England's lakeland. We wish we could give his description of Tintern Abbey, so characteristic is it of the writer's poetic sentiment kept sane by the humour of common things which constantly seasons his exuberant fancy. Here is part of it:

> "When I reached Tintern Abbey the moon had climbed over the woody ridges and shone on the grey walls with a brilliance that made the southern arch, seventy feet high, look as dark as the mouth of a cave. Close by the ruin stood one of those clean and beautiful little inns special to England. They gave me a well-furnished bedroom, though one so small that the honeysuckles which made their way through the open window trailed on to the bed. Very soon I sallied out to see the ruins. The gates were locked, but I was left free to walk round and round the building and get glimpses into the interior through the long windows the traceries of which cast their ebony bars over plats of grass whitened by moonbeams. The wind sighed in the ivy, and the river murmured close by; and there was no sound beside, except that of an old white horse that cropped his meal in the churchyard, and left an occasional sigh on the sward."

Mr. de Vere passed several days under Wordsworth's roof, which he regards as the greatest honour of his life. They rose early and went to bed early. "Each night prayers were read by Mrs. Wordsworth in a voice full of reverence and sweetness. He (Wordsworth) knelt near with his face hidden in his hands. That vision is often before me." "Rich and rare" must have been the burden of their conversation during those days, for the harvest of a quiet eye and ear has treasured a store of good things that will make the lover of Wordsworth greatly a debtor to Mr. de Vere. Wordsworth showed him the scenes to which he was most attached, and recorded many incidents connected with them. During their walks together Wordsworth's chief theme, next to Nature, was poetry. He did not think very highly of our modern poets except Coleridge, of whom he affirmed that no other poet had ever had so exquisite an ear, and that if he had gone on writing poetry for ten years more he must have been the greatest poet of the modern world. In a letter of Wordsworth to Mr. de Vere there is this delightful dictum:

> "Certain it is that old men's literary pleasures lie chiefly among the books they were familiar with in their youth; and this is still more pointedly true of men who have practised composition themselves."

Again he writes:

> "Publication was ever to me most irksome: so that if I had been rich I question whether I should ever have published at all, though I believe I should have written."

Later in these reminiscences, Mr. de Vere tells us that several friends looking upon the face of Wordsworth as he lay on his bed of death, were deeply impressed by the resemblance which his face then bore to that of Dante, as preserved in the best portraits, a resemblance which they had never noted before.

But space fails us to tell of Hartley Coleridge, who "could do everything but keep his footing" and who "wandered like a breeze;" of Sir Henry Taylor, with whom Aubrey de Vere travelled in company, chiefly in Italy, when (1843–44) the former was ordered South on account of ill health; of his travels in Switzerland and in Scotland; of Cardinal Newman and Cardinal Manning. The chapter on Manning especially commends itself to the reader by its staunch tribute to the disinterested character of the man. A very fine and appreciative portrait is that of Cardinal Newman, showing us glimpses of the man under the wearer of the Red Hat. The metaphysical or theological may care to read the chapter, "My Submission to the Roman Catholic Church;" but for us we passed hastily to the more edifying one which follows it recounting the political changes witnessed between 1848 and 1895. A concluding chapter on "Some of My Poems, their Aims and Objects," brings the volume to a close.

You will remember that we quoted Mr. de Vere at the beginning of this review as setting out to "amuse" and "interest" others by describing the persons and places he had himself seen in his lifetime. If every other reader who peruses this volume of recollections gets as much amusement out of it and is as keenly interested in its recital as we have been he will have nothing to complain of. Immensely readable for its story of incidents, its pictures of celebrated places, and for its well-drawn portraits of eminent men of whom the world never tires hearing, Aubrey de Vere's *Recollections* merits a wide recognition. Few books of reminiscences have been published for some time which equal this one in value and interest.

James MacArthur.

"SARACINESCA FISHES FOR PAGLIUCA."*

An artist may compose a great novel in one of two ways. He may surrender himself, mind, body, soul and conscience, to the inspiration, regarding the setting forth of whatever vision or dream has come to him as the one great necessity, to which must give way all conceivable duties either to God or man. Or he may welcome the creative impulse with a burning heart, it is true, yet a cool brain, and carry out its behests not because it commands, but because he himself wills it, and with a hand so steady, and so invincible a determination, that neither interruption, adverse criticism nor even the deadening influence of unsympathetic surroundings can do more than perhaps slightly to delay the progress of his work toward completion.

Of the first psychological condition most workers in any art know something; the second is peculiar to the great artist alone, and in him is the result of a long and arduous training. When we have added that the latest work of Mr. Marion Crawford bears the unmistakable stamp of having been precisely so wrought out, it will at once be evident what rank we are inclined to claim for the author among American novelists.

And we should claim for him the very highest, had he never written anything but *Corleone.* Unfortunately, he is a writer most unequal in execution, heavily handicapped by his enormous popularity, so that his work is not always even conscientious; at times it is meretricious, at times deliberately *scamped;* so that we can hardly credit that the same brain evolved the utter futility of *Adam Johnstone's Son*, and the lame and impotent conclusion of *A Rose of Yesterday*, and (for an example on the other side) the sane strength and virility of the Saracinesca trilogy, to which *Corleone* has now added a fourth chronicle of that noble house.

It is, however, not through its sanity that Corleone will appeal to the average novel-reader, who—under breath be it spoken—is not averse to a touch of hysteria. The mere story is of absorbing interest, and possesses the transcendent merit that even a blasé and veteran reviewer is altogether unable to foresee the conclusion. And yet the sequence of events is of absolute necessity, following one upon the heels of the other with that inevitability which in itself betokens the hand of the master workman. Beginning in Rome, thence shifting to Sicily, and so back and forth, the mere local colour of the scene of action is of a depth and variety to excite an ordinary writer to extravagance of diction, to enthusiasm, at least, of description; the plot is highly dramatic, not to say sensational; but Mr. Crawford's manner from first to last is that of the impartial historian; not once is he moved to apostrophe or invective; he distinguishes as calmly between ignorance and innocence in the case of the young Vittoria as he analyses the nervous tension produced in Tebaldo Pagliuca by his wilful and deliberate assassination of Francesco, his brother. "He had not the sort of real timidity under a superficial recklessness which begins to feel remorse almost as soon as the irrevocable deed is done. But little by little . . . a kind of stealing horror surrounded him, and would not leave him . . . the horror . . . *of having destroyed at a blow, something to which he had been accustomed all his life.*" The italics are ours; they mark a depth of cold, clear insight, which — shall we speak the truth?—rather repels one as almost unhuman.

The motto which we have placed at the head of this review was one way of reading certain letters, engraved on the floor of the little Sicilian Church of Santa Vittoria. Begun at another point

* Corleone. By F. Marion Crawford. New York: The Macmillan Co. $2.00.

—for it ran round a circle like a disk—it made a sense very different; no one knew what might be the true reading, but there existed a superstition that when it should come true the last Corleone should die, and the Pagliuca d'Oriani should end. And now, once again, an ordinary writer would have made this Sibylline sentence the keynote of his tale, or at least would have caused it to fulfil itself. Mr. Crawford views it as a curious and interesting superstition, but it has no shadow of influence either upon himself or the events which he narrates, and its fulfilment is merely a singular coincidence.

In the manner of death of one of these Pagliuca, our author has created one of the strongest situations with which we are acquainted, either in the novel or the drama. The murderer of his brother in this same old Church of Santa Vittoria, finding that he has unwittingly had the young priest Ippolito Saracinesca for a witness, communicates the crime to him, without loss of a moment, under the seal of confession. Then, caring not, knowing not, whether his astounded auditor has absolved him or not, he straightway leaves the church, locking the door behind him, and denounces Ippolito to the authorities as the murderer. The ingenuity of it baffles belief in its invention by mortal mind. Surely it must have happened! Of a similar nature is Concetta's denunciation of the same rather unlucky young priest, who has just rescued her from the violence of Francesco. "And you thought I would turn and accuse a Corleone when I could accuse a Saracinesca? You do not know us," says Concetta.

Truly we may confess it without shame we do not know the Sicilians, if these are they; and we may add without a blush that we do not want to! Mr. Crawford probably does; at least his calm, dispassionate narrative compels belief. Certainly the national character as depicted by him is thoroughly self-consistent; even that charming and childlike villain, "the Moscio," is in his hands more entirely comprehensible than one's dearest friends and nearest relations. That Aliandra should be attracted by this delightful person is perfectly intelligible, and may contain the seed of another Sicilian tale; in the mean time, if Mr. Crawford's presentment of the island, with its mixed Saracen and Greek ancestry, be as voracious as it appears, if the Mafia be "not a band . . . but a sentiment, a feeling, a sort of wild love of our country," then he has rendered an important service to social science, in addition to creating one of the strongest and most delightful novels of our century.

John Lennox.

NATURE IN DANTE.*

As a rule the Dante monograph, like other special treatises, is apt to prove caviare to the general. Dante's theology, his philosophy, his politics are not subjects which appeal strongly to the layman. But every one, old and young alike, who has once come under the spell of Florence, and has felt the witchery of Tuscan skies, must have some curiosity to know what emotions these same aspects of nature awoke within the poet who is of all others most closely identified with the life of mediæval Italy. And for this reason Professor Kuhns's unpretentious but thoroughly scholarly little volume ought to appeal warmly to the general reader as well as to the student of Dante.

It has the sterling merit of being written in a broad spirit of impartiality; the author has sought to collect and sift down all the passages in the *Divina Commedia* that in any way bear upon his subject, together with whatever side lights the *Vita Nuova* or *Canzoniere* afford; and this he seems to have accomplished with commendable thoroughness, and has presented his results in a style at once lucid and entertaining. Taken as a whole, the book cannot be said to throw any especially new light upon Dante's attitude toward nature, but rather to confirm previously accepted views. "My object," he says, "has not been to deny Dante's claim to be considered a close observer and a genuine lover of Nature—for this I believe to be true of him in an eminent degree—and I fully concur in the opinion of Burckhardt and Humboldt, who consider him the first poet to show the modern appreciation

* The Treatment of Nature in Dante's Divina Commedia. By L. Oscar Kuhns, Professor in Wesleyan University, Middletown, U. S. A. New York: Edward Arnold. $1.50.

of the world in which we live" (p. 44); but at the same time he finds that "when compared with modern writers, Dante seems narrow in the use he makes of nature; the poet and the painter of to-day manifest a deep and wide sympathy for all manifestations of life, and for all variety of scenery. . . . The feeling for the sublime and wild in Nature, which is entirely lacking among the ancients, is also lacking in Dante." In their attitude toward nature there is a close analogy between Dante and the early Florentine painters, beginning with Cimabue and Giotto, as has been well brought out by Mr. Ruskin, in his delightful chapters on "The Mediæval Landscape" (*Modern Painters*, Part IV., chaps. xiv., xv.), to which Professor Kuhns has frequent occasion to acknowledge his indebtedness; in poet and painter alike we see the same effort to emancipate themselves from their classical or Byzantine models; but the trammels of tradition were not to be thrown off in a single generation. One of Professor Kuhns's most interesting chapters is that on "Dante's Conventional Treatment of Nature," in which he shows Dante's extensive indebtedness to the Bible and to classic writers, Vergil, Ovid, and others, for stock phrases and metaphors, many of which have become the common property of poets in all ages. "The only wonder," he concludes, "is not that Dante has so many conventional references to nature, but that, in spite of the artificiality of his times, he gives such striking evidence of close personal observation of the world about him" (p. 19). And he cites the many phases of Nature which Dante was the first to introduce into poetry, "such as the hand bathed and smoking in winter, the change of colour in burning paper, the lizard flashing across the sunlit road, and especially the phosphorescent glow on water at night" (p. 186). What seems to impress him especially is Dante's topographical accuracy, and he dwells upon the exactness and minuteness of the poet's descriptions of the course of the Arno (Purg. XIV., 16 sq.), and of the location of Mantua (Inf. XX., 61 sq.). But notwithstanding Dante's keen powers of observation and accuracy of detail, the most casual reader of Professor Kuhns's book cannot fail to note the absence in the *Divina Commedia* of all that we are in the habit of thinking of as the salient features of an Italian landscape—the blue sky, the blue waters of the Mediterranean, the matchless scenery of the Riviera, the olive groves and vineyards, with all the busy life attending the vintage and the gathering of the olives—all, in short, which in modern parlance goes to make up the *milieu*, is lacking. "We must confess," admits Professor Kuhns with visible reluctance, "that the direct evidence in the *Divina Commedia* of an appreciation of the natural beauties of Italy in any way comparable to that shown by modern writers is very small;" and in almost every chapter he is forced to show his surprise at such a want of appreciation. For example, "in all references to the sea there is a strange absence of colour in the descriptions. . . . The waters of the Mediterranean are very beautiful, and show every shade of colour, according to circumstance. But of all this there is not one word in the *Divina Commedia*" (p. 87). Or again, "There is not the slightest evidence in the *Divina Commedia* of a love for the simple, wild, uncultivated flowers, those which are found in the fields and along the wayside" (p. 116); that "as in the case of flowers, the number of different trees is surprisingly small, and forms a striking contrast with Vergil and even Ovid" (p. 123); that the "most common birds used by troubadours and minnesingers are the nightingale and lark. . . . It is rather singular that Dante has so little reference to them" (p. 135); and similarly, in regard to places, that "of all the beauty which hovers about Venice, floating on the bosom of the Adriatic, not a trace can be found in the *Divina Commedia*." A similar comment has been made by Ruskin of Dante's apparent lack of appreciation of the magnificent panorama of the Val d'Arno and the purple range of the mountains of Carrara, which one commands from the hill of San Miniato. Of course it is unwise to build too much upon the omission of certain phases of nature from the *Divina Commedia*, and Professor Kuhns is quite justified in being persuaded that "in spite of the above facts, Dante did appreciate the beauty of his native land." But the tendency of his book is to leave a vague sense of doubt and disillusion.

How many good books are marred by an unsatisfactory index! The present one might have been considerably amplified with profit, while a table of passages cited, without detracting from the popular character of the book, would have greatly increased its value to the specialist.

Frederic Taber Cooper.

THREE PARTNERS.*

In the chastened words of Whisky Dick, we wish to offer our congratulations and felicitations to Mr. Harte on his having written so delightful a story, and one that embodies so distinctly the noble qualities, and their defects, which have made his personality the force it has been in American literature. There is here the same gift of lucent narration, the same deft selection of incidents and love of unravelling mysteries, the same plucky determination not to blink the tragic and irreparable facts of human conduct, which have always informed his writing, and these, as usual, threaten to play the very mischief with his dramatic instinct and his delineation of character. No one but a genuine artist in intent could emerge so creditably from such a *mêlée* with himself, or indeed be under the constant and harassing necessity of essaying so many things at once. If it should be found that the book before us lacks wholeness and symmetry and abounds in clever artificial situations—"curtains," grand entrances and exits; that its four central figures are Dickensian incarnations of a single trait or characteristic, and its minor personages, being less strongly accentuated, are more complex and human, though less appealing, because the targets of the author's gentle satire; and that its humour, founded upon truth rather than exaggeration, and taking its hue from the complications of the plot, alone remains intact before the surge and undertow of conflicting ideals, let us yet be thankful for those ideals, and lenient toward one who has attempted much and been unable to weld into complete harmony the intricacies of his design.

The three partners who carved their fortune out of Heavy Tree Hill were Stacy the practical, Demorest the contemplative, and Barker the impulsive. Stacy got them away in time from the ill-fated cabin, in three years became a rich banker, and curbed the others' *penchant* for wildcat investments. Demorest, in his all-night vigil before they packed off to Booneville and ever afterward, brooded on the vision of a fair young girl whom he had abandoned, in obedience to a malicious forged letter, that he might remove the reproach of his poverty. Now it was the sight of a stagecoach, now of a photograph, that reminded him of his buried past. We leave him happy in the discovery that the loved one was not dead, as he had been informed, and gloomily wondering if she had "grown stouter and more complacent." Barker, who always believed in everybody until they believed in themselves, and then "shook" him, who was not only open to deceit, but seemed to invite it, to whom "all women were either virgins or married saints," wedded a vulgar little fool who carped at his enthusiasms, talked loudly in hotel dining-rooms, and berated hotel clerks, and finally eloped with her broker. Barker drifted into chimerical but lucky speculations. He fell effusively in love with a Mrs. Horncastle, of infelix reputation, who in his eyes was "as noble as she was generous and handsome." And when his wife, deserted by the lover of her money, drove up in a buggy, dirty and dishevelled, he incurred her everlasting contempt by tenderly assuming that she had been to the Divide looking after the money he had given her. Each one of the trio is drawn with firm, broad strokes, and stands out unrelieved by lights or shadows. Nor is our old friend Jack Hamlin, who hovers about like a good angel, guarding their treasure and visiting wrath upon the robber and murderer in their midst, conceived differently. He is a buoyant soul with "not a crease in his white waistcoat nor a speck upon his varnished boots." That is all.

Every one of these characters is essentially simple. While you are under the glamour of the romance, they are all momentarily convincing. You fancy that you have met a Barker, a Demorest, a Stacy, if not a Hamlin. Yet I venture to say that in real life they are far outnumbered by the Van Loos, the Mrs. Horncastles, and the Steptoes.

* Three Partners; or, The Big Strike on Heavy Tree Hill. By Bret Harte. Boston: Houghton, Mifflin & Co. $1.25.

Not that defaulters, and claim jumpers, and cutthroats, and adventuresses are in the majority (*pas du tout!*), but that almost everybody is a bundle of inconsistencies, actuated in each deed by a confluence or clash of motives, as were Clive Newcome, Silas Marner, Sir Willoughby, and Diana of the Crossways. You can think of no one of *them* as a personified trait. But eliminate Barker's impulsiveness, or Demorest's lovesickness, and he is a cipher. And Hamlin's immaculateness is a mere external ticketing, like Carker's display of his teeth, or Mrs. Gamp's or Mr. Micawber's favourite speech.

Perhaps their very simplicity renders them the more pliable in the construction of telling scenes. Why does Barker arrive at the hotel the very moment Van Loo is expected by Mrs. Barker? Why does Mrs. Horncastle receive calls, on the same afternoon and in the same room, from her brutish husband, from whom, as Barker said, "all California would gladly see her divorced;" from the fibbing wife whom she had warned against eloping with a swindling hypocrite; and from the only man in the world she ever cared for? Why does the dishevelled Mrs. Barker drive up when her husband has just confided to Mrs. Horncastle: "If I had loved her truly I could not have touched *your* lips"? Why does Demorest torture himself with the thought of his sleeping "in the same bed lately occupied by the mother of the man who was suspected of having forged his name"? Why, indeed, unless Mr. Harte makes his characters dance attendance on contrasted effects and theatric climax?

As if it were not enough, like one of his own stage-drivers, to hold two pairs of reins, Mr. Harte has given us in this story a couple of ghastly enigmas. While Demorest sat dreaming of his sweetheart on the night before the partners' evacuation of their shanty, he heard "a gentle brushing of some yielding substance" in the corner where the gold nuggets lay concealed. Lifting the blanket, he beheld a human hand reaching in between the logs, which he promptly jabbed with his bowie knife, amputating two of the fingers. Whose hand this was, is a sealed mystery for some three hundred pages. It haunts one's imagination like the hand Tom Sawyer saw in the cave or the single footprint Robinson Crusoe spied on the beach. Then there is the question, who forged that heart-breaking letter, and how the photograph of Demorest's *fiancée*, standing on Mrs. Van Loo's mantel-shelf, could have been taken and dated two years after her death.

Altogether, it is a story of thrilling and diversified interest. Mr. Harte has given us of his best. His humour is—thank Heavens!—more like Irving's and Thackeray's than Mr. John Kendrick Bangs's—"subtle and pervasive," as they say, rather than jestful and distorted. "Armorous tryst," by the way, is an excellent misprint. But why, O Mr. Harte, this carnival, one might almost say *Moulin Rouge*, of split infinitives?

George Merriam Hyde.

A SISTER OF THE SAINTS.*

Nearly five centuries ago there was born in a little village, among the Vosges Mountains, to Jacques d'Arc and Isabel Romée, his wife, a girl, who was, perhaps, considering her education and what she accomplished, the greatest military genius whom the world has ever seen. Born of pure and strong peasant parents, living the simple, free peasant life, she was healthy and vigorous both in mind and body. At the age of about seventeen she exhibited, in addition to military genius (in itself not unaccountable, under the mysterious law of prenatal influence), a purity or sexlessness not infrequently found at that age in girls of unusually vigorous mental gifts and a moral character so noble and lofty, combined with so rare a spirituality as to overshadow all her other qualities, and cause her to be considered, in her own day and in ours, "The Sister of the Saints."

Now, it happens, singularly enough, that in three important historical novels which have recently appeared three views have been presented of this character of Jeanne d'Arc which are distinctly progressive in relation to one another. The first of these, *Personal Recollections of Joan of Arc*, said to be from the pen of her page and secretary, Louis de Conte, and really written by Mark

* The Days of Jeanne d'Arc. By Mary Hartwell Catherwood. New York: The Century Co. $1.50.

Twain, or Mr. Clemens, bears the stamp of inaccuracy on its title-page in the name "Joan of Arc;" which impresses the judicious reader with a grief as sincere as if the late Lord Beaconsfield were termed "Mr. Benjamin of Israel." The name is, moreover, precisely typical of the book, in which, at the expense of vast study and an immensity of manual labour, Mr. Clemens has succeeded in travestying Jeanne d'Arc and her time. Probably this opinion of ours will tend to an emptying of the vials of wrath on the part of the millions of admirers who have been won to Mark Twain by his undoubted genius; but genius is only permitted to transgress all the received canons of a given art when the result is demonstrably a success. In the present case Mr. Clemens was handicapped by his professional position as a humourist; and perhaps we can best appease his friends, lovers, and especially his countrymen, by defining that typically American trait of which he is the best exponent. American humour in its origin is largely the faculty of making the best of things, united to a distaste for stage effect or "making a scene;" it avoids apparent egoism by a belittling of the really heroic features of any story which it undertakes to tell, and exaggerates details which would otherwise be sufficiently commonplace, with a final result obviously grotesque. Now all this is well enough in its own place—for example, in *A Connecticut Yankee at the Court of King Arthur*—but the user of this method becomes himself as insensible to its effects as if it were any other nerve excitant; and evidently Mr. Clemens is perfectly unconscious in his *Joan of Arc* of an incongruity which to the reader is even acutely painful. And yet we could forgive his slipshod Connecticut English—*e.g.*, "arrived back," or to do a thing "evenings;" we could overlook the fact that his *Paladin* is simply a cheap American edition of Daudet's *Tartarin;* we could almost pardon his utter inability to understand any point of view except that of a nineteenth century Protestant of Hartford, Conn.; what we can never forgive in Mr. Clemens is his invincible ignorance of the true nature of inspiration, which, while he recognises Joan's purity of thought and intention, leaves him content with his private theory that she "imagined" her visions, while he tries to hoax the reader into a firm belief in them, in her, and in the alleged author. Mr. Clemens's *Joan of Arc* is a not unattractive though a trifle masculine, American girl, who keeps the reader awake all the time by her "smartness" and stirred with wonder at her powers of endurance; even the author dimly recognises in her a certain spiritual something which he values, no doubt, but has not the slightest desire to possess in and for himself.

Upon this ideal of our heroine the Jeanne d'Arc of Mr. Andrew Lang, in *A Monk of Fife*, is a distinct advance. Needless to dwell upon the historic setting, upon the delicacy of characterisation, upon the beautiful and poetic diction, or the absolute correctness of the point of view which is always that, not of the author, but of the Monk of Fife, once a brave soldier of Jeanne la Pucelle, and the faithful lover of Maid Elliot. But the Jeanne d'Arc of Mr. Lang is not the inspired deliverer sent from heaven. How should she be? She is rather an impossible Vala maid, pure, lofty, courtly in manner, tender of heart, even childlike, and possessed in a pre-eminent degree of that mysterious second sight, in the existence of which Mr. Lang's Scottish birth will not permit his agnosticism entirely to lose faith.

Now turn to Mrs. Catherwood's *The Days of Jeanne d'Arc*, and we find ourselves at once in the company of the "Sister of the Saints." This is the distinguishing mark; for the rest, she is a peasant as other peasants, nor very far above the best of them, such as her own parents, her brother Pierre, and the lovely and radiant petite Mengette. Only Jeanne is the sister of the saints, sharing with them in divine communion and fellowship. And it is well to note just here that in her preface the author confesses, "at the risk of provoking a smile," that her book is the "result of a divine hint." For which word in itself we feel rather sorry, though it be the outcome of a divine modesty; for the divine commands, impels or inspires; it never hints.

But the result to the book is to place the author at once *en rapport* with her heroine; she does not merely describe her as the inspired maid; she herself feels in her own soul the burning of the same inspiration. From this truth of feeling results, first of all, a singularly delicate and dignified reserve and self-control; an avoidance of the vulgar heaping up of marvellous details, and a tendency to attribute as much as is possible to the working of natural laws, which is very like the supernaturalism of Scripture, and very unlike that of the *acta sanctorum*.

"But," says the *fin de siècle* reader, beginning a plea against enforced faith, if not in visions *per se*, at least in visions of the rabbinical St. Michael, and the more than half-mythical saints Catharine and Margaret; "but if these names stood to the peasant Jeanne for the fullest concept of the divine battle power, of royal authority, of immaculate virginity, then we know of a certainty that she was inspired and directed by precisely these forces and by none other. It becomes, in fact, an added wonder that the voices claimed to belong rather to these abstract conceptions than to characters more easily proven historical."

But let us pass from the soul of the story to its body, and observe its methods of construction; for Mrs. Catherwood's technique is scarcely equalled, certainly unexcelled in modern literature. She is by no means an impressionist; rather, her manner is that of the line engraver; her backgrounds are clear, distinct, accurate, full of detail, full of atmosphere, against which her figures stand out in a significant grouping that of itself tells the story. For indeed the story is told in a series of dramatic incidents rather than in a continuous narrative. A selection from these will help us to understand the author's method of getting her effects. First of all there is the peasant interior, the home of Durand Laxart; outside, the moonlight on the Mouse Valley; France, England and Burgundy at war in the far distance; in the foreground, the Angelus, and "his wife's cousin, Jeanne d'Arc, came out of the oven shed with a huge ring of bread in her hands. She slipped the ring upon her arm and joined her palms, bending her forehead to them. While the Angelus rang no man could speak a word to little Jehannette." The Man, the Woman, the Angelus! It is Millet! At once the reader is *en rapport;* more, he himself is a part of the scene. But this is not plagiarism, it is not clap-trap; it is the result of study as faithful as Millet's own," of journeys over the maid's country . . . in voitures, on foot, in carts."

Again, even Andrew Lang fails to see that a miraculously recovered sword is a necessity for the divinely commissioned warrior of heaven; yet the old legends might have taught him this, though treated simply as myths, from King David to Siegfried, the hero. To be sure, he describes the finding of the old sword in a historical sort of way. Mrs. Catherwood brings Pierre d'Arc, wounded and weary, to the church of St. Katherine of Fierbois, and shows him the yawning dark gap in the wall beneath the feet of the statue, whence the sword had been taken.

Or how does she let us learn that at the Maid's intercession, refusing for herself any gift at all, the tax was taken forever from Domremy and Greux? There is discontent in Domremy because of the exaltation of the D'Arc family; there is the attempted drowning of Choux—a marvellous bit of drawing, by the way—with his hump, his red woollen cap, "his stealthy, hyena-like odour," and his boyish-voiced familiar. There is the defence of the cripple by Mengette; and finally, in the dimly lighted church, the voice of the curé, like a sword flashes across the people's penitence, "The king takes the burden of tax off Domremy and Greux. I have no more to say. Go home." And then the congregation weeping, "like one great sorrowful child."

Or, last of all, the martyrdom, where the unshrinking realism is yet softened by reflection in the mirror of Bertrand de Poulengy's mystically sympathetic experiences. The interview with D'Aulon, which immediately follows; the vow of Bertrand, understood, not distinctly related; the meeting with the executioner, and the floating out to the sea of the faithful squire with the ashes of his lady and mistress—is not this indeed a romance of the fifteenth century that we read? Hardly can one believe that the words are not in black letter upon vellum!

Mrs. Catherwood has done more than merely to revive for us the real Pucelle d'Orleans, living, breathing, and inspired, though this is much; for many years she has been the apologist, the interpreter of the Gallic character. *The Days of Jeanne d'Arc* is simply a further advance along the same lines. The

Frenchman is not, as has been said, "half monkey and half tiger." Doubtless the tiger is there, perhaps the monkey also; but our author teaches us that there exists yet a third element—that he is a trinity, not a dualism; and that the third person in this trinity is sister to the saints.

August Max.

THE FANTASTIC FICTION; OR, "THE INVISIBLE MAN." *

I am very glad to see that there is now a chance of Mr. H. G. Wells acquiring the popular vogue and celebrity to which he is entitled. He has for some time been known as a remarkable and ingenious artist, and there were great things in his cycling story, *The Wheels of Chance.* But his effects have not been palpable and violent enough to win for him a great constituency of readers. In *The Invisible Man*, and still more in *The War of the Worlds*, now being published in the *Cosmopolitan*, he has written books which should be read eagerly and generally. My one fear for him is that he is going to write too much. There are by far too many paragraphs in the literary papers about forthcoming stories of his. Let me beseech him to hold his hand, to write few books, to write them as well as he can, and not to make them too short.

Such a kind of literature as that of which *The Invisible Man* is a specimen is inevitable. We are living in an age of inventions. The conditions of life are being more or less modified by these. It is very natural to imagine the development of invention; very natural also to ask whether the world will be any happier for it. Mr. Wells has remarkable literary abilities. He has also had a good scientific training, and he is saved alike by his sense and knowledge from the insanity which might easily wreck such attempts as these. *The Invisible Man* is not so good a book as it might have been and ought to have been, but it is decidedly striking and original, and what is rare in such books, it is also provocative of thought. The story is of a man who by following up certain scientific principles, which are carefully and plausibly explained, found that he could make himself invisible. He saw, not unnaturally, great possibilities in the discovery, possibilities of wealth beyond the dreams of avarice, and a power even greater than the power which goes with wealth. But he found when his goal was reached that it was not a paradise. In the first place, although invisible, he was not intangible. In the second place, although his body was invisible, his clothes were not. Consequently, in order to enjoy the full privileges of his invisibility, he had to go naked, which is uncomfortable in this non-Edenic climate. He found, further, that if he took food he was visible until it was assimilated, and of course the dishes on which it was contained were seen mounting to the unseen mouth. Mr. Wells has thoroughly worked out his plan in his own mind, and the result is decidedly amusing. It follows from the facts that the invisible man had to provide himself with a false face. He might, by dint of huge overcoats, disguise the absence of a visible body, but something had got to be done with his head. He develops, like all monsters, a cruel and murderous tendency, and is ultimately run to death after doing a great deal of mischief. The story is slight, and might be passed as a curiosity, but it suggests something of the limits of invention.

We are always reading about the great things Mr. Edison is to do. He has done nothing, so far as I can make out, for a long time. He is said to be continually experimenting and inciting hopes that at last he will begin. The fact is the limits of invention are apparently marked. We have inventions given us sufficient to maintain our social life amid growingly complex conditions. We could not live with the contrivances which served our grandfathers. The population of the world has increased so enormously that we have to make more haste, or to find means which will accelerate our work, and so we have railways, telegraphs, phonographs, telephones, and the like. But will anybody say that life has been made any easier by these inventions? Have they done more than keep pace with our steadily increasing needs? Is it easier for the average man to earn his living now than it was eighty years ago? I doubt it very much. Furthermore, has the happiness of life been materially increased by these inventions? Here again I doubt. We can travel much further and at a cheaper rate than our fathers,

* The Invisible Man. By H. G. Wells. New York: Edward Arnold. $1.25.

but do we get out of our journeys the intense relish and enjoyment they did out of theirs? We have postal cards, and alas! that it should be said, people who are willing to use letter-cards, and the penny post, of course, but have we more pleasure from our correspondence than those who wrote more rarely, but who filled their letters with news and kindness? I am not certain. We seem always to be on the verge of some invention that will really alter the moods and complexions of human life, but an invisible hand seems to stay us, and we remain in the old circle of experiences.

Is it difficult to see the reason for this? There are certain inventions and discoveries which, if attained by man, would totally destroy the moral basis of life. Suppose, for example, that the secret of invisibility was discovered. Suppose it was discovered in a way not exempt from the limitations of Mr. Wells. Suppose whatever we were doing some one could come in through the closed doors, invisible, intangible, the witness of all we did, would not our whole moral life be overthrown? As I write these words, I know what is in my room. But suppose I wrote them with the haunting consciousness that the room might be peopled, what then? Would not the reason reel? Would not the supports of an ordinary life be suddenly struck away? There are strange approximations, like that of the Roentgen rays; but, after all, what do the Roentgen rays come to? They give some amusement at first, rather ghastly and short-lived amusement. They may possibly help doctors a little, though I now hear not much about that. But if it had been made possible to see the soul, how different would all things have been then! We have gone, as some think, dangerously far in the direction of hypnotism, but think how it might have been if one human will could totally subjugate and dominate another. The moral personality would be annihilated; in fact, every idea belonging to morality and religion would be gone, but "the abysmal secret of personality" has been kept, and will still be kept.

Happily there are no invisible men, and never will be any invisible men. But we are not ill-pleased that there is a Mr. H. G. Wells to beguile us by his ingenious fancies of what might be.

Claudius Clear.

STEVENSON'S "ST. IVES."*

That our palate was not keyed up to a proper enjoyment of this late unfinished romance of Stevenson's was a most vexatious discovery. While we enjoyed it as we have relished few tales of adventure published in the last few years, we recall how much more intense was our satisfaction in *Treasure Island* and *David Balfour*. The decrease of appetite for Stevenson's adventurous romances, which we reluctantly admit, is the effect of having been sated with his imitators. To Stevenson as the maker of modern romance we owe an allegiance that his followers can only crave. *St. Ives* deserves to be warmly regarded as a masterpiece of the adventurous school, and we hope that there are those who still keep their early zest for this phase of art to get its highest expression and aroma from these pages. It is one of the chief misfortunes of genius that it has to contend against that reaction which springs from the popularisation of its virtues. The success of Stevenson's exploitations has become the cause of general surfeit.

St. Ives must prove a grateful legacy to all Scotch lovers of Stevenson, not only because it is marked with some of the most characteristic and persuasive qualities of his art, but also because in its choice of material it seems like a homecoming of his spirit. In this unfinished romance, written some few months before his death, Stevenson binds his heart to the heather of his native land with a warmth that the long sojourn of his fancies elsewhere appears only to have increased. Coming at an interesting juncture in the literature of Scotland, when a new school is at its height, *St. Ives* offers in its distinctive treatment of native subject-matter an artistic protest of great liveliness. Those at least to whom the recently homely and dialectic fiction of that land has ever remained an unpalatable haggis will regard its local note as a relief after a bondage to difficult colloquialism and russet sentiment.

The buoyant temper of *St. Ives*, untouched as it is by any stress of gloom, is an affecting proof of the indomitable cheerfulness which cast its gage in the face of disease and death. The exhilaration of the book is in fact one of

* St. Ives. By Robert Louis Stevenson. New York: Charles Scribner's Sons. $1.50.

its chief fascinations. Nor can its joyous character, artistically considered, be regarded as a mere factor of entertainment or of manner. It is manifest to even the casual reader that it is the serenity of real inner graciousness, a blitheness of spiritual conviction, which in a day of pessimistic constraint is a precious gift indeed. Perhaps no one in these latter decades has petitioned for this nobler phase of mind with such glow of zeal as has Stevenson in the expression of his sane and wholesome art. It is this hidden criticism of life that compounds a spiritual tonic in such frank vehicles of amusement as *Treasure Island* and *Kidnapped.*

The pith of *St. Ives* is the characterisation of the hero, the Vicomte Anne de Keroual. In the Vicomte Anne, Stevenson has given us a study of the most insinuating flavour, such as is not likely soon to elude one's consciousness. His humanness has that positive stamp of the complete delineation. The Vicomte convinces with a readiness that phrases a high commentary on Stevenson's acuteness of portrayal. As the fine gentleman of mind as well as of manner, he is worthy of association with Thackeray's select types and the rare few of all time that literature has produced. French to the last conceit of character, his aristocratical intonations would admit him without parley to the Faubourg de St. Germain. Lightness of spirits, readiness of wit, an aptitude for every situation—all that makes up the composition and conscience of the gallant soldier and courtier of the France of yesterday has full echo in *St. Ives.* A tale of such personal interest as the present one could have no better style of narrative than the monologue form, which in Stevenson's hands shows unusual plasticity and responsiveness. It may in the present instance afford the hero a little too much leisure for telling his story, and the reader, to whom incident is the salt of fiction, has some reason to quarrel with the Vicomte over his soliloquising before a mental mirror, but for the real Stevensonian these pauses will represent the conspicuous beauties of the romance.

The concatenations of accident in *St. Ives* do not illustrate the full range of Stevenson's ingenuity in the construction of plot. The excitements are of a less vigorous character than those of many of his earlier tales, holding the attention without blinding it to the frequent analytic touches and consummate turns of style which make *St. Ives* a masterpiece in a minor key. And it is this perfect balance that goes far to make it rank with the more classic literature of adventure, of which *Tom Jones* is an example, rather than with the breathless school of Jules Verne.

Flora Gilchrist, the cynosure of St. Ives's adoration, should by right of importance take her place next to the hero in the interest of the reader. Her power of assertion is not, however, of that commanding quality which distinguished Catriona's claim on the heart, and with the memory of that high-strung and thoroughly delightful Highland maid warm upon us, Flora seems by contrast a vague and unsuccessful portraiture. St. Ives wears his sentiment somewhat carelessly, we think, and in spite of a fine amorous fire which inspired his return to Edinburgh, voluble with dangers, for the sake of a token of his mistress's fidelity, one is half persuaded to the opinion that the actual incentive was an unruly appetite for adventure. Many of the less conspicuous characters, who mainly furnish pegs on which to hang the Vicomte's hopes and fears during his wanderings, are admirable thumbnail impressionisms rich in humour and dry psychological discernment. Few may seem to hold an incontestable patent of novelty, but in minor idiosyncrasies and spice of speech they have that which baptises them to a fresh regeneracy. Of these it would be an unmerited slight indeed not to mention Rowley, valet and esquire to the hero. In Alain and Major Chevenix, the two characters of the book who hold the main vials of ill fortune for the Vicomte, there is little display of that vigorous originality common to Stevenson's creations of villainy. Seriously considered, these etchings are without great value in the larger sense. They strike no urgent note of emotion. They disclose nothing new of the intricacies of human nature. Humour is for the most part their rôle. It is, however, the humour of characteristics rather than of character. As a psychological performance, *St. Ives's* claim rests on the delineation of the hero ; the remainder of the book is recess after study-hour.

To speak of the delicate peach-bloom

smoothness and exquisite modulations of Stevenson's style, as shown in *St. Ives*, is to reiterate a platitude concerning what must ever be his strongest appeal to remembrance, a charm that has no rival among contemporary writers. In the present tale that charm asserts itself throughout, in spite of distracting incidents; it is in itself an ample reward for a reading of the book. One almost fancies that the vintage of Stevenson's manner has grown a trifle mellower with the reserve of time, that it has taken to itself a more ingratiating savour. In no work of his, outside of his essays, does the vesture of his language seem to clothe so exactly the sense of his personality or deck his fancy with such variable and becoming attire. Delightful as is the style of *David Balfour*, we are inclined to think it is in *St. Ives* that Stevenson erects his true monument as a master of narrative style.

Mr. Quiller-Couch's part in the composition of *St. Ives* deserves cordial praise. He has shown, in weaving the story to a finish, a surprising aptitude at imitating Stevenson's whimsical methods and vivacity. Many of Stevenson's partisans doubtless resent the alien hand, and would have preferred the story as a torso to its present completed form; but beyond a question of choice in this matter there is little material for serious grievance. Mr. Quiller-Couch, in the episode of the balloon voyage, has given the closing chapters a dramatic force that would, we believe, have met with the hearty approval of Stevenson himself.

Edward O. Uffington Valentine.

THE STORY OF AN UNTOLD LOVE.*

Every wide reader of fiction has often been struck by the fact that while love is the subject of ninety-nine out of a hundred novels, a story that really throbs with the feeling is one of the rarest things in literature. So rarely, indeed, has an author been able to imprison in his pages the very spirit of passion—as the ruby holds the flame in its heart—that such a work seems always to win a place apart and to live as though the power were in itself one of the elements of immortality. There is no need to mention the titles of the few famous books of which this is true. Everybody knows *Manon Lescault* and *Paul and Virginia*, and the rest of these immortals, and they are only referred to in this connection because Mr. Ford's new novel is a striking illustration of the love story that is not a love story.

The opening pages appeal, it is true; the feeling of the first and second chapters is peculiarly warm and tender, having an intimacy that may come by reason of the author's method; for the use of the first person seems more susceptible of such effects than any other manner that a writer can employ. But the fine, soft touch is lost almost as soon as felt, and the excellence of Mr. Ford's good work bends forthwith in an entirely different direction.

It bends, in truth, in several different directions; so that while the book is full of interest, it is rather formless as a work of art. For example, the exquisite tenderness of the introductory pages changes abruptly to the keenest dissection of a literary career. The lover who tells the story leaves off love-making with an abruptness that no woman worth wooing would tolerate for a moment, and begins to describe in minutest detail the instincts of the literary temperament, the difficulty of following them, the bitter struggles at the foot of the ladder, and the perils of the ascent. As has been said already, it is all most interesting. It is, indeed, so interesting to every man and woman of letters that it would be hard for one of them to judge the work for the unprofessional reader. One of its searching questions is whether a writer may in honour allow his work to appear above another's signature. Most professional writers have been confronted by this problem, and have perhaps usually settled it—as the man of the story settles it—according to the pecuniary stress of the moment. Another—a clearer and still more vital question, lying closer to a wider world than that of literature—is the moral responsibility involved on the buyer's side—for there are many more such buyers than the uninitiated might suspect. The buyer in this case is a business man, and arguing apparently that all is fair in love, publishes as his own a

* The Story of an Untold Love. By Paul Leicester Ford. Boston: Houghton, Mifflin & Co. $1.25.

book which another man has written, in order to commend himself to an intellectual woman who disdains the merely commercial. Of course the real author loves the same beautiful woman, and one wishes his scruples had asserted themselves before he knew why his rival had paid a fabulous sum for a dry manuscript. It must, however, be admitted that it was rather hard upon him to learn that the book had convinced the woman in the case that the other man was not a mere minting machine, but nobler, finer than he seemed, "that no man but one of noble character and fine mind could write from such a standpoint."

So much for the professional departure from the direct line of the story. It is perhaps unnecessary to follow the innumerable other divergencies, entertaining as most of them are, even when one does not subscribe wholly to the sentiments advanced, as in the long dissertation upon the higher education of women. It may be true that "women who know much of books know little of men, and that's why intellectual women always marry fools;" but one must have time to think about it. There would seem to have been exceptions, say Sappho for example, or George Sand, or George Eliot, or Mrs. Browning, or Mary Godwin, or a good many others. The proposition that "the cables have done more to aid the brotherhood of man' is simpler, although not perhaps in its connection more conducive to the artistic symmetry of the work.

And where, with all the brilliant paragraphs, ranging the largest fields of morals, and literature, and education, and manners, and religion, and politics—where is the spirit of love that has nothing, nothing, nothing in the world to do with any of these? And more incomprehensible of all, why the story of an *untold* love? For it is told many times—whenever, in fact, the lover happens to think of it amid the turmoil of many distracting interests. Told not only to the reader between epigrams on miscellaneous matters, and through letters to the lady, but *vis-à-vis*. The avowal is convincing to the lady, but hardly to the reader. Ah, well, one should not expect too much! After all, it may be almost as difficult to grasp love's real wings in modern fiction as to hold fast to them in real life. Mr. Ford's book, it ought to be added, has the excellent quality of being eminently readable, which characterises all his work.

George Preston.

QUEEN OF THE JESTERS.*

The Impregnable City won for Mr. Max Pemberton an American audience which has grown with each of his subsequent books. The growth may have been less rapid than that of certain contemporary English authors, but, on the other hand, it has been more steady and still advances. Strength was more marked than beauty in *The Impregnable City*; beauty in turn claimed *The Little Huguenot* and *Christine of the Hills*, and now comes the *Queen of the Jesters* to take a place between the two, as the nearest approach to the ideal union that the author has yet achieved.

There is a strong masculine element in the feeling of the eight stories which make up this volume, and which narrate adventures of the most stirring description, but the ruling power supreme over all is the "Queen of the Jesters," as womanly a little woman as ever "went wrong" in the phrase of the world which has so often and so cruelly misjudged her kind.

It might, perhaps, judge more justly, or at least with clearer understanding if it could ever come to believe—as this new book of Mr. Pemberton's seems to argue—that a woman may be at once fine and frail; that she may be as feminine and as weak as Nell Gwynne, yet hold, as poor Nell held, and as many great men have held, that all nobility is not bounded by virtue, and that all meanness does not belong to vice.

This, looking from a man's point of view may, of course, be admitted only in extenuation. Certainly it cannot be safely urged with any sort of directness. Mr. Pemberton as a true artist says not one word bearing directly upon the subject. He merely tells these charming stories, of which Corinne de Montesson, the king's favourite, is the central figure, showing her in every instance as the friend of the helpless, of justice, of mercy, of honesty and truth, always using her unlimited influence for good. Yet her aims are usually reached with such gaiety and laughter as cover the real

* The Queen of the Jesters. By Max Pemberton. New York: Dodd, Mead & Co. $1.50.

intent, for this little woman possesses a large masculine sense of humour, which separates her still further from her own sex.

The tales have a semi-historical colouring, and are of the Old Paris of 1761. Mr. Pemberton knows France—and indeed several other countries—as well as he knows his own land, and he has consequently succeeded perfectly in creating the French atmosphere, and in maintaining it with unusual uniformity throughout the volume. It would be hard to say which of the stories is best. They are all distinctively of the period and of the race. The provincial scamp of the first story and the Parisian dwarf of the last story are equally French, and the work is filled throughout with the sights and the sounds of the city of the Seine. "A Prison of Swords" is one of the vividest sketches, so weirdly horrible, that the foot-note is needed to prove not only the artistic probability of the tale, but its historical accuracy. This note says:

"The Bombec Tower, it may be well to point out, was that tower of the *Conciergerie* prison in Paris, in which torture was generally inflicted. I have added nothing in this story to the historical descriptions of the cells in this horrible place. It was not until the end of the last century that these sunless dungeons were altered radically. At that time the swords in the walls, and the loathsome creatures which the Seine washed into the cells were still the talk of the curious."

Through these gruesome romances of prisons and daggers and duels and poisons, wherein life seems a hand-to-hand combat and force the only law, the Queen of the Jesters treads her perilous, merciful path. "The very air about her was laden with roses. Her girlish face was like the face of one of the Madonnas which the great masters had painted," and surely to one who loves humanity as Corinne de Montesson loved it much shall be forgiven.

It is a tribute to Mr. Pemberton's art that this is felt. There is less readiness to believe in the good heart of the woman who "goes wrong" than to accept the story of the "Prison of Swords" from which it has rescued some fellow-sinner. Yet his art convinces. He teaches charity to frailty as no sermon could preach it, while he deepens scorn of what is cruel and false. And it all looks so simple, too, on the surface—merely a group of dashing tales of adventure without purpose other than amusement. But what so simple as art! For this book seems the efflorescence of that seed which budded in *The Impregnable City*.

Nancy Huston Banks.

TWO FAMOUS SCOTS.*

These volumes are, in spite of certain defects both of plan and of style, useful and readable biographies, and worthy of the places they hold in the Famous Scots Series. It is plain that both Mr. Leask and Mr. Smeaton are enamoured of their subjects. They do not quite say, indeed, that there are no specks upon their suns. Mr. Leask could hardly even carry the *lues Boswelliana* so far as to claim perfection for the marvellous combination of moral weakness and genuine, if limited, intellectual capacity that wrote the *Life of Johnson*. Smollett also confessed so freely and fully to that sin of temper which marred his career, that Mr. Smeaton could not have ignored this side of his hero's life had he been so minded. Otherwise both writers are very ready with praise where that is possible, and with apologies where nothing else is available. On the whole, too, both may be allowed to have taken the right views of their heroes. There must have been a certain power of inspiring love in poor Boswell, in spite of his vanity—though that has been rather exaggerated by Macaulay and other critics—and in spite even of his lamentable infirmity, which often brought him not only to the ground, but into the gutter. But for his temper, or what Mr. Smeaton rather extravagantly terms "the vitriolic acidulousness as well as the saturnine bitterness of his nature," Smollett's life would not have been "a long-drawn-out epic of anguish from the cradle to the grave." Even as things were, the author of *Roderick Random* was not without his moments of personal ecstasy or his periods of domestic happiness. As for the literary judgments passed by Mr. Leask and Mr. Smeaton, they are very much the same as the verdicts passed by all competent critics in the past. Mr. Leask does well to quote as a specimen

* James Boswell. By D. Keith Leask. Tobias Smollett. By Oliphant Smeaton. Famous Scots Series. New York: Charles Scribner's Sons. Each, 75 cts.

of Boswell's art at its best his admirable rendering of the interview between the two old Pembroke men, Johnson and Oliver Edwards, and to say that "No fool with a note-book, no tippling reporter, as the shallow critics say, could have written this." Mr. Smeaton may be allowed also to have grasped the true significance of Smollett's power as a realist when he says, "Smollett's genius was by no means of that purely imaginative, highly spiritual type from which great poetical conceptions are to be expected. He was rather an unsurpassed observer, who, having noted special characteristics of mind as being produced by the fortuitous concourse of certain incidents, straightway proceeded to expand and idealise them." In other words, Smollett was a second-rate Balzac. There are some evidences of hasty writing in both these volumes. Mr. Leask ought not to have put into the mouth of Horace Walpole one of the most famous sayings of Sydney Smith, or credited Mr. Gladstone instead of Mr. Disraeli with having proposed a Parliamentary vote of thanks to Lord Napier for having "planted the Standard of St. George upon the Mountains of Rasselas."

William Wallace.

MR. ANDREW LANG AND "THE BRONTËS: FACT AND FICTION."

To the Editors of THE BOOKMAN :

SIRS : In discussing that part of my book, *The Brontës : Fact and Fiction*, which treats of Charlotte Brontë's relation to M. Héger, Mr. Andrew Lang says, "there can be only one reason for discussing that problem," and this, he hints, is the desire to pry into "the mechanism of genius." I am afraid that Mr. Lang has not read carefully the essay he criticises, and I may perhaps be allowed to point out to your readers that my purpose was not "to pry into" anything. I introduce the subject with these words :

> "Let me state at the outset that I think this subject should never have been publicly touched upon. . . . It was a secret which Charlotte kept hidden from her dearest friends in her lifetime. It does not, as I shall attempt to show, affect, though it confirms, our estimate of her character, and the knowledge of it is not necessary to the appreciation of her art. It should have been left alone."

I go on to point out, however, that it has not been left alone, but has been frequently discussed during the last twenty years ; that lately the evidence in support of it has become to many minds irresistible ; and that it is now hinted that the story, if true, is discreditable. My purpose, therefore, is quite different from that imputed by Mr. Lang ; it is by substituting frank discussion of the subject for that "treatment by dark hints and significant nods" which has been hitherto accorded it to save the character of Charlotte Brontë from aspersion, and to show that she truly was *in any case* not only one of the most gifted, but one of the noblest of women. I repudiate with indignation the implied charge that I have written what could justly give offence to surviving friends. Indeed, so great is my admiration both for the character and genius of this great writer that I honestly believe few would be more pained by any attack upon her fame than I should.

Mr. Lang's correspondence with Dr. Wright in the *Academy* I did not see till after my book was printed. The doubts therein expressed are of a hesitating kind, and relate only to the first part of the Irish romance. On the other hand, his review in the *Illustrated London News* was enthusiastic, and so late as February of this year Dr. Wright speaks of himself as indebted to Mr. Andrew Lang "for valuable criticisms both public and private." Under these circumstances no ordinary weight attaches to Mr. Lang's acknowledgment that my book "confirms his doubts," and that "the origin of these legends seems to need exploration."

On one point Mr. Lang suggests a possible excuse for Dr. Wright, but this excuse is based on a misquotation, and as this affects the question under discussion I may be allowed to point it out. Mr. Lang's words are as follows :

> "When Hugh III. is made to say that his grandfather Hugh I. suffered somehow under George III., we may suspect a misprint. George I. must be intended if any George, and if so some anachronisms will disappear and some miracles with them."

But it was not Hugh III., but Hugh II. who in Dr. Wright's book *twice* makes the assertion alluded to. Now Hugh II. was fifteen years old when George III.

ascended the throne, and he could never have spoken of events which occurred long before his birth as happening in that monarch's reign. This confirms the conclusion I had arrived at from other data—viz., that *Hugh II. cannot possibly have been the real author of the myths.* It needs some one much nearer our own time to confuse George III. with Queen Anne! I am, etc.,

Angus M. Mackay.

NOVEL NOTES.

MARGOT. By Sidney Pickering. New York: G. P. Putnam's Sons. $1.00.

Those who enjoy a graphic sketch of Parisian *pension* life, with a "peekneek" to Versailles and plenty of gossip, with a maiden who exclaims, "Oh, why can't people let me alone!" and a young Englishman in quest of a rich French marriage, that he may rehabilitate his ancient manor, and a trio of innocently shady characters who are mixed up with the political intrigues of Russian refugees, will find this a sufficiently well-written story to merit their perusal. Every one visiting the *pension* had something on his mind, the disclosure of which is for the most part reserved till the romp-in at the finish. Esdale had come to Paris that he might learn something of Margot Lee, the illegitimate daughter of an English gentleman, whom he served as private secretary, and who was dying of an incurable disease. Miss Lee has been secretly and, as she did not know, illegally married to Count Ernroth, who was passing his days in Siberia in administrative exile. Olga Keller, who without the knowledge of the other had been Ernroth's mistress, indulged a spiteful hatred for Margot, although herself ignorant of the latter's relation to Ernroth, and placed under deep obligation to her by her kindness. Petroff, the Russian doctor who befriended Margot when she fled from Esdale's love (obviously for other reasons than that he had been sent to pry into her affairs), although bluntly saying, in answer to her query why he was so good to her: "Don't you know that you are one of those pretty, delicate little women who can extract chivalry even from an old bear?" likewise knew more than for a long time he was disposed to divulge; and if he did not from the first win Margot's confidence he would be put down by the reader as an arrant scoundrel. Indeed, all the minor characters are shrouded in mystery until, as in every-day life, we have formed various conflicting opinions of them, based on seeming inconsistencies of conduct. Margot herself, despite her fainting spells and yearnings for solitude, is free from suspicion, since she is manifestly a person of cultivation and fine moral sensibility. Saved from suicide and a threatened shooting, which with less adroit handling would savour of the police court calendar, at the moment of her disillusionment she is given by the good Samaritan Petroff into the arms of Esdale. The happy ending seems logical, and the melodramatic undercurrent of the tale does not obtrude. Margot's *penchant* for literary criticism, too, is kept within reasonable bounds for one who tramped to Montmartre to lay flowers on Heine's grave, and could repeat from memory "The Lady of Shalott." Several of the contemporaneous allusions, however, conspicuously that to May Yohe, seem inappropriate.

THE HISTORY OF THE LADY BETTY STAIR. By Molly Elliot Seawell. New York: Charles Scribner's Sons. $1.25.

Miss Seawell's little story of the Comte d'Artois's sojourn in Holyrood Palace in the year 1798 is an agreeable *soufflé* with just the slightest fruit flavour of history to enhance its bubbling sentiment and airy simplicity. Among the gentlemen and ladies in waiting to Marie Thérèse and the future Charles X. of France, four appear picturesquely in this novelette—Lady Betty, "one of the sweetest creatures that ever lived;" the Abbé de Ronceray, who had a wonderful and disastrous capacity for keeping secrets; the arrant scoundrel, Bastien, whom Lady Betty struck in the face with her green fan, threatening to report his kiss to the princess; and De Bourmont, who, when he was not yearning consumedly to join the Vendeans, "claimed sanctuary" from his creditors in the palace, and was on the verge of falling in love with two women at once. How Lady Betty gained the ascendency in De Bourmont's heart, and they were victimised and separated by the wiles of Bastien, we will let the reader find out for himself. Toward the end the scene shifts to Algeria, the lovers again meet on the battlefield, and an attempt is made to infuse more movement into what would otherwise merit the name of a sketch. Once, on the explosion of a shell at her feet, when she fell "bleeding from a dozen wounds," the heroine is in dire peril of extinction; but on the next page we read with a sigh of relief that after many months she is "quite well." Thus the coast is cleared for a happy, pathetic ending.

"Quite well" illustrates aptly Miss Seawell's most pronounced literary failing. So does the sentence "She and Angus openly kissed each other quite warmly at parting." She has a little way of understatement which produces the effect of self-consciousness. In this respect, however, *The History of the Lady Betty Stair* is a decided improvement on *The Sprightly Romance of Marsac*, and in every respect a more refined piece of work. Indeed, nothing can be urged against its selection of incidents or the texture of its descriptions; and it is instinct with an atmosphere of delicate feeling, such as few historical romances possess

A NORWAY SUMMER. By Laura D. Nichols. Boston: Roberts Brothers. $1.25.

Even a Loti or Hopkinson Smith finds it by no means easy to embody his observations of foreign lands in a story, the picturesque and the human interest are so sure to militate against each other. In the note-book of her Ellen, Miss Nichols has made a feeble and necessarily futile attempt to sketch Norwegian customs and scenery in conjunction with the inevitable love story. In the midst of a prosy itinerary of the guide-book order, which includes such diverting names as Hønefos, Røros, Tromsø, and Lake Mjøsen, Ellen and Sidney meet amorously on a pier, "she not knowing that he was holding both her hands." Such a manifest absurdity should startle the reader, but does not, since Ellen and Sidney are the merest puppets, used ineffectually to dole out colourless information about the author's summer in Norway. However, the photographic touches given to these paper dolls savour naïvely of New England villageousness. Ellen "had stood well in her classes," and finding that abroad everybody drank wine, "learned to touch her lips to her glass and take as little as possible," lest she violate the precepts of her childhood. The impressions she records, on the voyage and thereafter, are readable for a reason obviously not intended by the author. The volume is interleaved with photographs in half-tone which are of extraordinary interest.

THE EYE OF ISTAR. By William Le Queux. New York: Frederick A. Stokes Co. $1.25.

Following in the wake of Mr. Rider Haggard and of Dr. W. Starbuck Mayo, whose *Kaloolah*, hingeing upon the discovery of a white tribe in the heart of Africa, was much read nearly a half century ago, but with conventionally modern properties and in the light of recent exploration, Mr. Le Queux has written a mazy, diverting tale, the slender plot of which is inflated by a vast amount of mighty palaver, which may easily be mistaken for what Mulvaney called "the power of the tongue." It is justly estimated as one part Midway Plaisance and two parts natural history and theosophy. It has, however, the saving grace of a contagious enthusiasm.

Zafar-Ben-A'Ziz, the dervish in "loose cotton unmentionables," whose love for Lalla Azala, the Princess of Sokoto, inspired him to unravel the Mystery of the Asps branded upon each of their bosoms, was himself one of the bodyguard of the Great Mahdi, Khalifa Abdullah of Omdurman. He met her most romantically. The sole survivor from a fight with the Tuaregs, or Veiled Men of the Desert, he awoke in the harem of the Sultan of Othman, whither, wounded and unconscious, he had been spirited by the princess dressed as a female slave. It is needless to say that he found rich solace there. Till he arrived, Azala's bejewelled breasts had been heaving and falling in many a long-drawn sigh, from fear that no one could be found to solve the riddle of the asps. Indeed, we are informed that unhappiness, like a cankerworm, ate into her heart. Zafar was just promising to go on an expedition to the Rock of the Great Sin, whence a cavernous path led to the Land of No Return, and consult Istar, Queen of Ea, concerning the asps, when a gigantic eunuch named Khazneh turned informant and caused his expulsion from the Sultan's domains. After many hairbreadth escapes he reached Omdurman, and, on telling the Khalifa of his exploits, was made the chief of his *mulazimin*. Thereupon, the Khalifa receiving an invitation to visit the Sultan, Zafar was enabled to combine business with pleasure and imprint some more passionate caresses [*sic*] on Azala's white, sequin-covered brow. Again discovered in the harem, he got away with the dwarf Tiana, and was permitted to pursue his theosophical researches in peace. How he emerged from the Forest of Perpetual Night and swam to the sinful rock in the Lake of the Accursed, and descended to the Kingdom of Myriad Mysteries, and read Assyrian tablets, and first served as the footstool and then as the beloved of Istar, who also had the mark of the asps, and, rather than lose him, eventually pressed a little live asp to her breast, like Cleopatra; and how he returned from the Land of No Return to put his prospective father-in-law on the track of a new conquest, the reader must decipher for himself. It strikes us that Zafar was something of a fool to tell the Queen of Ea about Azala. And we should by all means have named the story *The Foot of Istar*.

THE MAN OF THE FAMILY. By Christian Reid. New York: G. P. Putnam's Sons. $1.25.

"Oh, to be free from this intolerable slavery of debt!" exclaimed Madame Prévost of New Orleans, after an unsatisfactory interview with her landlord, the son of her father's overseer, who was not content with the interest and threatened to foreclose unless she arranged a *mariage de convenance* between the two families. "If he asks for the money, the end is come. We are ruined!" Thus does Mrs. Fisher provide a melodramatic portico for her unpoetical variant of the time-honoured Viola-Cesario incident. In the next chapter, happily, a package of papers, in the handwriting of a great-grandfather (or a "great-great-grandfather," as is subsequently stated), is found, labelled "Titles of Estates in Santo Domingo," and with it a full description of the spot where the money and jewels were buried. Rather than permit the barter of her sister Diane for the discharge of a debt, Yvonne, who had always supplied the masculine element in a family altogether feminine, put on boy's dress, and took the Clyde steamship from New York for Hayti. Then we are introduced to Herbert Atherton, a wealthy young man in ill-health, who was also booked for Hayti. Of course he met Yvonne masquerading under the name of Henri de Marsillac, and wondered what kind of a youngster this could be. As they neared their destination Henri "shrank from the unknown and difficult, now that they were close at hand." Till then their hands had never met, and Herbert noticed how slender and delicate Henri's were. They hobnobbed together for two weeks, and succeeded in unearthing not only a diamond necklace and $150,000 in coin, but a large quantity of gold-bearing quartz to boot. While treading the historic soil of Hayti on a certain occasion Henri imagined himself to be one of his ancestors, and that he was "handed into a carriage by a gentleman with a powdered wig." He also fainted, and was carried away insensible on witnessing a Vaudoux dance. But Herbert never "caught on." He only fancied that

Henri's sister Diane must be very attractive, and asked for an introduction to her. In compensation for his friendly services he would accept only a ruby, the emblem and symbol of passion. The bags of gold, surrounded by quartz, passed through the custom-house unexamined. Then Henri tried to put himself out of the other's life. But Herbert visited New Orleans, and blundered about an unconscionable length of time identifying his friend. Yvonne was so fond of her masculine rig that she finally planned a tea-party, where she should be announced as M. de Marsillac, to Atherton's joy and the general scandalisation. Meanwhile Diane had found an Adrien who loved to serve her family without reward. The only remaining question was whether Atherton could "ever forget" that his Yvonne had masqueraded in mannish attire. "I can never wish to forget it!" he replied nobly.

The dialogue is rather stilted, and the characters evince their personality in the author's description of them rather than in speech and action.

THE STATUE IN THE AIR. By Caroline Eaton Le Conte. New York: The Macmillan Co. 75 cents.

The vision of a magical chasm, "prodigious," "tremendous," "cursed," "murderous," in which dwelt Troglodytes, the demon of cold and darkness, fell upon the soul of Heliophanes, who with his daughter Leanira and the divine Euphorion lived in Eucarpia; and with the vision was revealed the coming of a deliverer who should slay Troglodytes. The oracle was confirmed by words graven on a stone in the Cave of Love:

"When a prophet, the father of one daughter, has a vision, and when in accordance with his vision the hero steps to the pool, and plucks from its bosom the sacred flower, and the same day arrives in the palace a five-year-old child, the statue of Eros,—that very day Troglodytes is slain, and the chasm closed forever."

How all this came about, through the wondrous love of Euphorion for Leanira, amid the crash of thunderbolts and the surge of incandescent vapours and the swooping of harpies and the shrieks of Melanion, the vengeful son of a human mother by the omnivorous monster of the abyss, is the burden of this little phantasy, which, in a high and well-sustained key and a consistently grand style of locution, that rarely lapses into fine writing, deals with the old Greek fable of the conflict of sunlight and love with icy darkness and hate. The author has taken her cue from neither the cosmic myths of Plato nor those of Hesiod, but apparently from some Egyptian source, opposing Eros, son of Earth and Heaven, to one of the vasty Troglodytæ, cave-dwellers on the shores of the Red Sea. The story is of the kind which it is impossible to paraphrase without seeming travesty. To feel its full poetic beauty and dignity, one must read it at a single sitting, and submit graciously to its spell. It lures one away from the present age to the majestic isolation and otherworldliness of antiquity. It is of the texture from which used to be woven the libretti of grand opera, and from which, by a slight change of tone, it is easily possible for some flippant mind to construct a dreary mythological extravaganza of the *Nature* species. We hope that it will be spared such irreverent treatment, and that, above all, it will not come under the eyes of Mr. John Kendrick Bangs.

THE WAY OF FIRE. By Helen Blackmar Maxwell. New York: Dodd, Mead & Co. $1.25.

The readers of *The Bishop's Conversion*, one of the most notable and popular novels of its kind, will be glad to hear that the author's later book lies within the same environment. For India has a charm which invests any well-written story with fascination, and Mrs. Maxwell's new novel is more than well written. It is quiet work; there are no attempts at striking effects, no approaches to a dramatic crisis, yet the story appeals and the interest is uniform throughout. The subject can scarcely be called new—hardly as new as that of the author's first book. Many novelists have dealt with the unfortunate early marriage, in which the husband outgrows the wife, so that she comes to appear his social and intellectual inferior. We have all seen such sad cases, too, in real life, but without the interesting *dénouement* that Mrs. Maxwell works out through *The Way of Fire*. In real life the wife usually stays where she has stopped or goes back still farther. Domestic cares, child-bearing, natural limitations—many causes conspire to prevent her overtaking her freer and stronger mate in the race of life. In Mrs. Maxwell's story things are ordered more as they should be, were life less wrong than it is. The wife goes away, which is natural enough, since the husband is not usually clamorous for her presence under the circumstances. In England, under the direction of an elegant and intelligent woman, she begins to learn all that she should have learned before marriage. There have been many versions of the story, though it is not often so gracefully told as Mrs. Maxwell tells it, and the situation is complicated by the presence of a fine, noble-souled woman, who cares enough for the husband to befriend his wife, and through whose unselfish efforts their happiness is finally regained. The character drawing of the work is good as a whole, but the women are more distinct than the men.

A CHILD IN THE TEMPLE. By Frank Mathew. New York: John Lane. $1.50.

This was meant to be an exquisite little story. A good deal of it is exquisite as it stands. Mr. Mathew has a wayward imagination, a still more wayward sense of humour, and they served him well in that far too little appreciated book, *The Wood of the Brambles*. In this much slighter thing they have led him less happily. The child in the temple should have stopped there, or should have gone home in poverty to Ireland. He should have grown wise in the society of his dog, and with the tangled affairs of Kitty and Kilmorna and the others to unravel, for of course they would have come to him. But he should not have, even once, gone out into the world and used that revolver; he did not; the little braggart was lying to Mr. Mathew. He would have grown old and wise, grown into a kind of Charles Lamb, we imagine. He would certainly never have grown up. But that rowdy day at the end, with the anarchists, and the runaway peer and the repentant magdalen and the penitent nobleman. at the convent gate, and the "child" mixed up in it all, is a nightmare. And to dismiss the wise "child" at the end with an estate and a decent income is to treat him most undeservedly as a Philistine.

THE BOOKMAN'S TABLE.

TALKS ON THE STUDY OF LITERATURE. By Arlo Bates. New York and Boston: Houghton, Mifflin & Co. $1.50.

This volume, made up from a course of lectures delivered under the auspices of the Lowell Institute in 1895, is a further contribution to the literature that gathers about the discussion and criticism of literature *per se*. It goes on the principle: Once make a youth fall in love with a good book, and you open the door wide to a noble company and a goodly fellowship. A passage from the lecture on "The Study of Literature" will at once aptly indicate the author's aims and sympathies. "By the study of literature," he says, "can be meant nothing pedantic, nothing formal, nothing artificial. I should like to call the subject of these talks, 'Experiencing Literature,' if the verb could be received in the same sense as in the old-fashioned phrase 'experiencing religion.' That is what I mean. The study of literature is neither less nor more than experiencing literature—the taking it to heart and the getting to its heart." These talks are the more helpful and suggestive in their treatment, inasmuch as they do not confine themselves to the discussion of abstract theories concerning the study of literature. Concrete examples are cited and used as illustrations, the reader is brought into close and fond intimacy with "the classics," "new books and old," "fiction," "poetry;" and the living touch of an imagination that perceives the relation between literature and life vivifies and spiritualises the mind and heart to a warm and true appreciation of "the works of genius," which have ever "been the delight of mankind," according to Lowell. An index is provided—a provision too seldom furnished in books of this class.

NATURE'S DIARY. Compiled by Francis H. Allen. New York and Boston: Houghton, Mifflin & Co. $1.25.

This is quite a unique book. Mr. Allen describes himself on the title-page as "a minstrel of the natural year," and his work may be further explained by a quotation from Thoreau as "a book of the seasons, each page of which should be written in its own season and out of doors, or in its own locality, wherever it may be." The original idea, which is carried out in this natural year-book, is "to have each selection fit its day as exactly as possible, avoiding all generalities," and to insure scientific accuracy and poetic value in doing so. Then on the right-hand page is given a calendar of the birds that arrive and the flowers that bloom on those dates, and blank space is left for the student or lover of nature to record his own notes and observations. So many new books have appeared recently with monotonous regularity on Nature in all her diverse forms of life, that it is a pleasure to single out *Nature's Diary* as a work of practical value and a book whose method is original and most attractive. Its attractiveness is further enhanced by a number of beautiful illustrations, evidently reproduced from photographic nature studies.

BESIDE OLD HEARTH-STONES. By Abram English Brown. Boston: Lee & Shepard. $1.50.

The promoter of the series "Footprints of the Patriots," and the author of *Beneath Old Rooftrees*, has written another work of Revolutionary and patriotic interest in *Beside Old Hearth-Stones*, which sustains the reputation the author has attained through his former volumes. In this series it is the author's purpose to bring to light some of the obscure movements of the early patriots, and his diligent researches have yielded a rich harvest of results in gleaning where others have already reaped. Especially is this the case with that outer circle of the battlefield of the opening Revolution, where the footprints of the minute-men have escaped the eye of the tourist. Not only is this work replete with historical lore and with the traditions and memories that have clustered thick beside old hearth-stones, its invaluable product is made more intelligent and fascinating by the numerous fine fac-similes of documents and autographs and pictures of persons and places. Throughout New England the book is sure to command a wide popularity, as it deals with so much of its family history, as well as with its organic growth as an important factor in the making of a nation. What so enthralling as the stories told by firelight on the hearth of the sturdy patriots from whose loins we have sprung to inherit the blessings of peace and prosperity which they sowed in the blood-shed of war and adversity!

NATURAL HISTORY. The Concise Knowledge Library. New York: D. Appleton & Co. $2.00.

This authorised edition of a most useful and indispensable work at a moderate price ought to be welcome. For ready reference, accuracy of statement, and handiness of form it is unexcelled. The authors are specialists in their own departments, and are distinguished as authorities and as original investigators. There are upwards of five hundred illustrations in the text, reproduced from original drawings made expressly for this work. A concise systematic index is furnished at the outset, while at the end we find a full alphabetical index containing about ten thousand references. The book is substantially bound; there are nearly eight hundred pages in it, yet it is not bulky, nor is the typography too fine for ordinary use. It is one of the popular household compendiums of scientific information which "no home should be without."

2. Soldiers of Fortune. By Davis. $1.50. (Scribner.)
3. Pursuit of the House-Boat. By Bangs. $1.25. (Harper.)
4. Farthest North. By Nansen. $10.00. (Harper.)
5. Relics of Primeval Life. By Dawson. $1.50. (Revell.)
6. Equality. By Bellamy. $1.25. (Appleton.)

NEW HAVEN, CONN.

1. The Christian. By Caine. $1.50. (Appleton.)
2. Jerome. By Wilkins. $1.50. (Harper.)
3. Soldiers of Fortune. By Davis. $1.50. (Scribner.)
4. The Choir Invisible. By Allen. $1.50. (Macmillan.)
5. Quo Vadis. By Sienkiewicz. $2.00. (Little, Brown & Co.)
6. English Lands, Letters and Kings. Vol. IV. By Mitchell. $1.50. (Scribner.)

OMAHA, NEB.

1. The Christian. By Caine. $1.50. (Appleton.)
2. Quo Vadis. By Sienkiewicz. $2.00. (Little, Brown & Co.)
3. Honourable Peter Stirling. By Ford. $1.50. (Holt.)
4. Wolfville. By Quin. $1.50. (Stokes.)
5. Many Cargoes. By Jacobs. $1.00. (Stokes.)
6. Soldiers of Fortune. By Davis. $1.50. (Scribner.)

PHILADELPHIA, PA.

1. Quo Vadis. By Sienkiewicz. $2.00. (Little, Brown & Co.)
2. Jerome. By Wilkins. $1.50. (Harper.)
3. Massarenes. By Ouida. $1.25 (Fenno.)
4. A Rose of Yesterday. By Crawford. $1 25. (Macmillan.)
5. The Choir Invisible. By Allen. $1.50. (Macmillan.)
6. Pursuit of the House-Boat. By Bangs. $1.25. (Harper.)

PITTSBURG, PA.

1. John Marmaduke. By Church. $1.25. (Putnams.)
2. Soldiers of Fortune. By Davis. $1.50. (Scribner.)
3. Quo Vadis. By Sienkiewicz. $2.00. (Little, Brown & Co.)
4. The Choir Invisible. By Allen. $1.50. (Macmillan.)
5. Chevalier d'Auriac. By Yeats. $1.25. (Longmans.)
6. Wolfville. By Lewis $1.50. (Stokes.)

PORTLAND, ORE.

1. Quo Vadis. By Sienkiewicz. $2.00. Little, Brown & Co.)
2. Jerome. By Wilkins. $1.50. (Harper.)
3. The Choir Invisible. By Allen. $1.50. (Macmillan.)
4. Equality. By Bellamy. $1.25. (Appleton.)
5. Land of Snow Pearls. By Higginson. $1.50. (Macmillan.)
6. Soldiers of Fortune. By Davis. $1.50. (Scribner.)

ROCHESTER, N. Y.

1. The Christian. By Caine. $1.50. (Appleton.)
2. Quo Vadis. By Sienkiewicz. $2.00. (Little, Brown & Co.)
3. The Choir Invisible. By Allen. $1.50. (Macmillan.)
4. Chevalier d'Auriac. By Yeats. $1.25. (Longmans.)
5. Jerome. By Wilkins. $1.50. (Harper.)
6. Soldiers of Fortune. By Davis. $1.50. (Scribner.)

SALT LAKE CITY, UTAH.

1. The Choir Invisible. By Allen. $1.50. (Macmillan.)
2. Soldiers of Fortune. By Davis. $1.50. (Scribner.)
3. Rose of Yesterday. By Crawford. $1.25. (Macmillan.)
4. Checkers. By Blossom. $1.25. (Stone.)
5. Equality. By Bellamy. $1.25. (Appleton.)
6. Quo Vadis. By Sienkiewicz. $2.00. (Little, Brown & Co.)

SAN FRANCISCO, CAL.

1. Quo Vadis. By Sienkiewicz. $2.00. (Little, Brown & Co.)
2. The Christian. By Caine. $1.50. (Appleton.)
3. Wolfville. By Lewis. $1.50. (Stokes.)
4. Many Cargoes. By Jacobs. $1 00. (Stokes.)
5. Soldiers of Fortune. By Davis. $1.50. (Scribner.)
6. The Gadfly. By Voynich. $1.25. (Holt.)

ST. LOUIS, MO.

1. Soldiers of Fortune. By Davis. $1.50. (Scribner.)
2. The Choir Invisible. By Allen. $1.50. (Macmillan.)
3. Wolfeville. By Lewis. $1.50. (Stokes.)
4. The Christian. By Caine. $1.50. (Appleton.)
5. Sketches in Lavender, Blue, and Green. By Jerome. $1.25. (Holt & Co.)
6. Quo Vadis. By Sienkiewicz $2.00. (Little, Brown & Co.)

ST. PAUL, MINN.

1. The Choir Invisible. By Allen. $1.50. (Macmillan.)
2. Soldiers of Fortune. By Davis. $1.50. (Scribner.)
3. Quo Vadis. By Sienkiewicz. $2.00. (Little, Brown & Co.)
4. The Christian. By Caine. $1.50 (Appleton.)
5. From a Girl's Point of View. By Bell. $1.25. (Harper.)
6. Chevalier d'Auriac. By Yeats. $1.25. (Longmans.)

TOLEDO, O.

1. The Christian. By Caine. $1.50. (Appleton.)
2. Jerome. By Wilkins. $1.50. (Harper.)
3. The Choir Invisible. By Allen $1.50 (Macmillan.)
4. Equality. By Bellamy. $1 25. (Appleton.)
5. Soldiers of Fortune By Davis $1.50. (Scribner.)
6. The Martian. By Du Maurier. $1.75. (Harper.)

TORONTO, CANADA.

1. * The Christian. By Caine. 75 cts. and $1.50. (Morang.)
2. † In Kedar's Tents. By Merriman. 75 cts. and $1.25. (The Copp-Clark Co)
3. †With Edged Tools. By Merriman. 70 and 90 cts. (Smith, Elder & Co.)
4. † Farthest North. By Nansen. $1.50 and $2.00 set. (Macmillan.)
5. Quo Vadis. By Sienkiewicz. $2.00. (Little, Brown & Co.)
6. *Soldiers of Fortune. By Davis. 75 cts. and $1.25. (Copp-Clark Co.)

TORONTO, CANADA.

1. Soldiers of Fortune. By Davis. Paper, 75 cts.; cloth, $1.25 (The Copp-Clark Co., Limited.)
2. The Martian. By Du Maurier. Paper, 75 cts.; cloth, $1.25. (The Copp-Clark Co., Limited.)
3. The Chevalier d'Auriac. By Yeats. Paper, 75 cts.; cloth, $1.25. (Longman's Colonial Edition.)
4. A Fountain Sealed. By Besant. Paper. 75 cts.; cloth, $1.25. (The Copp-Clark Co., Limited.)
5. A Story Teller's Pack. By Stockton. Paper, 75 cts.; cloth, $1.25. (The Copp-Clark Co., Limited.)
6. Seats of the Mighty. By Parker. Paper, 75 cts.; cloth, $1.25. (The Copp-Clark Co., Limited.)

WACO, TEX.

1. The Christian. By Caine. $1.50 (Appleton.)
2. The Hon. Peter Stirling. By Ford. $1.50. (Holt.)
3. On the Face of the Waters. By Steel $1 50. (Macmillan.)
4. Quo Vadis. By Sienkiewicz. $2.00. (Little, Brown & Co.)
5. The Choir Invisible. By Allen. $1.50 (Macmillan.)
6. Old Ebenezer. By Read. $1.25. (Laird & Lee.)

WORCESTER, MASS.

1. The Christian. By Caine. $1.50. (Appleton.)
2. The Choir Invisible. By Allen. $1.50. (Macmillan.)
3. Soldiers of Fortune. By Davis. $1.50. (Scribner.)
4. Jerome. By Wilkins $1.50. (Harper.)
5. My Father as I Recall Him. By Dickens. $1.25. (Dutton.)
6. A Son of the Old Dominion By Harrison. $1.50. (Lamson, Wolffe & Co.)

* Canadian Copyright Edition.
† Colonial Library.

THE BEST SELLING BOOKS.

According to the above lists, the six books which have sold best in order of demand during the month are—

1. Quo Vadis. By Sienkiewicz.
2. Soldiers of Fortune. By Davis.
3. The Christian By Caine.
4. The Choir Invisible. By Allen.
5. Jerome. By Miss Wilkins.
6. Equality. By Bellamy

BOOKS RECEIVED.

AMERICAN BAPTIST PUBLICATION SOCIETY, Philadelphia.

The Isle that is Called Patmos, by William Edgar Geil.

AMERICAN PUBLISHERS' CORPORATION, New York.

Van Hoff of the New Faust, by Alfred Smythe.

D. APPLETON & CO., New York

The Story of Germ Life, by H. W. Conn.
French Stumbling Blocks and English Stepping Stones.
Natural History.
The Exploits of Myles Standish, by Henry Johnson.

BARBEE & SMITH, Nashville, Tenn

Southern Writers, Biographical and Critical Studies, by William M. Baskerville.

BELFORD, MIDDLEBROOK & CO., New York.

John L. Stoddard's Lectures, Vol. I.

BENZIGER BROS., New York.

The Football Game, by Francis J. Finn.
Illustrated Explanation of the Commandments.

A. I. BRADLEY & CO.

Bubbles, by Fannie E. Newberry.
Kent Fielding's Ventures, by I. T. Thurston.

THE BULLETIN PRESS, Norwich.

Bas' Theres, by Jean Porter Rudd.

THE BURROWS BROS. CO., Cleveland.

The Jesuit Relations and Allied Documents, edited by Reuben Gold Thwaites.

THE CENTURY CO., New York.

The Last Three Soldiers, by William Henry Shelton.
The Century Book of the American Revolution, by Elbridge S. Brooks.
A New Baby World, compiled from *St. Nicholas*, by Mary Mapes Dodge.
Master Skylark, by John Bennett.
The Scholar and the State, by Henry C. Potter.
Joan of Arc, by M. Boutet de Monvel.
An Artist's Letters from Japan, by John La Farge.
American Contributions to Civilisation, by Charles W. Eliot.
Fighting a Fire, by Charles T. Hill.
De Amicitia (On Friendship), by M. Tullius Cicero. Translated from the Latin by Benjamin E. Smith.
A Christmas Carol, by Charles Dickens.
Miss Nina Barrow, by Frances Courtenay Baylor.
Up the Matterhorn in a Boat, by Marion Manville Pope.

T. H. COATES & CO., Philadelphia.

In the Days of the Pioneers, by Edward S. Ellis.

G. W. DILLINGHAM CO., New York.

Near a Whole City Full, by Edward W. Townsend.

DODD, MEAD & CO., New York.

Constitutional Studies, by James Schouler.
The Missing Prince, by G. E. Farrow.
Witch Winnie in Venice, by Elizabeth W. Champney.
Hannah Ann, by Amanda M. Douglas.
Subject Index to Prose Fiction, by Zella Allen Dixson.
The Book of Parliament, by Michael MacDonagh (Isbester & Co., London).
The Green Guess Book, by Susan Hayes Ward and Mary L. McL. Watson.
The Romance of Colonisation, by G. Barnett Smith.
The Romance of the Irish Stage, by Fitzgerald Molloy, 2 vols.
A Dog of Constantinople, by Izora C. Chandler.
The Birthright, by Joseph Hocking.
The Gods Arrive, by Annie E. Holdsworth.
Queen of the Jesters, by Max Pemberton.
The Way of Fire, by Helen Blackmar Maxwell.
By a Hair's Breadth, by Headon Hill.
The Adventures of Mabel, by Rafford Pyke.

DOUBLEDAY & MCCLURE CO., New York.

Tales from McClure's, Romance, Humour.
How to Build a Home, by F. C. Moore.
Little Masterpieces, edited by Bliss Perry.

EDITOR PUBLISHING CO., Cincinnati.

Doctor Marks, Socialist, by Marion Couthouy Smith.

GOVERNMENT PRINTING OFFICE, Washington.

Report of the Commissioner of Education, Vol. I., 1895–96.

HARPER & BROS., New York.

White Man's Africa, by Poultney Bigelow.
My Studio Neighbours, by W. Hamilton Gibson.
Three Operettas, by Henry C. Bunner.

D. C. HEATH & CO., Boston.

The Arden Shakespeare, The Tempest, edited by Frederick S. Boas.
The Ancient Mariner, by Samuel Taylor Coleridge.

HOUGHTON, MIFFLIN & CO., Boston.

The Story of an Untold Love, by Paul Leicester Ford.
Talks on the Study of Literature, by Arlo Bates.
Three Partners, by Bret Harte.
The Young Mountaineers, by Charles Egbert Craddock.
The Federal Judge, by Charles K. Lush.
Gleanings in Budda Fields, by Lafcadio Hearn.
Uncle Lisha's Outing, by Rowland E. Robinson.
Varia, by Agnes Repplier.
Nature's Diary, by Francis H. Allen.
Diana Victrix, by Florence Converse.
France under Louis XV., by James Breck Perkins, 2 vols.

THE JEWISH PUBLICATION SOCIETY OF AMERICA, Philadelphia.

The Talmud, by Arsène Darmesteter.

WILBUR B. KETCHAM, New York.

Little Phil, the Engineer's Son, by George A. Warburton.

LAIRD & LEE, Chicago.

Yellow Beauty, by Marion Martin.

LEE AND SHEPARD, Boston.

Queer Janet, by Grace Le Baron.
The Blue and the Gray Series, At the Front, by Oliver Optic.

THE LEVYTYPE CO., Philadelphia.

The New Man, by Ellis P. Oberholtzer.

LONGMANS, GREEN & CO., New York.

The Professor's Children, by Edith Henrietta Fowler.
Rameau's Nephew, a Translation from Diderot, by Sylvia Hill.
Kallistratus, an Autobiography, by A. H. Gilkes.

THE MACMILLAN CO., New York.

The Faerie Queen, 2 vols.
Kroeh's French Course.
The Conception of God, Vol. I.
Bon-Mots of the Eighteenth Century, edited by Walter J. Errold (Dent & Co.)
The Rivals, by Richard Brinsley Sheridan (Dent & Co.)
Cousin Betty, by H. De Balzac.
Portrait Miniatures, by George C. Williamson (George Bell & Sons).

Poems of Thomas Hood, edited by Alfred Ainger, 2 vols.
The Life of Samuel Johnson, by James Boswell, Vol. III. (Dent & Co.).
The Essays of Michael Lord of Montaigne, translated by John Florio (Dent & Co.).
The Histories of American Insects, by Clarence M. Weed.
Christianity and Idealism, by John Watson, LL D.
A Dictionary of American Authors, by Oscar Fay Adams.
Wild Neighbours, by Ernest Ingersoll
The Seamy Side of History, by H. De Balzac.
A Political Primer of New York State and City, by Adele M. Fielde.
The Statue in the Air, by Caroline Eaton Le Conte.
Outlines of Elementary Economics, by Herbert J. Davenport.
Golden Treasury of Songs and Lyrics, Second Series.

M. F. MANSFIELD, New York.

A Batch of Golfing Papers.

A. C. McCLURG & Co., Chicago.

The Story of Language, by Charles Woodward Huston.
The Big Horn Treasure, by John F. Cargill.
The Campaign of Marengo, by Herbert H. Sargent.

DAVID McKAY, Philadelphia.

Prisoners of the Sea, by Florence M. Kingsley.

THOMAS B. MOSHER, Portland, Me.

The Story of Cupid and Psyche, Done out of the Latin by Apuleius by Walter Pater.
The Story of Amis and Amile, Done out of the Ancient French into English by William Morris.
The Child in the House, an Imaginary Portrait, by Walter Pater.
The Pageant of Summer, by Richard Jefferies.
The Centaur and the Bacchante, Two Prose Poems Done into English from the French of Maurice de Guerin by Lucié Page.
The Story Without an End, Translated from the German of F. W. Carove by Sarah Austin.
Sonnets from the Portuguese, by Elizabeth Barrett Browning.
Essays from the "Guardian," by Walter Pater.
Helen of Troy, Her Life and Translation, Done into Rhyme from the Greek Books by Andrew Lang.
Atalanta in Calydon, a Tragedy, by Algernon Charles Swinburne.
The Sonnets of Michael Angelo, translated by John Addington Symonds.
Long Ago, by Michael Field.
An Italian Garden, a Book of Songs, by A. Mary F. Robinson.

MUNN & Co., New York.

Magic, Stage Illusions and Scientific Diversions.

THE PILGRIM PRESS, Chicago.

Links of Gold, by Harriet A. Cheever.
A Son's Victory, by Fannie E. Newberry.

G. P. PUTNAM'S SONS, New York.

Ayrshire Homes and Haunts of Burns, by Henry C. Shelley.
Studies in Psychical Research, by Frank Podmore.
The Literary History of the American Revolution, by Moses Coit Tyler.

FLEMING H. REVELL Co., New York.

And She Got All That! by Cara Reese.
Seven Years in Sierra Leone, by A. T. Pierson, D.D.
Ruth Bergen's Limitations, by Marion Harland.
The Gist of Japan, by R. B. Peery.

CHARLES SCRIBNER'S SONS, New York.

Selected Poems, by George Meredith.
Adventures in Toyland, by Edith King Hall.
With Crockett and Bowie, by Kirk Munroe.
English Lands, Letters, and Kings, by Donald H. Mitchell.
The Golden Galleon, by Robert Leighton.
Lords of the World, by Rev. Alfred J Church.
American Nobility, by Pierre de Coulevain.
The American Railway.
Women of Colonial and Revolutionary Times, by Catherine Schuyler.
St. Ives, by Robert Louis Stevenson.
Will Shakespeare's Little Lad, by Imogen Clark.
Vasari's Lives of the Painters, edited by E. H. and E. W. Blashfield and A. A. Hopkins, 4 vols.

FREDERICK A. STOKES Co., New York.

Sheilah McLeod, by Guy Boothby.
The Eye of Istar, by William Le Queux.

F. TENNYSON NEELY, New York.

A Mountain of Gold, by Willis Steell.
A Son of Mars, by Sir George Rathbone.
Isidra, by Willis Steell.
The Dreamers, by Edward S. Van Zile.
Lunar Caustic, by Charles H. Robinson.

THOMAS WHITTAKER, New York.

How to Become like Christ, by Marcus Dods.
Toinette, by Barbara Yechton.
A Girl in Ten Thousand, by L. T. Meade.
Potters, their Arts and Crafts, by John C. L. Sparkes and Walter Gandy.
Founded on Paper, by Charlotte M. Yonge.

W. A. WILDE & Co., Boston.

The Romance of Discovery, by William Elliot Griffis.

WILLIAMS & WILKINS Co., Baltimore.

Rose-Leaves, Poems by Henry Clayton Hopkins. Drawings by Lee Woodward Zeigler.
'Twixt Cupid and Coresus; or, the Exhibits in an Attachment Suit, Compiled and Illustrated by Charles P. Didier.
R. S. V. P., a Novelette, by Charles P. Didier.

PRICE 20 CENTS

THE BOOKMAN

CHRISTMAS NUMBER

F.C.

DODD · MEAD & COMPANY

PUBLISHERS NEW-YORK

Peace on earth, good-will towards all.
Waterman's Ideal Fountain Pen
The Standard of the World.
A Gift Suitable, Serviceable, and Appropriate for all who write.
It is always ready, and writes continuously without shaking.
WATERMAN'S IDEAL FOUNTAIN PEN
X Mas
For Him Her
Very many men and women of great prominence have freely said good words for WATERMAN'S IDEAL FOUNTAIN PEN because of its sterling worth.
"This delightful fountain pen is to the literary worker as wings to a bird."
MARGARET E. SANGSTER, Lit. Ed. Harper's Bazar.
Made in plain, gold-mounted, solid silver, and gold designs, at prices according to their value.
The best writing instrument of the age. Sold upon merit. Absolutely guaranteed. Call on your dealer or send for holiday catalogue.
Chicago
Boston
St. Louis
L. E. Waterman Co.
155 & 157 Broadway, New York, N. Y.
Largest Fountain Pen Manufacturers in the World.
London
Paris
Berlin

THE BOOKMAN

A LITERARY JOURNAL.

VOL. VI. DECEMBER, 1897. No. 4.

CHRONICLE AND COMMENT.

The Editors of THE BOOKMAN *cannot undertake to return rejected manuscripts, whether stamps are enclosed or not; and to this rule no exception will be made.*

Oscar Wilde has written a new French play called *Pharaon*, and a poem of a hundred stanzas dealing with a painful experience.

Apropos of the much-reviled *Christian*, we have seen no reference to Oscar Wilde's *jeu d'esprit* on Hall Caine in his clever paper, "The Decay of Lying." It is too good to be lost sight of. "Mr. Hall Caine," he says, "aims at the grandiose; he writes at the top of his voice. He is so loud that one cannot hear what he says."

Mr. Hall Caine is now engaged in dramatising *The Christian*. The author, we understand, is uncertain about the predominance of the hero or the heroine in the dramatic form; but it appears that he has provided for either emergency. If John Storm prove to be the leading character, the play will go to Mr. E. S. Willard, who is now here on a tour with Mr. Henry Arthur Jones's new play, *The Physician*. But in case Glory Quayle should be in the ascendant, Mr. Caine has arranged that Miss Olga Nethersole shall produce it. By the way, is there not a Hall Cainesque echo in the title of a drama announced to appear as *From Rogue to Christian?*

We are not expressing any opinions about the recent municipal elections in Greater New York, but we feel that we must publish the following letter from Mrs. Annie Nathan Meyer because of the amusing literary coincidences which it points out.

To the Editors of THE BOOKMAN:

There have been many false prophets during the late campaign for the election of the first mayor of Greater New York. How will the advent of a new prophet be hailed? Here comes Robert Browning with a poem entitled "WARING." I shall quote some of the lines to prove the keenness of his prophetic vision.

> "What's become of Waring?"

it begins. The fourth verse runs:

> "Meantime, how much I loved him,
> I find out now I've lost him.
> I who cared not if I moved him
> Who could so carelessly . . .
> . . . . get free
> Of his . . . company."

Here is the fifth verse:

> "Oh, could I have him back once more,
> This Waring, but one-half day more."

The sixth begins:

> "Ichabod, Ichabod,
> The glory is departed!
> Travels Waring East away.
> . . . . happy Waring,
> Having first within his ken
> What a man might do with men."

It concludes:

> "Contrive, contrive
> To rouse us, Waring! . .
> Our men scarce seem in earnest now.
> . . . . 'tis somehow
> As if they played . . .
> . . . . like the games
> Of children. Turn our sport to earnest
> With a visage of the sternest!
> Bring the real times back, confessed
> Still better than our very best!"

ANNIE NATHAN MEYER.

Something over a year ago we mildly criticised what we regarded as a touch of amateurishness in some departments of *Harper's Weekly*. As a matter of fairness we think we ought to say that now for a long time we have read that very able journal with unalloyed admiration. It is really surprising to observe so high a standard of literary and artistic excellence united with the freshness, timeliness, and point that belong to ideal journalism. One recent bit of enterprise has struck a good many readers, and that is the promptness with which the *Weekly* was able to publish photographic views of the Klondike region after it came into such sudden prominence. It appears that credit for this is to be given to Mr. Nelson, the editor. As soon as the Klondike craze began, he telegraphed to a correspondent in San Francisco, "Interview every person arriving from Klondike and get photographs if any." In an incredibly short time the photographs were secured, and *Harper's Weekly* gave them to an interested public.

❀

A laborious piece of translation has recently been completed. This is an English version of the great Sanskrit epic, the *Mahābhārata*, which was undertaken by a learned Babu of Bengal, Pratāpa Chandra Roy, many years ago, and published in parts, of which the hundredth and last appeared early in the year. The history of the work of translation is the history of a life's devotion to a single idea. The Babu in question was a poor man and with no influential friends; but he set about the task with the most self-sacrificing devotion and enthusiasm, and included in his plan the *gratuitous* distribution of the work to scholars in all countries who applied for copies. His efforts secured in the end a good deal of recognition; the government of India gave him a grant of 11,000 rupees, and many private individuals contributed. Mr. Roy died before the translation was finished, and it was carried on through other scholars whom the zealous interest of Mr. Roy's widow, Sundari Bāla Roy, secured for the task. In completing it as a memorial work to her late husband, she has incurred a considerable debt, to discharge which contributions may be sent to her manager, No. 1 Rājāh Gooro Dass' Street, Calcutta.

❀

In the last part appears a long narrative by the lady, giving some account of the inception and progress of the work, and of the efforts made to secure subscriptions to carry it on. Her devotion to her husband's memory and to his life-work is touching; her quiet slaps at those who subscribed and never paid are very feminine and amusing, not less so because of the quaint English in which she writes. She mentions the delinquents (they are native Hindu magnates) by name, and with a delicious assumption of respect proceeds to lay them out. It is sad to read how "an eminent Zemindar of Bengal," the Maharajah Lal Roy, "having promised to aid the work with a contribution of 5000 rupees, forgot all about it after paying only 500." She adds: "More than a decade ago, when the offer of this distinguished person was noticed in the *Saturday Review* (of England), that journal spoke of him as 'a Maccenas hailing from Rungpore.' My husband waited several times on him, but the balance somehow remains unpaid to this day." It appears also that Sir Gajapati Rao had also promised to contribute a good sum; but this person, whom the late Dr. Sambhu C. Mookerjee, as we read, dubbed "the premier nobleman of Bengal," did not pay up. His fair critic gently says: "The fault must be in my husband and myself." Else how could he fail to do what had been done "by many who were his superiors in respectability"? This is rather hard on Sir Gajapati Rao. Other natives, however, with euphonious names were more honourable. The chiefs of Jummoo, of Bhownaggar, of Cooch-Behar and Jodhpore, and all the Mookerjee family stood by the Babu nobly. Mrs. Roy notes also with warm gratitude the assistance and encouragement given to her husband and herself by two Americans—Professor C. R. Lanman, of Harvard University, and Mr. William Emmette Coleman, of San Francisco. The end of the Prefatory Note is very touching in its quaint simplicity, and may be commended to the brawling American woman of to-day:

> "I wish to bid my final adieu to the public in order to enter that life of privacy and retirement which is ordained by the Scriptures I believe in for one of my sex and condition."

❀

While Mr. Anthony Hope is appearing on the platform in the United States his *confrère*, Mr. Zangwill, is delivering his lectures on the Ghetto, in the United Kingdom. There is rumour of an American lecture tour to be arranged for Mr. Zangwill, but at the moment nothing definite is known. Mr. Zangwill has been working hard in Paris until a few weeks ago, when he returned to England. He was present at the Zionist Congress at Basle, which was convened by Dr. Herzl of Vienna for the purpose of considering the arrangements necessary to permit the scattered Jews in all lands to return in a body to Palestine. The idea of Palestine as a Jewish kingdom has, it appears, aroused extraordinary interest in Jewish circles. Mr. Zangwill was deeply impressed by the enthusiasm displayed at the congress. Max Nordau's speech, he says, summed up the condition of the Jews all over the world in a sympathetic and masterly manner, and was one of the chief events of the meeting.

❀

Mr. Daniel Frohman has in hand a new four-act comedy by Mr. Anthony Hope. He has also acquired the dramatic rights to produce a play based on the sequel to *The Prisoner of Zenda*, which begins its serial appearance in the current number of *McClure's Magazine* and the *Pall Mall*.

❀

There was no more strikingly original book published by a new author last year than *Nancy Noon*, by Benjamin Swift. The genius and personality of the author were expressed with a force and wealth of power that were unmistakably emphatic. And in spite of the fact that *The Tormentor*, his second book, which has just been published by the Messrs. Scribner, will press its harrowing title home to the minds of most readers, the evidence of its author's individuality is as strongly marked as ever. We should not wonder if Benjamin Swift were as great a puzzle to his friends as he is to his critics. There is something very baffling and also insoluble about the morbid impressions of life reflected in these books which would seem to have been affected by the writer's imagination. We still believe in Benjamin Swift and that he will yet achieve something worthy of his undoubted gifts. Meantime, we must bear with him, critics must scold, and readers, for the most part, perhaps, avoid him until he has passed through the *Sturm und Drang* of his literary apprenticeship. We say avoided by most readers, for only an imaginative mind of a psychological cast will take any pleasure in following the evil machinations of his modern Machiavellian Faust in *The Tormentor*. We happen to know that, as a matter of fact, it was written and much of it rewritten during illness and against the physicians' orders, and it does not take much insight to perceive that the

pessimism of a sick man and the suppressed agony of a sufferer have affected the writer's point of view. We are sorry to see that the title of his next book is to be *The Destroyer;* a title which, to say the least, does not promise much relief. To Benjamin Swift, who is still midway in the twenties, and who is now announced as the author of a third book almost within a year, we would recall the adage that "too swift arrives as tardy as too late." We reproduce from Mr. Zangwill's literary *causerie* in the November *Cosmopolitan* the pictorial accompaniment to his remarks on *The Tormentor*, which are of the same tenor as our own. The artist's *jeu d'esprit* is very felicitous.

❀

Tom Hall's second collection of verse, humorous and otherwise, with the title *When Love Laughs*, has just been published by Messrs. E. R. Herrick and Company. It is beautifully printed on hand-made paper, with ragged edges and gilt top, and has border design decorations and title-page in colour by Frank M. Gregory. The cover design is peculiarly happy in its conception. There is also a limited edition on Japan paper, bound in Japanese silk, numbering one hundred copies. The character of Mr. Hall's work is well known from

his numerous contributions to the periodical and magazine press. No better companion for a light hour, "when love laughs," could perhaps be had than Tom Hall s little volume. Browning said he never intended his work to be read over a cigar—here Tom Hall has decidedly the advantage.

❀

Arrangements have just been concluded as we go to press to produce a dramatisation of Ian Maclaren's famous stories *Beside the Bonnie Brier Bush*, *The Days of Auld Lang Syne* and *Kate Carnegie*. The play is entitled *Beside the Bonnie Brier Bush*, and is the work of Messrs. James MacArthur and Tom Hall. When Dr. Watson was in this country a year ago Mr. MacArthur submitted a synopsis of the play to him, and received his full consent and permission to make the dramatisation. During the last few months Mr. MacArthur and Tom Hall have been busily engaged collaborating on the play, and it is now in a New York manager's hands, and will be produced in this city immediately after the holidays.

❀

We reproduce herewith the humorous pen drawing prefixed to the table of contents in *Chimes from a Jester's Bells*, by Robert J. Burdette, just published by the Bowen-Merrill Company. The drawing is, we understand, from the pen of Mr. Burdette's son, and is considered a very good likeness of the humourist at work. Mr. Burdette first became famous in this country as "The Hawkeye Man." About a dozen years ago he was editor of the Burlington (Ia.) *Hawkeye*, and his amusing sketches were widely copied by the press all over the country. He has been a constant contributor of articles to the periodical press for many years, and his book, *The Rise and Fall of the Moustache*, had a wide sale. His greatest success, however, has been gained on the lecture platform, where, as it is written, "this Physician of the Merry Heart has dispensed his Good Medicine in answer to over three thousand calls." Mr. Burdette has always been a great admirer of the *Rollo* books, by Jacob Abbott; Rollo and Jonas striking him as immensely funny characters. *Chimes from a Jester's Bells* opens with a travesty on these books, which runs through a dozen chapters. This is followed by twelve stories and sketches of mingled humour and pathos. The cover design is also from the pen of Robert J. Burdette, Jr., to whom the book is thus dedicated by his father: "To my best friend, gentlest critic, trustiest comrade, Robert, the son of his mother."

❀

The portrait of Mr. Kipling presented on the next page is taken from one of the celebrated coloured woodcut lithographs which Mr. W. Nicholson has been making for the *New Review*, published by Mr. Heinemann in England. These portraits lithographed in colours from wood blocks have been mounted on gray cardboard and published by Mr. R. H. Russell, at $1.00 each. The subjects now ready are Queen Victoria, Sara Bernhardt, Lord Roberts, Mr. Whistler, and Mr. Rudyard Kipling.

RUDYARD KIPLING.

Of the portrait of the Queen, when it first appeared in the *New Review*, Mr. Joseph Pennell wrote in the London *Daily Mail*: "The portrait truly is a masterpiece of its kind, for it reveals: the sitter with character; . . . the artist with a point of view of his own, Mr. Nicholson having had eyes to see for himself, without the aid of dull camera or the spectacles of other men." And Mr. Whistler has characterised Mr. Nicholson as one of the greatest artists that England has produced since Hogarth. Mr. Russell also publishes an alphabet with a colour plate for each letter, and an *Almanac of Twelve Sports for 1898*, with colour prints reproduced in Mr. Nicholson's original method. Mr. Rudyard Kipling, we understand, has written a set of verses to accompany the pictures of the latter.

❀

The most attractive holiday catalogue of the season is issued by Mr. R. H. Russell, of New York, and is the work of Mr. Will Bradley, of the Wayside Press, Springfield, Mass. It is worth having, as a curiosity.

We understand that Mr. Kipling declined payment from the *Times* for his poems "Our Lady of the Snows" and "The Recessional." His reason was that he would not take payment for patriotic poems. He sent to the *Times* after the appearance of "The Recessional" a poem entitled "The Destroyers," which described the action of torpedoes. For this he would have accepted the usual honorarium, but the editor of the *Times* considered that it would clash with the fine and stately piece of verse which had gone before it, and it was not accepted.

At the close of an unsigned article on "Lord Tennyson" in the November *Blackwood*, the present position in the realm of poetry is described as not dissimilar from that in which Christopher North found himself five-and-sixty years ago. With a silence of indifference regarding the present Laureate, which casts a withering contempt on Lord Salisbury's sad blunder, the writer passes from the pre-eminent poets who have left us—Mr. Swinburne alone survives—to Mr. Kipling as the repository of our secret hopes. "We venture to predict that English poetry will be permanently enriched by Mr. Kipling's pen more signally than by that of any other living writer." True, he has made us wince under "a thousand needless flippancies, a thousand gratuitous deviations from good taste." His almost diabolical cleverness and dangerous versatility, and the fine qualities conspicuous in the "Flag of England" thrill us with shocks of delight and admiration, but it is not upon these we build our hopes. "We turn to that memorable 'Recessional,' which alone of all the poems that have appeared since the late Laureate's death made an instantaneous and a deep impression on the public intellect and conscience; and, unless we mistake the matter, there we find precisely that nobility of sentiment, that weight, that sense of responsibility with which the finest of Lord Tennyson's patriotic effusions were indelibly stamped, and which that poet must needs possess in full measure who aspires to be called great."

We are tempted here to quote a passage from an article by Mr. James Lane Allen in the October *Atlantic*, apropos of Mr. Kipling's poem "Recessional," "probably his noblest and most enduring poetic achievement," says Mr. Allen. The analysis which follows shows upon what a strong basis the critic in *Blackwood's* builds his claim for Kipling's succession to Tennyson:

"It is virile—nothing that he ever wrote is more so; yet is refined—as little else that he has ever written is. It is strong, but it is equally delicate. It is massive as a whole; it is in every line just as graceful It is large enough to compass the scope of the British Empire: it creates this immensity by the use of a few small details. It may be instantly understood and felt by all men in its obviousness; yet it is so rare that he alone of all the millions of Englishmen could even think of writing it. The new, vast prayer of it rises to the Infinite; but it rises from the ancient sacrifice of a contrite heart."

Mr. Merriman's novel *In Kedar's Tents*, which is concluded in this number, and is reviewed on another page, has met with instantaneous success. No previous novel published by this author has been received with such quick appreciation. Published only a few weeks ago, it is now in its fourteenth thousand. In his new novel, entitled *Roden's Corner*, Mr. Merriman has further extended his widely travelled itinerary by placing the scenes for the most part in the Hague. The Messrs. Harper, who published *The Sowers*, have secured this story as a leading serial for their magazine, beginning in January. *Roden's Corner* will afterward be issued in book form by the same firm next autumn.

The Federal Judge, by Charles K. Lush, a first novel by a new writer, has gone into a second edition within a few weeks of its publication, and the publishers, Messrs. Houghton, Mifflin and Company, report a steadily increasing demand for the book. *The Federal Judge* is a good story, but it seems to us it would make a better play with W. H. Crane as the honest, rugged old judge. Again, when we think of the dramatic value of the railway magnate's part, Richard Mansfield in *Doctor Jekyll and Mr. Hyde* comes before the mind's eye. But what an impossible combination—W. H. Crane and Richard Mansfield! On the other hand, two plays might be constructed out of the book, one for Crane with the federal judge as the hero, and one for Mansfield with Gardwell as the principal character.

Dr. S. Weir Mitchell's great novel of the American Revolution, *Hugh Wynne*, is now in its twenty-fifth thousand. The story proved a most successful serial feature in the *Century* during the past year, and a new work by the same author, entitled *The Adventures of François*, has been secured, and will shortly appear in the same magazine. Dr. Mitchell returned a few weeks ago from a trip to Paris

Ibsen is going to Berlin next spring, on invitation, for the celebration of his seventy-first birthday. It is expected that this occasion will be made the opportunity for an important Ibsenite demonstration.

A curious incident reported to us as happening during the printing of *Brokenburne* furnishes corroborative testimony to our claim made last month that this story of the old South is equal to the best of Mr. Page's work in *Marse Chan* and *Meh Lady*. The copy for the title-page is usually handed in to the printer after the book is set up, and upon submitting this for *Brokenburne* at the De Vinne Press, where Mr. Page's stories have also been printed, the reader, who is quite an old-time *littérateur*, with a surprised look said, "Oh, I thought this book was by Thomas Nelson Page!"

Mrs. Virginia Frazer Boyle, the author of *Brokenburne*, is fairly well known to magazine readers by her poems and short stories. The first time we remember noticing her name was as the writer of a story called "Uncle Bias's Vision," published in the *Century*, if we mistake not, three or four years ago. Last year Mrs. Boyle received by unanimous vote the prize over one hundred and forty-seven contestants for the best poem written upon the occasion of the celebration of the Tennessee Centennial. Mrs. Boyle is descended of Scotch, Irish,

MRS. VIRGINIA FRAZER BOYLE.

and English settlers in North Carolina and Virginia, but her immediate parentage was of Mississippi, and her home has always been in Memphis, Tenn. A review of *Brokenburne*, one of the best stories ever told of the old South and the war, appears on another page.

One of the most popular books in Sweden is King Oscar's volume of poems, and this because the poems are liked, not because the poet is a king. The book has been a great commercial success, which is uncommon in Sweden, where literature and journalism are poorly remunerated.

Count Tolstoy has been expressing himself very severely on Wagner and

EVERT VAN MUYDEN.

One of the illustrators of *Quo Vadis*.

Wagner's music. Wagner, according to Tolstoy, was a *décadent* who made up in trickery what he lacked in inspiration and idea. He had no notion of melody, and loved noise. He was incomprehensible to the mass, and he, Tolstoy, vastly preferred to Wagner's most pretentious compositions the simplest popular tunes.

❀

Mr. Dan Beard has drawn some very spirited illustrations for a book which has just been published by Messrs. Lamson, Wolffe and Company ; indeed, we think these ten full-page pictures represent the best work in half-tone illustration that Mr. Beard has yet done. The book is an historical novel of the Civil War, entitled *A Hero in Homespun*, by William E. Barton, and we understand that the artist accompanied the author during the summer on a tour through the picturesque mountain region of Kentucky and Tennessee, where the scenes of the story lie, and that his pictures are based on photographs and studies of the actual historical scenes reproduced in the story. It is a tale of the loyal South ; the author, who knows the country well and understands the feelings of the people from a long sojourn among them, has been at work on this novel for twelve years. In calling forth the homespun hero of the southern Appalachians from his obscurity, the author has sought to make him better known, that he may be loved the more, and more fully recognised for his manliness, his patriotism, his heroism beneath the rough, plain homespun. A review of the book appears on another page.

❀

The great popularity of *Quo Vadis*, resembling that achieved by *Ben Hur* some years ago, would seem to indicate that there is something vital, after all, in the argument that scenes and characters borrowed from the times of Christ and the early Christian Church take tremendous hold of the imagination of the people when utilised by an author of stirring narrative powers. Reports have shown that for some months past *Quo Vadis* has gone away ahead of every other book in point of sale. The publishers, Messrs. Little, Brown and Company, believe evidently that a handsome holiday edition of the work will be appreciated, for they have just issued a beautiful edition in two volumes, with maps, photogravure illustrations, and reproductions from ancient sculptures. It is bound in royal purple, and printed from new type. The original pictures contributed to these volumes have been drawn by Howard Pyle, Edmund H. Garrett, and Evert Van Muyden. We give a portrait of this famous Dutch artist and etcher from a new photograph, and also a new one of Sienkiewicz, taken expressly for this edition, and reproduced here through the courtesy of the publishers.

❀

Messrs. Little, Brown and Company have in the press a volume of short stories translated from the Polish of Henryk Sienkiewicz by Mr. Jeremiah Curtin, whose authorised translations of the previous works of Sienkiewicz have given genuine satisfaction, and have won for their author a wide reputation outside of his native country. One story in this collection, called

"Let Us Also Follow Him," will be of great interest to the readers of *Quo Vadis*, as in this story lies the germ of the greater volume. *Hania*, as the book is entitled, will, we understand, be published at once.

❀

Messrs. Dodd, Mead and Company have just published a new edition of Mr. Hamilton W. Mabie's attractive volumes of literary studies. The edition is printed from new plates, and contains seven volumes, each volume having a frontispiece in photogravure. Mr. Mabie recently returned from England, where he spent most of the summer; and some interesting results of his sojourn abroad will be visible in two series of articles to be published in the *Outlook*. The first of these will be a finely illustrated paper on "The Lake Country as the Background of Wordsworth's Poetry." Mr. Mabie spent some days at Grasmere, and it was while there that he wrote the article published by him in the November *Atlantic* on "The Life of Tennyson." Mr. Mabie will also give personal impressions of some of the great English schools, such as those at Eton College, New College, Oxford, and the University of Edinburgh, institutions which have done much to mould and fix the character of the Briton. These articles, we understand, will be accompanied with illustrations made from photographs.

HENRYK SIENKIEWICZ.

From a new photograph of the author of *Quo Vadis*.

❀

Mr. Henry H. H. Cameron, to whose photographic studies of eminent literary people we referred last month, treasures many interesting and curious letters written to his mother, Mrs. Julia Margaret Cameron, during her lifetime. There is a characteristic letter of George Eliot's from which we may quote a few paragraphs to throw a side light on her much-discussed personality. The letter was written in 1871, in response to one accompanying a number of Mrs. Cameron's photographs:

"The love which you have so prettily inscribed on the beautiful present which you have sent me is the more precious because it is given for the sake of my books. They are certainly the best part of me—save in the power which my fleshly self has of returning love for love and being grateful for all goodness. . . . I thank you with all my heart. Wise people are teaching us to be sceptical about some sorts of charity, but this of cheering others by proofs of sympathy will never, I think, be shown to be harmful; at least, you have done me good.

"You are happy in being far away from under the London blanket, with a sight of the sky above you. I suppose you will some time return to the uglier world here, and in that case I may hope that the kindness which sent the photographs may bring you to me in your own person. . . ."

Then there is another letter written in 1858 by Thomas Carlyle, in which he says:

"I work all day and all days, riding abroad a little in the dusk like a distracted ghost, trying if I can keep alive till the thing gets done, and gloomily returning to my den again. If I can live about a year at this rate I hope to be free, and for the rest of my life, whatever that may amount to."

It was only by chance that Mrs. Cameron contrived to take the portrait of Carlyle, which we reproduce, for it was not easy to induce him to make

THOMAS CARLYLE.

From a photograph by Julia Margaret Cameron.

an appointment. However, taken it was, and on receiving it Carlyle wrote back :

"Has something of likeness, though terrifically ugly and woebegone ! My candid opinion.
"T. CARLYLE."

❀

Sartor Resartus was originally published in 1831, and ten years later we find George Eliot writing to an early school friend :

"Have you, dear Patty, read any of T. Carlyle's books ? He is a grand favourite of mine, and I venture to recommend to you his *Sartor Resartus*. I dare say a barrister of your acquaintance has it. His soul is a shrine of the highest and purest philanthropy, kindled by the live coal of gratitude and devotion to the Author of all things. I should observe that he is not 'orthodox.'"

The playful touch of the last sentence recalls the late Professor Drummond's humorous sally when, in naming the first books that found a place on his student's shelf—Ruskin, Emerson, George Eliot, Channing—he said that one day it suddenly struck him that all these favourite authors of his were heretics, that these books were regarded by many good people as dangerous books ! Himself a Scotchman, it is a curious fact that he could not tolerate Carlyle. "After wading through a page of Carlyle I felt as if I had been whipped. Carlyle scolded too much for my taste, and he seemed to me a great man gone delirious."

❀

If Carlyle had married a sweet-tempered woman how very different life might have been, and how far better things might have gone with him. One's mind naturally reverts from such a reflection to the beautiful story of Carlyle's first love in *Sartor Resartus*. Some interesting particulars have come to light recently concerning Carlyle's "Blumine" in an exceedingly interesting book entitled *Aberdeen Awa'* by Mr. George Walker, published by Messrs. A. Brown and Company, Aberdeen, Scotland. Dr. Guthrie of London, the author of a celebrated treatise on gunshot wounds, married a lady who had two daughters, one of whom was Margaret Gordon, Carlyle's "Blumine." Mr. Walker saw her in 1833 when she was married to a notable Aberdonian, Sir Alexander Bannerman. He remembers her again in 1851, "fair in looks, handsome in person, and accomplished in manner," and a niece of Lady Bannerman says that she had the sweetest of tempers. Lady Bannerman accompanied her husband to his various governorships in the colonies. He died in 1862 from an accident while he was preparing to return to his native city. After his death his wife retired to a villa in Hampstead, where, being childless, she lived a solitary life and died there about 1886. She never alluded to her early relations with Carlyle, but talked freely of his character and of his works, especially the essays on Burns,

Goethe, Scott, and other articles in his *Miscellanies*. But it is said that she talked even more of Edward Irving, who had been her tutor in mathematics. Lady Bannerman's sister survives her and is still living at a very advanced age. So "Blumine" lived silently through the great Carlyle controversy, and died even more alone than the famous man who was once her lover.

❀

An appreciative and sympathetic paper on "Mrs. Cameron, Her Friends and Her Photographs," by V. C. Scott O'Connor, appears in the *Century* for November. Several beautiful reproductions of photographs taken by Mrs. Cameron are given, and also a fine portrait of this gifted woman from a painting by G. F. Watts, R.A.

❀

A Roman Catholic writer in England, Dr. Maurice Francis Egan, has been characterising some modern writers. Marie Corelli puzzles him, but he succeeds in getting rid of the following sentence:

> "The English, whose taste in novels largely dominates ours, have borrowed from France the idea of making their works of fiction into tremendously philosophical treatises. In fact, the French schools, to which we owe the later Henry James and the new methods of Harold Frederic, have permeated Hardy and Meredith, Mrs. Humphry Ward, Mr. Grant Allen, and half a dozen others."

Of Mrs. Humphry Ward he says:

> "She is pagan rather than positivist, a rather conventional pagan, studying in the breakfast-cap of the British matron the sports of the arena. She could have taught Marcus Aurelius much that would have opened his eyes. One is sure, however, that her head would have been cut off early in the week if she had pre-existed as the story-telling princess of *The Arabian Nights*."

❀

A collection of dignified essays by the late George William Curtis has been published by the Harpers under the title *Ars Recte Vivendi*. No one, it has been very well said, who reads these essays can conceive of the author, as an undergraduate, committing, aiding, or abetting any of the strange category of departures from good form, order, courtesy, and justice. Interest in this important phase of Mr. Curtis's mind and character will be heightened by an article on "George William Curtis at Concord," which will appear in the Christmas number of *Harper's Magazine*, from the pen of Mr. George Willis Cooke. The paper will consist for the most part of letters written by him at the age of twenty. They are a revelation of Mr. Curtis's early manhood, disclosing even at this early date his passionate interest in life, and the deep thoughtfulness pervaded by the charm of the man of letters which made him so characteristic a figure in our literary and social American world.

❀

Mr. William Le Queux, whose African adventure story, *The Eye of Istar*, was recently published by the Messrs. Stokes, has just completed a new novel entitled *The Day of Temptation*, which will first appear serially in America and England during 1898. The chief character, we understand, is an Italian adventuress called "La Funaro," whose cunning and recklessness give scope for many thrilling scenes in Florence, Rome, and London. Mr. Le Queux, who has for nearly a year past taken up permanent abode in Italy, may be said to know Italian life thoroughly, as many years of his youth were passed in the vicinity of Genoa. He now lives in Leghorn, and has for his friend and neighbour Pietro Mascagni, the well-known composer of the *Cavalleria Rusticana*.

❀

Mr. Le Queux's novel *Whoso Findeth a Wife*, which appeared serially in America, England, and Australia in the spring, has now been issued in book form in London, and has run through three editions in as many weeks. The American rights have been secured by Messrs. Rand, McNally and Company, who will issue it immediately. The story deals with diplomacy in various European capitals, and has been pronounced by a critic in the *British Weekly* as "one of the most remarkable novels of the season." For some time past Mr. Le Queux has had contracts with an English syndicate for serials until 1901, but a few weeks ago he signed one to write a novel for publication in 1903!

❀

Mr. H. B. Marriott Watson, the author of *Galloping Dick*, has finished the novel on which he has been engaged for some months. It is a story of adventure pure and simple, and it will next year be published serially in a well-known periodical before it appears in book form.

Thomas Bailey Aldrich.

The new Riverside Edition of Mr. Thomas Bailey Aldrich's works announced by us some months ago is now published. It makes the most attractive set of books we have seen this autumn, its artistic book-making vying with the literary value of the work and assuring this edition a final place among our standard authors. Several poems are included which only appeared during the year, one of which is the sonnet "On Reading William Watson's Sonnets entitled 'The Purple East,'" published in THE BOOKMAN, and another the recent "Ode on the Unveiling of the Shaw Memorial on Boston Common." Two portraits reproduced in photogravure appear as frontispieces, one of which is herewith reproduced through the courtesy of the publishers.

❀

The first acquaintance which the writer made with Mr. Aldrich's work occurred some ten years ago, when it was told him that the copy of Mr. Aldrich's poems which lay on a table in the parlour of his home had on a fly-leaf the inscription, "To my wife, Lilian, after seventeen happy years with her. November 28th, 1882," and on the next blank page were written the lines:

"Two things there are with Memory will abide,
Whatever else befall, while life flows by:
That soft, cold hand-touch at the altar side;
The thrill that shook you at your child's first cry."

The lines, which were indelibly graved on the memory of the reader, appear on page 202 of Volume I. in the new edition under the title "Memories." They stamped the author, whoever he might be, as a poet of fine feeling and distinction, and ever since then the writer has been grateful to the friend who introduced him to one with whose writings in poetry and prose he can now boast a wider and deeper intimacy. Another quatrain touched with the same pathos and artistic reserve is "A Child's Grave," which is also a favourite:

"A little mound with chipped headstone,
The grass, ah me! uncut about the sward,
Summer by summer left alone
With one white lily keeping watch and ward."

His poem to Tennyson, it may not be uninteresting to note at the present moment, gives unmistakable expression to his high opinion of the late Poet Laureate's genius and rank among poets. "Shakespeare and Milton," he asks,

"what third blazoned name
Shall lips of after-ages link to these?
* * * * *
Others shall have their little space of time,
Their proper niche and bust, then fade away
Into the darkness, poets of a day;
But thou, O builder of enduring rhyme,
Thou shalt not pass! Thy fame in every clime
On earth shall live where Saxon speech has sway."

Some late publications of Messrs. Dodd, Mead and Company include *The Spanish Maid*, by L. Quiller-Couch, a sister of Mr. A. T. Quiller-Couch, or "Q.;" *Over the Hills*, by Mary Findlater, a sister of Jane Findlater, whose story *The Green Graves of Balgowrie*, published a year ago, impressed us by its strong if sombre power. Jane Findlater has herself a new novel coming out with her sister's, entitled *A Daughter of Strife*, and competent critics, who felt the promise of greater work in her former novel, declare her new book to be one of the strongest novels that they have read in the past few years. The same firm has also a new book about the late war between Greece and Turkey—namely, *With the Conquering Turk*, by Mr. G. W. Steevens, and as this volume is from the clever pen of the author of *The Land of the Dollar*, published last spring, it will be welcomed as the work at first hand of an acute observer and a brilliant writer. Other volumes being issued by this firm are *Bye-ways of Life*, a volume of short stories by Mr. R. S. Hichens, and *The Children of the Sea*, a tale of the forecastle by Joseph Conrad. Mr. Conrad is a new writer of recent years, whose work has been steadily gaining ground for him in the estimation of the literary world. He has a marvellous power of word painting, and there is a description of a storm at sea in this story which is the finest thing of the kind we know of outside of Loti's *Iceland Fisherman*.

CHARLES MACOMB FLANDRAU.

❀

The first large edition of *The Invisible Man*, by Mr. H. G. Wells, was exhausted within a few days of publication. Mr. Grant Allen's *An African Millionaire* has also run into a second edition. Both books are published by Mr. Edward Arnold.

❀

Mr. Charles Macomb Flandrau, whose portrait we give on this page, is the author of seven stories of Harvard life, written from the point of view of a recent graduate, and portray in an entertaining manner the Harvard man of to-day. *Harvard Episodes* is not to be hastily ranked with the college story-book, which, so curiously amusing to insiders, is as curiously deceptive to outsiders. The publishers, Messrs. Copeland and Day, have a serious pride in issuing this volume, not only as an entertaining series of stories characteristic of Harvard college life, but as a book that will appeal to the inner sense of those who look upon a great college as a fit training-school for life, and not simply as a finishing institution to previous educational studies.

❀

George Egerton (Mrs. Clairmonte), whose portrait is given on the next page, inaugurated the Keynotes Series with her first volume of stories called *Keynotes*. This was followed by *Discords*; later, only a few months ago, this was succeeded by *Symphonies*, and now a new book entitled *Fantasias* will make its appearance shortly through Mr. John Lane, who publishes the Keynotes Series. This

GEORGE EGERTON.

author, with a curious penchant for musical titles, is an Australian, whose maiden name was Dunn. Her first husband died a year after marriage, and in 1891 she was wedded to Mr. Egerton Clairmonte, a Nova Scotian. Mr. Clairmonte is fairly well known in South Africa and in London press circles, and has even enjoyed the amenities of an editorship. Mrs. Clairmonte, after travelling over most of the world, now lives quietly in retirement at Notting Hill.

❀

At the request of an enterprising editor of a London magazine, Mrs. Clairmonte recently wrote the following concerning her method and rate of writing: "I have no average, nor do I work every day; nor if I did would it be possible for me to work daily by rule of thumb—so many hours, so many words. No writer of temperament or inspiration could possibly do so. Moreover, it irritates me to have to consider how many words there are in anything I write. I write just as many as I need, no more, no less—always less if possible. I have no idea how many words are contained in any story I have written, nor which book the longest or shortest to write. Some have been written straight off at a sitting; some have been begun and laid aside for weeks."

❀

Dr. H. H. Furness keeps steadily at work on his Variorum Edition of Shakespeare's Plays. It is reported that he has completed another volume, *A Winter's Tale*, which the Messrs. Lippincott will publish within a few months.

❀

Mr. Paul Leicester Ford, the author of *The Honourable Peter Stirling*, contributes an exceedingly interesting and instructive article to the current *Atlantic* on what elements go to constitute historical fiction, with especial application to the American historical novel. The term, though one in common use, he finds to be a very loosely applied expression, and that a satisfactory definition is by no means a simple matter. After some preliminary skirmishing Mr. Ford pins down this decision which we submit as a definition of the historical novel in a nutshell:

"The great historical novel in the past, and, as the writer believes, in the future, is not and will not be great because of its use of historical events and characters, but because of its use of an historical atmosphere, such as Scott created in his *Ivanhoe* and Thackeray in his *Esmond*. . . . In other words, in each case the atmosphere of the book is correct, falsify or pervert history as it may, and, therefore, as already said, each satisfies the imagination of the reader. For a like reason *The Scarlet Letter* and *The Deerslayer* have done the same. The reader breathes Puritanism throughout the first. It is not merely the descriptions of Massachusetts life that give the book this wonderful quality. Dimmesdale's conscience and the intellectual cruelty of his tormentor are truer historically than what in the book purports to be actually reconstructed from documentary sources. *The Deerslayer* is a description of an isolated outpost struggle between white and red—a series of adventures that Cooper might have placed at almost any date, and in almost any spot in this country. Yet the world over it has been accepted as the classic of the wonderful two hundred and fifty years' struggle between two races for the possession of a continent."

In closing, Mr. Ford laments the existence of certain serious defects in our contemporary novelists—an entire disregard of the big elements of American life and an over-accentuation of the untypical ; an almost universal silence on all that has given us distinct nationality. "Who in reading American fiction has ever brought away a sense of real glory in his own country?" Disregarding the great issues and struggles of our national movements, the novelist has turned to the petty in American life ; we are overburdened with dialect stories, with novels of locality that pass as typical and not exceptional, and all this in a country where the people are the most homogeneous in both thought and language in the world. "We are almost submerged with what may be styled the Afternoon Tea Novel." It is the old feud between the utilitarian and the spiritual elements in our national life that Mr. Ford dwells upon with the concluding presage, that "when our people produce as good literary workers as mechanical engineers, when the best of our imagination turns from the practical to the ideal, there will be no lack of an American fiction."

❀

We requested an American writer to name the best twenty books for boys, and in submitting the following titles, he says that he has considered them "from the adviser's standpoint, yet from the boy's standpoint also :"

Westward Ho.	By Charles Kingsley.
Ivanhoe.	" Scott.
Phaeton Rogers.	" Rossiter Johnson.
Treasure Island.	" Stevenson.
The Spy.	" Cooper.
Tale of Two Cities.	" Dickens.
Hoosier Schoolmaster.	By Eggleston.
Hans Brinker.	" Mary Mapes Dodge.
The Prince and the Pauper.	" Mark Twain.
Tales from Shakespeare.	" Lamb.
Boy's Froissart.	" Lanier.
Wreck of the Grosvenor.	" Clark Russell.
Henry Esmond.	" Thackeray.
Silas Marner.	" George Eliot.
Ben Hur.	" Lew Wallace.
Two Years Before the Mast.	" Dana.
St. George and St. Michael.	" George Macdonald.
The Wonder Book.	" Hawthorne.
Historic Boys.	" Elbridge S. Brooks.
Little Women.	" Alcott.

—the last being one of the few "girls' books" that all boys will read, even if they do it on the sly or in a corner.

❀

An English writer names the following titles in a list of the best twenty books for a boy's bookshelf :

Treasure Island.	By Stevenson.
Kidnapped.	" "
Dead Man's Rock.	" Q.
Tom Cringle's Log.	" Michael Scott.
Michael Strogoff.	" Jules Verne.
Beric the Briton.	" G. A. Henty.
The Battery and the Boiler.	" Ballantyne.
The Three Midshipmen.	" Kingston.
The Jungle Books.	" Kipling.
Tom Brown's School-days.	" Thos. Hughes.
Westward Ho!	" Kingsley.
David Copperfield.	" Dickens.
Pickwick.	" "
Lorna Doone.	" Blackmore.
The Pirate.	" Scott.
Ivanhoe.	" "
The Talisman.	" "
The White Company.	" Doyle.
Robbery Under Arms.	" Boldrewood.
The True Story Book.	" Lang.
The Story of the Iliad and the Æneid.	" Church.

After all, such lists are largely a matter of personal taste and inclination. *Treasure Island*, *Kidnapped*, and *Ivanhoe* are indisputable. *Tom Cringle's Log* has the weight, we believe, of Mr. Kipling's authority ; *Tom Brown's School-days* has long been a favourite—especially in England ; but *Dead Man's Rock*, by "Q.," though well known there, has yet to be discovered by the American boy. As for *Pickwick*, what boy is there who, having gone through his Dickens, does not end with a second reading of the immortal *Pickwick?* *Robinson Crusoe* is omitted by this writer as belonging to the category of "elementary stories."

❀

But of all books in the world, *Don Quixote* is the book for an English-speaking boy. "There is a time in his boyhood," said a writer some time ago in the *Atlantic Monthly*, "while the sun of life throws a long shadow behind him, when, after he has read the Waverley Novels, Cooper, and Captain Marryat, he pauses, hesitating between Thackeray and Dickens. . . . It is at that moment of hesitation that *Don Quixote* should be put into the boy's hands," and he puts forth a plea for a good translation of this classic for the boy. "The boy wants two qualities in his books, enthusiasm and loyalty; and here he has them jogging on side by side through four good volumes." One would not wish to select as typical boys young Thackeray, who fed on Dumas, yet thousands of boys feast on *Monte Cristo*, in which their imagination finds expansion in untrammelled fields; nor yet the young Dickens, who nearly read himself into a second Tom Jones, but whose essentially robust and manly character might shame much that is now written for boys and finds shelter in many homes; nor even young Macaulay, who when twelve was discussing Plutarch's *Lives;* and yet of all books we cherish the fondest memories of dear old Plutarch, and would fain see a copy of his book in the hands of every boy.

❀

Max Pemberton, whose *Queen of the Jesters*, recently published, seems to have taken hold of the public, is reported in an interview published in the November *Young Man* as saying that *The Little Huguenot* is his favourite among his own works, and that the Americans prefer it to his other books. "It is an odd thing," he goes on, "that the books which I feel contain my best work go best in America, and not so well in this country (England). I think the Americans attach more importance to finding what I may call 'heart' in the work. Anything that is human and simple seems to go well in America. I don't think they care so much for the fanciful—I mean, for the scientific romance."

❀

For the benefit of the journalistic aspirant we quote in full Mr. Pemberton's plain and practical discussion of the possibilities of success for beginners in journalism, particularly as applied to young writers, and of the difficulties of the editorial position in dealing with them. Mr. Pemberton, we may add, is the editor of *Cassell's Magazine*.

"My experience is that in work of this kind the demand exceeds the supply. In my own case—and I suppose it is the experience of every magazine editor—the difficulty of getting anything readable from those who are not known—from people, I mean, outside the office—can hardly be exaggerated. If, in sketching out my programme, I had to rely upon the work of outsiders, my contents-page would be nearly a blank. Out of all the matter sent in, I do not get more than one acceptable story or item in a month. Of course, when I say that the demand exceeds the supply, I refer to work of a fair standard of merit. There is a great supply of men who can't write at all well, and, naturally, there is no demand for their services; but for young men who can write English, and know how to make the subject they are treating attractive, there is a better opening nowadays than there ever has been, and, granted the beginner has a few ideas of his own, there is nothing to prevent him becoming successful. But then, as you know, the gift of writing is much rarer than people imagine. Journalism is the great open profession, and every man at his wit's end to earn a living turns his hand to it. Out of one hundred men who start writing, I should say ninety-eight per cent have no gift for writing whatever; and I think they are a terrible weight upon the two per cent, the two just ones who are trying to start with them. When there is such an inrush of rubbish, one's editorial inspection is necessarily rather cursory. If you only had to look at the contributions of the two just ones, their work would naturally come in for still closer scrutiny."

"Characterisation, the understanding of humanity, and the ability to make other people understand it, is undoubtedly the highest form of literary art." Such was the terse definition of successful fiction-writing thrown off by Mr. Pemberton during this interview. He very modestly described his adventure stories as being told in the market-place, where people becoming interested step out to listen and then pop home again.

❀

When Mr. James Bowden left the firm of Ward, Lock and Bowden to go into business for himself, his first venture was Mr. Coulson Kernahan's famous booklet, *The Child, the Wise Man and the Devil*. With the exception of *God and the Ant*, by the same author, no book of its kind has made such a stir within recent years. Mr. Bowden has sold over fifty thousand copies of this book in London, and he has now commemorated the event by issuing an *édition de luxe*, limited to five hundred copies, signed and numbered by the author. The book

great house in Portland Place. Although it was in the month of July, they were gathered around a little open fire, for Mrs. Burnett is an ardent member of the sect of fire-worshippers, and the damp, penetrating chill of a July rain in London made the smouldering glow quite endurable.

Midnight came, and the big house was still. They talked quietly by the fire of old times and old friends, and heard the last distant window and door bang as they were closed for the night.

"Now," said Mrs. Burnett, "let us go."

She lit a candle—the effect would be ruined, she explained, by any light but that of one solitary candle—and they went downstairs. As in most London houses, the first floor is the dining-room, and below that is the kitchen and an elaborate system of pantries, housekeeper's quarters, servants' dining and sleeping-rooms, etc. Passing through long, narrow passages, they left all this behind, and their guide opened a door, through which a sudden chill draught of air struck them, nearly extinguishing the candle. Mrs. Burnett closed the door behind them, and they followed her along what seemed an interminable winding passage, with cold stone under their feet.

THE AUTHOR OF "A LADY OF QUALITY."

Mrs. Burnett opened door after door on one side and the other, holding the flickering candle high to show one wine-cellar and vault after another, bleak, empty caves stretching out in a mysterious labyrinth. Each one would seem to be the last, when the winding passage would take an unexpected turn and another would open before them. Finally, by devious ways they came to the end. The passage terminated at a small cupboard door. Lifting the old-fashioned lock, they peered into the little triangular closet, and recoiled from its damp chill.

"You must go in," said the autocrat with the candle.

Only one at a time could get in, but following Mrs. Burnett they entered, turned sharply to the right, and beside the door opening into the closet, and quite concealed by it, they saw another door. Groping their way through that, they went down a step, and found themselves in a round, vaulted room, as remote, as secret, as hushed as if it were a thousand miles away from busy London. Where they were, how far they had come they could not guess. They only knew that far behind them somewhere was a warm, cheerful house, bright with electric lights, and that, sounding muffled over their heads, was the ceaseless living roar of the streets of London.

The candle was lifted high. Around them were damp, stone walls shut in like a tomb, through which no ray of daylight had ever penetrated.

"Here," said Mrs. Burnett, and she waved the candle dramatically—too dramatically, for it flickered out in the close air, and left them for a minute in absolutely impenetrable blackness—"here," she resumed after relighting the candle, "the *Lady of Quality* was born! When I first leased this house I explored these subterranean recesses several times before I discovered this hidden vault.

SIR JOHN OXON (EDWIN ARDEN) AND CLORINDA (JULIA ARTHUR) IN THE ROSE GARDEN SCENE.
From a photograph by Pach Brothers.

When I did, it fascinated me with its mysterious remoteness. What was it for? Why was it ever excavated? What dark purpose might it have served in the distant past?—for the house is very old and has a long history. Of course, you know, I just had to have something happen to fit this vault, and so Clorinda was born and lived out her destiny, and in her strong arms brought the body of John Oxon here, where no eye would ever see it. It is perfectly obvious, you see—in fact, it was inevitable after I had once stood in this room."

❀

Every one concerned about legitimate drama has watched with interest to see what success would attend the dramatisation of *A Lady of Quality*. In adapting this strong and dramatic novel to the stage, Mrs. Burnett has had the assistance of Mr. Stephen Towneshend's stage knowledge. The result, while not by any means such a brilliant achievement as Mr. Lorimer Stoddard's dramatisation of *Tess*, is nevertheless on the whole successful. Some cutting may be done with profit. With fewer lines, in some strong situations, Clorinda would be more convincing. The criticism of practical playwrights will probably guide Mrs. Burnett in making these changes. Alteration is much needed at the close of the play, where the dramatic effect flattens out calamitously. The audience should surely not be suffered to become interested in putting on their wraps just when the gravest issues of life and death are occupying the stage before their eyes. Miss Julia Arthur's performance is always interesting. Her beauty and charm are unfailing. She holds the audience from first to last, but never does she sweep them off their feet in a torrent of passion. The audience never quite forgets how extremely well she is doing her part. Among her supporters, Sir Geoffrey Wildairs and Lady Betty Tantillion deserve commendation. Theirs are minor parts, but given with a finish and adequacy which win them prominence.

❀

The Christmas issue of the *Art Amateur* will be the finest number that has ever been published. It is a Rembrandt number, and besides the other art features which comprise engravings from the famous pictures of the Dutch artist, there will be a Rembrandt supplement containing engravings of his famous paintings now in the possession of Americans. Since the *Art Amateur* changed management last July there has been a marked improvement and advance in the tone of the magazine.

❀

The Macmillan Company will publish at once an authorised edition of *The Letters of Elizabeth Barrett Browning* in two volumes, edited by Frederic G. Kenyon.

FORGET ME, DEATH!—O DEATH, FORGET ME NOT!

Forget me, Death, as from the meadowland
  I rise with wayside song and bounding feet,
  While far below me fades the valley sweet
And far above, the beckoning summits stand.
Halt me not midway up, where the dim band
  Of those who watch below shall see us meet
  And mark Thee cut me down in the full heat
Of my soul's mounting purpose. Stay Thy hand
  As I climb on, climb on—always more nigh
The sacred heights where lovest Thou to be,
  My heart an eagle-brood of hopes that cry
To those lone crags of storm and majesty.
  The eaglets gone, my heart their empty nest,
  Strike me, quick Death, into my warm deep rest!

O Death, forget me not, till I descend!
  Take not Thy place behind me, as with slow
  And slower steps, a waning shape, I go
Toward the silent valley and the end.
Lest midway down I turn with rage and send
  A curse at Thee, nay, seize thy blade and mow
  Myself down at Thy feet, and with the snow
Of those deep years let my heart's summer blend.
  O Mighty One! How were it meet for Thee
To set Thy foot upon the vanquished head,
  To wrest from Age a stingless victory
Whence Joy and Song and Love long, long have fled!
  Await me on the peaks of heavenward strife!
  Slay me, great Death, on the young peaks of Life!

James Lane Allen.

LIVING CONTINENTAL CRITICS.

VI.—N. K. Michailovsky.

The methods of literary criticism in the empire of the Czar differ essentially from those employed by the literary guides of liberal European countries. Owing to the peculiar conditions of the intellectual and literary life of Russia,

N. K. MICHAILOVSKY.

it has been neither possible nor desirable to emancipate the criticism of letters from the criticism of life—social and political. The Russian literary critic is generally a political leader in the theoretical sense. There being no freedom of political discussion and opinion, and no formal and recognised division of the educated elements into definite political parties with frankly avowed principles, writers have perforce had to cultivate the art of giving a literary form to their political propaganda. The inevitable result has been to invest even purely literary criticism with a political significance. Scratch a Russian critic, and you will find the champion of a social philosophy, of a governmental policy.

In no country is the doctrine of "art for art's sake" so unpopular as it is in Russia. How is opinion to be directed and influenced, how is thought on moral and political subjects to be stimulated if not through art? Art for art's sake in a free country need not necessarily hamper the fullest development of the ethical, social, and political life of the nation; but where artists are the only teachers and leaders, their indifference to vital practical questions, their unwillingness to assume the burden of a social mission must naturally cause apprehension among the lovers of progress. Social service is exacted of every artist in Russia, especially of the literary artist. Beauty is regarded as a means to an end, and perfection of form without regard to the moral value of the content is almost inconceivable. The literary critics of Russia have been the relentless censors of the moral government, the vigilant sentinels and dictators whose authority could not be evaded.

In estimating the work of an English, French, or German critic, it would hardly occur to us to ask whether he is a radical, liberal, or conservative; whether he is a socialist or *bourgeois*, a popular tribune or an opportunist and time-server. In Russia this question is not only deemed proper and relevant, but absolutely unavoidable. We must, therefore, in sketching Michailovsky's career and activity define his position as a social reformer and his relation to the various schools of political science.

Michailovsky is the legitimate successor of the greatest critics Russia has had—Bielinsky, Dobroluboff, and Pisareff. Even his most vigorous opponents will not question his right to the mantle of those moulders of Russian thought. Doubtless his influence on the youth of his generation is not as profound, but this is not due to any intellectual or moral shortcoming in him, but to the changed conditions of national life. Bielinsky was Russia's first great critic and publicist, and he was the product of peculiar conditions. At first his philosophy was distinguished by a certain tendency to fatalism and quietism, which has characterised so many other Russian writers, and which is really the undertone of Count Tolstoy's pleas for non-resistance and Christian anarchism. Bielinsky was an ardent Hegelian at the outset, but he utterly misinterpreted that German metaphysician. In his first contributions to the *Saveremennik* (the *Contemporary*) he taught the gospel of self-sacrifice and love. The purity and vigour and brilliancy of his style made him a fascinating and powerful advocate, and it is not improbable that, if he had not radically modified his philosophy of life, he would have proved a dangerous though unconscious enemy of Russian progress. But he soon discovered his fundamental error, and became an apostle of freedom and emancipation. In an intellectual sense he was as great a revolutionist in the second period of his activity as Herzen or Tchernishevsky. The direct discussion of political questions being out of the question, Bielinsky had to inculcate his ideas by means of literary and æsthetic and abstract philosophical essays. Literary criticism in a strict technical sense was often but secondary and incidental to a discussion of principles and tendencies as represented by a novelist's types and characters.

Bielinsky's successor was the comrade and co-worker of Tchernishevsky, Dobroluboff. As a literary critic he was far superior to Bielinsky, but as a metaphysician and philosopher distinctly inferior. Dobroluboff was a socialist of the French school, and he laid stress on the necessity of transforming social and industrial conditions rather than on the importance of improving individual character. So keen and comprehensive was he as a critic, however, that the aggressive and influential Tchernishevsky avoided literary topics in order to save himself from the result of comparisons which he felt would be adverse to his claims. After Dobroluboff came Pisareff, the Bazaroff of Russian letters. Pisareff sympathised with reform, but to him physical science was supreme. He urged Russians to neglect poetry and the fine arts and devote themselves to the study of the exact sciences. The hero of Tourgénieff's *Fathers and Sons* was his ideal, and his short-sightedness carried him to the extreme of ridiculing the unique satirical productions of the Russian Rabelais, Saltikoff. "In science lies salvation," was Pisareff's message; and he was attracted to Auguste Comte's positivistic philosophy (though not to his "religion of humanity") by its "scientific" label and the pretence of absolute precision of the methods of that school. Yet in most of his literary judgments Pisareff was acute and sound. He had a passion and talent for polemics, and he was successful and brilliant as a controversialist. His style was remarkable for its clearness, limpidity, and lucidity. To read him is a liberal education in the richness and capacity of the Russian language, so clumsy and awkward when used by the ordinary writer.

Michailovsky is inevitably compared by every Russian of culture with his predecessors. He can hardly be grouped with any one of the three, but he occupies the same position in the literary world and sustains the same relation to the progressive and reformatory circles. So far as education and true scientific training are concerned, he is the best-equipped critic Russia has had. No branch of knowledge is foreign to him, but he has no illusions with regard to the all-sufficiency of science as a civilising agent. He is a radical and a reformer, and his proclivities, so far as they have found expression, are undoubtedly socialistic, but he is not a revolutionist or a visionary. His many-sidedness protects him from fanaticism. He realises, with Emerson, that it is possible to state a truth too strongly, and that almost every proposition in ethics or scientific politics needs qualification and proper restriction. Unlike the majority of Russian radicals, he does not deride liberalism and liberal institutions. He has always respected and sympathised with that school of Russian thought admirably represented by the *Viestnik Evropy* (European Messenger), whose editor, Stassulevitch, and chief critic and writer, Slonimsky, have long and ably fought the narrow slavophile cult in the name of the culture and progress of Western Europe. Michailovsky does not share the veneration of these liberals for the parliamentary institutions of England and France; and the adoption of those institutions does not appear to him to contain the ultimate solution of Russia's political problem. It is, of course, hardly necessary to say that Michailovsky in no way endorses or countenances the extravagant and pseudo-patriotic notions of the extreme slavophiles. For the preposterous claim that "holy Russia" has a sacred and peculiar mission"—the mission, namely, of teaching "effete Europe" that *bourgeois* liberty, parliaments, universal suffrage, constitutional safeguards, etc., are nothing but a mockery and snare, and that absolutism tempered by religion and a Christian conscience is the true and permanent form of government—for this claim Michailovsky has as profound a contempt as the most intense lover of republicanism can feel for it. But Michailovsky is at one with Dobroluboff and Tchernishevsky in regarding certain rooted Russian institutions as the germ and promise of an industrial order fundamentally different from that existing in republican and "free" governments. In a word, he is a radical, using the term in its peculiar Russian sense, not in the sense in which Sir Charles Dilke or Labouchère are called Radicals in England, and not in the sense in which revolutionists are generally designated as radicals. In Russia a radical is one who has advanced beyond the parliamentary notions of Europe and is not satisfied with "political freedom" in the constitutional sense; one who leans toward socialism and is not opposed to government interference in behalf of the working classes and peasants; one to whom political liberty—the freedom of speech, press, and agitation—is merely the means to an end.

So far nothing has been said about Michailovsky as a critic; but the close connection between Russian literature and politics renders necessary these introductory observations. Michailovsky's judgments of books, writers, and literary tendencies are naturally determined by his philosophical views of man, society, and government. The fact that, although generally admitted to be the greatest contemporary publicist and critic, his influence on his generation is by no means proportioned to his scientific and literary authority, can only be explained in the light of his relation to the political movements of the present day. Liberalism has made great gains in Russia of late, while radicalism has not even held its own. The "stream of tendency" is against Michailovsky, and the wonder is not that he is not as powerful as Bielinsky was in his day, but that he is still the most respected and admired of Russian writers. His conclusions are not always accepted, but his strength and authority are cheerfully recognised.

Michailovsky's literary career opened in the seventies, but he became a power in the early eighties. His first important work was of a sociological character. He contributed to the *Annals of the Fatherland* a series of profound articles on Darwinism and Spencerian discoveries and generalisations. In *What is Progress?*—a general title for several essays, now published in a separate volume—he discussed with great acuteness and evidence of learning Spencer's law and formula of progress. It is a pity that these criticisms are not known to the English-speaking world. The great philosopher of evolution himself might have found the criticisms of his Russian opponent, highly suggestive and forcible. These articles established Michailovsky's reputation as a scientific writer on sociological topics. Other essays dealing with cognate subjects were: "The Method of Analogy in Social Science," "The Natural Order of Things," "The Darwinian Theory and Social Science," "The Struggle for Individuality," and so on.

It is hardly necessary to say that Michailovsky is an evolutionist, but he revolts against the extravagant and superficial deductions drawn by certain apologists for social inequality from the doctrine of natural selection. As a humanitarian and socialist, he naturally repudiated the contention that the present social order exemplified the law of the survival of the fittest, and that defeat in the struggle for existence indicated mental or moral inferiority. Several years ago, when Daudet's "Darwinian" play was brought out, and the term "struggle for life-er" coined to designate those unscrupulous, criminal, and vicious schemers and egoists who deny that morality is a "natural" condition of social existence, who claim that success at any cost is legitimate under the "cosmic" process of development, Michailovsky returned to the discussion of the true bearing of evolutionism on social relations. It is strange, however, that Michailovsky has really never grasped the Spencerian ethical philosophy. Those of us who know that Mr. Spencer is the most uncompromising apostle of individualism of this epoch, the champion *par excellence* of the rights and liberties of "man" as against the "State," will smile at Michailovsky's persistent harping upon the assertion that the Spencerian conception of society as an organism involves undue subordination of the individual and loss of personal dignity and importance.

In his capacity of publicist, Michailovsky has treated numerous subjects of general interest, and several volumes of essays on political, historical, sociological, and economic questions, originally contributed by him to magazines, have been published. The latest edition of his essays exhibits a remarkably wide range of study. We have essays on Karl Marx and his economic and political doctrines, on Voltaire as a man and a thinker, on Bismarck, on heroes and hero-worshippers, on pathological magic, etc. In these volumes are also found the author's first attempts at systematic literary criticism. There is a study of the "experimental novel"—on the realistic tendencies in fiction and the elements introduced by Zola and his followers. There is an elaborate study of Tourgénieff, an appreciation of Eliel Ouspensky, the great novelist and painter of peasant life, and reviews of the productions of minor Russian and foreign writers.

"Realism" has always been strong in Russia, but in Michailovsky it has had a formidable and influential foe. He has attacked the fundamental claim of Zola and other writers that fiction should be "scientific" and "exact." He has endeavoured to show that there are radical differences between the requirements of the scientific method and the requirements of the artistic method; that "scientific" fiction is a self contradiction, an anomaly, and an absurdity. Of late he has had to fight the decadent tendencies in fiction, the fashion of moral "indifferentism," and the attempted rehabilitation of the doctrine of art for art's sake.

Among Michailovsky's larger critical works are: *Count Leo Tolstoy*, *Stchedrin* (the pen-name of Saltikoff, the satirist mentioned above), and *Ivan the Terrible in Russian Literature*. Like Tourgénieff, Michailovsky deplores Tolstoy's abandonment of the sphere of true literary art and pursuit of theological and ethical problems. He has never regarded Tolstoy as a philosopher or profound thinker, but he looks upon him as the greatest novelist of the age. Tolstoy's recent fiction Michailovsky characterises as possessing a dual character, as being more didactic than artistic. The sensational *Kreutzer Sonata* was reviewed in a masterly manner by Michailovsky, and both its weakness as an argument and its defects as a story were ably and clearly pointed out.

Very valuable and readable are Michailovsky's comments on current topics and events. His monthly *causerie* has long been the most interesting feature of the periodicals with which he has been connected. At present he conducts a "Life and Letters" department in the most advanced monthly published in Russia, called *Russian Treasure*. A glance of his work of the past year will show that nothing noteworthy in philosophy, political science, fiction, art, the drama, and practical social affairs is likely to escape his attention. The work of Professor Drummond and Benjamin Kidd receives due consideration and analysis, because ethics and philosophy still remain favourite fields of exploration with him, but literature is not neglected. Only a few months ago Michailovsky entered upon a comprehensive study of Ibsen's plays and their social and artistic significance.

Nowhere has Michailovsky defined his method as a literary critic, but logical inference would appear to justify the statement that he would accept Taine's philosophy of literary criticism with considerable qualifications. Michailovsky is not unmindful of the influence of surroundings and the environment, but he sets great stress on the importance of the individual. He has been called a "subjectivist," and he has not cared to disavow the designation. He is opposed to the attempt at excusing indifference to the requirements of moral duty by vain phrases regarding the "operation of natural forces," the "necessary cause of development," and so on. He believes that human ideals of truth, justice, and beauty have no small share in shaping social relations. He expects the intellectual leaders of mankind to *lead*, to be in advance of their time, to proclaim and fight for new truths and discoveries. He insists on the social function of art and literature, and strenuously combats the notion that beauty is independent of morality. He once rather paradoxically expressed this idea in discussing the old-fashioned conception of the dramatist's duty to compensate us for the flagrant injustice of the real world by picturing the possibilities of an ideal world. "Why," he asked, "is it improper to represent virtue as triumphant and selfishness or vice as doomed to failure and defeat? Why should the dramatist necessarily copy things as they are, and not show us things as they ought to be and as it is our duty to strive to make them?" Of course, this raises the large question of the purpose of the drama; but Michailovsky does not intend to beg it by assuming that naturalism is necessarily illegitimate. He simply reminds us that imagination and idealism have their place and value.

In any other European country a critic like Michailovsky would receive official recognition and be called to a chair in a leading university. In Russia, the great critics have always been in the "opposition," while mediocre and narrow-minded men have filled the positions of public trust and responsibility. This has injured the universities, but it has strengthened literature and journalism. Michailovsky keenly feels the disadvantages under which Russian writers labor, but his practice has always conformed to his belief in doing what is possible while trying to enlarge the sphere of literary freedom. As he has recently said: "The aim of the writer, the real 'born' writer, is to induce in his readers the sentiments and ideas which he believes should be entertained and felt with regard to the subject treated, and to prompt corresponding action —if not to-day, then to-morrow, although the 'to-morrow' may be at the end of many, many years. Such a true, born writer cannot put away his pen even when he has become convinced of the utter uselessness of his work, in the sense of immediate practical results. Despair is of course possible, but one cannot prevent his mind from thinking on matters which occupy and interest one, and to the born writer 'to think' is almost synonymous with 'to write.' And if he cannot write about great things, he will write about small things, but with the same methods and in the same manner which, under different conditions, he would employ in the treatment of great things."

Michailovsky has written on great things as well as on small, and while he has never preached contentment, he has wasted no energy on futile complaints. His work is not known to foreigners, but he certainly ought to find a place in our best prose anthologies. Every lover of Tolstoy and Tourgénieff would read with interest and profit what the most cultivated Russian critic has to say about their qualities and literary rank. European writers who have studied Russian literature pay willing tribute to the vigour and profundity of Michailovsky's work. Thus Georg Brandes, in his *Impressions of Russia*, refers to Michailovsky as "the celebrated and influential critic," who is inclined in his style to the imitation of the satirical tone of Saltikoff, who is "audacious and wily," and "who is capable of placing a not inconsiderable store of learning and remarkable ingenuity at the service of the opposition." Brandes, however, is mistaken with regard to the style of Michailovsky. There is no conscious imitation of Saltikoff, although long and intimate association with that great writer may have influenced Michailovsky's polemical methods.

Michailovsky is not a stylist. He is not a brilliant writer, but he is direct, forcible, incisive, and clear. He is fond of the homely Russian proverbs, and uses them with great effect. He is never pedantic or pompous, and possesses the art of exposing the hollowness and emptiness of pseudo-scientific propositions or arguments advanced by the "official" representatives of the science-of-the-chair.

V. S. Yarros.

THE ABUSE OF THE SUPERNATURAL IN FICTION.

The primary object of the story-teller is to attract our attention. He sits down by the fireside and begins to recount something. If it seems to be amusing or thrilling, we listen ; if not, we go away. But nowadays there are so many tellers and so many tales that the anxiety of the novelist becomes almost painfully apparent. He is so afraid that we shall not attend to him that he uses every subterfuge to excite us at the outset. If he is a realist, he puts in the squalid details on his first page ; if he is a romanticist or a satirist, he tries to do the tricks of his business the very moment that he catches our eye. And as the ground becomes more and more crowded, and the novel situation taken from real life more and more difficult to find, the writer of fiction is tempted to return to the congenial hunting-ground of his forefathers, and try to interest us in what never was and never could be. Within the last two or three years we have seen a revival among us of the supernatural in fiction ; we have had quite a crop of noticeable books the plots of which run counter to all existing experience. There is no objection to this practice in principle, but some of the novelists do not seem to perceive what the rules and limitations of it are.

The first law of romantic invention must be not to overstep the boundaries of belief. In the Ages of Credulity it was easy to keep this law. The world was so wide and dim, man's knowledge of it so imperfect, nature still so mysterious, that if a specially bold man said that he had seen a green dragon chewing little children in his jaws, and puffing flames from his nostrils, he was widely credited. I suppose that there were always some sceptics, but they were likely to be of the class of the sailor's mother, who easily believed in mountains of cake and rivers of rum, but was not to be persuaded that there were fishes which could fly. It was just the absolutely impossible which found an easy path to the mediæval imagination. As experience became wider and calmer, preposterous fancy obtained less and less ready entrance into the mind, but its extravagances lingered among the ignorant. To this very day, in the wilder parts of Ireland, the people will tell you that fairies and witches exist and do marvellous things ; they will sometimes aver that they themselves have seen such beings. Here is the mediæval condition in full survival ; and to these people, if their fancies were properly approached, nothing too monstrous could be told. They would believe the magic wonders with the simplicity of children. We have to remember that, up to three or four hundred years ago, every one, except a few learned men, was in this condition, in order to realise how facile an appeal was made to terror and awe by the hotch-potch of supernatural romance in the Middle Ages.

But to-day people abide no longer in this ignorance. Science has invaded every section of the world, and there is scarcely a dark corner left into which the imagination can flit like a bat and rest itself in the twilight. Nevertheless, the use of supernatural or extra-experimental elements increases in fiction, and is accepted without demur. Why is this ? Primarily, of course, it is because we have accepted the convention of being interested in a story even though we are perfectly aware that it cannot be "true." For instance, there are incidents familiar to every reader of Hawthorne which are outside the limits of prosaic belief. But no reader objects to these, or to the brilliant flights of Oriental magic in Mr. George Meredith's *Shaving of Shagpat*, or to the monstrous adventures of Mr. Frank Stockton's heroes. The reason is that these authors have the art to awaken in us the curious condition of mind which we may call temporary credence. That is to say, they form such an atmosphere around their creations, and make the movements of the latter so consistent and in such harmony with one another that we resign ourselves, as in a dream, to complete belief as long as the story lasts.

With this must not be confounded the treatment of the Unexplained in fiction. Some of the stories which we most naturally think of in connection with the supernatural really belong to this class, and most prominently the blood-curdling tales of the once famous Mrs. Radcliffe, who has lately found in Professor Walter Raleigh so able a defender. In the awful romances of this lady everything which appeared to be mysteriously sinister was always comfortably cleared up on natural grounds in the last chapter of the book. In the thrilling productions of the first Lord Lytton there is usually a pretence of explaining away or of suggesting a loophole for explanation. But his real successes, and particularly *A Strange Story*, with its splendid invention of the Skinleka or luminous banshee vision, sail boldly away from these safer shores. When I was a child, the author who was most in request for giving readers "the creeps" was Mrs. Crowe. I suppose that if we were now to read *The Night Side of Nature* and *Light and Darkness* in the garish light of middle life we might find them poor enough. But they thrilled us in the early sixties, and they were pre-eminently stories of the Unexplained. Mrs. Crowe went the length of pretending that they were all "founded on fact," and she usually left herself a chance of escape on physical grounds. Even as a child, I remember being much more impressed by her when she was mysterious than when she made a coarse use of the palpably and revoltingly impossible.

The subterfuge of the Explainable Mysterious has not found much favour among recent English novelists. The great objection to it is that a romance which accepts its aid is obliged to be built up on the lines of a detective story. Under the influence of Gaboriau and Conan Doyle we have come to prefer detective stories that are straightforward tales of crime or social embarrassment. Every now and then the newspapers present us in real life with humble imitations of *The Castle of Otranto*, in which spoons are snatched out of old ladies' hands and coals are showered on babies' cradles by an unseen force. These events, styled "The Macclesfield Mystery" or "Panic in a Shropshire Village," usually turn out in the course of a few days to be the work either of naughty little girls or of rats. They have grown somewhat too obvious and vulgar for the modern romance writer, although they were quite good enough for those old-fashioned favourites of the public, *St. Leon* and *The Mysteries of Udolpho*. Our idealists and romanticists of to-day are anxious to press the genuine supernatural into their service, but they are not all of them sufficiently considerate of the laws that govern this difficult province of constructive art. It is not enough for me, while I am telling a story of middle-class life in Bayswater, because I feel that the plot is getting a little dull, suddenly to say: "As Maria was leaving Mr. Whiteley's shop, with two small brown-paper parcels under her arm, she was somewhat surprised to see that a large blue Unicorn was threading its way between the omnibuses, and that, as it caught her eye, it touched its horn." Yet Miss Marie Corelli is hardly less artless than this in her appeal to the impossible as an exciting element in fiction. The error of this *naïveté* can perhaps be best comprehended by a reference to its opposite, an artful and successful appeal to the incredible.

A little book has just come into my hands which strikes me as exemplifying the right use of the supernatural to a remarkable degree. It is a story by that very interesting young novelist Mr. H. G. Wells, and it is called *The Invisible Man*. This is a pure extravaganza—a young adventurer of science hits upon a plan by which his own living tissues are made absolutely undetectable by human vision. The mode in which the invention of Mr. Wells has worked is obviously this. He has created the notion of a man made chemically invisible by a scientific discovery, and then he has considered how a man in such a condition would act. The poor wretch has no protection for his naked body. He catches a violent cold; he is knocked over in the street; dogs sniff at him and track him; he has to steal clothes and food like a savage, and the clothes he puts on can never hide him sufficiently, even though he wears a false nose, whiskers, blue goggle spectacles, a wig, and copious bandages. Mr. Wells rightly sees that such an existence, though comical at the outset, must become infinitely painful, and must end tragically. So, in fact, we are quickly led to a scene of murderous violence which ends in the death of the Invisible Man, who slowly comes to sight as his life ebbs away.

Nothing of the supernatural order could run more violently counter to experience than this. No man has been or ever will be invisible ; the idea is absolutely grotesque. But the author commands our belief while we read, by the consistency and inevitability of his details. We have to grant him one admission—and, of course, it is a huge one—namely, that any chemical action could make the flesh of a living and healthy person inappreciable to vision. But, having made that demand upon us, he makes no more ; for the rest of the story he accepts all the responsibility. We are asked to believe no other impossibilities, but, on the contrary, everything is made as easy to belief as possible. Just the same is true of those delightful, grotesque romances of Mr. Frank Stockton, *The Transferred Ghost* and *Negative Gravity*. The imagination has to accept one monstrous outrage upon experience, and then all is perfectly straightforward.

But other modern novelists who use the supernatural do not seem to perceive the importance of thus keeping to the rules of the game. That delightful writer, Stevenson, in a little book which has had hundreds of thousands of readers, *Dr. Jekyll and Mr. Hyde*, missed this initial simplicity. You were asked to believe in the possession of two bodies by a single soul, the good qualities of it inhabiting the handsome frame, the bad ones that which was loathsome and hideous. I do not say that so outrageous a supposition might not have been supported, but I do say that it was not. The little work is beautifully written, and it has a fascinating moral fervour, and it teems with mystery. But that mystery is not legitimately supported. All the cleverness of the author does not make us absolutely credit the occurrences ; and when the final explanation comes we reject it. No, we reply as we put down the book, that is no real way out of the extraordinary difficulties which the narrator has raised. The overpowering improbabilities have only been evaded, not really faced, as Mr. Wells, for instance, would have faced them.

A more recent case of the abuse of the supernatural occurs in a clever novel which has been widely read this summer—*Flames*, by Mr. Hitchens. Here we have what purports to be a story of middle-class life in London to-day. There are two friends, one of whom is older and more authoritative than the other, of a cooler temperament, and possessing a will more fully under control. For a reason ill-explained they get weary of the conditions of their friendship and determine to "exchange souls." For this purpose they shut themselves up in a dark room and perform a sort of table-turning on successive occasions, until at last there is a violent nervous crisis, and small blue flames cross the floor in the silence of the night, and we are asked to believe that these are the "souls" of the two young men changing house, like two soldier-crabs in a tidal pool, each creeping into the shell the other has just left. Then follow excited scenes, and a plot, the intrigue of which depends on the temperament expected from the one man manifesting itself in the other, and *vice versa*. I will not charge Mr. Hitchens here with what I think a fatal lack of simplicity, and therefore of credibility, in the succeeding evolution of his story, but I will venture to maintain that this initial incident is an abuse of the supernatural. Why should the temperament—for that is all that Mr. Hitchens means by "the soul"—take the form of a little flame ? There is absolutely no reason suggested. And why should this "soul" be limited to one or two of the infinitely complex qualities of which the moral nature of a man is composed ? To these questions, and to many others, there is given no reply. We are left vaguely, sceptically, to endeavour to believe that all souls are like blue flames, and could be detached by an effort of the will in a dark room. The initial principle by which an abnormality can be made credible to the imagination—namely, insistence on its being definitely abnormal, has been neglected. The result is that while the careful reader firmly believes in Mr. Wells's *Invisible Man* and shares the agonies of that poor creature's existence, he is apt to toss Mr. Hitchens's *Flames* aside as the mere caprice of a clever, hasty writer.

But no more striking example of the abuse of the supernatural in fiction can be pointed to than is to be found in a book which has just been placed in everybody's hand—*The Martian* of George Du Maurier. In this story a being from the planet Mars is introduced into realistic scenes of every-day life in London and Paris, and is represented as able to endow her favourites with every species of personal charm and executive talent. After she has lived for some years as the wife of one of the characters, whom she has made the most eminent English (and also French) author of his time, she chooses to become reincarnated in the ninth baby of one of her husband's friends, and she starts on another career of fatuous disturbance of the laws of nature and of art. For my own part, I do not see why Mr. Du Maurier should have limited himself to the moral vagaries of his creation. If he had presented to us an image with three heads or a luminous monster without any limbs whatever, we should have been neither more grateful to him nor less. For our belief, our temporary intellectual credence would have been untouched, as it remains untouched by the preposterous Martia. We should have skimmed the pages and have put them down absolutely unenthralled. Yet Mr. Wells and Mr. Stockton, describing things quite as completely foreign to experience, carry us captive with them wherever they will.

A wise novelist will be very cautious how he makes use of supernatural agency to help himself out of a difficulty. No one will blame him if, to heighten the effect of his fable and give it intensity, he introduces what we call incredible incidents with success; only he must remember that we, his readers, will judge success by the degree in which at the time he makes his marvels credited by us. In the old Greek criticism the poets were forbidden to represent the coming of storms in the halcyon days, on the ground that "it would be an affront to the power of the gods to ascribe to them such a force as contradicts poetical probability." Once admit, for special purposes, that such a force as "negative gravity" exists, and there is no contradiction to poetical probability in describing what the effects of its exercise would be on ordinary human beings. Once admit that the tissues of a living man can be made transparent (which seems scarcely more fabulous than the exercise of the Röntgen rays would have seemed two years ago), and there is nothing poetically improbable about the discomforts and adventures of a man reduced to that condition. But to be so unskilful as to have to produce a personage from Mars in order to account for the sudden celebrity of a commonplace man, this is to sin against the laws of supernatural machinery, and to show real poverty of invention.

Perhaps a safe rule would be: Never use supernatural agency to gain an effect which could with the exercise of more ingenuity be produced by natural agency. And a rider on this would be, Never employ a supernatural agency without having thoroughly made up your mind what you mean its exact action to be. Whether you take the reader into your confidence about this limit of action is a matter for your own judgment, but that you should understand it yourself is unquestionably necessary. Many of our latter-day purveyors of the mysterious seem to be as doubtful about the nature of the bogeys they introduce as the most credulous of their readers can be.

Edmund Gosse.

A HUNDRED BOOKS FOR A VILLAGE LIBRARY.

Asked to name what I think the best hundred books for a village library, I am at a somewhat different standpoint from one who would name the best hundred books that literature has given us. This latter task would be but to put on paper the name of volume after volume that no one now reads, that no one today would derive any profit from reading. Sir John Lubbock once named the hundred books that he thought most interesting and most desirable of study, and he was addressing a workingman's club. If Sir John Lubbock has read all of these himself, he has read some sad trash. One of them is the *Nibelungen Lied*, which it may be presumed he did not expect the workingmen he addressed to study in Old German or Modern German. The book is available in English only in an absurd translation. If he had quietly mentioned Carlyle's essays as a source from which an English reader can obtain some knowledge of those delightful legends, he would have shown less pretentiousness. Is it anything but an affectation, further, which flings together Smith's *Wealth of Nations*, Butler's *Analogy*, Locke *On the Human Understanding*, Hesiod, Descartes, Spinoza's *Tractatus Theologico-Politicus*, and the *Ramayana* and the *Mahabharata*, as books which a workingman should study? Every one of these books should, of course, be rigidly avoided by every intelligent man outside of purely scholastic circles. Their perusal would make him a terror to his neighbours. And a recommendation of Hume's *History of England* is to be blind to the historical studies of half a century.

It is not in the least difficult to make a list of a hundred books perfectly "understanded of the people" which not only workingmen, but all of us might profitably read and re-read every ten years or so. In such a list I object to put Shakespeare in bulk, now that the Messrs. Dent and Mr. Gollancz have so adequately provided us with Shakespeare's plays in separate volumes. Each one of Shakespeare's greater plays has furnished forth a library of criticism, and is entitled to rank as a separate book. Besides this, many a beginner is liable to be repulsed by a recommendation so formidable as the whole of Shakespeare's plays, perhaps in one more or less ill-printed volume, implies. If, say, half a dozen plays have been read with pleasure, the reader will be sure to turn to the others. The same criticism applies to Scott, to Dickens, or whoever may be the writer. One or two typical works open the door to the study of the author who most attracts the particular individual; and temperament and taste are so at variance that one man is repulsed by Dickens, but finds in Omar Kháyyám a profound affinity; another delights in Dickens, and is bewildered by the praise which FitzGerald's paraphrase of Omar has secured in our day.

The hundred best books for a village library are not necessarily the hundred best books in the language. Mr. James Payn said that the reading of Sir John Lubbock's hundred books would make a man a hopeless prig. It would do more—it would make him a hopeless dullard. I cannot see what Sir John was driving at. He could not have intended to suggest the hundred best books in the world's literature, although he named numbers of classical books, much talked about and never read, and, indeed, impossible of modern consumption! He would surely not have included works by Bulwer Lytton and Charles Kingsley in such a list, and have ignored Jane Austen. Lytton and Kingsley may fairly be included in any suggested hundred books for a village library, but their works are not among the world's great classics.

Here, then, is my list of a hundred books. It contains many that I do not pretend to call classics, but it contains nothing that will in the least bore any intelligent man or woman. My list does not include any books merely of information: scientific research or ordinary travel, for example. Literature I conceive to mean books presenting life in an artistic form. No man of science has ever been an artist, although some, as, for example, Darwin and Huxley, have been believed by their friends to have been such. One or two travellers have been artists—Borrow, for example. The Bible, of course, is taken for granted.

1. Homer's Iliad. Pope's translation.
2. The Odyssey. Butcher and Lang's translation.
3. Dante's Inferno. Translated by J. A. Carlyle.
4. The Purgatory of Dante. Translated by A. J. Butler.
5. The Paradise of Dante. Translated by A. J. Butler.
6. The Rubáiyát of Omar Kháyyám. Translated by Edward FitzGerald.
7. Cellini's Autobiography. Symonds's translation.
8. The Pilgrim's Progress.
9. Robinson Crusoe.
10. Gulliver's Travels.
11. Sterne's Sentimental Journey.
12. Goldsmith's Vicar of Wakefield.
13. Bryce's Holy Roman Empire.
14. Letters of Cowper in the Golden Treasury Series.
15. Colvin's Selections from Landor in the Golden Treasury Series.
16. Palgrave's Golden Treasury of Songs and Lyrics.
17. Thackeray's Vanity Fair.
18. " Esmond.
19. Dickens's Pickwick.
20. " David Copperfield.
21. Fielding's Tom Jones.
22. Boswell's Life of Johnson.
23. Gibbon's Decline and Fall of the Roman Empire.
24. Gibbon's Autobiography.
25. Prologue to Chaucer's Canterbury Tales, being vol. 1 of Morris's Chaucer in the Aldine Poets.
26. Shakespeare's Hamlet.

27. Shakespeare's King Lear.
28. " Macbeth.
29. " As You Like It.
30. " Much Ado About Nothing.
31. " Merchant of Venice.
32. Pepys's Diary.
33. Milton's Paradise Lost.
34. Dowden's Shakespeare Primer.
35. Stopford Brooke's Life of Milton.
36. Hans Christian Andersen's Fairy Tales.
37. Johnson's Rasselas.
38. Arnold's Selections from Johnson's Lives of the Poets.
39. Charlotte Brontë's Jane Eyre.
40. Mrs. Gaskell's Life of Charlotte Brontë.
41. " Cranford.
42. Carlyle's Past and Present.
43. " Hero Worship.
44. Macaulay's History of England.
45. " Essays.
46. George Eliot's Silas Marner.
47. Ruskin's Sesame and Lilies.
48. Matthew Arnold's Selections from Wordsworth. (Golden Treasury Series.)
49. Matthew Arnold's Selections from Byron. (Golden Treasury Series.)
50. Stopford Brooke's Selections from Shelley. (Golden Treasury Series.)
51. Scott's Waverley.
52. " Guy Mannering.
53. " Ivanhoe.
54. " Heart of Midlothian.
55. " Marmion.
56. " Lady of the Lake.
57. The Arabian Nights.
58. Jane Austen's Pride and Prejudice.
59. Borrow's Bible in Spain.
60. Sheridan's School for Scandal.
61. Burns's Poems. (Globe Library.)
62. Moore's Irish Melodies.
63. Goethe's Faust. Anster's translation.
64. Schiller's Wallenstein. Coleridge's translation.
65. Coleridge's Poems.
66. Keats's Poems.
67. Trevelyan's Life of Macaulay.
68. Don Quixote.
69. Gray's Elegy.
70. Tennyson's Maud.
71. " Idylls of the King.
72. Browning's Selected Poems.
73. Plutarch's Lives. Long's translation.
74. Dryden's Virgil. (Chandos Classics.)
75. The Greek Anthology. (Blackwood's Ancient Classics for English Readers.)
76. Horace. (Blackwood's Ancient Classics for English Readers.)
77. Southey's Life of Nelson.
78. Motley's Dutch Republic.
79. Prescott's Mexico.
80. " Peru.
81. Tolstoy's Anna Karénina.
82. Green's Short History of the English People.
83. Lewes's Life of Goethe.
84. Lockhart's Life of Scott. Unabridged edition.
85. Rousseau's Confessions.
86. George Meredith's Evan Harrington.
87. Stevenson's Treasure Island.
88. Sir Walter Besant's Rabelais.
89. Taine's French Revolution. Translated by Durand.
90. De Quincey's Confessions of an Opium-Eater.
91. Hawthorne's Scarlet Letter.
92. Charles Kingsley's Westward Ho!
93. Henry Kingsley's Geoffrey Hamlyn.
94. Balzac's Le Père Goriot.
95. Dumas's Monte Cristo.
96. Charles Reade's Cloister and the Hearth.
97. Longfellow's Poems.
98. Tourguéneff's Virgin Soil.
99. Lamb's Essays of Elia.
100. Ibsen's Master Builder.

Clement K. Shorter.

HELOISE TO ABELARD.

The wild rose that you pressed between
  The vellum of my Book of Hours
Hath left a stain of rust and green
  To mark the joy that once was ours.

Not so the flowers unplucked, whose scent
  Sufficed us as we wandered on ;
The sweetness of them is not spent,
  Nor is their stain, though they be gone.

Thomas Walsh.

OLD BOSTON BOOKSELLERS.

III.

Of the coterie of old Boston booksellers still living whose association with the book trade of Boston began in the second third of this century, none has a richer fund of reminiscence than Alexander Williams and William Lee. And none of them was more active in the trade during the periods of Boston's leadership than these two comfortable old gentlemen.

Alexander Williams comes of a bookselling family. His father, an uncle, and his mother's half-brother were booksellers before him. The father and uncle were together as R. P. and C. Williams from about 1812–36. The uncle, Charles, was earlier associated with the mother's half-brother, Elam Bliss. Later Mr. Bliss moved to New York, where he became the friend of Bryant, and published *The Talisman*, that brilliant "Annual" written by Gulian C. Verplanck, Robert C. Sands, and Bryant, subsequently issued in three volumes of *Miscellanies*. Bliss was that bookseller whom Duyckinck characterises as "of great liberality and worth ; a gentleman by nature." Robert Pearce and Charles Williams started their bookselling business in a little shop on State Street, on the site of the first meeting-house of the Puritan settlers of Boston, where now is rising a modern "sky-scraper." Their place became the headquarters of the Episcopalian book-buyers of the town, and they dealt in much theological and solid general literature. From State Street they moved to Cornhill Square, occupying a shop in Joy's Building, which stood in front of Young's Hotel.

It is curious that Episcopacy and bookselling were associated with State Street more than a century earlier, for John Checkley had his shop opposite the head of the street on the present site of Sears' Building, and here he published things hateful to Puritan Boston which had him fined, in 1724, for "scandalous libel," to the tune of fifty pounds.

In his father's shop Alexander Williams began work as a boy of twelve (he was born in 1818 on old "Fort Hill," long since levelled), but not altogether without experience, for when but eight years old he was about the shop during his school vacation, selling that steadfast New England publication the *Old Farmer's Almanac*. From his fourteenth to his eighteenth or nineteenth year he was in New York in Elam Bliss's shop, learning the trade under excellent conditions. Mr. Bliss had good literary connections, and the lad here came close to a number of the *littérateurs* of the time. In going about among other booksellers he made friends, in some cases lasting friendships, with several young men who afterward became leaders in the New York trade. During the panic year of 1836 his father's firm failed, and subsequently the family moved from Boston to St. Louis. Thereupon he left New York and joined them. About a year later, however, he returned to Boston and entered trade on his own account.

It was a small and modest beginning with newspapers and periodicals, in partnership with George W. Redding, whose name was long familiar in New England as attached to "Redding's Russia Salve." They had a box of a shop with a single "two-foot" counter, on the north side of State Street, opposite the Old State House. They continued together for fifteen years, during that time considerably expanding their mixed business. Then Mr. Williams sold his interest to Mr. Redding and bought out William P. Fetridge, who had the showiest book and periodical shop at that time in Boston. It was on Washington Street about where the *Advertiser* newspaper building stands, close upon the site of the dwelling and shop of James Campbell, bookseller and postmaster, who in 1704 issued the *News-Letter*, the first permanently established newspaper in Boston. Here Mr. Williams developed a large trade, adding fresh books to the stock, and made his shop the chief resort especially of buyers of periodical literature. He was the agent for *Harper's Magazine* when it was in fact the *New Monthly*. Spurred to extra efforts in its behalf at starting, by the promise of a bonus of a new suit of clothes if he should bring its circulation in the Boston market up to ten thousand copies, he so advanced it that he won not only the new suit but a gold-headed cane. He was the first to introduce the regular sale of foreign newspapers in America. He began with small lots of London papers brought out to him by pursers of the steamships. These finding ready sale, in less than a year he had established direct connection with English newspaper and periodical publishers. He addressed himself to this department of his business with such activity and zeal that it increased rapidly, and before very long his London accounts were averaging £350 a month. His progress attracted the attention of dealers elsewhere, notably in New York, and organisations followed which were forerunners of the modern news companies. He himself became in later years the father of the New England News Company. The story of the development of the news company of to-day, in the early stages of which Alexander Williams figures prominently, is a chapter by itself.

In the autumn of 1869 Mr. Williams moved to the cherished "Old Corner Bookstore," succeeding here Messrs. E. P. Dutton and Company, now so well known among New York booksellers, who had themselves succeeded Messrs. Ticknor and Fields at the ancient stand. Shortly after, he took as partners Messrs. Charles L. Damrell, Henry M. Upham, and Joseph G. Cupples, under the firm name of A. Williams and Company. In the spring of 1883 he withdrew, disposing of his interest to his associates, from whom have evolved the present firm. He has since lived in retirement, but still in touch with trade, having regular hours "down town," clinging to the habit of the methodical man of business, so that he does not grow rusty.

Mr. Williams recalls with entertaining detail the booksellers and bookselling methods of his father's time and his own younger days. When his father kept the Joy's Building shop the most prominent Boston booksellers were Messrs. Hilliard and Gray, the trade ancestors of Messrs. Little, Brown and Company. In near neighbourhood were Messrs. Munroe and Francis, the first publishers of Shakespeare's works in the country. Opposite them was John Parker, a former partner, whose issue of the Waverley Novels filled all Boston with astonishment. Above the "Old South" was the little stationery shop of Ebenezer Clapp, father of Mr. Charles A. Clapp, of Messrs. E. P. Dutton and Company, over which was the antiquarian book-shop of Otis Clapp. In the Old Corner Bookstore were, first, Robert H. Carter and Charles J. Hendee, as Carter and Hendee, and after 1833, John Allen and William D. Ticknor. Where the *Herald* Building now stands were Weeks and Jordan. Near by was Samuel T. Armstrong, who became Lieutenant-Governor of the State in 1836, and Mayor of Boston in 1837. Armstrong had been bred a printer with Samuel Etheridge of Charlestown, afterward partner of Elam Bliss before the latter's removal to New York. In 1837 he was the oldest bookseller in the town. He printed for the Andover Theological Seminary. From his concern the long-time firm of Crocker and Brewster sprung. Then, nearly opposite the "Old Corner," was James Spear Loring, scholar, publisher (he brought out the *Hundred Boston Orators*), in 1852, and dealer in rare old books. And near by was Henry B. Greene of the "Bible and Crown," who published *Brownson's Quarterly Review* in the forties.

When Mr. Williams was a boy in his father's shop most of the books there were bound in sheep and morocco, and he looked with admiration upon Cooper's Novels as they appeared bound in boards with white label. This was an innovation in bookbinding. Then came Harper's Family Library bound in linen. Messrs. R. P. and C. Williams obtained their supplies of foreign books through an "elegant salesman by the name of Jackson," whose coming at intervals with samples was an event. There were no rapid sales in those days—no cheap novels ; it was a slow business with fair profits. One feature of the trade was exchanges between booksellers of different and widely separated cities. It was not unusual for a Northern bookseller to journey South, and exchange his old stocks for stocks of Southern booksellers, containing importations new to the Northern market.

At the Old Corner Mr. Williams was essentially the bookseller. The shop became again a bookselling shop rather than a publishing house. He gave the customer the freedom of the shop, allowing him to browse among the books, and lead himself into the temptation of buying. Although Ticknor and Fields had their inviting "Author's Room" in their new Tremont Street store, Little and Brown's was the headquarters of scholars of various kinds, and other shops had become gathering-places of literary workers, the Old Corner still continued a favourite haunt for bookmen. Holmes was a regular *habitué* to the last days of his life. Parkman's was a familiar figure. Motley, after his final return home from the English mission, sat in the Old Corner by the front window and remarked that it was the one natural spot he had found, for so changed had the town become that he felt himself almost a stranger in it.

William Lee was also born in Boston, at the old North End. He began as a boy in Samuel G. Drake's antiquarian bookshop at the age of eleven, for one dollar a week, with hours from six in the morning to nine at night. That was in 1837. He was the son of a sea captain who had just died, leaving the mother with slender means and a family of six children, of whom William was the eldest. He was two years with Drake; then three years on a farm in Sturbridge, Worcester County, where he managed to get a schooling which fitted him for college. Returning to Boston, he entered as clerk with Oliver L. Perkins, who had been a partner of Drake, now engaged in selling books at auction in New England towns. After two years of this experience, in which he displayed the keen sense of the trader, and distinguished himself as a successful seller from the auctioneer's chair, he got a place with Phillips and Sampson, then a rising firm, and was soon on the road to prosperity. Evening auction sales were at that time a feature of the Boston book trade; and young Lee was given charge of the evening sales which Messrs. Phillips and Sampson were carrying on. His success was so marked that at the age of eighteen he was receiving a salary of seven hundred and fifty dollars—unusually large for a young man in those times. In his twenty-first year he was admitted to a share in the profits of the house. At twenty-four he was an equal partner. Seven years later he retired with what he then deemed almost a competence, selling his interest to his partners for sixty-six thousand dollars. Then he set out on a leisurely European tour, which covered five years.

This was pretty rapid progress in twenty years for a bookseller, and William Lee was accounted in the trade most fortunate. But the ebb soon came to this prosperous tide. In the midst of his travels he received word first of the death of Mr. Sampson, then of Mr. Phillips, then of the embarrassment of the house. Having taken the promissory notes of his late partners instead of cash for the larger part of his interest, he hastened back to Boston. He found his claim against the firm disallowed by the assignees on the ground that it lay against the personal property of the dead partners. Thereupon, giving the widows a release, he brought suit against the assignees, and received about half of the face value of his notes. Then, with this sum and what little cash he had in hand, he started again, buying an interest in the firm of Crosby and Nichols, the name of which was thereupon changed to Crosby, Nichols, Lee and Company. This was in 1860. The business was enlarged, and spread especially in the West and South. But with the coming of the Civil War heavy losses fell upon the house, and during 1861 Mr. Lee withdrew with the loss of his interest.

Now literally without a dollar, and the book trade deranged by the war, he spent several gloomy months in looking for new opportunities. One day he chanced to meet on the street Mr. Charles A. B. Shepard, who had not long before suffered a similar disaster, his firm—a young venture—having failed through the war, leaving him dollarless. Mr. Lee suggested that they unite their forces and start a business based on experience rather than capital. This idea struck Mr. Shepard as happy, as it was novel. Accordingly they straightway repaired to Mr. Lee's lodgings and arranged preliminaries. They hired at low rent the street floor of an ancient building on Washington Street, opposite the head of Milk Street, then known as the "Old Chelsea Dye House." This bore a sign, "Oldest

House in Boston," which they obliterated, and in place of it printed in very antique letters :

Books in all the departments of Literature	LEE AND SHEPARD	The oldest house in Boston

in this cheerful way they launched their enterprise. This was the beginning of the house of Lee and Shepard, of which Mr. Lee in his rugged old age is still the active head.

The partners began not only without a bank account, but without bookkeeper, clerk, or porter, themselves constituting the firm and the force. But they had credit, wide acquaintance, the confidence of the trade, reputation as able and shrewd buyers and sellers, and a thorough knowledge of all details of the business. Mr. Shepard had been for some years, prior to the venture in his firm, with John P. Jewett, the famous publisher of *Uncle Tom's Cabin*, while Mr. Lee had been recognised as a force in the house of Phillips and Sampson during its most prosperous period. Their intent at first was to engage in bookselling, as retailers and jobbers only. But shortly after they had got under way Samuel C. Perkins, the then surviving partner of Phillips, Sampson, and Company, offered them the stereotype plates of some books of "Oliver Optic" (the late William T. Adams) and other good-selling authors, all at that time new. Purchasing these at a bargain, they ventured a few editions. Meeting with unexpected success, "Oliver Optic" was engaged for further work. Other authors were in time added to their list, and from the start to the present the imprint of Lee and Shepard has appeared on two thousand different works. Mr. Shepard died in 1889.

In the house of Phillips and Sampson Mr. Lee was the partner who, perhaps, best knew the bookselling trade. He influenced the venturing of some of its most important publications, which proved to be good selling ones. But he advised against one work which brought fortune to another. This was *Uncle Tom's Cabin*, which Mrs. Stowe first offered to his firm. Mr. Lee earnestly counselled against it because of the effect its publication would have on the Southern trade of the house, which at that time was large and profitable. He looked at it from the business point of view entirely ; for personally he was an anti-slavery man. The house, however, published all of Mrs. Stowe's subsequent works issued during its existence. One of the most notable enterprises of Phillips and Sampson was the starting of the *Atlantic Monthly*, of which Mr. Lee and Francis H. Underwood were the originators so far as the publishers were concerned.

Mr. Lee relates the experience of the house with Prescott, the historian, substantially as Derby in his *Fifty Years* tells it. Learning, through Mr. Underwood's intimate relations with the Harvard literati, that Prescott's contract with the Harpers for his *Ferdinand and Isabella* and *The Conquest of Mexico* had run out, and that he had a new work in preparation—his first two volumes of *Philip II.*—Mr. Phillips called upon him to make a proposition. Mr. Prescott observed that while he felt bound in courtesy to give the New York house an opportunity to renew the contract, there was nothing to prevent him from entertaining any proposal from another house for a new contract, and for the publication of the new work. The Harpers were paying him fifty cents per volume copyright on each book sold, he furnishing the stereotype plates. Mr. Phillips thereupon offered to take the old works and pay Mr. Prescott fifty cents a volume on all copies sold, while for the *Philip II.* he proposed to guarantee a sale of twelve thousand sets within a specified time with a payment to Mr. Prescott of six thousand dollars when the two volumes were published and six thousand more at the end of six months from the day of publication.

Most truly yours
William Lee

He added a proviso that in case the number guaranteed was not sold within the specified time the loss should fall on the firm. Mr. Prescott wrote the Harpers asking if they desired to renew the old contract, and with respect to the new work stating his wish for a proposition guaranteeing the sale of a specified number of copies. To this the Harpers replied that they would gladly renew the old contract, and would undertake the new work, devoting to it their best energies, but they did not feel that it was necessary for them to guarantee any fixed number of sales. Then Mr. Prescott turned to Mr. Phillips, and the contracts as the latter had proposed them were executed and signed.

Now comes the feature of the transaction which reflected such credit upon Mr. Prescott. After *Philip II.* was out and selling, Mr. Prescott one day came into the store and asked Mr. Phillips to allow him to look at the contract once more, remarking that he wished to suggest a slight change. It was handed to him, and when he returned the paper it was found that he had added a note to the effect that in case the full number of twelve thousand copies was not sold within the time specified, the publishers should not pay the copyright agreed upon till it had accrued by actual sales. The sales fell a little short within the period fixed, but the publishers met the conditions of the contract.

An idea of the wide circulation of *Philip II.* is conveyed in a note of Prescott's given in Ticknor's *Life* of the historian. This note was written six months after the publication of the first two volumes :

> "A settlement made with my publishers here last week enables me to speak of the success of the work. In England, it has been published in four separate editions, one of them from the rival house of Routledge. It has been twice reprinted in Germany, and a Spanish translation of it is now in course of publication at Madrid. In this country, 8000 copies have been sold, while the sales of the preceding works have been so much improved by the impulse received from this that nearly 30,000 volumes have been disposed of by my Boston publishers, from whom I have received $17,000 for the *Philip* and the other works the last six months. So much for the lucre !"

CHARLES A. P. SHEPARD.

Alexander Williams
1893.

It seems to be quite forgotten in the trade that Prescott's *Ferdinand and Isabella* was first issued by The American Stationers' Company; and few are found to-day who have ever heard of the existence of this association of author-publishers. It was organised in Boston in the autumn of 1836 by a number of leading literary men and lawyers, with considerable capital. Samuel G. Goodrich defines its object to have been "the publication of original American works of high character, and in such a way as to render due compensation and encouragement to authors." The *Ferdinand and Isabella* was one of the first works issued by this association. The contract as described by Prescott, made in April, 1837, stipulated for the use by the company of the stereotype plates and the engravings already prepared at the author's charge; an edition of twelve hundred and fifty copies, the company to find the paper and all other materials; and a payment to the author of one thousand dollars. Prescott regarded this offer as a liberal one. "It insures," he wrote, "the zealous and interested co-operation of a large and somewhat influential body in the sale and distribution of the work," through its "agencies diffused through every part of the United States." Another of its publications was Hawthorne's *Twice Told Tales*, Goodrich giving a bond to indemnify the company against loss, the only condition upon which it would be undertaken.

This early authors' enterprise ended in disaster despite its elaborate organisation. In the financial crash of 1838 the company, says Goodrich, was "precipitated into the gulf of bankruptcy with thousands of others. Though I was a hesitating and reluctant subscriber to the stock, and, in fact, was the last to join the association, I still shared largely, I may say, fatally, in its misfortunes."

Edwin M. Bacon.

THE WANDERER.

For one astray, behold
The Master leaves the ninety and the nine,
Nor rest till, love-controlled,
The Discord moves in Harmony divine.

John B. Tabb.

Drawn by Mélanie Elisabeth Norton.

Romance revives! Once more we read
Of bold adventure, daring deed,
Of valiant knight and lady fair,
Of secret hoard of treasure rare,
Of hero's pluck and villain's greed.

A GARDEN IN NEW ORLEANS.

suspended any other occupation and struck attitudes all over the place and listened. Mr. Shelby was a fine figure of a man. He wore jack-boots and white duck trousers, while Mrs. Shelby at 3 P.M. appeared in a low-necked dress and a tiara of precious stones. When it subsequently transpired that the Shelbys were deeply in debt, and that the white marble mansion was mortgaged up to its fastigium, I couldn't help thinking that Mrs. Shelby might have raised a little money on her tiara instead of weakly consenting to the sale of George Harris and Eliza, and of poor Uncle Tom, all of whom presently appeared while the hands were singing their seventh hymn. George Harris was undoubtedly a typical mulatto slave, because the play-bill said so; but if I had seen him anywhere else I should have taken him for Albert Chevalier doing a coster turn. Uncle Tom was nice and black. When he was summoned to appear, in order that he might be informed that he had been sold to the heartless Haley, he came directly from working in the fields, and he had white cotton gloves on, such as were doubtless always worn at the South by the better class of slaves when hoeing corn and digging sweet potatoes. He had a fine deep voice and a rich Whitechapel accent; and when he was informed that he had been sold to Haley, he observed with some emotion that it was very 'ard. But there was no help for it; so he had to go, but not before he, too, had sung a hymn, and listened to the rendering of still another by his fellow-slaves.

George and Eliza, however, had more spirit than Uncle Tom; for they resolved to run away; and they did so while Haley was obligingly looking at the inland sea and the gondolas, and perhaps composing poetry; for he failed to hear a word of their intention, though it was discussed by them in a loud and carrying tone of voice. When he did discover it, they had already gone, and then he promptly called for bloodhounds and set off in hot pursuit, waiting, however, to hear the field hands give a rendering of one final hymn, and also the encores for which the audience very kindly called, perhaps to give Eliza and her child a better start.

The beginning of the second act revealed a tavern on the banks of the Ohio River, to which place Eliza had succeeded in escaping. The tavern was simply but sufficiently furnished with one deal table and two chairs, and it had a large window which commanded a sweeping view of the river. And here one discovered a remarkable fact as to the variations.

dear Julia," replied the general soothingly.

"But they think she is here. The people are in the streets. Look out of the window. They are in the plaza."

"I know it, my dear," said the general.

"They are armed ; they are going to attack this house . . ."

"I am aware of it."

"Their plan is to murder the Queen."

"So we understand," said the general gently. He had a horror of anything approaching sensation or a scene, a feeling which Spaniards share with Englishmen. "That is the Queen for the time being," added Vincente, pointing to Estella.

Julia stood looking from one to the other, a self-contained woman made strong by love, for there is nothing in life or human experience that raises and strengthens man or woman so much as a great and abiding love. But Julia was driven and almost panic-stricken. She held herself in control by an effort that was drawing lines in her face never to be wiped out.

"But you will tell them. I will do it. Let me go to them. I am not afraid."

"No one must leave this house now," said the general. "You have come to us, my dear, you must now throw in your lot with ours."

But Estella must not take this risk !" exclaimed Julia. "Let me do it."

And some woman's instinct sent her to Estella's side, two women alone in that great house amid this man's work and strife of reckless politicians.

"And you and Señor Conyngham," she cried ; "you must not run this great risk."

"It is what we are paid for, my dear Julia," answered the general, holding out his arm and indicating the gold stripes upon it.

He walked to the window and opened the massive shutters, which swung back heavily. Then he stepped out on to the balcony without fear or hesitation.

"See," he said, "the square is full of them."

He came back into the room, and Conyngham, standing beside him, looked down into the moonlit plaza. The square was, indeed, thronged with dark and silent shadows, while others, stealing from the doorways and narrow alleys, with which Toledo abounded, joined the group with stealthy steps. No one spoke, though the sound of their whispering arose in the still night-air like the murmur of a breeze through reeds. A hundred faces peered upward through the darkness at the two intrepid figures on the balcony.

"And these are Spaniards, my dear Conyngham," whispered the general—"a hundred of them against one woman. Name of God, I blush for them !"

The throng increased every moment, and withal the silence never lifted, but brooded breathlessly over the ancient town. Instead of living men, these might well have been the shades of the countless and forgotten dead, who had come to a violent end in the streets of a city where Peace has never found a home since the days of Nebuchadnezzar.

Vincente came back into the room, leaving shutter and window open.

"They cannot see in," he said, "the building is too high. And across the plaza there is nothing but the cathedral, which has no windows accessible without ladders."

He paused, looking at his watch.

"They are in doubt," he said, speaking to Conyngham, "they are not sure that the Queen is here. We will keep them in doubt for a short time. Every minute lost by them is an inestimable gain to us. That open window will whet their curiosity, and give them something to whisper about. It is so easy to deceive a crowd."

He sat down and began to peel a peach. Julia looked at him, wondering wherein this man's greatness lay, and yet perceiving dimly that against such as he men like Esteban Larralde could do nothing.

Concha, having supped satisfactorily, was now sitting back in his chair, seeking for something in the pockets of his cassock.

"It is to be presumed," he said, "that one may smoke, even in a palace."

And under their gaze he quietly lighted a cigarette, with the deliberation of one whom a long solitary life had bred habits only to be broken at last by death.

Presently the general rose and went to the window again.

"They are still doubtful," he said, returning, "and I think their numbers have decreased. We cannot allow them to disperse."

He paused, thinking deeply.

"My child," he said suddenly to Estella, "you must show yourself on the balcony."

Estella rose at once, but Julia held her back.

"No," she said; "let me do it. Give me the white mantilla."

There was a momentary silence, while Estella freed herself from her cousin's grasp. Conyngham looked at the woman he loved while she stood, little more than a child, with something youthful and inimitably graceful in the lines of her throat and averted face. Would she accept Julia's offer? Conyngham bit his lips and awaited her decision. Then, as if divining his thought, she turned and looked at him gravely.

"No," she said; "I will do it."

She went toward the window. Her father and Conyngham had taken their places, one on each side, as if she were the Queen indeed. She stood for a moment on the threshold, and then passed out into the moonlight alone. Immediately there arose the most terrifying of all earthly sounds, the dull, antagonistic roar of a thousand angry throats. Estella walked to the front of the balcony and stood, with an intrepidity which was worthy of the royal woman whose part she played, looking down on the upturned faces. A red flash streaked the darkness of a far corner of the square, and a bullet whistled through the open window into the woodwork of a mirror.

"Come back," whispered General Vincente. "Slowly, my child, slowly."

Estella stood for a moment looking down with a royal insolence, then turned, and with measured steps approached the window. As she passed in she met Conyngham's eyes, and that one moment assuredly made two lives worth living.

CHAPTER XXIX.

MIDNIGHT AND DAWN.

> "I have set my life upon a cast,
> And I will stand the hazard of the die."

"Excellency," reported a man, who entered the room at this moment, "they are bringing carts of fuel through the Calle de la Ciudad to set against the door and burn it."

"To set against which door, my honest friend?"

"The great door on the plaza, excellency. The other is an old door of iron."

"And they cannot burn it or break it open?"

"No, excellency; and, besides, there are loopholes in the thickness of the wall at the side."

The general smiled on this man as being after his own heart.

"One may not shoot to-night, my friend. I have already given the order."

"But one may prick them with the sword, excellency," suggested the trooper, with a sort of suppressed enthusiasm.

The general shrugged his shoulders, wisely tolerant.

"Oh, yes," he answered; "I suppose one may prick them with the sword."

Conyngham, who had been standing half in and half out of the open window listening to this conversation, now came forward.

"I think," he said, "that I can clear the plaza from time to time if you give me twenty men. We can thus gain time."

"Street-fighting," answered the general gravely, "do you know anything of it? It is nasty work."

"I know something of it. One has to shout very loud. I studied it at Dublin University."

"To be sure; I forgot."

Julia and Estella watched and listened. Their lot had been cast in the paths of war, and since childhood they had remembered naught else. But neither had yet been so near to the work, nor had they seen and heard men talk and plan with a certain grim humour, a curt and deliberate scorn of haste or excitement, as these men spoke and planned now. Conyngham and Concepcion Vara were altered by these circumstances—there was a light in their eyes which women rarely see—but the general was the same little man of peace and of high domestic virtue, who seemed embarrassed by a sword which was obviously too big for him. Yet in all their voices there rang a queer note of exultation, for man is a fighting animal, and (from St. Paul down to the humblest little five-foot-one "recruit") would find life a dull affair were there no strife in it.

"Yes, said the general after a moment's reflection, "that is a good idea, and will gain time. But let them first bring their fuel and set it up. Every moment is a gain."

At this instant some humourist in the crowd threw a stone in at the open window. The old priest picked up the missile and examined it curiously.

"It is fortunate," he said, "that the stones are fixed in Toledo. In Xeres they are loose and always in the air. I wonder if I can hit a citizen."

And he threw the stone back.

"Close the shutters," said the general. "Let us avoid arousing ill-feeling."

The priest drew the jalousies together, but did not quite shut them. Vincente stood and looked out through the aperture at the moonlit square and the dark shadows moving there.

"I wish they would shout," he said; "it is unnatural. They are like children. When there is noise there is little mischief."

Then he remained silent for some minutes, watching intently. All in the room noted his every movement. At length he turned on his heel.

"Go, my friend," he said to Conyngham; "form your men in the Calle de la Ciudad, and charge round in line. Do not place yourself too much in advance of your men, or you will be killed, and remember the point. Resist the temptation to cut—the point is best."

He patted Conyngham on the arm affectionately, as if he were sending him to bed with a good wish, and accompanied him to the door.

"I knew," he said, returning to the window and rubbing his hands together, "that that was a good man the first moment I saw him."

He glanced at Estella, and then, turning, opened another window, setting the shutters ajar, so as to make a second point of observation.

"My poor child," he whispered, as she went to the window and looked out, "it is an ill fortune to have to do with men whose trade this is." Estella smiled a little whitely and said nothing. The moon was now shining from an almost cloudless sky. The few fleecy remains of the storm sailing toward the east only added brightness to the night. It was almost possible to see the faces of the men moving in the square below, and to read their expressions. The majority stood in a group in the centre of the plaza, while a daring few, reckoning on the Spanish aversion to firearms, ran forward from time to time and set a bundle of wood or straw against the door beneath the balcony.

Some, who appeared to be the leaders, looked up constantly and curiously at the windows, wondering if any resistance would be made. Had they known that General Vincente was in that silent house, they would probably have gone home to bed, and the crowd would have dispersed like smoke.

Suddenly there arose a roar to the right hand of the square, where the Calle de la Ciudad was situated, and Conyngham appeared for a moment alone, running toward the group with the moonlight flashing on his sword. At his heels an instant later a single line of men swung round the corner and charged across the square.

"Dear, dear," muttered the general; "too quick, my friend, too quick!"

For Conyngham was already among the crowd, which broke and swayed back toward the cathedral. He paused for a moment to draw his sword out of a dark form that lay upon the ground, as a cricketer draws a stump. He had at all events remembered the point. The troopers swept across the square like a broom, sending the people as dust before them, and leaving the clear, moonlit square behind. They also left behind one or two shadows, lying stark upon the ground. One of these got upon his hands and knees, and crawled painfully away, all one-sided, like a beetle that has been trodden underfoot. Those watching from the windows saw, with a gasp of horror, that part of him —part of an arm—had been left behind, and a sigh of relief went up when he stopped crawling and lay quite still.

The troopers were now retreating slowly toward the Calle de la Ciudad.

"Be careful, Conyngham!" shouted the general from the balcony; "they will return."

And as he spoke a rattling fire was opened upon them from the far corner of the square, where the crowd had taken refuge in the opening of the Calle del Aico. Immediately the people, having noted that the troopers were few in number, charged down upon them. The men fought in line, retreating step by step, their swords gleaming in the moonlight. Estella, hearing footsteps in the room behind her, turned in time to see her father disappearing through the doorway. Concepcion Vara, coatless, as he loved to work, his white shirt-sleeves fluttering as his arm swung, had now joined the troopers, and was fighting by Conyngham's side.

Estella and Julia were out on the balcony now, leaning over and forgetting all but the breathless interest of battle. Concha stood beside them, muttering and cursing like any soldier.

They saw Vincente appear at the corner of the Calle de la Ciudad and throw away his scabbard as he ran.

"Now, my children!" he cried, in a voice that Estella had never heard before, which rang out across the square, and was answered by a yell that was nothing but a cry of sheer delight. The crowd swayed back as if before a gust of wind, and the general, following it, seemed to clear a space for himself, as a reaper clears away the standing corn before him. It was, however, only for a moment. The crowd surged back, those in front against their will, and on to the glittering steel, those behind shouting encouragement.

"*Caramba!*" shouted Concha, and was gone.

They saw him a minute later appear in the square, having thrown aside his cassock. He made a strange, lean figure of a man, with his knee-breeches and dingy purple stockings, his gray flannel shirt, and the moonlight shining on his tonsured head. He fought without skill and heedless of danger, swinging a great sword that he had picked up from the hand of a fallen trooper, and each blow that he got home killed its man. The mettle of the man had suddenly shown itself after years of suppression. This, as Vincente had laughingly said, was no priest, but a soldier.

Concepcion, in the thick of it, using the knife now with a deadly skill, looked over his shoulder and laughed. Suddenly the crowd swayed. The faint sound of a distant bugle came to the ears of all.

"It is nothing," shouted Concha in English—"it is nothing! It is I who sent the bugler round."

And his great sword whistled into a man's brain. In a moment the square was empty, for the politicians who came to murder a woman had had enough steel. The sound of the bugle, intimating, as they supposed, the arrival of troops, completed the work of demoralisation which the recognition of General Vincente had begun.

The little party, the few defenders of the Casa del Ayuntamiento, were left in some confusion in the plaza, and Estella saw, with a sudden cold fear, that Conyngham and Concha were on their knees in the midst of a little group of hesitating men. It was Concha who first rose and held up his hand to the watchers on the balcony, bidding them stay where they were. Then Conyngham rose to his feet, slowly, as one bearing a burden. Estella looked down in a sort of dream and saw her lover carrying her father toward the house, her mind only half comprehending, in the semi-dreamlike reception of sudden calamity, which is one of Heaven's deepest mercies.

It was Concepcion who came into the room first, his white shirt dyed with blood in great patches, like the colour on a piebald horse. A cut in his cheek was slowly dripping. He went straight to a sofa covered in gorgeous yellow satin and set the cushions in order.

"Señorita, . . ." he said, and spread out his hands. The tears were in his eyes. "Half of Spain," he added, "would rather that it had been the Queen, and the world is poorer."

A minute later Concha came into the room dragging on his cassock.

"My child, we are in God's hands," he said, with a break in his gruff voice.

And then came the heavy step of one carrying sorrow.

Conyngham laid his burden on the sofa. General Vincente was holding his handkerchief to his side, and his eyes, which had a thoughtful look, saw only Estella's face.

"I have sent for a doctor," said Conyngham; "your father is wounded."

"Yes," added Vincente immediately, "but I am in no pain, my dear child. There is no reason, surely, for us to distress ourselves."

He looked round and smiled.

"And this good Conyngham," he added, "carried me like a child."

Julia was on her knees at the foot of the sofa, her face hidden in her hands.

"My dear Julia," he said, "why this distress?"

SALEM CUSTOM-HOUSE.

From *The Century Magazine* by permission.

boy, as he was a man of uncommon physical beauty. But an accident to one of his feet, while he was playing at "bat-and-ball" one day, rendered him quite lame for a portion of his youth, in which he acquired voracious habits of reading, and fortunately the English classics were the books within his reach. An event of even more important influence was the early removal of his family to Raymond, Me., where his mother's people owned a large tract of land. "It was there," said Hawthorne in later life, "that I first got my cursed habits of solitude." The woods about Sebago Lake, the ice that covered it in winter time, gave him free foot for solitary excursions under sun and stars. He lived, he said, like a bird of the air. But his mother, for all her own seclusion, would not have the boy grow up in complete separation from men, and sent him back to Salem, where a private instructor prepared him for entrance to Bowdoin College. Longfellow was one of his classmates, though not of his intimates in college. Horatio Bridge, afterward Paymaster-General of the Navy, was both, and, moreover, was acknowledged by Hawthorne as the friend who was responsible for his becoming an author. In the class above him was Franklin Pierce, a lifelong friend, of whom Hawthorne could write when both were growing old, "I do not love him one whit the less for having been President." At his graduation, in 1825, Hawthorne's college rank was eighteenth in a class of thirty-eight, but especially in "the humanities" he had acquired some sound learning, and in his long walks and frank intercourse with his best friends, he had doubtless gained a knowledge of himself and of them that would stand him in good stead.

As a period of human companionships Hawthorne's four years at college stand out in bright relief He had come there from a solitary boyhood, and emerged into a manhood still more solitary. While all his friends were taking up active pursuits, he established himself with his mother and sisters at Salem, whither they had returned to live in the house of his grandfather Manning. Instead of undertaking any recognised work, "year after year," he said, "I kept on considering what I was fit for." But he had known for a long time. Even as a boy he had written from Salem to his mother in Maine: "How would you like some day to see a whole shelf full of books, written by your son, with 'Hawthorne's Works' printed on their backs?" In pursuance of this idea he seems to have made up his mind in college to adopt the profession of authorship; once committed to it, and conscious of the powers within him, he would not permit himself or others to turn them cheaply to account. His first book, *Seven Tales of My Native Land*, he burned in manuscript. His second, *Fanshawe*, a novel, he made every effort to disown and suppress. What he desired above and beyond any immediate success was to do only such work as he felt to be worthy of him.

It was a strange apprenticeship to which he bound himself. It is hard to think of another writer whose young manhood is not to be regarded in the light of its outward circumstances. Nearly all the circumstances of Hawthorne's life for some years after his leaving college were inward. Though possessed of such beauty of person that an old gipsy woman, meeting him suddenly in the woods, exclaimed, "Are you a man or an angel?" and though sought out for a time by the "good society" of his native town, he kept himself resolutely to himself. "For months together," to repeat his own words, "I scarcely held human intercourse outside of my own family, seldom going out except at twilight, or only to take the nearest way to the most convenient solitude, which was oftenest the seashore. . . . Once a year or thereabouts I used to make an excursion of a few weeks, in which I enjoyed as much of life as other people in the whole year round." He doubted whether so many as twenty persons in Salem were aware of his existence. Within his mother's

FAC-SIMILE OF HAWTHORNE'S AUTOGRAPH AS SURVEYOR.

house, his cloistral habits were not infringed upon. For months at a time he scarcely saw his older sister, who was almost as strict a recluse as his mother. Both of these ladies had their meals brought to their separate rooms. Indeed this was Mrs. Hawthorne's unbroken custom from the time of her husband's death. In the evening she and her younger daughter would come down to the little parlour and sit with Hawthorne. Love and respect seem to have gone out from each corner of the curious personal quadrangle to each and all of the other corners, but the life of the family could not have been such as to make amends in any way for the dearth of human influences from without.

Hawthorne, to be sure, maintained a certain contact with mankind through correspondence with his college friends, and by means of his occasional excursions into the world. It marked him as a man of uncommon mould that by looking merely into himself, and drawing forth what he found there, he could produce so much that was worth producing, for this is not the usual result of such a process. In his room at Salem, which has been well called "the antechamber of his fame," he read and wrote incessantly. The results of this labour were published in the magazines of the day, and in Goodrich's annual, *The Token*, where Willis's first efforts were rapidly winning him fame, while Hawthorne's attracted so little attention that he could call himself with some truth, "the obscurest man of letters in America." It was twelve years after his graduation from college—that is, in 1837—that the first collection of *Twice-Told Tales* brought together the best of his work for this period. Longfellow wrote an appreciative review of it for *The North American*, and so moved Hawthorne, who complained because for lack of approbation he had "always written with benumbed fingers," that he despatched a hearty letter to his old classmate, saying: "Whether or no the public will agree to the praise you bestow on me, there are at least five persons who think you the most sagacious critic on earth—viz., my mother and two sisters, my old maiden aunt, and finally—the sturdiest believer of the whole five—my own self." He could not have been blind to the relation between his life and his *Tales* even before 1851, when he wrote in the preface of a new edition: "The book, if you would see anything in it, requires to be read in the clear, brown, twilight atmosphere in

STENCIL-PLATE NOW IN THE SALEM CUSTOM-HOUSE.

which it was written; if opened in the sunshine, it is apt to look exceedingly like a volume of blank pages."

Hawthorne had come out from his twilight atmosphere for a short time before the publication of *Twice-Told Tales* to edit an ill-fated *American Magazine of Knowledge* in Boston, and would have stood in a still more glaring light if his desire to be appointed historian of a Government expedition to the South Polar seas had been fulfilled. He gained no glory by the anonymous writing of *Peter Parley's Universal History* (1837). Two events which soon took place, however, brought about all-important changes in the course of his life, and saved him from the dangers of continuing longer in his career of solitude. The one was his appointment by George Bancroft, in 1839, as weigher and gauger in the Boston Custom-House; the other was his engagement to Miss Sophia Peabody, of Salem, which occurred at about the same time.

It will not be imagined that the life Hawthorne had been leading could naturally bring him to matrimony. But for his writings it is to be doubted whether his path would ever have crossed that of the Peabody family. The three sisters of that name, however, had read and admired certain fugitive pieces of writing which they had succeeded in tracing to their townsman, and through the rather difficult mediation of his sisters, they made his acquaintance. This was in 1837, and neither Hawthorne's reserve nor Sophia Peabody's invalidism could have given promise of the result. Uninterruptedly from her twelfth year she had been afflicted with an acute nervous headache. She had felt that she must never marry, yet her illness had served to heighten all the beauties of a nature inherently beautiful, and Hawthorne recognised for what she was; nor did she fail, early or late, to see in Hawthorne the incarnation of all her ideals. When they became conditionally engaged she said to him, "If God intends us to marry, He will let me be cured; if not, it will be a sign that it is not best." It was not only possible for them to marry in 1842, but from that time forth her malady never returned.

It was an abrupt transition for Hawthorne from the quiet of Salem to the noisy unlading of coal-schooners at the Boston wharves. But he toiled faithfully at his work of supervision, and did not let the opportunity of observing keenly the ways of men and of his own heart pass unimproved. His next change of surroundings provided him with contrasts no less striking, for in 1841 he joined his fortunes with those of the Brook Farm community. Here he toiled like a veritable Hodge, and stored his mind and his *Note-Books* with many impressions which found their way into the *Blithedale Romance* ten years later. Emerson summed up the drollery of the Brook Farm experiment when he wrote: "The ladies again took cold on washing-days, and it was ordained that the gentlemen shepherds should hang out the clothes, which they punctually did; but a great anachronism followed in the evening, for when they began to dance the clothes-pins dropped plentifully from their pockets." Hawthorne had so clear a vision for the humour of things, that he could not take himself and his "brethren in affliction," as he called them, altogether seriously in their new life. The eight cows and the "transcendental heifer belonging to Miss Margaret Fuller" were never complete realities to him, though he worked hard in the barnyard. There was, however, sufficient reality in the loss of his custom-house savings, which he had invested in the community, and in his failure to satisfy himself that the farm would be the best place for him to begin his married life.

He could not have chosen a better place for this purpose than the Old Manse at Concord, where he and his bride took up their abode in the summer of 1842. The introductory paper to the *Mosses from an Old Manse* (1846) tells with inimitable charm as much as Hawthorne was willing to tell of the delight of his new life. He frankly declared himself to be not "one of those supremely hospitable people who serve up their own hearts, delicately fried, with brain sauce, as a tidbit for their beloved public." One cannot help feeling that something like this has been done in the publication of Mrs. Hawthorne's intimate letters written at this time. But the life which they reveal was filled with ideal beauty, the more to be prized because it remained unchanged till the end. In these early days Hawthorne is seen raising vegeta-

Nathaniel Hawthorne.

From a wash drawing by G. Reynolds after a daguerreotype believed to have been taken in the last year of his life. Now reproduced for the first time.

bles, which acquire from his care a flavour unknown before on earth ; nobly cooking and washing dishes in domestic emergencies ; and rejoicing his young wife with long evenings of reading aloud. How shrewd an eye she herself possessed, a single bit of winter landscape-drawing will show : "One after-

HAWTHORNE AT 36.

noon Mr. Emerson and Mr. Thoreau went with him down the river. Henry Thoreau is an experienced skater, and was figuring dithyrambic dances and Bacchic leaps on the ice—very remarkable, but very ugly, methought. Next him followed Mr. Hawthorne, wrapped in his cloak, moved like a self-impelled Greek statue, stately and grave. Mr. Emerson closed the line, evidently too weary to hold himself erect, pitching headforemost, half lying on the air." The deeper spiritual understanding constantly shown in these letters of Mrs. Hawthorne's made her a wife in whose comradeship her husband could not suffer again from loneliness. The birth of his daughter Una at Concord made Hawthorne's home still more completely the centre of his life. The scene, however, was not to remain long unchanged, and late in 1845 the little family left the Manse, and moved to Salem, where Hawthorne soon received President Polk's appointment of surveyor in the Custom-House. The ability thus shown, for the second of three times, to plunge efficiently into the life of a political officeholder is best explained by the presence of a strong practical quality in the structure of Hawthorne's mind. It was doubtless allied to the quality of saneness which robbed his earlier solitary life of half its dangers.

It is hardly surprising that the prosaic duties of the radically new surroundings were not productive at once of literary results. But when three years had passed, in which his son was born, his mother died, and Hawthorne himself suffered political decapitation, the time was come for showing the world that the years had not passed in vain. His wife hailed the release from office as the opportunity for writing his book, and to her husband's amazement brought forth a sum of money which she had been saving against a rainy day. His mind was doubtless full of *The Scarlet Letter*, for it took him only six months to write it, amid the distractions of his mother's fatal illness and his own personal sufferings of care and pain. James T. Fields has told with what difficulty he forced Hawthorne, when the book was done, even to admit that he had been about such a piece of work, and to surrender up the manuscript. The publisher's delight in the story as a work of art seems to have exceeded his belief in it as a commercial venture, for as soon as the first edition of five thousand copies was printed the type was distributed. In ten days the entire edition was sold, and all the printers' work had to be done over again. The book was published in 1850, and won the world's instant recognition, at home and abroad, of Hawthorne's consummate literary skill and penetrating vision into the mysteries of the human soul. Thenceforth his fame was secure.

Thenceforth, also, his physical powers were as those of a man no longer young. With the hope that change might be of benefit, he moved in 1850 with his family to Lenox, and lived for a little more than a year in a small red farmhouse, which bore to his eyes the aspect of the Scarlet Letter. Here his youngest child was born, and here he wrote *The House of the Seven Gables*—which he frankly called "a more natural book for me to write than *The Scarlet Letter* was"—and also *The Wonder Book*, projected some years before, it appears, as a thing to be done in collaboration with Longfellow. Here, too, he is seen in intercourse with friends and his children, which showed him to be something other than the brooding mystic of his books and the moody, inaccessible creature of common report. His son tells of his own boyish delight in the nutting excursions in which the father, standing beneath a great walnut-tree, would bid the children turn their backs and cover their faces, till they heard a shout above them, when they would look up to see Hawthorne, "a delightful mystery and miracle," in the topmost branches. Such are the brighter glimpses of the Lenox life, from which an increasing spirit of unrest bore Hawthorne with his family, before the end of 1851, back to the neighbourhood of Boston. The winter that followed was spent in the house of Mrs. Hawthorne's brother-in-law, Horace Mann, at West Newton, and here the *Blithedale Romance* was written between the first of December and the end of April. The three years brought thus to a close are almost without parallel in the importance of their productiveness.

HAWTHORNE AT 46.

The time had come for Hawthorne to establish himself more permanently in one place, and Concord, the town of his happiest days, was naturally chosen. From Alcott he bought the house known as "Wayside," standing a little farther from the village than Emerson's dwelling upon the same road. It was told of Hawthorne in Lenox that when in his walks he saw the approach of any one to whom he might have to talk, he would suddenly leave the road and take to the pasture beside it. This aversion to promiscuous intercourse kept him in Concord from taking any such part in the village life as Emerson took. Alcott, his next-door neighbour, has told how difficult it was to see him except as a hare vanishing in the shrubbery on the hill behind his house. Here he would walk to and fro for hours under the larches in the path which he called "the only remembrance of me that will remain." Emerson's son has recorded the only formal visit paid by Hawthorne to his father's house, on a certain Sunday evening, when the caller, to cover his shyness, began looking at pictures in a stereoscope. He asked what the scenes were, and was much surprised to hear that they were the Concord Court and Town House and Common, all of which his body must have passed, at least occasionally, though his thoughts were elsewhere. Another resident of Concord, the clear-sighted Henry James, Sr., in writing to Emerson of a Saturday Club dinner at which Hawthorne was present, said: "He has the look all the time, to one who doesn't know him, of a rogue who finds himself suddenly in a company of detectives." Hawthorne himself knew that the dinner-table of any house but his own was

HAWTHORNE AT 56.

the Liverpool consulate. This criticism had its sufficient answer, for Hawthorne and for all minds capable of generous judgment, in the friendship between him and Pierce, long before his presidency and long after it. The outward episode revealed less of Hawthorne than an anecdote related by Pierce. When he was nominated, "Hawthorne came to see him, sat down by him on a sofa, and after a melancholy silence, heaving a deep sigh, said, 'Frank, *what* a pity!' Then, after a pause, 'But, after all, this world was not meant to be happy in—only to succeed in!'"

Hawthorne succeeded well enough at Liverpool, where he performed the duties of consul from 1853 to 1857. For three years after his resignation he moved about Europe, especially in Italy and England, enjoying some of the most satisfying friendships of his life, and writing or preparing to write the books which fixed his fame more firmly from year to year, even after his death, when the Passages from his various Note-Books were published. The literary result of sojourns in Europe would furnish forth a chapter by itself in any account of American writers. The effect of foreign lands upon Irving, Cooper, Willis, and a score of others were no unfruitful theme. Here it suffices to be thankful for its provocation of Hawthorne's *Marble Faun*. His *Italian Note-Books* show how the scenes of Italy were preparing him to write the *Romance of Monte-Beni*. Outside of Florence he made the first sketch for the book. In the summer of 1859 he returned to England to write it, and chiefly at Redcar, on the Yorkshire coast, and at Leamington the work was done in time to be published by March

not the best place for him, and once said: "I have an almost miraculous power of escaping from necessities of this kind. Destiny itself has often been worsted in the attempt to get me out to dinner."

That such a man, after two experiences of political office, should have been removed again from private life was one of the anomalies of his career. The writing of the *Tanglewood Tales* soon after his removal to Concord was more what might have been expected of him than any mingling in a presidential campaign. But his friend Pierce had been nominated for the Presidency, and Hawthorne hastened to his support with the offer of any service in his power. This, he was told, might best be a campaign life of the candidate. When it was written, and Pierce was elected, of course it was said that the book paid the price of the good appointment to of 1860. The London publishers insisted upon giving it the name of *Transformation*, against Hawthorne's wish. It was his preference also not to write for the second edition the "Conclusion" which is now joined to the last chapter. But there were objections of vagueness, and Hawthorne was willing to meet half way the suggestion of Motley: "To those who complain, I suppose that nothing less than an illustrated edition, with a large gallows on the last page, with Donatello in the most pensile of attitudes—his ears revealed through a white night-cap — would be satisfactory." Longfellow found "the old, dull pain in it that runs through all Hawthorne's writings," but he found it also "wonderful;" and so did the world.

HAWTHORNE AT 58.

When Hawthorne came back to America and re-established himself at "Wayside," in 1860, the country stood on the threshold of war. As a friend of Pierce he was, to say the least, not a friend of the Northern party which was readiest for the struggle. But when it began, the consciousness that he had a country stirred him to regret that he was too old to carry a musket; the compensating joy was that his son was too young. A War Democrat like Hawthorne was not precisely the person from whom one would expect an article "Chiefly About War Matters" for the vigorously Northern *Atlantic Monthly*. Yet a paper under this title, signed "By a Peaceable Man," was the result of a visit to Washington in the spring of 1862. The foot-notes which accompanied it protested against the disloyalty of some of the writer's words. "Can it be a son of old Massachusetts who utters this abominable sentiment? For shame!" So read one of the notes, representative of all. Donald G. Mitchell detected Hawthorne's touch in the article, and wrote to him as one "ready to swear at the marginal impertinences. Pray, is Governor Andrew editor?" The truth, revealed some years later, was that Hawthorne himself, requested by James T. Fields to make certain omissions, had made them, at the same time writing the foot-notes and befooling the public with the remonstrances against himself. The incident is worth recording as one of the lighter passages in the darkening days of Hawthorne's last years.

The strain of the almost fatal illness of Una Hawthorne in Rome had seriously sapped her father's strength. Neither his physical condition nor the mental state, induced by the war, was propitious for literary production. Yet in the few years that followed his return from Europe he wrote, in the quiet tower added to the "Wayside" house, the papers which filled the volume of *Our Old Home*, besides the fiction which has been published since his death, under the titles of *Septimius Felton*, *The Dolliver Romance*, and *Dr. Grimshawe's Secret*. True to a constant friendship, he insisted, against all the protests of his publisher, upon dedicating *Our Old Home* to Franklin Pierce, whose unpopular name was sure to excite hostility against the book. However fully the publisher's fears were borne out, Hawthorne's own name is memorably the brighter for his devotion to a friend. In England, it must be said, the book gave other cause for offence, in that Hawthorne, speaking of the English woman in her riper years and portlier dimensions, made bold to say, "You inevitably think of her as made up of steaks and sirloins." Yet the book has not been unknown even in recent years to do service in England akin to that of *The Marble Faun* in Rome—a prosaic test, if you will, to apply to a work which does not make utility its first aim.

FIELDS, HAWTHORNE AND TICKNOR.
From an old daguerreotype.

Happily it is not needed here to follow Hawthorne closely through all the days of failing strength. More than a year before the end came Longfellow made the record, "He looks gray and grand, with something very pathetic about him." In March of 1864 his health was so broken that a journey to Washington was attempted with hopes of improvement. His travelling companion was his friend and publisher, William D. Ticknor. Hawthorne was gaining in strength, when, with appalling suddenness, Mr. Ticknor died in Philadelphia. Instead of being the object of care, Hawthorne found himself borne down by the most sorrowful of responsibilities. He returned to Concord far worse than he had left it. This was in April. In May another attempt was made to restore him by means of a driving tour with Franklin Pierce through the White Mountains. The travellers went only as far as Plymouth, in New Hampshire, and here it was to Hawthorne, asleep, that death came in the darkness before the sunrise of May 19th. His burial, at Sleepy Hollow, in Concord, took place on May 23d. Within a few days his wife, who needed no human consolations, wrote with gladness: "There can be no death nor loss for me for evermore. . . . God gave me the rose of time; the blossom of the ages to call my own for twenty-five years of human life."

The variety of the attempts to apply epithets of accurate definition to Hawthorne and his writings recalls the fate of a bust for which he sat in Rome. The clay, a good likeness, was finished, and handed over to the marble-cutters to be reproduced in stone. While this process was going forward an American, who might have known better, directed the workmen, on his own responsibility, to make certain changes in the lower part of the face, with the result that the finished bust, in the words of Hawthorne's son, "looks like a combination of Daniel Webster and George Washington." Something like this happens when words like "glimmering" and "cobweby," good enough as far as they go, are too freely used to describe the attributes of Hawthorne. Different eyes see different things in his books, just as the man differed in the circles of intimacy and of the outer world. The remodelled bust doubtless suited the interfering critic better than the truer likeness. Mr. Howells, when he had met the man face to face, said, "Hawthorne's *look* was different from that of any picture of him that I have seen." And so it may be said of his writings that the terms used for their definition never quite define them. To characterise the obvious is easy enough. But there are personalities and works of art about which the last word in modification of any confident statement is far to seek. To a certain degree it defines them merely to make this assertion with regard to them. Let us be satisfied with making it of Hawthorne and of his books. What he is, in our heritage from his pen, is immeasurably more important than any words about him. It is enough that the stony soil of New England could bear such fruits of the imagination as he has garnered for our wonder and delight.

M. A. De Wolfe Howe.

The subject of the next paper in this series, to appear in the January BOOKMAN, *will be "Walt Whitman."*

LONDON LETTER.

At the date of writing, matters are proceeding quietly and prosperously in the publishing trade. But since the issue of *The Christian* no very conspicuous success has been secured. The general feeling among critics against *The Christian* has grown, and Mr. Andrew Lang has written possibly the severest attack that has yet appeared on the book. This has been published in *Cosmopolis*. But the circulation goes on well, and has been very greatly stimulated by the fact that many ministers are delivering sermons about the volume to large audiences. There has been much bad feeling about the interviews which appeared, and threats are still held out in certain quarters of a fuller disclosure of Mr. Hall Caine's action. But it is to be hoped that this unpleasant controversy will be allowed to die down.

I should perhaps have said that the memoir of the late Lord Tennyson has been a conspicuous success. For so expensive a book the circulation has been very large, and there is general approval of the manner in which Lord Tennyson has performed his task. The criticism which one hears in private is that the whole portrait is idealised, and that Tennyson was by no means so heroic a figure as he appears in this record, but it has been well replied to this that if there had been anything to be ashamed of in Tennyson's life and character, it would have shown itself incidentally. It would have been impossible to keep it out altogether. In this view there appears to be much truth.

Mr. Kipling's *Captains Courageous* has sold well, the interest in him having been stimulated by his "Recessional," a poem which took a deeper hold of the general public than anything Mr. Kipling has hitherto written. The book itself is admitted to be brilliant, but in a measure disappointing, though every one gives credit to Mr. Kipling for the care with which he has studied his somewhat uninteresting subject. Mr. Kipling evidently still shrinks from the publication of a long novel, although years ago the beginning and more than the beginning of such a novel was safely lodged in his publishers' desk. Mr. Kipling has found it difficult to suit himself with an English residence, and the last thing I have heard on the subject is that he was thinking of taking a house beside Mr. Thomas Hardy at Dorchester. The beautiful idyllic poet, William Barnes, lived in the same neighbourhood, and if Dorchester is fortunate enough to secure Mr. Kipling, the quaint old town will have a new significance and perhaps a new interpreter.

Our critics are somewhat apt to have likes and dislikes in a body. Mr. Kipling at present is a great favourite with most; on the other hand, something like a dead set has been made on Mr. Crockett. His *Lads' Love* found hardly any one to say a good word for it, and the *Daily Chronicle*, which gave him generous welcome at first, made haste to criticise in the severest manner his new romance, *Lochinvar*. Something of this may, perhaps, be due to the fact that Mr. Crockett publishes normally about three books a year. I am much mistaken, however, if it does not turn out that one of his books written, though not published, is the best work he has done so far.

It is reported on good authority while I write that Mr. Jerome has relinquished the editorship of his paper, *To-day*, to Mr. Barry Pain. If so, I shall regret it, for Mr. Jerome seems to have hard measure dealt to him. He is a writer in his way of considerable originality, and is personally a man of open and generous nature. But there is no denying that his enterprises have been very unsuccessful. He founded the *Idler*, which had a large circulation at first, but which after numerous vicissitudes has passed out of his hands. He has produced various plays, but I do not think any of them have caught on. He put his whole force into a weekly paper called *To-day*, which had an excellent start, and which after the expenditure of a considerable capital seemed successful. The story is now that he is to start a penny weekly, but the market is so full that I am afraid this will be found almost impossible. Whether possible or not, there are many who are trying it. It is said that Mr. Hooley, the millionaire, wished to buy the business either of Messrs. Harmsworth or of Sir George Newnes. Failing in this, he is to attempt an enterprise of his own. The first paper to be published is called *Stories*. I have seen the first number. It is not an imitation of *Answers* and *Tit-Bits*, but contains long and improving articles, one, for example, by Sir Walter Besant on the rise of the Empire. Whether there is any chance for a paper of this kind, however well conducted, may be gravely doubted. It is not wonderful, however, that many should be tempted this way, for it is said that the profits of Messrs. Harmsworth on their various publications, which now include newspapers all over the kingdom, will amount this year to the large sum of £250,000. This is the largest newspaper income in Britain, that of the *Daily Telegraph* coming second.

The new paper, *Literature*, published by the *Times*, was bought by every literary person last Saturday, and by many who were not literary, and I believe more than 30,000 copies were disposed of. So far it does not promise much. I turned first to the obituary notices, which are always a good test. They were simply bald summaries from the *Times* without a single fresh fact or attempt at characterisation. The news department is practically non-existent as yet, the paragraphs inserted being completely trite and vapid. Mr. Birrell was most unfortunate in the first signed article, which was in every respect one of his poorest productions. The reviews, though good-natured enough, are lacking in knowledge, brilliancy, and distinction. They seem to be mainly supplied by the *Times'* staff, and the strength of the *Times* does not lie in its criticisms of books. However, of course, first numbers are proverbially difficult, and the paper may improve, though it is not likely that it will so long as Mr. Traill is the editor. Mr. Traill is not in the least in touch with current literature, and is a journalist of a school that has gone by. It will interest your readers to know that Ian Maclaren has been engaged to contribute a monthly *causerie*.

Mr. Barrie's accident in falling from a platform at the Haymarket Theatre during the rehearsal of his play, *The Little Minister*, might have been very serious—in fact, it was thought at first that he was dead. Fortunately no great harm was done, and in a very few days Mr. Barrie was back again at the theatre. He is much exhausted by the personal care which he has given to every detail of the play, but will no doubt be compensated by its success. The play will have no very serious rival in London just at present, and much is hoped from Miss Winifred Emery's appearance.

Everybody is amused at the *Quarterly Review's* notice of our little Laureate. The *Quarterly* is the organ of Toryism, and Mr. Austin is nothing if he is not a Tory. He is, indeed, one of the leader writers in the *Standard*. The *Quarterly* mentions a number of minor poets, and concludes with Mr. Austin. It says he has said nothing, though he has said it nicely. "His philosophastering or martial strains are at best neutral, constantly insignificant in the extreme. He seems to us a ladylike painter in water-colours." Mr. Austin has been so much intimidated by the roars of derision with which every fresh attempt of his is received, that he has been comparatively silent since he became Laureate, and no one would grudge him his title or his money if that silence were absolute.

Mr. John Lane, the publisher, who is to be married to a charming and gifted American lady, has some notable books of poetry on his list. Chief of these is a book of poems by Mr. Theodore Watts-Dunton. Mr. Watts-Dunton is the leading critic and the chief attraction of the *Athenæum*. Whether one agrees with his judgments or not, his extraordinary knowledge of literature and his skill in calling up and marshalling parallels make all he writes instructive in the best sense. He has contributed also some poems to the *Athenæum*. They are never commonplace, but seem to lack the singing quality. However, we shall be better able to judge them now they are printed together. Many of us would prefer that Mr. Watts-Dunton should issue a volume of criticisms, and include in it the thoughtful essay on Poetry which appeared in the last edition of the *Encyclopædia Britannica*. Mr. Watts-Dunton is something of a recluse, and has never sought fame. He is a staunch friend, and has been a kind helper to many struggling young men of letters.

Mr. Le Gallienne has followed his *Quest of the Golden Girl* by a little pamphlet entitled *If I Were God*. He seems ambitious to keep up two publics, one of those who delight in indecent stories, and another of those who are interested in religious subjects. The attempt is perhaps not likely to succeed, and those who wish Mr. Le Gallienne well would be glad to see him attempt a third public, leaving the others alone.

W. Robertson Nicoll.

LONDON, October 29, 1897.

PARIS LETTER.

Men of letters have just had two important occasions of meeting each other here: one yesterday, in the palace of the Institute of France, the other the day before, in the charming Parc de Monceaux, where took place the unveiling of the monument erected to Guy de Maupassant. What a delight to be able to say that the monument is in every way worthy of the man! I had seen it already in the Salon des Champs Elysées last spring, and I think that I described then for the readers of THE BOOKMAN the tastefully dressed Parisienne who interrupts her reading and looks ahead dreamily, thinking of the pages that have just passed under her eyes. The book is *Fort Comme la Mort*. But the monument was incomplete then. Maupassant's bust, which was to crown it, was still missing. Now the Parisienne can look up toward the broad forehead, the manly face that belonged to her favourite author, and made him beloved by so many of her fair sisters. The location selected by the Société des Gens de Lettres and the city of Paris is an ideal one. It is in a charming spot of one of the most beautiful of the city parks, in the heart of the fashionable district where Maupassant used to live, almost under Flaubert's windows, and within three minutes' walk of the Place Malesherbes, where poor Dumas Fils will be looking toward the image of his illustrious father.

Poor Maupassant! We could hardly realise that twenty years ago his name was still all but unknown (his first successes belong to the year 1879), and that already six years have gone by since the sudden collapse of his brilliant intellect. Recollections were exchanged among us. Ollendorff, his publisher, told me how he called on him once, after the first performance of his play, *La Paix du Ménage*, at the Comédie Française, and handed him a copy of the play. Maupassant would not admit it was his. "Not by me, not by me," he said. On his visitor's insisting, he yielded one moment. "Yes, yes, by me!" Then suddenly, almost fiercely, "But no, I have not done that, I have not done that!" The poor fellow, when in Doctor Blanche's asylum, thought he was in a convent of Genovefan monks, and feared the monks wanted to poison him. He suffered but little, except during his last hours, which were frightful to behold.

The speeches at the unveiling were of the best. Far above the others rose those of Henry Houssaye, the President of the Société des Gens de Lettres, and of Zola, who spoke as a friend, and in very touching terms. Houssaye's speech contains about Maupassant's style a paragraph or two, which are gems of literary criticism.

The poet of the occasion was Jacques Normand, who had written a string of lovely quatrains, and his interpreter was Marthe Brandès. I tell you, the whole thing was one of those treats that can hardly be enjoyed outside of our dear Paris! Even the sun, which I must admit we do not see quite as often as we might like, was shining brightly over the face of our departed friend.

We had speeches also by Rouyon, the Directeur des Beaux Arts, who represented the Minister of Public Instruction, and a few others, and music by the incomparable band of the Garde Républicaine. All literary and artistic Paris was there. We shall not soon forget the day.

Twenty-four hours later almost the same crowd was gathered under the dome of the Palais Mazarin, where the Institute of France—that is, the great body consisting of the five academies, held its annual session. This event is always considered one of the great functions of the year, social as well as literary. The session was this year presided over by the representative of the French Academy, Albert Sorel, who delivered a beautiful eulogy on the members who died during the year, and especially of the Duc d'Aumale, the donor of Chantilly, whose marvellous collections will be thrown open to the public next May. I suppose you will be not a little surprised to hear that the honours of the day belonged to the city of Chicago. Professor Moissan, of the Faculty of Sciences of the University of Paris, who was the spokesman of the Academy of Sciences, read a paper on the foundation of the University of Chicago, and he put his interesting matter in a very entertaining form. The name of Rockefeller sounded to him, he declared, a little barbaric, but he none the less recommended the example of the American *milliardaire* to his European brethren.

The most successful of the plays I mentioned in my last letter has been *Jalouse*. I named to you only one of its authors, Bisson; I hasten to mention the other, a Belgian journalist, by the name of Leclerc, for fear I should have to pass through the same experience as our friend Sarcey. He had been, in his Monday *Chronique Théâtrale*, guilty of the same omission as I, when he received a bitter letter, in which the slighted playwright accused him of numberless breaches against literary honesty. Sarcey, who of late has shown a decided tendency to lessen his own literary labours by inserting in his articles the letters of his correspondents, forthwith gave to Leclerc's letter a place in the columns of the *Temps*, and had it followed by a paragraph or two of really witty castigation. But what was his dismay when he received from Brussels another letter, signed Leclerc, and in a very different handwriting, in which he was informed that the first letter was the work not of the co-author of *Jalouse*, but of some unknown practical joker! Bisson confirmed the authenticity of the second and the spuriousness of the first letter, and Sarcey had to apologise to Leclerc, which he did in one of his Sganarelle *Fagots*. But now he declares that he receives lots of communications declaring to him that both letters were really by the Belgian dramatist, who repudiated the first one only in order to crawl as graciously as possible out of an unpleasant hole. *Qui croire?*

Brieux's *Les Trois Filles de M. Dupont* was well received at the Gymnase. It is a decided advance over his last play, *L'Évasion*. He is one of the coming men. His ambition is to succeed Dumas Fils as the authoritative author of *pièces à thèse*.

The big failure of the month is that of Lytton's *Richelieu*, at the Odéon. The adaptation, by Charles Samson, is well done. But no one could really expect that the French could take an interest in a Richelieu so different from the one they know. Ginisty, the manager of the Odéon, ought to have stuck to his original idea, which was to have Richelieu presented in one of his Thursday matinées, after an explanatory lecture. There its fate would have been a little less cruel.

We are still awaiting the first performance of Silvestre's *Tristan*, and it is announced that Abel Hermant has just dramatised his *Transatlantiques*, of which I wrote to you a few months ago. I doubt whether he will duplicate with them his success with *La Carrière*.

Now *the* book of the month, and there

is no mistake, is *Le Mannequin d'Osier* (the willow dummy), by Anatole France. It is even better than *L'Orme du Mail*, of which it is a continuation. It is France at his best, and at his best he is far from bad, as you know. But I do not recommend his books to those who are in search of solid arguments on which to base their moral or social convictions. Side by side with France's scepticism Montaigne's utterances sound almost like the most old-fashioned fanaticism.

Women are all taken by the *Lettres d'Amoureuses*, published over the as yet rather unknown signature of Broda. The lovers of Loti are treated to a book in his style, which is not by him, but by an imitator, André Chevrillon. The title is *Terres Mortes; Thébaïde, Judée*. Dead places seem more interesting to Chevrillon than live ones, it seems. I am told, and I can vouch for the truth of the story, that something like two years ago he decided upon a visit to the United States. He went no farther than New York though. He was so bewildered by the incessant din and noise of the great American metropolis, that he hastened back to Europe by the same steamer on which he had sailed from Havre. So here is at least one traveller who will not write a book on America. Chevrillon, by the way, is a nephew of the late Hippolyte Taine.

I must mention a good historical book, *L'Alliance Autrichienne*, by the Duc de Broglie. It is a continuation of his studies on the diplomatic history of the eighteenth century, and is fully up to the level of the former volumes.

Two good volumes on art have appeared, *La Peinture Française du IXe au XVIe Siècle*, by Paul Mantz, in the Bibliothèque d'Enseignement des Beaux Arts, and *Les Collections de Monnaies Anciennes*, by Babelon. Mantz's book, unfortunately, is marred by incorrectly designated illustrations. The text is excellent.

Hugo's executors have just given us one more volume of his posthumous works. It is a series of letters written by him to his wife during a voyage to the Alps and Pyrenees. The trip came to a sudden end on Hugo's being called back home by the announcement of his daughter's and son-in law's terrible death in the Seine.

A curious volume of *fin de siècle* poetry by Jean Rictus, *Les Soliloques du Pauvre*, will be welcomed by those who take pleasure in the productions of Aristide Bruant.

The National Library has just issued the first volume of its general catalogue of printed books. Thus far it had published only a catalogue of books on French history. The new volume relates solely to the novel and the drama. The plays mentioned in it reach the total of 33,993, and the novels rise to 116,824! And still we are told of people who have "read everything."

In the *Revues* the most notable things have been an article of Th. Beutzon (Madame Blanc) in the *Revue des Deux Mondes* on Communism in Fiction, in America, and a collection of letters of Lamennais to Montalembert in the *Revue de Paris* of October 15th.

Finally, a daily paper, *Le Journal*, has begun the publication of Zola's *Paris*.

You see that the month has not been a barren one, and for the near future we are promised *La Sève*, by Bourget; *Quinze Ans de Mariage*, by Daudet; *L'Ile d'Amour*, by Anatole France, and *Deux Jeunes Filles*, by Ludovic Halévy. You see that there will be a few more numbers to be added soon to the 116,824 novels of the Bibliothèque Nationale!

Alfred Manière.

NEW BOOKS.

REPUBLICAN FRANCE.*

Americans have a traditional love for France. This is in part inherited from the days when France stood side by side with us in our first struggle against Great Britain; yet it is in part, and perhaps in a much higher degree, the result of a subtle sympathy which has its root in certain temperamental coincidences that can be found to exist in the point of view which Frenchmen and Americans alike maintain. We as a people owe so much to French art, we have read so much of French literature, and our civilisation has derived so many of its nicer touches from French elegance and taste, that the American feeling for France is largely independent of political considerations. Yet there is a political sympathy also which we as republicans must feel for a people who to-day are making the same great experiment that we have made, and under circumstances more adverse than any that we in our fortunate isolation have had to face and conquer. Nevertheless, the existence of this very real sympathy can blind no thoughtful person to the fact that the republican experiment under one set of conditions may be very far from achieving or from meriting the success which another and an entirely different set of conditions has made possible and easy.

The book before us, written with unusual fairness and philosophic insight, is one that will be read with the intensest interest by every friend of France, and by all who are concerned with the history of national and constitutional development. It gives in a concise and lucid form a history of the Third Republic, from September 4th, 1871, and the outbreak of the Commune, down to what the author styles "the triumph of the Republic" in the practical consummation of the Franco-Russian Alliance and to the death of Sadi Carnot. It covers, therefore, a period of something more than twenty years, and it touches upon those critical days when France had still the terror of Bismarck before its eyes, when the monarchists were still venomously active, when the Republicans themselves were disunited, when foreign complications hampered and confused domestic policy, and when the power of the Church was actively exerted to bring discredit on the statesmanship of the new régime. It contains chapters also on the educational development of France in recent years, on the effect of universal military service upon the nation and upon the army, together with some very luminous and instructive criticism of the ideas and habits of the French people as modified by the republican idea. The final chapter deals with the social question and with the growth and spread among the people of economic theories whose ultimate effects can rightly be perceived only in the years to come.

The difficulty of passing judgment on the French experiment in republican government is seen in the almost inevitable confusion of mind, which leads one to ascribe those traits which are essentially and nationally French to the influence of a particular form of government. There have been witnessed in France since the end of the great war of 1870–71 so many splendid instances of patriotic sacrifices, of devotion to the national ideal, of self-restraint and patience and resourcefulness, that if one looks at these alone and ventures to assign their cause to the inspiration of republicanism, they must to him stand as a magnificent vindication of the Third Republic. But if, on the other hand, with deeper insight one finds in them only the nobler side of the French character working its way into action without reference to governmental forms, then there is but little left that can be made exclusively the glory of the Republic itself. The wonderful and, to the German mind, the startling rapidity with which the French people, from prince to peasant, blotted out their enormous debt to Germany, and in a few short months redeemed those portions of French territory that had been held by German troops as a guarantee for the indemnity, was indeed a very striking thing. But

* The Evolution of France under the Third Republic. By Baron Pierre de Coubertin. Translated from the French by Isabel F. Hapgood, with an Introduction by Dr. Albert Shaw. Illustrated. New York: Thomas Y. Crowell & Co. $3.00.

how can this be credited to the republican inspiration? Its cause was deeper far than this. It was the passionate revolt of France against the thought of foreign occupation, and it was stimulated by the brutal exactions of an alien race, who rode rough-shod over those whom they had conquered, and the very sight of whom, with their stiff and arrogant militarism, made no sacrifice seem too great that would expel them from the presence of a people who had never learned submission to a foreign enemy. The patience and discretion displayed by France in the face of the cold-blooded Bismarckian policy, which in 1875 seemed bent upon precipitating another war, was again only the national instinct of self-preservation aroused and active. And it may be truly said that the continuance of the republican government itself for nearly thirty years has been due far less to any fundamental love for democratic forms than to the division and the inevitable lack of unity among its enemies. It was no love for the Republic that saved France from the ignominy of a dictatorship in the days of Boulangisme, when whole provinces went mad over the rider of the black horse, and when hundreds of thousands of men wore the red carnation, and were ready at a word to storm the Houses of Parliament and fling the pettifogging deputies into the Seine. It was rather the indecision of the pinchbeck general himself and his eternal consciousness that he was strong only in the anticipation of power, and that in the very moment of a triumph he would be forced to choose his party from among the heterogeneous factions that supported him, that whether he emerged a royalist or an imperialist, the great mass of his supporters, who were neither royalists nor imperialists, would at once turn upon him, and that if he attempted the rôle of a Napoleon on his own account, then royalists and imperialists and republicans alike would hurl him down from a dictatorship which he had not himself alone the power to conquer. These things, then, are by no means to be ascribed to the credit of that government which France to-day possesses.

On the other hand, there is much that must condemn it and discredit it in the eyes even of its most ardent advocates. In the first place, its bareness and essential lack of all impressiveness are out of harmony with much in the French character that is fundamental. The Frenchman, half Latin and half Celt, loves not only power, but its visible manifestation. He likes to feel behind the form of government a great irresistible force, something splendid and vital and magnificent; and in the form itself he loves the pageantry that goes with imperialism and with royalty. His artistic sense, his imagination, his curiosity, his national vanity, are all appealed to by a brilliant court, by great palaces, by imposing châteaux, by stately ceremonial. Nor is it for himself alone that he demands these things. He feels that in them France itself is glorified, and that as its art, its literature, and its civilisation as a whole are conspicuous in the eyes of the world, so should its government also be something dazzling and overwhelming. It is hard for him to accept the control of a lot of provincial pettifoggers chattering eternally as deputies, or the shadowy government of a little hair-splitting lawyer like Thiers, or of a chuckle-headed old peasant like Jules Grévy, moping about in the halls where once a Louis Quatorze received the homage of the old *noblesse*, or where a Napoleon stood robed in the imperial purple and the golden bees, surveying haughtily that brilliant soldiery which had tamed the pride of kings and emperors, and planted the French tricolour in every capital of Europe. Even to the foreigner there is something melancholy to-day in the externals of republican rule in France. An air of dilapidation broods over the palaces that have now become mere show places for the Cook's tourist. There is a musty, dusty smell about them, an air of having seen better days, a pervasive shabbiness that is, in a way, intensely typical. Whatever else France may have gained, she has undoubtedly lost distinction. The trail of the *bourgeois* is over everything. Paris is the only great capital in Europe where one may walk for hours without encountering a single group of men who have the air of gentlemen, and where alike in café and cathedral one sees eternally reproduced the type of face that suggests nothing higher in the social scale than the prosperous greengrocer and the *dame du comptoir*.

But it is not merely in distinction alone that France has lost since monarchy in some form or other was swept away. She has lost in her public men that fine integrity that was, at any rate, the prevailing rule in the days of aristocracy. It is pitiful to enumerate what every one remembers, the scandals commercial, political, and personal that rise like a mist throughout the history of the Third Republic. A President such as Grévy, whose nearest relatives corrupted the one Order that has survived all other changes, selling decorations and trafficking in honours, a parliament half bribed and half blackmailed into supporting the most gigantic swindle of the age, and even an army in which trusted officers can be found to betray their country's secrets to their country's deadliest enemies — these things, at least, are not national, but are directly traceable to republican rule.

The chief danger that attaches itself to democracy is found in the fact that its true meaning is so often misunderstood. For democracy really means that all shall have an equal opportunity to rise; it does not mean that all shall rise. In other words, it is equality. of opportunity and not equality of attainment that it promises. Under an aristocratic system, on the other hand, there is no equality of opportunity, and the great mass of human beings accepting this as inevitable, will remain contented with their lot whatever it may be, thus giving to the State tranquillity and a substratum of popular repose. The few bold spirits whose creative vigour can defy all obstacles and break through all restraint will, under this system as truly as under a democratic one, hew out a path to eminence even though the task be harder; so that in the end the aristocratic system is in reality the better one, for it attains the same results as the democratic, while avoiding the instability which is inseparable from any system that propagates and stimulates a general discontent. Those who are fitted to rule will always rule; but the State under a true aristocracy escapes the discredit, the confusion, and the experimental grotesqueness of attempts at government by those who are unfit.

Now in France under the Republic those classes who by tradition and heredity possess the loftiest ideals and the greatest capacity for statecraft are, in the main, excluded from any share of political power; and their place is taken by a horde of corrupt, ambitious, and incompetent persons who believe that opportunity and ability alike are theirs, and who thus give the world a specimen of republican rule, discreditable alike to the democratic theory and to France itself. And so we have kaleidoscopic changes of ministry, an aimless vacillation in public policy, and a total absence of coherence and of confidence. Because the Church was linked in sympathy, as in history, with the old régime, the Church was forced by men like Gambetta into the attitude almost of a national enemy. Its conservative influence has been estranged, and its teachings, which are those that make for national security, have been blotted out of the education of modern France. The result is seen each year with more and more distinctness, and is a shocking example of what a purely secular training for the young can lead to; since scepticism in religion has broadened and festered into scepticism in everything else —in patriotic ideals, and in the domain of personal honesty and honour. The mistrust of man by man is the canker that is blighting every day the nation's strength. Should a great war again call Frenchmen under arms, this universal feeling of mistrust would hamper the efforts of the ablest leaders. A single defeat would demoralise all those forces which in any other country could be banded together in an invincible unity for the national defence. The cry of treason by whomsoever raised would be echoed by a million voices, and half of France would believe that an unsuccessful general had been either bribed or was spontaneously disloyal. A French army would not only have to meet the public enemy in front, but the more insidious private enemy forever threatening the rear.

Baron de Coubertin does not attempt to minimise much that is grievous and much that is ominous in the life of France to-day. He notes the dangers of democracy, the tendency toward political and personal immorality, the fact that history and literature and statistics also justify the most rigorous judgment of the modern French republicans. He recognises the dangerous results that spring from the French system of inheritance which leads to a practical adoption of the theory of Malthus, so that the population of France is standing still while that of its most hated enemy is progressing by leaps and bounds; and he does not deny that under the Republic, the love of luxury and the sway of baser motives have set their mark upon the men who govern. He is, on the whole, however, willing to see a brighter side to all this picture, and he marshals such facts as seem, in his opinion, to justify the general conclusion that France under the Republic will ultimately regain its political and social health, and again resume its leadership among the nations of the Continent. We wish that we could summarise his optimistic argument, which is, however, not presented as an argument; but the space at our disposal will not allow this, and we must refer the reader to the book itself.

For weal or for woe, there is no doubt that France has definitely accepted a republican form of government. It is conceivable that as the result of a great war fought to a triumphant end by some brilliant soldier, a military chief might once more seize upon supreme power and found a new imperial dynasty. But short of this it seems impossible that France should ever again revert, even temporarily, to a monarchical system. The fact that a quarter of a century has now passed away since the Second Empire fell, and that a whole generation of Frenchmen has grown up with no personal knowledge of any form of government but that which now exists, and that the republican idea has at last leavened the whole mass of the population, supports this view. But there are some indications that the present constitution may sooner or later be modified in such a way as to give some real and tangible power to the President of the Republic whose functions hitherto have been those of the merest figurehead. It was a hopeful sign when after President Faure's return from Russia, where he secured from the lips of the Czar himself a formal admission of the reality of Russia's league with France, a proposition was seriously advanced for strengthening the presidency by giving to the President a share of real responsibility. If this shall at any time be done, it will in some way satisfy the French desire for personal rule; for it will give to the nation as a whole a representative who will actually represent, it will do away with something of the weakness and uncertainty of a government that now possesses no genuine chief magistrate, and it will make the unity of the nation to be both felt and seen.

Miss Hapgood's translation of the book is fair, but nothing more. It is weakest in those portions that relate to matters exclusively political, and there it justifies an opinion which we set forth some time ago to the effect that the translation of a legal or political or military work should never be entrusted to a woman, save when she has a male collaborator.

H. T. Peck.

MR. MEREDITH'S POETRY.*

There is no reason to quarrel with Mr. Meredith's selection from his poetry. We may miss a few favourite pieces, but there is hardly a characteristic note it does not sound. His compass in poetry is less than in prose, but there are depths that have never been made manifest save in his verse. In prose he has touched the tragic sometimes, but rather shyly; his desires and interests are all far removed from the wild and the frenzied. The morbid is to him forbidding and accursed; and though there is a good deal of wholesome cant spoken of the sanity of the great reflectors of the humankind, the tragedians have always looked over the borders of the sane and dwelt there for a space. Only in his poetry, and that seldom, does he ever grapple with the abnormal, the dark and terrible; and if "The Nuptials of Attila" be a fine experiment in this, "The Song of Theodolinda" is a great and singular achievement. This passionate outburst of religious frenzy is the one real glimpse of the terrible he shares with us.

It is of far other things he elsewhere sings, though of the strife behind the kindly veil of Nature he tells in "The Woods of Westermain." The common refreshment of earth and sky is his best inspiration. He is above all the poet of the woods—

"No Paradise is lost for them
Who foot by branching root and stem,
And lightly with the woodland share
The change of night and day."

He loves the cheery, the grateful, the

* Selected Poems. By George Meredith. New York: Charles Scribner's Sons. $1.75.

young, the unconscious things; for music, the lark's song—

> "The song seraphically free
> From taint of personality."

He is the sincerest observer; not Tennyson was more so. But his is too often the slow, cumulative effect of the naturalist rather than the vision-flash of the artist. There is excellent stuff, for instance, in such a poem as "The South-Wester," but it is a laborious pleasure you get from it. Yet after enduring much, out of respect to a man who never writes a line of sounding rubbish, you are rewarded by bursts of genuine lyric beauty, lines that paint once and forever the Nature-sensitive—

> "The breast of us a sounded shell,
> The blood of us a lighted dew;"

unforgettable pictures, like that of the sunset-star—

> "Remote, not alien; still, not cold;
> Unraying yet, more pearl than star;
> She seems a while the vale to hold
> In trance, and homelier makes the far;"

happy verses, like the song to water, "Water, first of singers," in "Phœbus with Admetus;" like those that sing the sweetest of all country girls, the morning-light maiden of "Love in the Valley"—

> "Deals she an unkindness, 'tis but her rapid measure,
> Even as in a dance; and her smile can heal no less;
> Like the swinging May-cloud that pelts the flowers with hail-stones
> Off a sunny border, she was made to bruise and bless."

But if his verse have that much-desired thing, a "message," it is not a call merely to the woodland, but a warning to the sensitive idealist, that wisdom does not grow rich in green fields alone, or in the press of men alone—

> "It hangs for those who hither, thither fare,
> Close interthreading nature with our kind."

There never was a less languorous, a robuster poet. The common, healthy man would heartily approve him if he would but make his speech a little plainer—for though he mostly drops his mannerisms in verse, his syntax is often maddening. He hates the "totter-kneed," the whiners, "who feed upon a breast unthanked." His belief in brains, "Sky of the senses!" in the delight of struggle, in manly, clear-eyed acquiescence with the trend of things, is as visible in his verse as in his prose. He has not, as some prose writers have done, used verse for the expression of his feebler, sicklier hours. Sanity amid beauty, courage amid the ruin of it, is for him earth's secret.

> "We fall, or view our treasures fall,
> Unclouded, as beholds her flowers
> Earth, from a night of frosty wreck,
> Enrobed, in morning's mounted fire,
> When lowly, with a broken neck,
> The crocus lays her cheek to mire."

A. M.

A MODERN GREEK ROMANCE.*

Whatever one may hear of the literary activity of modern Greece, one is not usually in the way of knowing much about it. Accordingly, when the Professor of European History in Amherst College translates a novel which he defines in his preface as the "greatest romance of contemporary Greece," it is not unnatural to take his word for it, and to draw conclusions of one's own about modern Greek literature in general. In the light of these circumstances, there are two ways of regarding *Andronike*, the romance which presents itself with so strong an endorsement. The one is, in its relation to the ancient literature of Greece, that it may be seen how the children carry on the work of their fathers, the work which provides us with most of our standards for the art we call "classic," in whatever age and through whatever medium it may be produced. The other way is to consider the book as an expression of national life in this present century of Greek history.

Before looking at the book in either of these aspects, it will be well to see what it is in itself. The Greek struggle for independence, beginning with the slaughter of the bishops in Constantinople in 1821, and ending with the battle of Navarino in 1827, gives the author not only his background, but many of his characters and incidents. The chief personal interest of the narrative is vested in a youth and a maid, ardent Greek

* Andronike, the Heroine of the Greek Revolution. By Stephanos Theodoros Xenos. Translated from the original Greek by Edwin A. Grosvenor. Boston: Roberts Bros. $1.50.

patriots, who meet and pledge each other their love two years before the war begins, pursue separate courses of astounding adventure through seven years, and meet at last in the doomed Misolonghi. Thrasyboulos, the hero, has just suffered the amputation of one of his legs, and survives only for a short time the sortie from the town. Andronike, wearied with grief and battle, in which she has more than once played a man's part, retires to a convent in Moscow, where she dies on the day of receiving the news that Greece is a kingdom and Otho its king. The evil machinations of Barthakos, the misshapen villain who keeps the lovers apart, enter largely into the scheme of the book. Something of interest is contributed by the personal presence of Markos Botsaris and Lord Byron, both of whom die before the reader's eyes. As the book extends to the length of five hundred and twenty-seven large pages, it is manifestly impossible to give more than the merest suggestion of its substance in the present space.

To apply the ordinary tests of classicism to this romance is to meet with disappointment. Unity is perhaps inevitably absent from a tale which demands from its readers an equal, or almost equal, interest in two characters who are separated for seven years. When one of them is brought to what seems the climax of his or her adventures, the reader is suddenly transported to the other, and is reminded again and again that he is reading two stories and not one. There is a measure of success in identifying the persons of the drama with the actual scenes of history, but it must be said that the persons possess such reality as is due to the author's descriptions of them rather than to the reader's positive conviction that they exist. How far the translator is responsible for the feeling that the classic spirit has entered but slightly into the production of *Andronike* it is not easy to say. Certainly the English style of the book sometimes lacks the simplicity and beauty which result from the careful study of classic models. The most scrupulous of writers would not father such a sentence as, "Every door, through which provisions could be introduced by sea, were one by one wrested from the Greeks;" nor would he describe a villain as "drenched in a perspiration of shame and conscious infamy." The exclamation "Shake!" in sealing an agreement, the retort of reassurance, "You bet," and the taunt to a man of seeming verdancy, "Does your mother know you are out?"—all these may be literal translations from the modern Greek; but if they are, it would surely have been better to convert them into terms less strongly suggestive of the American small boy. If these are trivial objections, they are not without a larger significance, though it would not be quite fair to say of them, *Ex pede Herculem.*

When the book is considered in its second aspect, it becomes possible at once to speak of it in other terms, and to appreciate the high opinion of it entertained by a professor of European history. As a contribution to our knowledge of the Greeks and the immemorial conflict between Christians and Moslems in the East, the book has a positive value. In this very year it is well to gain a better understanding of the religious and patriotic motives which have fired the hearts of the Grecian people. Here we learn also the elements of the nation's weakness, the mingling of lower with higher impulses in some of the men from whom most has been expected. But whatever appears to the discredit of the Greeks is as nothing in comparison with the author's picture of the unspeakable Turk. His barbarous rapacity and thirst for blood, his utter treachery and scorn for what the Western races know as "honour," stand forth with hideous clearness. These qualities, to be sure, are drawn with the venom of an enemy, but the vigour of the hostile hand strengthens the reality of the picture. So, too, the most strenuous historical scenes of the book are the most effective merely in the light of art. The besieged Misolonghi and the bitter courage of the Greeks within it are memorably depicted. The battle of Navarino ceases to be a name, and becomes a reality of vastly tragic import.

"Battle, murder, and sudden death" is the burden of the story. If it be read merely for entertainment or as a specimen of the literary art of Eastern Europe, one may easily object to it as somewhat tedious and clumsy, and may remind one's self that Poland and Russia have both produced modern romances of war which appeal far more directly to the Western mind. If one is seeking a more vital historical knowledge of the foundations upon which modern Greece is built, of the people who dwell within it and of the enemies round about it, *Andronike* will serve well to shorten the search.

M. A. DeWolfe Howe.

"BROKENBURNE;" A SOUTHERN IDYLL.*

We have no hesitation in claiming for *Brokenburne* an honourable place among the best stories that have gathered around the old South since the war. It is with Thomas Nelson Page that Mrs. Boyle will inevitably invite comparison and classification more than with any of the other Southern writers. Her manner is not unlike his, though one perceives easily that it is her own and owes its likeness to the delicacy and grace, the subtle flavour of the soil, and the fineness of touch characteristic of both. In matter there is a stronger resemblance, which, however, must not be mistaken for reminiscence. The background is the feudal magnificence of plantation life in ante-bellum times in lower Mississippi. The story is of strained relations, broken happiness, and sundered loves, lighted at the end with a sunset ray of peace. But the characters and setting are indigenous to their own section of the South in *Brokenburne;* they retain their individual charm and make a distinct impression on the imagination. Mississippi has reason to be proud of Mrs. Boyle, as Virginia may well be of Mr. Page, for in *Brokenburne* she has opened a new field in the South—a field as rich in romance as any in our country. Mississippi may have retrograded in recent years, but she was a grand old State, and played her part bravely and nobly in the struggle for the South. And though evil winds have blown roughly over the broad and fertile lands of that golden time in which "Aunt Bene" glories, many an old landmark still stands, a loving guardian over deserted fields that now and again tempt dusky harvesters; a crumbling monument to the glad and sorrowful memories that have sought a more enduring memorial in literature. Such a memorial is *Brokenburne*, recording in quick succession the gradual transformation from a scene of happy plantation life to the tragedy that, God knows, was common enough in the days of the war. Many a story has Mrs. Boyle listened to from such old mammies as "Aunt Bene," and there is more truth than fiction in *Brokenburne.* Many an old mansion remains tottering on its rotten piers, forgotten and forsaken, its doors unlocked and oftentimes lying open, waiting for those who have been absent in foreign lands so long, or in that land from whose bourne no traveller returns, that their record has passed away. As a child Mrs. Boyle, awed but inquisitive, has entered such a house, peeped through the glass of cupboards, where, within the soft depths of the shadows, fine china and dainty linen lay, has crept through the musty rooms and sat in the stiff brocade chairs, until frightened out of her childish wits at the unearthly stillness she has rushed wildly into the yard, somewhat reassured by the commonplace aspect of the reality of things in broad daylight. The light of the old loves and graces clustering about these dwellings has fallen upon the author's imagination, which from a child has fed upon the ever-recurring tales of the days that have fled—fled leaving behind them the ghostly heritage that is restored to something of its pristine freshness and glory in the pages of this story, more real in its seeming than the reality.

The character of Virginia Balfour is one of the most pleasing and fascinating portraits preserved for us from among the high-spirited, the beautiful, and passionate creatures of the warm and luxuriant South. In her creation we see the treasures of the author's childhood unfolded in the maturer mind of the woman. Around the slender, poetic figure of Virginia are centred the delicate fancies of youth and the sentimentalism of the time. A clearly defined and intensely human figure, Virginia Balfour, or "Jinny" in the old auntie's narrative, wins the sympathy of the reader and holds it to the end. The strained affection for her lover, snapped by a chivalric devotion to family and to principle, changes comedy to tragedy, and reaches a climax in the last interview between Virginia and Phillip, not un-

* Brokenburne; An Old Auntie's War Story. By Virginia Frazer Boyle. Illustrated. New York: E. R. Herrick & Co. $1.50.

like that in Longfellow's *Evangeline*, that has in it the tears of things. No more pathetic figure moves across the record of the immemorial past before and during the war. The old time pride and beauty of life, the tender grace and noble sensitiveness, the high patriotism and love of honour which rose above the prevalent sentimentalism and found expression in true sentiment and brave deeds, the pity and the irony of it all—these are enshrined in the idyllic pages of *Brokenburne*, and set apart from the throng of the vulgar by the beauty of pathos and artistry that lies upon them.

But chief among Mrs. Boyle's achievements in *Brokenburne* is that she has a story to tell, and that she can tell a story. Was it not Sir Walter Scott—who knew the secret of story-telling so well—who resolved in *Waverley* to throw the force of his narrative upon the characters and passions of the actors?—those passions common to men and women in all stages of society, and which have alike agitated the human heart, whether it throbbed under the steel corselet of the fifteenth century, the brocaded coat of the eighteenth, under the blue and the gray uniform of this present century, or in the breast of Virginia Balfour and of Aunt Bene. The great book of Nature is the same in all climes and in all tongues; now and again a fresh chapter is reproduced which, whatever its external characters, finds entrance into the universal heart. *Brokenburne* makes this wide appeal; it entertains and compels interest even while its pathos moves and pierces emotion. All the changing incidents of the time, as seen through the eyes of Aunt Bene, are unconsciously dramatic. Poignant as are the feelings which the recital awakens, it is rather a reminiscent sadness that, gleaming like the aftershine on troubled waters, pervades the story and lingers in the memory. Its pathos, too, is plaintive rather than piercing—plaintive as the note of the wild bird that haunts those surroundings and fills the air with the mournful, far echoing cadence of its cry. An old, old story, you will say, but ah, how fond we are of hearing it told over and over again!

A word of praise must be passed to the artist who has added to the interest of the printed tale by his pictured pages. He has caught the spirit of the time and has restored several of the scenes of the story with such verisimilitude as betokens a careful study of his background and a sympathetic appreciation of its dramatic value. The book is beautifully made, and will present an inviting appearance during the approach of the festive season. *Brokenburne*, however, is not a book of the day to be cut down at even, but is of the class that calls for a wide and an enduring recognition.

James MacArthur.

THE PERSONAL EQUATION *

The "personal equation," I take it, to which Dr. Harry Thurston Peck refers in the title of his interesting volume lately added to Harper and Brothers' series of "American Essayists," is the more or less problematic relation of an author's personality to his published works, and, again, this matter of personality and expression as it affects readers—that is, you and me, gentle or ungentle reader (since we are all apt to be misguided as to our gentleness or other traits).

What I like about the book is its clarity of thought and style, its marked directness and simplicity of utterance, which turns out to be the very best medium for subtle, discriminating and precise appreciations. Nothing more comprehensive, delicate, and discerning has ever been written about Howells (for whose earnestness, beauty, and lovableness of character and sincerity of work I must ask to be allowed to say I have the greatest admiration) than Dr. Peck's essay, in which he traces quickly and clearly the composite influences of Mr. Howells's Welsh ancestry, Ohio birth, New England temperament, Massachusetts envelopment, and New York development and puzzling experience. Much of truth, also, is conveyed in the statement that Howells, after a while, "began to abuse his gift of observation. Instead of going always swiftly and unerringly to the very heart of things, he sometimes seemed to consider it sufficient to accumulate a multiplicity of trivial details, and to let a microscopic fidelity take the place of a

* The Personal Equation. By Harry Thurston Peck. New York and London: Harper & Bros. $1.50.

broader sympathy." The essayist's characterisation of Boston is very true, clever, and amusing—to those who do not have to live in or near or swear by Boston. Most happy, also, is his remark upon Marcel Prévost, that his style has the great facility and charm of George Sand's, but that "with him this fluency does not, as hers did, pass into fluidity." Dr. Peck says very wisely of Prévost, that "his conception of idealism makes it to be not so much a thing apart from real life and quite beyond it, as an essential feature of that life itself. . . . And in this he is far wiser than Mr. Howells, for instance, who, while kindly granting to the Romantic an actual existence in our psychical and even in our material experience, does hold it to be so utterly exceptional as to rule it out of literary use."

The chapter on Prévost also touches some points of curious interest regarding the relations of men and women and married life, and brings out strongly the true conception of loyalty in the institution of marriage—beautiful, sad, strange as it may be in particular instances, yet always noble when entered upon and followed in the right spirit. After reading this essay, I wish that some one would depict in fiction the man's side of marriage. Wedding is nearly always treated as a purely feminine affair ; yet surely it is quite as important when viewed as a masculine experience, with its effect upon the man and upon the race. The male being, who has feelings of his own, and a purity of his own, and trials and temptations far more numerous than those which afflict women, still exists, and ought to be considered. Novelists should be able to tell a good deal about the idealism, the self-sacrifice, the devotion of the average man, and the sorrows that come to him through marriage. But at present he seems to be of no account. Fiction is given over mainly to the largely fanciful trials and morbid introspections of women. Who ever thinks of the lifelong griefs and burdens of a simply loyal married man?

Dr. Peck's view is broad enough to take in many diversities of imaginative work and various phases of thought ; so that, despite his sharp differences with the English novelist, George Moore, he still finds it in his heart and his pen to say that Moore, notwithstanding his subtlety and coarseness, refinement and ineffable vulgarity, is, "with all his limitations and perversities, the greatest literary artist who has struck the chords of English since the death of Thackeray." This breadth of his enables him to give us a most interesting summary of Huysmans's novels and to conclude, with regard to the book called *En Route*: "It is full of deep instruction in revealing with startling force the secret of the power of that wonderful religious organisation which has made provision for the needs of every human soul, whether it requires for its comfort active service or the mystical life of contemplation. . . . There is something reassuring in the contemplation of the one great Church that does not change from age to age, that stands unshaken on the rock of its convictions, and that speaks to the wavering and troubled soul in the serene and lofty accents of divine authority."

The essay entitled "Some Notes on Political Oratory" contains many suggestive criticisms and hints, which for my part I wish could be further emphasised and carried out. I cannot do justice here to Dr. Peck's other papers in this volume, on "The New Child and its Picture Books," "President Cleveland," and "The Downward Drift in American Education." But I would like to say, and must say most distinctly, as conveying my own impression, which I hope will be shared by many others, that his volume is distinguished not only by a thorough and accomplished survey of the subjects he treats, but also by a sincerity and an uplifting purpose which ought to bring gratification to every candid man and woman into whose hands it may come. The author carries his survey of the "personal equation" up to the heights of sublime faith. Not limiting himself to the man and the author, or the author and the public, he goes on to intimate the relation of the person to the universe and the infinite ; ending with this majestic refrain or *envoi*, in *Quod Minime Reris*: "That which stands immutable and quite secure is the great tradition and the mighty system that perpetuate whatever is best and highest in the human aspiration and belief."

A man who writes such essays as these, full of research and reflection, with such wealth of immediate knowledge of his subjects, so many resources of comparison, so clear and helpful a faculty of judgment, and in so clear and delightful a style as Dr. Peck's, confers a personal favour and does an act of friendship to the sympathetic reader and to the reading public.

George Parsons Lathrop.

MR. MERRIMAN'S CASTLE IN SPAIN.*

"*The Prisoner of Zenda,*" some one said a while ago, "is not literature." "No," said this reviewer, "but it is a good bit better reading than a great deal that *is* literature."

It must be confessed, however, that the novel of adventure, like other things and people in this naughty and troublesome world, has the defects of its qualities; for its primary necessity being the "story," the sequence of hair-breadth escapes by flood and field, sharpness of line in character drawing becomes not only a secondary consideration, but probably, at times, absolutely a hindrance; since one's *dramatis personæ*, when really alive, are apt to take matters into their own hands, and shape the plot to suit their own convenience. For this reason there is a distinct temptation to the story-teller to keep practically to the same staff, or stock-company, varying the names and costumes to suit the climate, the Anno Domini, or the station in life to which it pleases him to call his *corps dramatique;* and as thus they become to him types, rather than persons, he is the better able to depend upon them to attend strictly to business under the most exciting circumstances, and never, under any temptation, to lapse into self-analysis or introspection.

The method which we have thus indicated is, we must admit, very largely that of Mr. Henry Seton Merriman (Hugh S. Scott), whose *In Kedar's Tents* has been familiar to the readers of THE BOOKMAN for the past year. Whether he locates his drama amid the frozen steppes of Russia, on India's coral strand, or where African rivers roll down the plague, the "sleeping sickness," and crocodiles galore, the *personæ* who are affected by these incidents are very apt to be recognised as old acquaintances by the discerning reader.

There is, for example, always a bold, bad, beautiful woman, to whom we are invariably grateful for being less bad than she gave us reason to anticipate; there is a large young man for the leading gentleman; an astute man of the world, who is sometimes the heavy father, and at others merely a confidant in correct evening dress; and there is always a pure, cold English maiden, with abnormal powers of concealing her emotions, especially that one which, like a cough, is said to be non-concealable by man or woman. Out of these characters and others who appear less certainly in his pages, Mr. Merriman gets, we confess with joy, very excellent work; they have been thoroughly drilled in stage business and are letter-perfect in their lines; the author has never for a moment a touch of Mr. Puff's difficulty in getting them off the stage at the right time; on the contrary, the action is always rapid, the plot never falters in interest, though one must admit that the mechanism is occasionally slightly clumsy, and the execution apt to reveal the mark of the tool.

The truth of the matter is that Mr. Merriman has always been capable of even better things; that his stock-characters have never entirely contented him. *The Sowers* showed a decided advance in this respect, for "Prince Paul," though still a large young man, was decidedly more individualised than any of his predecessors in that rôle, while Steinmetz was a real characterisation, if not quite a living human being. And the present book notes a growth still more encouraging; for while Conyngham, Estella, and General Vincente still retain a vague flavour of reminiscence, the Padre Concha is a real creation, and Concepcion Vara is very much alive indeed. In the construction of the plot also there is a genuine growth in power; the story takes hold of one from the beginning, centring as it does around one small pink and scented letter, which, before the final catastrophe occurs, the reader is as anxious to read as is Conyngham himself.

Mr. Merriman is quite aware, we must add, of the peculiar flavour imparted to a novel of adventure by a feather from Freedom's bird; but it does not seem to signify very greatly, in his opinion,

* In Kedar's Tents. By Henry Seton Merriman. New York: Dodd, Mead & Co. $1.25.

whether his hero takes sides for or against the special reform under consideration; in truth, it signified very little to Conyngham, who in England called himself a Chartist, and in Spain served under the banner of Queen Christina. Conyngham is rather a reckless variety of the large young man; and his complaisance in accusing himself of complicity in a Chartist riot, and taking upon his own shoulders the death of Alfred Pleydell, in order to save his not very courageous friend, Geoffrey Horner, is the prologue to the real story. With the same polite readiness to oblige, this large young man, who runs away to Spain with Geoffrey's guilt on his devoted head, next proceeds to save two ladies from a very disagreeable situation, and undertakes to carry a letter for Estaban Larralde, a handsome and untrustworthy Carlist conspirator. What the letter contains, and what befell our hero because of it, be it far from this reviewer to divulge; suffice it to say that it is not recovered, by any of the persons who are willing to hazard their lives in pursuit of it, until the very last chapter. Meanwhile the interest accumulates, at compound or geometrical ratio, which ever means most to the mathematician, and finally culminates in a glorious shindy in the Plaza del Ayuntamiento in Toledo, where Estella, on the stone balcony of the "Mansion House," personates the Queen, and Father Concha, unable to preserve the rôle of a man of peace, shouts "Caramba!" and is gone.

"They saw him a minute later appear in the square, having thrown aside his cassock. He made a strange, lean figure of a man, with his knee-breeches and dingy purple stockings, his gray flannel shirt, and the moonlight shining on his tonsured head. He fought without skill and heedless of danger, swinging a great sword that he had picked up from the hand of a fallen trooper, and each blow that he got home killed its man."

But we have failed to do Mr. Merriman justice by omitting all reference to the brilliancy of his manner of telling a story—a manner which at all times sparkles with wit, and includes not a few epigrammatic descriptions that print themselves on the memory. What, for example, could be better than this from *One Generation to Another*:

"A portentous standing lamp, six feet high in its bare feet, with a shade like a crinoline"?

Or this, a very different picture, but equally vivid:

"'Yes, it is the hollow hearts that make the most noise in the world,' said Concha, folding his handkerchief on his knee. He was deadly poor, and had a theory that a folded handkerchief remains longer clean."

Or Concepcion's inimitable adieu to his hostess of an hour:

"'It's better,' said Concepcion with a meaning and gallant bow to the hostess—'it's for my peace of mind. I am but a man.' Then he haggled over the price of the supper."

In *The Sowers* we are almost overwhelmed with epigram; but in this respect also the author shows in *Kedar's Tents* that he has himself and his subject very much better in hand; that his art has become far more a part of himself than in any former work. To quote the phrase of a friend, it is "a rattling good story;" if it should ever be dramatised we foresee in especial a rising of the audience in wild and sincere applause when Sir John Pleydell, coming to Spain to seek revenge for the death of his son, applies to our hero for assistance in kidnapping Frederick Conyngham; and Conyngham, presenting his card, assures him that he could not have come to a better man. Wherein this present critic and Mr. Merriman's readers in general will agree with Frederick Conyngham.

John Lennox.

BOOKS ABOUT THE STAGE.*

Mr. Fitzgerald Molloy resembles Mr. Percy Fitzgerald in more ways than one. The Irish writer, like the English, is pleasant and prolific, careless enough in style, no stickler for exact accuracy, swift to seize a picturesque episode, and

* The Romance of the Irish Stage, with Pictures of the Irish Capital in the Eighteenth Century. By Fitzgerald Molloy. 2 vols. New York: Dodd, Mead & Co. $4.00.

The English Stage, being an Account of the Victorian Drama. By Augustin Filon. Translated from the French by Frederic Whyte, with an Introduction by Henry Arthur Jones. New York: Dodd, Mead & Co. $2.50.

The Theatrical "World" of 1896. By William Archer. London: Walter Scott, Ltd.; New York: Charles Scribner's Sons.

La Préface de "Cromwell." Introduction, Texte, Notes. Par Maurice Souriau. Paris: Société Française d'Imprimerie.

Chronologie Moliéresque. Par Georges Monval. Paris: Librairie Flammarion.

to present it alluringly to the reader. Mr. Fitzgerald Molloy has already gossipped about *Some Famous Plays*; he has already told the sad life of Edmund Kean; he has already set forth the strange adventures of Peg Woffington, and now he gives us two briskly written volumes on the *Romance of the Irish Stage*, proffered perhaps as a pendant to Mr. Percy Fitzgerald's *Romance of the English Stage*. It would not be unfair to characterise Mr. Percy Fitzgerald's *Romance of the English Stage* as rather sensational and slightly meretricious; and it is agreeable to discover that Mr. Fitzgerald Molloy's *Romance of the Irish Stage* is altogether a better book. It is discursive, no doubt; indeed, Mr. Fitzgerald Molloy has raised discursiveness almost to the dignity of an exact science. In the present work he does not repeat his great feat in the biography of Peg Woffington, in which there are five consecutive chapters wherein even the name of the heroine is not a single time mentioned. In Mr. Fitzgerald Molloy's behalf it may be said that these extraneous chapters were quite as lively and quite as entertaining as any of the others more closely related to the subject of the book.

In the present work the author tells us on the title-page that he intends to describe Irish society as it was in the last century; and in his preface he declares that "no more splendid and varied panorama can be imagined than Dublin in its pre-Union days, with its state processions, its parliament, its court festivities, its reckless gambling, duelling, and abductions, its roystering and extravagance, the whole illumined by a gaiety that has become a tradition." The modes of this gaiety Mr. Fitzgerald Molloy brings before us with abundant anecdote only to confirm the sad impression of Irish life in the last century, which we have already derived from *Barry Lyndon* and *Charles O'Malley* and *Castle Rackrent*.

Among the interesting personalities that figure in Mr. Fitzgerald Molloy's pages are David Garrick, probably the greatest actor of all time; and Peg Woffington, the most charming woman of her day, although not the greatest actress; Thomas Sheridan, son of Swift's friend and father of the author of the *School for Scandal*, himself the initiator of a reform of the Dublin theatre not unlike that Macready was to accomplish in the London theatre in this century; George Anne Bellamy, a famous beauty who wrote her memoirs when her looks had left her—memoirs for which Thiers provided a preface when they were translated into French seventy or eighty years ago; and Quin of the biting witticisms; and Mrs. Abington, the original Lady Teazle; and Mossop, cleverly characterised in the *Rosciad* of Churchill; and Mrs. Siddons, the stately muse of tragedy.

It is well that M. Filon's admirable book on the English stage of this century should find an English translator, who has accomplished his task satisfactorily on the whole, although there are those who may think that he has carried over untranslated too many French words and phrases. The best history of Spanish literature is by an American, Ticknor, and the best history of English literature by a Frenchman, Taine; and now another Frenchman has given us the best history of the Victorian drama. As his own proverb says, every man has the defects of his qualities, and if M. Filon as a Frenchman has been able to get a more unprejudiced perspective of the British playmakers than any native could, he also has made a blunder or two an Englishman might not have made. For example, the *Octoroon* is not one of Boucicault's Irish plays; Robertson's *David Garrick* was not a failure; Mrs. Sterling was not the original Marquise in *Caste*. An Englishman would probably credit Sir Henry Irving with the substitution of Shakespeare's *Richard III.* for Cibber's, and M. Filon here follows the British authorities, although we Americans know that Mr. Booth discarded the Cibber perversion long before Sir Henry did.

But these are the merest trifles of hypercriticism. M. Filon's book is excellent, and no one who wants to understand the condition of the drama in England under Victoria can afford to neglect it. He clears the air when he cuts to pieces calmly and without any animosity the smug tragedy of *Virginius* and the ranting rhetoric of *Richelieu*. He suggests rather than declares the evil effect upon the serious drama of the inconsistent hypocrisy which is now a chief characteristic of the British social structure. He does not overestimate the increasing influence which the art of Ibsen has had upon the leading British dramatists of to-day, especially upon Mr. Pinero and Mr. Jones. He does full justice to *The Second Mrs. Tranqueray* (in some respects the strongest effort of the English stage in this century) and to the *Case of Rebellicus Susan* (in some respects the most intellectual of Mr. Jones's plays). He does not fail to give full credit for the change in the conditions of the British drama during the past ten years to Mr. William Archer, even going so far as to liken the effect of Mr. Archer's criticisms to that of the *Dramaturgie* of Lessing.

For the fourth time now Mr. Archer has gathered into an annual volume the articles in which he has criticised the plays of the year week by week, and with every succeeding volume the admiration of at least one reader grows. Mr. Archer is a born critic with an intense love for the theatre, a wide knowledge of its history, and a real understanding of its art. He has the logic of a Scotchman, the information of a German, and the wit of a Frenchman. He is not blinded by tradition—see, for example, his calm discussion of Marlowe's *Doctor Faustus*, as acted in London last year. He is no iconoclast either; he is modest; he is reverent really; he is sane always. To the present volume he has prefixed a plea for an endowed theatre, for a playhouse not dependent for its existence on a single performer or on long runs. Theatres of this kind exist in France and in Germany. Probably they will soon be established in Great Britain and the United States. Just how soon this will be depends on the length of time needed to lead Londoners and New Yorkers to take the theatre seriously.

Victor Hugo was victor in many fields, but it is in criticism that he was least successful. Two of his plays still keep the stage in France, and two at least of his novels are still read widely here in America; and nobody would deny that he was the greatest lyric poet that has illuminated the French language, more affluent than any other and more varied. For history and for criticism he was less fitted by temperament. Intensely personal in his views, seeing literature solely from the standpoint of his own achievement and of his own ambition, he was quite incapable of the detached and disinterested inquiry, which criticism must needs be if it is to command respect. When he published, in 1829, the unactablé play of *Cromwell*—planned perhaps for Talma's acting, but after the great tragedian's death turned into a mere drama for the closet—he prefixed to it an essay in which he laid down the laws of literary art as he wanted them to be obeyed. This preface to *Cromwell* was the Declaration of Independence of the revolting Romanticists, and as such its importance is far greater than that of the very juvenile play which it precedes. A French professor of literature, M. Maurice Souriau, has now treated this interesting literary document with the reverent affection it demands. He has edited it with all the care he would bestow on the treatise of Aristotle or the poem of Horace or the poem of Pope (with which indeed its kinship is closer). He prints the text of the preface (omitting wholly the play itself), revising this by the manuscript and the corrected proof sheets. He considers in an introduction the present value of Hugo's theories, the circumstances under which the essay was composed, and the various influences—Greek, Roman, Italian, Spanish, German, English, and French—which left their traces upon it. Then in notes to the text he verifies Hugo's quotations, explains Hugo's allusions, and elucidates Hugo's statements where more light seemed to be needed. The remorseless tooth of Time is already gnawing at Hugo's complete works, and few of them will escape altogether. But that one of his earliest writings, in a department of literature in which he is feeblest, should be edited now less than fifteen years after his death, as though it was to be ranked with the masterpiece of Boileau, this is proof enough, were any needed, of the towering position Victor Hugo holds in French literature.

Some day, it may be, a remote disciple will do for Hugo what has now been done by a pious hand for Molière. Some ten years ago, when the present writer was working in the archives of the Comédie-Française, he suggested to the learned librarian, M. Georges Monval, that a biographer of Molière would find his labour lightened if all the known facts and dates of the great

French dramatist's life and all the allusions to his acts were drawn up in chronological order. The editor of the *Molièriste* smiled and said, "*C'est fait!* I have it almost done." And what M. Monval had almost done ten years ago he has only now published. It is not too much to say that this little book is one of the most serviceable tools which has ever been put into the hands of a student of French literature, and that it is worth a dozen volumes of criticism and commentary. Chronology is the backbone of biography as of history, and to seize clearly the sequence of events in a man's career is a condition precedent to a proper understanding of his works. As M. Monval points out, there are still long years of Molière's life as to which we have scarcely any knowledge at all, in spite of the indefatigable research of ardent antiquaries; but after the great dramatist came back to Paris and performed before the king, it is easy to follow him almost day by day. This is what M. Monval has done, setting down every date with the most scrupulous exactitude, from the marriage of Molière's parents, in 1621, to the death of Molière's daughter, in 1723. Often the mere conjunction of dates is strangely suggestive, as when we see that the year of Molière's birth was the year when Richelieu became cardinal, when Corneille left school, and when Harvey made his great discovery. The method M. Monval has here employed most adroitly and skilfully to give us the skeleton of Molière's life will certainly be applied by other students to the lives of other great men. For Shakespeare the facts are too few, and perhaps for Dante also; but who will first attempt the chronology of Goethe?

Brander Matthews.

HIS GRACE OF OSMONDE.*

In giving a second version of this amazing tale, Mrs. Burnett has done a daring thing. Whether the result justifies her courage remains to be seen.

It is offered as the man's side of a story of which the woman's side has already been told, and should therefore be judged as nearly as possible from a new standpoint.

This seems at the outset to be easy enough. Anything more unlike the environment which from Clorinda's first hour crushes her "like an iron shroud" can scarcely be conceived. This man-child Roxholme is born of an ideal marriage, heir to the good that ought to be every human being's birthright; inheriting beauty and largeness of body and mind, with strength and sweetness of spirit, and so comes welcome and blessed into a world made safe and warm by goodness and love.

He stands, in a word, for the Perfect Man. He has all humanity's highest virtues, without the smallest of its vices. He holds his own great beauty as nature, regarding the ugliness of other men as disease. He is always the defender of the weak against the strong, and by the might of his giant strength he keeps even himself—even his own soul and body—unspotted from the world; and a greater thing than this surely no mortal man can do. Mere mention of it stirs memories of the greatest of all, the gentlest knight that ere sat in hall 'mongst dames and the sternest foe that e'er put lance in rest.

Having so conceded the supreme loftiness of the author's ideal, there may be fair question as to whether it has been attained. It almost seems so when Roxholme first steps out of the dark background of Clorinda's life and stands alone in the light. He has been drawn so big and with such bold strokes that one hardly realises at once how far off he really is. But gradually the gigantic figure becomes adjusted to its true perspective, and with Clorinda's reappearance it begins to recede, resuming by degrees its old subordinate place. Much continues to be said about him throughout, but he is never again actually seen or felt. Nor is his voice recognised in the many things that are said for him; so that after a very few pages this man's side of a story of which the woman's side has already been told becomes rather a Punch and Judy show.

Again, as before, the "Lady of Quality" dominates "His Grace of Osmonde," for whatever the questions concerning the

* His Grace of Osmonde. By Frances Hodgson Burnett. New York: Charles Scribner's Sons. $1.50.

character of Clorinda—moral and otherwise—there can never be any doubt of her vivid reality. And so it is that the new work soon assumes, notwithstanding the almost painfully strenuous efforts of the author, much of the feeling and many of the phrases of a twice-told tale. The work is firmer and perhaps finer than before; one usually does a thing better, if not more interestingly, the second time; but the divergencies from the familiar line of the narrative show slight seams and patches, and the most significant changes are rather too distinctly in the nature of concessions. Having once had the courage of one's convictions, it seems more consistent as well as more artistic to stand to one's guns. But Mrs. Burnett has either been shaken by the storm of protest or she has at last come to admit, as most women and many men have long ago admitted, that Clorinda might almost more readily be forgiven for killing her lover than her husband for not suspecting the truth. At all events, she yields, and in the new work he does suspect at an early stage. But he does not know, and the second important concession is letting him overhear Clorinda's confession beside her sister's deathbed. He does not flinch—that is, the voice speaking for him says he stands firm, justifying Clorinda in what she did; saying he could have found it in himself to have done the same. And then having but fairly entered the breech, the author's battery is silenced, and the whole battle floats off in smoke, leaving the real cause of the conflict untouched. For while Clorinda's forced confession and late repentance look a long way toward the solution of the problem of murder in sudden heat and passion, there is no nearer approach to the other great problem lying still deeper in the heart of the story—the problem of what a proud, honourable gentleman shall do when his wife comes to him in silence without womanhood's crown. Face to face at last with this burning question, the author, the Lady and His Grace recoil and fall dumb, as the wisest and the bravest have always done. So that, after all, nothing vital seems to have come from this hearing of the man's side of a story of which the woman's side has already been told.

George Preston.

A TALE OF COLONIAL NEW YORK.*

This new story by a new feminine writer (for the ambiguous signature cannot conceal the writer's sex) is a most welcome and refreshing addition to the romantic school of fiction which is once more appearing among us, and which almost deserves to be called a renaissance of healthy novel-writing. It is pleasant to be able to welcome and commend a new voice that speaks clearly and convincingly amid the inharmonious clamour of latter-day story-tellers. There is in Miss Rayner's manner of writing no suggestion of the halting and uncertain amateur. Her style is mature and definite, and she gives evidence of having satisfactorily mastered the technical and mechanical side of her art, of having conquered the difficulties of literary construction before she has chosen to elaborate her plot and characters and given them to the public as a finished piece of work. *Free to Serve* is most creditably free from the usual characteristics of a first book. It is more than "promising," for it fulfils many of the ideals of good novel-writing.

Miss Rayner has chosen a picturesque setting and period for her tale, the New York colonies in the early days of the eighteenth century. The scene opens dramatically, and almost in the manner of a prologue, in England, with swords and periwigs and all the eighteenth-century paraphernalia. The writer describes the departure of a brother and sister of gentle birth, who leave their dearly loved ancestral home to seek their fortunes across the seas in the New World. The brother, Fulke Nevard, is a wild young man about town, who has got himself so deeply in debt that it requires all the savings of his sister and himself to keep him from prison and enable him to sail away from his old life toward possible improvement in the American colonies. Through the weakness and secrecy of her brother in not confessing the full extent of his financial misfortunes, Aveline finds herself, on the arrival of their vessel in New York, forced to go into service as a bondwoman in order to pay the captain for her passage. Fulke tries every means to prevent this, but for once his self-con-

* Free to Serve. A Tale of Colonial New York. By E. Rayner. Boston: Copeland & Day. $1.50.

fidence is futile in its results, and Aveline, during her brother's absence in Albany in search of aid, is sold into bondage for a term of five years. She goes into the service of a Dutch lady, who, with her husband and two sons, lives in a manor-house on the banks of the Hudson. From them Aveline receives great kindness and affection, and is made to feel herself a daughter of the house rather than a maid. Both sons fall in love with her of course. They are rather of the fairy-story order of young men—the elder hot-blooded, impetuous, and unprincipled, the younger courageous, gentle, and good. Aveline bestows her affections on Helmer, the younger. Then follow many adventures, including the unjust accusation of Helmer for murder, his brother Geysbert's treachery, the death of their parents, the return of Fulke Nevard, and the final happy solution of all difficulties by the marriage of Aveline and Helmer, and the betrothal of Geysbert to his little Puritan cousin who has always loved him.

The close of the book suggests the ending of a play, which, though it has had melodramatic moments, is yet inevitable comedy. All the characters step to the footlights hand-in-hand, smiling and bowing. Sir Julian and Lady Betty Nevard, the uncle and aunt who had the early bringing up of their niece and nephew in England, come to America apparently for the express purpose of joining the happy group on the last page of the story. Fulke Nevard is sobered and softened by his trials, and may be considered a reformed character, while Geysbert Feljer, who at one time seemed almost competent to act the villain of the piece, vows repentance, is forgiven by all, and begins life over again. We do not much care whether these happy changes would have been wrought in real life or not. This story is not a psychological study, but a blending of the romantic and the probable, of the real and the unlikely; it is a story of adventure so well told that the conventional ending, "and they all lived happily ever after," seems the only fitting and consistent one.

The conditions of life in the old colonial days, the half-barbaric, half-poetic surroundings of the early settlers, are presented with picturesqueness and careful attention to historical correctness, and is something more than a mere background for incident and action. The character of Aveline Nevard is beautifully given, and her high spirit and courage and humanising humour make her a creature of flesh and blood; but occasionally the author, as well as the reader, forgets that her heroine dates from 1701, not from 1897. But these lapses are only occasional, and the spirit of the early colonial days pervades the book, though the robustness of life is somewhat softened by the delicacy and refinement of the feminine pen. If the book has a fault as a whole—and it is not easy to criticise a story which leaves such a pleasant impression—we should say that the 434 pages might, perhaps, have been condensed to a hundred or so less. It does not deserve to be called padded, and it is hard to say where the pruning-knife should be applied without our losing more than we should gain.

One of the great charms of this book is its unpretentiousness and sincerity. It contains no rhetorical fireworks or extravagant phrase-making from the happy title to the quietly dramatic ending. The style is in keeping with the simple strong days described, and by making no claim to be considered a Great Book, it may the more cordially be called—what is hardly less important in this era of fiction—a capital story, well told.

Fanny H. Quincy.

TENNYSON: A MEMOIR.*

So at last it has come to this. A great man is forced to publish his memoirs in self-defence. Not at all by way of apologia, or protest; but simply to forestall and countermine unauthorised versions. Tennyson, who all his life shrank from advertisement, nay, resented bitterly every intrusion on his privacy, wished that no life of him should appear. And this not merely from temperament, but probably from matured judgment. With his singular strong sense he must have felt that a life so private, so domestic, so reclusive, so uneventful, appealed to no lawful curiosity, and promised no commentary upon

* Alfred Lord Tennyson: A Memoir. By his son, Hallam Lord Tennyson. In 2 vols. New York: The Macmillan Co. $10.00.

his works beyond the bare fact that it was what it was, and what the world had long known it to have been. But he was powerless against the new Inquisition, and consented that his heir should publish his official *dossier*. "However, he wished," says his son, "that if I deemed it better, the incidents of his life should be given as shortly as might be without comment, but that my notes should be final and full enough to preclude the chance of further and unauthentic biographies." What was meant by "notes" is not quite clear, but the biographer, on whom rested the responsibility of a plenary discretion, has not followed strictly the poet's suggestion.

Now what should be the memoir of Tennyson which could satisfy him and his—for his we all are who love poetry and revere genius? This. Fifty pages—or at most a hundred—of prose fine as his verse, of prose simple, melodious, pure and purposeful—the prose of Goldsmith; and on this the "incidents of his life" should be strung with all the grace and charm of reverent sympathy, though "as shortly as might be, and without comment." So much for the Man, and no more; for the Poet an ampler portrayal. Without prying too much into the secrets of his craft, we would fain become conversant with every scene and incident which kindled and fed and tempered his poetic flame. All that may be known we would know of the purpose, the inspiration, and the working out of his greatest works; his bibliography and literary history should be handled finally and conclusively; the development of his own self-criticism traced side by side with that of his popularity. For criticism or interpretation of his poems no place remains; that is the province, not of the biographer, but of the critic.

Many of these elements will be found in Lord Tennyson's work, but embedded in a mass of trivial and, in our eyes, irrelevant gossip. We shall not presume to blame him. The public insists on knowing what the poet liked for breakfast, when he caught cold, and what casual remarks he and his callers made on weighty subjects about which their opinion is without special authority. And if Lord Tennyson did not supply these details, some one else would and with less veracity and good taste. A thousand pages—albeit the print is large—are overmuch; were they fewer, perchance some interloper would advertise a "full and complete Life." Perhaps, too, this wealth of domestic trivialities may render the publication of a "Real Lord Tennyson" impossible. The work has small pretensions to concinnity of structure or style. Though the author says, and no doubt truly, that he has tried to efface himself, he has not always succeeded. In the narrative chapters we are too often conscious of his inexperience or defective sense of proportion in the curtness and vagueness of the important sentence and the prolixity of the more trivial connecting matter. This vagueness—the preface is especially nebulous and empty—is partly due to his habit of weaving into his sentences scraps of his father's poems, which, apart from the context, are singularly confusing. Once upon a time our fathers who sat under the Kembles used to lard their style with scraps and orts of Shakespeare. The practice is happily extinct. Yet though it makes for obscurity, we do not upbraid the author with having learnt unconsciously to think in the words of his illustrious father, which to him are naturally more familiar and suggestive than to us. If the book as it goes on tends more and more to a *Tennyson and his Times* of the usual gossiping type, Professor Sidgwick and Professor Palgrave share the responsibility of "selection from upward of 40,000 letters." Many that appear from no point of view deserved printing in full with formal address and superscription. The copious extracts from the poet's and his wife's diaries and travel notes are often too trivial and domestic for publication. But the literary demerits of the work are, after all, its practical merits. Though the author and printer do not spare the paper, the varied and countless scraps of material succeed one another without joints or comments, in a stolid, business-like way that is really very convenient and comfortable. Lord Tennyson is always quite serious about it, and anxious to get as much as he can into his thousand pages. Some valuable papers on Tennyson contributed by various hands are printed in full as appendices. And finally the index is so excellent that we find it the pleasantest guide to the book. Infinite pains have been taken to render this labour of filial love, what it undoubtedly is, the final, full, authoritative life of the great Laureate. In the future many more brilliant, or sympathetic, or profound studies of that life may appear, but they can be only abridgments of this, nor will they dare to palter with its magisterial testimonies. For five years we have trembled for the poet's honour lying at the mercy of the *valetaille*; was it to be puffed up to shameful collapse, or vulgarised by sordid commonplace, or smirched by envious spleen? Lord Tennyson has devoted himself to spare us that pain, and we offer him the personal homage of our gratitude. Let him rest assured that he has let fall no word of enthusiastic veneration which has seemed too strong to one who, while upholding Tennyson's supremacy among modern poets, is perhaps more than most alive to his deficiencies, and for one phase of his work feels not only distaste, but positive repugnance. The book is no revelation. It only confirms and justifies the faith we had based upon the poet's writings. It is no plausible apology or artful panegyric. With nothing to conceal, nothing to explain away, the author is able without the least fail of seemly reverence to set just and reasoned limits to his enthusiasm. No judgment on Tennyson's life and character has ever been, or ever will be pronounced so judicious, so discriminating, so wise and moderate, and therefore so convincing as that suggested by the son, who of all living men knew the poet best, and whose whole life had moved under his controlling influence; nor shall our narrowing space prevent us from quoting it in full. "If I may venture," he says, "to speak of his special influence over the world, my conviction is, that its main and enduring factors are his power of expression, the perfection of his workmanship, his strong common sense, the high purport of his life and work, his humility, and his open-hearted and helpful sympathy."

The book is a mine of ore, some rich, some worthless. To throw up a few random spadefuls in this brief article were sorry work, when so many suggestive points are each tempting us to a lengthy essay. Tennyson's life we need touch at one point only, that which alone aroused criticism. The outcry against his peerage has died down; these memoirs should prevent its revival. The offer was Mr. Gladstone's idea; and his unrivalled experience and knowledge of what was fit and seemly should have been enough for the public. It was no question of a rubbishy "compliment to literature," like the baronetcies doled out to political journalists and pushing novelists. Nor was it a new-fangled "prize scheme" to encourage poetry. Mr. Gladstone never meant to fool the young recruit, slinking to the Row with his first epic, into the belief that he carried a coronet in his knapsack. Yet both these delusions were rife. Unchecked, to what would they tend? To a cry of injustice if a peerage were some day refused to an Otway, or Savage, or Goldsmith, or Burns of the future. We might easily have a poet of splendid genius and vast popularity who would be impossible as a peer; say a man of low birth, of disreputable or even criminal connections, with a wife who had "no marriage lines to show," and a progeny of neglected brats—the heir to the barony perhaps already in Holloway Gaol; a genial, tipsy visionary, unkempt, unwashed, innocent of politics and the great world, his great gains all squandered—in short, a splendid bankrupt in mind, body, and estate. Prime Ministers understand these matters better than the journalists. Lord Macaulay was not merely a popular writer, but a distinguished statesman and Indian official. Lord Tennyson was a man of good family and excellent connections, of the highest university breeding, of irreproachable and dignified life, an aristocrat of the best patriarchal type, yet a Liberal who had sympathised with and often voiced the progressive feeling of his day. He had ample means to support, and worthy descendants to transmit the title. The distinguishing favour of the Queen, and the confidence of some of her ablest statesmen were his; scarce one of the great men of England, nay, almost of the world, but sought and valued his acquaintance or friendship. Though gifted with no power of original or profound thought, he had a good practical head, and with his conscientious thoroughness had acquired a sound knowledge of most political and scientific questions. There was nothing, at least in his later days, visionary or hysterical in his opinions, which would probably have carried weight in either House of Parliament. True, he was a poet also, and in the public eye only and above all, a poet. But as such he had long held and illustrated an ancient office in the royal court, and somehow always seemed a great officer of State—the Queen's Poet, the Nation's Poet—rather than the Poet of the publishers and their customers. But what Mr. Gladstone probably saw, and was the first to see, was that Tennyson was not only a born poet, but a born noble. As a boy, the spell of *noblesse oblige* was laid upon him. His modest simplicity of heart, his self-respecting pride, his scorn of little ends and base means, his ardent thirst for achievement, his worship of the far-off ideal of pure and high and noble life, and his inspired faith that courage must at last attain it —what was all this but the spirit of the young knights of old? In any other calling this man could never have been less than great—as a sailor, a Nelson, as a soldier, a Gordon. And when he was grown famous, how lordly and dignified was his modest life. It was a real court he held at Farringford, the life which great nobles may enjoy in their private apartments, when the gorgeous state rooms are shut up. Not, indeed, an atmosphere overcharged with high-pressure intellect; no shrine of courtly elegance or brilliant wit; nor yet the sumptuous, soul-satisfying palace of our modern painter-princes. No, its stately dignity lay in that proud seclusion, that wholesome domesticity, that household order and decency, that marked our English territorial families, who, resting on their acres and pedigrees, could afford to live sanely and nobly, and follow their natural instinct. It is fine to notice that not only did Tennyson never think of pushing himself, but what is more, never once dreamt that he needed pushing. And then the man himself! that commanding figure, that stately mien, that noble, impressive face that would have graced the court of Elizabeth or Philip II., and inspired the brush of Velasquez! Yes, Mr. Gladstone was quite right.

Thus far a single point has led us, and no space left for other incidents of his life, such as his interesting correspondence with the Queen—nor even for his beautiful euthanasy. Of Tennyson's poetical career, of the many literary criticisms which this book has suggested, we have said nothing; some of them we may possibly treat hereafter. But before leaving his life, perhaps it should be pointed out that, so far as we know, gossip has busied itself with only three frailties of the poet. First, the cloak. Well, it was not good—too Spanish, and yet not Spanish enough; and it did not go well with the collar and tie. But let the cloak and hat drop for the present, though they are really food for an essay—they are hardly sins. Secondly, a certain "gruffness," or testiness of manner. Well, was not Johnson a little gruff at times? Tennyson's "gruffness" was a jest in early days with Hallam and FitzGerald, so it was no later affectation. It is plain that those who knew him, saw in it only a strain of British sincerity, like Carlyle's growls, and probably an occasional reaction from his over-strung poetical imagination. The charge disappears before the universal testimony to his warmth and tenderness of heart. Lastly, it has been said that he was a keen hand at a bargain, and no poet in money matters. But so was Shelley. And what of that? It is very well for the rich, bachelor poet who is alone in the world, to take no thought for the morrow, and despise lucre. Any thought of meanness or over-reaching was repugnant to Tennyson's whole nature, and if at any time he may have been a little hard to deal with, it must have been due to his constitutional suspicion of the trading classes (as shown in his *Maud* and elsewhere), to his passion for justice, and to an English tenacity in claiming his lawful rights. Against what great memory have so few charges, and so trivial, been brought? Tennyson was not half eccentric enough: he would have been more perfect if he had had more imperfections.

Y. Y.

A HERO IN HOMESPUN.*

The worst thing about this book is its preface. The author announces his work as a novel with a purpose, and that purpose not primarily, it would seem, to give its readers wholesome and artistic entertainment, but "to extend popular knowledge of the Civil War as it affected a large, but almost unrecog-

* A Hero in Homespun. A Tale of the Loyal South. By William E. Barton. Illustrated by Dan Beard. Boston: Lamson, Wolffe & Co. $1.50.

nised body of our people." He goes on to conscientiously warn off the enormously preponderating class of readers who read fiction for the sake of being amused, by declaring that "the form of fiction has been employed to permit a larger use of incident and personal experience, and to allow greater freedom of treatment;" all of which tends to prepare one for a mass of excellent history diluted with dull fiction, and for a group of wooden puppets stiffly endeavouring to move like a romancer's living characters.

Fortunately, however, few but professional critics and rival authors read a man's prefaces in these days. Still more fortunately, Mr. Barton has the true *raconteur's* enthusiasm, and his fiction carries his history along with it; his characters are live men and women; and the story would still be a good story if its history were all pure invention. When a purpose-novelist can fairly forget his purpose in the sweep of his narrative, then, and then only, can he afford to write with a purpose. The purpose becomes harmless. It may please those people who are pleased by that sort of thing; it may, incidentally, do a lot of good in one direction or another; but it ceases to trouble those readers who, reading for pleasure, are not concerned by problems. Mr. Barton, fortunately, after taking infinite pains to have his history, his background, and his local colour accurate, becomes so interested in his story and his characters, that he seems to forget his avowed purpose. In this way he has given us a story which seems to have been written for its own sake, and is to be read with delight for its own sake; while at the same time it succeeds in throwing new and vivid light upon events in American history which have been altogether too much ignored or misunderstood.

The hero in homespun is a splendid specimen of those mountaineers of Eastern Tennessee who have always been conspicuous for their patriotism, independence of character, and loyalty to the Union. When Tennessee joined the Southern Confederacy, the eastern section of the State remained stubbornly Federal in its sympathies. This was the region that supplied the Union with such indomitable and belligerent champions as Andrew Johnson and William G. Brownlow. Had the mountaineers been better understood by the Washington Government, had their loyalty been trusted as it deserved, Eastern Tennessee might have been, at the beginning of the trouble, set off as a separate State, like Western Virginia, and much bloodshed might have been spared. Longstreet's vain and ruinous assaults on Fort Sanders, the murderous struggle of Lookout Mountain, and several lesser but yet disastrous battles would in all probability have been averted. The overwhelming plurality of the Union votes in Eastern Tennessee should have indicated to the Washington Government the course to be taken in that district. All of which Mr. Barton shows us with convincing incisiveness.

The plot of the novel is a simple love affair between the hero in homespun and a pretty Kentucky girl, who appears upon the scene in the opening chapter, during the "Frolic at Hanson's," and safely marries her tall lover at the end of the last chapter. There is a dangerous rivalry which makes trouble from time to time, and there is also a rather unnecessary flirtation on the part of the hero, out of which he is extricated more smoothly than he deserves. But the love affair is kept in the background throughout long stretches of the tale, while the hero follows his star through innumerable adventures and perils, to win at last much honourable distinction, and a captain's rank before he wins his bride. Looking back upon the story, the critic perceives it to be loose in construction and somewhat awkward in evolution. But the interest is strongly sustained from page to page by the vividness with which the life of the mountaineers, their speech, their prejudices and passions, their customs, costumes, and personal appearance are brought before our view, a living, swiftly changing panorama. The book is crowded with battles, escapes, personal encounters, and all the lively incident that the reader can assimilate. It is pervaded, at the same time, by strong human feeling, pathos, and wholesome sentiment. There is a subtle suggestion of the first-mentioned quality in the following passage:

"They were not all saints, those East Tennesseeans, and now and then they looted a store When they did so, the first thing to be stolen, not even excepting the whiskey and tobacco, was the stock of baby shoes, which they tucked away in their knapsacks to take home to the little ones that rarely owned a shoe."

To sum up, *A Hero in Homespun* is a thoroughly interesting, red-blooded, virile story, and at the same time a historical document of the very greatest value. The author's conscientious investigation has cleared up points long under dispute. Historic characters, whose portraits cannot be spared from the nation's annals, are here delineated in vigorous strokes. A changing phase of life, conditions which are rapidly passing away, are here caught and crystallised. The author and artist together went over the scenes of the story, studying and questioning the people, and Mr. Dan Beard's spirited illustrations are no less trustworthy than Mr. Barton's narrative.

Charles G. D. Roberts.

BRANDER MATTHEWS'S SHORT STORIES.*

In the group of American fictionists who are doing earnest, honest, and skilful work in portraying the many phases of life to be found in New York City, Brander Matthews has come to occupy an honourable place. Both in the short story and the novel he has made studies that for quiet, unobtrusive truth and accurate yet atmospheric handling of the material, call for admiration. His latest contribution, *Outlines in Local Colour*, a dozen sketches of Manhattan, deepens one's sense of obligation to a writer who has steadily progressed in fictional art and broadened in his sympathies. Professor Matthews is a realist in the true sense of that hard-ridden word; his scenes and characters have the verisimilitude of actuality, with that selective instinct and sense of proportion which result in convincing the reader and charming him as well. It is impossible to go through this volume without being instructed in the great drama of human existence. It matters not at all that only glimpses and moments of life are presented, that commonplace folk are on the boards in the play, and that the detail is photographic. The little narratives are true, they are attractive; when that is said, all is said. The style is a model of ease, simplicity, and naturalness; it is, what it should be, a lucid medium to convey the idea. Next to never does a word like *lightsome*, which has a smack of literary self-consciousness, bring one up with a jar. The writer knows his New York thoroughly and loves it, too. Familiar with this *locale*, so rich for the purposes of the perceptive, sympathetic maker of fiction, he has the good sense to stick to it, sure that it is an exhaustless mine to work, and that he will extract therefrom his most precious ore.

A great variety of types is presented. We pass from the fashionable drawing-room to the corner bar-room; we hear the talk of upper society, of the horse-show, and that of the cook, the chambermaid, and the butler below-stairs. We see as through a peep-hole a suggestion of the work of the journalist, the playwright, and the actor. We are on Madison Square with a pair of up-town lovers, or on the Battery with lovers less exclusive, but quite as much in earnest. The street musician, the trained nurse, the homeless vagrant, and the Salvation Army shouter enlist our interest in turn, and are flesh-and-blood creatures all, fellows in the great fight. There is both light and shade, laughter and tears; the situations are never theatric, but, rather, inevitable with the unprejudiced inevitability of Life itself. In the best of these outlines—a word well indicating the author's method—in that very strong and truthful sketch, "The Vigil of McDowell Sutro," with its vivid description of a night spent perforce out of doors by a penniless Westerner; or "The Solo Orchestra," happy in title and delightfully heartful in feeling; or such things as "An Irrepressible Conflict" and "In the Watches of the Night," delicately conducted variants of the eternal love motive, Professor Matthews gives us fiction that is altogether satisfactory. To cavil at it argues, it seems to us, insensitiveness to the many-voiced appeal of humanity. The poetry of it all is just as evident as the realism. The dialogue, where dialogue is used, has the light touch and the accent of verity which give a colloquialism that is neither smart nor vulgar. Professor Matthews has learned a fact important to the novelist: that slang, so called, is idiom in the making. We can think of no stu-

* Outlines in Local Colour. By Brander Matthews. New York: Harper & Bros. $1.25.

dent of Eastern city life who is more the master of this adjunct of his art. The stories are done with such apparent ease, there is so little attempt at plot for plot's sake, that the careless or shallow may rise from a perusal of the book, thinking it a slight performance. A more grievous mistake could not be made. To suggest much in little is in fiction very difficult; *Outlines in Local Colour* does this and does it triumphantly. It is not realism in the narrow or unpleasant sense that we are given, but realism walking hand in hand with romance. Such fiction, based on the most careful, keen-eyed observation and study, controlled and shaped by a fine art, and warmed and humanised by a genuine democratic sympathy for all sorts and conditions of men, is of the finest efflorescence of the story-maker's craft. Professor Matthews is a worthy member of a school of which Mr. Howells is the natural head—a school which will receive its true praise and place only when some historian of the future discovers the value of the social documents left by these writers in revealing our age in its habit as it lived.

Richard Burton.

THE BETH BOOK.*

The uncovering of sewers may be endured when the temporary exposure looks toward lasting relief; but when there is no such justification, when merciful covers are ruthlessly torn off without the remotest prospect of improvement—or even of getting them back—it certainly seems time to protest.

It may therefore now be complained that again in *The Beth Book*, as before in *The Heavenly Twins*, Madame Grand makes an unjustifiable showing of uncleanness with scarcely a suggestion of remedy or so much as a claim to be giving information. No thinking man or woman need be told anything that *The Beth Book* tells. The loftiest soul aiming at the stars cannot go far along life's journey without gathering knowledge of these terrible things hidden by the way. A few are fortunate to see them only in the distance; many, less lucky, come close to them through bitter experience; the happiest may not hope to escape wholly, and the fuller the saddening acquaintance, the greater the shrinking from meeting in fiction horrors too well known in life. For those who think most deeply and work most earnestly for humanity's betterment do not, as a rule, march with drums.

The Beth Book makes such a noise that it almost stuns. There is an alarmed sensation of being overwhelmed by some huge, shifting mass, and smothered by a great cloud of dust. Gradually, however, it resolves itself into an hysterical statement of many undisputed truths relating mainly to the eternal sex problem, and accompanied by statistics belonging to a medical journal rather than to a work of fiction.

If the work may be considered as a novel, Beth stands of course at the centre, with her character and her career alone to bind the mass into something approaching a definite form. But the author has not realised her own evident conviction that Beth's character is rare, and that her career is typical. There is never a perfectly clear, steady view of her, it is true—there is too much dust—but such glimpses as are granted reveal an unpleasant and rather commonplace young woman whose trials are more often Life's just response to unwomanly hardness, morbid egotism, and cold-blooded selfishness than sex theorists, like Madame Grand, might be willing to admit. Why, Beth's brutal husband is more human than she! He wanders after strange gods only when she has repulsed him—as better men have done under similar circumstances—and no woman having half her pretentions to intelligence could have been surprised, however much she might have felt aggrieved. He is also brutally honest in this open transfer of his affections. There is none of the bloodless hypocrisy shown in Beth's own shameless philandering—a creepy travesty of passion. Well might it be said that "her pose is to reform men, to reform them away from their wives," as the book says of another woman however, for Beth is the only flawless pearl. There is something so monstrous about the whole situation that almost anything might be forgiven Beth if she would only once show warmth enough to endow a fish.

And is *this*, then, the Ideal Woman for

* The Beth Book. By Sarah Grand. New York: D. Appleton & Co. $1.50.

whom we have all been waiting since the advent of *The Heavenly Twins?* Is this really the emancipator who has arrived at last to strike off the shackles of sex, and to right all wrongs that women have suffered since Eve? And is this *how* it is to be done? By holding a lifelong grudge against her mother for having more children than she can care for, and never trying to help her; by being without affection for her brothers and sisters, regarding them as usurpers of her own rights; by being disliked by her schoolmates and dreaded by her teachers; by never having a friend of her own sex, and by making her interest in the "problem" offensively evident through her earliest association with boys; by marrying the first man who asks her, not because she loves him, but in order that she may have her own way; by turning against her husband for holding views that she does not approve; by scoffing at religion and most of the holy things which are women's surest safeguards; by seeking congenial companionship among men, not misled by love as far nobler women have been, but by a cold, cruel purpose, like a ghastly vivisection of sentiment; by being absolutely without the capacity for loving—without tenderness, or goodness, or gentleness, or patience, or unselfishness, or charity, or mercy, or any of the beautiful spirit of true womanhood.

If this be indeed the Modern Woman, this Beth, who "arose early and drew up the plan of her life," let us beg the antique woman to stay. Let us entreat on our knees, if need be, that she will go on living and letting men live according to the old plan that Nature, if anybody, drew! Meantime, pending the dreaded change, let us keep our social sewers covered as closely as possible until such time as we see our way to make them clean.

N. H. B.

DARIEL: A ROMANCE OF SURREY.*

It has been said that no one can write a love story beyond forty. Melody in music, and in literature love-songs go with youth; thus Wagner in his later days had to invent *leit motifs*, and the novelist resorts to humour to oil the dryness of his sentiment. We will suppose Mr. Blackmore a little (not much) beyond forty—and that is all that separates his *Dariel* from *Lorna Doone*. But a few years; and yet he views George Cranleigh's rapid passion more humorously than he would have done of yore.

Another difficulty than that of years has our romancer set himself—to make a romance out of Surrey, and in our own time. The attraction of locality is to readers very great; any Anglo-Saxon who has in his heart the love of the lay of the land cannot grow tired of good stories twining and growing about the denes and uplands of a goodly bit of country. If the tale be modern, so much the nearer home, and (the critic may say) so much the greater *tour de force*—for your bicycle girl will belittle a countryside as a railway grade dwarfs a slope of moorland. And no one since Scott has storied a countryside so well as Blackmore; if Scott was far the greater humanist, as his century made natural, Blackmore is better in the things of his own. For we of the nineteenth have grown a bit tired of people, since Di Vernon and the Dougal creature became extinct, and revive at the scent of the land and a touch of weather.

Yet even Blackmore can't quite invent a tale all Surrey for the century end. The scenery and the weather and the politics are all good Surrey, but the plot is of the Caucasus; and the only action takes place among the snows and eyries Verestchagin has painted, and we have here the impression they make on English eyes. Then there is a blood feud and some elegant fighting; and a capital fellow to do it, Strogue by name, and an excellent stock-broker who stays at home, Jackson Stoneman, and the hero himself to furnish the humour—for who but one that Mark Twain calls the "chuckle-headed hero of romance" (Mark makes it heroine, but they are not half so chuckle-headed as the men) would make possible a whole Caucasian revolution by going to a wedding at the other end of England the day after a Caucasian princess had accepted him, playing best man to a pretty bridesmaid for one whole week without so much as telegraphing the excuse of sudden death (there *was* a sudden death) or even writing to his newly won a daily letter?

The fact is, Mr. Blackmore is not quite so much in love with Dariel as John

* Dariel: A Romance of Surrey. By R. D. Blackmore. New York: Dodd, Mead & Co. $1.50.

Ridd was with Lorna Doone; nor is Surrey, despite its beechwoods and some goodly hills, quite the country that was Devonshire or even Yorkshire. The romance, then, is not quite so strong as that of *Lorna* or of *Mary Anerley*, perhaps the best of Blackmore's other stories. On the other hand, the book is full of a mellow humour. Dariel, we are told, "has not learned to make a Sect of sex;" and the statement endears her to us for life. The Lesghian chief, like Costigan as an old Roman, is immense, and the villain (Queen Marva—she is a woman) is all that a villain should be, and is shot at the end of the piece. We are glad he had the courage to do it. There is a lot of Surrey scenery, if little Surrey story.

But over all is the great charm of cleanly fresh air and honest, manly humour, and a feeling that is sane and a poetry that is sound. There does not have to be any religious problem in the story to make the parsons preach against it, for there is no indecency to make the public buy it. It is a good story, resting for its interest on no "problem" and on no provinciality. There is not a Scotchman, nor a minister, nor an hysterical woman in the whole book. And though we have not heard yet that its author is coming to America on a lecture tour (there must still be some provinciality in our letters, else why does not Mr. Howells or Mr. Davis go to lecture in England?) there is hardly another English author whom one would rather see in the flesh. For he is a scholar and a gentleman.

F. J. Stimson.

AN IDEAL CHILD'S BOOK.*

In the "Literary Note" (with which the publishers obligingly accommodate the weary critic nowadays) accompanying *The Adventures of Mabel*, it is stated that "these are simply stories told in such a way as really to interest children of five or six years of age," and, remarkable as it may seem, the statement is actually true. For why? Well, as a paterfamilias, we tried it on a five-year-old and a seven-year-old, and in each case the stories and pictures worked like a charm. It was noticeable, too, that each child had her own favourite story; the five-year-old preferring "The Giant's Castle," and the seven-year-old "The Animal Party." The reason for this is partly explained, we suppose, by the appeal of the Giant's talk, "writ large," to the quick perceptions and budding imagination of the younger, and in the case of the older the preference may have arisen from the quickened sympathy and love of pets aroused by the wonderful "animal party." To give an example of the former, this is how Mabel is greeted by the Giant:

> "WHAT HAVE YOU THERE?" he bellowed; and Mabel nearly fainted when she heard his tremendous voice.
>
> "A playmate for the Lady Elsie," answered Mabel's man.
>
> "OH!" roared the Giant; and he smiled a smile six feet long. He was evidently very much pleased.
>
> "GOOD!" he continued. "SHOW HER UP TO THE NURSERY." And he banged the window down again and went away.

Of course any ordinary, keen-eyed child, even if unable to read, has sufficient imaginative perception to recognise the Giant's big voice printed in capitals, and to have its fancy tickled by it as it follows the reader of the story. But the animal party!

> First of all came Rex, trotting down from the stable. . . . Scarcely had he taken his place when Towser trotted in, with his tail in the air. . . . Next came the Goat, and soon after the Gray Rat. . . . Presently the Mooly Cow walked in swishing off flies with her tail. . . . Next the Kitty-Cat pattered in. . . . Not long after, they heard a sharp trot, and the Little Pig ambled in. He was as clean as could be, and his tail was curled up tight over his back in his best party style. He went up to the Goat and began to talk to him about the weather. . . . Presently a sort of hippety-hop was heard, and the Green Frog appeared, his back shining in the sun. Mabel shook his damp claw and talked with him a moment, and then gave him a place next to the Grey Rat. . . . . It was nearly three o'clock.
>
> "Animals," said Mabel, "I think I ought to tell you that there is one other animal coming who will be here in a minute. . . . He is an old friend of mine, and you may be sure that he will be very, very good, so you needn't worry about him."
>
> The animals all pricked up their ears and looked interested. "Yes," added Mabel, "he will be here in a minute, and I will tell you who he is. He is a—Wolf." . . .
>
> The animals gave a big jump and looked greatly frightened . . . .
>
> "Here he is," cried Mabel . . . and just at that moment the great Wolf came moving through the grass in plain sight.

* The Adventures of Mabel. By Rafford Pyke. With illustrations by Mélanie Elisabeth Norton. New York: Dodd, Mead & Co. $1.50.

To convey the full effect of this tableau on a child's mind, the picture by Miss Norton which accompanies the text is most clever in its ingenuity, simplicity, and skill. We wish it were possible to have it reproduced here. And to a little girl of seven years of age who numbers among her pets a black cat and a gray one, a turtle and a bull-dog, who is always rescuing half-dead mice from the cruel trap, and whose home is a rendezvous for robins in summer and for stray cats and dogs innumerable in all seasons, the narrative of that animal party is as delightful a classic as was ever Greek ode or Latin oration to erudite scholar.

We must confess that with all the array and splendour of the new picture-books which are spread out in these *fin de siècle* days at this festive season for the delectation of children, we often look back with longing to the time—oh, so long ago!—when we rioted in the glory that was Bluebeard and the grandeur that was Cinderella! How our pennies were surreptitiously exchanged with a stolen delight for the cheap prints, "a penny plain and twopence coloured," setting forth the adventures of *Jack the Giant Killer, Little Red Riding Hood, Jack and the Beanstalk*, and all that glorious company! It seems as if we had only to shut our eyes to be in that storied country again where dwells the light that never was on land or sea. Too often it seems as if childhood was being robbed by our kindergartens, history picture-books, geography verses, and animal and vegetable catechisms, of its wondrous world of innocent delights and pleasures. After all, the closer we get to nature the better is it for a healthy-minded child, and the ideal child's book, both in story and in pictures, will be more like *The Adventures of Mabel* (it is for this reason we have given it prominence as an object lesson), keeping to the old themes or to themes that are not different in general spirit, while becoming more artistic in their execution. Here in these dozen stories we have our old friends, the horse, the wolf, the dog, the cat, the pig, the rat, the lizard, the brownies, the Giant, and moving among them with a charmed life "a little girl named Mabel, who lived in a cottage with her Grandma, and her brother Walter, and Jane the cook," and near them, of course, a large wood—the same old fables that have stirred the childish imagination of the individual and of the race since the world began. But into *The Adventures of Mabel* the author has infused a fresh spirit and insight, an originality of form and a subtle suggestive humour that cajoles the child into playing his little game of make-believe. For, as has been said, it is, in fact, the sub-consciousness of the fiction as fiction, the duality of thought, the underlying knowledge that the play is really nothing but a play, that so tickles a child's fancy and gives to the whole thing its greatest zest. For example, young seven-year-old rather staggered paterfamilias by proposing, after these stories were all read to her, that he should write a book like unto it and put her in "like the author did Mabel!"

As for the illustrations, they are delicious. How they excited desire and prompted a "tell me all about it" from the aforementioned five and seven-year-olds! Here, as in the text, we have an approach to an ideal child's picture-book, one whose illustrations will suggest the story that lies behind them, and at the same time will deserve respect for the adequacy of their execution. We congratulate the writer of these stories in finding so felicitous an artist to illustrate them. It may seem extravagant to say that what the Jungle Books have been to older children, *The Adventures of Mabel* should be to the little ones from five to eight years of age; but we are not afraid to have the stories stand the test. We could wish no better book to be found in the stockings of the youngsters on Christmas morning, and we submit the proposition to Santa Claus with profound respect.

Nicholas Brown.

CAPTAINS COURAGEOUS.*

We have met Mr. Kipling the educationist before now, but have never quailed under his eye for so long at a time. His latest story is addressed first to the young millionaire youth of America; but European youth with limited pocket-money cannot chuckle very loud,

* Captains Courageous. A Story of the Gr[illegible] Banks. By Rudyard Kipling. With illus[illegible] tions by J. W. Taber. New York: The Ce[illegible] tury Co. $1.50.

for some of them must certainly be included in the "unfortunate young people" who never in all their lives "received a direct order—never, at least, without long, and sometimes tearful, explanations of the advantages of obedience and the reasons for the request," and who are here warned by the tale of Harvey Cheyne, a soft-reared lad, taught the way he should go by hard living, hard work, and a rope's end. It is a new *Sandford and Merton.* Harvey—the millionaire's heir, saved from drowning by a fishing schooner—we like, as we always liked Tommy. Dan is a still smugger Harry: the amount of moral advice and virtuous example which that young man gives out is appalling. Granted that the discipline of the rope's end and hard living made a man of the spoiled child of fortune, yet the fisherman's son had evidently been frightened by an earlier course of the same into an excellence of conduct and a self-righteousness as ruinous as it was disagreeable. Disko Troop is the Mr. Barlow of an unphilosophical end of the century—an admirable preceptor, but one who finds his fists a shorter way than arguments to the reason of youth. The story is a pæan to what seems to be the strongest conviction that Mr. Kipling holds—the value of strict unreasoning discipline. It is a conviction many share, but one which, harped on outside the services, is dangerous—to discipline.

It is also a eulogy of the fishermen of the Great Banks, of the astuteness, the patience, the tenacity, the cool daring of their "Captains Courageous." We have no doubt that the book, tested by these, would prove a marvel of information and accuracy. The daily adventures in calm and gale, the slow apprenticeship to the work, the conversations of the men, the code of Bank laws, the technical phrases, are explained and described with a patience which, alas! is not contagious. If we had ever been on one of the schooners for a day, no doubt it would delight us to have the life reproduced photographically. But to outsiders it is more instructive than enticing. It all sounds very accurate; much of it is certainly very dull. The "actuality" of Mr. Kipling's former stories was not explained by mere technical correctness; imagination made his facts live, and imagination is left out here. Indeed, though the book must be the result of much difficult learning and hard experience, it has evidently no pretensions to be anything but a slight affair judged by literary standards. If it incites some lads to throw off the yoke of over-indulgent parents, and hunger after the toils that will make them men, it has hit its only mark.

BIBELOT ISSUES.*

Mr. Thomas B. Mosher, the well-known publisher of Portland, Me., is nothing if not consistent. As his manner of getting up his little volumes is unique among present-day publications, so is he unique in his manner of issuing them. Instead of giving us his choice volumes one at a time, as all other publishers do, Mr. Mosher denies us the pleasure of hearing from him during eleven months in the year, save by his little magazine, *The Bibelot,* only, however, to send us about the middle of October what is a whole year's output. If Mr. Mosher published the ordinary kind of book this method would be embarrassing to the reviewer who receives a set of Mr. Mosher's books for notice. But in this case the method suits the books.

To read the list of Mr. Mosher's books for this year must bring many recollections to a book-lover. The title of *Long Ago,* by Michael Field, in the Bibelot Series, recalls to the present writer many fruitless attempts to obtain the original edition of this rare book, as the little *Cupid and Psyche* brings back to memory the first time one read *Marius the Epicurean.* Then, again, there are Mrs. Browning's *Sonnets from the Portuguese,* Mr. Andrew Lang's exquisite poem *Helen of Troy,* which will come to Ameri-

* The Sonnets of Michael Angelo. Translated by John Addington Symonds.
Helen of Troy. By Andrew Lang.
Atalanta in Calydon.
Sonnets from the Portuguese. By Elizabeth Barrett Browning. The Old World Series. Vols. VII., VIII., IX. and X., $1.00 net each.
Long Ago. By Michael Field.
An Italian Garden. By A. Mary F. Robinson. Bibelot Series. Vols. IX. and X., $1.00 net each.
Essays from the Guardian. By Walter Pater. $2.50 net.
The Story of Cupid and Psyche Done out of the Latin of Apuleius. By Walter Pater.
The Story Without an End. From the German of F. W. Carova. By Sarah Austin.
The Centaur and the Bacchante. Two Prose Poems from the French of Maurice De Guerin. Brocade Series. Vols. IV., V. and VI., 75 cents net.

can readers almost as a new book, and a new book by Walter Pater! This last is the most interesting of all Mr. Mosher's new books. It is called *Essays from the Guardian*, and is the first volume of a series of Reprints of Privately Printed Books. In all respects the book is a fac-simile of the privately printed edition, limited to one hundred copies, which was issued in London in 1896. In addition the book contains the best portrait of Mr. Pater we have ever seen.

We have said that *Essays from the Guardian* is an interesting book, and we think no one will deny this, but at the same time we hope that it will not fall into the hands of any one who is not an ardent admirer of Pater. We should have been glad had Mr. Mosher printed on the cover of the book a warning to all would-be purchasers that only "Paterites" were allowed to buy. Then we could have given the book an unqualified welcome; for, as Mr. Edmund Gosse says in his introduction, "they are crumbs from the table of his delicate and never copious feast, and it is to the inner circle of his friends that they are here offered."

This was written to an audience which numbered but one hundred. Mr. Mosher has increased this audience by a possible four hundred and fifty, and we, for our part, are grateful to him. Nearly all of the nine essays contained in the volume have the work of a contemporary writer for their subject. Two of them treat of Mrs. Humphry Ward, one as translator, the other as the author of *Robert Elsmere;* while another is a review of Mr. Gosse's Poems. In his introduction Mr. Mosher gives a list of eleven unpublished essays by Mr. Pater. Their titles suggest that if collected they would make an even more interesting volume than the present one.

To say that a book is worthy of Mr. Mosher's imprint is sufficient recommendation to a book-lover, and none of the books before us fall below the high standard Mr. Mosher long ago set himself.

M. K.

SUB NOCTEM.

There used to be a simple song,
  A relic of the days gone by,
That in the years when we were voung
  We sang together, you and I.
It told of garden and of grove,
  Of blossoms bending on the bough,
And light, and life, and woman's love—
  Alas, we never sing it now!

For then, responsive to the strain,
  Our hearts took up its minstrelsy,
And echoed back the blithe refrain
  In all its mirthful melody.
We sang it in a careless mood
  Beneath a sunny southern sky,
While life still seemed supremely good—
  No more we sing it, you and I.

The youth that fanged its lines with fire,
  That youth has found in Time a tomb;
While slow the lagging years expire
  Like embers glowing in the gloom:
And now that life is nearly spent,
  And we are sitting here alone,
Its music seems a dumb lament,
  And tears are trembling in its tone.

H. T. P.

SOME HOLIDAY PUBLICATIONS.

The reissue in gala dress or holiday attire of the works of standard authors and of books that have gained the general suffrage of public favour is always a prominent feature in the output of publications at this season. These are quite numerous this year, and are for the most part deserving of special mention. In spite of the cut rates of the department stores and the increased enterprise in cheap and meretricious bookmaking, the workmanship bestowed on the holiday publications now before us shows no slackening of interest and care in producing the best results, often at a great and lavish expenditure, which makes one wonder sometimes with a utilitarian twist how it all pays. Foremost among these special editions ranks the new Parkman, eight volumes of which are issued, the remainder to follow at the rate of two volumes a month. That this complete edition of the works of Francis Parkman will supersede all former editions is evident when we remember that the historian revised and enlarged many of his histories up to the day of his death. The indexes have been remade, and the whole work as it will stand when completed will include each of the author's books in its final state, and thus become the definitive edition of all his writings. Portraits and pictures illustrative of the subjects of each work have been carefully reproduced in photogravure from authentic portraits, original paintings, and contemporary prints, several of which have not before been published. The bookmaking is excellent in every way, and does credit to Messrs. Little, Brown and Company, who are seeking to make in this edition an enduring memorial to the fame of America's greatest historian. Mr. John Fiske, the eminent living historian, has written an "Introductory Essay" of eighty-six pages, in which he discourses with characteristic charm and fulness of knowledge on Parkman and his work, and concludes with this noble panegyric :

"The book which depicts at once the social life of the Stone Age, and the victory of the English political ideal over the ideal which France inherited from imperial Rome, is a book for all mankind and for all time. The more adequately men's historic perspective gets adjusted, the greater will it seem. Strong in its individuality, and like to nothing else, it clearly belongs, I think, among the world's few masterpieces of the highest rank, along with the works of Herodotus, Thucydides, and Gibbon."

The work when completed will be in twenty volumes, and is issued by subscription ; there are two editions, a superb *édition de luxe*, limited to 308 numbered sets, at $10.00 per volume, and the Champlain Edition, to consist of 1225 numbered sets, at $3.50 per volume. We understand that this undertaking of the publishers has already met with a large and encouraging response.

The same firm has published a holiday illustrated edition of the book of the hour, *Quo Vadis*, reference to which has been already made in "Chronicle and Comment," where we have also reproduced the new portrait of the author, which accompanies the book. This edition will, in view of the great popularity of the work, prove an acceptable gift-book during the holidays. It is in two volumes, bound in purple cloth and richly adorned with new letter-press, with twenty-seven fine photogravure illustrations and several maps of ancient Rome and Italy, and reproductions from ancient sculptures. (Price, $6.00.) This house has also issued an illustrated edition of Mrs. Goodwin's pleasing romances of colonial Virginia—namely, *The Head of a Hundred* and *White Aprons*. The two volumes come neatly together in a box. (Price, $3.00.) To them also we owe a welcome popular edition of that mirth-provoking chronicle of an Oxford Freshman's adventures, to wit, *Verdant Green*, by Cuthbert Bede, with etched frontispiece and nearly two hundred drawings by the author. (Price, $1.50.)

Most attractive among the new editions brought out this autumn is the Riverside Edition of the complete works of Mr. Thomas Bailey Aldrich, from the press of Messrs. Houghton, Mifflin and Company. Reference has also been made at some length to this edition in "Chronicle and Comment," and a portrait of Mr. Aldrich given. In its general features the edition resembles the Riverside Edition of John Burroughs's works published last autumn, and so highly praised as one of the most satisfactory examples of the art of bookmaking in America. (In eight volumes. Price, $12.00.) From the same house we have a holiday edition of Mr. John Fiske's volume on *The Critical Period in American History 1783-1789*, illustrated in the same manner as his *American Revolution* published last year. There are 170 portraits, maps, fac-similes, and other reproductions intended to bring out the historical significance of the period. Those who have seen the holiday edition of *The American Revolution* need not to be told that these volumes are admirably finished in every respect, and make a noble ornament as well as a valuable literary addition to the library. (Price, $4.00.) Encouraged by the reception of the exquisite edition of Thoreau's *Cape Cod* issued last autumn, this firm has brought out the same author's most famous book, *Walden*, also in two volumes, and beautifully illustrated with thirty full-page pictures. (Price, $5.00.) One of the most exquisite gift-books of the season, however, will undoubtedly be the charming holiday edition of Longfellow's *Evangeline*. Ten of the most picturesque and dramatic scenes of the poem have been chosen for treatment in colour by two pupils of Mr. Howard Pyle—Miss Violet Oakley and Miss Jessie Willcox Smith. The conception and treatment of the work in colour have been highly praised by several well-known artists, and the designs, we understand, have been very faithfully reproduced in colour after careful experimenting in printing. Miss Alice M. Longfellow has written a pleasant introduction. We take pleasure in recommending this book to our readers, not only because of its seasonable attractiveness, but because of its intrinsic beauty and unique interest. (Price, $2.00.) Mr. Charles Dudley Warner's *Being a Boy*, which has gone on peacefully for over twenty years making new friends, has received the illuminating touch of Mr. Clifton Johnson's camera, and makes its entrance into the book mart once more in the green freshness of a verdant cover. Mr. Johnson's "sun-pictures" reflect the real life and heart of New England, and greatly enhance the interest of the volume. (Price, $2.00.) Another work of interest which has been brought down from the shelf and given a fresh start by Messrs. Houghton, Mifflin and Company is *Our Poetical Favourites*, a selection from the best minor poems of the English language. The new edition contains two volumes in one, and embellished with portraits and other illustrations. There is an index of first lines as well as a table of contents. Into 540 pages have been packed the poetical favourites in our tongue that from one generation to another have clung to the memory and become dear to affectionate remembrance. The book is substantially bound, and is printed in clear type on good paper. (Price, $2.00.)

A work upon which the publishers have lavished great thought and pains in making one of the most beautiful holiday productions of the season is Tennyson's *In Memoriam*, with illustrations by Mr. Harry Fenn. The poem touches so many points in foreign lands, and is so suggestive of Nature in her varying moods and seasons, that there is no lack of variety in the artistic treatment of the themes handled by the artist. The work of engraving these pictures, which are scattered over the pages in profusion, has been done with delicacy and precision. The clearness of outline, the softness of expression, the atmospheric effect of the pictures, have been rendered with execution and finish that match the unerring touch of the artist. To the engravers, the New York Engraving and Printing Company, as well as to Mr. Fenn, we are indebted for a work in which the quiet beauty of the world is reflected. Dr. Henry van Dyke, whose well-known volume on *The Poetry of Tennyson* has just been issued by the Scribners in the Cameo Edition, has written an introduction to the poem, and speaking of the peculiar character of this edition, he says: "There could be no better notes and illustrations to *In Memoriam* than the pictures of hill and meadow and garden, stream and tree and flower, which have been drawn for this volume by the hand of one whose devotion to art is the fruit of his intimacy with Nature, for he has lived with her long and loved her well." It is published by Messrs. Fords, Howard and Hulbert in a sumptuous style. (Price, $3.50.)

Besides his volume on *The Poetry of Tennyson*, the Messrs. Scribner have included Dr. van Dyke's *Little Rivers* in the Cameo Edition. Other volumes just added to this charming series are

Mr. Barrie's *Auld Licht Idylls* and *A Window in Thrums.* (Price, $1.25 per volume.) Dr. van Dyke's delightful story of *The First Christmas Tree* has also been issued in a special edition, with illustrations by Howard Pyle, and bound in an ornate cover. (Price, $1.50.) The same firm has brought out the best of Mr. Cable's work, *Old Creole Days*, in a most elaborate and beautiful form. There are eight full-page illustrations by Albert Herter, reproduced in photogravure, and the cover design is from a drawing by the same artist. Mr. Cable's finest work deserves the tribute which it has received in this special edition, and it is sure to be a favourite among the holiday books of this year. The price is $6.00, and there is also a special limited edition of 204 numbered copies on Japan paper at $12.00 net. Another book that will figure largely among this firm's holiday productions is Mr. C. D. Gibson's *London*, in a large folio 12 x 18 inches. The price of this edition is $5.00, but there is also an *édition de luxe* limited to 250 first impressions, to be sold at $10.00 net.

A second series of *Life's Comedy*, by various artists, containing nearly 150 drawings from *Life*, ought to meet with the success of the first. It is printed as handsomely and affords us an opportunity of studying and enjoying the work of some of the best-known illustrators in this field. (Price, $1.50.) Our old friend "Pomona," who owes her creation to Mr. Frank R. Stockton, has come out in a new dress in two of the books in which she cuts her capers. *Rudder Grange* and *Pomona's Travels*, illustrated profusely by Mr. A. B. Frost, have been issued in a new and cheaper edition at $1.50 each.

In the early autumn we had the pleasure of recognising the beauty and merit of the late William Hamilton Gibson's *Eye Spy.* Now we have another work before us, which, under the title of *My Studio Neighbours*, has all the valuable characteristics of his other works, and is rendered as picturesque and fascinating by the author's graceful fancy, keen observation, and the charm of his illustrations. (Price, $2.50.)

The Century Company has published an attractive work in Mr. John La Farge's *An Artist's Letters from Japan.* Mr. La Farge's fame as an artist of striking originality and power has given him a high standing in his profession, and in his latest work we see the trained eye, the eager imagination, the sincerity of simplicity in the vivid word painting and in the work of the brush. The book extends to 300 pages, and contains 48 illustrations by the author. It is richly bound and very attractively printed. (Price, $4.00.) A new edition of *The Autobiography of Joseph Jefferson*, with a supplementary chapter, brings this popular book of the stage, one of the most notable of its kind, to the front again. The work is profusely illustrated with portraits and other illustrations, and is a mine of anecdote, grave and gay, anent the stage, partaking of its comedy and tragedy. (Price, $4.00.) The Century Company has also published a reproduction of Boutet de Monvel's *Joan of Arc*, a special study in coloured pictures and in story of the "little sister of the saints." The book has had a great success in France, where it was originally produced. It is a most charming art gift-book, especially to the youth who can intelligently appreciate the work. (Price, $3.00.)

In another column we have commented on Mr. R. H. Russell's reproductions of Mr. William Nicholson's work in lithographed colour prints from wood blocks. Mr. Russell has increased his store of good things and seasonable beyond previous occasions, and all his publications are marked by good taste, excellent workmanship, and by attractive and meritorious qualities. His list this year includes a portfolio of six large photogravures and copper etchings of the best-known characters from Dickens, drawn by Mr. C. D. Gibson, and entitled *The People of Dickens.* These are printed on heavy deckel-edge plate paper measuring 16 x 20 inches. (Price, $5.00.) Also an *édition de luxe* of 150 copies on Japan paper, each print signed by Mr. Gibson, at $10.00. *Drawings by Frederic Remington*, illustrating the whole field of wild life in America, in which Mr. Remington is an accredited master, is sumptuously produced in large folio 12 x 18 inches with a picturesque cover. (Price, $5.00. *Édition de luxe*, limited to 250 copies, $10.00.) Mr. E. W. Kemble is represented this year in *The Blackberries*, composed of 32 humorous drawings in colour with descriptive verses. This book, which is full of irresistible fun and frolic at the expense of the "blackberries," is sure of success. But Mr. Kemble's *Coon Calendar* has some of the finest character sketching he has ever done. There are seven water-colour drawings of darkeys printed on heavy cardboard, and the portrayal of the figures in each sitting is so delightful and so characteristic that it is deserving of the highest praise. Kemble's *Coon Calendar* will, no doubt, fill this want wherever it exists in preference to all other calendars for 1898. (Price, $1.50.) *The Autobiography of a Monkey* is a laughable farce in drawings and verse—the drawings by Mayer and the verse by Albert Bigelow Paine—which reverses the Darwinian theory and makes the monkey descended from man. (Price, $1.25.) *Phil May's Sketch-Book* contains 50 full-page cartoons representing this clever artist's work in *Punch*. (Price, $3.00.)

Messrs. T. Y. Crowell and Company have published the University Edition of *The Poetical Works of Matthew Arnold*, for which Mr. Dole has written a biographical introduction. This volume claims to be the most complete yet published, and includes a number of his youthful poems, notably the prize poems, "Alaric at Rome" and "Cromwell." The book is beautifully printed and substantially bound. (Price, $1.50.) In their popular Faïence Series, published year by year, and including many of the most beautiful classics of the world's literature, the Messrs. Crowell have published *Colomba*, from the French of Prosper Mérimée, by Rose Sherman; *The Epic of Hades*, by Sir Lewis Morris; *The Crime of Sylvestre Bonnard*, from the French of Anatole France, by Arabella Ward, and *The Scarlet Letter*, by Nathaniel Hawthorne. This series is very daintily bound and printed with gilt top and ornate cover design. (Price per volume, $1.00.) The Doubleday and McClure Company has published a handsome volume entitled *Bird Neighbours* — an introductory acquaintance with 150 birds commonly found in the gardens, meadows, and woods about our homes, by Neltje Blanchan. Mr. John Burroughs has written a commendatory introduction "to second so worthy an attempt to quicken and enlarge the general interest in our birds." Mr. Burroughs vouches for the reliability of the book, which, he says, "is written in a vivacious strain and by a real bird lover, and should prove a help and a stimulus to any one who seeks by the aid of its pages to become better acquainted with our songsters. There are 50 large coloured plates prepared by the Nature Publishing Company. The bookmaking is a good piece of substantial work not without a certain amount of attractiveness. (Price, $2.00.) The J. B. Lippincott Company has published a new handy edition of *The Confessions of Rousseau*, with illustrations after Maurice Leloir. Printing and paper are very good, and the volumes are tastefully bound for library use. The Lippincott Company has also issued Mr. Charles C. Abbott's delightful books, *Travels in a Tree-top* and *The Freedom of the Fields*, in a dainty illustrated holiday edition. The two volumes come together in a box. (Price, $3.00.)

Messrs. G. P. Putnam's Sons have issued Washington Irving's *Astoria* in two handsome volumes, to be known as the Tacoma Edition. Type, paper, binding are excellent, and the whole work is finished in a most superb style. There are numerous illustrations beautifully reproduced, and the pages are embellished with decorative borders. It is in the truest sense an *édition de luxe*. (Price, $6.00.) Messrs. Putnam's Sons have also made a beautiful book of Marion Harland's *Some Colonial Homesteads and Their Stories*. There is a romantic flavour about the work—as the author says in her preface, the task has been a labour of love, and her sympathy wins the reader and relieves the treatment of the subject of anything like prosiness. There is certainly no monotony in these pages. The whole book in its workmanship is most charming and effective. The illustrations are beautifully reproduced. *The Ayrshire Homes and Haunts of Burns*, by Henry C. Shelley, makes a strong bid to the lover of the land of brown heath and shaggy wood. It is illustrated throughout with numerous reproductions of photographs of the haunts and scenes made famous by Burns. The photographs were taken by the author himself, so that they fit into the scheme of the book as a whole, and are not simply stuck in to help out its attractiveness. It is also published by the Messrs. Putnam. (Price, $1.25.) *Short Sayings of Famous Men*, issued by the Putnams, in two attractive volumes, collected by Helen Kendrick Johnson, is a happy idea, and will prove useful to many readers and students.

Last Christmas Mr. Charles P. Didier caused a great deal of amusement to ripple over the country with his unique story *'Twixt Cupid and Crœsus*, which displayed the exhibits in an attachment suit in a manner that was novel and artistic. He has followed this success up with *R. S. V. P.*, a novelette told in pen and pencil and issued in the same form. Mr. Didier has a happy talent for combining illustration and text, and his new story is touched with the qualities of refined sentiment, skilful characterisation and delicate fancy, which single it out for especial praise. The Williams and Wilkins Company of Baltimore publish this volume also, which is made in a very attractive style. (Price, $1.50 net.) If the sincerest form of flattery is imitation, then Mr. Didier ought to be gratified by the publication of *Cupid's Game with Hearts*, which is another tale of troubled love told by documents. Like its prototype, the new book is amusingly clever, and discloses a pretty love story. It comes bound in white cloth with blue and gold design, and is published by the Dodge Book and Stationery Company of San Francisco. (Price, $1.50.) Another work of interest of a very different character reaches us from San Francisco, and is issued by Mr. William Doxey, "publisher of the *Lark* and other good things." *The Wild Flowers of California*, their names, haunts, and habits, is an exquisite souvenir of the great Western State, with its wild luxuriance of floral beauty. The descriptive part has been contributed by Mary Elizabeth Parsons, and the illustrations by Margaret Warriner Buck. There are 150 full-page illustrations; the binding is in buckram, with an appropriate cover design. (Price, $2.00 net.) There is also an *édition de luxe* with coloured plates done by hand and printed on hand-made paper, limited to 150 copies and sold at $25.00 net.

A large illustrated volume that has already attracted a good deal of attention, and which is deserving of it, is *Sunlight and Shadow*, a book for photographers, amateur and professional. It is the work of Mr. W. I. Lincoln Adams, and the exquisitely printed pictures of nature which appear in profusion have been taken from original photographs. Mr. Adams is known by a former work, *Amateur Photography*, which was designed for the beginner. The present volume is an advance on that, and follows the progress made, presumably, by his readers. Were it only for the sake of possessing the fine illustrations which are published in the book, it would be well worth having, apart from its technical and scientific interest. It ought to command a large sale during the holidays. Published by the Baker and Taylor Company. (Price, $2.50.)

Three dainty little volumes have been published by the F. A. Stokes Company which will make a very suitable gift to the thoughtful or studious reader. *Pensées of Joubert* has been selected and translated by Henry Attwell; De Quincey's *Lyrics in Prose* is collated by R. Brimley Johnson, and *Pen Portraits*, from Carlyle, by the same scholar. Each volume has a portrait of the great man represented; the covers are very chastely designed, and the form is of the pocket-book size. (Price, 75 cts. per volume.)

Mr. Thomas Whittaker has published a marvellously cheap edition of Shakespeare at $1.50 net, and has issued three more volumes in the Apollo Poets Series, which we have already had occasion to commend. The poets now included in this edition are John Milton, Lord Byron, and William Wordsworth. (Price, $1.75 per volume.) The first volume of the *International Studio* has just been published by Mr. John Lane, and makes a finely illustrated art book. The *International Studio* is far and away the finest magazine of its kind, and the bound volume makes a very beautiful book and a very seasonable one.

BOOKS FOR BOYS AND GIRLS.

Quite a number of books in colour for the "littlest ones" have been produced against the needs of Christmas, 1897. A brief account of those that have reached us so far are herewith given. The Frederick A. Stokes Company, which yearly provides for the clamorous wants of these little people in a generous fashion, has sent out three pretty books with numerous full-page colour-plates after paintings in water-colours by Maud Humphreys, for which Elizabeth S. Tucker has written stories and verses. Messrs. Laird and Lee have issued *Jupiter Jingles, or a Trip to Mystery Land*, by Annetta Stratford Crafts, with illustrations adaptable either to the home information bureau for children or to the kindergarten. (Price, 50 cents.) *Just a Little Boy* is a series of "stories about Willie," by Alice Ashworth, which can be readily appreciated by children of five or six. It is charmingly illustrated by Lee Woodward Zeigler, and published by Messrs. Frederick Warne and Company. (Price, 75 cents.) Messrs. Longmans, Green and Company have no "Golliwogg" book this year, but they have issued in uniform style two books which will give as much pleasure. *The Adventures of the Three Bold Babes*, by S. Rosamond Praeger, and *The Vege-Men's Revenge*, by Florence K. Upton and Bertha Upton, are characterised by the same delicious humour and bright, mischievous fancy which endeared the Golliwoggs to all the children. A compilation of stories, rhymes, and pictures from the brightest pages of *St. Nicholas* has been done into book form by Mary Mapes Dodge, under the title *A New Baby World*, and published by the Century Company. *Baby World*, which has appeared in various editions, has been so popular and so widely appreciated that this fresh compilation is sure of a warm welcome. Pictorially and in all other respects the new volume is excellent, and deserves to be in every home where the "little folk everywhere," to whom it is dedicated, brighten the family life. (Price, $1.50.) Of the same order is Edith King Hall's *Adventures in Toyland*, illustrated in pen and ink and in colour by Alice B. Woodward, and published by the Scribners. Author and artist have combined to make one of the most attractive books of its class; they know that "the Toy World is a very real world indeed," and have entered with genuine pleasure into the make-believe of a child's world. It has a very "catchy" cover. (Price, $2.00.) The same firm has made a beautiful *Stevenson Song Book*, uniform with the *Field-DeKoven Song Book*, published last year. The verses have been taken from Stevenson's *A Child's Garden*, and set to music by various composers. It is very beautifully bound and printed. (Price, $2.00.) The Macmillan Company has also published *Singing Verses for Children*, the words being by Lydia Avery Coonley and the music by several composers. The verses are set in a series of coloured pictures by Alice Kellogg Tyler; and upon turning the rather sombre cover, one is immediately met by bright flashes of colour that greet the eye like sunlight suddenly let into a darkened room. The border designs and pictorial features give an exceedingly sunny and winsome appearance to the pages and ought to tempt the young singers to carol their sweetest. (Price, $2.00.)

Mr. James Barnes is becoming known to us by his voluminous product of tales of adventure and daring with a background of American history. Messrs. D. Appleton and Company publish a new book of his, entitled *Commodore Bainbridge*, which is a sea story narrating the events in the life of the hero from the gun-room to the quarter-deck. It contains some illustrations by George Gibbs and others. (Price, $1.00.) Mr. William O. Stoddard has a story of the American Revolution, entitled *The Red Patriot*, which is illustrated by Mr. B. West Clinedinst, published by the same firm. Mr. Stoddard is an old favourite of the boys and needs no further recommendation. (Price, $1.50.) Mr. Hezekiah Butterworth's new volume for boys this year is a tale of the boyhood of Franklin, and is entitled *True to His Home*. His latest story is based on history and includes the most interesting and picturesque episodes in the home life of Benjamin Franklin. This makes the seventh volume in Mr. Butterworth's Creators of Liberty Series, based for the most part on real events. It is also illustrated, and is published by the Appletons. (Price, $1.50.) The American Book Company send us a copy of their *Gems of School Songs*, selected and edited by Carl Betz, a choice collection of songs suitable for children of all ages and for schools of different grades. (Price, 70 cents.) *Kent Fielding's Venture*, by I. T. Thurston, the author of several books for boys, is published by Messrs. A. I. Bradley and Company, of Boston. It contains a frontispiece illustration. (Price, $1.25.) Messrs. T. Y. Crowell publish *The King of the Park*, by Marshall Saunders, the author of *Beautiful Joe*. In a previous story the dog finds a sympathetic friend and historian, and in the one now published Mr. Saunders has in the same spirit taken up "the harmless, necessary cat." The story is a delightful one, breezy and wholesome and not surcharged with pathos, and deserves to reach the little folks for whom it is intended. It is beautifully printed, and contains several half-tone illustrations. (Price, $1.25.) *Among Meadow People*, by Clara Dillingham Pierson, published by Messrs. E. P. Dutton and Company, is a collection of stories written for the little ones of the kindergarten. It is daintily illustrated with drawings from the pen of Mr. Frederic C. Gordon.

In *Fighting a Fire*, by Charles Thaxter Hill, with thirty illustrations by the author, the boys are told how the fire department of a great city is organised; how the firemen are trained; how fire alarms are transmitted by telegraph, and everything, in fact, connected with "fighting a fire." The book will surely be one of inviting interest to the boys, and the girls too for that matter; and in the chapter devoted to "Peter Spots, Fireman," they will be delighted with the account of a pet dog of one of the engineers that has attended almost all the large fires in recent years with all the zest of a uniformed member of the force. (Price, $1.50.) The Century Company, which publishes *Fighting a Fire*, has also issued a new book by Frances Courtenay Baylor, called *Miss Nina Barrow*, which, according to the dedication, is a

"Tale to show how growing things
Learn by mistakes and get their wings."

It contains a frontispiece illustration. A very interesting and instructive book published by the same firm is *Master Skylark: a History of Shakespeare's Times*, by John Bennett. It is profusely illustrated by Reginald B. Birch, and is packed with nearly four hundred pages of reading matter. (Price, $1.50.) Mr. William Henry Shelton, whose book of short stories, entitled *A Man Without a Memory*, gave us a good deal of pleasure two summers ago, also publishes through the Century Company a story of the Civil War, called *The Last Three Soldiers*. The dedication is worth quoting: "With an apology to the little sister that the plot is not more blood-curdling and harrowing, this story of what might have been is affectionately dedicated to his young friends, Gussie and Genie Demarest, by the author." It is copiously illustrated, and, like all books published by the Century Company, is handsomely bound and printed.

Messrs. Henry T. Coates and Company send us the third volume in the Boone and Kenton Series, entitled *In the Days of the Pioneers*, a sequel to *The Phantom of the River*, by Edward S. Ellis, with frontispiece illustration. (Price, $1.25.) The same firm publishes a book for girls by Lucy C. Lillie, entitled *A Girl's Ordeal*. This book also contains a frontispiece illustration which bears the legend, "A tall, quiet, young Englishman was conversing with Helen." A glance at the picture will satisfy the reader that it is *not* by Gibson.

Messrs. Dodd, Mead and Company publish a new book by Amanda M. Douglas in the Sherburne Series, entitled *The Children at Sherburne House*; also a sequel to *A Little Girl in Old New York*, entitled *Hannah Ann*. The new Witch Winnie book is one of the best that has been published in this series; it is entitled *Witch Winnie in Venice*. The historical background which Mrs. Elizabeth W. Champney has taken in this book is that of the Italian Renaissance. It is illustrated with a number of pictures evidently taken from photographic scenes. It is regrettable that the book has no index to the illustrations, as by their very nature they are closely associated with the text. Mrs. Champney has also given us a new juvenile after the style of *Paddy O'Leary and His Learned Pig*, which was successful two years ago. The new book is entitled *Pierre and His Poodle*, the scenes of the story in this case taking the reader to France. It is delightfully illustrated with pen-and-ink drawings by F. D. Steele. Another juvenile published by this firm attracts at once by its very handsome cover, which is one of the best we have seen among juveniles this season. The inside of the book is no less attractive, with its beautiful, clear type, on fine paper, interspersed with delightful illustrations drawn by Minna Brown. The story itself is a capital one for the "little lads whom I love," to two of whom the book is dedicated. Miss Lyda Farrington Krausé, who has been known for some years as a popular and pleasing writer of stories for boys and girls, under the pseudonym "Barbara Yechton," is the author of this new story, entitled *Derick*. Those boys and girls who have read her stories always ask for more; and we know older people who enjoy Miss Krausé just as well. To those readers who have not made Barbara Yechton's acquaintance in these stories we heartily recommend *Derick* as a beginning. They will find that her books are among the most wholesome, the kindliest, and the most entertaining of stories for young folks. (Price, $1.50.)

Messrs. Harper and Brothers publish a new story for boys and girls, entitled *Alan Ransford*, by Ellen Douglas Deland. The story has its scene laid in a suburb of Philadelphia, and the fun of the book arises from the collision of two contiguous households, one of which includes five boys and the other an only daughter who has several girl friends in the neighbourhood. Perhaps the most engaging personality in the book is the bachelor uncle who acts as guardian to the boys. There is a description of a false alarm of fire and of a football match between Harvard and Pennsylvania, and also of Class Day at Harvard, which brings the story to a happy conclusion. It is illustrated by Harry C. Edwards. (Price, $1.50.) *The Story of the Rhine-Gold*, by Anna Alice Chapin, is an account of Wagner's *Nibelungenlied* for young people; but older people will doubtless find the book just as interesting. (Price, $1.25.) Kirk Munroe contributes a new volume this year to the Messrs. Harper's juvenile library. *The Painted Desert* is a story of adventure for boys, the scene of which is laid in Arizona. It is profusely illustrated, and has a very picturesque cover. (Price, $1.25.)

Messrs. Houghton, Mifflin and Company have made a beautiful book of Frank Dempster Sherman's *Little Folk-Lyrics*. The illustrations, by Maude and Genevieve Cowles, are exquisitely conceived in the spirit of a child's humour, and are beautifully reproduced in the text. Mr. Sherman's book will appeal to older readers as well; indeed, it is likely that it will be a greater favourite of the older children than of the younger. (Price, $1.50.)

The Lothrop Publishing Company have as usual a goodly array of attractive books for boys and girls. Mr. Kirk Munroe publishes with them a story of boys, boats and bicycles, fire brigades and fun, called *The Ready Rangers*, with a half dozen illustrations. (Price, $1.25.) Then we have a collection of child verses by Miss Mary E. Wilkins, entitled *Once Upon a Time*. The drawings scattered over the pages by Miss Etheldred B. Barry are full of humour and vivacity. Miss Wilkins has been very happy in her illustrator. The preface to which Miss Wilkins affixes her autograph runs:

> "Trusting to the sweet charity of the little folk
> To find some grace, in spite of halting rhyme
> And frequent telling in these little tales,
> I say again, '*Now, once upon a time!*'"

Margaret Sidney has given us in *Phronsie Pepper* the story of the last of the "five little Peppers." Like many popular juvenile series, the Pepper Library grew out of the pressure from without made by the author's many importunate readers to know "some more about Mamsie and Polly, Ben, Joel, David, and Phronsie." The book is generously illustrated, and is bound in a very attractive cover. (Price, $1.50.) *His First Charge*, by Mrs. Foster, who, under the pen-name of "Faye Huntington," has written a number of serious stories of the "Pansy" type, is an earnest attempt to solve the question of responsibility regarding the drink question. The book, it will be seen, is one that is intended for Sunday-school purposes. (Illustrated, price, $1.25.) Pansy's new volume this year is entitled *Overruled*, and contains several illustrations. (Price, $1.25.) The story which Miss Sophie Swett has written this year for boys and girls is entitled *Tom Pickering of 'Scutney*, and is illustrated by H. D. Young. (Price, $1.25.) *The Great Island, or a Castaway in Papua*, by Willis Boyd Allen, who has written a number of books for boys, is a story of the adventure order, and has several illustrations. (Price, 75 cents.) Isabel Hornibrook has written a story of the Maine woods, called *Camp and Trail*, which takes two English boys and an American collegian into the woods of Maine to hunt deer and moose. The book is intended for young people between the ages of twelve and eighteen. It is illustrated by George Foster Barnes. (Price, $1.50.) The above books are all issued by the Lothrop Publishing Company.

To the famous War of 1812 Series, published by Messrs. Lee and Shepard, Mr. Everett T. Tomlinson has added a new book, entitled *Guarding the Border, or the Boys of the Great Lakes*. This is the fifth volume in the series, and gives an interesting historical account of many incidents of the War of 1812, which is woven around a story intended to excite the interest and instruct the mind of the young American. (Price, $1.50.) The posthumous book by Oliver Optic in the Blue and Gray Series is also the fifth in its series, and is entitled *At the Front*. It is a continuation of the narrative contained in the preceding books, and the personal adventures of the characters introduced in those volumes are continued in the present volume. The battle of Stone River is described by the author in a remarkably effective and interesting manner, and the whole story is one of the most stirring of the series. (Price, $1.50.) Another book written by the late Oliver Optic, and published through the same firm, is called *Pacific Shores, or Adventures in Eastern Seas*, which makes the twelfth volume, and now the last, in All-Over-the-World Library. These three books contain full-page illustrations. (Price, $1.25.) Messrs. Lee and Shepard also publish a story for the younger boys and girls, called *Queer Janet*, by Grace Le Baron, who is known in private life as Mrs. Upham, and abroad by her success in *The Hazelwood Stories* published by the same firm. (Price, 75 cents.) *On Plymouth Rock*, by Colonel Samuel Adams Drake, has also been issued by this firm, that the young people may become acquainted with the story of our Pilgrim Fathers. This he has done through the medium of a simple and touching story which will impress itself upon young minds by keeping in close touch with the spirit of Bradford and Winslow's narratives. (Price, 60 cents.)

Messrs. Little, Brown and Company publish a charming book of stories for little girls called *Ten Little Comedies*, "Tales of the troubles of ten little girls whose tears were turned into smiles." The stories are written by Gertrude Smith, and there are ten full-page illustrations by E. B. Barry. (Price, $1.25.) In uniform binding the same firm publishes *Miss Belladonna*, "a child of to-day," by Caroline Ticknor, very cleverly illustrated by L. J. Bridgman. This book has made quite a stir in Boston, and many of the papers there and in other cities have devoted columns of generous praise to the exceedingly clever story which Miss Ticknor has written. It is a book that will probably win older readers, and be more highly appreciated by them than by the younger generation. The following books have been published by the J. B. Lippincott Company, all of them attractively bound, well printed and embellished with full-page illustrations, namely: *Hunted Through Fiji, or 'Twixt Convict and Cannibal*, by Reginald Horsley; *From Fag to Monitor, or Fighting to the Front*, by Andrew Home; *The Rover's Quest*, a story of foam, fire and fun, by Hugh St. Leger; *The Lost Gold of the Montezumas, or the Story of the Alamo*, by the popular juvenile author, William O. Stoddard; and *Meg Langholme*, by Mrs. Molesworth. All these books, with the exception of Mr. Stoddard's, which is $1.50, are priced at $1.25.

Messrs. A. C. McClurg and Company have several juveniles on their list which include a new story entitled *A Little House in Pimlico*, by Marguerite Bouvet, with illustrations by Helen Maitland Armstrong; *The Big Horn Treasure*, a tale of Rocky Mountain adventure, by John F. Cargill, with illustrations (price, $1.25); *Fairy Starlight and the Dolls*, by Elizabeth S. Blakeley, illustrated with pen-and-ink drawings by Lucy F. Perkins. (Price, $1.00.) Messrs. Longmans, Green and Company publish a new story of child life called *The Professor's Children*, by Edith Henrietta Fowler, the author of a book entitled *The Young Pretenders*, which was very much favoured last Christmas. The illustrations—there are twenty-four of them—by Ethel Kate Burgess, greatly enhance the interest of the book. They are so full of childish humour and fancy that we should be tempted to purchase the book for the sake of the drawings alone. Mrs. Molesworth publishes through the Macmillan Company one of her delightful volumes of stories for children called *Miss Mouse and her Boys.* It is illustrated in a very spirited manner by Leslie Brooke. The Peter Paul Book Company of Buffalo, N. Y., publishes a little book entitled *Mannie Brown and Edward Kennedy*, by Mildred Rutherford. Mannie is a school-girl and Edward a college boy whose experiences in school life are woven into a simple story, simply told.

From the Pilgrim Press of Chicago we have received a half dozen volumes, containing stories for boys and girls, which are prettily bound and printed and contain several illustrations. The titles are: *A Son's Victory*, a story of the land of the honey-bee, by Fannie E. Newberry; *Links of Gold*, by Harriet A. Cheever; *A Young Capitalist*, by Linnie S. Harris; *The Benhurst Club*, a story of the doings of some girls, by Howe Benning; *A Genuine Lady*, by I. T. Thurston; and *Redmond of the Seventh, or the Boys of Ninety*, by Mrs. Frank Lee. The last-named story appeared originally as a short serial in the *Youth's Companion*, and has now been enlarged and expanded in book form. (Price, $1.25 per volume.) The Messrs. Putnam are the importers of a beautiful book of verse for children of all ages, published in England by Messrs. Blackie and Company, and entitled *Red Apples and Silver Bells.* The illustrations are drawn, after the manner of the new decorative school of art, by Alice B. Woodward. The verses are written by Hamish Hendry. The book is very beautifully bound, with gilt edges, and has a frontispiece and title-page in two colours. Messrs. Rand, McNally and Company publish a new story by the popular writer for boys, Mr. George Manville Fenn; the title is *Cursed by a Fortune*, and the book has been given a very picturesque cover. Another juvenile published by the same firm, very daintily bound, is *The Evolution of Dodd's Sister*, a tragedy of every-day life, by Charlotte Whitney Eastman.

Messrs. Roberts Brothers are well represented in the juvenile literature of the season. There is a sequel to a favourite of last year, *Nan at Camp Chicopee*, by Myra Sawyer Hamlin. The new book is entitled *Nan in the City, or Nan's Winter with the Girls*, and is prettily illustrated by L. J. Bridgman. (Price, $1.25.) Then there is a new book by Evelyn Raymond, called *The Little Red School-House*, written for "all the lads and lassies, the mistresses and masters of our blessed country schools." The illustrations, which are very well done, are by Victor A. Searles. (Price, $1.25.) In the Young Puritan Series we have a new volume by Mary P. Wells Smith, called *The Young Puritans of Old Hadley.* The story is an attempt, based on historical facts, to make more vivid to the children of to-day the hardships endured by the builders of the nation. The illustrations in this book are also by L. J. Bridgman. A story of sweet simplicity for the little ones is *Wanolasset*, by A. G. Plympton, with illustrations by the author. (Price, $1.25.) *Rich Enough*, by Leigh Webster, illustrated by Elizabeth S. Pitman, is a pleasant girl's story. A book of exciting interest for boys, with numerous illustrations, is a tale of the Big Horn, by William Shattuck, entitled *The Secret of a Black Butte, or the Mysterious Mine.* (Price, $1.50.) Mr. John Trowbridge, Professor of Physics at Harvard University, contributes an electrical story for boys, called *The Resolute Mr. Pansy.* (Price, $1.25.) *The Story of Mollie* has been written for little children by Mary M. Bower. (Price, $1.00.) *In Indian Tents*, "stories told by Penobscot, Passamaquoddy, and Micmac Indians to Abby L. Alger," is an interesting collection of legends and tales which the author has gathered from time to time when in the neighbourhood of Indians. The woman whose likeness appears on the cover of the book was a famous story-teller; the cover, by the way, is very prettily designed. *Torpeanuts, the Tom-Boy*, is an illustrated story about animal life on a New England farm-house by a favourite writer, Lillie F. Wesselhoeft. (Price, $1.25.)

From the Messrs. Scribner we have three boys' books handsomely bound and illustrated—one, by Robert Leighton, entitled *The Golden Galleon*, being a narrative of the adventures of Master Gilbert Oglander, and of how, in the year 1591, he fought under the gallant Sir Richard Grenville in the great sea fight off Flores, on board Her Majesty's ship *The Revenge* (price, $1.50) ; the second is a tale of Texas by Kirk Munroe, *With Crockett and Bowie* (price, $1.25) ; the other volume being *Lords of the World*, a story of the fall of Carthage and Corinth, by the Rev. Alfred J. Church (price, $1.50).

What would Christmas be for the boy without a new Henty book ? As a matter of fact, Mr. Henty's usual average with the Scribners is three books a year. The trio this time consist of *With Frederick the Great*, a tale of the Seven Years' War ; *A March on London*, a story of Wat Tyler's rising, and *With Moore at Corunna*, a story of the Peninsular War. Each book is fully illustrated, and the quality of the book-making is already familiar from his previous volumes. (Price, $1.50 each.) *Will Shakespeare's Little Lad*, by Imogen Clark, illustrated by Birch, is a happy attempt to familiarise youth with Stratford life in Shakespeare's day, the boy-hero being the son of the great dramatist. (Price, $1.50.) A new and cheaper edition, but most attractive withal, of Mrs. Burnett's famous juveniles has been issued, printed from new plates, but with all the original illustrations and a beautifully designed cover by R. B. Birch. There are five volumes, comprising *Little Lord Fauntleroy ; Two Little Pilgrims' Progress ; Piccino, and Other Child Stories ; Giovanni and the Other ;* and *Sara Crewe, Little Saint Elizabeth, and Other Stories.* (Price, $1.25 each.)

Messrs. Frederick Warne and Company publish a new story by Silas K. Hocking, entitled *In Spite of Fate*, and a book for girls, called *Mona St. Claire*, by Annie E. Armstrong ; also two volumes of fairy tales, *The One-Eyed Griffin and Other Fairy Stories*, by Herbert E. Inman, and *Icelandic Fairy Tales*, translated and edited by Mrs. A. W. Hall. These two books are profusely illustrated by E. A. Mason. The two books previously mentioned are also illustrated. The binding of these volumes is excellent, and print and paper are everything that could be desired. (Price, $1.50 each.)

Messrs. W. A. Wilde and Company of Boston have a number of excellent stories for boys and girls. *Over the Andes* is a tale of travel and adventure by Hezekiah Butterworth, and is illustrated by Henry Sandham. *Sue Orcutt*, by Charlotte M. Vaile, is a sequel to *The Orcutt Girls*, which was very favourably received last year, and continues the story of the fortunes of the central figure in that story. The illustrations are by Frank T. Merrill. Ellen Douglas Deland writes *A Successful Venture*, Mr. William Drysdale contributes a new story, *The Beach Patrol*, a story of the life-saving service, to the Brain and Brawn Series, and Mr. Everett T. Tomlinson narrates the story of the New Jersey campaign under the title *Washington's Young Days.* Both these books are illustrated by the well-known artist Charles Copeland. (Price, $1.50 per volume.)

Mr. Thomas Whittaker has, as usual, a number of good books by well-known authors for boys and girls. *Founded on Paper, or Up Hill and Down Hill Between the Two Jubilees*, is by Charlotte M. Yonge ; *A Girl in Ten Thousand* is from the pen of L. T. Meade. (Price, $1.00.) *'Toinette and Other Stories* is by an old favourite, Barbara Yechton, with some pretty pictures by Minna Brown. (Price, 75 cents.) *Old Tales from Greece*, by Alice Zimmern, and *Rome*, by Mary Ford, published in the Children's Study Series, present to youthful readers the gods and heroes who played so large a part in the ancient world of Greece and Rome. (Price, 75 cents each.)

In the Children's Favourite Classics, daintily bound and illustrated, the Messrs. Crowell have reprinted the famous "Rollo" books, by Jacob Abbott, *Rollo at Work* and *Rollo at Play ;* also *Tales from Hans Andersen*, and Hawthorne's *Tanglewood Tales for Boys and Girls.* Each book has a pretty coloured frontispiece. (Price, 75 cents.) Mr. James Otis, who gave the children *How Tommy Saved the Barn* a year ago, has now written for them a bright little story which will win their sympathy, called *The Wreck of the Circus*, with frontispiece. (Price, 50 cents.)

Mr. Andrew Lang favours the young people this year with *The Pink Fairy Book*, which has been edited and accompanied with numerous fine pictures that give to this latest collection all the charm that pervaded the previous books. (Price, $2.00.) Messrs. Longmans, Green and Company also publish a book that is full of fun and comicality in *Here They Are!*—more stories by J. F.

Sullivan. The mirthfulness of both stories and pictures is contagious in the highest degree, and a fund of merriment has been packed within the picturesque covers that would be hard to beat in the same volume among the juveniles of the season. (Price, $1.50.) *Aaron in the Wildwoods*, with Oliver Herford's fascinating illustrations, is the title of a new volume in which Mr. Joel Chandler Harris has added to the delight of his young readers, who look out eagerly, year after year, for his wonderful tales of adventures. "If you imagine," writes Mr. Harris, "that the book called *The Story of Aaron (so named), the Son of Ben Ali* [published last year], tells all the adventures of the Arab while he was a fugitive in the wildwoods, you are very much mistaken." Whereupon Mr. Harris proceeds to rectify the mistake in a most charming and entertaining manner. (Price, $2.00.)

One of the most fantastic books of the season is *The Bad Child's Book of Beasts*, which is to be followed shortly by another of the same sort. The drawings are not more ridiculous and mirth-provoking than the verses which accompany them. It must be seen to be fully appreciated. (Edward Arnold, price, $1.25.)

THE BOOK MART.

For Bookreaders, Bookbuyers, and Booksellers.

EASTERN LETTER.

New York, November 1, 1897.

October has been a very busy month in the trade. The publishers continue to deluge the market with new books, and every bookseller must be at his wits' end to find space for their display.

Hugh Wynne, by S. Weir Mitchell, has been the leading book of the month, and has sold remarkably well. *The Story of an Untold Love*, by Paul Leicester Ford; *Paste Jewels*, by John Kendrick Bangs, and *Captains Courageous*, by Rudyard Kipling, are also in much demand. *Corleone*, by F. Marion Crawford; *Dariel: A Romance of Surrey*, by R. D. Blackmore; *Fabius the Roman*, by Dr. E. Fitch Burr, and new books by Amelia E. Barr, Mary J. Holmes, Maurus Jokai and Blanche Willis Howard, are among the month's output.

The Beth Book, by Sarah Grand; *His Grace of Osmonde*, by Frances Hodgson Burnett, and *The First Christmas Tree*, by Henry Van Dyke, are announced for early publication.

A considerable number of the illustrated books for the holiday season are now ready, notably *Drawings*, by Frederic Remington; *The People of Dickens*, by Charles Dana Gibson, and *Bird Neighbours*, with an introduction by John Burroughs, while *Sunlight and Shadow*, a work for amateur photographers, edited by W. I. Lincoln Adams, and profusely illustrated, is particularly attractive.

Aaron in the Wilderness, by Joel Chandler Harris; *The Pink Fairy Book*, by Andrew Lang, *Stories and Sketches for the Young*, by Harriet Beecher Stowe, are new juveniles, and *The Blackberries*, illustrated by E. W. Kemble, will be found amusing to both young and old.

In miscellaneous literature *Alfred, Lord Tennyson*, a memoir by his son, has been especially well received, and, for so expensive a book, is having an unusual sale. *Happiness*, by Horace Fletcher, and *Spain in the Nineteenth Century*, by Elizabeth Wormley Latimer, are likely to be in good demand as they become known.

Ian Maclaren's *Year Book* and *The Potter's Wheel*; *The Theology of an Evolutionist*, by Lyman Abbott, and *A Good Start*, by F. B. Meyer, are additions on religious subjects.

That out-door books are not reserved for the spring trade alone is illustrated by the publication of *Game Birds of North America*, by D. G. Elliot; *Whip and Spur*, by George E. Waring, Jr., and *Song Birds and Water Fowl*, by H. E. Parkhurst.

Quite a number of poetical works are among the recent publications. *Colonial Verses*, by Ruth Lawrence, and *Poems Now First Collected*, by Edmund Clarence Stedman, may be mentioned; but there is no large demand for the new things, the old-time favourites still maintaining their popularity.

Small-sized books seem likely to be very much in favour this season. This applies not only to the various editions of popular sixteenmos, but to the Temple edition of Shakespeare and the newly announced Temple edition of the Waverley Novels; also such dainty books as the Little Masterpieces, Tales from *McClure's*, and the Thumb Nail Series.

Trade in general for the past month has been very good. The sales have been largely from the popular books of the day, although out-of-town trade buyers in the city have purchased liberally of the new holiday stock. The reports from the country trade and of the travelling salesmen all indicate expectations of an unusually busy season.

A list of the popular books of the month in their order of sale follows, and will be found to contain many of the titles of previous months' reports:

Quo Vadis. By Henryk Sienkiewicz. $2.00.

Hugh Wynne. By S. Weir Mitchell. 2 vols. $2.00.

The Choir Invisible. By James Lane Allen. $1.50.

Captains Courageous. By Rudyard Kipling. $1.50.

The Christian. By Hall Caine. $1.50.

Story of an Untold Love. By Paul Leicester Ford. $1.25.

Soldiers of Fortune. By Richard Harding Davis. $1.50.

Paste Jewels. By John Kendrick Bangs. $1.00.

Equality. By Edward Bellamy. $1 50.

The Honourable Peter Stirling. By P. L. Ford. $1.50.

Alfred, Lord Tennyson. By his son. 2 vols. $10.00 net.

Corleone. By F. Marion Crawford. 2 vols. $2.00.

The King's Highway. By Amelia E. Barr. $1.25.

Jerome. By Mary E. Wilkins. $1.50.

The Sowers. By Henry Seton Merriman. $1.25.

Trix and Trixy. By John Habberton. 50 cents.

WESTERN LETTER.

CHICAGO, November 1, 1897.

October business was brisk from the beginning of the month to its end, and an excellent demand for current books and holiday stock was remarkable for its steadiness and uniformity. One of the most satisfactory features to be seen in trade this fall is the way in which practically everything is selling. In fact, there is hardly anything that is not going well. This gratifying state of things must be attributed in part to the excellence of the publishers' lines this year.

The Christian still leads the van as a seller, but is followed very closely by *The Choir Invisible*. The latter work is having a remarkable sale in the West.

Sales of technical books and works treating of the practical sciences are exceptionally good this autumn. The demand for this class of books furnishes a reliable criterion to judge current business in general by. When times are bad or business is fluctuating the demand is poor and irregular, but just as soon as the country is on the road to prosperity the demand increases in the same ratio.

There is no diminution in the sale of sixteenmos this year, and the little books are as popular as ever. Good copyright lines, such as the Phœnix Series, are meeting with the most success, chiefly on account of their being non-competitive.

Hugh Wynne met with an exceedingly good reception last month, and its success as a seller during the holidays has been assured. *St. Ives* also went well, and so did *Captains Courageous*.

The various lines of small quarto editions of famous hymns, poems, songs, etc., show as usual a falling off in their sales. These have been declining for several years, and it is evident that they will soon lose their place on publishers' lists, and the trade will know them no more.

The Federal Judge, by Charles K. Lush, promises to have a fair run, calls for it being very frequent last month.

New books are now coming in so fast that it is very hard, indeed, to get even fairly well acquainted with them. Some three hundred or so reached the trade last month, without counting paper-covered novels and re-issues, and the indications point to a still larger number this month.

In addition to those already mentioned, the following were among the most successful publications of last month: *Dariel*, by R. D. Blackmore; *Stories from Italy*, by G. S. Godkin; *The King's Highway*, by Mrs. Barr; *Paste Jewels*, by J. K. Bangs, and *The Story of an Untold Love*, by P. L. Ford.

New juveniles are selling well so far, and appearances point to a successful season for this class of books. A goodly number was received last month, the best of them being *A Little House in Pimlico*, by Margaret Bouvet; *The Pink Fairy Book*, by Andrew Lang; *The Lost Gold of the Montezumas*, by W. O. Stoddard, and *The Children at Sherburne House*, by Amanda M. Douglas.

For so expensive a book the sale of Tennyson's memoir, by his son, was very good last month, and the work ought to have considerable vogue during the holidays. It is to be regretted that the book had to be published at so high a price, which of course materially reduces its chances of having a popular sale.

Publishers' agents are arriving here for their usual ante-holiday visit. Every one speaks of business as having far surpassed his expectations, and making due allowance for the usual optimism of the travelling man, there is no doubt that business in all parts of the country is much ahead of last year.

The Ian Maclaren Year Book should meet with a good sale among the many admirers of the author's works. The demand for *Beside the Bonnie Brier Bush* and the other books is still very good, and they all rank high as sellers.

Fall books are remarkable this year for their all-round excellence, and the number of really notable books to be found in each class. In fiction, history, biography, art, etc., books of the highest rank are to be found, and even the most fastidious bookbuyer should be satisfied this year.

An examination of last month's sales shows that the following books led the demand, the position of the first four being exactly the same as last month:

The Christian. By Hall Caine. $1.50.

The Choir Invisible. By James Lane Allen. $1.50.

Quo Vadis. By H. Sienkiewicz. $2.00.

Soldiers of Fortune. By R. H. Davis. $1.50.

Hugh Wynne. 2 vols. By S. Weir Mitchell. $2.00.

Equality. By E. Bellamy. $1.25.

Captains Courageous. By Rudyard Kipling. $1.50

Law of Psychic Phenomena. By Thomson J. Hudson. $1.50.

Trix and Trixy. By John Habberton. 50 cents.

The Hon. Peter Stirling. By P. L. Ford. $1.50.

The Pursuit of the House-Boat. By J. K. Bangs. $1.25.

St. Ives. By Robert L. Stevenson. $1.50.
The Story of an Untold Love. By P. L. Ford. $1.25.
Jerome. By M. E. Wilkins. $1 50.
On the Red Staircase. By M. I. Taylor. $1.25.
In Kedar's Tents. By H. S. Merriman. $1.25.

ENGLISH LETTER.

London, September 20 to October 23, 1897.

The autumn season is certainly a good one, and the same may be said of the prospect of the winter campaign. A good deal, but not all, depends on the weather. What is wanted is foggy or wet evenings, such as drive the reader indoors to a comfortable fireside, at once the delight of the booklover and the friend of the bookseller. Business with the colonies and foreign parts generally is fairly satisfactory, although the wholesale bookseller will not be thoroughly happy until this branch of the trade is wholly in his hands, a contingency which is more remote each year.

At the risk of repetition the fact must be recorded that the 6s. novel still reigns supreme. In all directions are evidences of the favour with which this form of issuing original fiction is regarded by publisher, bookseller, and reader. *The Christian* and *St. Ives* are the favourites of the moment. The great success of *On the Face of the Waters* has brought into existence several works founded upon incidents of the Indian Mutiny. It is astonishing to find how keen the interest still is in stories of that sad time. The advent of Trafalgar Day and its celebration brought a considerable demand for Nelson literature, by the attention thus directed to the subject. The Tennyson memoir by his son has sold remarkably well, especially when one considers the price (36s. net).

Sir Walter Scott's novels seem to be increasing in popularity. Mr. J. C. Nimmo's re-issue of the Border Edition in 3s. 6d. volumes is a marvellous production, and deservedly a favourite this season.

There has been considerable inquiry for the 3s. 6d. issue of Dr. Smiles's works. Twelve of the volumes will appear immediately, and large orders are being booked already.

At the present moment there is no single book which can be classed as the success of the season. But it is early yet for such a fact to be evident.

Among juvenile books, a large quantity of fairy tales have been issued. The earth appears to have been ransacked for them, the scope of their native lands ranging from Iceland to Australia—a pretty wide sweep. Messrs. Blackie and Son's 6s. and 5s. boys' books by such writers as Fenn and Henty are having a great sale. The titles selected for these books are most unique.

Rudyard Kipling is as great a favourite as ever. His *Captains Courageous* has been well received, a large issue being sold out at once. A limited edition of his works in twelve volumes, price £6 6s. net, is to be published. All the copies are sold, and some have been re-sold at from forty to fifty per cent premium.

The issue of new books and new editions is greater than ever, fifty, sixty, and even seventy *per day* being no uncommon event. It is simply impossible for the retail bookseller to keep in stock one half of the publications that he is sure will be wanted. This statement is made on the authority of one of the leading West End booksellers.

The enormous and ever-increasing output of magazine literature still finds a purchasing, and let us hope reading, public. There are no new comers of any importance. The best-selling ones are the *English Illustrated*, *Strand*, *Pearson's*, *Woman at Home* (better than ever), *Quiver*, *Cassell's*, *Windsor*, *Good Words*, *Pall Mall*, and *Chambers's Journal*.

The appended list contains the titles of the popular books of the hour. The subjects will be found to be comprehensive, to say the least of them. Theological literature seems to be neglected. As has often been remarked, the arrangement of the list has no significance.

The Christian. By Hall Caine. 6s.
The Choir Invisible. By J. L. Allen. 6s.
In Kedar's Tents. By H. S. Merriman. 6s.
St. Ives. By R. L. Stevenson. 6s.
The Gods Arrive. By A. E. Holdsworth. 6s.
Soldiers of Fortune. By R. H. Davis. 6s.
What Maisie Knew. By H. James. 6s.
Jerome. By M. E. Wilkins. 6s.
Wayfaring Men. By Edna Lyall. 6s.
Sunset. By B. Whitby. 6s.
Sweethearts and friends. By M. Gray. 6s.
Ordeal of Richard Feverel. By George Meredith. 6s.
The Sign of the Cross. By W. Barrett. 6s.
At the Cross Roads. By F. F. Montrésor. 6s.
Liza of Lambeth. By W. S. Maugham. 3s. 6d.
Sleep. By M. de Manacéine. 3s. 6d.
The Invisible Man. By H. G. Wells. 3s. 6d.
Founded on Paper. By C. M. Yonge. 3s. 6d.
The Pomp of the Lavilettes By G. Parker. 3s. 6d.
The City of Refuge. By W. Besant. 3s. 6d.
The Benin Massacre. By Captain A. Boisragon. 3s. 6d.
Forty-one Years in India. By General Roberts. 36s.
Pot-Pourri from a Surrey Garden. By Mrs. C. W. Earle. 7s. 6d.
The Jubilee Book of Cricket. By K. S. Ranjitsinhji. 6s.
Strength. By E. Sandow. 2s. 6d. net.
Mrs. Wood's Novels. 2s. edition.
With Moore at Corunna. By Henty. 6s.
Quo Vadis. By H. Sienkiewicz. 4s. 6d. net.
History of French Literature. By E. Dowden. 6s.

SALES OF BOOKS DURING THE MONTH.

New books in order of demand, as sold between October 1, 1897, and November 1, 1897.

We guarantee the authenticity of the following lists as supplied to us, each by leading booksellers in the towns named.

NEW YORK, UPTOWN.

1. Captains Courageous. By Kipling. $1.50. (Century Co.)
2. The Christian. By Caine. $1.50. (Appleton.)

3. The Choir Invisible. By Allen. $1.50. (Macmillan.)
4. Hugh Wynne. By Mitchell. $2.00. (Century Co.)
5. In Kedar's Tents. By Merriman. $1.25. (Dodd, Mead & Co.)
6. St. Ives. By Stevenson. $1.50. (Scribner.)

NEW YORK, DOWNTOWN.

1. Quo Vadis. By Sienkiewicz. $2.00. (Little, Brown & Co.)
2. In Kedar's Tents. By Merriman. $1 25. (Dodd, Mead & Co.)
3. Captains Courageous. By Kipling. $1.50. (Century Co.)
4. The Christian. By Caine. $1.50. (Appleton.)
5. Hugh Wynne. By Mitchell. $2.00. (Century Co.)
6. The Choir Invisible. By Allen. $1.50. (Macmillan.)

ALBANY, N. Y.

1. In Kedar's Tents. By Merriman. $1.25. (Dodd, Mead & Co.)
2. Hugh Wynne. By Mitchell. $2.00. (Century Co.)
3. The Christian. By Caine. $1.50. (Appleton.)
4. Story of an Untold Love. By Ford. $1.25. (Houghton, Mifflin & Co.)
5. Captains Courageous. By Kipling. $1.50. (Century Co.)
6 Paste Jewels. By Bangs. $1.00. (Harper.)

ATLANTA, GA.

1. Story of an Untold Love. By Ford. $1.25. (Houghton Mifflin & Co.)
2. The Christian. By Caine. $1.50. (Appleton.)
3. Hon. Peter Stirling. By Ford. $1.50. (Holt.)
4. Quo Vadis. By Sienkiewicz. $2.00. (Little, Brown & Co.)
5. The Choir Invisible. By Allen. $1.50. (Macmillan.)
6 Sowers. By Merriman. $1.25. (Harper.)

BALTIMORE, MD.

1. Quo Vadis. By Sienkiewicz. $2.00. (Little, Brown & Co.)
2. In Kedar's Tents. By Merriman. $1.25. (Dodd, Mead & Co.)
3. The Story of an Untold Love. By Ford. $1.25. (Houghton, Mifflin & Co.)
4. Hugh Wynne. By Mitchell. $2.00. (Century Co.)
5. The Choir Invisible. By Allen. $1.50. (Macmillan.)

BOSTON, MASS.

1. Hugh Wynne. By Mitchell. $2.00. (Century Co.)
2. Captains Courageous. By Kipling. $1.50. (Century Co.)
3. In Kedar's Tents. By Merriman. $1.25. (Dodd, Mead & Co.)
4. St. Ives. By Stevenson. $1.50. (Scribner.)
5. The Christian. By Caine. $1.50. (Appleton.)
6. Alfred, Lord Tennyson. By His Son. $10.00 net. (Macmillan.)

BOSTON, MASS.

1. Captains Courageous. By Kipling. $1.50. (Century Co.)
2. In Kedar's Tents. By Merriman. $1.25. (Dodd, Mead & Co.)
3. Hugh Wynne. By Mitchell. $2.00. (Century Co.)
4. Alfred, Lord Tennyson. By His Son. $10.00 net. (Macmillan.)
5. Farthest North. By Nansen. $10.00. (Harper.)
6. Forty-one Years in India. By Roberts. $10.00. (Longmans.)

BUFFALO, N. Y.

1. The Choir Invisible. By Allen. $1.50. (Macmillan.)
2. The Christian. By Caine. $1.50. (Appleton.)
3. Quo Vadis. By Sienkiewicz. $2.00. (Little, Brown & Co.)
4. Story of an Untold Love. By Ford. $1.25. (Houghton, Mifflin & Co.)
5. In Kedar's Tents. By Merriman. $1.25. (Dodd, Mead & Co.)
6. Two Captains. By Russell. $1.50. (Dodd, Mead & Co.)

CHICAGO, ILL.

1. The Christian. By Caine. $1.50. (Appleton.)
2. The Choir Invisible. By Allen. $1.50. (Macmillan.)
3. Quo Vadis. By Sienkiewicz. $2.00. (Little, Brown & Co.)
4. Soldiers of Fortune. By Davis. $1.50. (Scribner.)
5. Hugh Wynne. By Mitchell. 2 vols. $2.00. (Century Co.)
6. Captains Courageous. By Kipling. $1.50. (Century Co.)

CINCINNATI, O.

1. Hugh Wynne. By Mitchell. $2.00. (Scribner.)
2. The Choir Invisible. By Allen. $1.50. (Macmillan.)
3. Captains Courageous. By Kipling. $1.50. (Century Co.)
4. Jerome. By Wilkins. $1.50. (Harper.)
5. Story of an Untold Love. By Ford. $1.25. (Houghton, Mifflin & Co.)
6. Alfred, Lord Tennyson. By His Son. $10.00 net. (Macmillan.)

CLEVELAND, O.

1. Hugh Wynne. By Mitchell. $2.00. (Century Co.)
2. The Christian. By Caine. $1.50. (Appleton.)

3. Captains Courageous. By Kipling. $1.50. (Century Co.)
4. The Choir Invisible. By Allen. $1.50. (Macmillan.)
5. In Kedar's Tents. By Merriman. $1.25. (Dodd, Mead & Co.)
6. Quo Vadis. By Sienkiewicz. $2.00. (Little, Brown & Co.)

DETROIT, MICH.

1. Story of an Untold Love. By Ford. $1.25. (Houghton, Mifflin & Co.)
2. Hugh Wynne. By Mitchell. $2.00. (Century Co.)
3. The Christian. By Caine. $1.50. (Appleton.)
4. Captains Courageous. By Kipling. $1.50. (Century Co.)
5. In Kedar's Tents. By Merriman. $1.25. (Dodd, Mead & Co.)
6. Soldiers of Fortune. By Davis. $1.50. (Scribner.)

INDIANAPOLIS, IND.

1. Roach & Co. By Fuller. $1.25. (Bowen-Merrill Co.)
2. The Army Mule. By Captain Castle. $1.25. (Bowen-Merrill Co.)
3. Equality. By Bellamy. $1.25. (Appleton.)
4. The Choir Invisible. By Allen. $1.50. (Macmillan.)
5. Quo Vadis. By Sienkiewicz. $2.00. (Little, Brown & Co.)
6. Bolanyo. By Read. $1.25. (Way & Williams.)

KANSAS CITY, MO.

1. Quo Vadis. By Sienkiewicz. $2.00. (Little, Brown & Co.)
2. The Christian. By Caine. $1.50. (Appleton.)
3. The Poets' Poet. By Quayle. $1.25. (Curts & Jennings.)
4. The Choir Invisible. By Allen. $1.50. (Macmillan.)
5. St. Ives. By Stevenson. $1.00. (Scribner.)
6. Soldiers of Fortune. By Davis. $1.50. (Scribner.)

LOS ANGELES, CAL.

1. Hugh Wynne. By Mitchell. $2.00. (Century.)
2. The Choir Invisible. By Allen. $1.50. (Macmillan.)
3. The Christian. By Caine. $1.50. (Appleton.)
4. Quo Vadis. By Sienkiewicz. $2.00. (Little, Brown & Co.)
5. Captains Courageous. By Kipling. $1.50. (Century Co.)
6. Soldiers of Fortune. By Davis. $1.50. (Scribner.)

LOUISVILLE, KY.

1. The Christian. By Caine. $1.50. (Appleton.)
2. Bolanyo. By Read. $1.25. (Way & Williams.)
3. Quo Vadis. By Sienkiewicz. $2.00. (Little, Brown & Co.)
4. The Choir Invisible. By Allen. $1.50. (Macmillan.)
5. A Rose of Yesterday. By Crawford. $1.50. (Macmillan.)
6. Soldiers of Fortune. By Davis. $1.50. (Scribner.)

MONTREAL, CANADA.

1. Captains Courageous. By Kipling. $1.50. (Century Co.)
2. The Christian. By Caine. $1.50. (Appleton.)
3. Quo Vadis. By Sienkiewicz. 75 cts. and $1.50. (Morang.)
4. In the Swing of the Sea. By Oxley. $1.00. (Nisbet.)
5. In Kedar's Tents. By Merriman. $1.25. (Dodd, Mead & Co.)
6. St. Ives. By Stevenson. $1.50. (Scribner.)

NEW HAVEN, CONN.

1. Hugh Wynne. By Mitchell. $2.00. (Century Co.)
2. Captains Courageous. By Kipling. $1.50. (Century Co.)
3. In Kedar's Tents. By Merriman. $1.25. (Dodd, Mead & Co.)
4. Story of an Untold Love. By Ford. $1.25. (Houghton, Mifflin & Co.)
5. St. Ives. By Stevenson. $1.50. (Scribner.)
6. Alfred, Lord Tennyson. By His Son. $10.00 net. (Macmillan.)

NEW ORLEANS, LA.

1. Quo Vadis. By Sienkiewicz. $2.00. (Little, Brown & Co.)
2. The Choir Invisible. By Allen. $1.50. (Macmillan.)
3. Soldiers of Fortune. By Davis. $1.50. (Scribner.)
4. The Christian. By Caine. $1.50. (Appleton.)
5. In Kedar's Tents. By Merriman. $1.25. (Dodd, Mead & Co.)
6. Chevalier d'Auriac. By Yeats. $1.50. (Longmans.)

PHILADELPHIA, PA.

1. Hugh Wynne. By Mitchell. $2.00. (Century Co.)
2. The Choir Invisible. By Allen. $1.50. (Macmillan.)
3. Quo Vadis. By Sienkiewicz. $2.00. (Little, Brown & Co.)
4. Story of an Untold Love. By Ford. $1.25. (Houghton, Mifflin & Co.)
5. In Kedar's Tents. By Merriman. $1.25. (Dodd, Mead & Co.)
6. Chevalier d'Auriac. By Yeats. $1.25. (Longmans.)

PITTSBURG, PA.

1. Hugh Wynne. By Mitchell. $2.00. (Century Co.)
2. Captains Courageous. By Kipling. $1.50. (Century Co.)
3. Story of an Untold Love. By Ford. $1.25. (Houghton, Mifflin & Co.)

4. St. Ives. By Stevenson. $1.50. (Scribner.)
5. The Choir Invisible. By Allen. $1.50. (Macmillan.)
6. Quo Vadis. By Sienkiewicz. $2.00. (Little, Brown & Co.)

PORTLAND, ORE.

1. Quo Vadis. By Sienkiewicz. $2.00. (Little, Brown & Co.)
2. Captains Courageous. By Kipling. $1.50. (Century Co.)
3. St. Ives. By Stevenson. $1.50. (Scribner.)
4. The Sowers. By Merriman. $1.25. (Harper.)
5. Seven Seas. By Kipling. $1.50. (Appleton.)
6. Wolfville. By Lewis. $1.50. (Stokes.)

ROCHESTER, N. Y.

1. Hugh Wynne. By Mitchell. $2.00. (Century Co.)
2. Captains Courageous. By Kipling. $2.00. (Century Co.)
3. Quo Vadis. By Sienkiewicz. $2.00. (Little, Brown & Co.)
4. The Choir Invisible. By Allen. $1.50. (Macmillan.)
5. St. Ives. By Stevenson. $1.50. (Scribner.)
6. The Christian. By Caine. $1.50. (Appleton.)

SALT LAKE CITY, UTAH.

1. Soldiers of Fortune. By Davis. $1.50. (Scribner.)
2. The Choir Invisible. By Allen. $1.50. (Macmillan.)
3. Hugh Wynne. By Mitchell. $2.00. (Century Co.)
4. The Christian. By Caine. $1.50. (Appleton.)
5. The Federal Judge. By Lush. $1.25. (Houghton, Mifflin & Co.)
6. The Honourable Peter Stirling. By Ford. $1.50. (Holt.)

SAN FRANCISCO, CAL.

1. Quo Vadis. By Sienkiewicz. $2.00. (Little, Brown & Co.)
2. The Christian. By Caine. $1.50. (Appleton.)
3. St. Ives. By Stevenson. $1.50. (Scribner.)
4. Soldiers of Fortune. By Davis. $1.50. (Scribner.)
5. In Kedar's Tents. By Merriman. $1.25. (Dodd, Mead & Co.)
6. The Lark. Books I. and II. $3.00 each. (Doxey.)

ST. LOUIS, MO.

1. The Choir Invisible. By Allen. $1.50. (Macmillan.)
2. Soldiers of Fortune. By Davis. $1.50. (Scribner.)
3. In Kedar's Tents. By Merriman. $1.25. (Dodd, Mead & Co.)
4. Captains Courageous. By Kipling. $1.50. (Century Co.)
5. Quo Vadis. By Sienkiewicz. $2.00. (Little, Brown & Co.)
6. The Christian. By Caine. $1.50. (Appleton.)

ST. PAUL, MINN.

1. Quo Vadis. By Sienkiewicz. $2.00. (Little, Brown & Co.)
2. The Christian. By Caine. $1.50. (Appleton.)
3. Soldiers of Fortune. By Davis. $1.50. (Scribner.)
4. St. Ives. By Stevenson. $1.50. (Scribner.)
5. Hugh Wynne. By Mitchell. $2.00. (Century Co.)
6. Captains Courageous. By Kipling. $1.50. (Century Co.)

TOLEDO, O.

1. The Christian. By Caine. $1.50. (Appleton.)
2. Jerome. By Wilkins. $1.50. (Harper.)
3. Hugh Wynne. By Mitchell. $2.00. (Century Co.)
4. The Choir Invisible. By Allen. $1.50. (Macmillan.)
5. Captains Courageous. By Kipling. $1.50. (Century Co.)
6. In Kedar's Tents. By Merriman. $1.25. (Dodd, Mead & Co.)

TORONTO, CANADA.

1. * St. Ives. By Stevenson. 75 cts. and $1.25. (Copp-Clark Co.)
2. Clash of Arms. By Bloundelle-Burton. 50 cts. and $1.00. (D. Appleton & Co.)
3. † By Stroke of Sword. By Balfour. 75 cts. and $1.25. (Methuen & Co.)
4. † Lawrence Clavering. By Mason. 75 cts. and $1.25. (Macmillan.)
5. Quo Vadis. By Sienkiewicz. $2.00. (Little, Brown & Co.)
6. * In Kedar's Tents. By Merriman. 75 cts. and $1.25. (Macmillan and Copp-Clark Co.)

TORONTO, CANADA.

1. St. Ives. By Stevenson. Paper, 75 cts.; cloth, $1.25. (The Copp-Clark Co., Limited.)
2. In Kedar's Tents By Merriman. Paper, 75 cts.; cloth, $1.25. (The Copp-Clark Co., Limited.)
3. Soldiers of Fortune. By Davis. Paper, 75 cts.; cloth, $1.25. (The Copp-Clark Co., Limited.)
4. The Two Captains. By Russell. Paper, 50 cts.; cloth, $1.00. (The Copp-Clark Co., Limited.)
5. The Martian. By Du Maurier. Paper, 75 cts.; cloth, $1.25. (The Copp-Clark Co., Limited.)
6. Chevalier d'Auriac. By Yeats. Paper. 75 cts.; cloth, $1.25. (Longmans' Colonial Edition.)

WACO, TEX.

1. The Christian. By Caine. $1.50. (Appleton.)
2. Quo Vadis. By Sienkiewicz. $2.00. (Little, Brown & Co.)
3. Dariel. By Blackmore. $1.75. (Dodd, Mead & Co.)
4. The Story of an Untold Love. By Ford. $1.25. (Houghton, Mifflin & Co.)

* Canadian copyrights.
† Colonial Libraries.

5. The Vice of Fools. By Taylor. $1.50. (Stone & Co.)
6. Eat Not Thy Heart. By Gordon. $1.25. (Stone & Co.)

WORCESTER, MASS.

1. Hugh Wynne. By Mitchell. 2 vols. $2.00. (Century Co.)
2. Captains Courageous. By Kipling. $1.50. (Century Co.)
3. St. Ives. By Stevenson. $1.50. (Scribner.)
4. Son of the Old Dominion. By Harrison. $1.50. (Lamson, Wolffe & Co.)
5. Alfred, Lord Tennyson. By His Son. 2 vols. $10.00 net. (Macmillan.)
6. Romance of Isabel Lady Burton. By Herself. 2 vols. $7.50. (Dodd, Mead & Co.)

THE BEST SELLING BOOKS.

According to the above lists, the six books which have sold best in order of demand during the month are—

1. Quo Vadis. By Sienkiewicz.
2. The Choir Invisible. By Allen.
3. The Christian. By Caine.
4. Hugh Wynne. By Mitchell.
5. Captains Courageous. By Kipling.
6. In Kedar's Tents. By Merriman.

BOOKS RECEIVED.

AMERICAN BAPTIST PUBLICATION SOCIETY, Philadelphia.

The Baptist Principle, by William Cleaver Wilkinson, D.D.
A People's Commentary, Harmony of the Acts of the Apostles, by George W. Clark, D.D.
Heroic Stature, Five Addresses, by Nathan Sheppard.

AMERICAN BOOK CO., New York.

Round the Year in Myth and Song, by Florence Holbrook.
A School History of the United States, by John Bach McMaster.

AMERICAN PUBLISHERS' CORPORATION, New York.

In "God's Country," by D. Higbee.

D. APPLETON & CO., New York.

Children's Ways, by James Sully.
A History of French Literature, by Edward Dowden.
Baboo Hurry Bungsho Jabberjee, B.A., by F. Anstey.

EDWARD ARNOLD, New York.

The King with Two Faces, by M. E. Coleridge.
Style, by Walter Raleigh.
An African Millionaire, by Grant Allen.
Rome, the Middle of the World, by Alice Gardner.
Job Hildred, by Dr. Richards, edited by Ellen F. Pinsent.
Fire and Sword in the Sudan, by Rudolf C. Slatin Pasah, translated by Colonel F. R. Wingate. New and cheaper edition.
The Son of a Peasant, by Edward McNulty.
Memoir of Anne J. Clough, by Blanche Athena Clough.

RICHARD G. BADGER & CO., Boston.

The Right Side of the Car, by John Uri Lloyd.

THE BAKER & TAYLOR CO., New York.

Sunlight and Shadow, edited by W. I. Lincoln Adams.
A Colonial Witch, by Frank Samuel Child.
Fabius the Roman, by E. F. Burr.

BENZIGER BROTHERS, New York.

Moral Principles and Medical Practice, by Rev. Charles Coppens.
A Round Table of the Representative Irish and English Catholic Novelists.

BONNELL, SILVER & CO., New York.

The Sacrifice of a Throne, by H. Remsen Whitehouse.

THE BOWEN-MERRILL CO., Indianapolis.

Chimes from a Jester's Bells, by Robert J. Burdette.

THE CENTURY CO., New York.

Life of Napoleon Bonaparte, by William Milligan Sloane, Vol. IV.

THE CHAMBERLIN PRESS, Buffalo.

Verse Vagaries, by George Austin Woodward.

H. T. COATES & CO., Philadelphia.

A Girl's Ordeal, by Lucy C. Lillie.

CONTINENTAL PUBLISHING CO., New York.

Through the Invisible, by Paul Tyner.
Free Banking a Natural Right, by James A. B. Dilworth.

COPELAND & DAY, Boston.

Free to Serve, by E. Rayner.
Of Dandyism and of George Brummell, translated from the French of J. A. Barbey D'Aurevilly, by Douglas Ainslie.
Memorial Day and Other Poems, by Richard Burton.

T. Y. CROWELL & CO., Boston.

If I Were God, by Richard Le Gallienne.
Self-Cultivation in English, by George H. Palmer.
The Coming People, by Charles F. Dole.

DAMRELL & UPHAM, Boston.

Rhymes, by Edith Leverey Dalton.

DODD, MEAD & CO., New York.

Shakespeare Kalendar.
The Ian Maclaren Kalendar.
The Ian Maclaren Year Book.
Irish Idylls, by Jane Barlow.
The Potter's Wheel, by Ian Maclaren.
The Children of Sherburne House, by Amanda M. Douglas.
Dariel, by R. D. Blackmore.
Derick, by Barbara Yechton.
Pierre and His Poodle, by Elizabeth W. Champney.
The King's Highway, by Amelia E. Barr.
The Son of Ingar, by Katharine Pearson Woods.
Lawrence Clavering, by A. E. W. Mason.
The Two Captains, by W. Clark Russell.

DODGE BOOK & STATIONERY CO., San Francisco.

Cupid's Game with Hearts, illustrated by Stella A. Wittram.
Fifty Songs of Love.

DOUBLEDAY & MCCLURE CO., New York.

True Detective Stories, from the Pinkerton Archives, by Cleveland Moffett.
Whip and Spur, by George E. Waring, Jr.
Thro' Lattice Windows, by W. J. Dawson.
Peter the Priest, by Maurus Jókai.
Tales from *McClure's*, The West.
Taken from Life, Verse.
Prince Uno, Uncle Frank's Visit to Fairyland, illustrated by W. D. Stevens.
Bird Neighbours, by Neltje Blanchan.
Little Masterpieces, edited by Bliss Perry, Nathaniel Hawthorne, Washington Irving, Edgar Allan Poe.

WILLIAM DOXEY, San Francisco.

Yermah the Dorado, by Frona Eunice Wait.

R. F. FENNO & CO., New York.

The Dagger and the Cross, by Joseph Hatton.
The Cedar Star, by Mary E. Mann.
The Man Who Was Good, by Leonard Merrick.
Jasper Fairfax, by Margaret Holmes.

FUNK & WAGNALLS, New York.

The Epic of Paul, by William C. Wilkinson.
Sermon Stories for Boys and Girls, by Louis Albert Banks.
The Encyclopædia of Social Reform, edited by William D. P. Bliss.

HARPER & BROTHERS, New York.

The Personal Equation, by Harry Thurston Peck.
John Leighton, Jr., by Katrina Trask.
Outlines in Local Colour, by Brander Matthews.
Ars Recte Vivendi, by George William Curtis.
Celebrated Trials, by H. L. Clinton.
Paste Jewels, by John Kendrick Bangs.
Alan Ransford, by Ellen Douglas Deland.
Stuart and Bamboo, by Mrs. S. P. McLean Greene.
The French Revolution, Justin McCarthy, Vol. II.
Lorraine, by Robert W. Chambers.
Marchesi and Music, by Mathilde Marchesi.
Unkist, Unkind! by Violet Hunt.

FRANCIS P. HARPER, New York.

Game Birds of North America, by Daniel Giraud Elliot.

B. HERDER, St. Louis.

Beauties and Antiquities of Ireland, by T. O. Russell.

HENRY HOLT & CO., New York.

The Evolution of the Aryan, by Rudolph von Ihering. Translated from the German by A. Drucker, M.P.
Journeys Through France, by H. A. Taine.
The Italians of To-day, from the French of René Bazin. Translated by William Marchant.
The Evolution of the Idea of God, by Grant Allen.
Phil May's Graphic Pictures.

HOUGHTON, MIFFLIN & CO., Boston.

Hawthorne's First Diary, by Samuel T. Pickard.
A Browning Courtship and Other Stories, by Eliza Orne White.
The Revolt of a Daughter, by Ellen Olney Kirk.
Aaron in the Wildwoods, by Joel Chandler Harris.
Inequality and Progress, by George Harris.
Poems Now First Collected, by Edmund Clarence Stedman.
Correspondence of Emerson and Sterling.
Being a Boy, by Charles Dudley Warner.
The Ruins and Excavations of Ancient Rome by Rodolfo Lanciani.
An Unwilling Maid, by Jeanie Gould Lincoln.
Seven on the Highway, by Blanche Willis Howard.
The Theology of an Evolutionist, by Lyman Abbott.
Prose and Poetical Works of Thomas Bailey Aldrich, 8 vols.
Little Folk Lyrics, by Frank Dempster Sherman.
King Arthur and the Table Round, by William Wells Newell, 2 vols.

WILLIAM R. JENKINS, New York.

Un Drama Nuevo, by John R. Matzke, Ph.D.
A Brief Italian Grammar with Exercises, by Hjalmar Edgren.

WILBUR B. KETCHAM, New York.

Plain Living and High Thinking, by T. T. Munger.
A Vision of the Future, by F. B. Meyer.
Joy, Rest and Faith, by Henry Drummond.
Art and Morality, by Washington Gladden, D.D.
The Ministry to the Congregation, by John A. Kern, D.D.

The Story of a Church Bonnet, by Charles F. Deems, D.D.
True Manhood, by F. W. Farrar, D.D.
Christ Enough, by Hanna W. Smith.

LAIRD & LEE, Chicago.

Hours with the Ghosts; or XIX. Century Witchcraft, by H. R. Evans.

LEE AND SHEPARD, Boston.

Pacific Shores, by Oliver Optic.
On Plymouth Rock, by Samuel Adams Drake.
Dreams in Homespun, by Sam Walter Foss.
Guarding of the Border, by Everett T. Tomlinson.

J. B. LIPPINCOTT Co., Philadelphia.

Barbara, Lady's Maid and Peeress, by Mrs. Alexander.
The Yersin Phono-Rhythmic Method of French Pronunciation, Accent and Diction, by M. and J. Yersin.
Dead Selves, by Julia Magruder.
The Hermit of Nottingham, by Charles C. Abbott, M.D.
A Damsel Errant, by Amélie Rives.
Chalmette, by Clinton Ross.
The Epic of Sounds, by Freda Winworth.
A Queen of Hearts, by Elizabeth Phipps Train.
The Life of Charles Jared Ingersoll, by William M. Meigs.
The Lost Gold of the Montezumas, by W. O. Stoddard.
The Rover's Quest, by Hugh St. Leger.
The Flame Flower, by James F. Sullivan.
The Works of François Rabelais, translated by Sir Thomas Urquhart and Peter Motteux, 5 vols.
From Fag to Monitor, by Andrew Home.
Hunted through Fiji, by Reginald Horsley.
The Pride of the Mercers, by T. C. De Leon.
With Feet to the Earth, by Charles M. Skinner.
Meg Langholme, by Mrs. Molesworth.
Travels in a Tree-Top, by Charles C. Abbott, 2 vols.
Richard Wagner, by Houston Stewart Chamberlain. Translated from the German by G. Ainslie Hight, and revised by the author.
The Confessions of Jean Jacques Rousseau, 4 vols.
The Story of an Irish Sept, by a member of the Sept.
History of the United States, by Charles Morris.

LITTLE, BROWN & Co., Boston.

Miss Belladonna, a child of to-day, by Caroline Ticknor.
How to Know the Shore Birds, by C. B. Cory.
Romance and Reality of the Puritan Coast, by Edmund H. Garrett.
The Adventures of Mr. Verdant Green, by Cuthbert Bede.
Flint, His Faults, His Friendships and His Fortunes, by Maud Wilder Goodwin.
Ten Little Comedies, by Gertrude Smith.
Romances of Colonial Virginia, by Maud Wilder Goodwin, 2 vols.

LONGMANS, GREEN & Co., New York.

The Vege-Men's Revenge, pictures by Florence K. Upton, verses by Bertha Upton.
The Water of the Wondrous Isles, by William Morris.
The Pink Fairy Book, edited by Andrew Lang.
The Diary of Master William Silence, by Right Hon. D. H. Madden.
The Adventures of the Three Bold Babes, by S. Rosamond Praeger.
Here They Are! More Stories, by J. F. Sullivan.

THE MACMILLAN Co., New York.

The Household of the Lafayettes, by Edith Sichel.
Biblical Masterpieces, edited, with an introduction and notes by Richard G. Moulton, M.A.
Social and Ethical Interpretations in Mental Development, by James Mark Baldwin.
The Study of City Government, by Delos F. Wilcox.
The Temple Dramatists, Fletcher's Faithful Shepherdess.
The Temple Dramatists, Sheridan's The Critic.
A Forest Orchid, by Ella Higginson.
The Torrents of Spring, by Ivan Turgenev. Translated from the Russian by Constance Garnett.
Singing Verses for Children.
Practical Idealism, by William De Witt Hyde.
A Handbook of Greek Sculpture, by Ernest Arthur Gardner.
The Growth of the French Nation, by George Burton Adams.
Undine, by F. De La Motte Fouqué.
In the Permanent Way, by Flora Annie Steel.
Corleone, by F. Marion Crawford, 2 vols.
Miss Mouse and Her Boys, by Mrs. Molesworth. Illustrated by L. Leslie Brooke.
Captain Mansana and Mother's Hands, by Björnstjerne Björnson.
The Battle of Harlem Heights, by Henry P. Johnston, A.M.

A. C. McCLURG & Co., Chicago.

Love's Ways and Other Poems, by Martin Swift.
Stories from Italy, by G. S. Godkin.
A Little House in Pimlico, by Marguerite Bouvet.

METHODIST BOOK CONCERN, New York.

The Picket Line of Missions, Sketches of the Advanced Guard.
The Christ Brotherhood, by Louis Albert Banks, D.D.
Life on High Levels, by Margaret E. Sangster.

MEYER BROTHERS & Co., New York.

Tales of the Heart, by Roland B. Hennessy.

THE OPEN COURT PUBLISHING CO., Chicago.

Darwin and After Darwin, by the late George John Romanes.
Karma, by Paul Carus.

THE PILGRIM PROGRESS, Boston.

The Young Capitalist, by Linnie S. Harris.
The Benhurst Club, by Howe Benning.

JAMES POTT & CO., New York.

Bishop Cobbs and His Contemporaries, by the Rev. Greenough White, A.M.

G. P. PUTNAM'S SONS, New York.

Red Apple and Silver Bells, by Hamish Hendry.
Short Sayings of Famous Men, collected and edited by Helen Kendrick Johnson, 2 vols.
The Fall of the Sparrow, by M. C. Balfour.
Pratt Portraits, by Anna Fuller.
Robert E. Lee and the Southern Confederacy, by Henry Alexander White.
Astoria, by Washington Irving. Tacoma Edition, 2 vols.
American Ideals and Other Essays, by Theodore Roosevelt.
Chronicles of Tarrytown and Sleepy Hollow, by Edgar Mayhew Bacon.
Little Journeys to the Homes of Famous Women, by Elbert Hubbard.
In Search of a Religion, by Dennis Hird.
Nippur, or Explorations and Adventures on the Euphrates, by John P. Peters, D.D., second campaign, Vol. II.
Some Colonial Homesteads and Their Stories, by Marion Harland.
Modern English Prose Writers, by Frank Preston Stearns.
Elementary Jane, by Richard Pryce.
The Colloquy.
Poetical Sermons, by William E. Davenport.

FLEMING H. REVELL CO., New York.

The Gist of Japan, by R. B. Peery.
Christian Missions and Social Progress, Vol. I., by the Rev. James S. Dennis, D.D.
The Growth of the Kingdom of God, by Sidney L. Gulick.
The Pew to the Pulpit, by David J. Brewer, LL.D.

ROBERTS BROTHERS, Boston.

The Little Red Schoolhouse, by Evelyn Raymond.
The Procession of Flowers in Colorado, by Helen Jackson.
Rich Enough, by Leigh Webster.
Torpeanuts the Tomboy, by Lily F. Wesselhoeft.
Nan in the City, or Nan's Winter with the Girls, by Myra Sawyer Hamlin.
The Resolute Mr. Pansy, by John Trowbridge.
The Young Puritans of Old Hadley, by Mary P. Wells Smith.
Molière, translated by Katharine P. Wormeley. Vol. V.
History of Dogma, by Dr. Adolph Harnack. Translated from the third German edition by Neil Buchanan. Vol. III.

ROLLINGPIN PUBLISHING CO., St. Louis.

Log Cabin Poems, by Commodore Rollingpin.

HAROLD ROORBACH, New York.

A Night Off, by Augustin Daly.
Seventy-Twenty-Eight, by Augustin Daly.
All the Comforts of Home, by William Gillette.

R. H. RUSSELL, New York.

The Slambangaree, by R. K. Munkittrick.
An Alphabet, by William Nicholson.
The Blackberries, by Edward W. Kemble.
The Autobiography of a Monkey, by Hy. Mayer and Albert B. Paine.
Drawings by Frederic Remington.

CHARLES SCRIBNER'S SONS, New York.

Literary Love-Letters, by Robert Herrick.
This Country of Ours, by Benjamin Harrison.
Berquin, a Drama, by Elizabeth G. Crane.
William Blackwood and His Sons, by Mrs. Oliphant, 2 vols.
The Poetry of Tennyson, by Henry van Dyke. Cameo Edition.
Song Birds and Water Fowl, by H. E. Parkhurst.
A Romance in Transit, by Francis Lynde.
The Stevenson Song Book.

SILVER, BURDETT & CO., Boston and New York.

Reading Courses in American Literature, by Fred Lewis Pattee.
The Plant Baby and its Friends, by Kate Louise Brown.
Southey's Life of Nelson, edited by Alexander S. Twombly.
Shakespeare's Macbeth, edited by Fred Lewis Pattee.
Burke's Speech on Conciliation, edited by Francis R. Lane.
Macaulay's Essay on Milton, edited by Alexander S. Twombly.
Coleridge's Rime of the Ancient Mariner, edited by Alexander S. Twombly.
Addison's Sir Roger De Coverley Papers, edited by Alexander S. Twombly.
Macaulay's Essay on Addison, edited by Alexander S. Twombly.
De Quincey's Revolt of the Tartars, by Alexander S. Twombly.
Webster's First Bunker Hill Oration, edited by Alexander S. Twombly.
Elements of Constructive Geometry, by William Noetling.
Polyhymnia, for Male Voices, by John W. Tufts.
Stepping-Stones to Literature, by Sarah L. Arnold and Charles B. Gilbert.
First and Second Readers.

FREDERICK A. STOKES CO., New York.

The God Yutzo of B. C. 763, by Lord Gilhooley.
Collection of "Masterpieces," Robert Burns.
The Skipper's Wooing, by W. W. Jacobs.
A Great Lie, by Wilfrid Hugh Chesson.
The Charm and Other Drawing-Room Plays, by Walter Besant and Walter Pollock.
Old Youngsters, by Maud Humphrey and Elizabeth S. Tucker.
Make-Believe Men and Women, by Maud Humphrey and Elizabeth S. Tucker.
Little Grown-Ups, by Maud Humphrey and Elizabeth S. Tucker.
Lyrics by De Quincey, selected from his works, by R. Brimley Johnson.
Pensées of Joubert, selected and translated by Henry Attwell.
Pen Portraits by Thomas Carlyle, found in his works and correspondence, by R. Brimley Johnson.
Fac-similes of Water Colours, by Paul de Longpré.
Goldsmith's Comedies, edited by Joseph Jacobs.

H. S. STONE & CO., Chicago.

For the Love of Tonita, by Charles Fleming Embree.
Phyllis in Bohemia, by L. H. Bickford and Richard Stillman Powell.
Eat Not Thy Heart, by Julien Gordon.
Happiness as Found in Forethought Minus Fearthought, by Horace Fletcher.
What Maisie Knew, by Henry James.
The Vice of Fools, by H. C. Chatfield-Taylor.
Literary Statesmen and Others, by Norman Hapgood.

THE TEMPLE PRESS, Denver.

The Captain's Dream, by Paul Tyner.

F. TENNYSON NEELY, New York.

Urania, by Camille Flammarion. Translated by Augusta Rice Stetson.
An Army Wife, by Captain Charles King.
Smoking Flax, by Hallie Erminie Rives.
Seven Smiles and a Few Fibs, by Thomas J. Vivian.
Among the Dunes, by Rhone.
That Noble Mexican, by T. B. Connery.
Her Physician, by Andrew D. Spurgeon.

THOUSAND ISLANDS PUBLISHING CO., Clayton. N. Y.

Folk Stories of the Northern Border.

WAY & WILLIAMS, Chicago.

The Story of Ab, by Stanley Waterloo.
Paul Travers' Adventures, by Sam T. Clover.

WESTERN UNITARIAN SUNDAY-SCHOOL SOCIETY, Chicago.

The Growth of Christianity, by Joseph Henry Crooker.

THOMAS WHITTAKER, New York.

History of France, by Mary C. Rowsell.
History of Rome, by Mary Ford.
Old Tales from Greece, by Alice Zimmern.
The Message and the Messengers, by the Rev. Fleming James, D.D.
The Facts and the Faith, by Beverley E. Warner, D.D.
The Poetical Works of John Milton.
The Poetical Works of Lord Byron.
The Poetical Works of William Wordsworth.
Shakespeare's Works, Falstaff Edition.
Character Through Inspiration, by T. T. Munger, D.D.

W. A. WILDE & CO., Boston.

Over the Andes, or Our Boys in New South America, by Hezekiah Butterworth.
A Successful Venture, by Ellen Douglas Deland.
Sue Orcutt, by Charlotte M. Vaile.
Midshipman Jack, by Charles Ledyard Norton.
The Beach Patrol, by William Drysdale.
Washington's Young Aids, by Everett T. Tomlinson.

JOHN C. WINSTON & CO., Philadelphia.

Uncle Tom's Cabin, by Harriet Beecher Stowe.

J. H. YEWDALE & SONS CO., Milwaukee

Harp of Milan, by Shepperson.

THE BOOKMAN

A LITERARY JOURNAL.

VOL. VI. JANUARY, 1898. No. 5.

CHRONICLE AND COMMENT.

The Editors of THE BOOKMAN *cannot undertake to return rejected manuscripts, whether stamps are enclosed or not; and to this rule no exception will be made.*

There is a literary critic on the *Mail and Express* of this city who needs enlightenment. In reviewing a book recently he found the expression "Italian vinegar" coupled with the mention of "Attic salt." This struck him as very absurd, and he devoted a whole paragraph to displaying his own ignorance of what "Italian vinegar" meant. We like to enlighten persons of this sort, and so we will inform him that Italian vinegar (*Italum acetum*) was an expression used by the Romans to denote their own rude native wit as contrasted with the more urbane and polished wit of the Athenians (*sal Atticum*). For this elementary information we make no charge.

❀

We hear that Lord Charles Beresford and his collaborateur, Mr. Wilson, have discovered over a hundred hitherto unpublished letters of Nelson's, with which they will enrich the work upon the great seaman on which they are engaged.

❀

That the forthcoming *Enfant Terrible!* will not, like the *Lark*, eschew satire, is shown by its advance sheets, which contain, among other things, "The Bohemians of Boston"—a Bab Ballady poem evidently directed at the "League of the White Rose," the latest toy of the ultra-Anglomaniacs, who uphold the Jacobite pretension, and drink to the bonnie Prince Charlie—over the water. Among this cult are Louise Imogen Guiney, Alice Brown, Bliss Carman, Herbert Stone of the *Chap-Book*, Ralph Adams Cram, Herbert Copeland, and others. Of the Infant's "Orchid Club" it is said that

> "Fitz Willieboy was so *blasé*
> He burned a *Transcript* up, one day!"

and the accompanying sublime illustration pictures the climax of the Boston orchid's notoriety, when

> "Fitz-Willieboy McFlubadub,
> The Regent of the Orchid's Club,
> Had written on the window sill
> This shocking legend—
> 'Beacon H—ll!'"

The enterprising editor of the English magazine, *The Young Man*, presents in his December number a very interesting interview with Mr. Phil May, who succeeded Du Maurier on *Punch*. Mr. May, we learn, was born at Wortley, near

PHIL MAY.

Drawn by himself.

Leeds, England, thirty-three years ago. His career has been a very varied and serious one, and began when as a boy of twelve he was thrown upon his own resources. His first regular work was done on the now defunct *St. Stephen's Review* fourteen years ago, after which he went out to Australia in 1885. He worked there for the Sydney *Bulletin*, and came back to London in 1888. The publication of *The Parson and the Painter* in 1891 was the beginning of his success, when a writer in the London *Daily Chronicle* spoke in the highest terms of his work, and gave three columns to a criticism of it. During the last five or six years this brilliant young artist, after surmounting more difficulties than most men are obliged to encounter, has been recognised as the most gifted black-and-white artist of our time. He is now exclusively retained by *Punch* and the *Graphic*, so that his days as a free lance are over. He is anxious that it should be widely known that any sketches which appear in other papers are sketches which were done by him years ago, and are being republished with his signature left in and the date taken off without his permission. He would also like to put right the prevalent impression that he "dashes off" his sketches. Sketching, he says, is much more serious work than that. For every sketch of his which is published he makes a dozen studies which never see the light.

❀

Mr. May was asked why it is that one occasionally finds some of his original drawings on sale, and he replied characteristically, "That I don't know; they must be sketches which I have given to friends and have been sold by them. Terrible thought, isn't it? But that is the only explanation. It reminds me of the Liberal politician I once heard of—"

"What was that?" asked the interviewer, on the alert for a good story.

"Oh, it was the same sort of thing—only more so. It seems this man was an ardent Liberal—no, there is no political bias in this story! He got into correspondence with Mr. Gladstone, who gave him some of his works with his autograph on the fly-leaf. Nothing remarkable about that! No, but what was the sequel? That man went and sold those autograph books, and on the proceeds of the sale he went down into the country to vote against the Gladstonian candidate! Cynical sort of proceeding, wasn't it?"

❀

Mr. May works best when he is out of London. Besides his regular work for *Punch* and the *Graphic*, he has an engagement to illustrate an *édition de luxe* of Dickens's works which Mr. George Allen is to publish some time during the year. "I am never tired of reading Dickens," he says; "I can never find a dull page in his books. I think my favourite is *Oliver Twist*, and after that *David Copperfield*. I have been busy looking around for my types. and have met a good many of his characters. Wonderful genius for characterisation! He had the observant faculty as few men ever have it. The illustrations will be quite a labour of love, and therefore all the more arduous."

The two literary women who have been most talked about during the last decade have published almost simultaneously a new work in fiction. Madame Sarah Grand's *The Beth Book* appeared in November, and Mrs. Craigie's *The School for Saints*, first announced as *Saints and Sinners*, came out a few weeks later. To the curious and those versed in the black art of chirography we submit facsimiles of the manuscripts of both these books on the next page. The contrast is very striking. The new portrait which we give of Mrs. Craigie is taken from a photograph of a painting by Schmalz.

Mrs. Craigie works in a spacious study at the top of her parents' beautiful English home at Lancaster Gate. Book collecting is her great hobby, and she has some three thousand volumes, many of them rare and exquisite editions. Sarah Grand finds people and, above everything, a free, quiet life in the country more interesting than books. In winter the Riviera attracts her, and during the past spring and summer she lived in the most complete retirement at the Hermitage of Jean Jacques Rousseau in the Forest of Montmorency, where she wrote her new book. Her method of work is to write the story first with pencil, whenever an idea seizes her, and then to rewrite and polish what she has written, after which it passes to her secretary to be typewritten. Mrs. Craigie, on the other hand, is not a laborious writer. She spends several hours sometimes in meditating on a portion of a story, and it may be that only a few lines are the result. But when she comes to the actual writing she does it very quickly. It is to be noted that she says that her characters do not usually express her views. "Some people seem to hold me responsible for everything that I have put into the mouths of the people in my books, but I never describe living characters, and have never attempted to write what is commonly called 'a society novel.' My aim is to write about human nature—not about the peculiarities of an individual or the manners of a season."

A STUDY BY PHIL MAY.

Mrs. Craigie confesses that she has a growing love for the writing of history and biography, and thinks it not improbable that she may in future devote herself largely to that branch of literature. If she does, the romantic and stirring history of her own Puritan and Revolutionary forefathers will afford her interesting subject-matter. For though Mrs. Craigie has had no continuing city, but is, as she laughingly calls herself, a citizen of the world—she began her travels at the age of three—Boston is her native place, and the blood of Puritan divines and Tory politicians mingles in her veins. She is proud of the fact that she is a Daughter of the Revolution.

In studying her life it would be as foolish as it is useless to say that she should or would have done this, that, or the other thing at critical times. It is not what she should have done according to our judgment, nor what she would have done in our opinion, but what she actually did do, and the why and wherefore of her actions, which concerns us, and must be considered if we honestly wish to comprehend her, to arrive at the motives, principles, and impulses to which she was

FAC-SIMILE OF MANUSCRIPT FROM "THE BETH BOOK," BY SARAH GRAND.

But, said I, it may be that the two-fold abandonment of all natural hopes & affections comes from vanity — the ambition to be which we are yet not, like the angels of God. And while I might be tempted to feel exalted at my resignation, God, Who cannot be deceived, should know that it were not from virtue, but from a cultured inhumanity. Does our Blessed Lady in Heaven forget the Song she sang at Karim, or the anguish of [illegible] at Calvary? I cannot say then — 'Take my happiness. I do not need it. I am better off without it. Before the year is past, I shall have reason to be glad that it is no longer with me.' Oh, no! But I can say, 'Take it if it be Thy Will to take it. It is my life. When it has gone, I may [illegible] be calm, because my capacity for grief — or for any other feeling — will have gone also.' Self-absorbed & self-sufficient

FAC-SIMILE OF MANUSCRIPT FROM "THE SCHOOL FOR SAINTS," BY JOHN OLIVER HOBBES.

It is curious that both these women should have chosen *noms-de-guerre* as authors, and that they should have been actuated by different but distinctly characteristic motives. When it was suggested to Mrs. Craigie that her own name of "Pearl" would have suited her much better, she replied with a smile, "I adopted the name of John Oliver Hobbes to keep me from being sentimental." "I wanted," says the author of *The Beth Book*, "a name that would be simple; I dislike fanciful pen-names. I had no idea at the time that a real

John Oliver Hobbes.

From the photograph of a painting by Schmalz.

Sarah Grand had ever existed, but shortly after the publication of *The Heavenly Twins*, a gentleman said to me at dinner one evening, 'I am surprised that you should have taken the name of Sarah Grand. Possibly you are not aware that she was a notorious and beautiful woman, who ended eventually as the wife of Talleyrand.' I certainly had never heard this before, and have ever since been deeply interested in tracing the original Sarah Grand's history, but have discovered very little of it so far." She has now permanently adopted this *nom-de-guerre* as her real name, and Mrs. Chambers McFall, that once was, is now ushered into the London drawing-rooms as "Madame Sarah Grand."

❀

The censorious critics of the Kailyard in fiction will hail with delight what seems in two notable instances to be a return to the historic romance of the Stevensonian type. First on the field was Mr. William McLennan with *Spanish John*, which began as a serial in the October number of *Harper's*. The author's intimacy with the Scottish Highlands shows him no stranger to the heather, the loch, and the Ben, as his selection of themes denotes his knowledge of the salient features in Scottish romance. The second newcomer is Mr.

NEIL MUNRO.

Neil Munro, whose *John Splendid* will appear throughout the year in *Blackwood's Magazine* in England, and in THE BOOKMAN in this country. The first instalment is published in this number.

❀

Mr. Munro is a Highlander of the Highlanders. He was born at Inverary, and comes of a farming and shepherd stock who have lived for centuries in Glenaray and on the shores of Loch Awe. He barely escaped the prospect that has been the lot of his forefathers—herding sheep, harvesting in the yellow fields, and thinning turnips for the Duke of Argyle. The parish minister was Mr. Munro's "Domsie" at this critical time, who had him set to the law. But he turned his back on law and started to woo letters. After some journalistic experience, he sent his first story to the *Speaker*, and it was accepted. He sent a second to Mr. W E. Henley, who printed it in the *National Observer* in May, 1893, and took an opportunity thereafter to praise the author for his work. Then followed his connection with Mr. Blackwood, which began with the rejection of one story and the acceptance of the next sent to him. "Send me anything else you do," wrote Mr. Blackwood to the young author. *The Lost Pibroch*, which took him nearly a twelvemonth to put together, was the result. Of this volume Mr. Andrew Lang and other able critics have written in the highest terms of praise.

❀

His novel, *John Splendid*, is his first long-sustained effort, and is a remarkable performance, recalling the best of Stevenson, and succeeding where Stevenson failed, in portraying a womanly heroine with a glamour of witchery that wins the reader from the start. Mr. Munro disclaims the Celtic gloom. The Celt, as he knows him, is not gloomy at all, though something of a fatalist, and readily responsive to the pathos of life and nature, and unwilling to frivol with the large issues of existence which some races make jokes about in the comic papers. In half his moods he is riotously funny, with a vivid sense of the humorous, and a most beautiful zest in his little comforts and casual amusements. The story, like *Spanish John*, is autobiographic in form. *John Splendid*, we are certain, will prove to be one of the leading serials of the year.

❀

Pierre Loti's new volume, *Figures et Choses qui Passaient*, is a collection of scraps from a note-book, mostly written when he was staying in the Pays Basque preparing the matter for his novel *Ramuntcho*. His new book certainly contains examples of his finest writing. It would be difficult to find in any of his novels a more exquisite chapter than "Messe de Minuit," the description of a midnight mass in a small village in the Pyrenees.

The newest compilation of Ruskin enthusiasts is nearly ready. It is called *The Bible References of John Ruskin*. Miss M. and Miss E. Gibbs have selected and arranged the passages, by permission of the author. The publisher is, of course, Mr. George Allen.

It is proposed to issue Scandinavian, Dutch, Italian, Spanish, and even Greek supplements to *Cosmopolis* during the year.

The name of Dora Sigerson is not altogether unfamiliar and unnoted on this side of the water as a mark of genuine poetry. Some of her poems have appeared in the pages of this journal. Her genius is akin to that of Katharine Tynan Hinkson, Jane Barlow, and W. B. Yeats—the sweetest singer of them all, perhaps the sweetest singer living—and, like them, her imagination is rooted and grounded in Ireland. We have been eager to see her first volume of verse, which is now published by Mr. John Lane under the title *The Fairy Changeling, and Other Poems*. We hope to give more space to a review of the work in our next number; meanwhile, let us quote here what Dr. W. Robertson Nicoll has just written of the quality of these verses:

> "They are not written as so many books of verse are written—that their author's poetic conscience may be stroked and pleased; they are full of the spirit of a genuine emotion, of strong pathos and originality, of high purity of feeling, and often marked by a grave and graceful sweetness. There is not a line which breathes the spirit of bitterness or cynicism, or even a final despair, and there are many passages for the sake of which it will be a real pleasure to keep the book at hand, and occasionally to turn over its pages. This is surely the highest praise that can be given to a young writer."

Dora Sigerson was married in July, 1896, to Mr. Clement K. Shorter, the vivacious and genial editor of the *Sketch*, the *Illustrated London News*, and the *English Illustrated Magazine*.

ELIZABETH BARRETT BROWNING.

From the marble bust by W. W. Story.

On another page will be found a review of *The Letters of Elizabeth Barrett Browning*, which has just been published in two volumes by the Macmillan Company, also a fac-simile of Mrs. Browning's manuscript taken from an essay called "An Opinion on Tennyson," written by her in 1843, and unearthed by the editors of *Literary Anecdotes of the Nineteenth Century* (Vol. I.). In THE BOOKMAN for March, 1896, were published pictures of Mrs. Browning's monument in the cemetery at Florence, and the Casa Guidi, where she lived and died. Here we reproduce an oval portrait from the photogravure of the beautiful marble bust, by W. W. Story, which forms the frontispiece to the first volume of the *Letters*.

Florence, the place of Mrs. Browning's death, had already raised her tribute to the poet's memory before it was discovered with certainty where her exact birthplace was. But an explicit entry in a parish register clears away all doubt, and now the quiet little English country church of Kelloe Parish, so near the old hall where Mrs. Browning's life began, has paid its meed of service. A few weeks ago a marble tablet to the memory of Elizabeth Barrett Browning was unveiled in this church by the Dean of Durham. Mrs. Browning was born at Coxhoe Hall, which is near Kelloe. The illustrations showing the Hall and the tablet are taken from the *Sketch*.

FAC-SIMILE OF MARBLE TABLET IN MEMORY OF MRS. BROWNING IN KELLOE PARISH CHURCH.

❀

The London *Spectator* is usually so reasonable and just in its comment upon persons and things, that we are surprised to find a recent number of it speaking of the oratory of President Faure of France as being *bourgeois* and commonplace. Now, as a matter of fact, nothing could be more unfair. President Faure is a remarkably able speaker. No better proof of this could be found than that which is afforded by the perusal of the addresses made by him during his recent visit to the court of the Russian Czar. Under most trying circumstances, M. Faure acquitted himself oratorically in a manner that was simply perfect. His speeches were models of tact, of grace, and of dignity, and every Frenchman ought to have been proud of his very unusual talent for saying the right thing at the right moment. If the *Spectator* really wants some inimitable specimens of oratory that is *bourgeois* and commonplace, it should look up the various speeches made by the Prince of Wales during the last twenty years. Nothing more platitudinous and void of thought could very well be found. And only last June, when the Queen received some local tradesmen who for the moment were in some official position, she made an address which was about the dullest and flattest thing that we have ever seen. But what did the *Spectator* say about this? Why, it observed that it was difficult to conceive of anything more instinct with loftiness and stateliness. Yet any judge of oratorical form, if he had these different speeches set before him, with the names of their authors suppressed, would have picked out those of the Queen and the Prince of Wales as the productions of the ex-tanner, and those of President Faure as the deliverances of a monarch.

COXHOE HALL, WHERE MRS. BROWNING WAS BORN.

❀

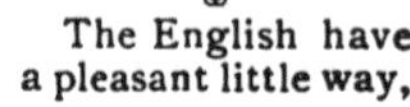

The English have a pleasant little way,

whenever they reprint an American book, of removing from its title page all possible indications of its source. We said something about this two years ago, and several English publishers at once took umbrage at our remarks, and the ubiquitous Mr. Andrew Lang rushed into print to defend his employers. But here are two recent instances of how the thing works. A new edition of the Latin-French Dictionary of Quicherat has just appeared, and in it the Latin Dictionary of Lewis and Short, which is a purely American publication, is credited to "two English scholars." This is because the Clarendon Press, which reprinted the book, after Oxford had adopted it as a standard, let it go forth as a purely British publication. Much the same thing happened in the case of one of Captain Mahan's works last summer. The English published it, suppressing the fact that its author was an officer of the United States Navy. Consequently, the *Temps* of Paris spoke of Captain Mahan as an English naval officer, and Lieutenant Fitch, the American naval attaché at the embassy in Paris, had to write a letter to the *Temps* in order to make it correct this false ascription. As we said about two years ago, this sort of thing is neither just nor even honest, and we hope that American authors whose books find favour in English eyes will insist upon appearing as Americans, and thus gain for their country a credit which the English invariably begrudge it.

❀

Mr. Mackenzie Bell has been so fortunate as to secure for his forthcoming book on Christina Rossetti a striking portrait of the poet, painted by James Collinson, and a drawing of her by Dante Gabriel Rossetti, neither of which has been published before. The book will also contain a photograph of Christina and her mother which was taken so long ago as 1863 by "Lewis Carroll" (the Rev. Charles Lutwidge Dodgson), as well as numerous letters from Christina Rossetti which throw an intimate light upon her personality.

❀

Mr. A. J. Butler, who is so well known in the varied capacities of a translator of Dante, a translator of Marbot's *Memoirs*, as an Alpine climber, and as an Inspector of Schools, is now engaged in translating a German book of ethnology. The illustrations will be a curious revelation to many students.

❀

Mr. George Gissing, who has been in Italy for some weeks past, staying at Siena, is at present at Naples. He is on his way to Sicily, where he will stay for some time. Mr. Gissing's next novel will be entitled *The Town Traveller*.

❀

Mr. W. W. Jacobs, whose first long story, *The Skipper's Wooing*, was recently published by the F. A. Stokes Company, is engaged in writing one more novel with the flavour of the sea. When that is finished, he purposes, in succeeding work, to make a determined effort to get away from boats and sailors and salt water.

❀

Mr. Frank Mathew, the brilliant young Irish novelist, has written a new romance under the title of *A Lady's Sword*. Mr. Mathew is a grandson of the famous "Father Mathew," and a nephew of the well-known judge of the same name.

❀

The publishers are sometimes able to gauge the effects of reviews upon the sale of their books in a somewhat humorous way. Not very long ago Mr. Edward Clodd's *Primer of Evolution* was published by Messrs. Longmans in England and the Appletons in New York, and was reviewed in a contemporary under the title of "From Gas to Genius." Orders poured in very rapidly from all quarters, most of them asking for a book entitled *From Gas to Genius*. In some cases embarrassment was caused by a bookseller's collector emphatically declining to accept a book bearing so different a title as *A Primer of Evolution*.

❀

That truth is stranger than fiction is daringly exemplified in the case of Mr. Walter A. Wyckoff, who six years ago left behind him the ease and quiet dignity of a college graduate's life at Princeton, and plunged incognito into an unknown and untried sphere of life, and adopted the obscure and inglorious rôle of a day labourer. The story is re-

WALTER A. WYCKOFF.

lated of him that while at a house party in the summer of 1891 he was expounding his social theories one evening at dinner, when an older man of the thoroughgoing business type retorted that he knew nothing of the actual conditions of the labouring class. Starting out a few days later without a penny in his pocket and only one change of clothes, he at once set out to adjust himself to the life of the labourer, and for two years he worked as a gang labourer, farm hand, hotel porter, lumberman, etc. At the expiration of these two years he rested and went abroad, arranging the notes he had made during his strange experiences and getting them in shape for publication. These experiences have been related in the autumn numbers of *Scribner's Magazine*, and are now published in book form, entitled *The Workers: an Experiment in Reality*. The book purports to tell the truth about the workingman from actual observation and knowledge gained while submitting to the conditions that govern his class. We have had many sociological novels, but none, we will dare to say, containing so unvarnished a picture of reality—a picture at once of the most profound scientific and romantic interest, if we accept Mr. Wyckoff's experiment as belonging to the romance of human life.

❀

But according to Mr. Wyckoff, the half has not yet been told, and the present work is only an introduction to that which he will disclose in the pages of *Scribner's* some time during the year. The second part will deal with his more arduous experiment in the West, where this modern Don Quixote of the social realm came near to starving on the streets of Chicago as a member of the army of the unemployed. He lived in tenement-houses, associated with sweat-shop workers, attended anarchists' meetings, and dived into the labyrinth of the abnormal and diseased organisms of decivilised life in the large and overcrowded cities. Mr. W. R. Leigh, who illustrated the first series, is now sketching in Chicago among the scenes of Mr. Wyckoff's experiences. Mr. Wyckoff is a Fellow of Princeton, and is at present a lecturer in the Sociological Department. The portrait herewith given is the only authentic one yet published.

❀

Messrs. Small, Maynard and Company, of Boston, have issued the first volume of their new edition of the works of Walt Whitman, being *Leaves of Grass*, including posthumous additions under the heading "Old Age Echoes," and also the poet's "Backward Glance O'er Travel'd Roads" in prose from *November Boughs*. The frontispiece is a fine portrait of Whitman in 1890 with his autograph. The book is printed on light hand-made paper, and is tastefully bound and stamped with a neat, ornamental design on back. The event was celebrated by a window exhibit of Whitman editions, manuscripts, portraits, curious relics, etc., during the closing weeks in November. The exhibition was exposed in one of the capacious windows of Messrs. Dodd, Mead and Company's bookshop, fronting

A WHITMAN WINDOW EXHIBITION IN NEW YORK.

Fifth Avenue, and was an object of interest to a continuous crowd of foot passengers during the days of its display. A photograph of the window was taken, which is herewith reproduced, and accompanying the article on Walt Whitman, on another page, are numerous reproductions from the curious contents of this window, obtained by the courteous permission of Whitman's executors.

❀

Dr. Benjamin E. Smith, who is preternaturally wise and good, has been saying things in the *Critic* about THE BOOKMAN's views of "Fonetik Retawrm." He observes:

"'Why,' asks Professor Peck as a clincher, 'when the compilers of the Century Dictionary wrote *honor* and the like, did they not also write *Savior?*'"

Professor Peck asked nothing of the sort. Then Dr. Benjamin E. Smith, who, as we remarked before, is preternaturally wise and good, concludes as follows:

"Since stupidity generally goes with vulgarity, it is to be feared that most of the reformers will never find out that their pet humbug has been exploded, and will go on working just the same. But what does it matter to persons of refinement and discrimination what such people may do?"

Well, it doesn't matter a little bit.

❀

"If you see it in the *Sun*, it's so." Not always. For example, the distinguished New York clergyman of West Fifty-seventh Street Baptist Church might take exception to a statement made last month by one of the *Sun's* bright young men that, "Ian Maclaren's *Bonnie Brier Bush* had been dramatised by Dr. MacArthur." The statement was evidently accepted as veracious by the Evening *Post*, which printed the item on the same day. Nevertheless, we hope that when the play is produced Dr. MacArthur, if he witness it, will feel that no indignity has been put upon him.

We are now able to give some further information about this dramatisation, which may not be without interest to Ian Maclaren's numerous admirers. The story of the play keeps close to the various episodes in the books, which have been drawn into dramatic perspective; in the constructive process the atmosphere of pathos and comedy intermingling in the stories has been preserved; unity has been given to the scenes, and the human interest sustained and made cumulative to the end. The principal characters appear in the play, and Mr. J. H. Stoddart, one of the greatest "old man" actors on the stage, and an old Scotchman to boot, will take the part of Lachlan Campbell. Scottish part songs with a humorous musical arrangement, not familiar in this country, will be introduced by a trained male quartette, appearing as haymakers, street singers, etc., and will be quite an attractive feature. The production is in the hands of a first-class management, Messrs. Frank L. Perley and Fred M. Ranken, who are sanguine of its success, and are sparing no pains or expense to make it one of the finest presentations of its kind that has ever been produced. It will appear in New York about the beginning of February.

We have received the following letter from Professor Edwin A. Grosvenor of Amherst College:

AMHERST COLLEGE, AMHERST, MASS.,
December 2, 1897.

The Editors of THE BOOKMAN.

DEAR SIRS: In my version of *Andronike*, on page 451, last paragraph in Chapter XI., occurs the following sentence: "The islands Vasiladi, Dolma, Poros and Anitolicon in the Gulf of Misolonghi, in a word, every door through which provisions could be introduced by sea, were one by one wrested from the Greeks." Here evidently "The islands," etc., is the grammatical subject of "were."

In the December BOOKMAN, page 347, bottom of first column, the reviewer of *Andronike* criticises the "English style" of the version as follows: "The most scrupulous of writers would not father such a sentence as 'Every door, through which provisions could be introduced by sea, were one by one wrested from the Greeks'"

That is to say, in order to make this criticism he omits part of the sentence including the original subject, changes the small *e* of "every" to a capital *E*, so as to render "Every door" the subject of a plural verb, and also inserts a comma after "door." In other words, he mangles my sentence by three changes, encloses the mangled residuum in quotation marks, and criticises it. I submit that such procedure on the part of a reviewer is dishonest and dishonourable.

Very respectfully yours,
EDWIN A. GROSVENOR.

The reviewer submits, in reply, his sincere regret that the unfortunate passage was not printed entire, and without an error in punctuation. This should certainly have been done, not only in fairness, but also to show in full why the most scrupulous of writers would not father such a sentence.

The January part of *Chambers's Journal* will contain an article tracing "The Fate of Sir Walter Scott's Manuscripts" through the hands of their various possessors, such as Constable, Cadell, and others, with the various sums paid for each when they changed hands.

The monument recently erected in Paris to Guy de Maupassant has revived the old controversy as to his position in literature. It would seem that Frenchmen still hesitate to give him the high place that has been accorded to him across the Channel. Rémy de Gourmont, one of the best known of the younger critics, speaks of him sarcastically as an amusing but monotonous writer possessed of a purely mechanical talent.

Mr. F. Marion Crawford was to have returned to Europe in February, but his popularity as a lecturer has grown so great under the management of Major Pond, that a tour through the Southern and Middle States to the Pacific Coast, which has just been arranged, will detain him until the month of May. Mr. Crawford's new novel, *Corleone*, is meeting with the success it so well deserves, and is having an immense vogue. The portrait given on the next page is taken from a new photograph presented by Mr. Crawford to Major Pond, to whose courtesy and the permission of Falk, the photographer, we are indebted for its appearance in our columns.

Copyright, 1897, by B. J. Falk, New York.

To my good friend Major J. B. Pond,
F. Marion Crawford.
Nov. 12. 1897

Publishers as well as authors are evidently being lured to the platform by Major Pond. Another lecturer, whose remarkable success is a surprise to himself, but was foreseen by the omniscient Major, is Mr. W. W. Ellsworth, of the Century Company. Mr. Ellsworth's subject belongs to the fascinating period of the Revolution, and is called "From Lexington to Yorktown." The procession of events during those years of our history is graphically described, with a panoramic accompaniment of views from photographs taken by the lecturer himself while touring over the historical ground covered in the lecture. We congratulate Mr. Ellsworth upon the success he has won in his new rôle.

F. A. Steel.

The Macmillan Company have just published another volume of short stories by Mrs. Steel, the author of *On the Face of the Waters.* This is the second collection that has been made since the publication of her novel of the Indian Mutiny about a year ago. But publishers and public have been responsible for this, and not the author. Mrs. Steel's success has not carried her away, and it will be some time, she says, before she puts forth another book. *In the Permanent Way*, the new book of short stories, has a decided advantage over *In the Tideway*, which was issued in the summer. In the latter she went to Scotland for her material, and Mrs. Steel always makes her admirers nervous when she wanders beyond her proper limits. The volume just published, however, takes us with boldness and sureness to India. Here the author is at home, and her stories of Indian life, its mystery, its inexplicability, its alien virtues and creeds, impress us, as heretofore, with her keen insight, her appreciation of racial instincts and differences, her sympathetic treatment of "her own people." Readers will compare this favourably with her first collection published a few years ago, *From the Five Rivers*, which, we still think, shows Mrs. Steel's work at its highest artistic level. The accompanying portrait is from a photograph taken at Turiff, Aberdeenshire, near which town Mrs. Steel's country retreat, Dunlugas, is situated.

❀

Mrs. F. A. Steel contributes the leading story to the Christmas number of the *Illustrated London News.* The Christmas issues of this perennially interesting weekly and of the *Graphic* are laden with seasonable treasure-trove for pleasure-seekers in fiction and pictorial fun. Among the contributors are Max Pemberton, Stanley J. Weyman, S. R. Crockett, H. G. Wells, W. W. Jacobs, Sir Walter Besant, and Bret Harte, each of whom seems to have been ordered to write in the vein he has made peculiarly his own. The large coloured illustrations are, as usual, an added attraction. *The Lady's Pictorial* and the *Figaro* in English are also out in Yule-tide splendour. The International News Company are the American publishers.

❀

Catulle Mendès, whose dramatic criticisms perhaps constitute his best work, has just published the second volume of *L'Art au Théâtre*, a collection of criticisms contributed to various papers. Mendès's judgments in dramatic matters now carry quite as much weight as those of Sarcey or Lemaître. He is more in harmony with new ideas than either of the older writers.

❀

Early this year the Kelmscott Press will be closed. Some books will be turned out before then, among others an account by William Morris of the foundation of the Press, and a collection of early German woodcuts. On the whole it is well that the business should be given up, now that its master-spirit can no longer inspire and control it.

❀

A new book, entitled *Millions of Bubbles*, by Gertrude Atherton, the author of *Patience Sparhawk*, is now in press.

THE LIONS OF BOSTON.

(The old Boston Public Library is now occupied by a menagerie.)

A Literary Zoo !
Whe———ew !
I had heard of this in Boston, but now I see it's true !
A Library of wonders, a collection all in cages,
Full of Literary Lions with their pens in inky rages.
And all on exhibition at a very moderate fee—
Oh, stockings blue of Boston, *do*—please come along and see !

A Literary Zoo !
A Spectacle to view !
Boston used to keep them private, but now they'll roar for you.
Now they name 'em and they tame 'em, and they shame 'em and they brand 'em,
And in spite of guttural dialect, a child can understand 'em.
Here's a Panther with a Purpose and a Problematic Tail,
And mark these neat poetic feet ! An Educated Snail !

A Literary Zoo !
So really clever, too !
Ah, what ghostly authors shudder from the shelves that once they knew !
In the alcoves that the sometime Literary Lights invaded,
Now the plagiaristic monkey thinks he does as well as they did,
And the Unenlightened Publishers assemble here to gaze
While the anaconda swallows undiscriminating praise !

Gelett Burgess.

LOVE'S LABOUR LOST.

I sent up my thoughts like roses
  To climb to the casement of Love,
But no face ever shone in the darkness,
  No whisper e'er beckoned above.

And now that the casement stands open,
  And now that the door stands wide,
'Tis no longer a man, warm and breathing,
  But a shadow that flits outside.

I. Zangwill.

THE CHICAGO PUBLIC LIBRARY.

LIBRARIES AND LIBRARIANS.

Of the world's libraries, the National Library of France is the largest, containing over 2,600,000 bound volumes, and about half that number of pamphlets.

The British Museum has, however, the largest collection of manuscripts in the world, and probably the largest and most valuable collection of Bibles, although the library at Stuttgart has hitherto been supposed to possess that honour. Its Shakespeariana are the most complete in the world, as, too, are its Caxton imprints. Its Chinese books alone number 27,000 volumes. Its great printed catalogue, begun in 1881, is not yet completed.

Our own Library of Congress, or National Library, as it ought more properly to be called, stands *fifth* in the list of the world's libraries in the number of its volumes; but the libraries of the United States contain more books than those of France, Great Britain, and Germany combined. There are here, according to the most recent report (1893), 3804 libraries supported wholly or in part by public moneys. In 1850, the year in which the free public library movement began, the estimated number of such institutions—very few without a subscription fee—was 694, which shows the enormous increase in less than fifty years. The libraries founded by bequest during that time, the Astor, Lenox, and Tilden, in New York; the Newberry and Crerar institutions at Chicago; the Carnegie Libraries at Pittsburg and Allegheny; and the Enoch Pratt Library at Baltimore, are merely prominent examples from the long catalogue of private munificence. The Boston Public Library, for example, spends an annual income of $240,000; and other libraries are in receipt of contributions in money and books, the aggregate value of which is enormous. It needs but the merest surface examination to discover what an important feature of our municipal and social life the public library has become.

The father of the subscription library in this country is Benjamin Franklin, to whose suggestion is due the existence of the present Library Company of Philadelphia, numbering 188,000 volumes and some 30,000 pamphlets. Mr. James G. Barnwell, formerly in charge of the library of the University of Pennsylvania, has been at its head since 1887. Mr. Barnwell graduated from a Philadelphia high school in 1850, and for thirteen years taught school in that city. He and Samuel J. Randall were the youngest members who ever sat in the Common Council. His innate love of books is illustrated by the fact that he is the possessor of a valuable private library, and his enthusiasm as a biblio-

MELVIL DEWEY,
Head of Albany Library School.

In the year preceding the call for the meeting that resulted in the establishment of the Mercantile Library, its present librarian, John Edmands, was born on a farm in Massachusetts, served an apprenticeship as a house carpenter, and in 1847 graduated from Yale. It was while at Yale that he received his first introduction to library work; and the system of references to subjects in magazines and reviews, which he prepared at that time, was the germ which was afterward developed into Poole's Index, so indispensable a help to writers and students.

Other important Philadelphia libraries are the Apprentices', the Athenæum, the Drexel Institute, and the University of Pennsylvania.

. . . . . We can speak but briefly of University libraries; oldest and most notable of these, the great library of Harvard, famous for its Americana; of Princeton, soon to possess a magnificent home; of Cornell, with its 159,000 volumes; of Columbia, with its 175,000 volumes, rich in political economy, and remarkable for its rapid accumulation, a collection which, though designed primarily for the use of the University, is open, under certain restric-

HERBERT PUTNAM,
Librarian Boston Public Library.

phile may be gathered from his contributions, continued for a long period of years, to that unique English publication, *Notes and Queries*.

This library, sometimes called the Philadelphia Library, is not to be confounded with the Philadelphia Free Public Library, of which John Thompson is librarian, and which has branches in various parts of the city. The latter institution is said to have a larger circulation than any similar library in this country or England. It is the youngest of the great libraries of Philadelphia, having been opened in 1892. Among the popular subscription libraries of Philadelphia is the Mercantile. It is not so old as the Philadelphia Library Company, it having originated in 1821 from a notice inviting the merchants and merchants' clerks, and those friendly to the formation of a Mercantile Library Association, to meet in the Mayor's Court Room; and in January of the following year, the rooms of the second story at 100 Chestnut Street were engaged at a rental of $150 per year, and a librarian at a salary of $100 per year, from which it will be seen that the public estimate of the value of a librarian's services has risen somewhat in seventy years, though the highest rewards of the profession are still inferior to those of the best class of French cooks.

WILLIAM H. BRETT,
President American Library Association and Librarian Cleveland (O.) Public Library.

Charles K. Bolton,
Brookline, Mass.

Alfred S. Collins,
Rochester, N. Y.

John Edmands,
Mercantile Library, Philadelphia, Pa.

George F. Winchester,
Paterson, N. J.

James K. Hosmer,
Minneapolis, Minn.

James J. Barnwell,
Philadelphia, Pa.

Caroline M. Hewins,
Hartford, Conn.

E. S. Wilcox,
Peoria, Ill.

Willis A. Bardwell,
Brooklyn, N. Y.

E. H. Anderson,
Pittsburg, Pa.

William M. Stevenson,
Allgheny, Pa.

Willis K. Stetson,
New Haven, Conn.

Samuel S. Green,
Worcester, Mass.

Mrs. Agnes Hills,
Bridgeport, Conn.

tions, to the public; and the libraries of many other colleges, religious and secular, and which have grown by generous bequests to enormous proportions in the lapse of years. Nor can we allude in detail to State libraries; to the many special governmental collections; to libraries of the Historical, Geographical, Genealogical, and Archæological Societies, many of them of great value.

Among the first of State libraries must be named our own State Library at Albany, with its 314,543 volumes, nearly a quarter of a million manuscripts, and a large pamphlet collection. Established in 1818, it is one of the first State libraries in time, and is easily the first in resources. A feature of this institution is its travelling libraries, a system which enables small localities in the State to receive the benefit for six months of the circulation among its population of a limited number of the best and latest books. Any town may obtain this privilege by a petition bearing the signatures of twenty-five resident taxpayers. Over three hundred of these travelling libraries are now being moved about the State. The director of the first State library in the Union is a man who is generally considered the first of librarians, Mr. Melvil Dewey. It is not easy to exaggerate the importance of the position in library circles which Mr. Dewey occupies. He comes to librarianship from the educational, not the bookish side. Twenty-five years ago he became imbued with the idea that libraries were the necessary complement of the schools in any satisfactory scheme of public education. The realisation of this ideal he chose as his life work, and this accounts for the fact, to which attention has often been called, that for almost a generation he has been the pioneer in nearly all the movements and organisations for promoting general library interests.

First in time and importance is the American Library Association, of which mention will be made hereafter, and which is Mr. Dewey's conception of a national society of those most interested in the modern library idea. For fifteen years he was its secretary and executive officer. When he insisted on retiring he was elected president, and again took the helm for the ten days international meeting at Chicago, during the Columbian Exposition.

Of the *Library Journal*, which won and has held its place for twenty years as the leading library periodical of the world, he was editor for the first five years. In June, 1886, he started the cheaper library quarterly, *Library Notes*, of which he has always been editor. January 5th, 1887, he opened the first school for the training of librarians in the world at Columbia, and is still its director, it having been transferred from Columbia University to the State, soon after Mr. Dewey's removal to Albany. In 1892 he drafted the law which was passed by the New York Legislature, and which is considered the most comprehensive and far-reaching library law yet placed upon the statutes of any State or nation, for in it the library is for the first time fully recognised as taking its place beside the public school, as a part of the State's educational system. Mr. Dewey is the author of the famous Dewey system of classification, which has enormously simplified the work of the librarian.

Among public libraries, that of Boston ranks first—the noblest institution of its kind in America, and the largest free circulating library in the world. On its shelves are many volumes of great rarity relating to American colonial and national history, a nearly unequalled collection of works on the fine arts, and many original manuscripts of much value. The total number of its volumes in over 600,000; and under Mr. Herbert Putnam, now its librarian, and formerly librarian of the public library at Minneapolis, is a force of assistant librarians and clerical assistants of over two hundred. The library building ranks next to the library of Congress (so called), the noblest home of books in the country, and in its interior decorations surpasses that of the National Library. The severely classic beauty of its architecture, rising amid the more picturesque and showy, but less impressive structures of Copley Square, is emblematic of the enduring character of that knowledge and learning to the service of which this magnificent temple is dedicated. One cannot but regret the necessity of dismissing with these few lines, the brevity of which is made necessary by a plan that shall comprehend a general survey of the subject, a library which is inclusive of so much, and which is in a general way, in the character and greatness of its aim and scope, typical of all others.

The ownership of the Boston Athenæum library of 188,000 volumes is vested in 1049 shareholders, who, with their families, have the use of the library and the privilege of sharing its use to a certain extent with friends. Strangers are permitted access to its shelves under certain restrictions. The Athenæum's librarian, Mr. William C. Lane, was assistant librarian of Harvard College from 1887–93, in which year he assumed the position he now fills.

There are a number of highly important public libraries in Massachusetts in the three hundred or more outside of the city of Boston. Massachusetts is, indeed, the banner State. Worcester possesses a library of nearly a hundred thousand volumes, and a librarian, Samuel Swett Green, who is known far and wide for his successful efforts in an important special field. It is generally conceded that the close association of the public library and the public school has been greatly stimulated throughout the country by the action of the Worcester Library. A later development along these lines has been the establishment of classes for the study of subjects by those who wish to avail themselves of such opportunity. Mr. Green was born in 1837, graduated from Harvard in 1858, became a director of the Worcester Library in 1867, and librarian in 1871. He was one of the founders of the American Library Association, and in 1891 was its president.

The citizens of Springfield might object to having the library of Worcester mentioned before theirs, for the former contains 90,000 volumes, and is estimated as ranking *eighth* among the public libraries of the country, and *first* in the number of volumes to population. Its venerable librarian, Dr. William Rice, who died in his seventy-sixth year on August 17th, was an old anti-slavery leader, and in 1853 received the degree of M.A. from the Wesleyan University, and in 1876 the degree of D.D. from the same institution. He had held the position which he occupied at the time of his death since 1861.

Brookline, Mass., said to be the richest community for its size in the United States, has a library, and a librarian who is among the youngest in the country, being under thirty. But Charles K. Bolton has already won a deservedly high place by his writings on subjects connected with libraries and library management, and by a profound sense of the responsibility of his office. Mr. Bolton, whose mother is the well-known writer, Sarah Knowles Bolton, is himself the author of several books, among which are *The Wooing of Martha Pitkin*, which has passed through three editions, and *The Love Story of Ursula Wolcott*.

Taunton has a public library of about 45,000 volumes. Mr. Joshua E. Crane, formerly in charge of the Y. M. C. A. Library at Albany, the father of all Y. M. C. A. libraries in this State, is its administrator. Mr. Crane was for several years instructor in the Protestant College in Syria, and later instructor in the classics at the Albany Academy.

Several of the cities of Connecticut have large public libraries. New Haven has a free public library, over which Mr. W. K. Stetson has presided since 1887. Hartford has a public library of some prominence, with a woman well known in library circles at its head—Miss Caroline M. Hewins. Miss Hewins is a lecturer on children's literature to the New York State Library School. Her library work was begun at the Boston Athenæum at a time when the famous Dr. W. H. Poole was its librarian, an association the benefit of which no one would admit more eagerly than Miss Hewins. Bridgeport has a library of some 30,000 volumes, of which Miss Agnes Hills is librarian; and Waterbury has a library with a collection considerably larger.

The Providence, R. I., Library of over 75,000 volumes has a famous librarian for its head—William E. Foster.

Among the benefactions of Andrew Carnegie must be named the great library at Pittsburg, and the smaller one at Allegheny. Mr. E. H. Anderson, the librarian of the first named, is a Western man, and was formerly a cataloguer in the Newberry Library at Chicago. The library has but 26,000 volumes, with a shelf capacity of 300,000; it has, however, been opened to the public only a little more than a year, and the popularity of the institution has gone beyond the most sanguine expectations of the founder. The Carnegie Library at Allegheny has 29,000 volumes, but is increasing its collection rapidly. Mr. William M. Stevenson, its librarian, when taking charge, had no previous library experience, and was obliged—in common, in fact, with all his assistants—to learn from the beginning the details of library work.

One of the most important events of the near future will be the bringing together in the New York Public Library of the Astor, Lenox, and Tilden foundations. Ever since its beginning the Astor Library has closed its doors at the only hours when it can be used by those to whom public libraries are of the most value. As for the Lenox, that is an institution which recalls the traditions of the time when the books of public libraries were chained to the cases. Of course it will be said that the Lenox is not a library of general reference ; that its works are rarities, and often of great value ; yet it does seem that its usefulness might be increased by some more liberal opportunities of access. It remains to be said, however, that there has been an improvement in the management of the Lenox in recent years, and that this criticism is happily losing its force. The Astor and the Lenox are too much a part of New York to be spoken of slightingly. The Egyptology of the first and the Americana of the second are nearly unrivalled. S. Austin Allibone, the author of the *Dictionary of Authors*, was once a librarian of the second ; Frederick Saunders, author of *Salad for the Solitary*, at one time an extremely popular book, and now by no means wholly forgotten, was for thirty-five years at the Astor, and has only the other day, at the age of *eighty-nine*, retired from his librarianship, which he has honoured for so many years. And now that these libraries are to be merged in one, let us cease to think unkindly of their imperfections, and recall only the delightful features of their management which have made them of inestimable value to writers and students.

New York had no free circulating library until what is sometimes called the Bond Street Library—its real name being the New York Free Circulating Library—was born, the Mercantile and Apprentices' being subscription libraries. The Y. M. C. A. Library is not free, the use of its books being conditioned upon the payment of a small annual fee. Its collection of works on architecture and the fine arts would probably surprise those not aware of its value.

The Brooklyn Library has 127,000 volumes. Stephen B. Noyes, whom old Brooklyn book lovers remember with gratitude, was succeeded by Mr. Willis A. Bardwell, the present incumbent. There are few libraries so generally used for reference as this one, its theological and musical collections being especially abundant, and its general works of ample and liberal selection. This library is not free, but its subscription fee is small, and its membership shows a slight yearly increase. Brooklyn, however, has a free circulating library in that of the Pratt Institute, founded by the munificence of Mr. Charles Pratt. It has a collection of 61,000 volumes, and is one of the few libraries, if not the only one, where children too young to read may draw books—which in this case, of course, are picture books. The children, too, have a library and reading room "all their own." This especial consideration for the young is due, perhaps, to the fact that its librarian is a woman, Miss Mary W. Plummer, a graduate and former teacher in the New York State Library School.

A word as to library schools. The calling of a library assistant is an occupation requiring far more technical knowledge and training than is commonly supposed. During the last twenty years library work has been so systematised that a thorough instruction in all its branches necessitates years of laborious preparation. Library schools have therefore arisen in obedience to the need of carefully trained assistants ; and courses of library training have been introduced into the curriculum of many of our colleges. The New York State Library School at Albany, the first in time, in requirements for admission and graduation, and in repute, is now drawing pupils from every State in the Union, and to some extent from foreign countries.

It is quite impossible within the limits of a magazine article even to refer to the many libraries which for one reason or another merit extended notice. We have been, therefore, obliged to content ourselves with indicating a few of the more important. We are to remember that there are over 5000 public libraries in the United States, for they must at least have reached that number since the 1893 report was issued. There has been an enormous increase in the number of these institutions within a generation. This increase, however, is less significant than the enormous increase in the number of volumes in public libraries, an enormously increased circulation, and a very largely increased use of books confined to the reference room, wherever statistics are kept of such use. Every year adds to the importance of "the missions and the missionaries of the book," to adopt a happy phrase of Mr. J. N. Larned, late Superintendent of the Buffalo Public Library. It is calculated that the libraries of New York State possess 4,000,000 books, about one quarter of which are in free libraries. New York County has 997 books to every 1000 persons.

Outside of New York City, one of the most important libraries in the State is perhaps the Reynolds Library, so called from the name of its founder, Mortimer F. Reynolds, at Rochester, of which Alfred S. Collins is librarian.

New Jersey, though facetiously accused of being out of the Union, is very much in it in the matter of comparative library statistics. The public library at Jersey City, under the supervision of Miss E. Burdick, ranks *fourth* in circulation in proportion to population of all the libraries in the country, and has over 50,000 volumes. The Paterson Library was, however, the first free public library in New Jersey, founded under a law passed in 1884, a law which is considered among the best library laws of the various States. It possesses about 27,000 volumes, and is in charge of Mr. G. F. Winchester. Its former librarian, Mr. Frank P. Hill, is now at the head of the Newark Library, he having been called from the Lowell (Mass.) Free Public Library, where he had served as librarian for a number of years. A feature of interest connected with these three flourishing public libraries of New Jersey is their rapid growth in accessions and circulation.

The West, though behind the East in the number and value of its public libraries, is not, when measured by the youth and comparative poverty of its cities, so very far in the rear of the older and wealthier section. Chicago's Public Library is generally held to rank second only to that of Boston; and as early as 1852 San Francisco had taken the first step toward a municipal library in the formation of a Mercantile Library Association. Other libraries arose at the same time. To-day Oakland and Los Angeles possess public libraries, the fame of which has travelled far beyond those cities.

The Chicago Library is supposed to lead the world in the home circulation of its books, but it will be observed that a similar claim is made for the Philadelphia Free Public Library, and we are at present without data to estimate these conflicting claims. Comparative library statistics of circulation are not always reliable, since some are made to include items which in other estimates are excluded, such as the circulation of periodicals and the use of books in reference and reading room. So, too, the figures of circulation of libraries in cities where there are distributing branches will as a rule, other things being equal, surpass the circulation in cities where no such branches exist. Of the 1,173,586 volumes taken from the Chicago Library for home use, more than half were issued through its thirty-one delivery stations.

Chicago, besides its splendid free public library, has the Newberry, founded in 1882, of which William F. Poole was librarian. The Crerar bequest of $3,000,000 is another magnificent benefaction destined to add to the intellectual greatness of the metropolis of the West.

The Free Public Library of Peoria, Ill., is the largest public library, relative to population, of any west of New England, with a collection of 58,000 volumes. Its librarian, Mr. E. S. Wilcox, is the author of the Illinois State library law, which has served as a model for several other States.

The Public Library at Minneapolis has about 85,000 volumes, and is remarkable as having one of the largest *per capita* circulations. Herbert Putnam, its librarian in 1892, was succeeded in that year by James K. Hosmer. Mr. Hosmer has made several notable contributions to our historical literature in his "Lives" of Samuel Adams (American Statesmen Series), Sir Henry Vane, and Thomas Hutchinson, the old Tory governor of Colonial Massachusetts, works which are as interesting as romances. Mr. Hosmer was a trustee of the St. Louis Public Library up to 1892, when he passed, as he cleverly expresses it, "from the grub condition of the trustee into a beautiful librarian butterfly." Two other cities of the West, St. Paul and Milwaukee, have large and important public libraries.

The public library of Cincinnati has 215,596 volumes. Its circulation is very large, even relatively to the great number of its volumes. William F. Poole, who appears to have been associated in an official capacity with almost all the great public libraries at one time or another during his active and useful life, was once its librarian, but it is at present under the charge of A. W. Whelpley. Mr. Whelpley served an apprenticeship in Robert Craighead's printing office, corner of Fulton and Dutch streets, this city, where De Vinne was a fellow-workman. In this office Mr. Whelpley met many of the literary lights of old New York, some of whom posterity has chosen to forget, but a few of whom are still known to book lovers — the Duyckinks, Charles Fenno Hoffman, Tuckerman, Fenimore Cooper. It is interesting to note that the manuscript of *Salad for the Solitary*, Frederick Saunders's well-known book, passed through the young printer's hands on its way to the public "more years ago," says Mr. Whelpley, "than I care to remember."

Another public library of Ohio, of which mention should not be omitted, is that of Cleveland, in charge of Mr. William H. Brett, first president of the State Library Association of Ohio and now president of the American Library Association. Mr. Brett has compiled a catalogue of the Cleveland Library which those qualified to know pronounce one of the best ever issued.

Among Western public libraries, that of Omaha is a not unimportant one. The total number of volumes in this library is 52,000, in charge of Mr. W. H. Barrows. The highly creditable fact is to be remembered that this library, with an active and efficient management keeping pace with the needs of the community, is supported independently of any State library law by a city the population of which was returned in the census of 1890 at 140,000.

The South is behind the West in the number and importance of its public libraries. Yet the Library Society of Charleston, S. C., dates as far back as 1748. The Howard Memorial Library of New Orleans owes its existence to a gift of $350,000 from Mrs. Annie F. Howard. It possesses a wholly unique collection of works on Louisiana and many rare treasures. The Howard Library is in charge of Mr. William Beer.

Another Southern library of prominence is the Public Library of St. Louis, with about 100,000 volumes. Mr. F. M. Crunden, a former president of the American Library Association, is its progressive and enlightened head, and is recognised everywhere as one of the ablest librarians of the country. His services to "the higher life" of St. Louis merit more than this passing allusion. Memphis, Tenn., has a large free library, given to the city by the heirs of Frederick H. Cossett. The Enoch Pratt Free Public Library of Baltimore, with its 170,000 volumes, stands high in the list of free libraries of the South. Lewis H. Steiner, its first librarian, was succeeded at his death, in 1892, by his son, Bernard H. Steiner.

A word in conclusion of the American Library Association. Organised in 1876, it has grown year by year in membership and influence. Its first president was the late Justin Winsor, librarian of Harvard College, and associated with him were Lloyd P. Smith, A. R. Spofford, and William F. Poole, as vice-presidents. Mr. Melvil Dewey was its executive officer, and had charge of its offices for fifteen years. He is generally regarded as the real founder of the association. With the present administration of Mr. Brett are associated Mr. George Watson Cole, formerly librarian of the Jersey City Public Library, Hannah P. James, of the Osterhant Public Library, at Wilkesbarre, Pa., and J. C. Dana, of the Denver (Col.) Library, compiler of a well-known *Public Library Handbook*. The secretary of the American Library Association is Rutherford P. Hayes, son of the late ex-President Hayes. Mr. Hayes was for some time trustee of the Birchard Library, at Tremont, O., and in 1889 became a member of the American Library Association. This association has been the means of establishing intimate and cordial relations between the librarians of the country, and has enormously conduced to advance the practical efficiency of "the missions and the missionaries of the book."

Joseph Dana Miller.

ONE HUNDRED BEST BOOKS FOR A VILLAGE LIBRARY.

Although I have not been requested to suggest a list of a hundred best books for a village library, it so happens that I have long felt an interest in the subject, and have, at several times, considered how to make the best selection for the purpose. Consequently I cannot deem myself presumptuous in offering some remarks on the article of Mr. Clement K. Shorter in THE BOOKMAN for December, and in suggesting a modification of his list which, I think, may be an improvement.

It seems to me that the selection should be made in accordance with the following propositions :

1. Book-reading is one of the means of education.

2. The proper aims of education are also the proper aims of book-reading, as far as it can subserve such aims.

3. The proper aims of education are —to cultivate and improve the faculties of body and mind, and to store the mind with useful knowledge, so as to fit the individual for making the best of life.

4. To these purposes, therefore, book-reading ought to be subsidiary.

5. It follows also that book-reading should not be regarded merely as an amusement or a pastime.

If these propositions be true, it must appear that a list which does not contain any books "merely of information" must be seriously deficient.

Mr. Shorter is careful to point out that the hundred best books for a village library are not necessarily the hundred best books in the language ; but it is apparently needful also to remember that they are not those that happen to be comprised in an arbitrary definition of the term "literature."

To Mr. Shorter's definition of this term as a presentation of "life in an artistic form," must, I think, be added —the presentation of truth. To give to scientific discourses a literary or artistic form ought to be quite possible, and I believe, as a matter of fact, is often done. The sweeping assertion that "no man of science has ever been an artist," is one against which I feel bound to protest. Of the two men whom he names as examples, Huxley, in connection with his literary presentation of truth, is certainly entitled to be called an artist—a dictum which, I ought to add, is entirely independent of friendship. So, too, ought to be esteemed John Tyndal, Sir W. R. Grove, R. A. Proctor, and Sir R. S. Ball. These are only a few examples from our own literature, but does Mr. Shorter deny that Goethe was an artist ? And does any one assert that he was not a man of science ?

It is easy to understand the tendency in human nature to overestimate the value and importance of those subjects to which we have devoted our attention with cost of money, time, and pains, and to depreciate others of which we know either little or nothing. But we must beware of such an error in choosing books for a variety of other people, and we should think of their needs as well as their wants. They should have the opportunity of a wider and more beneficent culture than Mr. Shorter's list would afford. And if only a very small proportion of the readers should avail themselves of the books of information, that would be justification enough for their admission into the list. Nay, if they were not read at all for years (which is incredible), but only occasionally looked into, they would not be useless. Some intelligent person—a youth most probably—might, sooner or later, find in them the bread his soul was hungering for, and he might thereby be enabled to discover his life's vocation. And it is quite conceivable that if the novel which a reader wants may happen to be out, he may be induced to take, reluctantly perhaps, Clodd's *Story of Creation*, Laing's *Modern Science and Modern Thought*, or Huxley's *Physiology*, and for the rest of his life may bless the day on which he did so.

In suggesting the following books as needful for a village library, I do not mean that they should be simply added to Mr. Shorter's hundred, but that they should be substituted for a corresponding number in his list that can best be spared.

Even with this emendation, the reasonable claims of relaxation and recreation have not been forgotten, but it should be remembered that true recreation depends quite as much upon diversion as upon mere amusement.

W. Fleming Phillips.

List of books to be added to Mr. Shorter's selection for a village library, instead of an equal number to be removed.

1. The Story of Creation. By E. Clodd.
2. Modern Science and Modern Thought. By S. Laing.
3. Lessons in Elementary Astronomy. By Proctor.
4. School Manual of Geology. By Jukes-Brown. Or the smaller text-book of either of the Geikies.
5. Elementary Lessons in Botany. By Oliver.
6. Lessons in Physiology. By Huxley.
7. Physiography. By Huxley.
8. Lessons in Logic. By Jevons.
9. Elementary Physics. By Everett, or Balfour Stewart.
10. Elementary Chemistry. By Ramsay.
11. Elementary Biology. By Campbell.
12. Hygiene. By Dr. Whitelegge. Or Public Health. By Dr. Willoughby.
13. The Personal Care of Health. By Dr. E. Parkes.
14. My Schools and Schoolmasters. By Hugh Miller.
15. Cassell's Concise Cyclopædia.
16. This World of Ours. By Arnold-Forster.
17. The Laws of Every Day Life. By Arnold-Forster.
18. The Citizen Reader. By Arnold-Forster.
19. The Science of Every Day Life. By J. A. Bower.
20. A good, small, recent Geographical Atlas.
21. A good practical book of lessons on Drawing. (Ruskin's Elements of Drawing is not practical enough, and in some respects is out of date.)
22. Shakespeare's Plays in one volume.

The books that I suggest should be removed from Mr. Shorter's list in order to make room for the above-mentioned works are numbered by him as follows :

No. 4, 6, 8, 11, 13, 14, 15, 27, 30, 32, 34, 35, 36, 37, 41, 57, 62, 64, 75, 93, 94, 99.

To the Editors of THE BOOKMAN :

DEAR SIRS: My attention has been drawn to an article in THE BOOKMAN for December on the choice of books for a village library, and as I have been librarian to one ever since 1875, I think a few words of my experience may be useful.

During all these years I have given out the books myself, and have taken every opportunity of finding out what books are wished for. The village is small (600 inhabitants), but the people are fond of reading, and fairly intelligent, and although the library has been open twenty-two years, the average number keeps about the same, and most of the subscribers take out fresh books each week. After this long experience I have come to the following conclusions. Short histories (such as Green's) are liked, but anything like Motley's *Dutch Republic*, Bryce's *Roman Empire*, or Gibbon's *Decline and Fall* would not be read. Poetry is *never taken out.* Some biographies are liked, also bright, interesting books of travels. Novels and stories are the most popular, and I think it a good sign that really good novels are liked the best. Dickens, Mrs. Gaskell, C. Brontë, Stevenson, Miss Yonge, are most popular, but I fear the rural mind would never appreciate the satire in *Don Quixote*, *Gulliver's Travels*, etc., while Goethe's *Faust* and Dante's works would never be understood. Village intellects are not so quick as town ones, and take much longer to grasp the full inner meaning of a subject. I believe the list of a hundred books given in your number might be a good one for a town workmen's library, but not at all suitable for a village one.

Ellis Fane.

ONE HUNDRED BEST BOOKS FOR A VILLAGE LIBRARY.

...en requested ...t books

When I pour the hot, clean water from the kettle into the shiny dishpan, my spirits rise with the steam. When I dash the soap to and fro, and the wholesome heated smell arises, I find myself singing a little tune.

When dishes, knives, forks, pans, and, above all, butter dishes, have passed the boiling ordeal, and stand in cleanly rows on the table, I look — not at these, but into the dishpan. Alas! a murky liquidity with minute, circling globes of grease, crumbs and slowly cooking egg fragments. And as I look, I know that a spoon lies forgotten at the bottom, and that I must fish for it.

"JEST CUMFTUBLE CRAZY."

It is a mistake to object to this. The well-regulated mind should either rise superior or else accept the inevitable. I have tried both ways. I have become lost in thought over an illustration to be planned later in the morning—and wiped a frying-pan with a clean towel intended for the silver. When I tried to accept the inevitable, my mind wandered off to the different conceptions of the Fates, and as I couldn't possibly remember whether Lachesis cut or twisted the thread, I went off to the library to look it up, with the dish-towel under my arm.

In the light of these failures I have come to the rather sententious conclusion that the only way to do is to give my whole and undivided attention to the dishpan for the time being, and I am amazed and delighted with the result. I am saddened by the fact that

his literary presentation of truth, is certainly entitled to be called an artist—a dictum which, I ought to add, is entirely ...endent of friendship. So, too, ...d John Tyndal, Sir

people ... and Sir regulated minus are often monotonous. They are active enough, but they move along like a clock that keeps good time and strikes when it should. One of our clocks has just become vocally deranged. It points primly and reliably at the right hour, minute, and second, but at the quarter hours it tells the most awful fibs. It ought not to strike at the quarters at all, but at fifteen minutes past eight it blandly remarks that it is ten. Now there is a great difference between a quarter past eight and ten, for at ten the dishes would be done. I have begged them to leave that clock as it is, for whenever it strikes, I can wonder what I might be doing if it had spoken the truth. The beauty of it all is that the clock has a new suggestive lie for each hour, and is an unfailing spur to the imagination.

They were talking a day or two ago about "Lucindy" Cowles. "Lucindy" is just about as much deranged as our clock, and there is no more need of sending her away than there is of sending our clock to the jeweller's. The doctor wants to find a place for her in some "Home," but her mother protests.

"There ain't no harm in Lucindy," she said. "She's jest cumftuble crazy." And so Lucindy stays at home, has a "faculty" with flowers, and is content. She lives on the back road a little aside from the town—just as her should be remembered [illegible] tion depends quite as [illegible] sion as upon mere [illegible]

W. F[illegible]

List of books [illegible] ter's selection [illegible] stead of an [illegible] moved.

1. The Story [illegible]
2. [illegible]

[illegible] the wind [illegible] in, and went in to [illegible] Dragon—all but four [illegible] a Sea-Serpent! There were [illegible] ations, it is true. Sometimes he had fins, sometimes flippers—sometimes he was all tail. When he had fins he usually had teeth to match. When he was all tail he had large eyes, but he always lived in the salt water. Only one boy, and he was the parson's son, had the classic idea of a Dragon with scales, wings, and claws, and a fiery breath.

[illegible] ,' and [illegible] day after [illegible] approved of sunsets [illegible] and Observation of Nature, but found a certain monotony. Just then it was a quarter past nine, and the clock struck twelve. Under its imaginative inspiration he decided to give "Dragons" as the next subject.

Now our High School building stands on a hill by itself. Over the roofs of the town there is a splendid stretch of sea-line and a long yellow band of beach. Then dunes and the salt-marsh. I can see the children as they climb the stony road, and I know just how the sea-line rises to meet them as they gain the top, until at the door-step the world looks round and a thing to be conquered.

The High-School teacher was inclined to draw all kinds of intricate conclusions about environment, unconscious influence, and local colour. I heard only part of what he said, because I was planning how that Sea Serpent would look on paper in black and white—but I have no doubt it was most reasonable and intelligent.

"What," said the High-School teacher, "would be the effect if the same subject were given to a school on the plains? An enormous Jack Rabbit? Or still better, if the experiment were tried where the children had been brought up within sight and hearing of the Tammany Tiger! Words fail me!"

Mélanie Elisabeth Norton.

DR. JOHNSON'S POLITICS.

"Johnson, though a bigoted Tory," says Macaulay, "was not quite such a fool" as Croker would make him. In fact, Macaulay's restriction is somewhat superficial and demands much limitation. A bantering attempt was lately made to prove to the Johnson Club, meeting in Fleet Street, that Johnson was a Whig. His Toryism was carried on his sleeve, but it was too abstract and too conventional to be quite genuine. Every one knows his sayings that the first Whig was the devil; that in his parliamentary reports he took care that the Whig dogs did not get the best of it; that Burke was a cursed Whig, a bottomless Whig. What is there on the other side? Whigs and Tories were originally distinguished quite as much by ecclesiastical differences, by the bent of religion, as by politics. To the Tory a clergyman was an object of reverence, to the Whig of suspicion. The Lichfield bookseller, Johnson's father, was a Tory, but took the oaths, and his son's views of the non-jurors were as contemptuous as any Whig's. In theory he was a Tory, in practice hard experience dealing with the individual often made him a Whig. He wished the clergy to have considerable influence founded upon the opinion of mankind, but could not raise his own opinion of them to the requisite height. The Tory sat at their feet; Johnson was critical and often cold. Goldsmith took his religion from the priest as he took his coat from the tailor. "Sir," said Johnson, "he knows nothing; he has made up his mind about nothing." If nothing could make Johnson contradict a bishop, in practice he often did worse. He could sneer at Archbishop Secker and call Bishop Newton a gross flatterer. He went near to calling Bishop Keppel a whited wall, and Boswell is forced to surmise that he wist not it was the High Priest. Bishops *in posse*, deans and the like, were always suffering at his hands. Percy was driven from the table, Douglas tossed and gored, and Barnard forced to defend himself with a biting epigram. Worse than all, when Johnson was for founding an ideal university, he named no clergyman among his professors. He would trust theology to nobody but himself. On remonstrance he tossed practical divinity to Percy, throwing British antiquities in with it, and reserved theology as a science to himself. It is true that the professorships were to be limited to members of the club, but what living clergyman would Johnson have set above Percy? He would have faced a battery of cannon to restore Convocation to its full powers, but we feel that he would have had scanty respect for its ordinances. It is true that the bishops of his later life were chiefly Whigs, most of them, indeed, those creatures of the Duke of Newcastle, who deserted him on his fall, and for once made him a wit. "Even Fathers in God," said the old minister, "sometimes forget their maker." But even Johnson's own Tory divines were little to his mind. The ideal of a Tory bishop was Atterbury, yet he is mentioned but once, and that inevitably, in all Johnson's writings. Nor does he figure more in Boswell's biography. Possibly Atterbury's Jacobitism may have been outweighed in Johnson's eyes by the force of language with which he expressed it. Bishop of Rochester and Dean of Westminster though he was, "D——n it," he said, when Queen Anne died, "d——n it, there's not a moment to lose." The same objection may have lain against Swift, to whom Johnson would allow neither head nor heart. All his reverence went out toward Usher, of whom it was said that, had all churchmen been like him, there had been no Non-conformity. For a Non-conformist the true Tory could have no good word. Of Richard Baxter's works Johnson said: "Read any of them; they are all good." He praised Grove's essays, and he added to his publisher's list of poets the name of Isaac Watts, a convert to dissent, "whom every Christian church would rejoice to have adopted." The true Tory kept Fridays and all the days of Passion Week as fasts. Johnson regularly dined out; indeed the club met on Fridays. In one Passion Week he dined out twice, and each time with a bishop. Clearly there was no little of the Whig in him crossing the pure Tory strain.

There remains the question of Johnson's civil politics. If here he seemed to be a Tory, it was because he had a profound disbelief in the power of government for good or evil. Witness the couplet which he added to Goldsmith's "Traveller":

> "How small of all that human hearts endure
> That part which laws or kings can cause or cure."

He always harped on the same theme in prose. "I would not give half a guinea to live under one form of government rather than another. It is of no moment to the happiness of an individual. Sir, the danger of the abuse of power is nothing to a private man. What Frenchman is prevented from passing his life as he pleases?" This did not mean that he had no patriotic spirit. Against the foreigner he would have shouldered a pike as readily as Socrates. The independence of the nation he valued as highly as his own personal freedom. Of this he was, as Dr. Maxwell wrote, extremely jealous. He was against certain forms of government, but he had no fear of them. He was ready to assert that under an absolute prince men are governed by chance. There is no security for good government. But he held that the disease involved its remedy. "If a sovereign oppresses his people to a great degree, they will rise and cut off his head." It is needless to quote what Lord Auchinleck said to Johnson of Cromwell's great achievement. Of that Johnson always thought with indignation, but the Revolution he admitted to have been necessary. It is true that the Revolution found supporters among Tories of the type of Lord Nottingham, but it was a sad declension from Tory principles. Johnson said that it broke our constitution. It broke his Toryism as well. But for that he would hardly have described a courtier as one whose business it is to watch the looks of a being as weak and foolish as himself. He retained a sentimental affection for the Stuarts, but it would stand no test. He looked at the Jacobites with a Whig's eyes. When it was observed that the Highlanders in 1745 made surprising efforts, considering their immense wants and disadvantages, "Yes, sir," said he, "their wants were immense; but you have not mentioned the greatest of them all, the want of law." So in theory he was all for a Tory government, in practice he preferred to see the Whigs in power. Much as he hated, and rightly hated, government by corruption, he praised Sir Robert Walpole as a fixed star. When, forty years after Walpole's fall, Lord North was driven from power, Johnson solemnly thanked God. The instinct was right that made Lord North no friend to the author of the "False Alarm." What wonder that, with this general disregard for political parties, Johnson had no delight in talking of public affairs? What wonder that he was intimate with earnest Whigs? His oldest friend was Taylor, a Whig parson. The man he admired most was perhaps Burke; the physician to whom he entrusted his dying frame was Brocklesby, and Brocklesby's admiration for Burke's politics transferred thousands of pounds from his own purse to his friend's. In this spirit Johnson dictated to Boswell his views on parties. "A wise Tory and a wise Whig, I believe, will agree. Their principles are the same, though their modes of thinking are different. A high Tory makes government unintelligible; it is lost in the clouds. A violent Whig makes it impracticable; he is for allowing so much liberty to every man, that there is not power enough to govern any man." What is there here of Macaulay's bigoted Tory? In fact Macaulay had no appreciation of wrong, and his lack of this faculty made him ascribe bigotry to Johnson as it made him turn Horace Walpole into a gentleman usher.

There was, indeed, one matter in which Johnson showed such a monstrous perversity that even the faithful Boswell fell away from him. He could not away with the claims of America. *Taxation no Tyranny* is indeed a lamentable pamphlet, but it is not Toryism. A sentence here and there undoubtedly smacks of the Tory. "An English individual," he wrote, "may by the supreme authority be deprived of liberty, and a colony divested of its powers for reasons of which that authority is the only judge." Yet he admitted that the sovereign power is not infallible, for it may do wrong. The remedy is rebellion. He argued that England had a legal right to tax America, and the Whigs, except Chatham, held the same view. He did not see that it was a legal right which ought not to be enforced and against which America might and must rebel. In fact, much of the argument of his pamphlet is not so much wrong in itself as hopelessly beside the mark; and it is beside the mark not because Johnson was a Tory, but just because he was indifferent to the forms of government. Thus he was distracted from the main issue to subsidiary points, and at such a crisis subsidiary points could have no weight. The British army had protected America against the French; why should America not help to pay for the British army? If America were free, her own government would tax her above any possible taxation from England; was it not wicked to refuse to pay? Would the mere sound of freedom make the Bostonians abandon their homes? If so, let no man thereafter doubt the story of the Pied Piper. Clearly nothing would have made Johnson believe Burke's Philadelphian correspondent, who wrote that the plain farmer and even the plain Quaker was become a soldier, "a man of iron, armed at all points, despising danger, and praying for another frolic with Howe and his redcoats." His patriotism might have gained force upon the field of Marathon, but he could not understand a patriot that wielded the sword against a government of his own race. If blindness to the warnings of history is synonymous with Toryism, then undoubtedly Johnson was a Tory. Indeed, his state of mind made him as blind as Dean Tucker of Gloucester, who in ungrammatical frenzy had screamed to Necker that the future grandeur of America was one of the idlest and most visionary notions that ever was conceived even by writers of romance. The Whigs were perhaps right in doubting the political prescience of the parson. Johnson's name is great enough to have lived down his political pamphlets. Tucker's name and pamphlets are alike forgotten.

Johnson, then, was no party politician. In a small Northamptonshire church there is an epitaph to a member of the house of Fitzroy, which may be taken either as an antithesis or as a climax. "Through life a consistent Liberal, he died in the Lord." There is no political term that we can substitute for Liberal to make the epitaph serve as Johnson's. We *can* say that his life was like his death, and that his death was as the Northamptonshire squire's.

John Sargeaunt.

OTTO VON BISMARCK.

These are gray days for kings and for the art
  Of them that fawn and follow in their train;
Men are to-day grown serious of heart,
  And watch with naught but tolerant disdain
The purpled puppets prank their little part,
  Content to rule no more if left to reign.

Yet there are sovereigns still, uncrowned, who sway
  The lives of nations with imperious nod—
Kings of the mind whom other kings obey,
  Sue for their aid and kiss their chastening rod;
Such have we still among us e'en to-day—
  Monarchs anointed by the hand of God!

O hero soul, of courage all thine own,
  Who fearedst naught save only might divine,
Not in the German fatherland alone,

On storied height and by the rippling Rhine,
But wheresoe'er the German name is known,
Such power to stir the souls of men was thine.

The mild old man whose ill-defended throne
Found thee a champion unbribed, unbought—
Not his, but thine the wisdom which, unknown,
Met craft with craft and plot with counterplot.
Thou saw'st the goal and followedst it alone
When thine own kinsmen cursed thee, seeing not.

Not his but thine the grand imperial dream
To rear an empire out of nothingness ;
Not his but thine through anxious years to scheme ;
Not his but thine the strain, the storm, the stress—
And, in the hour of victory supreme,
Not his but thine the splendour of success.

When, at the last, the foe that blocked thy path,
Baffled and beaten in each dark design,
Dropped his poor mask to draw the sword of Gath,
Then thy right hand against his power malign,
Loosing the lightnings of a nation's wrath,
Flung the impetuous legions o'er the Rhine.

Then came the shock of conflict and the roar
Of black-lipped cannon and the flaming breath
Hot from the hell of battle—such before
War's grim recorder ne'er remembereth ;
While the gashed earth drank greedily of gore,
And swooned and sickened at the taste of death.

And the fair sinful city on her height,
Mirth's chosen home, the capital of Lust,
Ceased from her mockery and in affright
Watched thy stern host against her rabble thrust,
Till the gay wanton of a world's delight
Trailed her lascivious tresses in the dust.

Maker of monarchs ! Statelier than Rome,
Stands a great empire heralding thy name ;
While German hearts in every German home
Cherish the deeds with loyal love aflame,
That, like the stars in Heaven's majestic dome,
Blaze in the boundless firmament of fame !

Harry Thurston Peck.

STRAY PROPOSALS.

Authors of a coy and modest disposition, when called upon to describe the love affairs of youthful characters in their novels, have to face difficulties that cannot be estimated by folk who possess the ordinary share of effrontery. Some shirk the task altogether, and omit all references to affairs of the heart, with the result that their books are sneered at by lady readers, and justly condemned by all right-minded critics. The following samples of love-scenes are offered as likely to suit varied tastes, and bashful novelists are respectfully urged to give them a trial.

No. I.

The gifted young woman surveyed from the doorway at the side of the stalls the critics who had not taken advantage of the *entr'acte* to go out and quaff beverages. Only one of them looked grim; that one was her quondam admirer Clarence Walton. She went along the row of stalls and sank into the seat next to his.

"*Dear* Mr. Walton," she said, "I—" She hesitated.

"Beg pardon?" he said, coldly.

"I do so want to know what you think of the first two acts of my play. As a friend, now tell me your candid opinion."

"My opinion, Miss Gordon," he said, with reserve, "will appear to-morrow morning in the ——"

"I know, I know," she said, agitatedly. "But surely, Clarence, you can give me a hint."

"I am of opinion," replied Clarence Walton, cautiously, "that the pruning-knife will have to be used here and there. I think, too, that it shows traces of the feminine spirit. Also that one or two situations are distinctly conventional. Moreover—"

"Clare!" she interrupted, appealingly. She looked around; there was no one within hearing. "I have something to say to you. Do you remember that morning at Lucerne?"

He slapped his forehead with a gesture of pain.

"Shall I ever forget?" he asked, bitterly. "Why torture me with these memories?"

She blew gently at the feathered edge of her fan, and kept her eyes down.

"I have thought so often of that journey up Mount Pilatus," she said, gently.

"And I, too. I have never ceased to blame myself for offering my heart to a careless girl, who lightly spurned it. But, tush! A truce to—"

"That careless girl," said Muriel, softly and earnestly, "has grown into a sedate, thoughtful woman. She has changed her opinion on many things; she has learnt to value the affection of a noble, honest, true-hearted man."

"His name?" he asked, brusquely. "Tell me the name of this fortunate person."

"Clarry," she said, shyly, touching his sleeve, "can't you guess?"

"Muriel!"

"It is you, and you alone whom I have never ceased to admire; it is you, and you alone who—"

The orchestra had stumbled back, and was signalling the fact by tuning its instruments noisily. The occupants of the stalls returned, and a gruff critic on apparently a halfpenny paper demanded the seat of which Muriel had taken temporary possession.

"Till to-morrow, dear heart," said Clarence Walton to her, a light of great joy in his eyes.

"I shall look out for your notice," she said, gaily.

No. II.

"Miss Goodenough!"

"Captain Purleigh!"

"Our journey is nearly at an end. For three weeks I have had the inestimable privilege of seeing you daily. Just as this steamer has neared hour by hour the land of our birth, so my heart, hour by hour—"

"I suppose the time's getting on. What do you make it now by your watch?"

"I forgot to wind it up. I forget everything, dear Miss Goodenough, while you are near. Your fair presence—"

"Wonder how large the sea really is? Looks an enormous distance out there, doesn't it?"

"The sea, Miss Goodenough, unlike

my affection for you, has its limits. To walk thus with you on the deck of this steamer, to touch your hand, to hear your voice—all this to me is happiness that cannot be measured."

"Do you golf at all, Captain Purleigh?"

"I have no thought for any links but those which shall join our hearts and make them one. Miss Goodenough—Trixie! won't you say one word, that I may become the happiest of men?"

"Wonder how much one ought to give the stewardess?"

"Why will you not utter one brief word, loved one? You and I have noted sometimes on the voyage from South Africa how on a dark night the fair moon will suddenly peep through and illumine all—"

"I think I see my uncle's straw hat."

"So one word from you will lighten my heavy anxiety and tell me that content is in store. Miss Goodenough, may I, dare I, venture to hope?"

"How funny it will seem to be on land again."

"You will not answer me? You refuse to say the one word? Be it so, Miss Goodenough. Farewell! Some day, perhaps, when it is too late—"

"Captain Purleigh, stay! You must have seen—"

"Go on!"

"You must have seen that I—I care for you—very much indeed."

"My dearest, dearest, ever dearest life!"

No. III.

The guide Imobersteg took the golden coin and winked. Henri Bernard resented this inflection of the eyelid as something of an impertinence, but he could not protest, for he knew that he was in Imobersteg's power.

May Wheatley tripped up to them gaily, and Henri Bernard motioned to the Swiss to be prepared.

"*Soyez sage* (Be a sage)," commanded Henri.

"With whom do I ascend the mountain, good Imobersteg?" she asked, speaking the language of the country.

The guide stolidly pointed to M. Bernard, and the girl made a charming *moue*.

"I understood that *mon cousin* (my cousin) was to accompany me," she said, with delightful naïveté.

"The arrangements at the last moment have altered been," said the guide.

"I trust, Miss Wheatley," said Henri Bernard, advancing with a sneer, "that my presence will not entirely destroy the charm of the scenery."

"There won't be much left," she said.

"Miss Wheatley is pleased to be facetious," he said, constrainedly.

"Miss Wheatley is not pleased at all," she said. "Good Imobersteg, *vous connaissez les cordes* (you know the ropes). Do your duty."

"*Farceuse!* (Low comedy lady!)" remarked the guide, as he performed his duties. When they were securely roped to each other, the guide touched his hat and waited. She took no notice, but ordered him with an imperious gesture to proceed.

"*La belle dame sans merci* (The beautiful lady without a thank you)," muttered the guide.

"Have you no fear, *chère mademoiselle?* (dear miss)" asked Henri Bernard.

"A Wheatley," she said, proudly, "*a vingt joues* (has cheek enough for ten)."

Presently they approached a difficult part of the mountain, and it was then that Imobersteg, leading, quietly detached himself from the rope, and Henri Bernard's heart gave a bound of joy. Feeling the tension of the rope lessened, May gazed around. Below her was a yawning chasm; above her M. Bernard, seated by the one tree within sight, looked down at her. "*Parbleu!* (My goodness!)" she shouted. "The guide! *Où est-il?* (Where is he?)"

"The guide," says M. Bernard, with *sangfroid* (blood-cold), "has departed. We are alone. The others are out of ear-shot. Scream, if you will; naught but the blue sky above and the chasm below can hear you."

"*C'est dommage!* (It is a damage!)" she cries.

"*Mais ce n'est rien* (But it is not nothing)," he replies. "With me at hand, Miss Wheatley, you are safe. You have but to amend the answer that you gave me last evening at the Schweizerhof. I asked you then to be my wife; you spurned me. Is it not so?"

"*Oui!* (Yes!)" she answers.

"Now," he says, leaning down, "now I tell you—"

"Keep tight hold of that rope."

"Now, I tell you that you must and shall be mine. I love you with a passion that cannot and will not—"

"You let that rope slip," she repeats, warningly, "and I shall look silly."

"If I cannot be your *mari* (husband)," he hisses, "no one else shall be your *mari* (husband). Give your consent, enchanting girl, or at this moment, when all nature smiles, when—"

"*Jamais!* (Never!)" she says.

"*Sapristi!* (Bother!)" he cries, standing up and paying out the rope. "Thus, then, do I lower you to certain—"

"*Non!* (No!)" cries an honest young voice beside him, snatching the rope from his hands. "*Me voilà!* (Me see!)"

In less time than it takes to write these words, the half-fainting May Wheatley was hauled into safety by her handsome cousin. With a wild cry of disappointment, Henri Bernard untied the rope from his waist, and leaped into the chasm.

"I'm glad he's gone, dear," said May Wheatley. "He was beginning to be quite a nuisance."

W. Pett Ridge.

TOWARDS THE DEEP.

Let the lilies flaunt their graces,
Since the golden hearts which bide
In the folded buds' embraces
Will adorn a richer tide.
Statelier swans will sweep the lake
When the cygnets quit the brake
Where the Undines lave their faces
Unespied.

More melodious Junes are sleeping
In the lingering linnet's throat,
And a richer dawn is peeping
Where the sunset aureoles float;
When the plaintive minor dies
All the grand crescendos rise,
Deeper rapture onward sweeping
Note by note.

And, as Sulla's rebel minion
Vaunted more the rising sun,
Love may turn on listless pinion
When the zenith well is won,
Spelled by some diviner glow
Which affection yet may know,
Since through even hearts Hercynian
Danubes run.

Hence I wait till, through the hushes,
Which thy latent passions keep,
Like some rosy dream that blushes
On the russet bough of sleep,
Love shall leap and greet my own
With an ardour yet unknown,
As the deep-born river rushes
Towards the deep.

Charles J. Bayne.

AMERICAN BOOKMEN.

X.—Walt Whitman.

WALT WHITMAN IN 1884.

Instead of defining Walt Whitman as an "American Bookman," one might with greater justice describe him and his *Leaves of Grass*—for they are virtually one—as an American Book and a Man. It is merely a distinction of syllables, yet it has an important significance. The precise significance of Whitman, with relation to other poets, has never been more truly pointed out by an admirer than by Mr. John Burroughs in these words: "Just as ripe, mellowed, storied, ivy-towered, velvet-turfed England lies back of Tennyson, and is vocal through him; just as canny, covenanting, conscience-burdened, craggy, sharp-tongued Scotland lies back of Carlyle; just as thrifty, well-schooled, well-housed, prudent, and moral New England lies back of her group of poets, and is voiced by them, so America as a whole, our turbulent democracy, our self-glorification, our faith in the future, our huge mass-movements, our continental spirit, our sprawling, sublime, and unkempt nature lie back of Whitman and are implied by his work."

In the life of the man who proclaims himself the mouthpiece of these national qualities, it would be idle to look for the circumstances which enter into the making of other men who have made books, since books in any large measure expressive of these qualities have not hitherto been made. It must not be expected, therefore, to follow him through college and foreign travel, and into friendships and domestic relations which make conspicuously for what are called the refinements of life. He constantly spoke in his writings of the "literats" as a class distinct from himself. His book, he maintained, is not to be viewed as a literary performance, but merely as an attempt to put a Person "freely, fully, and truly on record." This person is of course Walt Whitman, not merely Walt Whitman the private citizen, but also Walt Whitman as he conceived himself, "a great, composite *democratic individual*, male or female," ready to "raise high the perpendicular hand" to every person and every experience to be found on earth. It is the first step toward any acceptance of Whitman to accept him in this double personality. Whether the "composite,

WHITMAN AT 36.
From frontispiece to first edition of *Leaves of Grass.*

democratic individual" is or is not a person to one's liking in every respect, the *Leaves of Grass* speak for him in unmistakable terms. For Walt Whitman, the private citizen, his life speaks with an equal clearness. There are few writers whose lives and whose writings are so completely at one. It is therefore more than commonly helpful, in arriving at a true estimate of Walt Whitman as a writer, to gain a clear knowledge of him as a man.

The poet of democracy has need to be born and bred of the people, and Whitman had all the fitness for his work which comes from such a birth and breeding. His father, Walter Whitman, was a skilful carpenter and builder, living on a farm at West Hills, Huntington Township, Long Island, which his father and grandfather had owned before him. Here his wife, Louisa Van Velsor, of a neighbouring Dutch family of farmers, also long established in the region, and famed for the raising of horses, bore him a son, Walter, the second of nine children, on May 31st, 1819. To distinguish the boy from his father, his name

and its owner did not permit the years to restore the lost syllable. He was not five years old when his family re-

the public schools, and "tended" in a lawyer's and doctor's office, until at the age of fourteen he was set to learn the printer's trade. Two years of this

round" in the neighbourhood of his birthplace. To this experience he owed some of his "deepest lessons in human

shore, which appear and reappear in his writings, show that he learned them well. In 1839 and 1840 he is seen in his native town of Huntington as the found-

WHITMAN IN 1855.
From a daguerreotype.

WHITMAN IN WAR-TIME.

WHITMAN AND HIS LITTLE FRIENDS KITTY AND HAROLD JOHNSTON.

it by his experiences in the civil war. Though his productions in prose and verse were printed in the magazines of the day, they were not distinguished for individual merit, and he took no uncommon place as a writer. It was rather as a compositor in printing-offices, and then as the editor of a daily paper, the Brooklyn *Eagle*, that he provided himself with his "nothing too much" of money. It was still more as the observer and sharer of the life about him that he passed his days. The spectacles of the harbour and Broadway were his delight. The pilots on the ferry-boats, in which he crossed from Brooklyn to New York over and over again for mere pleasure, were his friends. Talking on all manner of subjects with them, giving and taking, lending a copy of Homer to a youth who swabbed the deck, listening to long accounts of their work and thoughts, thus he passed whole afternoons and even nights.

er and publisher of a weekly newspaper, *The Long Islander*. For the most part his boyhood and younger manhood differed in few outward respects from those of youths who go on to be good mechanics and tradesmen, or rural teachers and editors. Nor did the years that followed his return to New York and Brooklyn, in 1840, conspicuously foretell what was to come. Yet it was mainly in the fifteen years that preceded the first publication of *Leaves of Grass*, in 1855, that Whitman was traversing the "long foreground" into which Emerson's keen eye pierced its way when the book appeared. The elements of this foreground were the permanent elements of Whitman's thought, except for the great additions that were made to

Of some of these friends he wrote at a later time, "When we meet we kiss each other (I am an exception to all their customs with others)." The drivers of the Broadway stages were equally his intimates. Sitting on the box beside them, their life for the time became his. One winter, in order to keep a disabled driver's place for him, he drove a stage himself. To museums and theatres, and especially the opera, he paid frequent visits. Then there were solitary days of walking, reading, and bathing at the seashore. In all these ways the multiform life about him was taken into himself and made a living part of his own nature.

Yet the "foreground" would have been incomplete if its horizon had not

WHITMAN'S MOTHER.

been spread beyond that of New York and its vicinity, for the national sense enters as strongly into Whitman's completeness as the spirit of "Manahatta my city." This enlargement of view was brought about in 1848 and 1849 by what Whitman called "a leisurely journey and working expedition" with his brother "Jeff" through the Middle States, down the Ohio and Mississippi, to New Orleans, where he served on the editorial staff of *The Crescent*. Thence he returned by easy stages up the Mississippi and Missouri, and home by the way of the Great Lakes and Lower Canada. Back in Brooklyn in 1850, he published and edited *The Freeman*, a newspaper of his own, for about two years, after which he undertook the business of building and selling small houses. It seems to have been the danger of growing rich that made him abandon this enterprise.

Still one important element seems needed to complete the foreground for *Leaves of Grass*—an active personal share, more than the portion of a mere observer, in many expressions of man's physical nature. The testimony of Whitman's friends is that he was essentially a temperate man in all respects. If in the years from 1840 to 1855 "he sounded all experiences of life," as one well-accredited biographer has said, he was not one to disown his conduct, for he empowered John Addington Symonds to publish his statement: "My life, young manhood, mid-age, times South, etc., have been jolly bodily, and doubtless open to criticism." It would be no less misleading, in considering Whitman, to withhold these facts than to interpret them in the light of his poems without remembering that Walt Whitman the individual and Walt Whitman in his imagined life of "the average man" are at many points distinct personalities. It is in his personality of the average man that he changes the old saying, "There, but for the grace of God, goes John Newton," into the new and unqualified, "There goes Walt Whitman."

We are told that the purpose of *Leaves of Grass* formed itself in Whitman's mind early in the fifties, and that in 1854 he began putting on paper the twelve poems which made up the book, published as a thin quarto in 1855. It is worth while to bring together two statements concerning him and his work at this precise time. One of his brothers makes the report: "Walt did not always dress in this present style. He was rather stylish when young. He started in with his new notions somewhere between 1850–55." So much for the adoption of the unconventional costume which marked him from this time forth. Concerning the mode of utterance which he adopted at the same time, his own words are: "I had great trouble in leaving out the stock 'poetical' touches, but succeeded at last." His own conception of his work and the best way to do it was clear to him, and he squarely faced what seemed to be demanded of him. His warmest admirers in later years are tempted to regard as fools and blind all those who did not immediately put a true value upon his book. Yet it was no more strange that it met with hostility than that "the average person," utterly ignorant of Wagner and his intentions, should not rejoice in a first hearing of the most "Wagnerian" portions of *Tristan and Isolde*, or that another person quite unacquainted with impressionist art should experience scant pleasure in finding himself in a room full of Monet's pictures. Whitman's very themes, regarded in the light in which he saw them, forbade a cordial welcome. "The main objects of his enthusiasm" have been defined by Symonds as "America, Self, Sex, the People." To treat these themes in a series of "slack-twisted" dithyrambic chants, apparently flying in the face of all poetic tradition, and written with a frankness and egotism and lack of humour which, after forty years of Whitman "in the air," are still detested by many, was inevitably to court the opposition of "persons of taste." The critics representing these persons fell upon the book with a savage fury. The writer of it was "a beast;" he "should be kicked from all decent society." To one London journal he appeared as "a wild Tupper of the West;" another, commenting upon a later edition, declared: "Of all writers we have perused, Walt Whitman is the most silly, the most blasphemous, and the most disgusting." The bitterest condemnations of the book were due to its many offences against "the proprieties." Most men could not possibly take its unfamiliar point of view immediately. After many years the New York *Tribune* echoed but faintly the first voices of denunciation when it said: "The chief question raised by this publication is whether anybody—even a poet—ought to take off his trousers in the market-place."

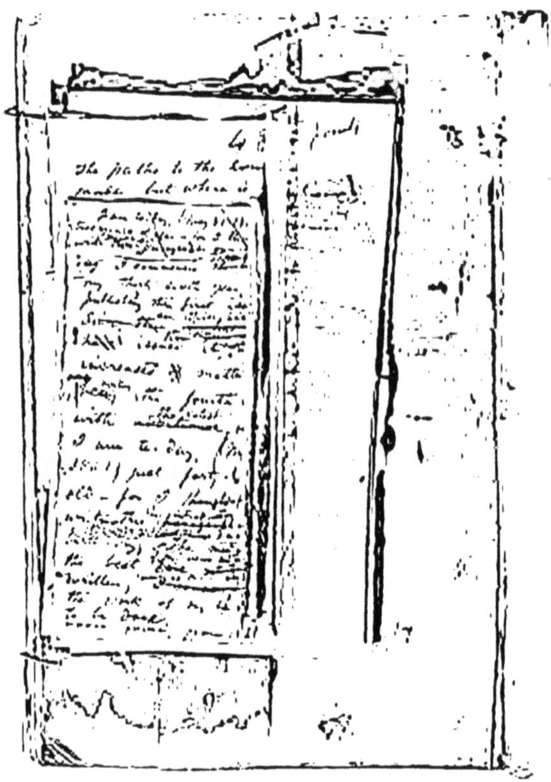

COVERS OF WHITMAN'S OWN COPY OF THE FIRST EDITION OF "LEAV

Such were the views most commonly held regarding the *Leaves of Grass*. But there were those, neither fools nor blind, who saw many other things in the book. In England, where Whitman has found many of his best admirers, a prompt word of appreciation was spoken by Richard Monckton Milnes (not yet Lord Houghton), in a letter to Hawthorne at the Liverpool consulate: "I wanted to see you mainly for your own sake, and also to ask you about an American book which has fallen into my hands. It is called *Leaves of Grass*, and the author calls himself Walt Whitman. Do you know anything about him? I will not call it *poetry*, because I am unwilling to apply that word to a work totally destitute of art; but, whatever we call it, it is a most notable and true book. It is not written *virginibus puerisque*; but as

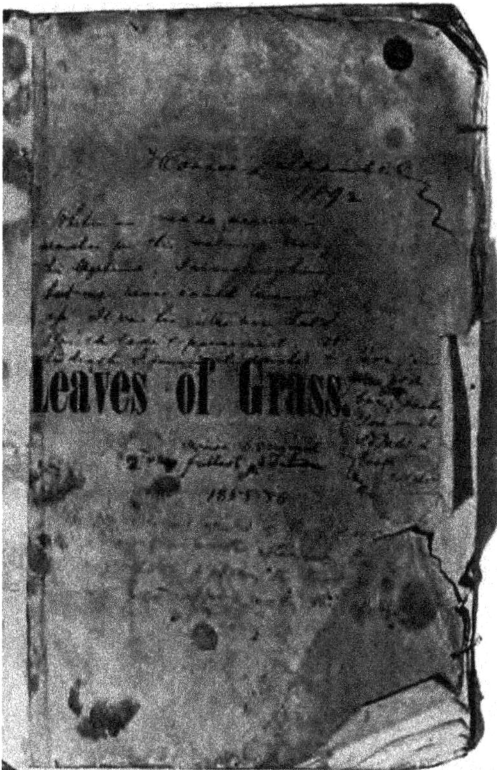

KASS," WITH AUTOGRAPH NOTES AND OTHER MEMORANDA.

Emerson took no account of it when he handed a copy of Whitman's book to a friend and said, "Americans abroad may now come home: unto us a man is born." He sent a copy of the book to Carlyle, not without misgivings, calling it "a nondescript monster, which yet had terrible eyes and buffalo strength, and was indisputably American;" and he added, "after you have looked into it, if you think, as you may, that it is only an auctioneer's inventory of a warehouse, you can light your pipe with it." There were no misgivings, however, in the words of thanks which he sent to Whitman himself for his gift of the book. "I find it the most extraordinary piece of wit and wisdom that America has yet contributed. . . . I find incomparable things said incomparably well, as they must be. . . . I greet you at the beginning of a great career, which must yet have had a long foreground somewhere, for such a start." (See fac-simile of Emerson's letter on page 435.) With a letter in his pocket from Emerson saying such words as these, Whitman, though needing no confidence but his own, could well afford to write, "Why should I hurry or compromise?" From the general storm of abuse which greeted his book, he did shield and recover himself in the summer and autumn of 1855 by going to the east end of Long Island. When he came back to New York it was, he said, "with the confirmed resolution to go on with my poetic enterprise in my own way, and finish it as well as I could."

I am neither the one nor the other, I may express my admiration of its vigorous virility and bold, natural truth. There are things in it that read like the old Greek plays. It is of the same family as those delightful books of Thoreau's which you introduced me to, and which are so little known and valued here." In America Whitman had the satisfaction of winning at once the highest opinion of the man whose good opinion was worth most at the time—namely, Emerson. It is said that Whitman knew nothing of Emerson's writings before producing the *Leaves of Grass*, yet if Emerson had withheld his hand from one whose practice so conspicuously reflected his preaching of the gospel of individuality, this preaching would have seemed a mockery. Wide as the gulf between the two men may have appeared,

The carrying out of this enterprise was Whitman's work for the rest of his life, for even his vivid share in the life of the war time may be regarded in the closest relation with his poetic purpose. It is not possible here to follow the book through all its fortunes and misfortunes of successive editions and gradual growth. When the second edition appeared in 1856, Emerson had good reason to be annoyed at finding his sentence, "I greet you at the beginning of a great career," printed in letters of gold over his name on the back of the volume. But he had the good sense to know that the standards of taste in Whitman's Brooklyn were different from those of his own Concord, and when Whitman came to Boston, in 1860, to superintend the issue of his third edition, Emerson took so great an interest in the undertaking that he walked for two hours up and down the Beacon Street mall of the Common, arguing with Whitman for the omission of many things in the "Children of Adam" poems. Whitman listened without contention, knowing, as he said, "I could never hear the points better put—and then I felt down in my soul the clear and unmistakable conviction to disobey all, and pursue on my own way." When the seventh edition of the poems was brought out in Boston, in 1881, the threat of official prosecution, on the ground of the objections urged by Emerson, caused the publishers, who had known well what they were doing, to abandon the book with incontinent haste. But publishers in Philadelphia were not slow to take it up, and after growing year by year, until Whitman's death, the book has returned to Boston, committed by the literary executors of the author to a young house which makes Whitman its first enterprise.

THE TOMB AT HARLEIGH, CAMDEN, N. J. DESIGNED BY WHITMAN HIMSELF.

It has been the present writer's fortune to see a few of the many note-books—simple, home-made things—in which Whitman jotted down his thoughts, and entered words and phrases that took his fancy, with their meanings and derivations. Here may be found such favourite terms of his own as "kosmos" and "literat" and "rondure," noted with a carefulness that would have seemed almost superfluous for a man without a certain consciousness that he was conducting his own education. Here the sentences which from time to time found their way into his chants are marked off as of no further use. We are told that these note-books were always with him, and that writing more literally with "his eye on the object" than most poets, his thoughts were put into their first form wherever he might happen to be. That their finished form was the result of offhand work is a mistaken idea, for his manuscripts show with what careful elaboration his lines were wrought. Mr. Stedman has called him "more formal than others in his non-conformity, and haughtier in his plainness than many in their pride." Certainly it is not without suggestion that the title which he chose for his first book defined all his subsequent work not in prose, and remains as the title of all that he did through nearly forty years. Few writers have maintained an identity so unvarying, so sure of its right to permanence. Time somewhat mellowed and broadened its expression. At first his cry was, "I sound my barbaric yawp over the roofs of the world." Later it became, "Over the tree-tops I float thee a song." But this was in his threnody for Lincoln, and the events of which Lincoln was the centre were the chief influences that brought the man and the poet to completeness.

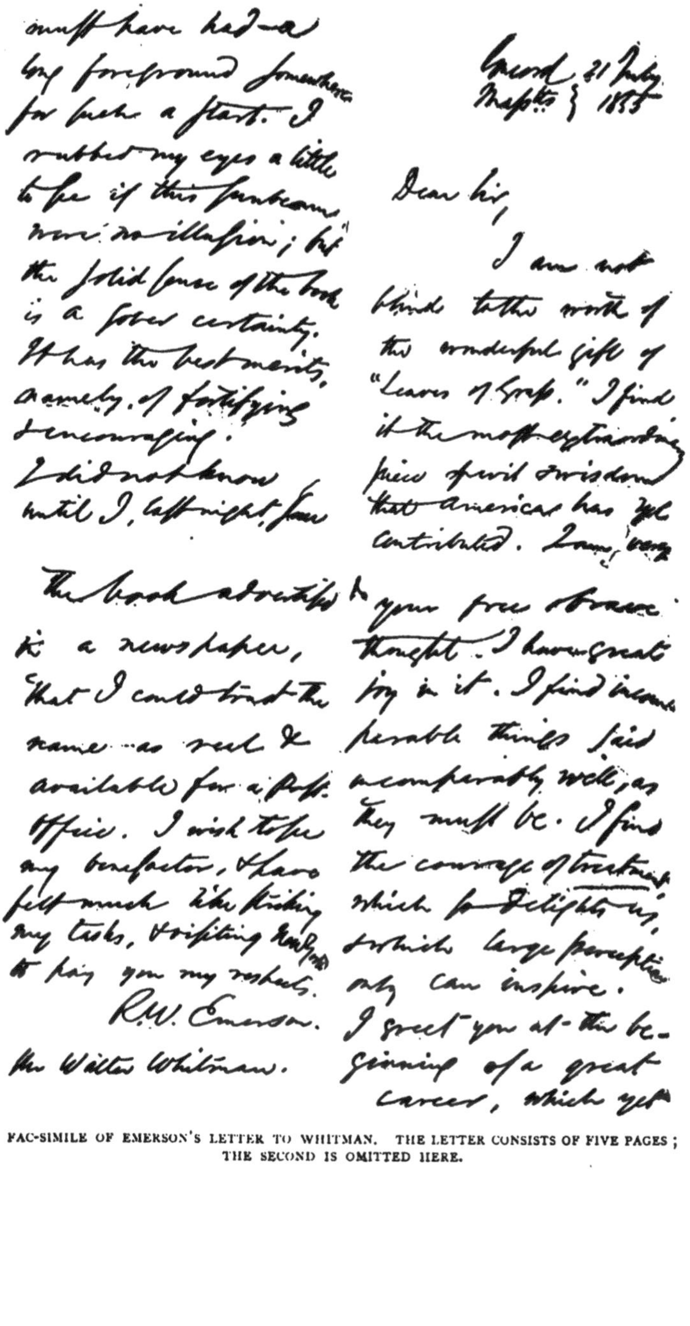

Concord 21 July
Mass'tts 1855

Dear Sir,

I am not blind to the worth of the wonderful gift of "Leaves of Grass." I find it the most extraordinary piece of wit & wisdom that America has yet contributed. I am very

your free & brave thought. I have great joy in it. I find incomparable things said incomparably well, as they must be. I find the courage of treatment, which so delights us, & which large perception only can inspire. I greet you at the beginning of a great career, which yet

must have had a long foreground somewhere for such a start. I rubbed my eyes a little to see if this sunbeam were no illusion; but the solid sense of the book is a sober certainty. It has the best merits, namely, of fortifying & encouraging.

I did not know until I, last night, saw the book advertised in a newspaper, that I could trust the name as real & available for a Post Office. I wish to see my benefactor, & have felt much like striking my tasks, & visiting New York to pay you my respects.

R. W. Emerson.

Mr Walter Whitman.

FAC-SIMILE OF EMERSON'S LETTER TO WHITMAN. THE LETTER CONSISTS OF FIVE PAGES; THE SECOND IS OMITTED HERE.

To understand the effect of the war in widening his poetic scope, national and human, it is necessary only to see how his life tallied with it—if one of his own phrases may be used. When his brother George, afterward lieutenant-colonel in his New York regiment, was wounded at Fredericksburg, in 1862, Whitman, at an hour's notice, started from Brooklyn to care for him. His wound was not severe, and the new-comer soon found himself in Washington caring for other Brooklyn soldiers sent thither in his charge. Gradually this care-taking extended itself to wounded soldiers in general, from both sides, in the army hospitals in Washington and at the front. In this capacity, rather of comforter than of nurse, Whitman gave of his best to the soldiers till the war was over. No man could have been better qualified for such a task. His habit of life had made him the comrade of all, especially the obscure. Unmarried—through an "overmastering passion," as he said, "for entire freedom, unconstraint"—he was checked by none of the ties which bind other men from holding their lives cheap. Blessed with a feminine gift of sympathy, which made children and weak persons instinctively trust in him, his touch and word were often what the wounded men needed most. His very physical presence was comforting. When Lincoln, looking from the White House window, saw Whitman pass, his word was, "Well, *he* looks like a man!" Six feet in height, of vigorous mould and carriage, ruddy of skin, bearded and gray of hair since thirty, given to frequent baths, the cleanest linen and simple clothes, he carried about with him an air of health and sunlight. By friends in Northern cities he was supplied with the means for bringing more tangible things to the hospitals. A friend who went his rounds with him once has told of what he saw, and a part of the record must speak for the whole of a beneficent service, a personal ministration, it has been estimated, to about one hundred thousand men. "From cot to cot they called him, often in tremulous tones or in whispers; they embraced him, they touched his hand, they gazed at him. To one he gave a few words of cheer, for another he wrote a letter home, to others he gave an orange, a few comfits, a cigar, a pipe and tobacco, a sheet of paper or a postage-stamp—all of which and many other things were in his capacious haver-sack. From another he would receive a dying message for mother, wife, or sweetheart; for another he would promise to go an errand; to another, some special friend, very low, he would give a manly farewell kiss. He did the things for them which no nurse or doctor could do, and he seemed to leave a benediction at every cot as he passed along. The lights had gleamed for hours in the hospital that night before he left it, and as he took his way toward the door, you could hear the voice of many a stricken hero calling, 'Walt, Walt, Walt, come again! Come again!'"

Before the war was over Whitman had the first illness of his life, an attack of "hospital malaria," induced by his labours, which converted him from a young into an old man. But the illness kept him only a short time from the hospitals, where all the time that he could spare from his new clerkship in the Department of the Interior was spent. This clerkship itself was short-lived, by reason of his dismissal as the author of *Leaves of Grass*. The incident brought forth W. D. O'Connor's flaming pamphlet, *The Good Gray Poet*, which provided Whitman with a permanent name better than anything he had lost. Another clerkship in the office of the Attorney-General was promptly secured, and there he worked till 1873, when an attack of paralysis, which had its first cause in his hospital service, incapacitated him for all regular labour. Thenceforth, until his death, on March 26th, 1892, he lived in Camden, N. J., in health of varying feebleness. At its best it permitted him to go about freely in the world, as in his journeys to Colorado and Canada. At its worst, it rendered him almost helpless. Yet his good cheer and courage never failed him. Living in one of the simplest houses in an unpretentious district, rejoicing, as of old, in the life of the ferries and the streets, and in all the aspects of nature, cared for by devoted friends, who gave him, among other things, a horse and buggy of his own, honoured by the recognition of the masters in literature, as the letters from Tennyson alone are enough to show, writing in prose the *Specimen Days*,

To those who've fail'd.

To those who've fail'd in aspiration vast
To unnamed soldiers fall'n in front, on the lead
To calm, devoted engineers — to over-ardent travelers — to pilots on their ships,
To many a song and picture without parturition — I'd rear a laurel-cover'd monument
High, high above the rest — to all cut off before their time,
Possess'd by some great spirit of fire,
Quench'd by an early death.

Walt Whitman

FAC-SIMILE FROM THE ORIGINAL MANUSCRIPT.

which Symonds called "the brightest and halest 'Diary of an Invalid' ever written," and singing in verse the ripened songs of one who has seen and suffered much, Whitman lived his old age so as to blur in no wise the picture of his life, but to work its fulfilment.

After all has been said about Whitman, there are good folk who ask, "But is not the whole Whitman attitude a monstrous pose? Why should catalogues be considered poetry? Why must all things be thought equally worthy of honour? Are the graces of humility, reverence, and proportion obsolete, that they should be thrown to the winds? This Whitman brings us no new discoveries, or very few—but barbarous declamation of commonplace in plenty: why should we listen to him?"

It is quite possible that for many persons these honest questions cannot be satisfactorily answered. The Whitmaniacs, as the renegade admirer Swinburne called Whitman's followers, sometimes answer such inquiries with a heat which is meant to warm, but burns instead. It would be idle to tell all men that they must accept Whitman entire or not at all. He has been called "an acquired taste"—and surely it is something different for which we turn to his book and to the books of the other poets; yet he need not displace, but supplement them. The things which most open-minded readers who turn to Whitman can accept and rejoice in are his large enthusiasm for mankind, especially in "these States," whose national spirit he utters as no one else has done; his elemental scorn, such as a cloud or a north wind might hold, for all but the real things; his faith and hope and love. With these watchwords he sets the spirit free, and accomplishes his definite purpose, of which he wrote: "The reader will have his or her part to do, just as much as I have had mine. I seek less to state or display any theme or thought, and more to bring you, reader, into the atmosphere of the theme or thought—there to pursue your own flight."

Persons of a casual temper read a page or two of Whitman, and ignorant of the truth set forth by Stevenson, that "no one can appreciate Whitman's excellences until he has grown accustomed to his faults," find it easy to toss him aside as an offender against all preconceived ideas of poetry, and therefore not a poet. It would be less easy for these persons to explain the effect his writings have had upon men and women whom they do not so readily dismiss. It is not necessary to enumerate the names of all his earlier and later admirers, at home and abroad. It is, however, worth while to repeat the deliberate statement of John Addington Symonds, surely a critical voice worth heeding: "*Leaves of Grass*, which I first read at the age of twenty-five, influenced me more, perhaps, than any other book has done, except the Bible; more than Plato, more than Goethe." If this was a personal rather than a critical estimate, a value of its own may be attached to his statement: that he was willing to pledge his reputation as a critic on the opinion that Whitman produced not only poetry, but "poetry of a very high order." Nor has the prophet been without honour in his own country, for the last and least faltering voice in his praise has been uplifted in a book, which confesses itself at the outset a panegyric, by John Burroughs, whose standards are pre-eminently those of sanity and nature. Before dismissing Whitman, it behoves the casual person to see what he brings to the minds of men like Symonds and Burroughs.

> "I charge you forever reject those who would expound me, for I cannot expound myself."

This was Whitman's command, and it cannot be said that his disciples have literally obeyed it. His own prose paper, *A Backward Glance O'er Travel'd Roads*, was in effect an exposition. His biographer, Dr. R. M. Bucke, who is also one of his literary executors, and yet another of these, Mr. Horace L. Traubel, have written many pages which serve to clarify the understanding of Walt Whitman and his book. Whether men call him a poet or a prophet or "a great composite, democratic individual," he is a figure which refuses to be passed by in the records of American letters; and the truest exposition of him, after all, is to be found in the *Leaves of Grass* itself.

M. A. De Wolfe Howe.

The subject of the next paper in this series, to appear in the February BOOKMAN, *will be "Whittier and Lowell."*

LET ME BELIEVE.

When boughs are shaken of bloom, and dead leaves drifting, too,
I would recall their first perfume, and the sunlight sifting through;
When fields lie barren without, and bitter frosts are come,
Bid me not hear the winds of Doubt, that with the darkness roam.

When hours grow dim and gray, and the song of the year is sung,
Leave me the thrill of the dawning day, in a heart that is young, is young!
Though Hope be a blossom whirled, and Time doth pillage and win,
Let me hearken the pulse of the World, and learn of Truth therein.

Ay, though my dreams shall pale, while night but an ember lures,
Let me believe, though its light shall fail, that Love, that Love endures!

Virginia Woodward Cloud.

A NOTE ON PROFESSOR HENRY DRISLER.

The newspapers and other periodicals have given with sufficient fulness the details of the official life of the late Professor Drisler, whose long and distinguished career as one of the leading classical scholars of this country came to an end with his death last month. Very little, however, has been published relating to his personality, although this, and not his professional work, is what will be most distinctly remembered by the great majority of his former students. For it is likely that most of these have long ago forgotten all the Greek he taught them, while their memory of the man himself is as fresh and vivid as when they took his hand for the last time on the day that marked the ending of their sojourn in the College halls.

By permission of Harper & Brothers.

PROFESSOR HENRY DRISLER.

Professor Drisler was not a handsome man, but he was, nevertheless, a man of most impressive aspect. Large and powerful of frame, his massive head surrounded by abundant, thick white hair, his keen and piercing but kindly eyes, and a certain suggestion of power that was conveyed in the strongly marked features of his face gave him a sort of leonine appearance that never failed to awe the student who for the first time came into his presence. His manner was one of calmness and repose, and this was characteristic of his methods and of his work. He never said anything for effect, and he never did anything for effect; and it was, in fact, rather difficult at times to get a glimpse of the rich treasures of learning that long years of unremitting labour had stored up in his mind. But modesty has its victories as marked as any that are won by self-assertion; and it was reserved for Professor Drisler to gain for American classical scholarship a triumph whose significance is as striking as the quiet way in which he won it is unusual.

When the two distinguished Oxford scholars, Dean Liddell and Dr. Robert Scott, put forth their great Greek-English Lexicon sometime in the forties, this work, the first of its kind, was hailed with a burst of enthusiasm, which was, in fact, deserved. As was natural, however, in the first edition of so comprehensive a thesaurus, much had been left undone, and some things that had been done had not been very accurately done. A subsequent criticism of the book found expression at Oxford in the following irreverent rhyme, which was widely circulated in the English universities, though never, I think, made public through the medium of print:

"This is the book of Liddell and Scott;
Some of it's good, and some of it's not.
That which is good is Scott;
That which is Liddell is not."

It was not long after the appearance of this monumental work that its authors began to receive from America occasional notes and courteously suggested criticisms signed with the name of Henry Drisler, at that time unknown outside of the United States. These notes were so valuable, and the criticisms were so acute and so indicative of an immensely wide range of reading, that Dr. Liddell requested his correspondent to favour him with more; and for many years Dr. Drisler continued to forward similar memoranda looking toward a future revision of the book. These showed a remarkable acquaintance with all periods of Greek literature and with the history of the language, covering not only the golden age of Greek literary creativeness, but extending down into the Alexandrian era and the Byzantine period. The notes contributed by him were of such exceptional value, and formed so large a mass of critical and supplementary material, that when in 1879 the augmented edition of the Lexicon appeared, its original editors, with that keen sense of justice and fair play which characterises the English gentleman, gave to Professor Drisler the unusual recognition of placing his name upon the title-page of the perfected work. When one considers the self-sufficiency of English scholarship and the low esteem which English classicists once had for all American learning, this compliment was as remarkable as it was well deserved.

Like most great teachers who have won the personal affection of their students, Professor Drisler had a number of pet likings and aversions which sometimes verged upon the whimsical, but which imparted to his character as a whole those little human touches that make a strong personality so delightful, and that appeal especially and with exceeding strength to the imagination of the undergraduate. He was, for instance, remarkably conservative, and this conservatism was seen not only in his general views of university education, but in many minor ways. He liked old traditions, old usages, and old customs, and he never voluntarily abandoned them. For instance, far back in the early days of his connection with the College, it had been the practice for a student when called upon for recitation to take his place at a table set apart for that purpose, upon which was placed a text of the Greek author in whose exposition the Doctor was engaged. This practice was ultimately given up; but twenty, thirty, and forty years after—in fact, down to the very end of his teaching career, the Doctor's formula of calling on a student to recite was couched in the words, "Place table!" This was a small matter; but many a student will remember his consternation on coming into the class-room for the first time to be greeted with the (to him) mysterious command, "Place table!" He saw no table, and he hardly understood what was expected of him; while the Doctor's evident displeasure at having to explain completed his discomfiture.

For some reason that no one has ever satisfactorily elucidated, the Doctor had a peculiar fondness for the second aorist tense of the Greek verb. This came to be a matter of tradition with the undergraduates, and it served a useful purpose in the lecture-room. Whenever a man had been called upon to recite and had done so, he felt reasonably safe for the rest of the hour; so seating himself beside some other equally lucky person, the two would engage in a quiet game of "go-bang." Sometimes, however, the Doctor would observe that one or the other of these men was not wholly intent on Greek; and, therefore, watching his chance, he would suddenly project at the offender some complicated question uttered in a loud voice. This always came like lightning out of a clear sky. The student never by any possibility understood what had been asked of him, nor could he have answered the question if he had known. But the College tradition had taught him what to do, and he invariably replied with a cheerful promptness, "Second aorist, sir!" This answer seldom had any bearing upon the question asked, and was sometimes absurdly wide of the mark; but the mention of his favourite tense always so mollified the Doctor that his face would at once relax into its usual expression of benignity, and the student would go on peacefully with his interrupted game.

Of all the pet aversions which the Doctor cherished, two were particularly marked. He always hated to see a student carrying a stick, and he hated even more to see him smoking. There is no reason to suppose that he had any objection to walking-sticks in the abstract, nor did he entertain any personal antipathy to tobacco ; but for some unaccountable reason he never liked to see a student with either one or the other of these two things about him. When any ill-advised undergraduate came into his presence carrying a stick, and began setting forth some petition or request, the Doctor would pay no attention whatever to the story, but would glare portentously at the cane. The student would see that something was wrong, and would become confused and stammer in his narrative, and finally be smitten with a panic terror, when at last the Doctor with his powerful voice would thunder out : "Sir, take that *thing* out into the hall and leave it there, and then come back and tell me what you have to say !"

And if the student happened to be a prudent person, he would, after going out into the hall, take himself off altogether and reserve his story for some other time ; since the Doctor's feelings were always so ruffled by such an occurrence as to make him for that occasion a most unsympathetic listener.

His other prejudice was even more accentuated, and sometimes showed itself in most amusing ways. On a certain occasion, a good many years ago, a number of Sophomores, of whom the present writer must reluctantly confess that he was one, inspired by a sudden impulse to which Sophomores are traditionally liable, had made a raid through the College grounds with much more energy than discretion. Their proceedings, however, had not escaped official notice, and the next day they were summoned to a grand *levée en masse.* When they had assembled, the Doctor strode into their presence like a sort of Jupiter Tonans, filled with indignation and giving a toss to his head that was decidedly Olympian. His comminatory eloquence when addressing a body of academic offenders was always couched in the vein of the immortal head-master in *Pendennis ;* and on this occasion he began his harangue in somewhat the following manner, the climax being deliciously suggestive of his pet aversion :

"Gentlemen, I am aware from my own observation and from the reports of the College officers, that you have been guilty of the most outrageous conduct. You have violated the promise which you made upon matriculation, and have broken all the rules of College order. You entered the College grounds fresh from a reprehensible orgy in a contiguous place, singing discordant songs, and emitting other sounds that were scarcely human. You interrupted the work of the whole institution. You broke several windows. You entered the bell-house of the chapel and removed from the bell an indispensable adjunct"—the Doctor would have died rather than call it "clapper"—"and you propelled with violence through the window of Professor S—— an animal—in fact, as I am informed, a—a cat. Moreover, you committed an unpardonable attack upon several unoffending Freshmen who were going quietly about their legitimate vocations ; and, seizing them by their lower limbs, you compelled them to stand for several minutes upon their heads, thereby endangering their lives and rendering yourselves liable to a charge of felonious assault, and perhaps of constructive murder. And finally, gentlemen"—this with very great impressiveness—"as I looked from my window I could see, even at that distance, that some of your number were smoking cigars !"

Professor Drisler was emphatically the defender of the student. When any man was in a scrape he always went to Dr. Drisler. He was sure to get a most tremendous lecture from him, but after this was over he knew that he had secured in him a very powerful champion. It is perhaps in this aspect that the majority of Columbia graduates today first think of him. They did not always understand his scholarship, though they accepted it as a fact ; but every man, even the most negligent, the least studious, and the most harum-scarum, could feel at once the illimitable kindliness and benignity of the man, and they will carry the recollection of it with them throughout their lives. To adopt the phraseology in which the University Council expressed its sense of grief at his death, Columbia's alumni retain for Dr. Drisler one universal sentiment—"a feeling of admiration for the scholar, of gratitude for the teacher, and of affection for the friend."

Harry Thurston Peck.

JOHN SPLENDID.

THE TALE OF A POOR GENTLEMAN AND THE LITTLE WARS OF LORN.*

By Neil Munro, the Author of "The Lost Pibroch."

CHAPTER I.

Many a time, in college or in camp, I had planned the style of my home-coming. Master Webster, in the Humanities, droning away like a Boreraig bagpipe, would be sending my mind back to Shira Glen, its braes and corries and singing waters, and Ben Bhuidhe over all, and with my chin on a hand I would ponder on how I should go home again when this weary scholarship was over. I had always a ready fancy and some of the natural vanity of youth, so I could see myself landing off the lugger at the quay of Inneraora town, three inches more of a man than when I left with a firkin of herring and a few bolls of meal for my winter's provand; thicker too at the chest, and with a jacket of London green cloth with brass buttons. Would the fishermen about the quayhead not lean over the gun'les of their skiffs and say, "There goes young Elrigmore from Colleging, well-knit in troth, and a pretty lad!" I could hear (all in my day dream in yon place of dingy benches) the old women about the well at the town Cross say, "Oh *lochain!* thou art come back from the Galldach, and Glascow College, what a thousand curious things thou must know, and what wisdom thou must have, but never a change on thy affability to the old and to the poor!" But it was not till I had run away from Glascow College and shut the boards for good and all, as I thought, on my humane letters and history, and gone with Cousin Gavin to the German wars in Munro's Corps of true Highlanders that I added a manlier thought to my thinking of the day when I should come home to my native place. I've seen me in the camp at night, dog-wearied after stoury marching on their cursed foreign roads, keeping my eyes open and the sleep at an arm's-length, that I might think of Shira Glen. Whatever they may say of me or mine, they can never deny but I had the right fond heart for my own country-side, and I have fought men for speaking of its pride and poverty—their ignorance, their folly!—for what did they ken of the Highland spirit? I would be lying in the lap of the night, and my Ferrara sword rolled in my plaid as a pillow for my head, fancying myself—all those long wars over, march, siege, and sack—riding on a good horse down the pass of Aora and through the arches into the old town. Then, it was not the fishermen or the old women I thought of, but the girls, and the winking stars above me were their eyes, glinting merrily and kindly on a stout young gentleman soldier with jack and morion, sword at haunch, spur at heel, and a name for bravado, never a home-biding laird in our parish had, burgh or land-ward. I would sit on my horse so, the chest well out, the back curved, the knees straight, one gauntlet off to let my white hand wave a salute when needed, and none of all the pretty ones would be able to say Elrigmore thought another one the sweetest. Oh! I tell you we learnt many arts in the Lowland wars, more than they teach Master of Art in the old biggin' in the Hie Street of Glascow.

One day, at a place called Nordlingen in the Mid Franken, binding a wound Gavin got in the sword-arm, I said, "What's your wish at this moment, cousin?"

He looked at me with a melting eye, and the flush hove to his face.

"'Fore God, Colin," said he, "I would give my twelve months' wage to stand below the lintel of my mother's door and hear her say 'Darling scamp!'"

"If you had your wish, Gavin, when and how would you go into Inneraora town after those weary years away?"

"Man, I've made that up long syne," said he, and the tear was at his cheek. "Let me go into it cannily at night-fall from the Cromalt end, when the boys and girls were dancing on the green to the pipes at the end of a harvest-day.

Them in a reel, with none of the abulziements of war about me, but a plain civil lad like the rest, I would join in the strathspey and kiss two or three of the girls ere ever they jaloused a stranger was among them."

Poor Gavin, poor Gavin! he came home no way at all to his mother and his mountains, but here was I, with some of his wish for my fortune, riding cannily into Inneraora town in the dark.

It is wonderful how travel, even in a marching company of cavaliers of fortune, gives scope to the mind. When I set foot, twelve years before this night I speak of, on the gabbard that carried me down to Dunbarton on my way to the Humanities classes, I could have sworn I was leaving a burgh most large and wonderful. The town houses of old Stonefield, Craignish, Craignure, Askaig, and the other cadets of Clan Campbell, had such a strong and genteel look; the windows, all but a very few, had glass in every lozen, every shutter had a hole to let in the morning light, and each door had its little ford of stones running across the gutter that sped down the street, smelling fishily a bit, on its way to the shore. For me, in those days, each close that pierced the tall lands was as wide and high as a mountain *eas*, the street itself seemed broad and substantial, crowded with people worth kenning for their graces and the many things they knew.

I came home now on this night of nights with Munchen and Augsburg, and the fine cities of all the France, in my mind, and I tell you I could think shame of this mean rickle of stones I had thought a town, were it not for the good hearts and kind I knew were under every roof. The broad street crowded with people, did I say? A little lane rather; and Elrigmore, with schooling and the wisdom of travel, felt he could see into the heart's core of the cunningest merchant in the place.

But anyway, here I was, riding into town from the Cromalt end on a night in autumn. It was after ten—between the twenty and the half-past by my Paris watch—when I got the length of the Creags, and I knew that there was nothing but a sleeping town before me, for our folks were always early bedders when the fishing season was on. The night hung thick with stars, but there was no moon; a stiff wind from the east prinked at my right ear and cooled my horse's skin, as he slowed down after a canter of a mile or two on this side of Pennymore. Out on the loch I could see the lights of a few herring-boats lift and fall at the end of their trail of nets.

"Too few of you there for the town to be busy and cheerful," said I to myself; "no doubt the bulk of the boats are down at Otter, damming the fish in the narrow gut, and keeping them from searching up to our own good townsmen."

I pressed my brute to a trot, and turned round into the nether part of the town. It was what I expected—the place was dark, black out. The people were sleeping; the salt air of Loch Finne went sighing through the place in a way that made me dowie for old days. We went over the causeway-stones with a clatter that might have wakened the dead, but no one put a head out, and I thought of the notion of a cheery home-coming poor Gavin had—my dear cousin, stroked out and cold under foreign clods at Velshiem, two leagues below the field of Worms of Hessen, on the banks of the Rhine, in Low Germanie.

It's a curious business this riding into a town in the dark waste of night; curious even in a strange town when all are the same for you that sleep behind those shutters and those doors, but doubly curious when you know that behind the dark fronts are lying folks that you know well, that have been thinking, and drinking, and thriving when you were far away. As I went clattering slowly by, I would say at one house front, "Yonder's my old comrade, Tearlach, that taught me my one tune on the pipe-chanter; is his beard grown yet, I wonder?" At another, "There is the garret window of the schoolmaster's daughter—does she sing so sweetly nowadays in the old kirk?"

In the dead middle of the street I pulled my horse up, just to study the full quietness of the hour. Leaning over, I put a hand on his nostrils and whispered in his ear for a silence, as we do abroad in ambuscade. Town Inneraora slept sound, sure enough! All to hear was the spilling of the river at the cascade under the bridge and the plopping of the waves against the wall we call the ramparts, that keeps the sea from thrashing on the Tolbooth. And then over all I could hear a most strange moaning sound, such as we boys used to make with a piece of lath nicked at the edges and swung hurriedly round the head by a string. It was made by the wind, I knew, for it came loudest in the gusty bits of the night and from the east, and when there was a lull I could hear it soften away and end for a second or two with a dunt, as if some heavy, soft thing struck against wood.

Whatever it was, the burghers of Inneraora paid no heed, but slept, stark and sound, behind their steeked shutters.

The solemnity of the place, that I knew so much better in a natural lively mood, annoyed me, and I played there and then a prank more becoming a boy in his first kilt than a gentleman of education and travel and some repute for sobriety. I noticed I was opposite the house of a poor old woman they called Kate Dubh, whose door was ever the target in my young days for every lad that could brag of a boot-toe, and I saw that the shutter, hanging ajee on one hinge, was thrown open against the harled wall of the house. In my doublet-pocket there were some carabeen bullets, and taking one out, I let bang at the old woman's little lozens. There was a splinter of glass, and I waited to see if any one should come out to see who was up to such damage. My trick was in vain; no one came. Old Kate, as I found next day, was dead since Martinmas, and her house was empty.

Still the moaning sound came from the townhead, and I went slowly riding in its direction. It grew clearer and yet uncannier as I sped on, and mixed with the sough of it I could at last hear the clink of chains.

"What in God's name have I here?" said I to myself, turning round Islay Campbell's corner, and yonder was my answer!

The town gibbets were throng indeed! Two corpses swung in the wind, like net bows on a drying-pole, going from side to side, making the woeful sough and clink of chains, and the dunt I had heard when the wind dropped.

I grued more at the sound of the soughing than at the sight of the hanged fellows, for I've seen the Fell Sergeant in too many ugly fashions to be much put about at a hanging match. But it was such a poor home-coming! It told me as plain as could be, what I had heard rumours of in the low country riding round from the port of Leith, that the land was uneasy, and that pit and gallows were bye-ordinar busy at the gates of our castle. When I left for my last session at Glascow College, the countryside was quiet as a village green, never a raider nor a reiver in the land, and so poor the Doomster's trade (Black George), that he took to the shoeing of horses.

"There must be something wicked in the times, and cheatery rampant indeed," I thought, "when the common gibbet of Inneraora has a drunkard's convoy on either hand to prop it up."

But it was no time for meditation. Through the rags of plaiding on the chains went the wind again so eerily that I bound to be off, and I put my horse to it, bye the town-head and up the two miles to Glen Shira. I was sore and galled sitting on the saddle; my weariness hung at the back of my legs and shoulders like an ague, and there was never a man in this world came home to his native place so eager for taking supper and sleep as young Elrigmore.

What I expected at my father's door I am not going to set down here. I went from it a fool, with not one grace about me but the love of my good mother, and the punishment I had for my hot and foolish cantrip was many a wae night on foreign fields, vexed to the core for the sore heart I had left at home.

My mind, for all my weariness, was full of many things, and shame above all, as I made for my father's house. The horse had never seen Glen Shira, but it smelt the comfort of the stable and whinnied cheerfully as I pulled up at the gate. There was but one window to the gable-end of Elrigmore, and it was something of a surprise to me to find a light in it, for our people were not overly rich in these days, and candle or cruisie was wont to be doused at bedtime. More was my surprise, when leading my horse round to the front, feeling my way in the dark by memory, I found the oak door open and my father, dressed, standing in the light of it.

A young *sqalag* came running to the reins, and handing them to him, I stepped into the light of the door, my bonnet in my hand.

"Step in, sir, caird or gentleman," said my father—looking a little more bent at the shoulder than twelve years before.

I went under the door-lintel, and stood a little abashed before him.

"Colin! Colin!" he cried in the Gaelic. "Did I not ken it was you?" and he put his two hands on my shoulders.

"It is Colin sure enough, father dear," I said, slipping readily enough into the mother tongue they did their best to get out of me at Glascow College. "Is he welcome in this door?" and the weariness weighed me down at the hip and bowed my very legs.

He gripped me tight at the elbows, and looked me hungrily in the face.

"If you had a murdered man's head in your oxter, Colin," said he, "you were still my son. Colin, Colin! come ben and put off your boots!"

"Mother," I said, but he broke in on my question.

"Come in, lad, and sit down. You are back from the brave wars you never went to with my will, and you'll find stirring times here at your own parish. It's the way of the Sennachies' stories."

"How is that, sir?"

"They tell, you know, that people wander far on the going foot for adventure, and adventure is in the first turning of their native lane."

I was putting my boots off before a fire of hissing logs that filled the big room with a fir-wood smell right homely and comforting to my heart, and my father was doing what I should have known was my mother's office if weariness had not left me in a sort of stupor—he was laying on the Spanish mahogany board with carved legs a stout and soldierly supper and a tankard of the red Bordeaux wine the French traffickers bring to Loch Finne to trade for cured herring. He would come up now and then where I sat fumbling sleepily at my laces, and put a hand on my head, a curious unmanly sort of thing I never knew my father do before, and I felt put about at this petting, which would have been more like my sister if ever I had had the luck to have one.

"You are tired, Colin, my boy?" he said.

"A bit, father, a bit," I answered, "tough roads you know. I was landed at break of day at Skipness and—Is mother—"

"Sit in, *lochain!* Did you meet many folks on the road?"

"No, sir; a pestilent barren journey as ever I trotted on, and the people seemingly on the hill, for their crops are unco late in the field."

"Ay, ay, lad, so they are," said my father, pulling back his shoulders a bit—a fairly straight wiry old man, with a name for good swordsmanship in his younger days.

I was busy at a cold partridge, and hard at it, when I thought again how curious it was that my father should be afoot in the house at such time of night and no one else about, he so early a bedder for ordinary and never the last to sneck the outer door.

"Did you expect any one, father?" I asked, "that you should be waiting up with the collation, and the outer door unsnecked?"

"There was never an outer door snecked since you left, Colin," said he, turning awkwardly away and looking hard into the loof of his hand like a wife spaeing fortunes—for sheer want, I could see, of some engagement for his eyes. "I could never get away with the notion that some way like this at night would ye come back to Elrigmore."

"Mother would miss me?"

"She did, Colin, she did; I'm not denying."

"She'll be bedded long syne, no doubt, father?"

My father looked at me and gulped at the throat.

"Bedded indeed, poor Colin," said he, "this very day in the clods of Kilmalieu!"

And that was my melancholy home-coming to my father's house of Elrigmore, in the parish of Glenaora, in the shire of Argile.

CHAPTER II.

Every land, every glen or town, I make no doubt, has its own peculiar air or atmosphere that one familiar with the same may never puzzle about in his mind, but finds come over him with a waft at odd moments like the scent of bog-myrtle and tansy in an old clothes-press. Our own air in Glen Shira had ever been very genial and encouraging to me. Even when a young lad, coming back from the low country or the scaling of school, the cool fresh breezes of the morning and the riper airs of the late afternoon went to my head like a mild white wine; very heartsome too, rousing the laggard spirit that perhaps made me, before, over-apt to sit and dream of the doing of grand things instead of putting out a hand to do them. In Glascow the one thing that I had to grumble most about next to the dreary hours of schooling was the clammy airs of street and close; in Germanie it was worse, a moist weakening windiness full of foreign smells, and I've seen me that I could gaily march a handful of leagues to get a sniff of the spirity salt sea. Not that I was one who craves for wrack and bilge at my nose all the time. What I think best is a stance inland from the salt water, where the mountain air, brushing over gall and heather, takes the sting from the sea air, and the two blended give a notion of the fine variousness of life. We had a herdsman once in Elrigmore, who could tell five miles up the glen when the tide was out on Loch Finne. I was never so keen-scented as that; but when I awakened next day in a camceiled room in Elrigmore, and put my head out at the window to look around, I smelt the heather for a second like an escapade in a dream.

Down to Ealan Eagal I went for a plunge in the linn in the old style, and the airs of Shira Glen hung about me like friends and lovers, so well acquaint and jovial.

Shira Glen, Shira Glen! if I was bard I'd have songs to sing to it, and all I know is one sculduddry verse on a widow that dwelt in Maam! There at the foot of my father's house, were the winding river, and north and south the brown hills, split asunder by God's goodness, to give a sample of His bounty. Maam, Elrigmore and Elrigbeg, Kilblaan and Ben Bhuidhe—their steep sides hung with cattle, and below crowded the reeking homes of tacksman and cottar; the burns poured hurriedly to the flat beneath their borders of hazel and ash; to the south, the fresh water we call Dubh Loch, flapping with ducks and fringed with shelisters or water-flags and bulrush, and further off the Cowal hills; to the north, the wood of Drimlee and the wild pass the red Macgregors sometimes took for a back-road to our cattle-folds in cloud of night and darkness. Down on it all poured the polished and hearty sun, birds chirmed on every tree, though it was late in the year; blackcock whirred across the alders, and sturdy heifers bellowed tunefully, knee-deep at the ford.

"Far have I wandered," thinks I to myself, "warring other folks' wars for the humour of it and small wages, but here's the one place I've seen yet that was worth hacking good steel for in earnest!"

But still my heart was sore for mother, and sore, too, for the tale of changed times in Campbell country my father told me over a breakfast of braddan fresh caught in a creel from the Garron River, oaten bannock and cream.

After breakfast I got me into my kilt for town. There are many costumes going about the world, but, with allowance for one and all, I make bold to think our own tartan duds the gallantest of them all. The kilt was my wear when first I went to Glascow College, and many a St. Mungo keelie, no better than myself at classes or at English language, made fun of my brown knees, sometimes not to the advantage of his headpiece when it came to argument and neifs on the Fleshers Haugh. Pulling on my old *breacan* this morning in Elrigmore was like donning a fairy garb, and getting back ten years of youth. We have a way of belting on the kilt in real Argile I have seen nowhere else. Ordinarily, our lads take the whole web of tartan cloth, of twenty ells or more, and coil it once round their middle, there belting it, and bring the free end up on the shoulder to pin with a *dealg*, not a bad fashion for display and long marches and for sleeping out on the hill with, but sometimes discommodious for warm weather. It was our plan sometimes to make what we called a philabeg, or little kilt, maybe eight yards long, gathered in at the haunch and hung in many pleats behind, the plain brat part in front decked off with a leather sporran, tagged with thong points tied in knots, and with no plaid on the shoulder. I've never seen a more jaunty and suitable garb for campaigning, better by far for short sharp tulzies with an enemy than the philamore or the big kilt our people sometimes threw off them in a skirmish, and fight (the coarsest of them) in their gartered hose and scrugged bonnets.

With my kilt and the memory of old times about me, I went walking down to Inneraora in the middle of the day. I was prepared for change from the complaints of my father, but never for half the change I found in the burgh town of MacCailein Mor. In my twelve foreign years the place was swamped by incomers, black unwelcome Covenanters from the shires of Air and Lanrick — Brices, Yuilles, Rodgers, and Richies—all brought up here by Gillesbeg Gruamach, Marquis of Argile, to teach his clans the art of peace and merchandise. Half the folk I met between the arches and the Big Barns were strangers that seemingly never had tartan on their hurdies, but settled down with a firm foot in the place, I could see by the bold look of them as I passed on the plain-stanes of the street. A queer town this on the edge of Loch Finne, and far in the Highlands! There were shops with Lowland stuffs in them, and over the doors signboards telling of the most curious trades for a Campbell burgh—horologers, cordiners, baxters, and suchlike mechanicks that I felt sure poor Donald had small call for. They might be incomers, but they were thirled to Gillesbeg all the same, as I found later on.

It was the court day, and his lordship was sitting in judgment on two Strathlachlan fellows, who had been brawling at the Cross the week before and came to knives, more in frolic than in hot blood, with some of the town lads. With two or three old friends I went into the Tolbooth to see the play—for play it was, I must confess—in town Inneraora, when justice was due to a man whose name by ill-luck was not Campbell, or whose bonnet-badge was not the myrtle stem.

The Tolbooth hall was, and is to this day, a spacious high-ceiled room, well lighted from the bay-side. It was crowded soon after we got in, with Cowalside fishermen and townpeople all the one way or the other, for or against the poor lads in bilboes, who sat, simple-looking enough, between the town officers, a pair of old *bodachs* in long scarlet coats and carrying *tuaghs*, Lochaber axes, or halberds that never smelt blood since they came from the smith.

It was the first time ever I saw Gillesbeg Gruamach sitting on the bench, and I was startled at the look of the man. I've seen some sour dogs in my day—few worse than Ruthven's rittmasters we met in Swabia, but I never saw a man who, at the first vizzy, had the dour sour countenance of Archibald, Marquis of Argile and Lord of Lochow. Gruamach, or grim-faced, our good Gaels called him in a byename, and well he owned it, for over necklace or gorget, I've seldom seen a sterner jowl or a more sinister eye. And yet, to be fair and honest, this was but the notion one got at a first glint; in a while I thought little was amiss with his looks as he leaned on the table and cracked in a humoursome laughing way with the panelled jury.

He might have been a plain cottar in Glen Aora side rather than King of the Highlands for all the airs he assumed, and when he saw me, better put-on in costume than my neighbours in court, he seemingly asked my name in a whisper from the clerk beside him, and finding who I was, cried out in St. Andrew's English—

"What! Young Elrigmore back to the Glens! I give you welcome, sir, to Baile Inneraora!"

I but bowed, and in a fashion saluted, saying nothing in answer, for the whole company glowered at me, all except the home-bred ones, who had better manners.

The two MacLachlans denied in the Gaelic the charge the sheriff clerk read to them in a long farrago of English with more foreign words to it than ever I learned the sense of in College.

His lordship paid small heed to the witnesses who came forward to swear to the unruliness of the Strathlachlan men, and the jury talked heedlessly with one another in a fashion scandalous to see. The man who had been stabbed—it was but a jag at the shoulder, where the dirk had gone through from front to back with only some loss of blood—was averse to being hard on the panels. He was a jocular fellow with the right heart for a duello; and in his nipped burgh Gaelic he made light of the disturbance and his injury.

"Nothing but a bit play, my jurymen—MacCailein—my lordship—a bit play. If the poor lad didn't happen to have his dirk out and I to run on it, nobody was a bodle the worse."

"But the law, man"—started the clerk to say.

"No case for law at all," said the witness. "It's an honest brawl among friends, and I could settle the account with them at the next market-day, when my shoulder's mended."

"Better if you would settle my account for your last pair of brogues, Alasdair M'Iver," said a black-avised juryman.

"What's your trade?" asked the Marquis of the witness.

"I'm at the Coillebhraid silver-mines," said he. "We had a little too much drink, or these MacLachlan gentlemen and I had never come to variance."

The Marquis gloomed at the speaker and brought down his fist with a bang on the table before him.

"Damn those silver-mines!" said he, "they breed more trouble in this town of mine than I'm willing to thole. If they put a penny in my purse it might not be so irksome, but they plague me sleeping and waking, and I'm not a plack the richer. If it were not to give my poor cousin, John Splendid, a chance of a living and occupation for his wits, I would drown them out with the water of Cromalt Burn."

The witness gave a little laugh, and ducking his head oddly like one taking liberties with a master, said, "We're a drouthy set, my lord, at the mines, and I wouldn't be saying but what we might drink them dry again of a morning, if we had been into town the night before."

His lordship cut short his sour smile at the man's fancy, and bade the officers on with the case.

"You have heard the proof," he said to the jury when it came to his turn to charge them. "Are they guilty, or not? If the question was put to me I should say the Laird of MacLachlan, arrant Papist! should keep his men at home to Mass on the other side of the loch instead of loosing them on honest, or middling honest Campbells, for the strict virtue of these Coillebhraid miners is what I am not going to guarantee."

Of course the fellows were found guilty—one of stabbing, the other of art and part, for MacLachlan was no friend of MacCailein Mor, and as little friend to the merchant burghers of Inneraora, for he had the poor taste to buy his shop provand from the Lamont towns of Low Cowal.

"A more unfriendly man to the Laird of MacLachlan might be for hanging you on the gibbet at the town-head," said his lordship to the prisoners, spraying ink-sand idly on the clean page of a statute-book as he spoke; "but our three trees upbye are leased just now to other tenants—Badenoch hawks a trifle worse than yourselves, and more deserving."

The men looked stupidly about them, knowing not one word of his lordship's English, and he was always a man who disdained to converse much in Erse. He looked a little cruelly at them and went on.

"Perhaps clipping your lugs might be the bonniest way of showing you what we think of such on-goings in honest Inneraora; or getting the Doomster to bastinado you up and down the street. But we'll try what a fortnight in the Tolbooth may do to amend your visiting manners. Take them away, officers."

"*Aberidh moran taing*—say 'many thanks' to his lordship," whispered one of the red-coat halberdiers in the ear of the bigger of the two prisoners. I could hear the command distinctly where I sat, well back in the court, and so no doubt could Gillesbeg Gruamach, but he was used to such obsequious foolishness and he made no dissent or comment.

"*Taing! taing!*" said one spokesman of the two MacLachlans in his hurried Cowal Gaelic, and his neighbour, echoing him word for word in the comic fashion they have in these parts; "*Taing! taing!* I never louted to the horseman that rode over me yet, and I would be ill-advised to start with the Gruamach one!"

The man's face flushed up as he spoke. It's a thing I've noticed about our own poor Gaelic men; speaking before them in English or Scots, their hollow look and aloofness would give one the notion that they lacked sense and sparkle; take the muddiest-looking among them and challenge him in his own tongue, and you'll find his face fill with wit and understanding.

I was preparing to leave the court-room, having many people to call on in Inneraora, and had turned with my two friends to the door, when a fellow brushed in past us—a Highlander, I could see, but in trews—and he made to go forward into the body of the court, as if to speak to his lordship, now leaning forward in a cheerful conversation with the Provost of the burgh, a sonsy gentleman in a peruke and figured waistcoat.

"Who is he, this bold fellow?" I asked one of my friends, pausing with a foot on the door-step, a little surprised at the want of reverence to MacCailein in the man's bearing.

"Iain Aluinn—John Splendid," said my friend. We were talking in the Gaelic, and he made a jocular remark there is no English for. Then he added, "A poor cousin of the Marquis, a M'Iver Campbell (*on the wrong side*), with little schooling, but some wit and gentlemanly parts. He has gone through two fortunes in black cattle, fought some fighting here and there, and now he manages the silver-mines so adroitly that Gillesbeg Gruamach is ever on the brink of getting a big fortune, but never done launching out a little one instead to keep the place going. A decent soul the Splendid! throughither a bit and better at promise than performance, but at the core as good as gold, and a fellow you never weary of though you tramped with him in a thousand glens."

The object of my friend's description was speaking into the ear of MacCailein Mor by this time, and the Marquis's face showed his tale was interesting, to say the least of it.

We waited no more but went out into the street. I was barely two closes off from the Tolbooth when a messenger came running after me, sent by the Marquis, who asked if I would oblige greatly by waiting till he made up on me. I went back and met his lordship with his kinsman and mine-manager coming out of the court-room together into the lobby that divided the place from the street.

"Oh, Elrigmore!" said the Marquis, in an offhand jovial and equal way; "I thought you would like to meet my cousin here—M'Iver Campbell of the Barbreck; something of a soldier like yourself, who has seen service in Lowland wars."

"In the Scots Brigade, sir?" I asked M'Iver, eyeing him with greater interest than ever. He was my senior by half a dozen years seemingly, a neat, well-built fellow, clean-shaven, a little over the middle height, carrying a rattan in his hand, though he had a small sword tucked under the right skirt of his coat.

"With Lumsden's regiment," he said. "His lordship here has been telling me you have just come home from the field."

"But last night. I took the liberty while Inneraora was snoring. You were before my day in foreign service, and yet I thought I knew by repute every Campbell that ever fought for the hard-won dollars of Gustivus even before my day. There were not so many of them from the West Country."

"I trailed a pike privately," laughed M'Iver, "and for the honour of Clan Diarmaid I took the name Munro. My cousin here cares to have none of his immediate relatives make a living by steel at any rank less than a cornal's, or a major's, at the very lowest. Frankfort, and Landsberg, and the stark field of Leipzig were all I saw of foreign battle, and the God's truth is they were my bellyful. I like a bit splore, but give it to me in our old style, with the tartan instead of buff, and the target for breastplate and taslets. I came home sick of wars."

"Our friend does himself injustice, my dear Elrigmore," said Gillesbeg, smiling, "he came home against his will, I have no doubt, and I know he brought back with him a musketoon bullet in the hip, that couped him by the heels down in Glassary for six months."

"The result," M'Iver hurried to explain, but putting out his breast with a touch of vanity, "of a private *rencontre*, an affair of my own with a Reay gentleman, and not to be laid to my credit as part of the war's scaith at all."

"You conducted your duello in odd style under Lumsden, surely," said I, "if you fought with powder and ball instead of steel, which is more of a Highlander's weapon to my way of thinking. All our affairs in the Reay battalion were with claymore—sometimes with targe, sometimes wanting."

"This was a particular business of our own," laughed John Splendid (for so I may go on to call M'Iver, for it was the name he got oftenest behind and before in Argile). "It was less a trial of valour than a wager about which had the better skill with the musket. If I got the bullet in my groin, I at least showed the Mackay gentleman in question that an Argile man could handle arquebus as well as *arme blanche* as we said in the France. I felled my man at thirty paces, with six to count from a rittmaster's signal. 'Blow, present, God sain Mackay's soul!' But I'm not given to braggadocio."

"Not a bit, cousin," said the Marquis, looking quizzingly at me.

"I could not make such good play with the gun against a fort gable at so many feet," said I.

"You could, sir, you could," said John Splendid in an easy, off-hand, flattering way, that gave me at the start of our acquaintance the whole key to his character. "I've little doubt you could allow me half a dozen paces and come closer on the centre of the target."

By this time we were walking down the left side of the street, the Marquis betwixt the pair of us commoners, and I to the wall side. Lowlanders and Highlanders quickly got out of the way before us and gave us the crown of the causeway. The main part of them the Marquis never let his eye light on, he kept his nose cocked in the air in the way I've since found peculiar to his family. It was odd to me that had in wanderings got to look on all honest men as equal (except Camp-Master Generals and Pike Colonels) to see some of his lordship's poor clansmen cringing before him. Here indeed was the leaven of your low country scum, for in all the broad Highlands wandering before and since I never saw the like! "Blood of my blood, brother of my name!" says our good Gaelic old-world: it made no insolents in camp or castle, but it kept the poorest clansmen's heads up before the highest chief. But there was, even in Baile Inneraora, sinking in the servile ways of the incomer, something too of honest worship in the deportment of the people. It was sure enough in the manner of an old woman with a face peat-tanned to crinkled leather who ran out of the Vennel or lane and bending to the Marquis his lace wrist-bands, kissed them as I've seen Papists do the holy duds in Nôtre Dame and Bruges Kirk.

This display before me, something of a stranger, a little displeased Gillesbeg Gruamach. "Tut, tut!" he cried in Gaelic to the *cailleach*, "thou art a foolish old woman!"

"God keep thee, MacCailein!" said she; "thy daddy put his hand on my head like a son when he came back from his banishment in Spain, and I keened over thy mother dear when she died. The hair of Peggy Bheg's head is thy door-mat, and her son's blood is thy will for a foot-bath."

"Savage old harridan!" cried the Marquis, jerking away; but I could see he was not now unpleased altogether that a man new from the wide world and its ways should behold how much he was thought of by his people.

He put his hands in a friendly way on the shoulders of us on either hand of him, and brought us up a bit round turn, facing him at a standstill opposite the door of the English kirk. To this day I mind well the rumour of the sea that came round the corner.

I have a very particular business with both you gentlemen," he said. "My friend here, M'Iver, has come post-haste to tell me of a rumour that a body of Irish banditti under Alasdair MacDonald, the MacColkitto as we call him, has landed somewhere about Kinlochaline or Knoydart. This portends damnably, if I, an elder ordained of this kirk, may say so. We have enough to do with the Athole gentry and others nearer home. It means that I must on with plate and falchion again, and out on the weary road for war I have little stomach for, to tell the truth."

"You're able for the best of them, MacCailein," cried John Splendid in a hot admiration. "For a scholar you have as good judgment on the field and as gallant a seat on the saddle as any man ever I saw in haberschone and morion. With your schooling I could go round the world conquering."

"Ah! flatterer, flatterer! Ye have all the guile of the tongue our enemies give Clan Campbell credit for, and that I wish I had a little more of. Still and on, it's no time for fair words. Look! Elrigmore. You'll have heard of our little state in this shire for the past ten years, and not only in this shire but all over the West Highlands. I give you my word I'm no sooner with the belt off me and my chair pulled into my desk and papers than it's some one beating a point of war or a piper blowing the warning under my window. To look at my history for the past few years any one might think I was Dol' Gorm himself, fight and plot, plot and fight! How can I help it—thrust into this hornets' nest from the age of sixteen, when my father (*beannachd leis!*) took me out warring against the islesmen, and I only in the humour for playing at shinty or fishing like the boys on the moorlochs behind the town. I would sooner be a cottar in Auchnagoul down there, with porridge for my every meal, than constable, chastiser, what not, or whatever I am, of all these vexed Highlands. Give me my book in my closet, or at worst let me do my country's work in a courtier's way with brains, and I would ask no more."

"Except Badenoch and Nether Lochaber—fat land, fine land, MacCailein!" said John Splendid, laughing cunningly.

The Marquis's face flamed up.

"You're an ass, John," he said; "picking up the countryside's gossip. I have no love for the Athole and Great Glen folks, as ye ken; but I could long syne have got letters of fire and sword that made Badenoch and Nether Lochaber mine if I had the notion. Don't interrupt me with your nonsense, cousin; I'm telling Elrigmore here, for he's young and has skill of civilised war, that there may in very few weeks be need of every arm in the parish or shire to baulk Colkitto. The MacDonald and other malignants have been robbing high and low from Lochow to Loch Finne this while back; I have hanged them a score a month at the town-head there, but that's dealing with small affairs, and I'm sore mistaken if we have not cruel times to come."

"Well, sir," I said. "What can I do?"

The Marquis bit his moustachio and ran a spur on the ground for a little without answering, as one in a quandary, and then he said, "You're no vassal of mine, Baron" (as if he were half sorry for it), "but all you Glen Shira folk are well disposed to me and mine, and have good cause, though that MacNaughton fellow's a Papisher. What I had in my mind was that I might count on you taking a company of our fencible men, as John here is going to do, and going overbye to Lorn with me to cut off those Irish blackguards of Alasdair MacDonald's from joining Montrose."

For some minutes I stood turning the thing over in my mind, being by nature slow to take on any scheme of high emprise without some scrupulous balancing of chances. Half-way up the closes, in the dusk, and in their rooms, well back from the windows, or far up the street, all aloof from his Majesty MacCailein Mor, the good curious people of Inneraora watched us. They could little guess the pregnancy of our affairs. For me, I thought how wearily I had looked for some rest from wars, at home in Glen Shira after my long years of foreign service: now that I was here, and my mother no more, my old father needed me on hill and field; Argile's quarrel was not my quarrel until Argile's enemies were at the foot of Ben Bhuidhe or coming all boden in fier of war up the pass of Shira Glen; I liked adventure, and a captaincy was a captaincy, but—

"Is it boot and saddle at once, my lord?" I asked.

"It must be that or nothing. When a viper's head is coming out of a hole, crunch it incontinent, or the tail may be more than you can manage."

"Then, my lord," said I, "I must cry off. On this jaunt at least. It would be my greatest pleasure to go with you and my friend M'Iver, not to mention all the good fellows I'm bound to know in rank in your regiment, but for my duty to my father and one or two other considerations that need not be named. But—if this be any use—I give my word that should MacDonald or any other force come this side the passes at Accurach Hill, or anywhere east Lochow, my time and steel are yours."

MacCailein Mor looked a bit annoyed, and led us at a fast pace up to the gate of the castle that stood, high towered and embrasured for heavy pieces, stark and steeve above town Inneraora. A most curious, dour, and moody man, with a mind roving from key to key. Every now and then he would stop and think a little without a word, then on, and run his fingers through his hair or fumble nervously at his leathern buttons, paying small heed to the Splendid and I, who convoyed him, so we got into a crack about the foreign field of war.

"Quite right, Elrigmore, quite right," at last cried the Marquis, pulling up short, and looked me plumb in the eyes. "Bide at hame while bide ye may. I would never go on this affair myself if by God's grace I was not Marquis of Argile and son of a house with many bitter foes. But, hark ye! a black day looms for these over home-lands if ever Montrose and those Irish dogs get through our passes. For twenty thousand pounds Saxon I would not have the bars off the two roads of Accurach! And I thank you, Elrigmore, that at the worst I can count on your service at home. We may need good men here on Loch Finneside as well as further afield, overrun as we are by the blackguardism of the North and the Papist clans around us. Come in, friends, and have your meridian. I have a flagon of French brown brandy you never tasted the equal of in any town you sacked in all Low Germanie."

CHAPTER III.

John Splendid looked at me from the corner of an eye as we came out again and daundered slowly down the town.

"A queer one yon!" said he, as it were feeling his way with a rapier point at my mind about his Marquis.

"Imph'm," I muttered, giving him parry of low quarte like a good swordsman, and he came to the recover with a laugh.

"Foil, Elrigmore!" he cried. "But we're soldiers and lads of the world, and you need hardly be so canny. You see MacCailein's points as well as I do. His one weakness is the old one—books, books—the curse of the Highlands and every man of spirit, say I! He has the stuff in him by nature, for none can deny Clan Diarmaid courage and knightliness; but for four generations court, closet, and college have been taking the heart out of our chiefs. Had our lordship in-bye been sent a fostering in the old style, brought up to the chase and the sword and manly comportment, he would not have that wan cheek this day, and that swithering about what he must be at next!"

"You forget that I have had the same ill-training," I said (in no bad humour, for I followed his mind). "I had a touch of Glascow College myself."

"Yes, yes," he answered quickly; "you had that, but by all accounts it did you no harm. You learned little of what they teach there."

This annoyed me, I confess, and John Splendid was gleg enough to see it.

"I mean," he added, "you caught no fever for paper and ink, though you may have learned many a quirk I was the better of myself. I could never even write my name; and I've kept compt of wages at the mines with a pickle chuckie-stones."

"That's a pity," says I, drily.

"Oh, never a bit," says he gaily, or at any rate with a way as if to carry it off vauntingly. "I can do many things as well as most, and a few other colleges never learned me. I know many *sgeulachdan*, from 'Minochag and Morag' to 'The Shifty Lad'; I can make passable poetry by word of mouth; I can speak the English and the French; and I have seen enough of courtiers to know that half their canons are to please and witch the eye of women in a way that I could undertake to do by my looks alone and some good-humour. Show me a beast on hill or in glen I have not the history of; and if dancing, singing, the sword, the gun, the pipes—ah, not the pipes—it's my one envy in the world to play the bagpipes with some show of art and delicacy, and I cannot. Queer is that, indeed, and I so keen on them! I would tramp right gaily a night and a day on end to hear a scholar fingering 'The Glen is Mine.'"

There was a witless vanity about my friend that sat on him almost like a virtue. He made parade of his crafts less, I could see, because he thought much of them than because he wanted to keep himself on an equality with me. In the same way, as I hinted before, he never, in all the time of our wanderings after, did a thing well before me but he bode to keep up my self-respect by maintaining that I could do better or at least as good.

"Books, I say," he went on, as we clinked heels on the causeway-stones, and between my little bit cracks with old friends in the by-going—"books, I say, have spoiled MacCailein's stomach. Ken ye what he told me once? That a man might readily show more valour in a conclusion come to in the privacy of his bed-closet than in a victory won on the field. That's what they teach by way of manly doctrine down there in the new English church, under the pastorage of Maister Alexander Gordon, chaplain to his lordship and minister to his lordship's people! It must be the old Cavalier in me, but somehow (in your lug) I have no broo of those Covenanting cattle from the low country; though Gordon's a good soul, there's no denying."

"Are you Catholic?" I said, in a surprise.

"What are you yourself?" he asked, *more Scottice* (as we say in the Humanities), and then he flushed, for he saw a little smile in my face at the transparency of his endeavour to be always on the pleasing side.

"To tell the truth," he said, "I'm depending on salvation by reason of a fairly good heart, and an eagerness to wrong no man, gentle or semple. I love my fellows, one and all, not offhand as the Catechism enjoins, but heartily, and I never saw the fellow, carl or king, who, if ordinary honest and cheerful, I could not lie heads and thraws with at a camp-fire. In matters of strict ritual, now—ha—um!"

"Out with it, man!" I cried, laughing.

"I'm like Parson Kilmalieu upbye. You've heard of him—easy-going soul, and God sain him! When it came to the bit, he turned the holy-water font of Kilachatrine blue-stone upside-down, scooped a hole in the bottom, and used the new hollow for Protestant baptism. 'There's such a throng about heaven's gate,' said he, 'that it's only a mercy to open two;' and he was a good and humoursome Protestant-Papist till the day he went under the flagstones of his chapel upbye."

Now here was not a philosophy to my mind. I fought in the German wars less for the kreutzers than for a belief (never much studied out, but fervent) that Protestantism was the one good faith, and that her ladyship of Babylon, that's ever on the ran-dan, cannot have her downfall one day too soon. You dare not be playing corners-change-corners with religion as you can with the sword of what the ill-bred have called a mercenary (when you come to ponder on't, the swords of patriot or paid man are both for selfish ends unsheathed), and if I set down here word for word what John Splendid said, it must not be thought to be in homologation on my part of such latitudinarianism.

I let him run on in this key till we came to the change-house of a widow—one Fraser—and as she curtsied at the door, and asked if the braw gentlemen would favour her poor parlour, we went in and tossed a quaich or two of aqua, to which end she set before us a little brown bottle and two most cunningly contrived and carven cups made of the Coillebhraid silver.

The houses in Inneraora were, and are, built all very much alike, on a plan I thought somewhat cosy and genteel, ere ever I went abroad and learned better. I do not even now deny the cosieness of them, but of the genteelity it were well to say little. They were tall lands or tenements, three storeys high, with through-going closes, or what the English might nominate passages, running from front to back, and leading at their midst to stairs, whereby the occupants got to their domiciles in the flats above. Curved stairs they were, of the same blue stone the castle is built of, and on their landings at each storey they branched right and left to give access to the single apartments or rooms and kitchens of the residenters. Throng tenements they are these, even yet, giving, as I write, clever children to the world. His Grace nowadays might be granting the poor people a little more room to grow in, some soil for their kail, and a better prospect from their windows than the whitewashed wall of the opposite land; but in the matter of air there was and is no complaint. The sea in stormy days came bellowing to the very doors, salt and stinging, tremendous blue and cold. Staying in town of a night, I used to lie awake in my relative's, listening to the spit of the waves on the window-panes and the grumble of the tide, that rocked the land I lay in till I could well fancy it was a ship. Through the closes of a night the wind ever stalked like something fierce and blooded, rattling the iron snecks with an angry finger, breathing beastily at the hinge, and running back a bit once in a while to leap all the harder against groaning lintel and post.

The change-house of the widow was on the ground-flat, a but and ben, the ceilings arched with stone—a strange device in masonry you'll find seldom elsewhere, Highland or Lowland. But she had a garret-room up two stairs where properly she abode, the close flat being reserved for trade of vending *uisgebaigh* and ale. I describe all this old place so fully because it bears on a little affair that happened therein on that day John Splendid and I went in to clink glasses.

The widow had seen that neither of us was very keen on her aqua, which, as it happened, was raw new stuff brewed over at Kames, Lochow, and she asked would we prefer some of her brandy.

"After his lordship's it might be something of a downcome," said John Splendid, half to me and half to the woman.

She caught his meaning, though he spoke in the English, and in our own tongue, laughing toothlessly, she said—

"The same stilling, Barbreck, the same stilling I make no doubt. MacCailein gets his brown brandy by my brother's cart from French Foreland; it's a rough road, and sometimes a bottle or two spills on the way. I've a flagon up in a cupboard in my little garret, and I'll go fetch it."

She was over-old a woman to climb three steep stairs for the sake of two young men's drought, and I (having always some regard for the frail) took the key from her hand and went, as was common enough with her younger customers, seeking my own liquor up the stair.

In those windy flights in the fishing season there is often the close smell of herring-scale, of bow tar and the bark-tan of the fishing nets; but this stair I climbed for the wherewithal was unusually sweet odoured and clean, because on the first floor was the house of Provost Brown—a Campbell and a Gael, but burdened by accident with a Lowland-sounding cognomen. He had the whole flat to himself—half a dozen snug apartments with windows facing the street or the sea as he wanted. I was just at the head of the first flight when out of a door came a girl, and I clean forgot all about the widow's flask of French brandy.

Little more than twelve years syne the Provost's daughter had been a child at the grammar school, whose one annoyance in life was that the dominie called her Betsy instead of Betty, her real own name; here she was, in the flat of her father's house in Inneraora town, a full-grown woman, who gave me check in my stride and set my face flaming. I took in her whole appearance at one glance—a way we have in foreign armies. Between my toe on the last step of the stair and the landing I read the picture: a well-bred woman, from her carriage, the neatness of her apparel, the composure of her pause to let me bye in the narrow passage to the next stair; not very tall (I have ever had a preference for such as come no higher than neck and oxter); very dark brown hair, eyes sparkling, a face rather pale than ruddy, soft skinned, full of a keen nervousness.

In this matter of a woman's eyes—if I may quit the thread of my history—I am a trifle fastidious, and I make bold to say that the finest eyes in the world are those of the Highland girls of Argile—burgh or landward—the best bred and gentlest of them I mean. There is in them a full and melting friendliness, a mixture to my sometimes notion of poetry and of calm—a memory, as I've thought before, of the deep misty glens and their sights and secrets. I have seen more of the warm heart and merriment in a simple Loch Finne girl's eyes than in all the faces of all the grand dames ever I looked on, Lowland or foreign.

What pleased me first and foremost about this girl Betty, daughter of Provost Brown, were her eyes, then, that showed, even in yon dusky passage, a humoursome interest in young Elrigmore in a kilt coming up-stairs swinging on a finger the key of Lucky Fraser's garret. She hung back doubtfully, though she knew me (I could see) for her old school-fellow and sometime boy-lover, but I saw something of a welcome in the blush at her face, and I gave her no time to chill to me.

"Betty lass, 'tis you," said I, putting out a hand and shaking her soft fingers. "What think you of my ceremony in calling at the earliest chance to pay my devoirs to the Provost of this burgh and his daughter?"

I put the key behind my back to give colour a little to my words; but my lady saw it and jumped at my real errand on the stair, with that quickness ever accompanying eyes of the kind I have mentioned.

"Ceremony here, devoir there!" said she, smiling, "there was surely no need for a key to our door, Elrigmore—"

"Colin, Mistress Brown, plain Colin, if you please."

"Colin, if you will, though it seems daftlike to be so free with a soldier of twelve years' fortune. You were for the widow's garret. Does some one wait on you below?"

"John Splendid."

"My mother's in-bye. She will be pleased to see you back again if you and your friend call. After you've paid the lawing," she added, smiling like a rogue.

"That will we," said I; but I hung on the stairhead, and she leaned on the inner sill of the stair window.

We got into a discourse upon old days, that brought a glow to my heart the brandy I forgot had never brought to my head. We talked of school, and the gay days in wood and field, of our childish wanderings on the shore, making sand-keps and stone houses, herding the crabs of God—so little that bairns dare not be killing them, of venturings to sea many ells out in tow-caulked herring-boxes, of journeys into the brave deep woods that lie far and wide round Inneraora, seeking the spruce branch for the Beltane fire; of nutting in the hazels of the glens, and feasts upon the berry on the brae. Later, the harvest-home and the dance in green or barn when I was at almost my man's height, with the pluck to put a bare lip to its apprenticeship on a woman's cheek; the songs at *ceilidh* fires, the telling of *sgeulachdan* and fairy tales up on the mountain sheiling—

"Let me see," said I; "when I went abroad, were not you and one of the Glenaora Campbells chief?"

I said it as if the recollection had but sprung to me, while the truth is I had thought on it often in camp and field, with a regret that the girl should throw herself off on so poor a partner.

She laughed merrily with her whole soul in the business, and her face without art or pretence—a fashion most wholesome to behold.

"He married some one nearer him in years long syne," said she. "You forget I was but a bairn when we romped in the hay-dash." And we buckled to the crack again, I more keen on it than ever. She was a most marvellous fine girl, and I thought her (well I mind me now) like the blue harebell that nods upon our heather hills.

We might, for all I dreamt of the widow's brandy, have been conversing on the stair-head yet, and my story had a different conclusion, had not a step sounded on the stair, and up banged John Splendid, his sword-scabbard clinking against the wall of the stair with the haste of him.

"Set a Cavalier at the side of an anker of brandy," he cried, "and—"

Then he saw he was in company. He took off his bonnet with a sweep I'll warrant he never learned anywhere out of France, and plunged into the thick of our discourse with a query.

"At your service, Mistress Brown," said he. "Half my errand to town to-day was to find if young MacLachlan, your relative, is to be at the market here to-morrow. If so—"

"He is," said Betty.

"Will he be intending to put up here all night, then?"

"He comes to supper at least," said she, "and his bidding overnight is yet to be settled."

John Splendid toyed with the switch in his hand in seeming abstraction, and yet as who was pondering on how to put an unwelcome message in plausible language.

"Do you know," said he at last to the girl, in a low voice, for fear his words should reach the ears of her mother in-bye, "I would as well see MacLachlan out of town the morn's night. There's a waft of cold airs about this place not particularly wholesome for any of his clan or name. So much I would hardly care to say to himself; but he might take it from you, madam, that the other side of the loch is the safest place for sound sleep for some time to come."

"Is it the MacNicolls you're thinking of?" asked the girl.

"That same, my dear."

"You ken," he went on, turning fuller round to me, to tell a story he guessed a new-comer was unlikely to know the ins and outs of—"You ken that one of the MacLachlans, a cousin-german of old Lachie the chief, come over in a boat to Braleckan a few weeks syne on an old feud, and put a bullet into a MacNicoll, a peaceable lad who was at work in a field. Gay times, gay times, aren't they? From behind a dyke wall too—a far from gentlemanly escapade even in a MacLa— Pardon, mistress, I forgot your relationship, but this was surely a very low dog of his kind. Now from that day to this the murtherer is to find ; there are some to say old Lachie could put his hand on him at an hour's notice if he had the notion. But his lordship, Justiciar-General, upbye, has sent his provost-marshal with letters of arrest to the place in vain. Now here's my story. The MacNicolls of Elrig have joined cause with their cousins and namesakes of Braleckan ; there's a wheen of both to be in the town at the market to-mor row, and if young MacLachlan bides in this house of yours overnight, Mistress Betty Brown, you'll maybe hae broken delf and worse ere the day daw."

Mistress Brown took it very coolly, and as for me, I was thinking of a tiny brown mole-spot she used to have low on the white of her neck when I put daisy-links on her on the summers we played on the green, and wondering if it was still to the fore and hid below her collar. In by the window came the saucy breeze and kissed her on a curl that danced above her ear.

"I hope there will be no lawlessness here," said she : "if the gentleman *will* go, he *will* go home ; if he bides, he bides, and surely the burghers of Inneraora will not quietly see their Provost's domicile invaded by brawlers."

"Exactly so," said John Splendid drily. "Nothing may come of it, but you might mention the affair to MacLachlan if you have the chance. For me to tell him would be to put him in the humour for staying—dour fool that he is—out of pure bravado and defiance. To tell the truth, I would bide myself in such a case. 'Thole feud' is my motto. My grand-dad writ it on the butt of his sword-blade in clear round print letters, I've often marvelled at the skill of. If it's your will, Elrigmore, we may be doing without the brandy, and give the house-dame a call now."

We went in and paid our duties to the good wife—a silver-haired dame with a wonderful number of Betty's turns in her voice, and ready sober smile.

(*To be continued.*)

PARIS LETTER.

I hope the readers of THE BOOKMAN do not expect me to have read all the works that have come from the French presses since my last letter. It has been one of the most prolific four weeks the French book trade has known, and fortunately these four weeks have been remarkable not simply for the number, but also for the quality of the books published. No masterpiece has appeared, to be sure, but a number of works which are decidedly above the average.

The first to be mentioned, perhaps, the one which will be most seriously discussed, is Maurice Barrès's new novel, *Les Déracinés*. *Uprooted!* might be a good translation of the title, and I suggest it to the translator, whoever he, or she, alas ! may be that will undertake to bring it before the American public. The attraction, the fascination exercised by Paris upon natives of the provinces has been more than once noticed, and sometimes deplored. It makes the main subject of Barrès's book, which is full of penetrating observations. It is freer from mannerisms than most of his former works, and the two sequels that are announced will be awaited with interest. *Les Déracinés* is only the first of a series, the general title of which is *Le Roman de l'Energie Nationale ;* the other two volumes will be *L'Appel au Soldat* and *L'Appel au Juge*.

Les Amants Bizantins, by Hugues Le Roux, is a very different book, a passionate love story, and will do much toward placing its author near the front rank of the younger generation of French writers. He is certainly one of the most indefatigable ones, and what he writes, whether in a serious vein, like his inquiries in the social conditions of modern French life, or in a lighter one, like his novels, is very seldom dull. Although he has of late published a volume, on an average, every fourth month, there is no sign of haste in his productions ; they strike the reader as something finished, over which a great deal of time has been spent. He is, perhaps, the most robust writer of his generation.

Whether the generation itself is quite as robust as it wishes to appear may, moreover, be questioned ; and the question is negatively answered in a very witty and curious book, *L'Age du Muscle*, by Mr. Riquet.

A prolific month would not be complete without a novel by George Ohnet. *Les Vieilles Rancunes* is neither better nor worse than a great deal which has come from the same source.

Figures et Choses qui Passaient, such is the somewhat strange and far-fetched title of Pierre Loti's last production. It will be welcomed by the class of readers that can endure Loti only in small doses. I confess that I am not far from belonging to that class.

Of course a great many more novels have been published, but I do not intend to give you a full catalogue of the good, bad, and indifferent. Zola's *Paris*, which is now appearing in *feuilleton*, certainly does not belong to the last category, and is followed with a good deal of interest.

More interest, perhaps, has been excited by another book, not fiction, but in many respects stranger than fiction, *Impressions Cellulaires*, by M. Baïhaut. Its author is the sorry politician who, when a cabinet minister, boldly levied 750,000 francs blackmail on the ill-fated Panama Company, and was sent therefor to the penitentiary. He now relates his impressions, while undergoing solitary confinement, which he had, as he had a right to by the law, chosen in preference to promiscuousness with the other prisoners. Strange times, in which a criminal, provided he can wield a pen, is enabled to derive money out of his very delinquencies !

To those who wish to know well the development of France in the last twenty-five years, I must mention a strong and, on the whole, very severe book, written by a very well-informed man who writes over the *nom de plume* of Ernest Charles. The title is *Théories Sociales et Politiciens ;* it discusses the career and ideas of seven public men, five of whom are still living, and even comparatively young—Messrs. Albert de Mun, Léon Bourgeois, Jules Guesde, Jean Jaurès, and Paul Deschanel. The other two are Léon Gambetta and Léon Say. In order to be anything like complete, the book ought to have contained also sketches of Jules Ferry and Georges Clémenceau. Still, as it is, it is and will remain worth consulting.

How shall we class General Carrey de Bellemare's book, *L'Empire, c'est la Paix ?* Is it poetry, is it history ? The general, who was one of the most conspicuous military figures during the siege of Paris, gives us there narratives of events in which he has borne a part ; but in order, so he says, to avoid prolixity and wordiness, he rejected prose, and his book is a book of verses ; a strange undertaking, to say the least !

With Mr. Arthur Chuquet we are entirely in the domain of history. His last volume, *La Jeunesse de Napoléon*, is sure to be very soon translated in English. It is a very important contribution to Napoleonic literature. Mr. Chuquet, who is the editor of *La Revue Critique*, is one of our most diligent and cautious investigators. Interesting comparisons are sure to be made between his book and the opening chapters of Professor Sloane's *Napoleon*.

Another book to be classed among Napoleoniana is Frédéric Masson's *Marie Walewska*. It forms an interesting addition to Masson's former work, *Napoléon et les Femmes*. By the way, do you know that one of the common descendants of Napoleon and Marie Walewska, one of their grandsons, was a son of Mademoiselle Rachel, whose letters to her teacher and friend, Samson, the great comedian, are just about to be published ? Samson, Mademoiselle Rachel ! "*Commediante, tragediante !*" that is just what Pope Pius VII. said of Napoleon !

Marie Antoinette, who has just found a new historian, was neither a comedian nor a tragedian, though there was a good deal of comedy in her life, and it ended in one of the most pathetic tragedies the world has known. *Marie Antoinette, Dauphine*, by Pierre de Nolhac, is certainly one of the best, as it is one of the least pretentious books written about the unfortunate wife of poor Louis XVI. Though decidedly favourable to the young princess, whose history it carries down to her accession to the throne of France, it is remarkably free from the sickly sentimentality one is almost sure to find in the panegyrics of a princess who is to-day condemned as severely by many as she is worshipped by others. M. de Nolhac's book, though short, gives the most vivid view we know of the court of France at the end of the reign of Louis XV. The same author had published formerly another volume on *Marie Antoinette, Reine de France*, so that he has now given us a complete history of his heroine, down to her downfall.

With *Napoléon III. et sa Cour*, of Imbert de Saint-Amand, and *Guillaume II. Intime*, of Maurice Leudet, we still remain among royalties. Both books are written in a light vein and give a good deal of anecdotical information.

Anecdotical information is not what will be looked for, and neither is it what will be found, in Ferdinand Brunetière's just published volume. It is his long-promised *Manuel de l'Histoire de la Littérature Française*, which is, unless I am greatly mistaken, to appear soon in an English, or rather an American translation, to be published by Houghton, Mifflin and Company. The first lines of M. Brunetière's preface contain an implied promise to write a longer and more exhaustive history of French literature. It is, indeed, an open secret that the great critic has been greatly dissatisfied by the bulky co-operative history of French literature which is now being published under the editorship of Professor Petit de Julleville, and that he has repeatedly given utterance to the sentiment that he could all alone easily beat the performance of the array of authors to whom its different chapters have been intrusted.

In the mean time he goes along carrying on his work as editor of the *Revue des Deux Mondes*, and does not seem to be greatly disturbed by the lawsuit in which he is soon to appear as defendant. The plaintiff is Mr. Alfred Dubout, who a few months ago had a tragedy, *Frédégonde*, acted at the Théâtre Français. The play was a failure. It displeased the public, it also displeased Jules Lemaître, who said it, and wittily, as is customary with him, in the *Revue des Deux Mondes*. M. Alfred Dubout's estimate of his own play is very different from Jules Lemaître's,

> "Et ma grande raison, c'est que j'en suis l'auteur !"

as Trissotin says in Molière, and he insists on having the *Revue* print a long answer of his to his critic's strictures. He appeals to the statute which gives to a man attacked in a paper the right to have placed at his disposal, for his defence, space twice as large as that given to the attack. Brunetière, of course, will take the ground that in presenting his play to the public M. Dubont invited, and in advance accepted, criticism, and it is announced that he will be his own counsel before the court. His defence is sure to be a masterpiece of witty and forceful reasoning, and his appearance in court will be one of the gala days in December.

In regard to the French courts, anybody who wants to know about them can learn much in a very entertaining and withal very serious book just now published, *La Cour d'Assises*, by Jean Cruppi. The book, the author of which is one of the State's attorneys before the Court of Appeals of Paris, is not simply an account, but also a criticism of the method of procedure of the French courts, and proposes remedies for existing evils.

I shall not close this review without mentioning the publication of an interesting volume of *reliquiæ*. I allude to the *Notes d'Art et de Littérature* of Joseph Capperon. The author died in 1896, when not quite thirty years of age. The little book, which has piously been put together by his friends, is made up of short, but very pithy contributions to the daily and weekly press. It makes one regret that their author was so prematurely snatched away.

We had a few days ago, on the 18th, the annual session of the Académie Française, the occasion of which Renan said that there is one day in the year in which virtue is rewarded. Jules Claretie read the report on the "Prix de vertu," and Gaston Boissier the report on the literary prizes. Among the latter I notice two that will be of special interest to Americans. They were awarded to *Les Américaines chez Elles*, by Thérèse Bentzon (Madame Blanc), and *La Société Américaine*, by Mademoiselle Dugard. Among the other prizes I shall mention two given, one to *La Maison de l'Enfance*, by Fernand Gregh, in spite of the novelties in versification accepted by the young poet, and the other to Frédéric Mistral, for his poem of the Rhone, in spite of its not being in French, but in Provençal. The old lady is making progresses ! as we say here.

Alfred Manière.

PARIS, November 23, 1897.

THE BOOKMAN'S LETTER-BOX.

There has been a painful and rather alarming activity among our correspondents since the November Letter Box appeared; and the batch of letters now before us is the largest that we have ever had to cope with at one time. We can, in fact, find space for only about one half of them in the present issue. Most of them are mild and serious. We are not afraid to answer them.

I.

A lady in Trenton, New Jersey, pleads with us to "do a little missionary work in behalf of 'awfully.'" She wants us to say something harsh about the use of such expressions as "awfully nice," "awfully sweet," and so forth. We should like to oblige her, but really we don't object to this particular colloquialism ourselves. It has, to our minds, a sort of classical flavour, recalling the familiar use in Latin of such adverbs as *misere* and *perdite*.

II.

Dr. Pierce Bailey of this city is grieved because we said in the last Letter Box that we had never heard of Sonyea, New York. He informs us that it is in Livingston County, that the name is Indian, and that there is a colony of epileptics in the place.

Well, we don't mind.

III.

This Sonyea business is troubling others also. Here is a postal-card in which the signature is multitudinously suggestive of a great popular uprising. It reads as follows:

"Let us be brighter than the man from Sonyea, and repeat his question without 'sarcasm.'
"OTHER READERS."

We always yield to a popular uprising, so we reprint herewith the question asked in November by the Man from Sonyea. It was this:

"DEAR EDITORS: I noticed in a recent issue of THE BOOKMAN that a writer had submitted some manuscript to you after he had received many favourable notices from well-known authors. Well, what I cannot understand is why he sent the manuscript to THE BOOKMAN at all."

Here is our answer: The aforesaid writer, who had submitted his manuscript to sundry well-known authors and had received favourable notices from them, sent it to THE BOOKMAN in order to discover whether the well-known authors were really justified in being so very favourable. And he found out.

IV.

Another postal-card, with no signature to it, quotes part of a sentence from an article of ours in the Christmas number, and puts an exclamation-point at the end of the quotation. The exclamation-point means that the writer of the card desires to fleer at our syntax. This is the quotation. We reproduce also the exclamation-point.

"Somehow or other, in the end, after everybody had used up all their cartridges!—*December* BOOKMAN, p. 315."

Now this person would have written "*his* cartridges." But we didn't, and for two reasons. First, we never object to the figure Synesis, and we think that "everybody" conveys here a distinct notion of plurality. Again, the party spoken of contained one woman; and if we had written "his," it would not have been technically true, and would besides have called attention to the fact that there is in English no pronoun of the common gender. And we always hate to uncover the nakedness of the English language.

V.

From Lawrence, Kansas, comes the brief inquiry:

"Please inform me if the following sentence is correct: 'Seven and five *is* twelve.'"

Not to our way of thinking; but some persons will justify it by saying that the expression "seven-and-five" is an entity, which they call a singular concept, and thus they use with it a verb in the singular number.

VI.

Mr. Edward W. Townsend writes us an amusing letter with regard to the *Chap-Book's* criticism of his last volume, *Near a Whole City Full*. We should like to print this letter, but we must stick to our precedents and not open our pages to animadversions on our literary contemporaries. And besides, what difference can it make to Mr. Townsend or to any one else what the *Chap-Book* said?

VII.

A Chicago lady who writes very pleasantly, and doesn't get into a huff over our rule about not returning manuscripts, asks this really pertinent question:

"I would like to know one thing. If a person has the temerity to send manuscripts to THE BOOKMAN, how does he (a woman wouldn't dare!) know that they are accepted? They are not sent back, and it may be months before they appear. What would be a reasonable time to wait before sending a copy of the manuscripts elsewhere?

"If this is not a reasonable question, don't answer it.

"It would take more than that to destroy my liking for the most delightful of magazines.

"Cordially yours."

Now this is the way to write to an editor when you want to convert him into a human being and make him do things for you! Well, about the manuscripts. If the writer is not notified of their acceptance in the course of a month, he (or she) may infer that they are not available for THE BOOKMAN'S purposes. Really, that was a very fetching letter. And the first part, which we refrain from printing, was better still.

VIII.

A legal gentleman in Atlanta, Georgia, writes us six pages of combined praise and good-humoured criticism. We must omit the praise and condense the criticism. These are the points he raises:

"1. Why did the author of the article on 'Fonetic Refawrm' in the November BOOKMAN use the editorial 'we' when writing, apparently, in an individual capacity?"

Because that is his way. Force of habit, probably.

"2. May not his remarks on the American Philological Association be regarded as due to a feeling of spite at not securing admission to that learned body?"

Hardly; as he has been a member of the Association for a good many years.

"3. Why is it any better to say 'some one's else' than to say 'Peter's the Great'?"

Because in the former expression the "else" is less essentially united with the "some one" than is the "Great" with "Peter."

"4. Why did Mr. G. M. Hyde, in a recent review, use the exclamation 'Great heavens!' Is there a plurality of heavens?"

We presume that Mr. Hyde meant this as the plural of excellence; and if so, he has the excellent authority of the Book of Genesis, which in the original Hebrew regularly speaks of heaven in the plural form.

IX.

A gentleman in Rahway, New Jersey, writes thus:

"Some time ago you stated, in answer to a correspondent, that there are no living American humourists who are doing good humourous work. Did you not overlook Mr. Frank Stockton?"

Well, of course there are those who rank Mr. Stockton among the great humourists of all time; but as for ourselves personally, we have always been able to read everything of his without bursting into loud guffaws.

X.

From Louisville, Kentucky, a correspondent, who signs himself "A *Times* Reporter," asks two questions.

"1. Will you kindly discriminate the meanings of 'farther' and 'further'?"

Popularly they are used as though they were identical in origin and meaning; but they are really not connected. "Farther" is, of course, the comparative of "far," while "further" is the comparative of "fore" and means "more to the front," the true superlative of it being "first."

"2. Can you give me an idea of the religious belief of Emerson? Not what he *was* (I know that), but the nature or a definition of his belief."

See Emerson's "Address to the Senior Class in Divinity College, Cambridge," delivered by him in July, 1838. To our mind this is a plea for extreme individualism, making the consciousness of each man the supreme judge of matters spiritual, and defying all traditional or dogmatic authority. But it would be well if our correspondent would read the "Address" for himself.

XI.

A Clear White Soul from Philadelphia, who loves peace, and is probably of Quaker ancestry, writes plaintively these words :

"I see that THE BOOKMAN, the *Critic*, and the *Chap-Book* are continually publishing little flings at one another. Is not this at variance with the spirit of literature, which ought to be serene and tolerant? Is there any justification for these displays of malice?"

Malice? Bless you! there is no malice. It is only a little amicable sparring to keep the editorial blood in circulation and prevent things from getting too dull in the literary world. We think a great deal of the *Critic*, and always read it with eagerness, especially when it is doing us up or calling us down. And as to the *Chap-Book*, which has a very nasty temper of its own, and which periodically accuses us of pretty nearly everything from plagiarism, vulgarity, and slander to ignorance and general imbecility—even the *Chap-Book* doesn't really mean anything by it. Whenever its editor visits this town we hope he will drop in and see us. We will take his battle-axes and poisoned darts and stack them up neatly in our umbrella-stand, and then talk shop with him for half an hour any day in the week. You see, we have a perfectly clear conscience and a remarkably good digestion, and it takes a very able person to get a rise out of us.

Some fairly belligerent letters have come in during this month, but they are inappropriate to the Christmas season; so we have locked them up in our fire-proof safe until the appearance of the next number.

NEW BOOKS.

AN AMERICAN EDITION OF CICERO'S LETTERS.*

The extremely limited amount of ancient classical literature available for teaching purposes in editions prepared by American scholars is again indicated by the fact that the *Selected Letters of Cicero* of Professor Abbott, of the University of Chicago, is the first acceptable American edition. Other editions of like scope are announced as in preparation by Professor Pease in the *Students' Series of Latin Classics*, and by Professor Platner in the recently initiated Allyn and Bacon's *College Latin Series*, and one for school use by Professor Dillard. Even if all these attain the high level of the edition before us, we shall not be surfeited; but future editors will especially deserve our gratitude by including in their volumes only such letters of Professor Abbott's selection as must needs find a place in any specimen of Cicero's correspondence. For the others, they can easily substitute the desired amount of text of altogether equal interest and value.

This very matter of the choice of letters for a small volume is probably the most difficult of decision with which the editor has to deal. Not only has he to determine what particular aspect of the correspondence he wishes to make most prominent—the language, the life and labour of Cicero as it impressed Cicero himself, his offhand account of current events that have become historic, the private life of the people of Rome, or the implied ethics—but he must, furthermore, make choice from a large number of letters of nearly equal value for his purposes. Our present editor has not thus confined himself to a particular aspect of the correspondence, but has chosen a hundred letters which are likely to be accepted as fairly representative of the whole. It may be questioned whether the choice could well be so free in the case of an edition for other than advanced students, inasmuch as minute historical knowledge and an intimate acquaintance with all sides of Roman public and private life is necessary for the intelligent reading of the entire correspondence. The range in time of Professor Abbott's selection may be seen from the fact that the initial letter is only the tenth of the extant correspondence, and the final letter the last left to us.

Of the letters given, seventy-one are from the so-called *Epistulæ ad Familiares*, twenty-five from the *Epistulæ ad Atticum*

* Selected Letters of Cicero. Edited, with Introduction and Notes, by Frank Frost Abbott. Boston: Ginn & Co.

(but three of these are enclosures), and four *Ad Quintum Fratrem*. The arrangement is, of course, chronological. Most of the more famous letters find a place in the volume, among them *Att.* i. 1, on the political situation and the writer's canvass for the consulship; *Att.* i. 16, descriptive of the trial of Clodius for violation of the rites of the *Bona Dea;* the naïve and *valde bella epistula* to Lucceius (*Fam.* v. 12); the somewhat hypocritical account of the games that celebrated the opening of Pompey's theatre (*Fam.* v. 1); the letter of condolence from Sulpicius (*Fam.* iv. 5); and his account of the murder of Marcellus (*Fam.* iv. 12); and Matius's manly statement of his feeling for the dead Cæsar (*Fam.* xi. 28). There is a good showing of letters not found in any edition in English suited to class-room use: *Fam.* viii. 15; ix. 8, 11, 15, 24; x. 12; xiii. 50, 72; xiv. 8, 11, 12, 15, 17, 19, 20; xvi. 4, 6; *Att.* iii. 4, 12, 22; xii. 16. The many long and in some instances rather tedious letters are happily balanced by an unusually large number of the short notes from Books XIV and XVI. *Ad Fam.* and by the *jeux de mots* and *jeux d'esprit* of a large portion of the correspondence with Trebatius and with Pætus. Half of the letters of the selection were written during the last five years of Cicero's life—sad years of political ineffectualness and of sorrow.

Professor Abbott has printed the newly constituted text of Mendelssohn for the *Epist. ad Fam.*, Wesenberg's for the *Epist. ad Att.* (except for Books XII. and XIII., for which Schmidt's text is given) and Müller's for the *Epist. ad Quint. Frat.* Wesenberg's emendations are frequently displaced, usually by a return to the manuscript reading. There may appear to be serious *a priori* objections to the use, side by side, of the texts of critical scholars of so opposite views, but a hurried examination has revealed no startling failure to harmonise differences. The writing of compounds is not altogether consistent, and we confess to a dislike for the abbreviated *res p.* together with the full form and the like variations in other than a critical edition.

It is difficult to imagine any useful purpose for the critical appendix, the *apparatus* being, on the one hand, too meagre for helpful textual criticism, and on the other, more extensive than is otherwise demanded. In the case of such a book there is need only of a list of important departures from manuscript tradition or from the text which is the basis of the edition. In this, as in several important particulars, the editors of the various volumes of the *College Series of Latin Authors* differ in their practice. At one extreme, Professor Greenough makes no mention of critical matters; at the other, Professor Merrill, finding his warrant in his independent collation of the *Codex Oxoniensis* of Catullus, prints a fairly complete *apparatus*.

The introduction supplies the necessary information of the public and the private life of Cicero, of the implements and the conventions of the Roman letter writer, of the history of Cicero's correspondence, and of its diction. The commentary is especially happy and helpful in supplementing the introductions on this last point. It is a little unfortunate that so large a proportion of the citations of common colloquial usages are from the letters *to* Cicero. Misleading inferences are likely to be drawn also from the too definite classification as colloquial of many usages that are sufficiently common in formal prose. This may be seen, for example, in the statement as to "extravagance in expression," which takes no account of the hyperbole of Cicero's other works and chargeable to the national temperament and the prevailing literary style. The citation of an example is sometimes made by reference to its place in the traditional arrangement, where the number of the letter in the present selection would be more helpful. In one case (p. lxvi. 83*a*) there is a reference to a note that does no more than itself refer to another note.

Both introduction and commentary are so nearly adequate that it may reasonably be considered ungrateful to demand more; but some account of the way of writing upon the wax tablet should have been given, where so much space was allowed for a description of the use of papyrus, the matter of the epistolary use of tenses should have been made clearer in the introduction (this deficiency is, however, made good in the commentary), and some will undoubtedly miss the arguments in support of certain confident assertions of the notes on moot points.

The phrase "in a large degree" is used loosely on p. xxi.; on p. xxii. "continued straight on toward his cherished purpose" is, perhaps, not strictly logical; there is an unfortunate use of either "other" or "affect" on p. lxix.; one may perhaps with propriety express a preference for *per cent* or *p. c.* over % in such a context as that of p. xxix. We who have heard nothing worse than, "Explain the whole business," wonder where "Tell me the whole business" may be in even vulgar use (p. 57). One is surprised at meeting the intangible Pseudodamasippus in such company as that of an index of proper names. The statement on p. lxi. that Greek did not directly influence colloquial speech is misleading in the light of the *sermo volgaris* of comedy. The editing of the collection *Ad Fam.* should be mentioned in the list of Tiro's literary undertaking (p. li.). The example cited for the colourless use of the compound with *per* (p. lxiv.) is not conclusive, for the phrase *quæ parcius frater perscripserat* certainly admits of translation as "which my brother had written in too little detail." To us the phrase *mihi ante oculos dies noctesque versaris* (p. 57) has no flavour of colloquial redundancy, but is the very idiom of formal prose. A casual reading has discovered few typographical errors: p. lvi., genitives in *ii*; p. lxiv., *benivolus*, although the preferable orthography stands in the text; p. 11 n., *Af-ricanum* for *A-fricanum*; *Sex* for *Sex.* in the third name of the index of proper names; in the name above, the use of the parentheses is inconsistent with the printing of other names of the list.

Professor Abbott has previously published in the *Archiv für lateinische Lexikographie* an earnest of independent work in this profitable field, and we are prepared to find throughout his edition the results of other investigations. These, however, are put forth so modestly side by side with the accepted views of the recent authorities, that it is easy to underestimate the substantial value of the book for the scholar. For teacher and student it is a veritable boon.

The index to the notes is made unusually serviceable by the classification of the matter of the commentary under such heads as "archaisms," "colloquial phrases," "popular expressions," and the like.

J. C. Kirtland, Jr.

MRS. BARRETT BROWNING'S LETTERS.*

Mr. Frederic G. Kenyon has edited, with biographical links, a large collection of letters by Elizabeth Barrett Browning, and has done his work carefully and with knowledge. He evidently feels that something has to be said in justification of his volumes. Put shortly, his defence amounts to this—that the Brownings, who were very sensitive to publicity in their own lives, recognised that the public had some claims with regard to writers who had appealed to and partly lived by its favour. I am not disposed to criticise this. We are the gainers by these volumes, though not to a great extent. Nevertheless, I am morally certain that Mrs. Browning would not have wished them published, and I feel more than ever that it is wise to destroy all letters. There may be and there are occasions when you wish you had them again, but the balance of advantage is enormously on the other side.

Of course we are no strangers to Mrs. Browning's letters. The volumes of Miss Mitford and R. H. Horne, not to speak of others, had given us a good deal of material. There are many fugitive letters which have not been collected here, and some of them are valuable. But it may be said at once that the editor is right in saying that there is nothing here to raise Mrs. Browning's reputation. She was not a great letter writer. In his very remarkable article on "Poetry," published in the *Encyclopædia Britannica*, Mr. Theodore Watts startled his readers by saying that Elizabeth Barrett Browning typifies in English literature the poets of energy. He said further:

> "The most truly passionate nature, and perhaps the greatest soul that in our time has expressed itself in English verse, is Elizabeth Barrett Browning. At least, it is certain that, with the single exception of Hood in the 'Song of the Shirt,' no writer of the century has really touched our hearts with a hand so powerful as hers."

And while admitting Mrs. Browning's metrical blemishes, he affirmed the splendour of her metrical triumphs at her best. These were startling words at the time, and they are still startling. The tendency of the best criticism has

* The Letters of Elizabeth Barrett Browning. Edited by F. G. Kenyon. New York: The Macmillan Co. 2 vols. $4.00.

been slowly but surely to lower Mrs. Browning's place in poetry. She lives now by the passion of her occasional verses, and I should much doubt whether even *Aurora Leigh* is very familiar to the readers of this generation. She was perhaps the greatest soul that in our time has expressed itself in English verse. The letters throw little light on the poetry, but much on the woman. Was she, then, the greatest soul among the poets of her age?

I take leave to doubt it. Mrs. Browning was essentially human. She had large and tender sympathies, was very faithful to her friends, bore with them even in their aberrations with much patience. But there are many women and some men who do as much as this. She was not in any proper sense of the word learned. It is amazing how few indications these volumes contain of anything like real culture. Every one is familiar with her Greek. But it was Greek of her husband's sort, Greek without accents, the kind of Greek that helps one to get at the meaning by the aid of cribs. In her early days of weakness she read a great deal and miscellaneously, but never, so far as we see, mastered anything. After she was married and went to Italy, she seems to have read just what other people read, Tennyson, Balzac, George Sand, Wordsworth, Miss Mitford, and the rest. There is no sign that during all the years of her marriage she had one serious intellectual interest, or pursued any fruitful course of study. Her mind was occupied mainly by two subjects, spiritualism and politics. Her letters on spiritualism are distressing, and the editor manifestly winces in printing them. They are written with no little heat and occasional anger. They chronicle impostures as dead as Agag. Then they are incoherent alike in form and in thought. It is very questionable whether they should ever have been revived. Has any fine mind ever touched that subject without sapping and contamination? I doubt it. On politics her let-

FAC-SIMILE OF MANUSCRIPT FROM "AN OPINION ON TENNYSON," BY MRS. BROWNING.

ters are even more distressing. I wish very much that the sentence about Mazzini had been omitted, and also that the whole series of shrill and feverish epistles which close the volume had been quietly put in the fire. The depth of Mrs. Browning's political instinct is shown by the fact that Napoleon III. was her demigod. Titania kissing the long ears of Bottom was an intelligible and respectable phenomenon when compared with Mrs. Browning kneeling at the feet of that most profligate charlatan among recent rulers. In both of these subjects we learn from many hints that Mr. Browning was opposed to his wife. She acknowledges that he behaved angelically, and I have no doubt that it was so. But the trial at times must have been considerable. Against these facts there is not much to set. Of course it goes without saying that many sentences here are turned with unconscious felicity. Mrs. Browning was undoubtedly a Christian. But what she believed and did not believe it is hard to say. There is very little to show that she depended in the least on any Christian sustenance. She does not seem habitually to have gone to church, or to have read the Bible, or to have studied religious or theological books. Like all of her kind she could lay down the law with great emphasis. She was a decided Nonconformist. She exceedingly disliked sacerdotalism in every form, but she had no sympathy with churches as a whole, and believed that they would pass away in the brightness of a new Christianity.

Well, then, how about her character? This is undoubtedly to be said, and it is a very great thing to say, that she was sweet. The note of personal rancour is completely absent here. Though she was well over forty when her first and only child was born, no young mother could have been more enthusiastic over her boy. To her husband she was also most affectionately devoted. Curiously enough, however, they seem to have worked apart, and to have known little of one another's work until that work was in print. She complains very much, and reasonably, that the English public did not do her husband justice, and he acquiesced in the popular judgment which put his wife above him. In fact, one's opinion of Browning is greatly heightened by this book. His magnanimity, his patience, his steadfast affection, his self-denying spirit, in a word his nobleness, are conspicuous everywhere, and the volume fittingly ends with his tenderly told story of her death. We hear, however, if it is not a shame to say so, of his frequent depression, and in spite of what Mr. Kenyon says there is plenty of evidence to show that the divergence between the two on spiritualism was real and acute. Mrs. Browning had no respect for intellectual authority in any form, and her husband does not seem to have influenced her in that way at all. If I must speak the truth, then, I must confess that Mrs. Browning seemed in her poetry a greater soul than she seems in these volumes, and that one can easily think of higher and nobler souls than hers. Yet she was, let it be cordially said, a very great woman and a very great poet.

I content myself with a very few notes on points in these volumes. A great deal might be said if the manuscript material available were used, but I presume the friends of the Brownings have resolved that this shall be the final publication. I hope it will be, for neither Mrs. Sutherland Orr's biography of Browning nor this collection of letters is quite to my mind.

In 1832 Miss Barrett, as she then was, writes:

"Bulwer has quite delighted me. He has all the dramatic talent which Scott had, and all the passion which Scott had not, and he appears to me to be besides a far profounder discriminator of character."

I leave it to Mr. Christie Murray and to Mr. Watts-Dunton to characterise this. More correctly, but not quite correctly, she draws the distinction between Wordsworth and Landor—great genius and eminent talent. There are few glimpses of her Nonconformist upbringing, but she refers once to Dr. Wardlaw, and to hearing Dr. Chalmers preaching in Glasgow.

"His eloquence was very great, and his devotion noble and grasping. I expected much from his imagination, but not so much from his knowledge. It was truer to Scripture than I was prepared for, although there seemed to me some want on the subject of the work of the Holy Spirit on the heart."

She says, "Everybody should read *Coningsby*. Disraeli, who is a man of genius, has written nevertheless books which will live longer and move deeper." There is, perhaps, a touch of true insight here. She refers to "an excellent refutation of Puseyism" in the *Edinburgh Review*, and wonders who was the author. The author was Henry Rogers. Mr. Kenyon should have quoted, in connection with the letters to Miss Mulock, the beautiful verses which Miss Mulock published in the *Athenæum* on Elizabeth Barrett Browning. They began, if I recollect aright:

"I know not that the cycle of strange years
Will ever bring thy human face to me.
Sister! I speak this not as of thy peers."

One is glad to find that she likes Elizabeth Wetherell. "Tell me if you have read *Queechy*, the American book of Miss Wetherell. I think it very clever and characteristic. Mrs. Beecher Stowe scarcely excels it after all the trumpets." She considers that Miss Gaskell's *Ruth* is "strong and healthy at once, teaching a moral frightfully wanted in English society." Lockhart in Rome she describes as "like a snow-man in complexion, hair, conversation, and manners." She does not like Alexander Smith, and cannot understand why he gets into a third edition. Of Miss Austen Mrs. Browning had "a very limited admiration." A curious feature is the excessive importance attached to the reviews in the *Athenæum*, for which Mrs. Browning wrote a good deal. Latterly Mrs. Browning became a Swedenborgian. She says that Mrs. Stowe's last words to her, when they parted, were, "Those who love the Lord Jesus Christ never see one another for the last time." The same saying appears in Mr. Philpot's *Pocket of Pebbles* in the finer form, "They who love God never meet for the last time." Luther, she says in her last days, was "a schoolman of the most scholastic sort, most offensive, most absurd, presenting an idea of old cerements to the uttermost." "Kossuth is neither very noble nor very wise." Her worst saying about Mazzini I will not quote.

The book teaches us not to expect too much of poor human nature. Mrs. Browning spent her days in Florence happily enough, in spite of her suffering. She appears to have read hardly anything except French novels. She was the best of wives and mothers. Beyond that, she was taken up with spiritualism and with the maddest notions about politics. As for her arguments for spiritualism, I will quote one: "By the way, a lady whom I know here writes Greek without knowing, or ever having known, a single letter of it. The unbelievers writhe under it." The unbelievers have been made to writhe again. If the Greek was anything like Robert Browning's Greek manuscripts, which I have frequently seen, there is no man, woman, or child in England who could not write a good imitation of it without the aid of any spirit, evil or holy.

Claudius Clear.

ADVENTURES IN CRITICISM.*

That Mr. Roosevelt is a good fellow, if you will pardon me for saying so, and means well, no one in his senses will doubt. To out-of-town residents he can talk, even entertainingly, about the three legislatures of which he was a member at Albany, the New York Police Department, and machine politics generally. Moreover, he has scholarship enough to grapple intelligently, when his turn comes, with such a book as Kidd's *Social Evolution*. On other occasions, like one of Mark Twain's characters, he needs a cross of big nails in his left boot-heel to keep off the devil. Pugnacity and an undefined, and undefinable, intense and fervid Americanism are his two dominant ideas, which he applies at random to every human situation and reiterates, in the manner of Cato rather than St. John, on nearly every page. Life is a battle, and every citizen is a soldier whose aim should be to "do or die." One must be of sufficiently coarse fibre to strike back, whenever opportunity offers. There is a certain lack of robustness in our educated men, to whom the State has a "right" to look for good service, which makes them shrink from contact with rough politicians. This is wrong. No man has any "right" to let politics alone. Instead of sitting by the fire and reading the evening paper, every one who is worth his salt should rush to the hurly-

* American Ideals, and Other Essays. By Theodore Roosevelt. New York: G. P. Putnam's Sons. $1.25.

Certain Accepted Heroes, and Other Essays in Literature and Politics. By Henry Cabot Lodge. New York: Harper & Bros. $1.50.

burly of the caucus and the primary. Above all, one must be imbued with "the American spirit." An educated man must not go into politics as such, but simply as an American. If one has religious prejudices, he must lay them, too, aside at the polls. A German-American or an Irish-American vote simply should not be recognised in a party platform. Elsewhere it is said that we must face the facts, but that does not matter. Nor does it occur to the writer that in whooping it up for "intense and fervid Americanism" he is echoing the vociferous demand for "reform," which, on another page, he says certain persons make as if it were a slice of something good to eat.

Of course Mr. Roosevelt incidentally damns "that flaccid habit of mind which its possessors style cosmopolitanism." There is danger of over-civilisation and over-refinement. The man who becomes Europeanised in the sense of losing his power of doing good work on this side of the water is a "silly and undesirable citizen." The American painter who lives in Paris forfeits all chance of doing his best work. Why doesn't he "strike out to rise or fall on a new line," renouncing the masters? The *émigré* may write graceful and pretty verses, essays, novels; but he will never compare with his brother who is "strong enough to stand on his own feet." The under-sized man of letters who flees his country — but enough. Let it pass. This is not a book of literary essays, and, on the face of them, such remarks are sufficiently ludicrous.

Mr. Roosevelt is a writer who sees only blacks and whites. He appears to be overpowered with the difficulty of drilling a little sense into decent people. His opponents he scores in unmeasured terms; they are always "those solemn prattlers" who are "utterly incapable" of something or other. But WE who, "however imperfectly, do the work of the nation," who "work honestly for what we think to be right," who "in two years did more to increase the efficiency and honesty of the police department than had ever previously been done in its history," what is the matter with US? Now I am not questioning if all this be so. As one of Mr. Roosevelt's readers, I am merely averse to being hide-bound and dragged about, like Hector, by his cloud-compelling personality. He says that the function of a mere critic is of very subordinate usefulness. May this critic say here that he would feel he had been supereminently useful if, the next time Mr. Roosevelt publishes a book, he should curb his braggadocio and condescension? Will it never stop ringing in one's ears? "The great writers have done much for us!" Ugh! Yet—be it said to Mr. Roosevelt's everlasting credit—the thought is clinched in one's mind, after an hour's reading, that it is an exceedingly difficult thing nowadays to be a good citizen—at least, good enough to please Mr. Roosevelt. If you don't vote, you're blackguarded; and if you do vote, you're blackguarded—for not doing more than vote. Mr. Thomas E. Watson's letter is an epitome of this book. "You merely obey a law of your nature," he wrote to Mr. Roosevelt, "which puts you into mortal combat with what you think is wrong." Let others obey the law of their natures, and all will be well, *n'est ce pas?*

Mr. Roosevelt has inscribed his book to Henry Cabot Lodge, the one person in the world who cannot receive any harm from it, because he has long since stopped at all the stations therein demarked, and recovered his manly equilibrium.

Mr. Cabot's manner is more dispassionate. When Chatterton or Dr. Holmes is his text it is in spots even judicial. He contributes a timely essay on the home of the Cabots, and adds a few words to Lowell's and Professor Brander Matthews's list of Shakespearian Americanisms. The papers on our foreign policy and the brutality and corruption of English elections aside, he is a partisan only in his selection of subjects, which means, merely, that it is the fashion nowadays to write essays from a particular point of view. "The Last Plantagenet" may be likened to Miss Guiney's "Inquirendo into the Wit and Other Good Parts of King Charles the Second," although the latter is in dialogue—because, I suppose, Miss Guiney didn't care to be responsible for her point of view. Assuming that Shakespeare's noble style has fooled generations as to the real characteristics of Richard III., which it hasn't at all, Mr. Lodge draws an interesting parallel between fiction and fact, showing that there is no more evidence of the king's deformity than of his monstrous birth; that the second stage murder, that of Henry VI., should in justice to history have been attributed to Edward and his cabinet council rather than to Richard; that Richard had nothing to do with the death of Clarence; and that, if one may judge from his successor's continuance of his policy, Richard was a wise statesman and great soldier, despite his known crimes and overmastering ambition. Assuming, again, that Achilles and Agamemnon and Odysseus have hitherto been accepted as heroes, although by his own admission there are many boys to whom they seem less manly than Saladin, Richard of the Lion Heart, and Leatherstocking, Mr. Lodge proves that Odysseus was an artful liar; that Agamemnon advised his followers to forego the peril of fighting single-handed; and that Achilles was a blatant skulk, who didn't avenge the death of Patroclus until his mother got him a suit of impenetrable armour, and who overtook the agile Hector only when Athena caused him to stand still, and after killing him dragged his body behind a chariot until the gods intervened. The whole lot of them, Mr. Lodge says, had the manners and morals of South Sea Islanders or of Zulus, and therefore should not be regarded as heroes. I venture to say that nobody ever so regarded them. They belong in the same category with Peregrine Pickle and Tartarin de Tarascon and Zagloba—morally. Because of their failings, however, which put them often in unsupportable situations, they shall ever be picturesquely endeared to memory. Yet Mr. Lodge's little game, so long as he will not consent to "do the legitimate," is well worth the candle. As he himself says of the translations, everything is so good it is invidious to grumble. However, it may be questioned if the same facts might not more convincingly have been marshalled in a mere study of Homer. *Daniel Webster*, in the American Statesmen Series, is of permanent value, I suspect, largely because it was not converted into a tilt-yard.

In the Phi Beta Kappa address, "A Liberal Education," earnestness is tinctured with the saving grace of humour. If a man is [illegible] good citizen, it boots little (to t[illegible] suppose Mr. Cabot means) whether he knows Latin and Greek. Americanism, in the right sense, should by no means repress wholesome criticism of what is wrong. There is not the slightest danger, however, that the supply of critics will run out; and the colleges should take care not to educate young men to be mere critics at the outset. No one is in any particular peril of overvaluing his own country; and in the broad sweep of a liberal education there is a tendency to lose the sense of proportion—that is (according to Mr. Cabot) to underrate our own place in the history and life of the world.

George Merriam Hyde.

THIS COUNTRY OF OURS.*

It is interesting to note the change in the character of books written on the subject of the Government of the United States. The older books on this subject, whether they were serious studies designed for students of the Science of Government, or popular works intended for general reading, dealt almost exclusively with the principles underlying our polity and with the history and construction of our Constitution. The greater number of the books recently published treat of what may be termed the mechanism of our government, the institutions of the country as they exist, the methods of their operation, and their advantages and defects. This change in the literature of the subject is of profound significance, because it indicates that the thinking and reading public are more interested in the practical effects of the institutions of government than in their history, and are applying the test of practical results to institutions rather than inquiring as to the theories of human rights on which they rest and the relations that underlie them.

The literature of England on the subject of its government reached this stage earlier than our own. Englishmen have long been possessed of a complete survey of the character and practical working of their institutions in the well-known book by Albany de Fonblanque,

* This Country of Ours. By Benjamin Harrison, ex-President of the United States. New York: Charles Scribner's Sons. $1.50.

entitled *How We are Governed*, which has passed through many editions, and has been re-edited from time to time as the administrative methods of the English government have changed; and in the well-known series entitled "The English Citizen," written by authorities on the subjects specially treated, they have had complete information as to the details of their government in all its departments.

With us, since the appearance of Professor Bryce's *American Commonwealth* and Professor Woodrow Wilson's *Congressional Government*, there has been a great multiplication of books treating of the practical operation of the departments of our Government. The last of these is by ex-President Harrison, and bears the somewhat ambiguous title *This Country of Ours*; but the number of such books recently published made it difficult to find a title that was truly descriptive that had not been appropriated. The title chosen suggests that of Professor Strong's well-known book, *Our Country*. It is, however, of an entirely different character and has a very different purpose.

The present book is entitled to serious consideration. Few persons have been in a position to write from such full knowledge and experience as ex-President Harrison, and the result is an extremely readable, entertaining, and suggestive volume. Besides being a full and complete exposition of the working of the various departments of our Government by one who has had the advantage of large, personal observation and experience, it has the charm of containing to some extent reminiscences of his experiences as Chief Executive of the Nation. This feature is not avowed, but it is very evident that ex-President Harrison has taken the public into his confidence and given them some leaves from his life in the White House.

The book is accurately described in the preface by the statement that, "it is a modest attempt to give the readers a view of the machinery of our National Government in motion, and some instructions as to the relation and uses of its several parts." It is written from the standpoint of optimism and with the high purpose of promoting "an intelligent patriotism and a faithful discharge of the duties of citizenship." The introduction is an earnest essay on the paramount importance of the cultivation of the virtue of patriotism by the American people, and a quickening of the conscience toward law. This is so impressively stated that the language should be quoted.

> "The real enemies of our country—the dangerous ones—are not the armed men nor the armoured ships of the great Powers. If there is too much exuberance in the thought that we can whip the world, it is a safe saying that we can defend our land and coasts against any part of the world that will ever be in arms against us. We are alert as to foreign foes—the drum-tap rouses the heaviest sleepers. But we are a dull people as to internal assaults upon the integrity and purity of public administration. . . . It has seemed to me that a fuller knowledge of our civil institutions and a deeper love of them would make us more watchful for their purity; that we would think less of the levy necessary to restore stolen public funds, and more of the betrayal and shame of the thing."

The earnestness and truth of these words command our attention, not only to this essay, but to the entire book, which throughout is characterised by the same high spirit and purpose.

The first chapter of the book explains the relations of the State governments to the Federal government under the provisions of the Constitution. It is only in this chapter that there is found any ground of criticism of the book for incompleteness or indefiniteness, but this chapter fails to make clear and leaves confused the subject, not popularly understood, of the limitations upon the powers of the Federal and State governments by reason of the prohibitions in the Federal Constitution.

Methods of legislation and procedure in the Senate and House of Representatives is next taken up and fully described. The most interesting part of the book follows, in the chapters which relate to the President, and which state his duties and explain the manner in which he performs them and attends to the social demands made upon him. Nearly one half of the book is taken up with this subject, and fortunately so, for it is very clear that these chapters are but the ex-President's experiences, and are reminiscences of the four years during which he was the Chief Executive of the nation. We know of no account to be found anywhere which so fully describes the official life of the President as these pages, and certainly some of the suggestions and criticisms as to the demands made upon the President's time, to the interference of the performance of his official duties, are worthy of thought and consideration.

A full statement of the practical workings of the departments of government, presided over by the secretaries forming the President's Cabinet, an account of the Smithsonian Institution, the Department of Labour, the Interstate Commerce Commission, the Civil Service Commission, and the Judiciary Department complete the book. In connection with the explanation of the mechanism of each of these governmental departments and their workings, there is a brief but lucid statement of the history of each department, and of the development of the present method of its administration.

The book should have a wide circulation, as it is highly interesting and instructive, and the American reading public owes a debt to ex-President Harrison for writing a book on this subject addressed to the general reader rather than to the student.

We note on page 144 a curious error, by which a quotation from Montesquieu is credited to Montaigne.

Edward M. Colie.

THE NEW GOLDEN TREASURY.*

Thirty-six years have passed since the publication of the *Golden Treasury*, and the judgment of two generations has not only confirmed the long series of judgments upon English poets and poetry which Professor Palgrave's work involved, but has accepted that work as a kind of original creation. The book is one of the English classics; and its quality and place are so marked and distinct that we have come to think of it as a contribution to English literature. Its individuality lies, however, entirely in the insight, the critical discernment and the taste which it illustrates. These are so nearly infallible that the mass of other men's work collected in the *Golden Treasury*, to which Professor Palgrave added not a line of his own, seems somehow to belong to the Editor.

A felicity of choices so complete that it constitutes a distinct achievement is not likely again to fall to any editor in the same field. For Professor Palgrave had several aids which will be denied those who come after him. He had, in the first place, the whole range of English poetry to draw upon, and he was, for the purpose he had in view, the first comer into that rich field. He had the bloom of the earliest harvest, and he had two invaluable helpers in making his choices—Time and Tennyson. Upon all the earlier poetry with which he had to deal the English people had already pronounced a judgment which, if not infallible, was the expression of the spiritual and poetic insight of many generations. That this long series of popular choices was of immense assistance Professor Palgrave implicitly confessed when he wrote in his preface to the first edition of the *Golden Treasury* that he had "found the vague general verdict of popular Fame more just than those have thought who, with too severe a criticism, would confine judgments on Poetry to 'the selected few of many generations.' Not many appear to have gained reputation without some gift or performance that, in due degree, deserved it." Tennyson's assistance was another great element in his success; for the trained instinct and insight of the Poet Laureate in matters relating to his art were well-nigh infallible.

The Second Series was prepared under very different conditions. The period covered was that which began with the year 1850, in the middle of the Victorian Age. The range of selection was therefore immensely reduced; and within this narrow field the public judgment was still in many cases unsettled. Professor Palgrave had much less material to choose from, and he had to trust, in large measure, to his own judgment. The matured opinion of Time could not be consulted, and Tennyson was no longer within reach. That the second *Golden Treasury* should fall below the standard of its predecessor in richness of material and in sureness of taste was inevitable; but it is a disappointment even to those who were ready to give full might to the change in conditions. Since the appearance of the volume the Editor has "passed to where beyond these voices there is peace," and his reputation rests safely on his earlier work; the later will never secure either the authority or the affection which belong of right to the original selection.

* Golden Treasury of Songs and Lyrics. Selected from the Best Songs and Lyrical Poems in the English Language, and Arranged with Notes. By Francis T. Palgrave. Second Series. New York: The Macmillan Co.

In the Second Series the critical judgment is far less consistent and certain, and there are singular inclusions and unaccountable omissions. In so small a collection ought the Duke of Argyle, John Clare, Henry C. Kendall, Sir Francis Hastings Doyle, George John Romanes, and John Campbell Shairp to have been included, while William Morris, Dobson, Watson, and Kipling are omitted? It may be questioned, moreover, whether too much space has not been given to Lord Houghton, to Frederick Tennyson, to Charles Tennyson-Turner, and to O'Shaughnessy. It is a pleasure to find the gifted and lamented Irish poet so generously recognised; but would not a truer perspective of judgment have been secured if two or three of the pages devoted to his work had been given to Yeats and some of the younger poets who are his successors? More space is given to O'Shaughnessy than to either of the Brownings, to Matthew Arnold, to either of the Rossettis! Landor is limited to a single poem, while William Barnes is represented by twelve selections. No one will quarrel with the admission of Coventry Patmore into this charmed circle; but why exclude Andrew Lang, who more than once struck a fine, high note? Such questions will come even to those who study the second *Golden Treasury* in the light of its preface, and with full appreciation of the difficulties of Professor Palgrave's task. If he is judged by the very highest standards, it is because he had already established those standards.

It must not be inferred, however, that this selection of recent English poetry is lacking in value and interest; on the contrary, it brings together a body of verse which it is a delight to have at hand in such a form, and it will do something toward the ultimate settlement of the claims of a group of poets whose work is part of the history of the last half century. It furnishes material, moreover, for a very interesting comparison of the poetry of the first and second halves of the century. The fourth book of the earlier *Golden Treasury* included the poets of the period between 1800 and 1850—Blake, Keats, Coleridge, Byron, Shelley, Scott, Wordsworth, Campbell, Moore, Southey, Hood. In the Second Series the great names are Arnold, Browning, Rossetti, and Tennyson. The standard has not fallen, but how small the company that carries it forward! Of the earlier group at least five—Keats, Shelley, Byron, Wordsworth and Coleridge—stand not only for poetic genius, which falls only a little short of the highest, but for new movements of thought and art, while the name of Scott is still a point of light amid these greater stars. Of the later group only two can be put forward as possessing the fountain quality of song—Tennyson and Browning. There are those who will deny Browning's claim to this equality with Tennyson; but when all deductions are made from the poet's work enough will remain, in quantity and quality, to assure his place, not only among the great thinkers, but among the great poets of the English race. Matthew Arnold was not mistaken in the interesting comparison of his work with that of Tennyson and Browning which he makes in one of his letters. He will not be excluded from their company, although his place will fall below theirs. It is safe to assume, too, that Rossetti and Mrs. Browning will not be forgotten when the great mass of contemporary writing has gone into oblivion.

The conclusion of the matter seems to be, that the great tradition of English poetry has been fully sustained during the last half century, but that there have been fewer voices of the farthest reach and fewer original notes. The stream runs as deep as it did in the first half of the century; but it is not so wide, nor is its current so swift and tumultuous. It would be interesting, if space permitted, to contrast the content of this later body of verse with that of the earlier poetry; such a contrast would bring out in a very striking way the movement of modern life, and would perhaps bring consolation to those who believe that the springs of song are running dry.

Hamilton W. Mabie.

THE POLYCHROME BIBLE.*

After seven years of eager expectation the day draws near for the appearance of one of the most brilliant and edifying books of modern times. In the circles where the scope and plan of *The Poly-*

* The Polychrome Bible. Judges. By Professor George Moore, of Andover: Psalms. By Professor J. Wellhausen, of Göttingen: Isaiah. By Professor T. K. Cheyne, of Oxford. New York: Dodd, Mead & Co.

chrome Bible have been understood one is reminded of the impatience with which men waited for the Revised New Testament of 1881. To have seen the advance sheets of the splendid work proceeding under the editorship of Professor Paul Haupt of Johns Hopkins University, and Dr. Horace Howard Furniss of Harvard University, is to have had one's intellectual appetite wondrously stimulated; and one feels almost a sense of personal gratitude to the broad-minded publishers who have undertaken to issue *The Polychrome Bible* in a form of suitable dignity and beauty.

For the information of such as have not had occasion to inform themselves touching the motive and spirit of this work, a few words of explanation may be permitted.

The book represents primarily an attempt to render the sublime documents of the Old Testament in a modern English translation which, being founded upon a critically verified text, is "literal" in the higher sense of the word—a true representation of the spirit of the original. The distinguished editor-in-chief of *The Polychrome Bible* would be the last to claim that the scheme of a modern English translation has occurred only to himself. The *Revised Version* was founded upon the same idea, and Professor Moulton's *Modern Reader's Bible* deserves and commands recognition as an expression of a similar purpose. But Professor Haupt, possibly because his life contains an old-world training at the feet of Delitzsch and Dillmann, blended with a new-world energy fostered in a great American university, has developed a threefold combination of excellency in *The Polychrome Bible*, which elevates that work to a station of unique and fascinating distinction. We may be permitted to point out these three features, by which the Book becomes to the Biblical student one of the "necessaries of life:"

First of all, one examines the text with a sense of security, founded in the fact that the modern masters of Old Testament study have issued it in the calm, clear light of exalted scholarship. The men to whom were committed, for translation, the several documents, are of that great brotherhood of scholars in which the study of the Word of God is a task

"Too great for haste, too high for rivalry."

Canon Driver, Professor Adam Smith, Professor Briggs, Professor McCurdy, Dr. Delitzsch, Canon Cheyne, Professor Francis Brown, Professor Curtis, Dr. Ward, and those other pure-minded and reverent men associated with them, entered upon this work for the truth's sake only. Incapable of wilful perversion of one "jot or tittle" of the Sacred Word, walking at liberty among the traditions of men, yet bound in the Spirit as the servants of God, they who have edited the several books of *The Polychrome Bible* have given to all men of all theological schools an instrument of precision with which to study the Holy Oracles. When one remembers, for example, that Canon Cheyne has devoted thirty years to the study of *Isaiah*, that he has already published three great books upon that subject, and that his whole life bears witness to his intellectual and spiritual honesty, the busy minister in his study, the private Christian in his daily Bible reading, may well feel a sense of security and of gratitude when he reads the superb text of *Isaiah* in *The Polychrome Bible*.

But in addition to the text we have the notes and the illustrations. When it is fully understood that these notes are not prepared in the interest of any school of denominational thought, that they are non-controversial, and that they are intended to be simply an expression of the translator's reasons for their translations, one may believe that all possible distrust of the critical motive lying back of *The Polychrome Bible* will vanish from honest minds. In the instructions to the contributors occur the following wholesome words: "Any thing that might tend to hurt the religious feelings of the reader must be avoided, provided that it can be done without any detriment to the truth. The contributors need not hesitate to state what they consider to be the truth, but it should be done with the *verecundia* due to the venerable documents which form the basis of our faith." An examination of advance sheets of the notes on *Judges* and *Psalms* bears out these instructions. Brief, concise, clear as crystal, sharply cut as with the tempered blade of one skilled to divide the Word of Truth, the notes exhibit a spirit of reverence all the more exalted because free from the zeal of theological partisanship. They leave the reader in the possession of his own liberty. They admonish him that he must think for himself. The illustrations are so beautiful in their spirit and design, so effectively selected and distributed, so finely wrought by generous publishers who stayed not the artist's hand, so obviously realistic, that one counts them of equal value with the notes. The faithful camera has been used unsparingly; and the man of the Western World who has never walked beneath the Syrian stars nor wandered amid the Holy Hills may rise from the examination of these sumptuous pages with all the enthusiasm of an Oriental traveller kindled within him.

To many persons, representing all shades of critical opinion, the supreme interest awakened by *The Polychrome Bible* will focus on that feature of its construction which gives to the book its distinctive title. It is a "polychrome"—a "many-coloured" Bible. Dr. Haupt and his distinguished associate, Dr. Furniss of Harvard University, may congratulate themselves upon a device as simple as it is effective for bringing to all minds an instantaneous appreciation of one of the problems of the Higher Criticism.

Those who accept and those who contest modern critical opinions on the authorship of Old Testament documents are equally concerned to know the nature and contents of those opinions. While it is everywhere understood that the Higher Critics incline toward the theory of the composite authorship of certain books of the Old Testament canon, the exhibition of such results as have been tentatively reached in this direction has not heretofore been possible in any form which would readily appeal to the eye. And it may be believed that mutual advantage will result to all schools of Biblical Criticism if the theory of composite authorship can find a mode of expression readily accessible to the public mind. The scheme of Professor Haupt to this end is simply a colour scheme. By making use of inks different in colour, and by identifying certain supposed authors with certain colours, an absolutely unmistakable exhibition is made of the present state of critical opinion on this line of research. A "polychrome" page of *Genesis* or of *Judges* gives in one instant of time to the average reader a more exact knowledge of one department of the work of Higher Criticism than can be given by volumes of technical explanation or by pages of acrimonious controversy. As a matter of information, as a *datum* of current opinion, *The Polychrome Bible* is of equal value to every scholar, clerical or lay, whatever his point of view toward the interesting literary questions now opened about the Sacred Scriptures. But even if a man have no interest whatever in the "polychrome" feature of the vast work now ripening toward its consummation under the general editorship of Dr. Haupt and Dr. Furniss, the other characteristics of the work to which we have referred make it one of the noblest of aids to the single-minded scholar.

Charles Cuthbert Hall.

NOVEL NOTES.

FLINT, HIS FAULTS, HIS FRIENDSHIPS AND HIS FORTUNES. By Maud Wilder Goodwin. Boston: Brown, Little & Co. $1.25.

In this new work the author has made a departure, carrying her charm from the historic into the modern field. Flint, the editor of a great daily, is as modern a type as our newest civilisation produces, and he is described as he has hardly been before. There is little personal description. What he says and what he does bring him before us. The very spot in which he first appears reveals him through its "inaccessibility and general lack of popular attractions;" his pessimism toward the real and his sympathy with the ideal are shown in his cynical words while under the spell of the sea. Prematurely old, as the editors of great dailies so often are, and hating his kind with a frankness that only the editors of great dailies seem to allow themselves, he comes to this isolated place to meet experiences that alter these views. Many sorts and conditions of men—and of women too—have loved where they did not approve, but the psychology of the situation has rarely been shown with such vividness. Flint resists, as if love were disgrace, and the woman, approving of him as little or less than he approves of her, is even more unwilling. Yet love, the red spider, binds them together closer and closer, despite their tugs at the intangible, unbreakable web. It is rather a relief to the woman to discover that the landlady's daughter has also fallen in love with Flint. It does not matter at all that he regards the girl simply as an agency for procuring food and towels, and that he does not know that his rolls are hotter and his coffee stronger than those of the other boarders. In a most amusing scene the woman takes him to task for his heartlessness to the girl. The man stammers, as any ordinary man not the editor of a great daily might stammer, under the accusation, and protests that he does not understand the girl, that he never understands people of that kind. "Have you ever tried to understand them?" asks the merciless fair one. "Haven't you always thought of them only as they ministered to your comfort like the other farm animals? Is it anything to you that this narrow-minded girl has conceived a silly, but none the less unhappy sentiment for you?" Some brilliant and decidedly new things are said in this connection about the saving influence of the "monogamous instinct of the Anglo Saxon race." There would seem to have been a rather widely accepted opinion to the contrary. Did not some one, speaking with authority, say not long ago that Man, regardless of race, was but an imperfectly monogamous animal? Had the woman held to the original line of her argument—the man's unfeeling fastidiousness—she would have stood upon more tenable ground, for it is only too often that fastidiousness stands to morals as a stone wall to a fog. But be this as it may, the episode of the landlady's daughter leads to the tragedy of the story, to its broadening and uplifting beyond the slight, almost trivial beginning. It can scarcely be necessary to comment upon the excellence of the workmanship, in view of the author's several notable successes. The epigrammatic quality of her work also shows to unusual advantage in this new story, which gives —perhaps by reason of its modernity—opportunities not afforded by her historical novels.

PHYLLIS IN BOHEMIA. By L. H. Bickford and Richard Stillman Powell. Chicago: Herbert S. Stone & Co. $1.25.

It seems reasonably certain that this little book is mainly a woman's work, notwithstanding that a man's name also appears on the title-page, and it is he who ostensibly tells the tale. The Bohemia described is distinctively a woman's Bohemia, that country wherein geniuses galore abide, wherein congregate "people on the verge of great careers," people who make the world—such a Bohemia as no man, perhaps, ever knew or imagined. Only one futile protest comes from the masculine point of view, declaring the real Bohemia to be filled with people who are always intending to do something, and who never do anything, and describing it as a wilderness of literary disappointments, musical failures, artistic mistakes, and nondescript freaks. It is, as usual, the woman who has her way, and who directs the entrance into this debatable land. She has no doubt that she has located it in a street full of pianos and a flat full of geniuses, but the reader finds nothing extraordinary in the situation, except the fact that Phyllis, most unsophisticated of country girls, settles among the geniuses, to live alone with her fiancé. It is all as inartistically innocent as a cup of milk and bread. It is two commonplace children playing at seeing the world, and the things that the geniuses say and do are the things that would appeal to such guileless lookers-on. There are bright bits here and there, as when one of the geniuses says, "Bohemia is a green acre in the heart of everywhere surrounded by a wall so high that none may climb—all must be born inside," and when another declares that "the difference between a roof garden and a Bohemian basement is not a difference of altitude—it is simply a difference of drinks;" but when the author goes on:

> "Engaged in commending this observation, followed by a gentlemanly discussion with the person sitting opposite who had appropriated a bottle of claret ordered for my side of the table, I was not made aware that another favourite son of Bohemia, born within the walls, was claiming attention until the enthusiast hissed fiercely. . ."

the reader closes the book, feeling that he lifts too heavy a club to brain too small a butterfly.

THE KING WITH TWO FACES. By M. E. Coleridge. New York: Edward Arnold. $1.50.

It would perhaps have been more specific had the title been *One of the Kings with Two Faces*, and certainly it would have been much to the story's advantage had it begun less like a riddle with A. saying this and B. saying that. But after passing the alphabet the tale marches steadily, though heavily, through its four hundred pages. In this, as in her earlier novel, *The Seven Sleepers of Ephesus*, Miss Coleridge groups the characters around historic incidents, taken in this case from the history of Sweden. The events relate to the struggle between Sweden and Denmark. Gustav III. sits on the throne of Sweden, and Madame de Staël is ruling the world as the Swedish ambassadress at Paris. "Of the ambassador nobody ever spoke; he was *tout bonnement le mari de sa femme*." In the company of the enchantress may be found many of the famous men and women of the time, who touch more or less closely the lives of Adolf and Tala, the young people whose love-story is the heart of the romance. It is a stirring tale of adventure, thrilling with hairbreadth escapes. All the elements of the orthodox novel of its kind are abundant in this. There is even a witch who tells the king that he will be slain by a man in a red coat, and out of the prophecy grows many of the hero's misfortunes and his ultimate victory.

A QUEEN OF HEARTS. By Elizabeth Phipps Train. Philadelphia: J. B. Lippincott Co. $1.25.

The author caught the public eye by means of two fresh books, *A Social Highwayman* and *The Autobiography of a Professional Beauty*, and there is something in the beginning of this new work that promises to hold the audience thus won. The personality of the queen of hearts—the actress who tells the story—is successfully realised. Her description of herself, from childhood to marriage, is full of restrained power. The scene in which her puritanical guardian finds her dancing in the garret stands out like a picture, and the narrative moves with surety up to the inevitable revulsion which such a nature must feel sooner or later in an uncongenial marriage. It is easy to understand the unhappy wife's powerlessness to resist when accident brings her in contact with her own kind. But from this point the work falls off, and indeed changes its style as completely as if another hand and mind took up the pen and the theme. Instead of the terse, nervous force of the earlier chapters, the later ones gallop along after a distinctively journalistic fashion, with apparently no other object than to "get over ground." And however admirable such speed may be in a newspaper, it is hardly in harmony with certain literary effects, and the reader of this story feels as if he had been rather too rapidly conducted when he is told of the first year's study for the stage, and the second year's experiences upon it, all within a single short paragraph. Nor is there any return to the composure of the opening pages, and the story which begins admirably, as well or better than other good things written by the author consequently hurries to a lame and impotent conclusion.

CHALMETTE. By Clinton Ross. Philadelphia: J. B. Lippincott Co. $1.50.

This new story is an addition to Mr. Ross's group of well-thought, well-written historical romances. The period selected is the beginning of the present century, the events are those associated with the battle of New Orleans, and the central historic character is Jean Lafitte, the famous pirate of Barataria, as picturesque a figure as may be found in any country's history. Miss King recently revived his dangerous fascination in her charming book on New Orleans, and Mr. Ross has hardly coloured the facts in framing them with fiction. The brilliant rascal so takes hold of the fancy, that one can scarcely keep it in mind that he came, followed by his desperate companions, to General Jackson's aid to save his own and their thievish necks from the halter. It were better he thought—like the shrewd scoundrel he was—to fight the British than to be hanged. And such fighting as they did has hardly ever been seen in this world. Their demoniac faces, red-turbaned, glaring out of the battle-smoke, are said to have been among the most terrible spectacles of that awful fight. No wonder that England's trained troops—the flower of her army, the very men, some of them, who met Napoleon's invincibles at Waterloo—quailed, feeling that they were fighting demons rather than human beings. A love-story of a sweet and wholesome kind runs through this, as through almost everything that Mr. Ross writes, but it is not the hero, Captain Robe, and his fictitious adventures that make the charm of the story. The actual career of the dazzling villain Lafitte is more romantic than any romance.

AMERICAN NOBILITY. By Pierre de Coulerain. New York: Scribner's. $1.50.

The writer's name is unfamiliar, and has, moreover, a made-up sound. It almost arouses a suspicion that another American author may be masquerading as a critic of his own countrymen and countrywomen. But a moment's reflection shows this to be unlikely. A writer who could "the giftie gie us," as it is given here would hardly give it in such an amateurish way. There is little if any skill in the construction of the work, which is much cleverer taken page by page than as a whole. Then the point of view seems so distinctively French that one feels bound to accept its nationality as genuine. No Anglo-Saxon true to his race would say to the girl whom he wished to marry, that drink and cards are worse than unfaithfulness in a husband, no matter what his private conviction might be. And certainly the "temptation to tell his wife all the griefs his mistress caused him" is one of the few temptations that never assails the married American. Balzac, it will be remembered, actually allows one of his fine gentlemen to do this, as the most natural thing in the world. The noble husband who figures in *American Nobility* resists the temptation, and it is his inamorata, the duchesse, who issues the shameless proclamation, without which no French liaison seems to be a success. The depravity dissolving France reveals itself with revolting candour in every part of the work, and yet, as said before, it abounds nevertheless in shrewd observation of American types and conditions. The angular, open-eyed uprightness of the French count's American wife realises a national type. One knows, too, just what he means when he says "she gave him the sensation of biting some beautiful fruit, sound and not yet ripe." Nor is he far from the truth when he says of a more common type of the American woman abroad, that "she is virtuous enough not to give entrance to the devil when at home, but she is enchanted to meet him elsewhere. In Paris she does not neglect to seek out the archfiend, first of all to see how he is made, and especially to be able to say she has seen him, and you may be sure he is never black enough." All this must be admitted, but American readers will draw the line at the statement that "all these things which might permanently disturb a French girl's mind and sully it forever" leave the American girl untouched, mainly because "she is as incapable of understanding depravity as holiness."

PRISONERS OF THE SEA. By Florence M. Kingsley. Philadelphia: David McKay. $1.25.

Among the historical facts and traditions which have held the imagination through many generations, none has a firmer grasp than the story of the man with the iron mask. Scarcely a season passes without the reappearance in fiction of this sphinx of the seventeenth century, and *Prisoners of the Sea* is its latest apparition. There is, indeed, such finality in the appendix accompanying this version of the romance that it almost claims to be the decisive reading of the riddle. The story opens with a shipwreck and the landing of the sufferers on a mysterious island which has once been the home of the man with the iron mask. Among the shipwrecked are two women, mother and daughter, and the sentiment of the tale surrounds the girl and the lover, who comes, of course, to the rescue. There is little to be said of a novel of this kind, one seems to have read it so often, and it goes along quite readably in the conventional way for the first two hundred pages—conventional, that is, so far as the general outline of the narrative is concerned, not otherwise, for it is certainly somewhat unconventional to find an English sailor—that most distinctive and unmistakable personality—talking sometimes like an illiterate Yankee and sometimes like the Yankee's idea of a negro, while the negro himself speaks a lingo never heard before on land or sea. Yet the story holds together fairly well till within perhaps a hundred pages of the end, when it gradually goes to pieces like a raft in the waves. When a dying man "raises his hand" and begins to tell a tiresome yarn that stretches through ten close-printed pages—but why say anything more of such 'prentice work?

THE SKIPPER'S WOOING. By W. W. Jacobs. New York: Frederick A. Stokes Company. $1.00.

Mr. Jacobs's humour is so much his own that, though he is a new-comer, we already recognise it with a distinctness that proves it to be, of its kind at least, first-rate. Its kind is good, too—very genial, very laughter provoking, very unaffected, in temper American rather than English. The slight mixture of sentiment here gives the foil which was wanting in *Many Cargoes*, and a hint of a promise that Mr. Jacobs may one day write a good novel, though we are far from suggesting that we are tired of his excellent fooling. The crew of the *Seamew* are the most delightful of companions, and the king of them all is that hopeful boy Henry. Henry must not be lost sight of. He should still serve both Mr. Jacobs and us on many future occasions. And something is owing to him, a day of triumph to wipe out certain indignities, notably that of his being used as a dumb-bell by the pretty young gymnasium mistress. A story of quite another stamp is thrown in at the end, "The Brown Man's Servant," quite successful as a horror.

MARRIETTA'S MARRIAGE. By W. E. Norris. New York: D. Appleton & Co. $1.00.

If Mr. Norris had but contrived to make this same spoilt Marrietta interesting or attractive; if she had had the germs of qualities for which it would have been worth her admirers' while to have suffered as they did on her account, we should have been better pleased. We must take the story as he has given it. A restless, querulous, mean-natured, practically clever and pretty woman, born to poverty and a Bohemianism distasteful to her luxury-loving nature, is transported into an atmosphere of ease, wealth and adoration, and is none the happier therefor till she has endangered her honour, made her husband miserable, and been the indirect cause of two grim tragedies. We have no great interest or belief in her alleged reconciliation to life; but we have the highest admiration for the excellent work, both brilliant and close, which Mr. Norris has put into the story. There is a group of vividly conceived characters. There is the breath of real life in the book.

LAWRENCE CLAVERING. By A. E. W. Mason. New York: Dodd, Mead & Co. $1.25.

There is some complaint to-day, and not too much, of how historical romance-writers scamp their work, their study of a chosen period and its great figures being of the flimsiest. No such reproach can be cast at Mr. Mason's newest book. The era of the earlier Jacobite troubles has found a close investigator in him. Without ostentation he shows his grip of the facts, and even gives us a hint of what the times felt like to those who were tossed about in their strife. The story is better than its hero, who contrives to be a dull fellow, even when he is courting, making his bed on the bracken, and facing death for honour. That is, he is never personally vivid; but his long struggle with his traitor cousin and rival, his part in the northern rising, his conduct at the trial of Herbert the painter, imprisoned for him, make stirring material for a narrative, which Mr. Mason has written in an excellent style. The light sketches, too, of Bolingbroke and Derwentwater are touched by a skilful hand.

THE BOOKMAN'S TABLE.

ROBERT E. LEE AND THE SOUTHERN CONFEDERACY. (Heroes of the Nations Series.) By Henry Alexander White. New York: G. P. Putnam's Sons. $1.50.

It is as a hero rather than as a man that the author treats the great Confederate leader. Far the greater portion of the book relates to the part he took in campaigns and battles, and comparatively little is said of his private life. Small blame to the author for this, however, since he is merely obedient to the behests of tradition, which in political biography requires that a hero shall stalk and be stately, revealing always the godlike in his gait. Privately we may believe that some heroes were pleasant, human sort of people, who during those long reaches in their lives when they were not occupied in scaling Olympus or permeating posterity, talked and laughed, and loved and hated, and enjoyed themselves much in the manner of us men with little souls. But if we think so, let us keep it to ourselves, blinking and gaping the while with due reverence at each new bit of biographical statuary.

The author of this book is thoroughly Southern in his sympathies, and has a good excuse for making his hero a trifle too statuesque. He writes in a vindicating spirit, and no wonder, when we think of some of our Northern histories of a few years ago. Even now one does not have to seek far to find a man who thinks the learned Von Holst a safe repository for his historical conscience, and who regards Lee as a sincere but misguided rebel. The self-complacent magnanimity of the North must be rather more irritating than the old-time bitterness. The very fact that the patriotism of a man like Lee requires any vindication at all shows how far we are from open-mindedness. What the South needs from us is an ability to appreciate the relativity of truth. What she receives is a virtuous charity which says, "You were very bad, but we are very forgiving."

In a chapter on "Secession and Slavery," Professor White reviews the whole question of State sovereignty. It is, of course, a meagre treatment of the subject, but it is sincere and forcible and interesting. One cannot read it without wondering whether the morality of confiscation would appear quite as evident if we were the persons whose property was forfeited. As to the good points of slavery, the author remarks: "With truth, perhaps, it may be said that no other economic system before or since that time has engendered a bond of personal affection between capital and labour so strong as that established by the institution of slavery." But he adds: "Slavery was a blight upon the economic development of the South. It repressed inventive talent; it paralysed Anglo-Saxon energy, and it left hidden in the earth the South's material resources."

On the whole, the book is a fine and not exaggerated tribute to Lee, and is agreeably written in spite of a few little mannerisms. The too frequent inversion of subject and verb betrays rhetorical self-consciousness here and there. "Unto the ships of New England the slave-carrying trade was transferred after the Revolution." "Into a whirlwind of passion against slavery did the erroneous portraiture in *Uncle Tom's Cabin* begin to sweep the people of the North." But this is a small matter.

THE CAMPAIGN OF MARENGO. By Herbert H. Sargent. Chicago: A. C. McClurg & Co. $1.50.

The author of this volume is a soldier, and shows the soldier's interest in the most minute details of a campaign. Nevertheless he has the faculty of grasping the entire situation and summing up results in a clear, comprehensive manner which is refreshing to the civilian reader. In his critical power and accuracy of detail he has been compared to Mr. John C. Ropes. Of the justice of this comparison the present reviewer, not being a military historian, is unable to judge. He knows, however, that in point of clearness and the power of compelling an appreciation of the difficulties in the way of military success, Lieutenant Sargent is far superior to many of the authors of general histories. In Sloane's *Napoleon*, for instance, the battle of Marengo is described with some detail, but the impression received from it is vague and confused, and the only grounds apparent in the text for belief in the magnitude of the conflict are the author's own statements to the effect that it was a very wonderful affair. Lieutenant Sargent makes one see how great a feat Napoleon's victory was, and just what means he employed to gain it. He gives an interesting account of the massing of the Army of the Reserve at Dijon, and the devices by which this movement was kept secret. So successful was Napoleon in this concealment that the Austrian General Melas did not learn of Napoleon's passage over the Great St. Bernard until May 21st, hardly more than three weeks before the battle of Marengo, and within a few days of the battle the French captured despatches on the way from the Aulic Council to Melas telling him that the Army of the Reserve was a mere myth. All the essential details of the operations in the plain of Marengo are clearly stated, and the author shows how complete was the victory of the Austrians before the French turned the tables on them and won the day. The greater part of the French cavalry had been destroyed, most of their cannon had been captured, and only a few of their infantry organisations remained. Yet the genius of Napoleon in a few hours converted this defeat into a victory which gave him at once the greater part of Northern Italy.

Commenting on the boldness of the general plan of this campaign, the author points out the caution which Napoleon showed in the carrying out of every detail. "No commander," he says, "has ever looked with more anxiety to his lines of retreat than did this great master of war." This is true of many of Napoleon's campaigns. Even at Austerlitz, where he was so sure of success that he issued beforehand a proclamation explaining the means by which the victory would be won, he had nevertheless provided a retreat through Bohemia in case of defeat.

In the author's estimate Napoleon was the foremost soldier in the world. "The fact that he was a great organiser, a great tactician, and a great strategist is the real reason why he was so successful in war. Among all other great soldiers of the world it would be difficult to select a single one who possessed in so marked a degree all these qualities."

LETTERS TO AN UNKNOWN. By Prosper Mérimée. New York, Chicago, Washington, Paris: Brentano's. $1.25.

Among the few books that stay while many come and go is this long-lived little volume of Prosper Mérimée's. The demand for it is as staple as for sugar and cotton, and an exquisite edition, bound in pale gray and gold, has just been published by Messrs. Brentano. The preface by the translator, Henri Pène du Bois, describes the author's interesting personality, and mentions the principal facts of his well-known career. He, the translator, quotes Goncourt as saying that Mérimée talked slowly, as if he were distilling words; that as he talked he made glacial coldness fall around him; that his irony was dry, wicked, astonishing, and domineering. He, the translator, goes on, however, to tell of Goncourt's dislike of Mérimée, and adds that Hugo, Gautier, Banville, and George Sand were equally prejudiced against him.

> "He found on George Sand's table one day, while he was waiting for her in her drawing-room, a portrait of him in prose, which she had written. George Sand, half dressed, rushed into the drawing-room and tore the manuscript from his hands. He said: 'These lines are true, perhaps, but they are not flattering. I confess I am sorry I was honest, and did not steal them. I would have burned them.'"

But no reader of his *Letters to an Unknown* will accept any such estimate of the character revealed between the lines, so tender, so loyal, so profoundly pathetic to the very end, for the last letter was written two hours before his death. Of the work itself there is nothing to say that has not been said many times by the lovers of the best in literature. It is interesting, however, to be reminded by the translator that Mérimée's apartments were burned by the Communists six months after his death, and that his paintings, books, medals, manuscripts, and letters were destroyed, which is supposed to be the reason why there are no letters from the Unknown.

RICHARD WAGNER. By Houston Stewart Chamberlain. Translated from the German by G. A. Hight. London: Dent & Co.; Philadelphia: J. B. Lippincott & Co. $7.50.

This magnificent volume, which is, on the whole, the most sumptuously printed book of the season, was written in German by Mr. Chamberlain, who also contributed an introduction to the translation made by Mr. Hight. The work is not a formal life of Wagner; for, as the preface says, the biography of the subject has already been done with exhaustive minuteness by Glasenapp; but the author has made it instead a study or, as he calls it, a "picture of the great composer. It consists, first of all, of an introduction which gives a general account of the position of Wagner in the history of modern music, with a summary of the views of his critics, both friendly and unfriendly, including Nietzsche; and then of three parts, the first giving succinctly the facts of the musician's life, the second an account of his writings and teachings, with a discussion of his religious views, his art doctrine, and his philosophy and poetry, adding a bibliography of his works; the third, treating of his art works; and the fourth containing an admirable and interesting description of Bayreuth and its theatre. An appendix contains other matter collaterally related to the general subject. The book is lavishly illustrated with superb portraits in photogravure, and is supplied with facsimiles, diagrams, and other Wagneriana. We know of nothing on Wagner yet published that is so beautiful and so complete, or that would be so acceptable a gift for any cultivated person with a special taste for music.

COLUMBIA VERSE. New York: W. B. Harrison. $1.00.

This little volume contains a selection from the verses that have appeared from time to time in the undergraduate publications of Columbia University—the *Spectator*, the *Morningside*, and the *Literary Monthly*. The choice has been made with a good deal of taste and discrimination, and the result is seen in the absence of anything amateurish or really commonplace. In fact, the verse included in the book is much better than what one usually finds in the magazines, and greatly superior to the general run of minor poetry that comes in multitudinous volumes from the presses of those publishers who are always experimenting with new writers. The subjects chosen show a wide range, and the literary manners are equally varied, gliding from Austin Dobson to Kipling without turning a hair. We can give space to only one or two short specimens, and we select these as showing a very admirable degree of technical skill. The first is by Mr. Robert Jermain Cole.

> Ah, sweet but unremembered days,
> I grope for you in twilight ways,
> As loiterers scent a faint perfume,
> But know not where the flowers bloom,
> In summer haze.

And this, in a different vein, by Mr. R. H. Loines, will appeal to many a victim of the typothete:

> A poet once wrote in an ode to Spring,
> Which he sent to the *Weekly Drum*:
> "My heart it throbs with a soulful joy
> Each year when the crocuses come."
>
> Thought he, "That couplet is grave and deep;"
> But he somewhat made things hum,
> When his favourite line appeared in print,
> "Each year when the *circuses* come!"

We are glad to see Mr. Wharton's lines on the Beardsley Ass preserved here in permanent form, for the Beardsley Ass easily ranks with the Purple Cow.

PRATT PORTRAITS. By Anna Fuller. New Edition. New York: G. P. Putnam's Sons. $2.00.

Those of us who have known the Pratt family in simpler guise are glad to welcome them in the luxury of a new illustrated edition, with broad margins and decorative covers. In none of Miss Fuller's later work is there more charm and delicacy and insight into character than in these early sketches. She has brought out the individuality of each of "Old Lady Pratt's" children and grandchildren, without eliminating the strong family traits they share. Their humour is as real as their pathos, and the only times when we can at all question Miss Fuller's sincerity as an interpreter of New England human nature are the semi occasional moments when sentiment glides into sentimentality. But the privilege of softening and sweetening the types she draws should, perhaps, be accorded to an artist who gives us not photographs, but portraits.

THE BOOK MART.

FOR BOOKREADERS, BOOKBUYERS, AND BOOKSELLERS.

EASTERN LETTER.

NEW YORK, December 1, 1897.

Publications continued to be very numerous during November, and maintained a high degree of attractiveness, particularly as to bindings and illustrations, in which there are marked improvements each year.

His Grace of Osmonde, by Frances Hodgson Burnett; *The Beth Book*, by Sarah Grand, and *Lorraine*, by Robert W. Chambers, are among the most popular of the month's output of fiction, while *Seven on the Highway*, by Blanche Willis Howard; *Queen of the Jesters*, by Max Pemberton, and *The Great Stone of Sardis*, by Frank R. Stockton, are also in good demand. Other recent novels selling largely are *The Story of an Untold Love*, *In Kedar's Tents*, *Hugh Wynne*, and *Corleone*.

The new books have not, however, by any means crowded out the favourites of longer standing, and the sale of *The Choir Invisible* continues unabated, while the publication of a competitive translation and the consequent reduction in price of the authorised edition of *Quo Vadis* has increased its sale enormously.

The successful playing of *A Lady of Quality* has caused a new demand for the book, and we have no doubt that the forthcoming presentation of a dramatisation from the works of Ian Maclaren will produce a similar result with his books.

Juveniles enter very largely into the sales at this time of year. In a pictorial way such books as *The Vege-Men's Revenge*, *The Bad Child's Book of Beasts*, and *The Blackberries* are very popular. *Sir Toady Lion*, by S. R. Crockett; *Phronsie Pepper*, by Margaret Sidney, and *The Century Book of the American Revolution*, by Elbridge S. Brooks, are new titles among the leaders, while recent books of such standard juvenile authors as Henty, Munroe, Martha Finley, and Alger are much sought after by the young people.

Illustrated books are another prominent feature of holiday trade, and the Gibson, Remington, and Wenzell illustrations are selling readily. These are the only large books in demand, and seem to be the successors to the old flat or table books once so much in vogue.

Old Virginia and Her Neighbours, by John Fiske; *The Letters of Elizabeth Barrett Browning*, by Frederic G. Kenyon, both published in handsome two-volume editions, are substantial additions of the month to miscellaneous literature. Other important books likely to be in good demand are *This Country of Ours*, by Benjamin Harrison; *The Life of Gladstone*, by Justin McCarthy; and a cheap edition of Motley's *Dutch Republic*.

Birdcraft, with coloured illustrations; *Sunlight and Shadow*; *Hamlet*, illustrated by Christy; *Bird Neighbours*, with coloured plates; *Some Colonial Homesteads and Their Stories*, are among the attractive books for the holidays. The *Wenzell*, the *Smart Set*, the *Sarony*, the *Coon*, and the *Hal Hurst Calendars* are very attractive for the coming year.

The Story of Jesus Christ, by Elizabeth Stuart Phelps-Ward; *Seven Puzzling Bible Books*, by Washington Gladden; *Christian Missions and Social Progress*, by the Rev. James S. Dennis, D.D., and the new Ian Maclaren books are already among the leading books in demand on religious subjects.

Sales for November continued heavy, comparing favourably with those of previous years. The outlook for a good holiday season is bright, and nearly all classes of literature will be used.

It is difficult, after the first two or three books are selected, to determine the order of popularity, as so many books at present are selling largely. The following list, however, is practically correct:

Quo Vadis. By Henryk Sienkiewicz. $2.00.

The Choir Invisible. By James Lane Allen. $1.50.

Hugh Wynne. By S. Weir Mitchell. 2 vols. $2.00.

His Grace of Osmonde. By Frances H. Burnett. $1.50.

Soldiers of Fortune. By Richard Harding Davis. $1.50.

The Honourable Peter Stirling. By P. L. Ford. $1.50.

The Beth Book. By Sarah Grand. $1.50.

The Christian. By Hall Caine. $1.50.

Story of an Untold Love. By Paul Leicester Ford. $1.25.

Captains Courageous. By Rudyard Kipling. $1.50.

Rubáiyát of Doc Sifers. By James Whitcomb Riley. $1.50.

A Lady of Quality. By Frances H. Burnett. $1.50.

In Kedar's Tents. By Henry Seton Merriman. $1.25.

Corleone. By F. Marion Crawford. 2 vols. $2.00.

Lorraine. By R. W. Chambers. $1.25.

WESTERN LETTER.

CHICAGO, December 1, 1897.

The booksellers' harvest time is now at hand, and the trade throughout the country are busily planning to meet the annual holiday rush, that is even now commencing. Christmas means much to nearly everybody, but to no one does it mean more than to the man who deals in books, for upon a successful or unsuccessful Christmas depends whether his books will show a profit or a loss for the year. The indications are that the rush this season will be as great as ever, if not greater, for the tendency to put off holiday purchases until the last minute, so prominent a feature during the last few years, is still evident.

Country business was good during November, library orders numerous and heavy, and the local demand very encouraging. In fact, as a whole, the month's trade was quite satisfactory.

Nearly everything in the way of stock is moving well nowadays. The term "Christmas books" is often used to describe literature supposed to be suitable for Christmas gifts, but in a strict sense the expression is a misnomer, for there is scarcely a volume upon the market that is not doing duty, or has not done duty, as a Christmas book at some time or other. In fact, the odds and ends that are called for at Christmas are a source of perplexity to the dealer.

New and cheaper editions of *Quo Vadis* made their appearance last month, including a paper-covered edition of the authentic translation by Messrs. Little, Brown and Company to retail at twenty-five cents. This places a remarkable book within everybody's reach.

A notable feature of the season's output is the number of valuable works, belonging to the class of biography and memoirs, that have appeared. Justin McCarthy's *Gladstone*, Tennyson's *Memoir* by his son, *The Life of Mrs. Stowe* by Mrs. Fields, and Mrs. Browning's *Letters* are all works that should live. *Spain in the Nineteenth Century*, by Mrs. E. W. Latimer, is a very timely book in view of the prominence of that country in international affairs at present, and it is also a very valuable addition to the Spanish histories, of which the number is very small. The work is selling remarkably well.

Illustrated editions of books especially designed for holiday trade are not very numerous this year, the demand for these having been on the wane for several years. What may be lacking in number, however, is more than made up in quality by such works as Cable's *Old Creole Days*, *Quo Vadis*, *The Critical Period of American History*, *Irish Idylls*, Gibson's *London*, D'Amici's *Morocco*, and Thoreau's *Walden*.

The death of Henry George was the cause of quite a run upon his books last month, *Progress and Poverty* being the work most frequently called for.

Last month's new books make a list which has probably never been surpassed for excellence and number. Space does not permit the mention of all those which met with prompt success, in a mercantile sense, but the best of them were *Corleone*, by Marion Crawford; *His Grace of Osmonde*, by Mrs. Burnett; *The Great Stone of Sardis*, by F. R. Stockton; *Lochinvar*, by S. R. Crockett; *The General's Double*, by Captain King; *An Imperial Lover*, by M. Imlay Taylor; *Social Life in Old Virginia*, by T. N. Page; *Gondola Days*, by J. H. Smith; *Old Virginia and Her Neighbours*, by John Fiske; *Spain in the Nineteenth Century*, by Mrs. Latimer; *The Story of Jesus Christ*, by Mrs. Phelps-Ward, and *The Rubáiydt of Doc Sifers*, by J. W. Riley.

Quo Vadis, *The Choir Invisible*, and *The Christian* have led the sales for the past month, as they undoubtedly will for the year. Outside of these the book most called for at present appears to be *Hugh Wynne*.

The best-selling books of the month were the following, but there are at least fifty others which deserve mention did space allow it:

The Christian. By Hall Caine. $1.50.
The Choir Invisible. By James Lane Allen. $1.50.
Quo Vadis. By H. Sienkiewicz. $2.00.
Hugh Wynne. By S. Weir Mitchell. 2 vols. $2.00.
Spain in the Nineteenth Century. By Mrs. E. N. Latimer. $2.50.
Soldiers of Fortune. By R. H. Davis. $1.50.
Captains Courageous. By Rudyard Kipling. $1.50.
Corleone. By F. Marion Crawford. 2 vols. $2.00.
An Imperial Lover. By M. Imlay Taylor. $1.25.
The General's Double. By Captain King. $1.25.
Equality. By E. Bellamy. $1.25.
Jerome. By M. E. Wilkins. $1.50.
His Grace of Osmonde. By Mrs. Burnett. $1.50.
The Hon. Peter Stirling. By P. L. Ford. $1.50.
St. Ives. By R. L. Stevenson. $1.50.
Dariel. By R. D. Blackmore. $1.75.
In Kedar's Tents. By H. S. Merriman. $1.25.

ENGLISH LETTER.

LONDON, Oct. 25 to Nov. 20, 1897.

Whether trade can be called good or not, one thing is certain—an enormous quantity of literature is being purchased by the reading public. In years gone by such a state of things would have meant fortunes to the publishers, but competition among them and among booksellers reduces the producing and selling of books to a bare living. Coming to the state of trade, this may be said to be satisfactory, as trade goes nowadays. At the beginning of the period under review it was very good, but, as is usual, fell off as November advanced. There is little alteration to chronicle in the colonial and foreign trade, which continues to be fairly active. It would gladden the heart of the statistician could he ascertain the number of tons avoirdupois of six shilling novels that have been sold since the commencement of this now popular form of publication. It is still *the* leading line of the bookseller. *The Christian* has been the favourite of late, but has now a serious rival (from a trade standpoint) in *The Beth Book*, which is the most popular work of the moment. There does not appear to be a third novel to approach these in the number sold. There is much need for improvement in the titles of books; not orthographically (although many are far from blameless in this respect), but as regards conveying some idea, to say the least, of the nature and contents of the book. Unfortunately, in many instances the title is absolutely no guide at all in this matter, and the bookseller has little time for examining the work to discover its object and scope. A monosyllable, such as, for instance, "Max" or "Styles," is no great help in this direction. A short subtitle would, in most cases, remove the difficulty in question.

Fairy tales of various kinds are being bought freely, but it is noticeable that the older ones are being passed over this year.

There is quite a craze for children's books with illustrations of oddities—impossible, nightmare-like creatures. Tenniel's *Mock-Turtle* (see *Alice in Wonderland*) is, comparatively, a respectable combination beside some of the more recent creations.

The old English classics and plays are just now receiving considerable attention. There is a fair demand for two new editions of the *Spectator*, and for the volumes of Dent's Temple Classics and Temple Dramatists. The Waverley Novels are not selling so freely as the inquiries of a few weeks back seemed to promise. Sixpenny novels are again to the fore. Editions in this form of *John Halifax*, *Lorna Doone*, and *The Wreck of the Grosvenor* have sold in large numbers.

The long-looked-for *Queen Victoria*, by R. R. Holmes, has now been issued. The orders had, in most cases, been booked for months in advance of publication. Many of the Christmas numbers of weekly periodicals have been published during the last few days. This means a tremendous amount of cartage and packing for a small return.

The December magazines are being issued in large quantities, many of them being double or Christmas numbers, which leads in some cases to an increased sale.

Subjoined is a list of popular books. The state of affairs in India may account for the appearance here of some works; the bulk of the remainder is fiction.

The Christian. By Hall Caine. 6s.
The Beth Book. By Sarah Grand. 6s.
In Kedar's Tents. By H. S. Merriman. 6s.
The Gadfly. By E. L. Voynich. 6s.
The Sign of the Cross. By W. Barrett. 6s.
The Beetle. By R. Marsh. 6s.
Jerome. By M. E. Wilkins. 6s.
Captains Courageous. By R. Kipling. 6s.
In the Permanent Way. By F. A. Steel. 6s.
On the Face of the Waters. By F. A. Steel. 6s.
Wayfaring Men. By Edna Lyall. 6s.
At the Cross Roads. By F. F. Montresor. 6s.
What Maisie Knew. By. H. James. 6s.
The Little Minister. By J. M. Barrie. 5s.
Musical Memories. By A. M. Diehl. 6s.
The Benin Massacre. By A. Boisragon, 3s. 6d.

All about Klondike. 1s.
Pioneers of the Klondike. By M. H. E. Haynes. 3s. 6d.
Poems. By A. L. Gordon. 6s.
Liza of Lambeth. By W. S. Maugham. 3s. 6d.
Quo Vadis. By H. Sienkiewicz. 4s. 6d.
Book of Verses for Children. By E. V. Lucas. 6s.
The Jubilee Book of Cricket. By K. S. Ranjitsinhji. 6s.
Strength. By E. Sandow. 2s 6d. net.
The Potter's Wheel. By J. Watson. 3s. 6d.
The Invisible Man. By H. G. Wells. 3s. 6d.
Women of the Old Testament. By R. F. Horton. 3s. 6d.
Letters of E. B. Browning. 2 vols. 15s. net.
Another's Burden. By J. Payn. 3s. 6d.
Baboo Jabberjee. By F. Anstey. 3s. 6d.
Under the Red Crescent. By C. Ryan. 9s.
Twelve Indian Statesmen. By G. Smith. 10s. 6d.
Forty-One Years in India. By Lord Roberts. 36s.

SALES OF BOOKS DURING THE MONTH.

New books in order of demand, as sold between November 1, 1897, and December 1, 1897.

We guarantee the authenticity of the following lists as supplied to us, each by leading booksellers in the towns named.

NEW YORK, UPTOWN.

1. His Grace of Osmonde. By Burnett. $1.50. (Scribner.)
2. The Beth Book. By Grand. $1.50. (Appleton.)
3. London as Seen by C. D. Gibson. $5.00. (Scribner.)
4. Letters to an Unknown. By Merimée. $1.25. (Brentanos.)
5. Yankee Ships and Yankee Sailors. By Barnes. $1.50. (Macmillan)
6. Gondola Days. By Smith. $1.50. (Houghton, Mifflin & Co.)

NEW YORK, DOWNTOWN.

1. Hugh Wynne. By Mitchell $2.00. (Century Co.)
2. The Christian. By Caine. $1.50. (Appleton.)
3. In Kedar's Tents. By Merriman. $1.50. (Dodd, Mead & Co.)
4. Quo Vadis. By Sienkiewicz. $2.00 and $1.00. (Little, Brown & Co.)
5. Story of an Untold Love. By Ford. $1.25. (Houghton, Mifflin & Co.)
6. The Choir Invisible. By Allen. $1.50. (Macmillan.)

ATLANTA, GA.

1. Story of an Untold Love. By Ford. $1.25. (Houghton, Mifflin & Co.)
2. The Kentuckians. By Fox. $1.25. (Harper.)
3. Quo Vadis. By Sienkiewicz. $2.00. (Little, Brown & Co.)
4. The Christian. By Caine. $1.50. (Appleton.)
5. Hon. Peter Stirling. By Ford. $1.50. (Holt.)
6. Smoking Flax. By Rives. 50 cts. (Neely.)

BOSTON, MASS.

1. Quo Vadis. By Sienkiewicz. $2.00. (Little, Brown & Co.)
2. Alfred, Lord Tennyson. By His Son. $10.00 net. (Macmillan.)
3. Letters of Mrs. Browning. Edited by Kenyon. $4.00. (Macmillan.)
4. Farthest North. By Nansen. $10.00. (Harper.)
5. Hugh Wynne. By Mitchell. $2.00. (Century Co.)
6. Captains Courageous. By Kipling. $1.50. (Century Co.)

CHICAGO, ILL.

1. Spain in the Nineteenth Century. By Latimer. $2.50. (McClurg & Co.)
2. The Christian. By Caine. $1.50. (Appleton.)
3. The Choir Invisible. By Allen. $1.50. (Macmillan.)
4. Quo Vadis. By Sienkiewicz. $2.00. (Little, Brown & Co.)
5. An Imperial Lover. By Taylor. $1.25. (McClurg & Co.)
6. Hugh Wynne. By Mitchell. $2.00. (Century Co.)

CINCINNATI, O.

1. Hugh Wynne. By Mitchell. $2.00. (Century Co.)
2. Quo Vadis. By Sienkiewicz. $2.00. (Little, Brown & Co.)
3. In Kedar's Tents. By Merriman. $1.25. (Dodd, Mead & Co.)
4. The Choir Invisible. By Allen. $1.50. (Macmillan.)
5. The Beth Book. By Grand. $1.50. (Appleton.)
6. His Grace of Osmonde. By Burnett. $1.50. (Scribner.)

DETROIT, MICH.

1. Hugh Wynne. By Mitchell. $2.00. (Century Co.)
2. Story of an Untold Love. By Ford. $1.25. (Houghton, Mifflin & Co.)
3. Dariel. By Blackmore. $1.75. (Dodd, Mead & Co.)
4. The Choir Invisible. By Allen. $1.50. (Macmillan.)
5. Farthest North. By Nansen. $10.00. (Harper.)
6. Alfred, Lord Tennyson. By His Son. $10.00. (Macmillan.)

INDIANAPOLIS, IND.

1. Chimes from a Jester's Bells. By Burdette. $1.25. (Bowen-Merrill Co.)
2. Roach & Co. By Fuller. $1.25. (Bowen-Merrill Co.)
3. Corleone. By Crawford. $2.00. (Macmillan.
4. The Choir Invisible. By Allen. $1.50. (Macmillan.)
5. The Christian. By Caine. $1.50. (Appleton)
6. Down Our Way. By Judah. $1.25. (Way & Williams.)

KANSAS CITY, MO.

1. Quo Vadis. By Sienkiewicz. $2.00. (Little, Brown & Co.)
2. The Christian. By Caine. $1.50. (Appleton.)
3. In Kedar's Tents By Merriman. $1.25. (Dodd, Mead & Co.)
4. St. Ives. By Stevenson. $1.50. (Scribner.)
5. Hugh Wynne. By Mitchell. $2.00. (Century Co.)
6. Virginia and Her Neighbours. By Fiske. $4.00. (Houghton, Mifflin & Co)

LOS ANGELES, CAL.

1. Hugh Wynne. By Mitchell. $2.00. (Century.)
2. The Christian. By Caine. $1.50. (Appleton.)
3. The Choir Invisible. By Allen. $1.50. (Harper.)
4. St. Ives. By Stevenson. $1.50. (Scribner.)
5. Quo Vadis. By Sienkiewicz. $2.00. (Little, Brown & Co.)
6. Captains Courageous. By Kipling. $1.50. (Century Co.)

LOUISVILLE, KY.

1. The Kentuckians. By Fox. $1.25. (Harper.)
2. Quo Vadis. By Sienkiewicz. $2.00. (Little, Brown & Co.)
3. The Story of an Untold Love. By Ford. $1.25. (Houghton, Mifflin & Co.)
4. The Christian. By Caine. $1.50. (Appleton.)
5. The Choir Invisible. By Allen. $1.50. (Macmillan.)
6. Hugh Wynne. By Mitchell. $2.00. (Century Co.)

MONTREAL, CANADA.

1. The Habitant. By Drummond. $1.25. (Putnam.)
2. Quo Vadis. By Sienkiewicz. $1.50. (Morang.)
3. With Frederick the Great. By Henty. $1.50. (Blackie.)
4. With Moore at Corunna. By Henty. $1.50. (Blackie.)
5. A March on London. By Henty. $1.50. (Blackie.)
6. Wayfaring Men. By Lyall. $1.50. (Longmans.)

NEW ORLEANS, LA.

1. In Kedar's Tents. By Merriman. $1.25. (Dodd, Mead & Co.)
2. Diana Victrix. By Converse. $1.25. (Houghton, Mifflin & Co.)
3. The Christian. By Caine. $1.50. (Appleton.)
4. Story of an Untold Love. By Ford. $1.25. (Houghton, Mifflin & Co.)
5. Corleone. By Crawford. $2.00. (Macmillan.)
6. Hugh Wynne. By Mitchell. $2.00. (Century Co.)

PHILADELPHIA, PA.

1. Quo Vadis. By Sienkiewicz. $2.00. (Little, Brown & Co.)
2. The Choir Invisible. By Allen. $1.50. (Macmillan.)
3. In Kedar's Tents. By Merriman. $1.25. (Dodd, Mead & Co.)
4. St. Ives. By Stevenson. $1.50. (Scribner.)
5. Dariel. By Blackmore. $1.75. (Dodd, Mead & Co.)
6. Story of an Untold Love. By Ford. $1.25. (Houghton, Mifflin & Co.)

PITTSBURG, PA.

1. Hugh Wynne. By Mitchell. $2.00. (Century Co.)
2. Captains Courageous. By Kipling. $1.50. (Century Co.)
3. The Latimers. By McCook. $1.50. (Jacobs.)
4. Story of an Untold Love. By Ford. $1.25. (Houghton, Mifflin & Co.)
5. Prisoner of Zenda. By Hope. 75 cts. (Holt.)
6. Dariel. By Blackmore. $1.75. (Dodd, Mead & Co.)

PORTLAND, ME.

1. Quo Vadis. By Sienkiewicz. $2.00. (Little, Brown & Co.)
2. The Christian. By Caine. $1.50. (Appleton.)
3. The Choir Invisible. By Allen. $1.25. (Macmillan.)
4. Jerome. By Wilkins. $1.25. (Harper.)
5. A Forest Orchid. By Higginson. $1.50. (Macmillan.)
6. The Massarenes. By Ouida. $1.25. (Fenno.)

ROCHESTER, N. Y.

1. Hugh Wynne. By Mitchell. $2.00. (Century Co.)
2. Quo Vadis. By Sienkiewicz. $2.00. (Little, Brown & Co.)
3. Captains Courageous. By Kipling. $1.50. (Century Co.)
4. The Christian. By Caine. $1.50. (Appleton.)
5. The Choir Invisible. By Allen. $1.50. (Macmillan.)
6. St. Ives. By Stevenson. $1.50. (Scribner.)

SALT LAKE CITY, UTAH.

1. Quo Vadis. By Sienkiewicz. $2.00. (Little, Brown & Co.)
2. The Christian. By Caine. $1.50. (Appleton.)
3. The Choir Invisible. By Allen. $1.50. (Macmillan.)
4. Soldiers of Fortune. By Davis. $1.50. (Scribner.)
5. Equality. By Bellamy. $1.25. (Appleton)
6. The Honourable Peter Stirling. By Ford. $1.50. (Holt.)

SAN FRANCISCO, CAL.

1. Wild Flowers of California. By Parsons-Buck. $2.00. (Doxey.)
2. Idle Hours in a Library. By Hudson. $1.25. (Doxey.)
3. Quo Vadis. By Sienkiewicz. $2.00. (Little, Brown & Co.)
4. Captains Courageous. By Kipling. $1.50. (Century Co.)
5. The Choir Invisible. By Allen. $1.50. (Macmillan.)
6. The Christian. By Caine. $1.50. (Appleton.)

ST. LOUIS, MO.

1. The Christian. By Caine. $1.50. (Appleton.)
2. Captains Courageous. By Kipling. $1.50 (Century Co.)
3. St. Ives. By Stevenson. $1.50. (Scribner.)
4. In Kedar's Tents. By Merriman. $1.25. (Dodd, Mead & Co.)
5. Hugh Wynne. By Mitchell. $2.00. (Century Co.)
6. Quo Vadis. By Sienkiewicz. $2.00. (Little, Brown & Co.)

ST. PAUL, MINN.

1. The Choir Invisible. By Allen. $1.50. (Macmillan.)
2. St. Ives. By Stevenson. $1.50. (Scribner.)
3. Hugh Wynne. By Mitchell. $2.00. (Century Co.)
4. Corleone. By Crawford. $2.00. (Macmillan.)
5. Story of an Untold Love. By Ford. $1.25. (Houghton, Mifflin & Co.)
6. Lochinvar. By Crockett. $1.50. (Harper.)

TOLEDO, O.

1. The Christian. By Caine. $1.50. (Appleton.)
2. Hugh Wynne. By Mitchell. $2.00. (Century Co.)
3. The Choir Invisible. By Allen. $1.50. (Macmillan.)
4. Quo Vadis. By Sienkiewicz. $2.00. (Little, Brown & Co.)
5. Jerôme. By Wilkins. $1.50. (Harper.)
6. Equality. By Bellamy. $1.25. (Appleton.)

TORONTO, CANADA.

1. * Quo Vadis. By Sienkiewicz. 75 cts. and $1.50. (Little, Brown & Co.)
2. * St. Ives. By Stevenson. 75 cts. and $1.25. (Copp-Clark Co.)
3. † Farthest North. By Nansen. $1.50 and $2.00 set. (Macmillan.)
4. Captains Courageous. By Kipling. $1.50. (Century Co.)
5. Dariel. By Blackmore. $1.75. (Dodd, Mead & Co.)
6. The Choir Invisible. By Allen $1.50. (Macmillan.)

TORONTO, CANADA.

1. St. Ives. By Stevenson. Paper, 75 cts.; cloth, $1.25. (The Copp-Clark Co., Limited.)
2. Dariel. By Blackmore. Paper, 75 cts.; cloth, $1.25. (The Copp Clark Co., Limited.)
3. Prisoners of the Sea. By Kingsley. Paper, 75 cts.; cloth, $1.25. (The Copp-Clark Co., Limited.)
4. His Grace of Osmonde. By Burnett. Paper, 75 cts.; cloth, $1.25. (The Copp-Clark Co., Limited.)
5. Wayfaring Men. By Lyall. Paper, 75 cts.; cloth, $1.25. (The Copp-Clark Co., Limited.)
6. Corleone. By Crawford. Cloth, 2 vols., $2.00. (The Copp-Clark Co., Limited.)

WACO, TEX.

1. Dariel. By Blackmore. $1.75. (Dodd, Mead & Co.)
2. On the Face of the Waters. By Steel. $1.50. (Macmillan.)
3. Captains Courageous. By Kipling. $1.50. (Century Co.)
4. The Christian. By Caine. $1.50. (Appleton.)
5. In Kedar's Tents. By Merriman. $1.25. (Dodd, Mead & Co.)
6. Quo Vadis. By Sienkiewicz. $2.00. (Little, Brown & Co.)

WORCESTER, MASS.

1. Hugh Wynne. By Mitchell. 2 vols. $2.00. (Century Co.)
2. Corleone. By Crawford. 2 vols. $2.00. (Macmillan.)
3. Alfred, Lord Tennyson. By His Son. 2 vols. $10.00 net. (Macmillan.)
4. In Kedar's Tents. By Merriman. $1.25. (Dodd, Mead & Co.)
5. Letters of Elizabeth Barrett Browning. Edited by Kenyon. 2 vols. $4.00. (Macmillan.)
6. Dariel. By Blackmore. $1.75. (Dodd, Mead & Co.)

* Canadian copyrights.
† Colonial Libraries.

THE BEST SELLING BOOKS.

According to the foregoing lists, the six books which have sold best in order of demand during the month are—

1. Quo Vadis. By Sienkiewicz.
2. The Choir Invisible. By Allen.
3. The Christian. By Caine.
4. Hugh Wynne. By Mitchell.
5. In Kedar's Tents. By Merriman.
6. Captains Courageous. By Kipling.

BOOKS RECEIVED.

W. L. ALLISON CO., New York.

Poor but Plucky; or, The Mystery of a Flood.
The Missing Tin Box, by Arthur M. Winfield.
The Young Auctioneers, by Edward Stratemeyer.

D. APPLETON & CO., New York.

Industrial Freedom, by David MacGregor Means.
Uncle Robert's Geography, edited by Francis W. Parker.
The Beth Book, by Sarah Grand.
The Freedom of Henry Meredyth, by M. Hamilton.
Miss Providence, by Dorothea Gerard.
At the Cross-Roads, by F. F. Montrésor.
A History of Dancing, from the earliest ages to our own times, from the French of Gaston Vuillier.
Punctuation, by F. Horace Teall.
Scientific Aspects of Christian Evidences, by G. Frederick Wright.
Bird-Life, by Frank M. Chapman.

EDWARD ARNOLD, New York.

Autobiography and Letters of Rt. Hon. J. A. Roebuck, by R. Eadon Leader.
More Beasts (For Worse Children). Verses by H. B. Pictures by B. T. B.

RICHARD G. BADGER & CO., Boston.

The Right Side of the Car, by John Uri Lloyd.

THE BAKER & TAYLOR CO., New York.

Oriental Days, by Lucia A. Palmer.

BENZIGER BROTHERS, New York.

Blossoms of the Cross, by Emmy Giehrl.
Aser, the Shepherd, by Marion Ames Taggart.
Bezaleel, by Marion Ames Taggart.
Illustrated Life of the Blessed Virgin, by Rev. B. Rohner, O.S.B.

J. W. BOUTON, New York.

The Private Library, by Arthur L. Humphreys.

BRENTANO'S, New York.

Colonial Verses (Mount Vernon), by Ruth Lawrence. Illustrated.

THE BURROWS BROS. CO., Cleveland.

The Jesuit Relations and Allied Documents, vol. ix.

Songs of Liberty, and Other Poems, by Robert Underwood Johnson.
Java, the Garden of the East, by E. R. Scidmore.
Impressions of South Africa, by James Bryce.
Forty-six Years in the Army, by Lieutenant-General John M. Schofield.
The Story of Marie Antoinette, by Anna L. Bicknell.

H. T. COATES & CO., Philadelphia.

Songs of Flying Hours, by Edward Willard Watson.

WILLIAM G. COLESWORTHY, Boston.

The White Ship, A Little Book of Poems, selected from the works of Dante Gabriel Rossetti.

COPELAND & DAY, Boston.

Victory, by Hannah Parker Kimball.
Vivette; or, The Memoirs of the Romance Association, by Gelett Burgess.
Middleway, by Kate Whiting Patch.
Out of the Silence, by John Vance Cheney.
Harvard Episodes, by Charles Nacomb Flandrau.
One Way to the Woods, by Evaleen Stein.
Shadows, by M. A. De Wolfe Howe.

T. Y. CROWELL & CO., Boston.

The Self-Made Man in American Life, by Grover Cleveland.
General Grant's Letters to a Friend, 1860–80, with Introduction and Notes by James Grant Wilson.

DODD, MEAD & CO., New York.

Success and Failure, by R. F. Horton.
Stories of Famous Operas, by H. A. Guerber.
Pictures from the Life of Nelson, by W. Clark Russell.
Victorian Literature, by Clement K. Shorter.
Portraits and Silhouettes of Musicians, by Camille Bellaigue.
A Lonely Little Lady, by Dolf Wyllarde.
Lumen, by Camille Flammarion.
A Daughter of Strife, by Jane H. Findlater.
A Spanish Maid, by L. Quiller Couch.
Over the Hills, by Mary Findlater.
Untold Tales of the Past, by Beatrice Harraden.
Hamlet, illustrations by H. C. Christy.

DOUBLEDAY & MCCLURE CO., New York.

Tales of the Real Gypsy, by Paul Kester.
Tales from *McClure's*.

WILLIAM DOXEY, San Francisco.

Yermah the Dorado, by Frona Eunice Wait.
The Voice of the Valley, by Yone Noguchi.
Petrarch, and Other Essays, by Timothy H. Reardon.
Idle Hours in a Library, by William Henry Hudson.
Sonnets of Heredia, Done into English by Edward Robeson Taylor.

E. P. DUTTON & CO., New York.

Hepworth Year Book.

EDITOR PUBLISHING CO., Cincinnati.

The Secret of Hamlet, Prince of Denmark, by South G. Preston
Some Common Birds, by P. M. Silloway.

R. F. FENNO & CO., New York.

The Dagger and the Cross, by Joseph Hatton.
Ramuntcho, by Pierre Loti.
Defiant Hearts, by W. Heimburg Translated by Annie W. Ayer and H. T. Slate.

FOREST & STREAM PUBLISHING CO., New York.

Men I Have Fished With, by Fred Mather.

FOWLER & WELLS CO., New York.

A Manual of Mental Science, by Jessie A. Fowler.

FUNK & WAGNALLS, New York.

The Reader's Shakespeare, by David Charles Bell. Vol. III., Comedia.

GINN & CO., Boston.

Specimens of Pre-Shakesperian Drama, by John Matthews Manly. Vol. I.
Poems by Wordsworth, a selection edited by Edward Dowden.
Selections from Morte D'Arthur, edited by William Edward Mead.
Annotated English Classics, Tennyson's The Princess, edited with introduction and notes by Albert S Cook.

HARPER & BROTHERS, New York.

The Great Stone of Sardis, by Frank R. Stockton.
The Shepherd's Calendar.
The Kentuckians, by John Fox, Jr.
Lochinvar, by S. R. Crockett.
School Boy Life in England, by John Corbin.
"All Hands," Pictures of Life in the United States Navy, by Rufus Fairchild Zogbaum.

FRANCIS P. HARPER, New York.

Early Long Island Wills of Suffolk County, 1691–1703, by William S. Pelletreau, A.M.

E. R. HERRICK & CO, New York.

The Old House, and Other Poems and Sketches, by Grace Duffie Boylan.
Brokenburne, by Virginia Frazer Boyle. Illustrated by William Henry Walker.
Childhood's Songs of Long Ago, with picturings by Blanche McManus.

HOUGHTON, MIFFLIN & CO., Boston.

The Juggler, by Charles Egbert Craddock.
Gondola Days, by F. Hopkinson Smith.
Seven Puzzling Bible Books, by Washington Gladden.
Old Virginia and Her Neighbours, 2 vols., by John Fiske.
The Critical Period in American History, 1783–89, illustrated holiday edition, by John Fiske.
Thoreau, Walden, illustrated edition.
Evangeline, Longfellow, illustrated holiday edition.
The Complete Poetical Works of Robert Burns, Cambridge Edition.
The Story of Jesus Christ, by Elizabeth Stuart Phelps.
Life and Letters of Harriet Beecher Stowe, edited by Annie Fields.
The Westward Movement, by Justin Winsor.
Poole's Index to Periodical Literature. Vol. IV., 1892–96.

Hudson-Kimberly Publishing Co., Kansas City.

Trialogues, by William Griffith.

George W. Jacobs & Co., Philadelphia.

Reasons for the Higher Criticism of the Hexateuch, by Rev. Isaac Gibson.

A Dear Little Girl, by Amy E. Blanchard.

The Latimers, by Henry Christopher McCook.

The J. M. W. Jones Stationery & Printing Co., Chicago.

We Mortals, a Play in Three Acts, by M. Salmonsen.

Charles H. Kerr & Co., Chicago.

Chalk Lines Over Morals, by Rev. Charles Caverno.

Wilbur B. Ketcham, New York.

Thou Remainest, by E. S. Elliot.

Wonderful Gifts, by Frances Ridley Havergal.

For All and for Each, by James Stalker, D.D.

Home Making, by Ian Maclaren.

Laird & Lee, Chicago.

Won by a Woman, by Edmondo De Amicis and translated by Signor Mantellini.

Lamson, Wolffe & Co., Boston.

Don Luis's Wife, a Romance of the West Indies, by Lillian Hinman Shuey.

Threads of Life, by Clara Sherwood Rollins.

John Lane, The Bodley Head, New York.

The Happy Exile, by H. D. Lowry.

New Essays Toward a Critical Method, by John M. Robertson.

The Coming of Love, by Theodore Watts-Dunton.

The Fairy Changeling, and Other Poems, by Dora Sigerson.

The Earth Breath, and Other Poems, by A. E.

Lee and Shepard, Boston.

The District School as It Was, By One Who Went to It, edited by Clifton Johnson.

Her Place in the World, by Amanda M. Douglas.

An Oregon Boyhood, by Louis Albert Banks.

The Happy Six, by Penn Shirley.

The Spinning-Wheel at Rest Poems by Edward Augustus Jenks.

Dorothy Draycott's To-morrows, by Virginia F. Townsend.

J. B. Lippincott Co., Philadelphia.

The General's Double, by Captain Charles King.

King Washington, a Romance, by Adelaide Skeel and William H. Brearley.

Three Pretty Maids, by Amy E. Blanchard.

Other People's Lives, by Rosa Nouchette Carey.

Little, Brown & Co , Boston.

Quo Vadis, by Sienkiewicz, illustrated edition, 2 vols.

Let us Follow Him, by Sienkiewicz.

Longmans, Green & Co., New York.

Wordsworth, by Andrew Lang.

Dreams and Ghosts, by Andrew Lang.

Iva Kildare, by L. B. Walford.

Rampolli, Translations New and Old, Chiefly from the German, by George MacDonald.

Wellington, His Comrades and Contemporaries, by Major A. Griffiths.

The Macmillan Co., New York

On Heroes, Hero-Worship, and The Heroic in History, by Thomas Carlyle.

Nature Study in Elementary Schools, by Mrs. Lucy L. W. Wilson, Ph.D.

William the Silent, by Frederic Harrison.

Yankee Ships and Yankee Sailors, by James Barnes.

The Life of Gladstone, by Justin McCarthy.

The Old Santa Fé Trail, the Story of a Great Highway, by Colonel Henry Inman.

Charles the Great, by Thomas Hodgkin, D.C.L.

The Life and Letters of Elizabeth Barrett Browning, edited by F. C. Kenyon.

Book of Old English Love Songs, with an introduction by Hamilton Wright Mabie and decorative drawings by George Wharton Edwards.

Poetical Works of Elizabeth Barrett Browning, with Portrait.

Maynard, Merrill & Co., New York.

Maynard's English Classic Series, The Princess, by Alfred, Lord Tennyson.

A. C. McClurg & Co., New York.

Men in Epigram, compiled by Frederick W. Morton.

Poems, by Henry D. Muir.

A Group of French Critics, by Mary Fisher.

With a Pessimist in Spain, by Mary F. Nixon.

The Lovers' Shakespeare, compiled by Chloe Blakeman Jones.

Spain in the Nineteenth Century, by Elizabeth Wormeley Latimer.

Thoughts and Theories of Life and Education, by H. L Spalding.

An Imperial Lover, by M. Imlay-Taylor.

Christianity the World Religion, by John Henry Barrows.

George Munro's Sons, New York.

Facts and Fakes about Cuba.

F. Tennyson Neely, New York.

Through Field and Fallow, by Jean Hooper Page.

The Invasion of New York, by J. H. Palmer.

The Strolling Piper of Brittany, by John W. Harding.

The Tragedy of Ages, by Mrs. Isabella M. Witherspoon.

The Peter Paul Book Co., Buffalo, N. Y.

The Chatelaine, by G. E. X.

Folly's Bells, a German Legend, by Anne Gardner Hale, illustrations by Lillian Hale.

G. P. Putnam's Sons, New York.

The American College in American Life, by Charles Franklin Thwing.

Anarchism, by E. V. Zenker.

Poetical Sermons and the Ballad of Plymouth Church, by William E. Davenport.

Historic New York, Being the First Series of the Half Moon Papers, edited by Maud Wilder Goodwin, Alice Carrington Royce, and Ruth Putnam.

Nullification and Secession in the United States, by Edward Payson Powell.

The Cruikshank Fairy Book.
The Man of Last Resort, or the Clients of Randolph Mason, by Melville Davisson Post.
The Central Italian Painters of the Renaissance, by Bernhard Berenson.
Pendennis, by W. M. Thackeray, illustrations by Chris. Hammond.
Shirley, by Charlotte Brontë, illustrations by F. H. Townsend.
The Venetian Painters of the Renaissance, by Bernhard Berenson. With twenty-four photogravure illustrations.
Ambroise Paré and His Times, 1510–90, by Stephen Paget.
The Protestant Faith; or, Salvation by Belief, by Dwight H. Olmstead.
Washington, a National Epic in Six Cantos, by Edward Johnson Runk.
On Blue Water, by Edmonde De Amicis, translated by Jacob B. Brown, illustrated.
The Habitant, and Other French Canadian Poems, by William Henry Drummond, M.D.
The Story of the Palatines, by Sanford H. Cobb.
The Cid Campeador, by H. Butler Clarke, M.A.
Teaching as a Business, by C. W. Bardeen.

RAND, MCNALLY & CO., Chicago.

A Colonial Dame, by Laura Dayton Fessenden.
The Sinner, by Rita.

ROBERTS BROTHERS, Boston.

Andronike, the Heroine of the Greek Revolution, by Stephanos Theodoros Xenos, translated from the original Greek by Edwin A. Grosvenor.
Antichrist, by Ernest Renan, translated and edited by Joseph Henry Allen.
The Quest of Happiness, by Philip Gilbert Hamerton.
Molière, VI. Translated by Katharine Prescott Wormeley.
The Christ of Yesterday, To-day, and Forever, by Ezra Hoyt Byington.

ROYCROFT PRINTING SHOP, East Aurora, N. Y.

On the Heights, a volume of verse by Lucius Harwood Foote.

R. H. RUSSELL, New York.

The Dumpies, by Frank Ver-Beck and Albert Bigelow Paine.
An Almanac of Twelve Sports, by William Nicholson, with words by Rudyard Kipling.

SCOTT, FORESMAN & CO., Chicago.

Principles of Vocal Expression, by William B. Chamberlain, A.M., and S. H. Clark, Ph.B.
A Parliamentary Syllabus, by Joseph T. Robert.

CHARLES SCRIBNER'S SONS, New York.

Mrs. Knollys, and Other Stories, by F. J. Stimson.
The First Christmas Tree, by Henry Van Dyke, illustrated by Howard Pyle.
Old Creole Days, by George W. Cable, illustrated by Albert Herter.
A Capital Courtship, by Alexander Black.
The Works of James Whitcomb Riley, Neighbourly Poems and Dialect Sketches. Vol. I.
Cinderella, and Other Stories, by Richard Harding Davis. New Edition.
Gallagher, and Other Stories, by Richard Harding Davis. New Edition.
His Grace of Osmonde, by Frances Hodgson Burnett.
London as Seen by Charles Dana Gibson.
Kirkcaldy of Grange, by Louis A. Barbé, Famous Scot Series.
Waverley; or, 'Tis Sixty Years Since, by Sir Walter Scott, 2 vols. Temple Edition.
Frederick the Great, by Thomas Carlyle, Vols. I. and II.
Taken by Siege, by Jeannette L. Gilder.
Gloria Victis, by J. A. Mitchell.
Social Life in Old Virginia before the War, by Thomas Nelson Page.
Lullaby-Land, by Eugene Field.

FREDERICK A. STOKES CO., New York.

Collection of Masterpieces, Oliver Goldsmith, She Stoops to Conquer.
Fairy Tales, by Thomas Dunn English.
The Second Book of Nursery Rhymes, set to music by Joseph Moorat, pictured by Paul Woodroffe.
Sir Toady Lion, by S. R. Crockett.
Little Homespun, by Ruth Ogden, with numerous original illustrations by Mabel Humphrey.
Lucile, by Owen Meredith, with twelve facsimiles of water colours by Madeleine Lemaire and one hundred illustrations in black and white by C. McCormick Rogers.
Lucile, edition de luxe of the same.
The School for Saints, by John Oliver Hobbes.

H. S. STONE & CO., Chicago.

The Fourth Napoleon, by Charles Benham.

THE TEMPLE PUBLISHING CO., Denver, Col.

The Living Christ, by Paul Tyner.

FREDERICK WARNE & CO., New York.

Mona St. Claire, by Annie E. Armstrong.
The One-Eyed Griffin, and Other Fairy Tales, by Herbert E. Inman.
In Spite of Fate, by Silas K. Hocking.
Icelandic Fairy Tales, translated and edited by Mrs. A. W. Hall.
George Malcolm, by Gabriel Setoun.

WAY & WILLIAMS, Chicago.

Like a Gallant Lady, by Kate M. Cleary.
The Teacup Club, by Elisa Armstrong.
Pippins and Cheese, by Elia W. Beattie.
The Muses Up to Date, by Henrietta Dexter Field and Roswell Martin Field.
A Night in Acadie, by Kate Chopin.
Down Our Way, by Mary Jameson Judah.
A Book of True Lovers, by Octave Thanet.
The Enchanted Burro, by Charles F. Lummis.
Mother Goose in Prose, by L Frank Baum.

THOMAS WHITTAKER, New York.

St. Francis of Assisi, by Knox Little.
The Facts and the Faith, by Beverley E. Warner, D.D.
The Message and the Messengers, by Fleming James.
Lessons from Life, with an introduction by Rev. Hugh Macmillan, LL.D.
History of the Episcopal Church, by S. D. McConnell, D.D., D.C.L. 2 vols.

THE BOOKMAN

A LITERARY JOURNAL.

VOL. VI. FEBRUARY, 1898. No. 6.

CHRONICLE AND COMMENT.

The Editors of THE BOOKMAN *cannot undertake to return rejected manuscripts, whether stamps are enclosed or not; and to this rule no exception will be made.*

At the suggestion of the editor of the *Youth's Companion*, of Boston, Mr. Bret Harte has recently completed the manuscript of an autobiographical sketch, entitled "How I Went to the Mines."

Mr. Frank R. Stockton is writing a new serial story for publication in one of the Messrs. Harper's weekly periodicals. It is at present entitled *The Associate Hermits*, and will, we understand, be published simultaneously in a London weekly.

We learn that the sales of Mr. S. R. Crockett's new book for children, *Sir Toady Lion*, are, considering the time it has been before the public, far ahead of the large number which was sold of his delightful *Sweetheart Travellers*.

Mr. Howe's article on Whittier and Lowell in the series of American Bookmen which should have appeared in this number has been held over until next month.

Mr. R. D. Blackmore holds to a considerable extent his place in the favour of the reading public, and the sales of his latest book, *Dariel*, have been larger than might be easily believed. Among novelists of his period he undoubtedly sells best.

It is announced that Max Müller's volume of reminiscences, reprinted from *Cosmopolis*, will be called *Auld Lang Syne*. This recalls the title of Ian Maclaren's second book, *The Days of Auld Lang Syne*. A novel was published many years ago by Mr. Clark Russell under the title *Auld Lang Syne*. It is not probable that either Ian Maclaren or Mr. Clark Russell will do anything to prevent Professor Müller's use of the title.

Readers evidently very much prefer to have their stories complete. Mr. Stevenson's *St. Ives* is by no means so able a book as *Weir of Hermiston*, yet it has been singularly successful in book form, with the continuation by Mr. Quiller Couch.

We understand that Mr. Rudyard Kipling proposes to stay in South Africa for four months, and that he means to take a holiday, and to do no literary work of any kind. He will be accompanied by his father, Mr. J. Lockwood Kipling.

It has now been arranged that Mr. Kipling's new volume of stories shall not be published, as at first contemplated, in the spring of this year. The book will be held over until September or October. The volume will contain, among other stories, "Bread Upon the Waters," and that delightful beast story, "The Maltese Cat." We have always felt that had "The Maltese Cat" been a jungle beast, this story would have taken a very prominent place in one or other of the *Jungle Books*.

The story goes that an enterprising American magazine editor lately instructed his English representative to obtain, through the Archbishop of Canterbury, "A live, brainy article" on home-life in the Vatican from the Pope. Presumably this is the same editor who some months ago returned a manuscript on the life of Christ to Mrs. Phelps-Ward with the answer: "It won't do; what we want is a 'snappy' life of Christ." Mrs. Phelps-Ward's manuscript, since published as *The Story of Jesus Christ*, is finding a wide appreciation. Over fifteen thousand copies have been sold within three months.

❀

The scene of Mr. Rider Haggard's recently completed story, *Elissa*, is laid in the centre of Africa about 3000 B.C. The serial rights of the story have been purchased by the proprietors of a new weekly, the first number of which it is expected will see the light in the early part of this month.

❀

Mr. Austin Dobson reached his forty-eighth year on January 18th. Few writers of our day have so rooted an objection to the intrusion of their personality in any public form as Mr. Dobson, and only a few weeks ago he could say that he had never been interviewed. During a recent Saturday afternoon talk with a contributor to THE BOOKMAN he spoke of this reticence, and said that in writing he has never been preoccupied by anything more than the desire to produce good work, though there are many subjects which he should instinctively refrain from treating at all. "If, as a whole, what I have done does not make for harmless pleasure, sympathy with humanity and things honest and of good report, it has missed its meaning. This is what I have tried to express in 'In After Days.'" Among the few personal pieces in the whole of his *Collected Poems*, recently issued in England, are the dedication, the stanzas "To One Who Bids me Sing," and the concluding rondeau, "In After Days." This new collected edition may be accepted now as practically final if we take the poet's word for it. "After five and-forty," he says, "a writer of familiar verse usually feels that he has said about all he can well say in that form, and in my judgment, unless he strike out an altogether new line, he had far better be silent. No doubt I shall still write pieces occasionally, but certainly the bulk of my verse is done."

❀

The record of Mr. Dobson's life, so far as it is of public interest, must be sought in his work. He quoted as applicable to his own case the sentence from Montaigne which, written in Mr. Dobson's ordinary handwriting, is given below. For the last forty-one years he has spent his days at the Board of Trade, and for nearly thirty of them has devoted his evenings to literary work. On returning from Whitehall, his usual habit after dinner is to read or listen to music until about ten o'clock, when he retires to his study and works until midnight. A Government office is not precisely a bed of roses, and he regards his literary work as recreation. One would imagine, from Mr. Dobson's poetry, that such prosaic work as that of the Board of Trade would be altogether foreign to his taste, and on inquiring whether he had never been tempted to relinquish his position there and devote himself entirely to literature he responded: "No; the one occupation balances the other in a very satisfactory and agreeable manner. Business habits are useful—even to a literary man."

❀

It was in *Temple Bar* that Mr. Dobson made his first appearance as a poet. In accepting "A City Flower," Edmund Yates wrote that he was delighted with it, and characterised it as "fresh, original, and very pretty." When *St. Paul's* appeared, Mr. Dobson became a frequent contributor, but it is a common error that he was "discovered" or brought out by Anthony Trollope through personal friendship. It is true they were both Government officials, but the young poet forwarded his pieces to Trollope as a perfect stranger, and, while he ac-

"Je ne puis tenir registre de ma vie par mes actions; fortune les met trop bas; je la tiens par mes fantaisies."
Montaigne, Essais, l. iii, ch.

cepted them with great cordiality, it was not until 1873, five years after he began to contribute, that Dobson met him, and they did not come into close personal relations until after Trollope had ceased editing *St. Paul's*. Mr. Dobson speaks enthusiastically of Trollope as an editor. "He was most prompt in answering letters, and took the keenest interest in one's work. He criticised freely and severely. Sometimes he would return a manuscript with queries to nearly every stanza, and I frequently made modifications in deference to his views. I have never known a magazine better edited than *St. Paul's* was, and I cannot understand why it was not a greater success."

AUSTIN DOBSON'S BOOK-PLATE.

❀

For the most part, Mr. Dobson lives in the atmosphere of the eighteenth century. His devotion to subjects of this period he attributes partly to temperament, partly to the influence of Thackeray (particularly his lectures on the English humourists), and partly to accident. He has edited many editions of the works of eighteenth-century writers, and written the lives of several, including Hogarth, Fielding, Goldsmith, Steele, and Horace Walpole, and a book on Thomas Bewick, the engraver, and his pupils. He has edited numerous editions of *The Vicar of Wakefield*, including a beautiful fac-simile of the original, with a bibliographical preface, and is engaged on another. He is now preparing a definitive edition of his *Life of Hogarth*, which is to be published in February, and is engaged upon a new series of *Eighteenth-Century Vignettes*. Asked whether he had any special preference for any one part of his literary work, Mr. Dobson said that writing his *Eighteenth-Century Vignettes*—little studies on out-of-the-way subjects—had given him peculiar pleasure. Hogarth has always been a passion with him, and Goldsmith he speaks of as a hobby. Almost as far back as he can remember he used to pore over Hogarth's prints in the *Penny Magazine*. The drawers of a table in his study are full of Hogarth prints, and he has a large number of books relating to the artist. Among the treasures in his study is A. E. Abbey's original drawing of Mr. Dobson's book-plate, reproduced herewith in fac-simile.

❀

In noticing the kindly intended criticism of *Yankee Ships and Yankee Sailors*, which appeared in the *Chap-Book* of December 15th, attention has been called to the infallibility of critics. Although the article in question quotes in part the author's preface, and acknowledges that the author says that in some cases he has "touched the fragile bric-à-brac of tradition with the feather duster of investigation," the critic goes on to italicise another extract and quotes these words: "It will not confuse our historical knowledge to accept it thus," the latter "it" referring to the contents of the book. At this the critic is up in arms, and, after picking out several instances in which he claims that Mr. Barnes differs in his historical statements from the well-known authorities, he himself makes statements without giving the source of his information, and challenges, at the end of his article, the writer of *Yankee Ships and Yankee Sailors* to prove his position. Thus says the *Chap-Book* critic in his last paragraph:

"But with due apologies, we beg to say that since Mr. Barnes has set out to alter the face of history as he has done (we apologise once more) in this work, it is incumbent upon him to do what he has not yet done, to give us something from his unpublished papers, and exceptional opportunities and special collection—at least some proof of what he appears to have written out of his personal knowledge only."

And now let us instance the *Chap-Book's* instances:

"Take, for example," says the critic, "the yarn of Allen of the *Chesapeake*. The American whose blood is not stirred by the story of the *Chesapeake* and the *Leopard* is a cur who ought to emigrate. Mr. Barnes retells this in a spirited fashion; but he says that Barron did not haul down the flag until after Allen with the famed live coal from the galley had fired a gun. All others say the flag was already at the rail. If Mr. Barnes is right, Mr. Barron is in a great measure rehabilitated."

Just before this the writer of the criticism has quoted as authorities Cooper and Maclay and "the careful Roosevelt." Cooper says, on page 151 of his *Lives of Distinguished Naval Officers* (Carey and Hart, Philadelphia, 1846), in detailing the adventurous life of Lieutenant John Templer Shubrick, who was a midshipman in Allen's division on the *Chesapeake*:

"He (Allen) then ran to the galley, procured a coal, and with that he succeeded in discharging one gun. It is doubtful whether this was before or after the order had been given to haul down the colors, the two things occurring almost at the same instant."

Maclay, on page 307 of his *History of the American Navy*, Volume I., follows Cooper closely:

"Just as the flag was coming down, Lieutenant William Henry Allen, who commanded the second division, seized a live coal from the galley fire with his fingers and discharged a gun."

But what does Allen, the man who fired the gun, say in regard to the matter? In a letter written by Allen immediately after the event, and published in January, 1814, in *The Portfolio*, occur these words:

"I was in the galley (the camboose), and, snatching a coal from the flames, fired the only gun, which went through the wardroom of the English ship. A shot came into us and struck a man on the breast—he fell at my feet, covering me with blood and splinters of bones. One of my guns suffered severely; one had his leg carried away, two an arm each, and two more were wounded severely—five out of eight. After one gun, one single gun, was fired, we struck, by order of the captain, who then called his officers into the cabin, and asked their opinions. My answer was, 'Sir, you have disgraced us.'"

This should be conclusive; but how strange! the critic apparently has not read his own authorities!

❀

Then the critic goes on to take exception to Mr. Barnes's account of the affair of the *Constitution* in the harbor of Portsmouth, Eng., when she carried the English deserter out from under the guns of the fleet of Sir Roger Curtis (the critic says, "with two frigates in chase"). Referring him to pages 36 and 37, Volume II., of Cooper's *Naval History* (Putnam, 1856), in which a number of mistakes of the Bentley and French editions were corrected, he will find that

"The ship (the *Constitution*) lifted her anchor, and stood over to Cherbourg, however, without being followed. There is no doubt that the prudence of Sir Roger Curtis alone prevented an engagement of some sort or other on this occasion."

The *Chap-Book* critic, in his review, gives a version of this affair for which there seems to be no authority. We have quoted one of the very authors he cites.

❀

In regard to his final objection—concerning the Dartmoor massacre—the critic could not have read Mr. Barnes's account very thoroughly, and is certainly all in a fog in regard to the facts. We beg to refer him to King and Larpent's report of the affair, to the report of the American committee, and the affidavits of American prisoners, especially those of Edward Coffin, Samuel Lowdy, and John Battice. For his information we take pleasure in telling him that he will find full accounts of the matter in a little volume of great interest, entitled *A Journal of Life, etc., at Dartmoor Pris-*

on, etc., published by Rowe and Hooper, Boston, 1816. This includes an accurate map showing the positions of the firing squads, and the killed and wounded where they fell and lay. He can compare this with the account to be found in *The American Cruiser*, by Captain George Little, which is the tale of an eye-witness; also, if he wishes to go further, to that delightful book, *A Green Hand's First Cruise*, the account of another prisoner, published by Messrs. Cushing and Brother, in Baltimore, 1841. With all of these Mr. Barnes agrees. In fact, we do not have to refer the *Chap-Book* to unpublished papers, but merely to history and record, whose face remains unchanged. A little knowledge is a dangerous thing, even in the critic.

FRED BARNARD'S FAMOUS PICTURE DRAWN FOR DICKENS'S "A TALE OF TWO CITIES."

❀

The announcement made in these columns last month that Mr. Phil May was engaged upon a series of black-and-white studies, to illustrate a new edition of Dickens in the hands of Mr. George Allen, is now further amplified by the news that the first volume will be *David Copperfield*, and will contain thirty-six illustrations. If Dickens is to be illustrated again from fresh types, we can imagine no better equipped or more sympathetic artist than Phil May. The enterprise has already aroused interest, and the outcome will be awaited with interest and expectancy.

❀

Dickens has had many artists and caricaturists, and the interest in these is still warm, judging by the letters which an illustrated article on a new collection of Dickensiana in the November BOOKMAN called forth. But of them all perhaps the most eminent, the most successful, and some would say the last delineator of Dickens's characters was the lamented Fred Barnard, whose sad and tragic death a little over a year ago is fresh in many minds. The greatest of his pictures, certainly the one which has always appealed pre-eminently to the imagination of Dickens's readers, is that which depicts Sydney Carton on his way to the guillotine in *A Tale of Two Cities*. The edition which contained this is now seldom seen, and we have heard inquiries made for it very frequently. For this reason the reproduction which is given on the previous page may not be without interest and value to a number of our readers.

❀

The volume of sketches by Dickens, hitherto unpublished in this country, brought together under the title *Old Lamps for New Ones*, by the New Amsterdam Book Company, shortly before the holidays, has met with a generous reception. The book has been so much in demand that, notwithstanding a first large edition, a second had to be prepared almost immediately. This edition is now ready, and is also being taken up rapidly. The same publishing concern has issued four volumes of its subscription edition of the works of Bulwer Lytton—namely, *The Last of the Barons*, in two volumes; *The Caxtons* and *Rienzi*. There was some delay, owing to the pressure of their holiday publications, in the regularity of the issue of these volumes, but the publishers now announce that two volumes will be published each month until the set is complete.

❀

We learn with interest that arrangements have recently been made with the author and his publishers for a translation into Japanese of some of the works of Mr. James Lane Allen. This is being done by Anne Heard Dyer, of Tokio, in collaboration with a native Japanese scholar. The translators are now engaged upon *A Kentucky Cardinal* and *Aftermath*. "These two little books are, I think," writes Mrs. Dyer to a correspondent in this country, "best suited to the delicacy and ideal tendency of the Japanese feeling for nature—the medium through which most of their emotions are transmitted. But I hope even in so pictorial and objective a language it will not be impossible to reproduce that pure literary and lyrical quality which so characterises them in their own. In regard to the former, it may not be uninteresting to you to hear the remark of one of Japan's most distinguished poets and art critics. 'My heart was won on the very first page,' he said, 'by the cricket.' After speaking most appreciatively of the book, he went on to tell us about a pet cricket of his own—I do not believe we have in America the bell cricket, which has such a peculiarly metallic and sweet note—and further about a Drama of Crickets, a famous old Chinese play of which he promised to make a translation in English for us." One could wish that it were possible for a Japanese artist to illustrate these editions of Mr. Allen's work. It would be rather curious to see their picturesque interpretation of his treatment of nature.

❀

It may not generally be known that the lines by George Eliot, beginning "Oh, may I join the choir invisible," which are given on the title-page of Mr. Allen's *The Choir Invisible*, and from which the title and *motif* of his book are taken, are engraved on George Eliot's tomb at Highgate Cemetery.

❀

Another translation now in progress is that of Miss Jane Barlow's *Irish Idylls* into German, by the widow of the late Professor von Helferich, of Dresden University. Messrs. Dodd, Mead and Company, who publish Miss Barlow's books in this country, have secured a new volume of stories by her.

❀

Authors, as a rule, are so dissatisfied with illustrations of their work, that it is worth while noting an exception when it occurs. Miss Jane Barlow, it appears, is very much pleased with the illustrations in the holiday edition of her *Irish Idylls*, recently published; the pictures, she says, are among the best she has seen of the West Irish country. This is a tribute to Mr. Clifton Johnson's photographic art, through whose camera this process of illustration has been so deftly done.

❀

Mr. James Breck Perkins, whose latest contribution to French historical research in *France under Louis XV.* is reviewed on another page, is an eminent lawyer in Rochester, N. Y., where he has practised his profession for over twenty-five years. In the pursuit of his historical studies Mr. Perkins has broken the routine of his professional duties twice during the last decade, living and studying in Paris, the second time remaining there for several years. He is now the author of five volumes on the history of France, beginning with the times of Louis XIV., which are published by Messrs. Houghton, Mifflin and Company. Notwithstanding his engrossing historical interests, Mr. Breck keeps up an active practice, and so successful is he in his profession that, despite his long visits abroad, he has always retained his old clients.

❀

The end of *Trilby* is evidently not yet come. We hear that a German professor of music has conceived the idea of making an opera out of it. Not a bad idea as it strikes us on reflection, and we should not be surprised if *Trilby* were to enjoy a triple success if the idea materialises on the stage. But why was it left to a German musician to think of this? Where are our musical wits? What a delightful theme for Reginald de Koven or Victor Herbert!

❀

We have received, through the courtesy of Professor F. N. Scott of the University of Michigan, a pamphlet containing the reprint of a paper by Dr. Willard C. Gore, entitled *Student Slang*. In a way we were disappointed by its perusal; not because of any defects in the paper itself, but because the title led us to expect something different from the actual contents. For the monograph does not treat of the slang that is peculiarly and essentially the students'—that is to say, of college slang as such—but with the slang of all sorts that students to-day employ. Yet we have been interested, none the less, in reading over the word-lists here arranged and classified with scientific accuracy; for they confirm a statement made by us last July to the effect that the racy, picturesque, and essentially academic slang of the old-time university is now corrupted and debased by an infusion of blackguard *argot* raked up from the gutters and the slums, just as the American university of to-day is itself being corrupted and debased by the influx of the utilitarian mob.

❀

Very little, comparatively speaking, of the slang here recorded is the product of the student mind. It reeks of the vulgarity that taints the non-collegiate cad; and Dr. Gore's collection is, therefore, rather depressing to a thoughtful reader. But there is much also to amuse, and to excite a healthy curiosity. We should like to know the origin of some of the expressions given, and we frequently wonder whether they originated at the University of Michigan or were imported into its halls from contiguous localities in the West. Thus *pruny* (cross) attracts us, as does *full of prunes* (*i.e.*, of mistakes). *Ding-dongs* (side-whiskers), *two-wheel house* (a two-dollar boarding-house), *take a harp* (die), *slam* (an uncomplimentary hint), *gone-some* (empty, hungry), *blug* (a swell), and *june around* (to be busily idle), are all very pleasing, though not, we think, originally academic as are *freshlet* (a young freshman), *dy over dx* (a failure to recite), *flossy* (stylish), *to make a stab* (to answer by guess-work), *crust the instructor* (make a good recitation), and *hen-medic* (a female medical student).

❀

We extracted some mild amusement, also, from the definitions, whose literary English is sometimes rather comical when placed side by side with the word defined. Any one, for instance, would be tickled by this:

"*Let her go, Gallagher*. An expression signifying a readiness to proceed."

We wish that we could spare the space for some general discussion of the whole subject of academic slang; but we shall reserve it until we write the introduction to our great *Dictionary of University Argot*—if we ever make one. Meanwhile we are indebted to Dr. Gore and to Professor Scott for giving us the pleasure of perusing these interesting lists.

❀

Early in the year Messrs. Dodd, Mead and Company will publish the most important contribution that has ever been made to the elucidation of a single period in the life of Burns. This is the correspondence between the poet and the friend and patron of the last ten years of his life, Mrs. Frances Wallace Dunlop. A considerable number of Burns's letters were handed over to his biographer, Currie, and have been included in all lives of the poet and all editions of his prose works. Mrs. Dunlop kept back, however, between thirty and forty of her friend's epistles, and only allowed the remainder to be published on condition of all her own being returned to her. Recently the unpublished letters of both were acquired from Mrs. Dunlop's descendants by Mr. R. B. Adam, of Buffalo, N. Y., and are about to be published with ample elucidations by Mr. William Wallace, editor of the latest issue of Robert Chambers's *Life and Works of Robert Burns.* We understand that the letters of the poet which are now about to see the light for the first time are of very great value. They throw a flood of light upon the last years of Burns's life, and indicate among other things that a serious effort was made to secure for him a position as a professor in the University of Edinburgh. They likewise state Burns's views upon religion with a precision which is not to be found in the letters that have hitherto been published. They also put in a new and unexpected light the "desertion" of Burns by his correspondent.

Mrs. Dunlop's letters, about a hundred in number, are also intensely interesting. They will show how little of a "patroness" and how very much of a devoted friend she was. At the same time she was a merciless critic; indeed, her letters constitute the one body of contemporary criticism of Burns which exists. They are also so full of references to the history of the time, and even of its literature, that Mr. Wallace's annotations, and an introduction in which he deals at length with the Wallace and Dunlop families, both represented by Burns's correspondent, form about a third of the volume. Mrs. Dunlop's letters also clear up many mysterious allusions in biographies of Burns, and rectify numerous mistakes which have been made by his editors, from Currie to Messrs. Henley and Henderson.

"THE PINES," PUTNEY, THE HOME OF THE POET SWINBURNE AND MR. WATTS-DUNTON.

Miss Grace King writes from New Orleans, dated January 5th, as follows:

Editors of THE BOOKMAN:

MY DEAR SIRS: Permit me to add some information to your article on Libraries and Librarians in the January number. Besides the Howard Library we have in New Orleans the very large and important circulating library, the Fiske Free and Public Library; the State Library, which contains the Law Library and the Historical Library of the State—the latter collected by Charles Gayarri when Secretary of State, and furnishes to students the complete list of Spanish and French authorities for our colonial history; the Tulane University Library, a fine working library, and a rich one in modern French authors. These last two are also practically circulating. The Howard Library is strictly a reference one.

I may add that the Fiske Free and Public Library was formed from the small, but very useful libraries whose foundation dates from some forty years ago.

Respectfully,
GRACE KING.

Both Anthony Hope and Stanley Weyman have made a departure from romantic Europe, and have delved into English history in their latest stories. *Simon Dale*, by Anthony Hope, is an historical novel of the times of Charles II., the merry monarch of England, and will be published shortly by the Messrs. Stokes. Mr. Weyman's new story is called *The Castle Inn*, and deals with the England of George III. The opening chapters appeared in *Munsey's Magazine* last month. Max Pemberton also begins a new novel, entitled *The Woman of Kronstadt*, in the same number. As the title would lead us to infer, it is a story of love and intrigue, in which a woman's wit is matched against the crushing military power of Russia.

The long-expected volume of poems by Mr. Theodore Watts-Dunton, the leading critic and chief attraction of the *Athenæum*, has just been published by Mr. John Lane. Mr. Watts Dunton was the intimate friend of Tennyson, Browning, William Morris, Meredith, and the house-mate of Rossetti and Swinburne. He was born in 1836, and received his education from private tutors at Cambridge. He was literary and artistic critic on the *Examiner*, under the editorship of Professor Minto, before his association with the *Athenæum*. He is the author of *Aylwin: a Poetic Romance*, and has contributed a number of thoughtful essays—especially interesting being the last one on Poetry—to the *Encyclopædia Britannica*, which many of his friends would like to see collected in a volume of criticisms. Mr. Coulson Kernahan, who contributes an article to the present number on Mr. Watts-Dunton and his poems, is perhaps the only one of the younger generation who knows him intimately, and this intimacy makes his article all the more interesting because of its special knowledge and insight. Mr. Watts-Dunton is something of a recluse, and has never sought fame. He is a staunch friend, and has been a kind helper to many struggling young men of letters. He and Swinburne live together at "The Pines," Putney, a suburb of London. Mr. Watts-Dunton is the shyest of men, and has never allowed his portrait to appear in public until now. We have the privilege of publishing an authentic portrait of him that has never appeared before.

The eighth anniversary of Robert Browning's death was celebrated on Sunday, the 12th of December last, in the Robert Browning Hall, Walworth, England. Mr. Augustine Birrell delivered an address, and the members of the Kyrle Society rendered several songs by the two Brownings, together with selections from Galuppi, Boison, and Verdi. Mr. Birrell, in the course of his remarks, said that "literature had a larger place in life than actual life itself. To night they were thankfully grateful and avowedly reverent for one who had entered into the lives of all who read him. Two things only commanded their reverence—first, a succession of great writers, and, second, the recollection of great, generous, and noble deeds. The obscure poet of the obscure 'Sordello' had an influence on literature which was indescribably majestic. Like Carlyle and Tennyson, he never bowed the knee to Baal. Poverty they knew, and depression of spirit, but not one of them abated one jot or tittle of his pretensions, or ever asked the people what they wanted; and so the people ceased to sneer and scoff, and the crowd—which is, after all, a docile crowd—became eager enough to pay its debt to them with compound interest. Browning's religious belief was not attained through the dark and mystical passage of the sacraments, but rather was the result of a firm belief in a personal God, and his strong faith in the soul of man."

A few months after the death of Robert Browning, in December, 1889, there

ROBERT BROWNING.

From a photograph by Julia Margaret Cameron.

appeared in an obscure English contemporary an article containing "A Young Man's Recollections," which recorded some good things worth repeating, but which is especially valuable for its fresh evidence of the poet's unfailing courtesy and great-hearted sympathy, particularly with would-be literary aspirants. We cull some extracts for our readers :

"I was taken up to his study and shown in. Huge heaps of books lay on the floor, the chairs, the table ; and at first I thought the room otherwise unoccupied. But suddenly a dapper little figure emerged from a huge arm-chair by the fire, and stepped briskly across the room. For a moment I was bewildered. The poet's face was familiar in photographs, but I had somehow imagined him a tall, gaunt man I recovered myself to find him standing before me, holding both hands, and saying : 'Now this is really very kind of you, to come so far just to see an old man like me.' Then he dragged up a companion chair and forced me into it, standing for some moments by my side, with his hand on my shoulder. Then he sat down and said : 'Well, tell me all about yourself. Have you not brought some of your poems to show me?' Of course I had not—I wanted to see him, and talk of his work. But for a while he would not let me do so. 'We'll talk about me later, if you like, though I'm rather tired of the subject,' he said ; and proceeded to question me pretty closely about my aims and work. Then he sat and thought awhile ; then came across to me again and said : 'Do you know that I was nearly fifty before I made any money out of my writings? That's the truth ; and you will understand my reluctance to advise any one to embark on such a cruel career. But—if you really mean to go in for it—I would do anything I could to shorten your time of waiting. So you just send me some of your work, that I may give you my candid opinion, if you think it's worth having.'

"A promise which seemed hard of fulfilment was that which I had made—to submit some of my poems to him. What he thought of them is nothing to the purpose ; I refer to the fact that I did so submit them to his criticism because I wish to quote a couple of significant sentences in the letter which contained his criticism. The first is a passing but pathetic reference to his own writing. 'With all your goodness to my own work,' he wrote, 'you know well enough how long it has been before the world, and how moderate a recognition of any sort of worth in it ever happened till lately ; so I dare say nothing as to chances of popularity which your poems are likely to attain.' That letter was dated December 6th, 1887 : two years later, when I heard of his splendid death at Venice, my memory went back to that sad phrase.

"The other noticeable sentence was one which seems to express an opinion curiously at variance with the views on the same subject generally imputed to him, and, indeed, appropriated by him in more than one poem.

"'If you determine to go on writing—as in this instance—poetry straight out of your own experience, I think you will easily attain the great and good end of affording help to a nobler bearing of sorrow, or firmer faith in eventual freedom from it.'

"The sentence gives but slight material wherefrom to construct a theory of any kind ; but I have always felt it an indication that

MATTHEW ARNOLD'S GRAVE IN LALEHAM CHURCHYARD.

Browning was sometimes ready to admit the defensibility of a theory of art which he had condemned so plainly. Which is to say that he was but a man.

❀

"A few weeks later I called again at the beautiful house in De Vere Gardens. The poet had just come in, he told me, from a meeting of the committee for the memorial to Matthew Arnold, and he was evidently very depressed by the sad thoughts which had come upon him of his 'dear old friend, Mat.' 'I have been thinking all the way home,' he said, 'of his hardships. He told me once, when I asked him why he had written no poetry lately, that he could not afford to do it; but that, when he had saved enough, he intended to give up all other work and go back to poetry. I wonder if he has gone back to it now.' Here Browning's voice shook, and he was altogether more deeply moved than I had ever seen him. 'It's very hard, isn't it?' he went on, 'that a useless fellow like me should have been able to give up all his life to it—for, as I think I told you, my father helped me to publish my early books—while a splendid poet like Arnold actually could not afford to write the poetry we wanted of him.'

"That morning Mr. Browning was in an unusually communicative mood. Generally he would say: 'Oh, I don't want to talk about my poems—they were quite enough trouble to write without talking of them.' But to-day he spoke of one and another, reciting scraps and chatting about their aims. I remember that among many others 'James Lee's Wife' was mentioned. 'Tell me,' I said, 'what is your private opinion of "James Lee's Wife"? Was she quite guiltless in the matter of her husband's estrangement? Or was he simply a shallow soul who would have got tired of her, or any other good woman, in time?' 'Well, I'm not quite sure,' he answered, and sat looking into the fire for some moments. 'I was always very fond of her, and I really believe that there are one or two bits of her history which are as good as anything I have done.' After a pause he suddenly began to recite part of that section of the poem entitled 'By the Sea,' with curious dramatic inflections of the voice. I had never till then quite realised the unutterable pathos of the woman's fate who sees her husband's love slipping away from her, tired by the excess of her own. He had got as far as the verse—

"'O love, love, no, love, not so indeed!
You were just weak earth, I knew;
With much in you waste, and many a weed,
And plenty of passion run to seed,
But a little good grain too.'

"There he stopped, and again paused a moment. By and by he said, 'Do you know, I think Mrs. Lee was a little to blame. I fancy she had not much tact, and did not quite know how to treat her husband. I think she worried him a little.'

❀

There is a pathetic reference among the recollections of Browning printed

THE NEW TOMB MARKING HEINE'S GRAVE AT MONTMARTRE, PARIS.

above to the slow recognition which was also Arnold's lot as well as Browning's. It is now nearly nine years ago since the apostle of sweetness and light was laid in his grave in Laleham Churchyard. And as Arnold himself cited Macaulay's comment on the waning influence of Wordsworth ten years after his decease, so in Arnold's case nearly the same period of time has brought about an opposite effect in the very remarkable and widespread growth of interest in his own poetry. Time has strangely altered his position in the world of letters, and it is not as a tractarian, controversialist, and critic that he is best known to-day, but pre-eminently as a poet and essayist. The splendid discernment of his *Essays in Criticism* will always preserve for him a place in English literature; and his verse, though it will never be popular in the common acceptation of that term, will always be appreciated and remembered by a "fit audience, though few." The reaction in favour of Byron at the present time calls to mind Arnold's partisanship and glorification of the poet, in defiance of Swinburne, by which he suffered much at the time with the literary public.

❀

We also give an illustration from the London *Sketch* of the new tomb marking Heine's grave at Montmartre, Paris. "I remember well the first time I visited Paris," writes a correspondent to this journal:

"It was in the month of September, and thus, when I went to the cemetery of Montmartre the force of Matthew Arnold's lines appealed to me in their full significance, as I stood viewing Heine's grave—

"'HENRI HEINE—'tis here!
That black tombstone, the name
Carved there—no more!'

Here Heine had lain since 1856, and when I visited it the monument was in a shocking condition. 'Trim Montmartre' was scarcely a fitting description to apply to the neglected little plot with the bald headstone, yet the place was just the same as when Arnold wrote

'. . . the faint
Murmur of Paris outside;
Crisp everlasting-flowers,
Yellow and black, on the graves.'

Yet this headstone, such as it was, formed all the memorial that Heine ever had, for neither Germany nor Austria has immortalised him thus.'"

The new monument which marks the lonely grave in Paris is the work of M. L. Hasselriis, a Danish sculptor in Rome.

❀

The conversion of John Oliver Hobbes, as manifested in her new novel, *The School for Saints*, is one of the topics of the hour in literary circles. The epigrammatic force of her style still remains, but purged of its steely cynicism and harsh edge, and chastened by a serious, even a profoundly, religious tone. In the midst of much that is dull, irrelevant, and didactic, there are flashes of originality, distinct power, and compelling interest in the romance of the inner life. Written in the manner of *John Inglesant*, recalling *Daniel Deronda* not infrequently, disclosing a remarkable knowledge of the Bible and the influence of Ouida in certain chapters, Mrs. Craigie has written a novel which commands respect for its thoughtfulness, its serious purpose, and its successful portrayal of the hero and heroine. There is to be a sequel, and we look forward with eagerness to learn how Robert and Brigit, after their brief moment of ecstatic union, bore their separation. We have a quarrel with Mrs. Craigie for calling her heroine by so unromantic a name as Brigit. To be sure it is Frenchified from Brigitte, but the association still remains. Not the least successful feature about Dr. Mitchell's *Hugh Wynne* is the name of his heroine. "Darthea" is eloquent of all the feminine graces, and weaves a spell on the page whenever she is introduced.

❀

The London *Literary World* declares that it has the best authority for saying that the statements made in several quarters as to the autobiographical character of Sarah Grand's latest work are misleading. The only foundation for them is the following allusion to *The Beth Book* by the author in an interview in *The Young Woman.* "In the story itself there will be a good deal of early experience among the peasantry in Ireland." All she has done is to use familiar scenes as a setting or background to her fiction ; but that is obviously not at all the same thing as using actual incidents in her own life. Taken as an autobiography, one is certainly repelled oftentimes by its extreme frankness, recalling the *Confessions* of Rousseau at many points. We are rather relieved by the denial set forth by the *Literary World*, for, to say the least, one cannot but be amazed and shocked at many things—for example, the choice of a name for the delinquent husband. However great one's respect may be for the sincerity and even the nobility of much that one finds in *The Beth Book*, it is impossible for her to escape the charge of coarseness, unconscious though she may be of this quality in her work. One thing is very certain : no one ever dwells long on such themes as are discussed in this public fashion and thrown open for solution over the tea-table without deterioration. It is impossible surely that Madame Grand can know how many of her readers will be affected by certain things in her book—things which stain the page without helping any argument in the least.

❀

It is reported in London that the allusion made by the late Poet Laureate (recorded in the *Memoir* by his son) to Tennyson's having smoked a pipe with Carlyle at the kitchen fireside of the latter in Cheyne Row, has attracted several visitors to the downstairs part of this well-known house, which has been as a rule neglected. Paul Bourget, who was accompanied on a recent visit to London by his daughter, is said to have exhibited a truly Gallic enthusiasm in his inspection of the various literary objects in each room, and Dr. Milburn, the blind chaplain of the United States Congress, and an old friend of Carlyle, displayed familiarity on the occasion of his visit lately with each corner of the house. While the interior of the building has undergone considerable renovation since Carlyle's decease, the kitchen fireplace and appurtenances remain as they were in 1852, and, indeed, appear as serviceable to-day as they ever did. Amid all the vicissitudes of time the following simple record remains indelibly engraven on a pane of glass, which singularly enough no Carlyle worshipper has disturbed : "John Harbert Knowles cleaned all the windows in this house and painted part in the 18 year of age, March 7, 1794"—more than a year before the birth of the man who was to render the old edifice famous for all time.

❀

In the January *Munsey* there may be seen a drawing which portrays the Rev. W. H. Milburn, the blind chaplain of the Senate, and his adopted daughter, who guides his footsteps. For fifty-two years Dr. Milburn has kept pace with the tide of Congressional life, and dur-

THE CHÂTEAU DE VELOR (EUGÉNIE GRANDET'S HOME).

ing that period Washington has grown around him out of a straggling village into a city of magnificent splendour.

❀

A correspondent from Paris sends us the accompanying photographs of the Château de Velor, at Avoine Beaumont, near Tours, which is celebrated as the home of the original "Eugénie Grandet." The château was at one time a hunting lodge of Charles the Seventh. It passed eventually by fraud into the possession of Père Nivelau, so that it became the home of his daughter Eugénie. Balzac lived in Tours at this time, and is said by local tradition to have fallen in love with the daughter, but to have been refused by old Nivelau on account of his poverty. The story, according to the present owner, the Marquise de Podestad, follows the facts very closely excepting that Eugénie's marriage was more actively unhappy than the novel represents it, and lasted long years instead of a few months. There were also several children, whereas in the story there are none, but Eugénie outlived them all, and died only some sixteen years ago. Many of her belongings are in the possession of the marquise, and the crucifix, at which old Grandet clutched while dying (because it was gilded) still hangs in the house. The moat surrounding the house is filled with water, but the story does not say whether or not it was so in Balzac's time. In the larger picture there is a glimpse of the chapel which Eugénie had decorated and which is just as she left it.

❀

Mrs. Gertrude Atherton has just finished the novel upon which she has been hard at work for several months. During the writing, Mrs. Atherton has been in France, living quietly in Bois Guillaume, Rouen, and will probably not return to London before March. The new story is entitled *The Americans of Maundrell Abbey*, and is understood to touch upon the question of international marriages. It is said to be the most important work that Mrs. Atherton has done, and there are reasons to believe that it fully sustains her reputation for daring frankness. Most of her books,

FRONT VIEW OF THE CHÂTEAU DE VELOR.

Patience Sparhawk particularly, aroused the resentment of many sensitive Americans, but in England the story has been cordially received. It has gone into a fifth edition, and is reported among the leading books at the libraries.

❀

On the morning of Friday, November 26th last, there passed away, in the seclusion of her quiet Yorkshire home, Miss Ellen Nussey, the life-long friend of Charlotte Brontë, and the chief, if not sole, personal link existing in connection with that gifted family. As a matter of incidental interest, Charlotte Brontë was born on April 21st, 1816—Ellen Nussey on April 20th, 1817, thus showing the very slight disparity between the ages of the two. Charlotte Brontë died at the age of thirty-eight—Ellen Nussey had completed her eightieth year. Lady Morrison, who enjoyed the close and confidential friendship of Miss Nussey for more than ten years past, contributes the following reminiscence:

❀

"In person Ellen Nussey was not striking, but she was sprightly, attractive — coquettish, no doubt, in her younger days—and intelligent; her manners charming; every word and gesture bearing emphatically the stamp of truth; while her voice, mellowed and modulated to a peculiarly gentle cadence, was exceedingly pleasant to hear. I have often sat beside her, and heard with unfeigned interest her sparkling talk about the Brontë family; have heard her relate incidents and anecdotes in the lives of the sisters, which seemed to me better than any information to be gathered from books; and I recall the unabated affection and zest with which she dwelt upon the ways and merits of her gifted friends, while the indignation with which she denounced any aspersion cast upon the memory of Charlotte Brontë and her sisters was, in its righteousness, beautiful to see. Miss Nussey told me that she considered Branwell, the brother, the cleverest and most talented of the whole family, and, but for his misused powers, he could, had he chosen, have outstripped his sisters in literature. Many of the incidents which she related go far to prove that Charlotte Brontë was keenly alive to humour, fun, and all the brighter aspects of life; that she eagerly enjoyed and participated in a joke; and that, until grave and distressing sorrows visited and clouded

ELLEN NUSSEY.

her life, she was at all times open to, and rejoiced in, its gaiety and sunshine. That Ellen Nussey is the prototype of 'Caroline Helstone' in *Shirley* cannot for a moment be doubted. It may be remembered that in one part of the book Caroline is described as wearing a brown dress with a pink bow. When I inquired of Miss Nussey if this also was taken from herself, she said that she *was* wearing that particular kind of attire at the time *Shirley* was written. It is to Ellen Nussey that the public is, and will ever be, indebted for authentic information with regard to the Brontë family. But for her, no history of these remarkable people could have gone forth to the world in a truthful and reliable form."

❀

Mr. Walter Raymond is just finishing a new book which he calls *A Man of the Mendify*—a title which his friends are right in urging him to change, as it is altogether too local. A well-known London critic who has read the manuscript says that it is the best thing that Mr. Raymond has written.

ALPHONSE DAUDET.

ALPHONSE DAUDET.

Alphonse Daudet is dead. In his death, which occurred on the 16th of last December, France has lost one of her brightest ornaments. He departed without one unkind word being uttered or one uncharitable thought being harboured by anybody, not even by the French Academy, in spite of his having written *l'Immortel*, not even by the Tarasconese, although he is the creator of the immortal Tartarin! And this universal kindliness around his open grave went to the writer no less than to the man, to the man no less than to the writer.

But what idea must we preserve of the latter? What will posterity say or think of him? What will remain of all that he wrote, to tell our descendants how he charmed us for a period of twenty or twenty-five years?

The first thing that must be noticed about him, it seems to me, the one feature which lies both at the surface of his works and in the very marrow of his nature, is that he was the one genuine *méridional* among the men of letters of his country. The course of history has given France such a strong, compact, national unity that we easily forget how discordant the elements were out of which French nationality has been formed. That there once was a Northern France and a Southern France which harboured none but feelings of enmity toward each other; that these two countries, wholly dissimilar in language, in institutions, in religious and ethical views, once fiercely rushed upon each other; that the Northern Frenchman was in the South hated as a ruthless conqueror, an ignorant and contemptuous destroyer of everything that was held dear and beautiful in the conquered country, is now all but forgotten, save by the close student of historical records. The South, it need hardly be said, gave to France afterward many a brilliant intellect, more, perhaps, than the North. But the sons of the South were taken hold of by the new nationality that resulted from the blending of the two halves, and are thought of simply as Frenchmen. Who thinks of the *méridional* in Thiers and Mignet, in Montaigne, in Montesquieu, in Guizot? Even Gambetta's exuberance is ascribed, and not unjustly, to his Italian father's more than to his Southern French mother's blood. In Daudet the Southerner, the Provençal, is discernible nearly in every line that he wrote. It is the sunshine of his native Provence that illumines his works and gives them the peculiar warmth which is one of their most attractive features. Oh, to be sure, he is a Southerner of a peculiar kind! He is not a Gascon; he does not, as the hero of the popular story, wonder that the river Garonne, or the Rhone, even, could give out enough water to fill all the seas and oceans. The Provençal that was in him had become a Parisian too, endowed with that keen sense of the ridiculous which is carried on the banks of the Seine farther than anywhere else, and sometimes altogether too far. The Parisianised Daudet could look from outside at the natives of his dear Provence, or else Tartarin never would have appeared. But his conception, if not of life itself, at least of that which makes life worth living, which makes it beautiful, remained Southern to the last; to the last his favourite music must have been the scraping of the *cigales'* wings, his favourite library, that *Bibliothèque des Cigales* of which he speaks in one of his most charming stories.

Then he was a poet, not a singer exactly, though *Les Amoureuses*, his first volume of verse, contains some of the prettiest poems written in France since the hushing of the three great poetical voices of the century, but a poet who had to draw music and harmony out of every sound of nature, out of every manifestation of social life. His saddest works, *L'Evangéliste* and *Sapho*, have their bit of brightness, their corner of repose, where the soul may rest a while from the stern tragedies of real life.

And yet those who call him a realist are not altogether wrong. He was not out of place in the famous quartette of writers of which he was a member together with Flaubert, Edmond de Goncourt, and his lifelong friend, Émile Zola. As soon as he found himself in Paris—and he was then only seventeen years of age—in 1857, he began to observe and to take notes. He saw quickly and noted accurately, with too great minuteness, perhaps, everything that he saw, and he soon acquired the gift of choosing the characteristic detail which must appeal to the eye and leave in the mind of the reader an indestructible image of the person described. Where is the reader of Daudet who has not before his eyes the standing silhouette of Monsieur Chèbe, Sidonie's father, who cannot accept any sitting business, and therefore has always to be up and doing—nothing?

A realist he undoubtedly was, but what sort of a realist? He was intensely interested in life; he loved to say what he had seen. We are not sure that this is not a Southern trait. His Numa Roumestan, a true Southerner, could not think except when speaking; but the reverse also is true of the *méridional;* what is in his mind and memory must come out, in talk or in print. And Daudet was as wonderful in his conversation as in his books. Life, the every-day events that he came across, were so interesting to him that he at times hardly dared to alter them when introducing them in his books. No one certainly could complain of poverty of imagination in the man who wrote the *Lettres de mon Moulin* and the *Contes du Lundi*, *Fromont Jeune et Risler Aîné*, and *Sapho*, and yet the same man has, perhaps, transferred bodily into his writings more actual events related in the newspapers, in the court-house, or in society, than any other writer of the present age; of some of his novels one hardly dares say that they are works of fiction; their characters are men and women of our time, we know their names, and they do in the book almost exactly what they had done in real life. Paris society was not a little amused once when, in a celebrated separation case, an incident was testified to by witnesses as having actually had for its heroine the woman in the case, which formed one of the most entertaining chapters of *Les Rois en Exil*, then the most recently published of Daudet's novels.

But this is not true of *all* of his books. We dare say it is not true of the best of them. Thus, for instance, it is hardly disputed by any one that *Port Tarascon* is decidedly inferior to the two preceding volumes of the Tartarin series, *Tartarin de Tarascon* and *Tartarin sur les Alpes;* and it is well known that the original of Port Tarascon was *Port-Breton*, a fantastic and swindling colonisation scheme, which brought poverty and ruin to hundreds of French families, and landed its originator in a French jail. *Le Nabab* belongs to the same class. Daudet himself did not, in fact, he could not, deny that the Duc de Mora was the Duc de Morny, by whom he had been employed as secretary; everybody in Paris, especially around the Chamber of Deputies, knew who was the original of Jansoulet, the nabob, and the same stories were read in the novel which had been related in the lobbies, and even in the open sessions of the House, when it had had to pass upon the credentials of the unscrupulous but good-natured adventurer. We could name here the physician, many said "the quack doctor," whom everybody then recognised in Dr. Jenkins; charity forbids. The same thing is true of *Les Rois en Exil.* In his *Souvenirs d'un Homme de Lettres* Daudet himself states, what everybody knew, moreover, that his Queen of Illyria was the ex-Queen of Naples, who had been living in Paris since the conquest of her kingdom by Garibaldi and Vittorio Emmanuele; everybody knew, not far from the Tuileries, the real estate agency which is so brightly described in the book, and the managers of which play such an important part in the development of the story.

The above features we single out not as merits, but as decided shortcomings in some of Daudet's novels. The explanation is obvious. Daudet did not write a history; he still clung to the idea that he was writing a novel. He conscientiously invented his plot, created some of the surrounding characters, but he had to make the whole fit in with every detail of the incidents which he had borrowed from real life, and which he had not previously transformed by the process of intellectual digestion, which is one of the necessary labours of the novelist. Those works of Daudet's are not unlike the panoramas, so popular in Paris and elsewhere a few years ago, where, between the spectator and the circular canvas, which was the work of the artist, were placed real material objects—trees, guns, carriages, etc.—intended to intensify the realistic effect. They did intensify it for a while, until close observation revealed the exact line where reality ceased and representation began. It seems to us that the same line is visible in such works as *Le Nabab*, *Les Rois en Exil*, and *Numa Roumestan.*

We are not sure that the same ought not to be said of *Le Petit Chose* also. The interest of the work lies in its autobiographical character, but it is not a simple autobiography, in which the author takes care to state nothing which is not true. The form is that of the novel, and the imaginary have to fit in exactly with the real incidents. Here, as in the above novels, it seems to us that the blending of the two elements has not been accomplished with perfectly artistic accuracy, and for the same reason, because the real incidents of the author's life are presented too much as they actually occurred. What would be a great merit in a historical work becomes thus a blemish in a work of fiction. How much more fascinating, because more convincing, the short chapters that constitute *Trente Ans de Paris* and the *Souvenirs d'un Homme de Lettres*, especially those that are headed *Histoire de mes Livres!* Here we have simple notes taken down almost day by day, where Daudet's marvellous accuracy of vision and power of delicate rendering stand out by themselves and interpose between us and reality nothing but the most deliciously translucid atmosphere.

Does this mean that Daudet was unable to create? By no means. When at his best he is a creator. In fact, he was essentially a creator, because a poet, but so curious of life in all its manifestations, that when he had held a portion of it under his observation he found it extremely painful to alter it in the smallest particular. That the public was quite ready to accept reality as transformed by his poetic imagination ought to have been made clear to him by the reception given to his first successful novel, which, perhaps, remains his masterpiece, *Fromont Jeune et Risler Aîné.* The characters in the novel were every one of them types, not individuals, or, rather, they were possibilities, not realities; they were almost truer than life, and at once Delobelle, the *cabotin* accepted by his family, and to a certain extent by himself, as a man of genius, poor self-sacrificing Mademoiselle Zizi, Sigismond Planus, the faithful cashier, Monsieur Chèbe, and, above all, the bewitching, scheming, and perverse Sidonie took their place among those products of human fancy, which we are hardly able at times to distinguish from our real acquaintances.

And, ten years later, in *Sapho*, we find the same achievement repeated, with less delicacy and less purity, perhaps, but with greater power of compact and logical construction. And here, we think, lies the greatest difference between Daudet and the great English writer to whom he has often been compared. Daudet's tragedies are of the simplest kind ; they spring from the natures of his characters ; they are every-day events, important for them alone ; we pass by them, and do not notice them ; they would hardly provide a newspaper with one paragraph ; no shipwrecking storms, no kidnappings, no murders ; and they are only the more real, the more heart-rending for their simplicity and homeliness. Give Jean Gaussin a little more strength of will, a little less susceptibility to sensuous enjoyments, and *Sapho's* tragedy disappears ; and the tragedy itself, what does it amount to ? A man overboard, that is all. It happens every day.

L'Evangéliste, in our estimation, ranks nearly as high as *Fromont Jeune et Risler Aîné* and *Sapho*. But here, again, a certain unreality is discoverable, due, no doubt, to the fact that the main incident was an event which had actually occurred in the family, if we are not mistaken, of the Daudet children's music teacher. In fact, the more Daudet trusts to his poetical faculty of transforming truth the more real he is

This is the secret of the extraordinary success of his short stories. There real occurrences had to be left out ; they would have taken too much room ; the artist dealt with possibilities, not with realities, and gave the most minute and convincing life to the dreams of his fancy. His two great faculties are both manifested in the highest degree in these earlier and, perhaps, most perfect products of his genius, the *Lettres de mon Moulin*, the *Contes du Lundi*, etc. Sometimes Daudet's fancy is fed by reality, as in *Le Siège de Berlin*, than which anything more realistic can hardly be imagined ; sometimes it is all poetry—the poetry of nature and love, the warm sunshine and the penetrating aroma of the fields of Provence, as in *Le Sous-Préfet aux Champs*. And whether realistic or poetical, his stories possess a charm which is due both to the author's inexhaustible sympathy with every form of life and to the accuracy of an unpretentious and self-restrained descriptive style.

This self-restraint Daudet does not always practise. In some of his larger works, in the *Nabab*, for instance, he once in a while allowed himself to be carried away by a desire of turning his pen into a brush, which has the invariable result of introducing vagueness of utterance. It may do well in other languages ; it does not in French. French style may be narrative, oratorical, descriptive, poetical to a certain extent ; but suggestiveness is not its province. When the outline is not clear, real good French is absent. How many of the French writers of the last thirty years are open to the above criticism ! Daudet is not altogether free from that fault, but with him it appears only here and there, in patches, as it were ; it is not a regular component of his literary nature. In fact, we would willingly say that no one was freer from it, with the exception of the lamented Guy de Maupassant.

Clearness and completeness of vision, perfect accuracy of statement, and sympathy, these are the qualities that made Daudet, perhaps, not only the novelist and story writer that he is, but also the first of French humourists. It has been said not seldom that the French have wit, but no humour. While true in general, we doubt whether an exception ought not to be made in favour of a few quite modern authors, at the head of whom Daudet stands pre-eminent. Who would realise the difference between humour and wit need only pass from the perusal of the Tartarin volumes to almost any of Edmond About's short stories. About's wit is simply irresistible, and laughter comes up to our lips and eyes whether we wish it or not. With Daudet it is simply an amused and kindly smile. We see this big Southern, fun-loving, bragging Tartarin uttering lies as big as houses, first among his own townspeople, whom he does not expect to believe him any more than he believes himself, then among other people, who first take him at his word, and whose contempt he cannot understand after they have found that his heroism is all Southern froth, and no more; all his ethical vagaries amuse us like the gambols of some big fishes. We do not want him to hurt himself; but we feel he is not exactly a man after our own likeness. Daudet knows all that and tells us: "Look at him, all the same. He is not useless; he'll bring into your life a ray of his Southern sunshine, provided you do not take him *au sérieux*." No wonder the Tarasconese never forgave him for making their small town the special home of this peculiar branch of the genus man!

On the whole, barring the terrible physical sufferings which in the last thirteen years of his life he endured with admirable fortitude—a fortitude made comparatively easy by the loving devotion of his wife—Daudet was a happy man. In one direction, however, he knew what disappointment was. It was one of his ambitions to be a dramatic writer, and he does not seem to have been meant for one. He who saw others so well was unable to gain the same accurate knowledge of his own nature. He wrote a good deal for the stage, and even before he published any of his novels. *L'Arlésienne*, which was not his first dramatic attempt, was performed when *Fromont Jeune et Risler Aîné* was not yet written. His dramatic writings are not without merit, and they did not go without a certain degree of success, but they lack the clear, rapid, logical development which is necessary on the stage. Daudet's great gift of accurate and complete vision here obstructed his path rather than helped his progress. He did not know what to set forth and what to omit. Indeed, he sometimes omitted what was most essential for dramatic emotion, so that the only thing to expect of his characters was the unexpected. There are beautiful scenes, though, in *L'Arlésienne*, in *La Lutte pour la Vie*, and especially in *L'Obstacle*, the one of his dramas which comes nearest to being a real play; but a string of scenes is not a drama. In Daudet's plays it always seems that we ought to have an interpreter, a guide, a chorus, to explain to us what is going on in the minds of the various characters before they get ready to take any definite action, and thus spare us the disappointed surprise which otherwise we are sure to feel when they do act before our eyes.

He remains, then, first of all, perhaps, a master of French prose, of a highly musical prose, lighted up with a dash of poetical radiance; a careful and interested observer and describer of life, of that inner life which is called fancy, as well as of the outer life by which we are uninterruptedly surrounded; a kindly and sincere humourist, and in many respects a creator of types. Posterity will lull itself in the mirth and poetry of his light sketches, read one or two, perhaps three, of his novels, and once in a while gaze with some wonder upon the features of the illustrious Tartarin de Tarascon's father.

Let us add here—for in forming an estimate of the man these facts ought not to be forgotten—that Daudet was not one of Fortune's *enfants gâtés*. His beginnings were as humble as well could be. It took him years of the hardest work so to master his natural gifts as to be able to turn them into agents of literary production. His first really great success he won when already thirty-four years of age, and ten years later he felt the first painful symptoms of the terrible ailment which has just carried him off. And yet he was a happy man, because he carried in himself, in his loving heart, and in his sympathy for everything that has received the inseparable gifts of life and suffering the source of his own and of his associates' happiness.

Adolphe Cohn.

IN CAPRICORN.

Around the shoulders of the sleeping hills
His ample robe the hands of Winter fold:
The muffled brook—a dream of tinkling trills;
In leafless woods the hazel's wrinkled gold.

Benjamin F. Leggett.

THEODORE WATTS-DUNTON.

Until quite recently the public, outside literary circles, had come to regard Mr. Theodore Watts-Dunton as a sort of literary "Mrs. Harris," as something between Mr. Stead's "Julia" and the critical spirit of the age personified. The minor poets—to their credit be it said—have never entertained atheistic doubts about the being of a Theodore Watts. Has not the name been used this last twenty years as a sort of bogey with which to frighten into silence the naughty little boys who would insist upon publishing verse? It is one of the first articles in their creed that on the watch-tower of that stern castle-keep of literature—the *Athenæum*—there lurks a dreadful ogre who lives upon suckling bards. In nine cases out of ten, when a critic with unraised visor sallies forth from these dreaded portals to administer a well-deserved castigation, or it may be only a gentle and salutary chastisement, the castigated person tells you that the hand which struck the blow was that of "Theodore Watts," little knowing—for there are not a score of poets all told, of whom Mr. Watts-Dunton has written in the *Athenæum*—that the critic in question has in all probability never so much as heard the victim's name.

So far from being the editorial ogre whose delight it is to rend and trample upon budding bards, the sober fact is that no living man of letters is more genuinely distressed to see a cruel and unjust review than he. More than one author of distinction has borne testimony to the fact that the hand which was outstretched to him in the hour of his direst need was the hand of the poet-critic of whom Rossetti once spoke as "a hero of friendship." It is true that, like his friend, George Borrow, Mr. Watts-Dunton will have none of your literary bagman who puffs his own wares. And it is true, too, that as he says in "Apollo in Paris,"

"He grieves when bastard-brows are crowned with flowers,
And Helicon grows noisier than a mart,"

but no one is more ungrudging and generous in his recognition of genuine merit. As a matter of fact, he writes comparatively few reviews of poetry in the *Athenæum*, and those few deal only with poets of distinction. "Reviews" is, indeed, hardly the word to apply to his contributions. They are essays pregnant with the fine gold of criticism—essays which display profound scholarship and intimate acquaintance with the literature of the world—but which deal more with the first principles of poetry than with any particular poet.

I remember once asking a well-known writer whether there was any likelihood of Mr. Watts-Dunton "doing" his new book for the *Athenæum*. "God forbid!" he replied. "He would write an article which would be more informing than a volume by any other critic—an article which in its mastery of the subject could be penned by no living hand except his own. But I should be only the peg upon which the rare and invaluable piece of critical workmanship would hang, and in all probability the only mention of my book would come in somewhere within the last half dozen lines." I replied that the writer who is reviewed, even in this way, by Mr. Watts-Dunton might consider himself peculiarly fortunate, for the readers of the *Athenæum*, who take English literature seriously, recognise Mr. Watts-Dunton's hand gladly, and read his brilliant and pregnant articles to the end. Our only quarrel with him is that what was meant for mankind should be given to the magazines. Mudie's knows him not, nor Smith's Library, and until recently one might vainly ransack the British Museum catalogue for his name on the title-page of a book. Rumours of a remarkable romance named *Aylwin* reached us—I am afraid to say how long ago—but though *Aylwin* has been actually in type for years, and a few intimate friends have been privileged to read it, the novel remains unpublished. Unpublished, too, and alas! unwritten is that Life of Rossetti—*the* Life of Rossetti—which only one living man, and that man Mr. Watts-Dunton, can adequately accomplish. And where is the Life of George Borrow for which we had fondly hoped? Where are the Reminiscences of Tennyson, Browning, Lowell, Morris, Jowett, and many another illustrious man with whom Mr. Watts-Dunton has been on terms of brotherly intimacy? Even his magazine articles have been, so to speak, "dragged out of him." Rossetti said of him long ago that he shunned publicity as persistently as other men sought it, and those who know the inner history of the volume of poems that he has at last published, or permitted to be published, know that Mr. Lane wrestled with Mr. Watts-Dunton for that work as Jacob of old wrestled for a blessing with the angel.

The volume takes its name from the longest and most important poem, but the name is in other respects singularly apt and inclusive, for the entire contents of the book might be ranged under the one title, *Love Poems*, with the following four subdivisions:

1. Poems dealing with the Love of Nature.
2. Poems dealing with the Passion of Love.
3. Poems dealing with the Love of Friends.
4. Poems dealing with the Love of England.

To Mr. Watts-Dunton Nature is not only the Great Mother, but the Great Mesmerist. No sorrow is too keen for a pass of her hand to soothe. He turns to her for consolation under bereavement or calamity as surely as his own stormy petrel turns, when liberated from its cage, to the sea.

" Away to sea! no matter where the coast,
The road that turns for home turns never wrong."

No doubt his capability of holding rapt commune with Nature, his readiness to respond to her every mood, is in part the result of the romantic experiences which brought him, in early life, into close association with that wandering people whose very existence in nineteenth-century England is an anachronism—the people to whom Emerson has given voice in rude and characteristic chant:

" The wild air bloweth in our lungs,
The keen stars twinkle in our eyes,
The birds gave us our wily tongues,
The panther in our dances flies."

The title-poem, "The Coming of Love," is the story of the passion of a "gorgio," or gentile, for a gipsy girl. It consists of a number of exquisite lyrics and sonnets, which, by the aid of what, for want of a better word, one must call "stage-directions" and interpolated descriptive passages, Mr. Watts-Dunton has woven together into an unconventional, but unique tragic drama. The difficulties—both in regard to sequence and to sustaining the narrative interest—which such a form presents must, in less skilful hands, have resulted in disastrous failure. To say that Mr. Watts-Dunton has achieved an unqualified success is to pay a high tribute to his ability as a dramatic poet. Only in one instance is its stage machinery obtrusive—that in which the poet watches, across a river, the death struggle between his lover and his rival:

" 'Tis he, my gipsy rival, by her side!
He lifts a knife. She springs, the dauntless girl,
Lithe as a leopardess! Ah! can she hurl
The giant down the bank?"

Is not this with the subsequent stage-directions—"He prepares to plunge into the river in order to swim to her" —dramatically weak? Surely, too, so passionate a lover, at the first hint of danger to his loved one, would have plunged into the river to her rescue! One finds it difficult to picture him standing tamely on the bank that he may act the part of chorus for the benefit of the audience.

But with this single exception, "The Coming of Love" is from first to last a success. The philosophy of the poem, and what Rossetti would have called the "fundamental brainwork," are what might have been expected from one of the most intellectual of living poets. The heart history of the rapt nature-worshipper, learning, by the purity of his love for a true woman, to read the secret of Natura Benigna, as in his loveless days he had never read it, is nobly conceived and nobly unfolded, and is faultless alike as poetry or as psychology. And when, after the tragic death of Rhona, Natura Benigna seems to the half-frenzied poet, wandering restlessly among the great mountains, to be Natura Benigna no longer, but Natura Maligna, the drama rises to a grandeur of lurid power that recalls Coleridge.

" The Lady of the Hills with crimes untold
Followed my feet with azure eyes of prey;
By glacier brink she stood—by cataract spray—
Where mists were dire, or avalanche echoes rolled.

At night she glimmered in the death-wind cold,
And if a footprint shone at break of day
My flesh would quail, but straight my soul would say,
''Tis hers whose hand God's mightier hand doth hold.'
I trod her snow bridge, for the moon was bright,
Her icicle-arch across the sheer crevasse.
When lo! she stood! . . . God made her let me pass,
Then felled the bridge! . . . Oh, there in sallow light,
There down the chasm I saw her cruel, white,
And all my wondrous days as in a glass."

Thence, through a succession of Blake-like pictures, the poem passes on to a fitting sunrise close, with its superb Natura Benigna morning anthem, which is quoted elsewhere in this paper.

The only point that calls for mention in connection with the poetic construction of the work is this: Mr. Watts-Dunton's friends are aware that the conception and scheme of "The Coming of Love" have been in his mind for years, and that each poem has been written as part of a component whole. But the fact that several of these exquisite lyrics have already been allowed to appear in print as separate poems, without any note to the effect that they were, as I have said, parts of a component whole; the fact that the public has been allowed to inspect as single gems some of the precious stones of poesy which are here found in their true setting, will cause the uninformed to ask whether the gems suggested the setting or the setting the gems; whether, to use another and somewhat Hibernian metaphor, Mr. Watts-Dunton has not raised a house, because he wished to enclose between four walls some previously built and beautiful rooms. He has done injustice to himself in letting the work appear without some note explaining the circumstances under which portions have already been published; and in view of the probability, or rather the certainty of other editions being called for, some such explanation might profitably be added.

In expressing one's admiration of "The Coming of Love," as a conception one must not forget to call attention to the many fine lyrics that round it into a single and sustained poem, but first we must congratulate Mr. Watts-Dunton on the success which has attended his curious experiment with Romany as a poetic medium. Many gipsy words—"chirikel" for "bird," "kollo" for "black," "gipsy magpie" for "water-wagtail," for instance—are so picturesque that they lend themselves readily to such an attempt, but to have written, in Romany, a love-letter which, while remaining Romany, passes into pure poetry, is a task which, perhaps, only such accomplished Romany scholars as Mr. Charles Godfrey Leland or Mr. Francis Hinde Groome can adequately appreciate. Rhona's piteous letter for forgiveness is heart-breaking in its pleading, and wherever Romany is introduced throughout, the result is as picturesque in effect as is the touch of red afforded by the handkerchief which a gipsy-girl's love of warm colouring prompts her to twine around her head or to thrust into her bosom.

Nor does Mr. Watts-Dunton omit to make impressive, even lurid, use of the gipsies' strangely superstitious belief in the "Dukkeripen," or omen. To them man's doom is pronounced by the stars, his destiny determined by the shape of a cloud in the sky, or by the very ripples on a river:

"The mirrored stars lit all the bulrush-spears
And all the flags and broad-leaved lily-isles;
The ripples shook the stars to golden smiles,
Then smoothed them back to happy golden spheres.
We rowed—we sang; her voice seemed in mine ears
An angel's, yet with woman's dearer wiles,
But shadows fell from gathering cloudy piles,
And ripples shook the stars to fiery tears.
What shaped those shadows like another boat,
Where Rhona sat and he Love made a liar?
There where the Scollard sank I saw it float,
While ripples shook the stars to symbols dire;
We wept—we kissed—while starry fingers wrote
And ripples shook the stars to a snake of fire."

Another signal achievement is the "Ode to a Caged Petrel." Nearly every bird has now its poet. Shakespeare, Shelley, Hogg, and Mr. Meredith have rivalled the lark with lyrics no less lovely than the carol which Richard Jefferies likens to "a waterfall in the sky." Keats has swooned into song more musical than the nightingale's plaining; Wordsworth has stayed the seasons as perpetual Spring with his cuckoo's cry; and Mr. Swinburne has sent floating sunward and southward after the swallow the very silver pollen of song.

The list might be multiplied indefinitely, as witness Mr. Phil Robinson's book, *The Poets' Birds*. But Mr. Robinson (much of whose work, by the by, appeared first in Mr. F. W. Robinson's memorable little magazine, *Home Chimes*, which counted among its contributors Mr. Watts-Dunton, Mr. Swinburne, Mr. Barrie, and many another distinguished man of letters) must add a new chapter to his next edition. Mr. Watts-Dunton is not the first English poet to write of the stormy petrel; but though posterity is a dark horse to lay money upon, one may give odds that posterity will rank his with the best. It is a noble poem, a poem rich

"In purple of billow, silver of ocean foam,"

and salt with the briny lash and sting of flying spray. As one reads, one's sight, like the sight of the poet's caged petrel,

"Is mocked with Ocean's horses—manes of white,
The long and shadowy flanks, the shoulders bright.
* * * * *
They rise, each foamy-crested combatant,
They rise and fall and leap and foam and gallop and pant,
Till albatross, sea swallow, and cormorant
Must flee, like doves, away."

The italicised line is masterly in its "representative art," and the whole poem is so fine that one may respectfully submit to the future editor of the *Golden Treasury* that here surely is work well worthy of inclusion in that standard anthology.

"The Coming of Love" is no less a love poem than a nature poem. It is, in fact, a love epic, opening with the coming of Love, passing on from the confession to the consummation of love on that sacred night

"When darkness seemed more dear than Eden's light,
Fragrant of Love's warm wings and Love's warm breath,"

and thence to the tragedy of Rhona's murder, after which all that is left of love to the poet-husband is a memory:

"Beneath the loveliest dream there coils a fear:
Last night came she whose eyes are memories now;
Her far-off gaze seemed all forgetful how
Love dimmed them once, so calm they shone and clear.
'Sorrow,' I said, 'has made me old, my dear,
'Tis I, indeed, but grief can change the brow:
Beneath *my* load a seraph's neck might bow,
Vigils like mine would blanch an angel's hair.'
Oh, then I saw, I saw the sweet lips move!
I saw the love mists thickening in her eyes—
I heard a sound as if a murmuring dove
Felt lonely in the dells of Paradise:
But when upon my neck she fell, my love,
Her hair smelt sweet of whin and woodland spice."

Another exquisite love poem is that entitled "A Sleepless Night at Venice," which occurs in the Sonnet-Sequence of "Prophetic Pictures."

"When hope lies dead—ah, when 'tis death to live,
And wrongs remembered make the heart still bleed,
Better are Sleep's kind lies for Life's blind need
Than truth, if lies a little peace can give.
A little peace! 'tis thy prerogative,
O Sleep! to lend it, thine to quell or feed
This love that starves—this starving soul's long greed,
And bid Regret, the queen of hell, forgive.
Yon moon that mocks me through the uncurtained glass
Recalls that other night, that other moon,—
Two English lovers on a grey lagoon—
The voices from the lanterned gondolas,
The kiss, the breath, the flashing eyes, and soon
The throbbing stillness, all the heaven that was."

There are in the volume other love poems no less beautiful, but in them, too, we find twin flames—the red flambeau of passion and the white taper of purity—burning on one altar.

And here I must pause to call attention to a characteristic of Mr. Watts-Dunton's work, both as poet and critic, which I do not remember ever to have seen commented upon—his innate love of purity and his uncompromising attitude toward everything like uncleanliness in literature. It is well for English literature that one who stands in her high places—one of whom so keen a student as Dr. Robertson Nicoll said recently (*Academy*, November 13th), "Mr. Theodore Watts-Dunton is undoubtedly the first of living critics, and perhaps the first of all English critics"—should thus jealously guard the honour of the mistress whom he serves. He is of the company of poets who, in his own words,

"Have for muse a maiden without scar,
Who knows how beauty dies at touch of sin."

He has kept unsullied the white shield of letters which has been entrusted to his care, and his influence for good upon the men and women of his own and a later generation is none the less real and lasting because it can never be estimated.

Pitfalls beset the feet of every poet of individuality and originality, and though no one walks more warily than Mr. Watts-Dunton, he is apt to wander perilously near to the steep and treacherous places of Mount Parnassus. When the successive lines of a sonnet have too great a similarity in rhythm and in fall of accent, the effect is peculiarly droning and humdrum to an ear so sensitive as his. Being keenly alive to this, he seeks occasionally, when writing a sonnet, to avoid monotony by the introduction of an extra syllable in some of the rhyming words. But his tendency to introduce the extra syllable has of late been so marked as to threaten to become a mannerism, as Mr. Watts-Dunton is possibly himself aware, for I observe that the sonnet on James Russell Lowell has been altered from the original reading in the *Athenæum*, so that the second and third lines now end with "years" and "pioneers" instead of with "story" and "hoary." As an example—a marked example—of a sonnet with lines containing extra syllables, the fourth of the second series of sonnets addressed to Rossetti may be quoted.

"Last night Death whispered: 'Life's purblind procession,
Flickering with blazon of the human story—
Time's fen-flame over Death's dark territory—
Will leave no trail, no sign of Life's aggression.
Yon moon that strikes the pane, the stars in session
Are weak as Man they mock with fleeting glory.
Since Life is only Death's frail feudatory,
How shall Love hold of Fate in true possession?'

"I answered thus: 'If Friendship's isle of palm
Is but a vision, every loveliest leaf,
Can knowledge of its mockery soothe and calm
This soul of mine in this most fiery grief?
If Love but holds of Life through Death in fief,
What balm in knowing that Love is Death's—what balm?'"

When it is done sparingly, the addition of an extra syllable gives what some sonnet-students may consider a pleasing variety to the lines, although personally I am strongly of opinion that Mr. Watts-Dunton's finest sonnets are those which are written in the more familiar form. Another sonnet to Rossetti—the first in the first series—may be instanced as a case in point. It is interesting to note, though the fact is not mentioned by Mr. Watts-Dunton in his volume, that the sonnet was originally addressed to Heine, though intended from the first for Rossetti.

"Thou knewest that island, far away and lone,
Whose shores are as a harp where billows break
In spray of music, and the breezes shake
O'er spicy seas a woof of colour and tone,
While that sweet music echoes like a moan
In the island's heart and sighs around the lake,
Where, watching fearfully a watchful snake,
A damsel weeps upon her emerald throne.

"Life's ocean breaking round thy senses' shore
Struck golden song, as from the strand of Day:
For us the joy, for thee the fell foe lay—
Pain's blinking snake around the fair isle's core,
Turning to sighs the enchanted sounds that play
Around thy lovely island evermore."

This is one of Mr. Watts-Dunton's most characteristic sonnets. He can concentrate into fourteen lines what many another poet could not cram into forty. The sonnet is noteworthy also as an illustration of his skilful treatment of elision, by the aid of which he gives some of his lines the confluent volume of sound and sonorousness of organ music. But much as one admires the fine effects he can attain in this way, the fact that his use of elision is fast merging into a mannerism must be patent to every one. It is true that elision, like alliteration, is a plant that blooms on Parnassus. But elision and alliteration are growths of strange quality. An odd blossom or two of either added here and there enriches a nosegay immeasurably, but pluck these treacherous flowers with reckless hand, and the chances are that your carefully culled posy turns to a handful of weeds.

Mr. Watts-Dunton's poems of friendship are numerous. The two sonnets addressed to Rossetti, that have already been quoted, bear witness to one of the most beautiful chapters in the history of literary friendships. Equally beautiful and brotherly is the affection that exists between himself and our one supreme living singer—the greatest lyric poet since Shelley—Mr. Swinburne. Indeed, to enumerate the distinguished men, from Tennyson downward, with whom Mr. Watts-Dunton has been on terms of intimacy would be to give a list of the most illustrious names in later Victorian literature.

Among the sonnets of friendship contained in *The Coming of Love*, there is one entitled "A Talk on Waterloo Bridge: the Last Sight of George Borrow," for which space must be found:

"We talked of 'Children of the Open Air,'
Who once on hill and valley lived aloof,
Loving the sun, the wind, the sweet reproof
Of storms, and all that makes the fair earth fair;
Till on a day, across the mystic bar
Of moonrise, came the 'Children of the Roof,'
Who find no balm 'neath evening's rosiest woof,
No dews of peace beneath the Morning Star.
We looked o'er London, where men wither and choke,
Roofed in, poor souls, renouncing stars and skies,
Yes, every voice that to their fathers spoke:
And sweet it seemed to die ere bricks and smoke
Leave never a meadow outside Paradise."

Mr. Watts-Dunton's two most important poems of the love of England are "Christmas at the Mermaid," occupying about sixty pages of *The Coming of Love*, and "Jubilee Greeting at Spithead to the Men of Greater Britain," which was published in the summer in a separate booklet. In "Christmas at the Mermaid" all the members of that historic club, with the exception of Shakespeare, whose love of meditation has caused him to forsake London for Avon, are assembled at the Mermaid Tavern, with Ben Jonson at the head of the table and Raleigh facing him. Raleigh, who fears that "the fine Elizabethan temper" is dying out in England, is anxious to reawaken public enthusiasm in favour of continuing the struggle with Spain, and he and his fellow-revellers vie with each other in retelling the glorious story of the Armada.

The most successful portion of the poem, with the exception of that fearsome and arresting bit of *diablerie*, the story of Gwyn, the galley slave and the golden skeleton, "God's Revenge," are not, however, the patriotic songs and narratives, but those relating to Shakespeare, "Mr. W. H.," Marlowe, and other literary subjects. It is possible that our recent surfeit of cheap patriotism of the manufactured and music-hall type has done something to spoil one's appreciation of the genuine article, though I am bound to confess that such a verse as the following, which Mr. Watts-Dunton puts into the mouth of Sir Walter Raleigh, leaves me unstirred:

"Wherever billows foam,
The Briton fights at home,
His hearth is built of water—water,
Blue and green;
There's not a wave of ocean
The wind can set in motion
That shall not own our England—own our
England Queen."

This seems to me too much in the style of "Rule Britannia"—on a copy of which Carlyle, according to tradition, once wrote "Cock-a-doodle-do!"—to be worthy of Mr. Watts-Dunton. How much "Rule Britannia" owes to its bugle-call music we shall never know. Its patriotism is of a somewhat gassy nature, and had Thomson lived a century or two later, one could readily have believed that, like many other articles for British consumption, it had been "made to order," and "in Germany," after a pattern designed by that well-meaning if ridiculous young man, William the Versatile. It is not when the British Lion is, in vulgar parlance, "doing a prance round," and inviting creation generally to "come in;" not when those who are the real "little Englanders"—since they would belittle England—scream, "*My* country: right or wrong!" not when Englishmen change the old battle-cry of "For God and England!" to "For England, and—unless otherwise inconvenient—God!" that the sturdy and splendid spirit of British patriotism leaps in our blood again. Rather is it when we see England as Mr. Watts-Dunton pictures her in the following fine sonnet, which shows how genuinely he can, on occasion, catch the true and ancient spirit of British patriotism.

ENGLAND STANDS ALONE.

"England stands alone: without an ally."—*A German newspaper.*

She stands alone! ally nor friend has she,
Saith Europe of our England—her who bore
Drake, Blake, and Nelson—Warrior Queen who wore
Light's conquering glaive; that strikes the conquered free.
Alone! From Canada comes o'er the sea,
And from that English coast with coral shore,
The old-world cry Europe hath heard of yore
From Dover cliffs: "Ready, aye ready we!"

"Europe," saith England, "hath forgot my boys!—
Forgot how tall in yonder golden zone
'Neath Austral skies my youngest boys have grown
(Bearers of bayonets now and swords for toys)—
Forgot' mid boltless thunder—harmless noise—
The sons with whom old England 'stands alone'!"

There are many equally noble and moving lines in the "Jubilee Greeting," but it seems to me that it is as a son and seer of nature, not as a writer of patriotic verse, stirring and virile though it be, that Mr. Watts-Dunton will live in English song. His patriotic poems are the handiwork of a master-craftsman whom long and patient study has taught every secret by which to "build the lofty rhyme." But his nature poems are of an entirely different order. "Natura Benigna," for instance, is less a sonnet than an incantation, like that by which Saul summoned to his presence the Witch of Endor. It is a spell, a wizard word, whispered in the poet's ear by the unseen lips, whence Coleridge and Wordsworth learned their lore—a spell that can at any time conjure the very spirit of nature before us.

"What power is this? What witchery wins my feet
To peaks so sheer they scorn the cloaking snow,
All silent as the emerald gulfs below,
Down whose ice-walls the wings of twilight beat?
What thrill of earth and heaven, most wild, most sweet—
What answering pulse that all the senses know,
Comes leaping from the ruddy Eastern glow,
Where far away the skies and mountain meet?

"Mother, 'tis I reborn: I know thee well,
That throb I know, and all its prophecies,
O Mother and Queen, beneath the olden spell
Of silence, gazing from thy hills and skies.
Dumb Mother, struggling with the years to tell
The secret at thy heart through helpless eyes."

Does not this noble sonnet, with its Wordsworthian sense of space, its Coleridgean grandeur and glamour of imagery, strike a new note in English poetry? Or rather, does it not strike an old note, the note which has been struck in varying degrees of majesty by every true poet from Chaucer to Swinburne?

Coulson Kernahan.

AT POMPEII.

At Pompeii I heard a woman laugh,
And turned to find the reason of her mirth,
Saw but the silent figure of a girl
That centuries had mummied into earth:

The running figure of a little maid
With face half hidden in her shielding arm,
Silent, yet screaming, yea, in ev'ry limb,
The cruel torture of her dread alarm.

At Pompeii I heard a maiden shriek
All down the years from out the distant past;
Blind in the awful darkness still she runs,
Death in the mould of fear her form has cast.

A little maid once soft and sweet and white,
Full of the morning's hope, and love and joy,
That Nature moving to the voice of Time,
Shook her dark wings to wither and destroy.

At Pompeii I saw a woman bend
Above this dead, pronounce an epitaph;
The mother of a child, it may have been,
O horrible! I heard a woman laugh.

Dora Sigerson Shorter.

THE PÆDAGOGICAL TYPE.

School-teachery is Haymarket Square among the professions, peculiarly liable to the explosion of bombs. There are enough teachers who manifest their first symptoms of unrest in "resignation" to give colour to the theory that their true prototype is Balzac's Athanase Granson, who was "likely to reach, through a series of emotions imperceptible to common souls, those sudden determinations which make fools say of a man, 'He is mad.'" As the searching analyst implied, the real "madness" appertains not to the imaginative soul that gives to the world only results, but to the public who wilfully overlook the difficulties under which he labours, and the stern facts with which he is in daily collision, and who are, therefore, startled at the unexpected.

A year or so ago, a Western superintendent of schools, who was admirably adapted by natural aptitude, educational training, and popularity with his associates to continue the good work he had begun, resigned a post worth $4000 per annum. He was led to this determination by no complaint or charge of incompetence. The only reason he gave was that he did not care to be longer identified with and responsible for the administration of the educational affairs of the city. A young man who had had several years of experience in teaching recently declined a good offer from the Brooklyn Boys' High School on the ground that he "didn't like the pædagogical type," and had decided to follow journalism instead. A brilliant woman of thirty-five, graduate of an Eastern college, after teaching for twelve years and attaining the headship of the classical department in an Ohio institution, quietly withdrew, and has since devoted her energies to humanitarian work in New York, preferring, she says, to meet society on a normal footing.

These, of course, are exceptional cases, and are cited in no spirit of special pleading. No brief is here held for the disgruntled or discouraged or changeling teacher. To say that these three had the courage of their convictions is far from implying that others have not. But the fact that thousands of teachers, from Maine to California, are plodding along with apparent content and, apparently, no serious thought of abandoning their vocation, does not deprive the examples presented of their striking suggestiveness. And if it were possible to ascertain the professional views held by the thousands whose lips are sealed, it might transpire that these were not isolated instances, of no particular significance, but rather straws indicating the current of hidden motives. There is certainly no harm in a frank discussion of the mental processes that lead occasionally to such astonishing decisions.

The last two pretexts given supplement each other as cause and effect. The fact that the public school-teacher meets society on an abnormal footing helps to accentuate the type toward which most teachers, both men and women, undeniably tend. This "type" looms up before them as a bugbear and kill joy, and sometimes appeals so strongly to their imaginations as to induce them to abandon teaching—while there is yet time. They doubtless observe that other occupations and professions leave as distinct an impress, that neither the lawyer, physician, business man, nor typewriter can long resist the subtle influence and indelible stamp of his calling. But there are types and types, and the teacher perhaps feels that his, when well emphasised, is quite beyond popular sympathy. And, alas! he is right. The teacher's reward, like that of many clergymen, is to be relegated to an isolated, unreal existence, with no vitalising outlook on the big bounding world or contact with it. His immediate environment fosters in him a narrow conceit, a talky shallowness, a worrisome primness and ethical-mindedness that would unbalance any ordinary mortal, and which compel the world, elbow deep in the batter of life, to make a special case of him. And there it ends; or rather, there his problem begins. What is a man to do when he is shelved socially and intellectually? He may live in the next world, or write his life-lines "to antiquity," but he does not live among his contemporaries.

It is true that he is in constant fellowship with his pupils. But they are not his contemporaries. They belong to another generation, to the world of the future. Discriminate as he will, their standards of conduct, or rather the standard of conduct he inculcates on them, becomes in time his own standard of conduct; and he finds himself living not according to principle, but by rule, precisely as, in the old college days, when he studied philosophy, he vowed that he never would. Moreover, police-duty vulgarises. To be a tool, a mere receptacle for others' determinations, degrades one who can come to his own. Reiteration dulls a bright mind. If, as an able critic once said, "acting is the lowest of the arts; and even if it were the highest, it would be brought low again by its infinite self-repetition," what can be the reflex influence of teaching, and where does teaching rank among "the arts"?

Against what odds must the teacher work! What blighting restraints are put upon his personality, and how he is handicapped in the free play of his individuality! The "superintendent" is usually an uncultured martinet, whose one thought is of his copper-ribbed "system," and whose knowledge of books is confined to the imprint of certain favoured publishers. The "principal" is usually of the jelly or weakfish variety, and manages to keep his balance between the superintendent and the teachers by acquiescing with every brain-cracked experiment of the former and by discouraging independence and spontaneity of thought among the latter. Knowing that his own invertebrate character is merely brought into strong relief by the light of a subordinate's ability or gentlemanliness, the principal is usually blind to merit and lavishes praise only on those who are frail enough to copy his own defects. Well may Mr. Zangwill exclaim, "O the scandal of a teacher's being guilty of originality!"

Then there are the parents to be reckoned with, all of whom, however crude their ideas of education or how superficial their judgments, the teacher must promptly please or the principal will persecute him. In fact, the principal prizes a teacher according as he saves him the necessity of sustaining any personal relations with parents. Moreover, the text-books are not of the teacher's choosing (a carpenter is permitted, I believe, to select his own hammer), and if "free," they are a whole corner-grocery by themselves, requiring a system of double-entry that would craze a peanut-vender or a pawnbroker, to either of whom it were better adapted. And there are likely to be other account-books to record attendance, "marks," vaccination, and so forth, all of which, absurdly enough, must balance as accurately as the entries of a head book-keeper. Whatever energy remains from these clerical duties and the "trimming" necessary to appease one's superiors is devoted to teaching. Under such conditions it is a curse to think. In fact, a thinking man will be least able to cope with the physical rack and mental boredom incidental to them. Circumstances well-nigh forbid that teaching should ever rise above the forced labour we call toil, to the level of real work; or that once attaining that level it should ever find the line of least resistance and be dignified—for the nonce, "art." Friction is a constant, dependable quantity, and must be allowed for always; and strong is the man or woman who, without becoming steel, can steel himself against the wear and tear of the upper and nether grindstone. For teaching, as the editor of an educational journal with unwitting felicity remarked, does "require effort." This effort is unremitting and is only consciously abated if the teacher fall into a rut; but then he becomes an automaton, and his pastime a far from harmless tampering with blank cartridges.

Naturally, when the pædagogical profession is noticed by the outside world, these side-tracked fossilised teachers are overlooked and attention is focussed on the active live teacher, the creature of forced labour, the untiring exerter of effort. One is tempted also to remark, Was there ever so much scrubbing with so little reflex polish? The circus girl gains an ease and grace. Of the teacher it may be said, Others he has helped, himself he cannot help. Mr. E. S. Nadal tells a story of a well-known poet who sat at table "with those who had taught others all their lives rather than themselves." This would be pathetic if it were not so common and prosaic.

It may be questioned if there is any romance about teaching at the best. John Addington Symonds wrote that he was "engaged in the husky task of lecturing to drowsy folk on topics which they neither understood nor cared to be instructed in." One does not have to read many of Lowell's letters, written when he was a professor at Harvard, to discover that he, too, was bored, and writhed right vigorously in the pædagogical harness. Yet between art and lecturing to college students the gap seems less wide. The bathos is rather in the transition from art to school-teaching. There is a pretty little story by Constance Fenimore Woolson, called "The Street of the Hyacinth," which tells how a Kansas "artist" settled in a narrow street back of the Pantheon, in Rome, with a determination to paint. She had come, much to his surprise, to be in the tutelage of Raymond Noël, an art critic, whose books she had secretly adored and memorised. He gave her over to an English artist, who from love of her overlooked her artistic failure and ministered to her false hopes till at his death she was disillusioned, and, Kansas girl once more, turned to teaching. The contrast is admirably worked out.

Without romance, without applause or other outward incentive, the teacher who does not misconstrue Emerson's advice to hold fast the illusions of one's youth will early decide upon one of two courses. On the one hand, he may boycott society even as he fancies he is boycotted, thereby depriving his work of a broad human interest and of "atmosphere," and seek what measure of comfort and congeniality is available within the pædagogical fold. In other words, he will court the companionship of teachers on all occasions. It is as easy as a snail's withdrawing within its shell or an ostrich's burying its head in the sand. Many choose this alternative in the ingenuous belief that it solves the problem. On the other hand, waging an unequal warfare against prejudice, he may determine to win a place with men of other professions. He will aspire to an acquaintance with the leading thinkers of his age, that his teaching may receive fresh stimulus outside of books. He will emulate the example of the late David Swing and Doctors T. T. Munger and Henry van Dyke, who, from the corresponding clerical standpoint, overcame the narrowing restraints of their profession by dint of literary ties. A few seize the latter alternative and nobly triumph. Many give it up, after an ineffectual trial, to their own detriment, or are forced into more congenial fields by a sense of social inadequacy. The last is no anomaly. In fact, most of those who appear to have used teaching as a stepping-stone to something else tried to make it their profession, but could not reconcile themselves to a steady diet of social ostracism and artistic penury, nor endure the dominance of "the machine," of which they were expected to be harmless, unnecessary cogs.

It is true that almost every wage-earner believes his task is the worst. In a private letter, from which I am allowed to quote, Mr. William Winter once wrote to a young man:

> "I should counsel you, or any other person asking advice on the same subject, to avoid both the Press and the Stage. Both are overdone. No vocation could be chosen more difficult, more thankless, or worse paid than that of a writer. Any industrial pursuit is preferable. Saw wood rather than undertake to earn your living with a pen. Above all, do not add to the flood of scribble with which the community is already afflicted about books and theatres."

No one could deny to Mr. Winter a sense of humour. It only shows how inevitably youthful exuberance gives way to conservatism and cynicism even in those who are ranked successful. To enjoin on young men not to renounce their "early visions" seems superfluous when Nature, in her economy, designed that each one of us should have just enough enthusiasm for the knock-down-and-drag-out fight of one life. Young men may well profit by the laconic replies elicited from those who have long been in the professions they are contemplating. The lesson appears to be: Take the line of work of which you will least weary, that of "the least resistance" if you please, for at best all is vanity, and little does the mountain rivulet know of the falls and eddies that will dissipate, as well as accelerate, its course toward the unknown ocean.

In spite of all that has been said, or may yet be said, it is possible to indicate what class of young men and young women may with least injury to themselves pursue teaching as a life-work. By noting the consequences that long-continued teaching carries in its train, we are the better prepared to detect the fallacy of *a priori* reasoning, and to take a sane and discriminating, and, above all, practical view. Any one can suffer himself to be induced to commence pædagogy; those alone make a safe choice who, as Keats said of friendship, first open their eyes to all its faults and drawbacks, and then, remaining passive, observe whether they are still insensibly drawn toward the object. One has no power to break the bonds of such a "call."

Who, then, should teach? And this is only another way of asking, Who can best resist the mordant fixative of the pædagogical type?

It has been well said that whoever takes in hand this great work of education must take it in all its parts. First and foremost is the physical strain. It is a truism that the ideal school does not exist. The following sketch of one is culled from a newspaper:

> "The students have no recess. There is no stated hour for instruction, although it is understood that the pupils are expected to be at their desks from 9 A.M. to 5 P.M. If one is tardy, no questions are asked. If he wants to be late or dilatory, he is the sufferer. There is no roll-call. There is no romping, no high jinks, at any time during the day. There is no sticking of bent pins into the seats of the other pupils; no pitching of the ball; no playing hookey. It is an earnest class. The teacher has never yet reprimanded one of his pupils."

Of course the school here described was in Utopia, or, as Carlyle would have said, in the village of Weissnichtwo. Every one knows that in most schools all the things here mentioned exist or have been perpetrated. The real question put to the teacher is not whether he has a love, and, I may say, the gift, of imparting knowledge, but whether he has such a love as will endure and be aggressive when

> "The etarnal bung iz loose."

It is not whether he has an affection for books, and can spout Emerson in the library or Thoreau in the woods to admiring friends, but whether he can maintain the same elevated view and inspiring grasp of literature in the class-room. It is not whether he can instruct the best students in congenial subjects, but whether he can teach dullards uncongenial subjects, and treat mischievous and sometimes malicious boys as if they were gentlemen, meanwhile not one jot abating his own scholarly zeal and aspirations. Can he be heart-whole against their seeming ingratitude, consent even to be caricatured, and *still* maintain a sympathy with them and with his subject, with no diminution of essential dignity or corroding self-consciousness or bitterness? From time immemorial it has been customary to make the pædagogue or the college professor, however illustrious, the butt of undergraduate jokes. Many of these are of such a "practical" nature as to occupy, in the course of years, a considerable part of his attention. It will be seen, then, that a strong physique is required. It is well to be either a steam-roller or an athlete in constant training. One may emerge exhilarated from buffeting the waves once or twice; but to contend each year with a new and mightier tide of youthful energy that is never quite gorged and sated, and that rises each morning to charge again its human barriers, presupposes an almost supernatural vigour.

No less important in coping with such odds are an even temper, a buoyant optimism, and lots of patience. The last two traits may be little more than a physical enthusiasm and a physical power of endurance, and so are not beyond youth to possess. While the truest optimism is usually the product of experience, few there are who thus attain to it; and a well-tried patience is quite as rare. It is difficult for people who have lived a while not to take what may be called the "middle-age" view of life, divested of every illusion and based on a rock-bottom of fact and common sense. The man who has reached this stage may be very well equipped for grappling with affairs, but he is not likely to succeed as a teacher. No melancholy Jacques who ever lived can inspire in scholars more than a picturesque interest, or support even that without great personal discomfort. One rather pities the students in a high school whose faculty is merrily described by one of its number as "full of cynics." Better far that the teacher be one of those round-faced, wrinkleless characters who proclaim their calling by their boyish ways and ebulliency. And patience, too—though Faust cursed it last among the virtues—at least, intellectual patience in dealing with the errors of others, may be a youthful acquisition. Some, from early years, are more charitable toward the defects of the world than are others. These are fitted by temperament or their own education to be teachers, for they will not be petulant and nagging when they are confronted by the shortcomings and stupidities of children who have "never had a chance." As to the other kind of patience, which is based on a knowledge of human nature, it will perhaps come with experience. It is absurd to expect inexperienced young people to be, morally speaking, other than impatient. But intellectual forbearance and physical enthusiasm are nowhere so widely diffused.

The teacher who is impatient with the infirmities and prejudices of others is very likely, without the knowledge of his peers, to be endowed with an artistic instinct, a creative impulse. Perhaps the converse is nearer the mark, that every creative soul is impelled to achievement by a "love of doing and a scorn of done" that make him at times as discontented with his environment as he is with himself. He never "settles down" to a low aim, and he cannot tolerate those who do. The satisfied man, in his opinion, is always the inferior man, and students who are inclined to choose ways that are lazy and thoughts that are hazy are pretty sure to irritate him. The ablest thinkers, consequently, are seldom the best teachers. From John Milton to Bret Harte it would be difficult to name a distinctively literary man who could patiently teach school. Such a man is quick to see that pædagogy puts him into a false position, and rather than sacrifice the serenity of his temper, he will at any cost resume his freedom. For him only tragedy lies in the direction of teaching. He may adopt it temporarily as a means of livelihood without serious detriment to himself or the community; but sooner or later he must choose between friction and art.

What is needed in the schools is the recreative impulse, that which will enable the teacher to sympathise and interpret rather than originate. He should be above all *a teacher*. He should cultivate that art of getting along with others which we call tact, and cherish definite aims and methods. He should have no inordinate thirst for κῦδος, the paths of which "lead but to the grave," and should be unharassed by the *cacoëthes scribendi* which is to-day bringing to the glaring light of publicity a varied assortment of immature and dreary views, and what is worse, is sadly interfering with the natural growth and efficiency of many of the holders of those views. The teacher's chief delight should be in his own work. He should have a serene confidence in the permanent value of that work, quite apart from public recognition. Getting himself well out of the way, he should esteem "exposition" the highest of all rhetorical norms. He will be more likely to succeed if his mind does not revel in poetic niceties or deep soundings, for students may generally be depended upon to miss subtleties. He will take especial pains not to be haunted by the theory that learning is valuable solely for the artistic use to which it may be put. He will reverence knowledge *per se*, and never, perceptibly, weary of facts. These, rather than principles, will find lodgment in the youthful mind, and must be driven home with unction. To this end the teacher will be incapable of being bored. He will regard literature, even, as something to be communicated, something to be implanted. It will not pall on him because of the association of great names with prosaic tasks. When masterpieces are dismembered; when Shelley's "Cloud" is paraphrased; when the metres of *L'Allegro* are labelled and its commas duly accounted for, he will have no disgust to choke down. He will consent to see beauty mangled that budding minds may acquire polish, and he will firmly believe that, once polished, they will "brighten to all eternity." These "tablets" are his κτῆμα ἐς ἀεί, and sympathy with stumbling humanity is his first duty.

It is plain, then, that the third qualification for teaching is interpretative skill. The teacher should be a telegraph-wire, not a post. He should not possess the artistic temperament.

Be his spiritual outlook that of the missionary rather than of the artist. At any rate, he must habitually take the ethical rather than the æsthetic view of life. This may rob him of attractiveness in the eyes of many, but in its superficial estimates the world is undoubtedly often wrong. As long as young people who are emerging from barbarism crave to have morality taught them no less than taste, the teacher must be able, by indirect preachment and example, to inculcate what is right as well as what is pleasing. "Child schools of ethical culture" has a heavy sound, but infants cry for these, and a consideration of the disorganising influences at work in many homes will leave one not ungrateful that they do. The teacher will find that in the class-room literature itself will inevitably be enveloped in an ethical atmosphere, owing to stubborn little centres of abnormal ethical development. It is difficult, for instance, to view Johnson's *Rasselas* except as it may be related to the last Sunday-school lesson, or to deal with Byron and *Don Juan* separately. The questions propounded indicate what aspect of literature the scholars and their parents are most interested in, and therefore expect you to be most interested in. Of course the trend of your mind will be ethical, and no doubt you will some day write a book claiming that the purpose of literature is "to unite into an organic unity a spiritual conception and a material form, to solemnise the nuptials of the finite and the infinite, to embody what may be in the terms of what is"!

Among the forces of which the pædagogical type of the present day is the resultant must be ranked the science of pædagogy. This is no longer merely one item in the teacher's presupposed outfit, like an acquaintance with the humanities, but it is an influence, and as such is the hall-mark of educationalism. The incipient teacher will reckon without his host if he does not imbibe or affect an interest in Herbart and Froebel. Hegel and Schopenhauer will not be received as collateral. One must hold his psychology of teaching, like a watch, in his hand, and be timekeeper to every circuit or movement of the youthful mind. The interest, the pose, is all-important. No one honestly pretends to an exact knowledge of the application of this science. Such questions as how much time a day should be devoted to writing or spelling, how many studies may be pursued simultaneously, or whether the classical and modern languages are equally disciplinary, are in a state of mellifluous uncertainty. But abstractions to the effect that "the Child's rest is in God" are cheap and elastic. Institutes discuss them, educational journals expatiate upon them. One must keep pace with the greatest. In order to teach, one must know not one system of education, but all systems of education, just as one must do homage to a whole World's Congress of Religions to be good. If the university graduate who has steeped his mind in philosophy and drunk deep of life is of the opinion that his co-workers are making a fetich of the word "pædagogy" and engaging in tiresome logomachies, he had better keep his opinion to himself. Pædagogy is *en l'air*. Once he has filled his lungs with it he will breathe easier. After all, man is a talking animal. In every vocation there is vapid ranting about something: in the ministry, theological quibbles; in the law, hair-splitting technicalities; in politics, free-trade and silver. Of course, no one knows what he is talking about. The Man Who Thinks will learn to keep a straight face with the rest. This is not hypocrisy, but courtesy. No one is asked what kind of a world he will be born into professionally.

Indeed, self-restraint and the timely assumption of that Atlas look which betokens an "outspoken interest" in these matters will be half the battle. Educational fads are not to be ignored by one who would retain his position. Fancy yourself an instructor in a high-school. A "progressive" Principal and School Board are subjecting it to all manner of experiments and innovations, each ostensibly representing somebody's age-end "apperception." At one time the Principal will insist that you take a boy's ability for granted; at another, that you harp on his salient defects and never fail to mention his weak point in a letter of commendation. One year the Board will believe in military rule and the subjugation of the individual; the next, in government by injunction or moral suasion. "Physical exercise" and singing, both probably conducted by the teacher who happens to be hearing the class recite at the time the gong rings, and various systems of "marking" will from time to time be introduced. These interruptions, it should be remembered, are not designed to make a clown of the teacher, but to keep it apparent that the school is forging ahead. The teacher is but a cog in a vast machinery, and will find it increasingly difficult to take himself seriously. It occurs to no one of his "superiors" that he is bestowing half the force of his fine intellect on calculating whether Tom, Dick, and Harry have earned a 7 or an 8 in recitation. It is difficult to imagine what would be the immediate effect on trustees and officers if Emerson should step in and say to the school: "It does not matter so much what you study as with whom you study," or if Garfield could retell the old story of Mark Hopkins and his log. There would certainly be a sensation. And the teacher, for the moment, would expand to the full stature of his manliness. Such a message, however, would be an intrusion on the present trend of things, and count as little as a penny placed upon a railroad track. The tendency in America is to glorify the institution, and reduce strong personalities to a dead level of uniformity and commonplace. Emerson's or Garfield's words would be far less likely to be heeded to-day than would the suggestion that, "in view of the enlargement and enrichment of its course of study, the Squashtown High School be renamed the College of Squashtown, and that a new building be constructed to emphasise its growth and expansion." This is latter-day Americanism, and the withering individual has no right to dispute the supremacy of stone and mortar. Are not granite and the Administration supreme in the Post-Office and the Custom House? And cannot the teacher taste the delights of obscurity along with the man who opens the trunks or handles the mail? Besides, he has his consolations. Chief among them is Pædagogy, the entering wedge of all this enlightenment. He no longer complains that it is expected of him socially. The chatter about Froebel and Sturm and "rest in God" becomes his grand resource. Without these tender affiliations he would be but a fraction of a man—how large a fraction he can now precisely calculate. This, again, is a diverting exercise and will be a welcome contribution to the Bureau of Statistical Information.

How important, then, that the young teacher should nestle up to Pædagogy! It was Dr. G. Stanley Hall who declared, at a "University Convocation," that this word included all that was dearest to him in the present life.

While the foregoing may be a truthful picture of the pædagogical situation, it cannot, I am well aware, be of any particular aid in enforcing the admonition that "nowadays one does what one can." Neither can it add dynamic stress to Mrs. Browning's lines:

"Better far
Pursue a frivolous trade by serious means
Than a sublime art frivolously."

The majority, in every age, prefer to find out the quicksands and rocks for themselves. Last fall, no doubt, scores of enthusiastic, sensitive youths, in delicate health, accepted principalships and instructorships, proclaiming that it was their intention to pursue teaching as a profession. Many a young college man turned his eyes in that direction who had never been known to keep his temper on the slightest provocation, or whose patience was frayed out at the edges in daily intercourse with his little sister. Many a fine spirit or timid talent, that recoiled from obstacles and shrunk before the least hostility, deliberately flung itself into the arena to wrestle with obstreperous boys rather than follow the leadings of its half-blown convictions. The thing is to fill up all the holes with pegs, whether square or round, and not be kept waiting. Many a potential preacher commences authorship, and many a potential author endeavours to teach literature to an ethical-minded community, and many a scholarly mind rejects pædagogy at the personal risk of its owner, who imagines that the appreciation of his pupils is all that is necessary to maintain him in his position.

Well, there are so many professions, we cannot all be hitting the mark. Neither can angelic foresight always be expected on life's threshold. It is only the young preacher who insists: "Be good—be good." The old preacher sagely says: "My dear friends, if you cannot be good, then be as good as you can." And for the traveller who has mistaken a wayside station for his final destination there are crumbs of comfort in the remonstrance of Epictetus: "Man, thou hast forgotten thine object; thy journey was not *to* this, but *through* this."

George Merriam Hyde.

NEW YORK NOCTURNES.

I.

A Nocturne of Exile.

Out of this night of lonely noise,
The city's crowded cries,
Home of my heart, to thee, to thee
I turn my longing eyes.

Years, years, how many years, I went
In exile wearily,
Before I lifted up my face
And saw my home in thee!

I had come home to thee at last.
I saw thy warm lights gleam.
I entered thine abiding joy—
Oh, was it but a dream?

Ere I could reckon with my heart
The sum of our delight,
I was an exile once again
Here in the hasting night.

Thy doors were shut. Thy lights were gone
From my remembering eyes.
Only the city's endless throng;
Only the crowded cries!

II.

A Nocturne of Trysting.

Broods the hid glory in its sheath of gloom
Till strikes the destined hour, and bursts the bloom,
A rapture of white passion and perfume.

So the long day is like a bud
That aches for coming bliss,
Till flowers in light the wondrous night
That brings me to thy kiss.

Then, with a thousand sorrows forgotten in one hour,
In thy pure eyes and at thy feet I find at last my goal;
And life and joy and hope seem but a faint prevision of the flower
That is thy body and the flame that is thy soul.

Charles G. D. Roberts.

ONE HUNDRED BEST BOOKS FOR A VILLAGE LIBRARY.

Editors of THE BOOKMAN :

I have read with much interest an article in the December BOOKMAN entitled "A Hundred Books for a Village Library," by Clement K. Shorter. I am curious to know what sort of village this writer had in mind when he prescribed his list. Was it the average American village, or an English village with a population made up of college graduates and retired professional men, whose book wants and needs he aimed to supply? I apprehend he had no thought of the American village, else he would have included in his list more than a paltry *four* American books out of one hundred.

If I may be permitted, I should like to offer a plea in behalf of the people of our American villages who are on the search for a hundred volume library. Mr. Shorter's criticism of Sir John Lubbock may be justly applied to his own selection, for a large portion would be as unwelcome in one of our village libraries as Butler's *Analogy* or the *Mahabharata;* besides, there is scarcely a modern book in his list. How many of our village people would ever read any of his first seven books, or Goethe's *Faust*, *Don Quixote*, Borrow, Horace, or Rousseau's *Confessions?* The proposition is to name a hundred books best suited to meet the requirements of the average village community. Mr. Shorter does not consider this point, as he admits that his list is limited to pure literature (and includes some thirty books of poetry). It occurs to me that such a library would fail of the chief benefits sought to be derived by a rural people from their village library. The American villagers, while intelligent, enterprising, and progressive, have not usually had their lives cast along literary lines exclusively, and they lack the opportunities for intellectual culture open to the people of our cities. A village library should consist of quite a variety of books outside of poetry; books that give information and mental strength; books of facts and principles; books that will enable youth to trace the rise and growth of houses, tools, governments, schools and industries, religions; books that teach men not only to think, but to see. This is a busy, hustling, practical age, and the battle of life is being waged with terrible earnestness. Time is too precious and life too short for the average villager to give much attention to poetry and the fine arts. It is more to his taste and station to study economics, politics, science, invention, biography, and history. These are matters of every-day service to him. There are boys and girls, young men and young women in our villages—shall the village library have nothing for them?

One would scarcely gather from Mr. Shorter's list even a hint that anywhere on earth there existed such a country as the United States of America. His list does not contain a line of American history or the biography of a single American. I am no Jingoist, but I believe in affording at least our young villagers the noble and inspiring examples to be found in the biographies of our own great men and women. A village library, however small, should contain a number of reference books, since these serve to explain and elucidate all other books. They are continually sought after for information on many topics. Our villagers will be allured into reading real history by reading some of the best historical novels, which give faithful pictures of life and society at various times and places. In the realm of fiction there is a vast wilderness of the good, bad, and abominable. The printing-presses are turning out tons of the last-named, and herein lies great danger to the indiscriminate reader. There are novels of great merit, healthful and instructive, which can be read without resorting to the so-called trash.

I subjoin a list of a hundred books for a village library, selected from the standpoint of my long acquaintance with the needs and capacities of a village population. Out of the thousands of good and suitable books, there could be chosen many lists of a hundred each. This list is a suggestion of the ground that ought, in my opinion, to be covered in forming a practical, working hundred-volume library for an American village.

1. The Bible.
2. The Standard Dictionary.
3. Hoyt Ward's Cyclopædia of Quotations (or Bartlett's).
4. Heilprin's Historical Reference Book.
5. Brewer's Dictionary of Phrase and Fable.
6. Smith's Bible Dictionary.
7. Atlas of the World.
8. History of English Literature. Taine.
9. History of the English People. Green.
10. The Age of Fable. Bullfinch.
11. Eighteen Centuries. White.
12. The Thirty Years' War. Schiller.
13. The Holy Roman Empire. Bryce.
14. The French Revolution. Carlyle.
15. Fifteen Decisive Battles. Creasy.
16. History of France. C. M. Yonge.
17. The Greeks and the Romans. George W. Cox
18. Student's History of Rome. W. W. How.
19. History of the United States. Ridpath.
20. American Lands and Letters. D. G. Mitchell.
21. Conquest of Mexico. Prescott.
22. Conquest of Peru. Prescott.
23. The Beginnings of New England. John Fiske.
24. The American Revolution. John Fiske.
25. Life of Nelson. W. C. Russell.
26. Plutarch's Lives of Illustrious Men.
27. Life of Oliver Cromwell. F. Harrison.
28. Life of Savonarola. William Clark, M.A.
29. Life of Columbus. C. K. Adams.
30. Life of Washington. Irving.
31. Life of Benjamin Franklin. James Parton.
32. Life of Lincoln. Noah Brooks.
33. Lives of Eminent Americans. Lossing.
34. Life of John Paul Jones. Abbott.
35. Life of Robert Fulton. R. H. Thurston.
36. Life of Dolly Madison. Maud Goodwin.
37. Captains of Industry. James Parton.
38. Girls who Became Famous. Sarah K. Bolton.
39. The Oregon Trail. Francis Parkman.
40. Views Afoot. Bayard Taylor.
41. Our Great West. Julian Ralph.
42. Self-Help. Samuel Smiles.
43. Pushing to the Front. O. S. Marden.
44. Homer's Iliad. Bryant's Translation.
45. Tennyson's Poems. Household Edition.
46. Longfellow's Poems. Household Edition.
47. Burns's Poetical Works.
48. Scott's Lady of the Lake.
49. Shakespeare's Hamlet. Rolfe.
50. " Merchant of Venice. Rolfe.
51. " Romeo and Juliet. Rolfe.
52. Milton's Paradise Lost.
53. Moore's Lalla Rookh.
54. Library of Poetry and Song. Bryant.
55. Farm Ballads. Will Carleton.
56. Kathrina. J. G. Holland.
57. Essays of Elia. Charles Lamb.
58. Emerson's Essays.
59. Ivanhoe. Sir Walter Scott.
60. Waverley. Sir Walter Scott.
61. Vanity Fair. Thackeray.
62. Pickwick Papers. Dickens.
63. David Copperfield. Dickens.
64. Zenobia. William Ware.
65. Lucile. Meredith.
66. Monte Cristo. Dumas.
67. Robinson Crusoe. De Foe.
68. Toilers of the Sea. Victor Hugo.
69. Jane Eyre. Charlotte Brontë.
70. Last Days of Pompeii. Edward Bulwer-Lytton.
71. Fairy Tales. Hans Christian Andersen.
72. Lorna Doone. R. D. Blackmore.
73. Scarlet Letter. Hawthorne.
74. Sketch Book. Irving.
75. The Cloister and the Hearth. Reade.
76. John Halifax, Gentleman. Miss Mulock.
77. Ben Hur. Lew Wallace.
78. Uncle Tom's Cabin. Harriet B. Stowe.
79. In Ole Virginia. Thomas Nelson Page.
80. Vicar of Wakefield. Goldsmith.
81. Autocrat of the Breakfast-Table. O. W. Holmes.
82. The Deerslayer. J. F. Cooper.
83. The Hoosier Schoolmaster. E. Eggleston.
84. Westward Ho! Kingsley.
85. Pilgrim's Progress. John Bunyan.
86. Tom Brown at Oxford. Hughes.
87. Little Women. Louisa M. Alcott.
88. The Boys of '61. C. C. Coffin.
89. Adventures of a Young Naturalist. L. Biart.
90. Boy Travellers in Great Britain and Ireland. T. W. Knox.
91. Ten Great Religions. J. F. Clarke.
92. Tools and the Man. Washington Gladden.
93. Fresh Light from the Monuments. A. H. Sayce.
94. Christianity and Social Problems. Lyman Abbott.
95. Life of Christ. A. Geikie.
96. Geological Sketches. A. Winchell.
97. Other Worlds than Ours. R. A. Proctor.
98. How Plants Grow. Grant Allen.
99. Beauties of Nature. Lubbock.
100. Books and Readings. Noah Porter. (A book about books.)

John W. Stone.

TOLEDO, O., December 18, 1897.

Editors of THE BOOKMAN:

Allow me the following criticism on an article appearing in your December number of THE BOOKMAN on "A Hundred Books for a Village Library."

The author says that if he should name the best hundred books that literature has given us, "this task would be but to put on paper the name of volume after volume that no one now reads, that no one to-day would derive any profit from reading."

Are not the writings of classic authors considered the best that literature can give us? I believe that there has never been a greater interest in real literature than at the present time. Good English translations of Homer's *Iliad* and *Odyssey* are read in English work in the high schools of the country, and Longfellow's *Evangeline*, *Hiawatha*, and like classics by school children below grammar grades. Does not the present idea of putting into children's hands choice complete stories and poems from our best writers, in place of scrap-book readers, show that interest in the best literature is very much alive?

I agree that much that would come under the classification of the best literature would not interest the majority of people demanding books of a village librarian; but I object to the thought that the *best literature* ever dies or reaches the stage where to read it would not be profitable. I believe, however, that the author's list for a village library is much too heavy, and would bore many intelligent frequenters of such a library. I do not question Sir John Lubbock's judgment in expecting workingmen to understand and enjoy the German Iliad, the *Nibelungen Lied*, as I do Mr. Shorter to expect the average readers in an ordinary village to appreciate or care to read Milton's *Paradise Lost*, the *Rubáiyát* of Omar Kháyyám, Cellini's *Autobiography*, or the Prologue to Chaucer's *Canterbury Tales*. I should consider it very bad form to criticise a list of books prepared by such a well-known worker in library fields as Sir John Lubbock without fully understanding the ground covered by such a list. I believe the list referred to was given as a *study list*, a very different thing to naming the best hundred books for a village library.

Why does the author speak of the *Nibelungen* as "sad trash"? The *Nibelungen Lied* is supposed to represent "the embodiment of German and hence English spirit," and it is therefore not only a good thing, but patriotic for workingmen to read these Teutonic legends. Many German workingmen would be familiar with it, as it contains much of the folk-lore of Germany. It is classed among the world's lasting literature, and forms the basis of many of our best known operas. As to translations, I have before me an edition prepared for young readers which has much interest for all classes of readers.

I note that Mr. Shorter objects to putting Shakespeare in bulk in such a library, "now that Messrs. Dent and Mr. Gollancz have so adequately provided us with Shakespeare's plays in separate volumes." The idea of putting into any public library a one-volume edition of Shakespeare has for some time been considered a bad policy, and a great many good single-volume editions may be obtained. A good American edition is one of six volumes by Richard Grant White. I should consider this a good edition for a village library, and should think it absolutely necessary to have all of Shakespeare's plays in such a library, for reference, even if some plays were never read.

In deciding as to the best hundred books for a village library, one must consider the hungry minds that are demanding food from a public library in a village or small town. We should give them books that are educating, but at the same time entertaining, and such as will make them love to read.

In the best hundred books for a village library, if it is best from all points of view, the children must not be forgotten. There must be good wholesome romance for the girls; books of adventure and travel for the boys; and interesting volumes for all classes of readers; and surely in this country, at least, a few carefully selected books on American history. I heard a librarian say recently that foreign-born patrons and their children call often for simple stories on American history.

I think that the editions given of the translations of classic authors in Mr. Shorter's list not the best. Do not the best authorities now give the following as the best translations—Bayard Taylor's *Faust*; Norton, Parson, and Longfellow's *Dante*; Bryant's *Iliad* and *Odyssey*; and would not these translations be preferred for a village library?

I sincerely believe that any honest thinker will agree with me that if the works recommended by Mr. Shorter were purchased and put on the shelves of a village library, in this country at least, two-thirds of them would not appeal to the frequenters of the library, and if all the books in the library were of the same nature, it would be impossible to develop in the public a love for good reading. The books are too heavy for any but good readers. Good readers, lovers of books, will read always, but the public libraries should have an educational influence in a community, and should aim to attract and interest the indifferent.

In creating a reading habit, by interesting the public in the best lighter literature, a love for good books is developed, which later on will carry the reader to the "fountains of perpetual life"—the writings of the classic authors.

Helene Louise Dickey.

4213 Ellis Avenue, Chicago, Ill.

JOHN SPLENDID.

THE TALE OF A POOR GENTLEMAN AND THE LITTLE WARS OF LORN.*

By Neil Munro, the Author of "The Lost Pibroch."

CHAPTER IV.

Writing all this old ancient history down, I find it hard to riddle out in my mind the things that have really direct and pregnant bearing on the matter in hand. I am tempted to say a word or two anent my Lord Marquis's visit to my father, and his vain trial to get me enlisted into his corps for Lorn. Something seems due, also, to be said about the kindness I found from all the old folks of Inneraora, ever proud to see a lad of their own of some repute come back among them ; and of my father's grieving about his wae widowerhood ; but these things must stand by while I narrate how there arose a wild night in town Inneraora, with the Highlandmen from the glens into it with dirk and sword and steel Doune pistols, the flambeaux flaring against the tall lands, and the Lowland burghers of the place standing up for peace and tranquil sleep.

The market-day came on the morning after the day John Splendid and I foregathered with my Lord Archibald. It was a smaller market than usual, by reason of the troublous times ; but a few black and red cattle came from the landward part of the parish and Knapdale side, while Lochow and Breadalbane sent hoof nor horn. There was never a blacker sign of the times' unrest. But men came from many parts of the shire, with their chieftains or lairds, and there they went clamping about this Lowland-looking town like foreigners. I counted ten tartans in as many minutes between the Cross and the kirk, most of them friendly with MacCailein Mor, but a few, like that of MacLachlan of that ilk, at variance, and the wearers with ugly whingers or claymores at their belts. Than those MacLachlans one never saw a more barbarous-looking set. There were a dozen of them in the tail or retinue of old Lachie's son—a henchman, piper, piper's valet, *gille-more, gille-cas-fleuch* or running footman, and such others as the more vain of our Highland gentry at the time ever insisted on travelling about with, all stout junky men of middle size, bearded to the brows, wearing flat blue bonnets with a pervenke plant for badge on the sides of them, on their feet deerskin brogues with the hair out, the rest of their costume all belted tartan, and with arms clattering about them. With that proud pretence which is common in our people when in strange, unfamiliar occasions—and I would be the last to dispraise it—they went about by no means braggardly but with the aspect of men who had better streets and more shops to show at home ; surprised at nothing in their alert moments, but now and again forgetting their dignity and looking into little shop-windows with the wonder of bairns, and great gabbling together till MacLachlan fluted on his whistle, and they came, like good hounds, to heel.

All day the town hummed with Gaelic and the round bellowing of cattle. It was clear warm weather, never a breath of wind to stir the gilding trees behind the burgh. At ebb-tide the sea-beach whitened and smoked in the sun, and the hot air quivered over the stones and the crisping wrack. In such a season the bustling town in the heart of the stern Highlands seemed a fever spot. Children came boldly up to us for fairings or gifts, and they strayed—the scamps !—behind the droves and thumped manfully on the buttocks of the cattle. A constant stream of men passed in and out at the change-house closes and about the Fisherland tenements, where seafarers and drovers together sang the maddest love-ditties in the voices of roaring bulls ; beating the while with their feet on the floor in our foolish Gaelic fashion, or, as one could see through open windows, rugging and riving at the corners of a plaid spread between them, a trick, I daresay, picked up from women, who at the waulking or washing of woollen cloth new spun, pull out the fabric to tunes suited to such occasions.

I spent most of the day with John Splendid and one Tearlach (or Charles) Fraser, an old comrade, and as luck, good or ill, would have it, the small hours of morning were on me before I thought of going home. By dusk the bulk of the strangers left the town by the highroads, among them the MacNicolls, who had only by the cunning of mutual friends (Splendid as busy as any), been kept from coming to blows with the MacLachlan tail. Earlier in the day, by a galley or wherry, the MacLachlans also had left, but not the young laird, who put up for the night at the house of Provost Brown.

The three of us I have mentioned sat at last playing cartes in the ferry-house, where a good glass could be had and more tidiness than most of the hostelries in the place could boast of. By the stroke of midnight we were the only customers left in the house, and when, an hour after, I made the move to set out for Glen Shira, John Splendid yoked on me as if my sobriety were a crime.

"Wait, man, wait, and I'll give you a convoy up the way," he would say, never thinking of the road he had himself to go down to Coillebhraid.

And aye it grew late and the night more still. There would be a foot going by at first at short intervals, sometimes a staggering one and a voice growling to itself in Gaelic; and anon the wayfarers were no more, the world outside in a black and solemn silence. The man who kept the ferry-house was often enough in the custom of staying up all night to meet belated boats from Kilcatrine; we were gentrice and good customers, so he composed himself in a lug chair and dovered in a little room opening off ours; while we sat fingering the book. Our voices as we called the cartes seemed now and then to me like a discourtesy to the peace and order of the night.

"I must go," said I a second time.

"Another one game," cried John Splendid. He had been winning every bout, but with a reluctance that shone honestly on his face; and I knew it was to give Tearlach and I a chance to better our reputation that he would have us hang on.

"You have hard luck indeed," he would say. Or, "You played that trick as few could do it." Or, "Am not I in the key to-night? there's less craft than luck here." And he played slovenly even once or twice, flushing, we could read, lest we could see the stratagem. At these times, by the curious way of chance, he won more surely than ever.

"I must be going," I said again. And this time I put the cartes bye, firmly determined that my usual easy and pliant mood in fair company would be my own enemy no more.

"Another chappin of ale," said he. "Tearlach, get Elrigmore to bide another bit. Tuts, the night's but young, the chap of two and a fine clear clean air with a wind behind you for Shira Glen."

"Wheest!" said Tearlach of a sudden, and he put up a hand.

There was a skliffing of feet on the road outside—many feet and wary, with men's voices in a whisper caught at the teeth—a sound at that hour full of menace. Only a moment and then all was by.

"There's something strange here!" said John Splendid, "let's out and see." He put round his rapier more on the groin, and gave a jerk at the narrow belt creasing his fair-day crimson vest. For me I had only the dirk to speak of, for the *sgean dubh* at my waist was a silver toy, and Tearlach, being a burgh man, had no arm at all. He lay hold on an oaken shinty stick that hung on the wall, property of the ferry-house landlord's son.

Out we went in the direction of the footsteps, round Gillemor's corner and the jail, past the Fencibles' arm-room and into the main street of the town, that held no light in door or window. There would have been moon, but a black wrack of clouds filled the heavens. From the kirk corner we could hear a hushed tumult down at the Provost's close-mouth.

"Pikes and pistols!" cried Splendid. "Is it not as I said? yonder's your MacNicolls for you."

In a flash I thought of Mistress Betty with her hair down, roused by the marauding crew, and I ran hurriedly down the street shouting the burgh's slogan, "Slochd!"

"Damn the man's hurry!" said John Splendid, trotting at my heels, and with Tearlach too he gave lungs to the shout.

"Slochd!" I cried, and "Slochd!" they cried, and the whole town clanged like a bell. Windows open here and there, and out popped heads, and then—

"Murder and thieves!" we cried stoutly again.

"Is't the Athole dogs?" asked some one in bad English from a window, but we did not bide to tell him.

"Slochd! slochd! club and steel!" more nimble burghers cried, jumping out at closes in our rear, and following with neither hose nor brogue, but the kilt thrown at one toss on the haunch and some weapon in hand. And the whole wide street was stark awake.

The MacNicolls must have numbered fully threescore. They had only made a pretence (we learned again) of leaving the town, and had hung on the riverside till they fancied their attempt at seizing MacLachlan was secure from the interference of the town-folk. They were packed in a mass in the close and on the stair, and the foremost were solemnly battering at the night door at the top of the first flight of stairs, crying, "Fuil, airson fuil!—blood for blood, out with young Lachie!"

We fell to on the rearmost with a will, first of all with the bare fist, for half of this midnight army were my own neighbours in Glen Shira, peaceable men in ordinary affairs, kirk-goers, law-abiders, though maybe a little common in the quality, and between them and the mustering burghers there was no feud. For a while we fought it dourly in the darkness with the fingers at the throat or the fist in the face, or wrestled warmly on the plain-stones, or laid out, such as had staves, with good vigour on the bonneted heads. Into the close we could not—soon I saw it—push our way, for the enemy filled it—a dense mass of tartan, stinking with peat and oozing with the day's debauchery.

"We'll have him out, if it's in bits," they said, and aye upon the stair-head banged the door.

"No remedy in this way for the folks besieged," thinks I, and stepping aside I began to wonder how best to aid our friends by strategy rather than force of arms. All at once I had mind that at the back of the land facing the shore an outhouse with a thatched roof ran at a high pitch well up against the kitchen window, and I stepped through a close further up and set, at this outhouse, to the climbing, leaving my friends fighting out in the darkness in a town tumultuous. To get up over the eaves of the outhouse was no easy task, and I would have failed without a doubt had not the strategem of John Splendid come to his aid a little later than my own and sent him after me. He helped me first on the roof, and I had him soon beside me. The window lay unguarded (all the inmates of the house being at the front), and we stepped in and found ourselves soon in a household vastly calm considering the rabble dunting in its doors.

"A pot of scalding water and a servant wench at that back-window we came in by would be a good sneck against all that think of coming after us," said John Splendid, stepping into the passage where we met Mistress Betty the day before—now with the stair-head door stoutly barred and barricaded up with heavy chests and napery-aumries.

"God! I'm glad to see you, sir!" cried the Provost, "and you, Elrigmore!" He came forward in a trepidation which was shared by few of the people about him.

Young MacLachlan stood up against the wall facing the barricaded door, a lad little over twenty, with a steel gray quarrelsome eye, and there was more bravado than music in a pipe tune he was humming in a low key to himself. A little beyond, at the door of the best room, half in and half out, stood the good-wife Brown and her daughter. A son of the house, of about eighteen, with a brog or awl was teasing out the end of a flambeau in preparation to light for some purpose not to be guessed at, and a servant lass, pock-marked, with one eye on the pot and the other up the lum, as we say of a glee or cast, made a storm of lamentation, crying in Gaelic—

"My grief! my grief! what's to come of poor Peggy?" (Peggy being herself) "Nothing for it but the wood and cave and the ravishing of the Ben Bhuidhe wolves."

Mistress Betty laughed at her notion, a sign of humour and courage in her (considering the plight) that fairly took me.

"I daresay, Peggy, they'll let us be," she said, coming forward to shake Splendid and me by the hand. "To keep me in braws and you in ashets to break would be more than the poor creatures would face, I'm thinking. You are late in the town, Elrigmore."

"Colin." I corrected her, and she bit the inside of her nether lip in a style that means temper.

"It's no time for dalliance, I think. I thought you had been up the glen long syne, but we are glad to have your service in this trouble, Master—Colin" (with a little laugh and a flush at the cheek), "also Mr. Campbell. Do you think they mean seriously ill by MacLachlan?"

"Ill enough, I have little doubt," briskly replied Splendid. "A corps of MacNicolls, arrant knaves from all airts, worse than the Macaulays or the Gregarach themselves, do not come banging at the burgh door of Inneraora at this uncanny hour for a child's play. Sir" (he went on, to MacLachlan), "I mind you said last market-day at Kilmichael, with no truth to back it, that you could run, shoot, or sing any Campbell ever put on hose; let a Campbell show you the way out of a bees'-bike. Take the back-window for it, and out the way we came in. I'll warrant there's not a wise enough (let alone a sober enough) man among all the idiots battering there who'll think of watching for your retreat."

MacLachlan, a most extraordinary vain and pompous little fellow, put his bonnet suddenly on his head, scrugged it down vauntingly on one side over the right eye, and stared at John Splendid with a good deal of choler or hurt vanity.

"Sir," said he, "this was our affair till you put a finger into it. You might know me well enough to understand that none of our breed ever took a back door if a front offered."

"Whilk it does not in this case," said John Splendid, seemingly in a mood to humour the man. "But I'll allow there's the right spirit in the objection—to begin with in a young lad. When I was your age I had the same good Highland notion that the hardest way to face the foe was the handsomest. *Pallas Armata* (is't that you call the book of arms, Elrigmore?) tells different; but *Pallas Armata* (or whatever it is) is for old men with cool blood."

Of a sudden MacLachlan made dart at the chests and pulled them back from the door with a most surprising vigour of arm before any one could prevent him. The Provost vainly tried to make him desist; John Splendid said in English, "He that maun to Cupar maun to Cupar," and in a jiffy the last of the barricade was down, but the door was still on two wooden bars slipping into stout staples. Betty in a low whisper asked me to save the poor fellow from his own hot temper.

At the minute I grudged him the lady's consideration—too warm, I thought, even in a far-out relative, but a look at her face showed she was only in the alarm of a woman at the thought of any one's danger.

I caught MacLachlan by the sleeve of his shirt—he had on but that and a kilt and vest—and jerked him back from his fool's employment; but I was a shave late. He ran back both wooden bars before I let him.

With a roar and a display of teeth and steel the MacNicolls came into the lobby from the crowded stair, and we were driven to the far parlour end. In the forefront of them was Nicol Beg MacNicoll, the nearest kinsman of the murdered Bialeckan lad. He had a targe on his left arm—a round buckler of *darach* or oak-wood covered with dun cow-hide, hair out, and studded in a pleasing pattern with iron bosses—a prong several inches long in the middle of it. Like every other scamp in the pack, he had dirk out. *Beg* or little he was in the countryside's byename, but in truth he was a fellow of six feet, as hairy as a brock and in the same straight bristly fashion. He put out his arms at full reach to keep back his clansmen, who were stretching necks at poor MacLachlan like weasels, him with his nostrils swelling and his teeth biting his bad temper.

"Wait a bit, lads," said Nicol Beg; "perhaps we may get our friend here to come peaceably with us. I'm sorry" (he went on, addressing the Provost) "to put an honest house to rabble at any time, and the Provost of Inneraora specially, for I'm sure there's kin's blood by my mother's side between us; but there was no other way to get MacLachlan once his tail was gone."

"You'll rue this, MacNicoll," fumed the Provost—as red as a bubblyjock at the face—mopping with a napkin at his neck in a sweat of annoyance; "you'll rue it, rue it, rue it!" and he went into a coil of lawyer's threats against the invaders, talking of brander-irons and gallows, hamesucken and housebreaking.

We were a daft-like lot in that long lobby in a wan candle-light. Over me came that wonderment that falls on one upon stormy occasions (I mind it at the sally of Lecheim), when the whirl of life seems to come to a sudden stop, all's but wooden dummies and a scene empty of atmosphere, and between your hand on the basket-hilt and the drawing of the sword is a lifetime. We could hear at the close-mouth and far up and down the street the shouting of the burghers, and knew that at the stair-foot they were trying to pull out the bottom-most of the marauders like tods from a hole. For a second or two nobody said a word to Nicol MacNicoll's remark, for he put the issue so cool (like an invitation to saunter along the road) that all at once it seemed a matter between him and MacLachlan alone. I stood between the house-breakers and the women-folk beside me—John Splendid looking wonderfully ugly for a man fairly clean fashioned at the face by nature. We left the issue to MacLachlan, and I must say he came up to the demands of the moment with gentlemanliness, minding he was in another's house than his own.

"What is it ye want?" he asked MacNicoll, burring out his Gaelic *r*'s with punctilio.

"We want you in room of a murderer your father owes us," said MacNicoll.

"You would slaughter me, then?" said MacLachlan, amazingly undisturbed, but bringing again to the front, by a motion of the haunch accidental to look at, the sword he leaned on.

"Fuil airson fuil!" cried the rabble on the stairs, and it seemed ghastly like an answer to the young laird's question; but Nicol Beg demanded peace, and assured MacLachlan he was only sought for a hostage.

"We but want your red-handed friend Dark Neil," said he; "your father kens his lair, and the hour he puts him in our hands for justice, you'll have freedom."

"Do you warrant me free of scaith?" asked the young laird.

"I'll warrant not a hair of your head's touched," answered Nicol Beg; no very sound warranty I thought from a man who, as he gave it, had to put his weight back on the eager crew that pushed at his shoulders, ready to spring like weasels at the throat of the gentleman in the red tartan.

He was young, MacLachlan, as I said; for him this was a delicate situation, and we about him were in no less a quandary than himself. If he defied the Glen Shira men, he brought bloodshed on a peaceable house, and ran the same risk of bodily harm that lay in the alternative of his going with them that wanted him.

Round he turned and looked for guidance—broken just a little at the pride, you could see by the lower lip. The Provost was the first to meet him eye for eye.

"I have no opinion, Lachie," said the old man, snuffing rapee with the butt of an egg-spoon and spilling the brown dust in sheer nervousness over the night-shirt bulging above the band of his breeks. "I'm wae to see your father's son in such a corner, and all my comfort is that every tenant in Elrig and Braleckan pays for this night's frolic at the Tolbooth or gallows of Inneraora town."

"A great consolation to think of," said John Splendid.

The goodwife, a nervous body at her best, sobbed away with her pock-marked hussy in the parlour, but Betty was to the fore in a passion of vexation. To her the lad made next his appeal.

"Should I go?" he asked; and I thought he said it more like one who almost craved to stay. I never saw a woman in such a coil. She looked at the dark MacNicolls, and syne she looked at the fair-haired young fellow, and her eyes were swimming, her bosom heaving under her screen of Campbell tartan, her fingers twisting at the pleated hair that fell in sheeny cables to her waist.

"If I were a man I would stay, and yet—if you stay— Oh, poor Lachlan! I'm no judge," she cried; "my cousin, my dear cousin!" and over brimmed her tears.

All this took less time to happen than it takes to tell with pen and ink, and though there may seem in reading it to be too much palaver on this stair-head, it was but a minute or two, after the bar was off the door, that John Splendid took me by the coat-lapel and back a bit to whisper in my ear—

"If he goes quietly or goes gaffed like a grilse, it's all one on the street. Outbye the place is hotching with the town-people. Do you think the MacNicolls could take a prisoner by the Cross?"

"It'll be cracked crowns on the causeway," said I.

"Cracked crowns any way you take it," said he, "and better on the causeway than on Madame Brown's parlour floor. It's a gentleman's policy, I would think, to have the squabble in the open air, and save the women the likely sight of bloody gashes.'"

"What do you think, Elrigmore?" Betty cried to me the next moment, and I said it were better the gentleman should go. The reason seemed to flash on her there and then, and she backed my counsel; but the lad was not the shrewdest I've seen, even for a Cowal man, and he seemed vexed that she should seek to get rid of him, glancing at me with a scornful eye as if I were to blame.

"Just so," he said, a little bitterly; "the advice is well meant," and on went his jacket that had hung on a peg behind him, and his bonnet played scrug on his forehead. A wiry young scamp, spirited too! He was putting his sword into its scabbard, but MacNicoll stopped him, and he went without it.

Now it was not the first time "Slochd a Chubair" was cried as slogan in Baile Inneraora in the memory of the youngest lad out that early morning with a cudgel. The burgh settled to its Lowlandishness with something of a grudge. For long the landward clans looked upon the incomers to it as foreign and unfriendly. More than once in fierce or drunken escapades they came into the place in their *mogans* at night, quiet as ghosts, mischievous as the winds, and set fire to wooden booths, or shot in wantonness at any mischancy unkilted citizen late returning from the change-house. The tartan was at those times the only passport to their good favour; to them the black cloth knee-breeches were red rags to a bull, and ill-luck to the lad that wore the same anywhere outside the Crooked-Dyke that marks the town and policies of his lordship. If he fared no worse, he came home with his coat-skirts scantily filling an office unusual. Many a time "Slochd!" rang through the night on the Athole winter when I dosed far off on the fields of Low Germanie, or sweated in sallies from leaguered towns. And experience made the burghers mighty tactical on such occasions. Old Leslie or "Pallas Armata" itself conferred no better notion of strategic sally than the simple one they used when the MacNicolls came down the stair with their prisoner; for they had dispersed themselves in little companies up the closes on either side the street, and past the close the invaders bound to go.

They might have known, the MacNicolls, that mischief was forward in that black silence, but they were, like all Glen men, unacquaint with the quirks of urban war. For them the fight in earnest was only fair that was fought on the heather and the brae; and that was always my shame of my countrymen, that a half company of hagbutiers, with wall cover to depend on, could worst the most chivalrous clan that ever carried triumph at a rush.

For the middle of the street the invaders made at once, half ready for attack from before or behind, but ill prepared to meet it from all airts as attack came. They were not ten yards on their way when Splendid and I, emerging behind them, found them pricked in the rear by one company, brought up short by another in front at Askaig's land, and harassed on the flanks by the lads from the closes. They were caught in a ring.

Lowland and Highland, they roared lustily as they came to blows, and the street boiled like a pot of herring; in the heart of the commotion young MacLachlan tossed hither and yonder—a stick in a linn. A half score more of MacNicolls might have made all the difference in the end of the story, for they struck desperately; better men by far as weight and agility went than the burgh half-breds, but (to their credit) so unwilling to shed blood, that they used the flat of the claymore instead of the wedge.

Young Brown flung up a window and lit the street with the flare of the flambeau he had been teasing out so earnestly, and dunt, dunt went the oaken rungs on the bonnets of Glen Shira, till Glen Shira smelt defeat and fell slowly back.

In all this horoyally I took but an onlooker's part. MacLachlan's quarrel was not mine, the burgh was none of my blood, and the Glen Shira men were my father's friends and neighbours.

Splendid, too, cannily kept out of the turmoil when he saw that young MacLachlan was safely free of his warders, and that what had been a cause militant was now only a Highland diversion.

"Let them play away at it," he said; "I'm not keen to have wounds in a burgher's brawl in my own town when there's promise of braver sport over the hills among other tartans."

Up the town drifted the little battle, no dead left as luck had it, but many a gout of blood. The white gables clanged back the cries, in claps like summer thunder, the crows in the beech-trees complained in a rasping roupy chorus, and the house-doors banged at the back of men, who, weary or wounded, sought home to bed. And Splendid and I were on the point of parting, secure that the young laird of MacLachlan was at liberty, when that gentleman himself came scouring along, hard pressed by a couple of MacNicolls ready with brands out to cut him down. He was without steel or stick, stumbling on the causeway-stones in a stupor of weariness, his mouth gasping and his coat torn well nigh off the back of him. He was never in his twenty years of life nearer death than then, and he knew it; but when he found John Splendid and me before him he stopped and turned to face the pair that followed him—a fool's vanity to show fright had not put the heels to his hurry! We ran out beside him, and the MacNicolls refused the *rencontre*, left their quarry and fled again to the town-head, where their friends were in a dusk young Brown's flambeau failed to mitigate.

"I'll never deny after this that you can't outrun me!" said John Splendid, putting by his small sword.

"I would have given them their kail through the reek in a double dose if I had only a simple knife," said the lad angrily, looking up the street, where the fighting was now over. Then he whipped into Brown's close and up the stair, leaving us at the gable of Askaig's house.

John Splendid, ganting sleepily, pointed at the fellow's disappearing skirts. "Do you see yon?" said he, and he broke into a line of a Gaelic air that told his meaning.

"Lovers?" I asked.

"What do you think yourself?" said he.

"She is mighty put about at his hazard," I confessed, reflecting on her tears.

"Cousins, ye ken, cousins!" said Splendid, and he put a finger in my side, laughing meaningly.

I got home when the day stirred among the mists over Strone.

CHAPTER V.

Of course Clan MacNicoll was brought to book for this frolic on Inneraora fair-day, banned by Kirk, and soundly beaten by the Dempster in name of law. To read some books I've read, one would think our Gaels in the time I speak of, and even now, were, and are, pagan and savage. We are not, I admit it, fashioned on the prim style of London dandies and Italian fops; we are—the poorest of us—coarse a little at the hide, too ready, perhaps, to slash out with knife or hatchet, and over-ready to carry the most innocent argument the dire length of a thrust with the sword. That's the blood; it's the common understanding among ourselves. But we were never such thieves and marauders, caterans bloody and unashamed, as the Galloway kerns and the Northmen, and in all my time we had plenty to do to fend our straths against reivers and cattle-drovers from the bad clans round about us. We lift no cattle in all Campbell country. When I was a lad some of the old-fashioned tenants in Glenaora once or twice went over to Glen Nant and Rannoch and borrowed a few beasts: but the Earl (as he was then) gave them warning for it that any vassal of his found guilty of such practice again should hang at the town-head as ready as he would hang a Cowal man for theftuously awaytaking a board of kipper salmon. My father (peace with him!) never could see the logic of it. "It's no theft," he would urge, "but war on the parish scale; it needs coolness of the head, some valour, and great genius to take fifty or maybe a hundred head of bestial hot-hoof over hill and moor. I would never blame a man for lifting a *spreadh* of black cattle any more than for killing a deer; are not both the natural beasts of these mountains, prey lawful to the first lad who can tether or paunch them?"

"Not in the fold, father," I mind of remonstrating once.

"In the fold too," he said. "Who respects Breadalbane's fenced deer? not the most Christian elders in Glenurchy; they say grace over venison that crossed a high dyke in the dead of night tail first, or game birds that tumbled out of their dream on the bough into the reek of a brimstone fire. A man might as well claim the fish of the sea and the switch of the wood, and refuse the rest of the world a herring or a block of wood, as put black cattle in a fank and complain because he had to keep watch on them!"

It was quaint law, but I must admit my father made the practice run with the precept, for more than once he refused to take back cattle lifted by the Macgregors from us, because they had got over his march-stone.

But so far from permitting this latitude in the parish of Inneraora, Kirk and State frowned it down, and sins far less heinous. The session was bitterly keen on Sabbath-breakers, and to start on a Saturday night a kiln-drying of oats that would claim a peat or two on Sabbath, was accounted immorality of the most gross kind.

Much of this strict form, it is to be owned, was imported by the Lowland burghers, and set up by the Lowland session of the English kirk, of which his lordship was ruling elder, and the Highlanders took to it badly for many a day. They were aye, for a time, driving their cattle through the town on the Lord's day or stravaiging about the roads and woods, or drinking and listening to pipers piping in the change-houses at time of sermon, fond, as all our people are by nature, of the hearty open air, and the smell of woods, and lusty things—like pipers playing old tunes. Out would come elders and deacons to scour the streets and change-houses for them, driving them, as if with scourges, into worship. Gaelic sermon (or Irish sermon, as the Scots called it) was but every second Sabbath, and on the blank days the landward Highlanders found in town bound to go to English sermon whether they knew the language or not, a form which it would be difficult nowadays to defend. And it was, in a way, laughable to see the big Gaels driven to chapel like boys by the smug light burghers they could have crushed with a hand. But time told; there was sown *in the land*ward mind by the blessing of God (and some fear of the Marquis, no doubt) a respect for Christian ordinance, and by the time I write of there were no more devout churchgoers and respecters of the law ecclesiastic than the umquhile pagan small-clans of Lochfinne and the Glens.

It is true that Nicol Beg threatened the church-officer with his dirk when he came to cite him before the session a few days after the splore in Inneraora, but he stood his trial like a good Christian all the same, he and half a score of his clan, as many as the church court could get the names of. I was a witness against them, much against my will, with John Splendid, the Provost, and some other townsfolk.

Some other defaulters were dealt with before the MacNicolls, a few throughither women and lads from the back-lanes of the burghs, on the old tale, a shoreside man for houghing a quay, and a girl MacVicar, who had been for a season on a visit to some Catholic relatives in the Isles, and was charged with malignancy and profanity.

Poor lass! I was wae for her. She stood bravely beside her father, whose face was as begrutten as hers was serene, and those who put her through her catechism found to my mind but a good heart and tolerance where they sought treachery and rank heresy. They convicted her notwithstanding.

"You have stood your trials badly, Jean MacVicar," said Master Gordon. "A backslider and malignant provan! You may fancy your open profession of piety, your honesty and charity, make dykes to the narrow way. A fond delusion, woman! There are, sorrow on it! many lax people of your kind in Scotland this day, hangers-on at the petticoat tails of the whore of Babylon, sitting like you, as honest worshippers at the tables of the Lord, eating Christian elements that but for His mercy choked them at the thrapple. You are a wicked woman!"

"She's a good daughter," broke in the father through his tears; but his Gaelic never stopped the minister.

"An ignorant besom."

"She's leech-wife to half Kenmore," protested the old man.

"And this court censures you, ordains you to make public confession at both English and Gaelic kirks before the congregations, thereafter to be excommunicate and banished furth and from this parish of Inneraora and Glenaora."

The girl never winced.

Her father cried again, "She can't leave me," said he, and he looked to the Marquis, who all the time sat on the hard deal forms, like a plain man. "Your lordship kens she is motherless and my only kin; that's she true and honest."

The Marquis said yea nor nay, but had a minute's talk with the clergyman, as I thought at the time, to make him modify his ruling. But Master Gordon enforced the finding of the session.

"Go she must," said he; "we cannot have our young people poisoned at the mind."

"Then she'll bide with me," said the father angrily.

"You dare not, as a Christian professor, keep an excommunicate in your house," said Gordon; "but taking to consideration that excommunication precludes not any company of natural relations, we ordain you never to keep her in your house in this parish any more; but if you have a mind to do so with her, to follow her wherever she goes."

And that sorry small family went out at the door, in tears.

Some curious trials followed, and the making of quaint bylaws; for now that his lordship, ever a restraining influence on his clans, was bound for new wars elsewhere, a firmer hand was wanted on the people he left behind, and Master Gordon pressed for stricter canons. Notification was made discharging the people of the burgh from holding lykewakes in the smaller houses, from unnecessary travel on the Sabbath, from public flyting and abusing, and from harbouring ne'er-do-weels from other parishes, and seeing it had become a practice of the women attending kirk to keep their plaids upon their heads and faces in time of sermon as occasion of sleeping, as also that they who slept could not be distinguished from those who slept not, that they might be wakened, it was ordained that such be not hereafter, under pain of taking the plaids from them.

With these enactments too came evidence of the Kirk's paternity. It settled the salary (200 lb. Scots) of a new master for the grammar-school, agreed to pay the fees of divers poor scholars, instructed the administering of the funds in the poor's-box, fixed a levy on the town for the following week to help the poorer wives who would be left by their fencible husbands, and paid ten marks to an elderly widow woman who desired, like a good Gael, to have her burial clothes ready, but had not the wherewithal for linen.

"We are," said Master Gordon, sharpening a pen in a pause ere the MacNicolls came forward, "the fathers and guardians of this parish people high and low. Too long has Lochfinneside been ruled childishly. I have no complaint about its civil rule—his lordship here might well be trusted to that; but its religion was a thing of rags. They tell me old Campbell in the Gaelic end of the church (peace with him!) used to come to the pulpit with a broadsword belted below his Geneva gown. Savagery, savagery, rank and stinking! I'll say it to his face in another world, and a poor evangel and ensample truly for the quarrelsome landward folk of this parish, that even now, in the more unctuous times of God's grace, doff steel weapons so reluctantly. I found a man with a dirk at his hip sitting before the Lord's table last Lammas!"

"Please God," said the Marquis, "the world shall come to its sight some day. My people are of an unruly race, I ken; good at the heart, hospitable, valorous, even with some Latin chivalry; but, my sorrow! they are sorely unamenable to policies of order and peace."

"Deil the hair vexed am I," said John Splendid in my ear; "I have a wonderful love for nature that's raw and human, and this session-made morality is but a veneer. They'll be taking the tartan off us next may be! Some day the old dog at the heart of the Highlands will bark for all his sleek coat. Man! I hate the very look of those Lowland cattle sitting here making kirk laws for their emperors, and their ill-bred Scots speech jars on my ear like an ill-tuned bagpipe."

Master Gordon possibly guessed what was the topic of Splendid's confidence, in truth few but knew my hero's mind on these matters, and I have little doubt it was for John's edification he went on to sermonise, still at the shaping of his pen.

"Your lordship will have the civil chastisement of these MacNicolls after

[illegible]

[illegible] ... while ... themselves ... In the heart of ... always ready ... steel ; ... Highlandman's ... punishing [illegible]

[illegible] MacCailein [illegible]

[illegible] ... except ... the Glens- ... is as safe as the heart ... You might leave ... anywhere ... Dyke with uncount- ... penny the poorer ... end ; there was never lock or bar on any door in any of the two ... locks, indeed, were a contrivance the Lowlanders brought for the first time to the town ; and the gardens lay open to all who had appetite for kail or berry. There was no man who sat down to dinner (aye in the landward part I speak of ; it differed in the town) without first going to the door to look along the highroad to see if wayfarers were there to share the meal with him and his family. "There he goes," was the saying about any one who passed the door at any time without coming in to take a spoon—"there he goes ; I'll warrant he's a miser at home to be so much of a churl abroad." The very gypsy claimed the cleanest bed in a Glenman's house whenever he came that way, and his gossip paid handsomely for his shelter.

It was a fine land this of ours, mile ... herds rolling in ... the seas, growing ... Highlands [illegible] and the rowan swelled grossly in a constant sun; the orchards of the richer folks were in a revelry of fruit. Somehow the winter grudged, as it were, to come. For ordinary, October sees the trees that beard Dunchuach and hang for miles on the side of Creag Dubh searing and falling below the frost; this season the frost stayed aloof long, and friendly winds roved from the west and south. The forests gleamed in a golden fire, that only cooled to darkness when the firs, my proud tall friends, held up their tasselled heads in unquenching green. Birds swarmed in the heather, and the sides of the bare hills moved constantly with deer. Never a stream in all real Argile but boiled with fish; you come down to Eas a-chleidh on the Aora with a creel and dipped it into the linn to bring out salmon rolling with fat.

All this I dwell on for a sensible purpose, though it may seem to be but an old fellow's boasting and a childish vanity about my own calf-country. 'Tis the picture I would paint—a land laughing and content, well governed by Gillesbeg, though Gruamach he might be by name and by nature. Fourpence a day was a labourer's wage, but what need had one of even fourpence, with his hut free and the food piling richly at his very door?

CHAPTER VI.

On the 27th of July in this same year 1644, we saw his lordship and his clan march from Inneraora to the dreary north. By all accounts (brought in to the Marquis by foot-runners from the frontier of Lorn), the Irishry of Colkitto numbered no more than 1200, badly armed with old matchlocks and hampered by two or three dozen camp-women bearing the bairns of this dirty regiment at their breasts. Add to this as many Highlanders under Montrose and his cousin Para Dubh of Inchbrackie, and there was but a force of 3500 men for the good government of Argile to face. But what were they? If the Irish were poorly set up in weapons, the Gaels were worse. On the spring before, Gillesbeg had harried Athole, and was cunning enough to leave its armouries as bare as the fields he burned, so now its clans had but home-made claymores, bows, and arrows, Lochaber *tuaghs* and cudgels, with no heavy pieces. The cavalry of this unholy gang was but three garrons, string, and bone. Worse than their ill-arming, as any soldier of experience will allow, were the jealousies between the two bodies of this scratched-up army. Did ever one see a Gael that nestled to an Irishman? Here's one who will swear it impossible, though it is said the blood is the same in both races, and we nowadays read the same Gaelic Bible. Colkitto MacDonald was Gael by birth and young breeding, but Erinach by career, and repugnant to the most malignant of the west clans before they got to learn, as they did later, his quality as a leader. He bore down on Athole, he and his towsy rabble, hoping to get the clans there to join him greedily for the sake of the old feud against MacCailein Mor, but the Stewarts would have nothing to say to him, and blows were not far off when Montrose and his cousin Black Pate came on the scene with his king's license.

To meet this array now playing havoc on the edge of Campbell country, rumour said two armies were moving from the north and east; if Argile knew of them he kept his own counsel on the point, but he gave colour to the tale by moving from Inneraora with no more than 2000 foot and a troop of horse. These regimentals had mustered three days previously, camping on the usual camping-ground at the Maltland, where I spent the last day and night with them. They were, for the main part, the Campbells of the shire: of them alone the chief could muster 5000 half-merkland men at a first levy, all capable swordsmen, well drilled and disciplined *soldadoes*, who had, in addition to the usual schooling in arms of every Gael, been taught many of the niceties of new-fashioned war, countermarch, wheeling, and pike drill. To hear the old orders, "Pouldron to Pouldron; keep your files; and middlemen come forth!" was like an echo from my old days in Germanie. These manœuvres they were instructed in by hired veterans of the Munro and Mackay battalions who fought with Adolphus. Four or five companies of Lowland soldiers from Dunbarton and Stirling eked out the strength; much was expected from the latter, for they were, unlike our clansmen, never off the parade-ground, and were in receipt of pay for their militant service ; but as events proved, they were MacCailein's poor reed.

I spent, as I have said, a day and a night in the camp between Aora river and the deep wood of Tarradubh. The plain hummed with our little army, where now are but the nettle and the ivied tower, and the yellow bee booming through the solitude ; morning and night the shrill of the *piobmhor* rang cheerily to the ear of Dunchuach ; the sharp call of the chieftains and sergeants, the tramp of the brogued feet in their simple evolutions ; the clatter of arms, the contention and the laughing, the song, the reprimand, the challenge, the jest—all these were pleasant to me.

One morning I got up from a bed of gall or bog-myrtle I shared with John Splendid after a late game of chess, and fared out on a little eminence looking over the scene. Not a soldier stirred in his plaid ; the army was drugged by the heavy fir-winds from the forest behind. The light of the morning flowed up wider and whiter from the Cowal hills, the birds woke to a rain of twittering prayer among the bushes ere ever a man stirred more than from side to side to change his dream. It was the most melancholy hour I ever experienced, and I have seen fields in the wan morning before many a throng and bloody day. I felt " fey," as we say at home—a premonition that here was no conquering force, a sorrow for the glens raped of their manhood, and hearths to be desolate. By-and-bye the camp moved into life, Dunbarton's drums beat the reveille, the pipers arose, doffed their bonnets to the sun, and played a rouse ; my gloom passed like a mist from the mountains.

They went north by the Aora passes into the country of Breadalbane, and my story need not follow them beyond.

Inneraora burghers went back to their commercial affairs, and I went to Glen Shira to spend calm days on the river and the hill. My father seemed to age perceptibly, reflecting on his companion gone, and he clung to me like the *crotal* to the stone. Then it was (I think) that some of the sobriety of life first came to me, a more often cogitation and balancing of affairs. I began to see some of the tanglement of nature, and appreciate the solemn mystery of our travel across this vexed and care-warped world. Before, I was full of the wine of youth, giving doubt of nothing a lodgment in my mind, acting ever on the impulse, sucking the lemon, seeds and all, and finding it unco sappy and piquant to the palate. To be face to face day after day with this old man's grief, burdened with his most apparent double love, conscious that I was his singular bond to the world he would otherwise be keen to be leaving, set me to chasten my dalliance with fate. Still and on, our affection and its working on my prentice mind is nothing to dwell on publicly. I've seen bearded men kiss each other in the France, a most scandalous exhibition surely, one at any rate that I never gazed on without some natural Highland shame, and I would as soon kiss my father at high noon on the open street as dwell with paper and ink upon my feeling to him.

We settled down to a few quiet weeks after the troops had gone. Rumours came of skirmishes at Tippermuir and elsewhere. I am aware that the fabulous Wishart makes out that our lads were defeated by Montrose at every turning, claiming even Dundee, Crief, Strathbogie, Methven Wood, Philiphaugh, Inverness, and Dunbeath. Let any one coldly calculate the old rogue's narrative, and it will honestly appear that the winner was more often Argile, though his lordship never followed up his advantage with slaughter and massacre as did his foes at Aberdeen. All these doings we heard of but vaguely, for few came back except an odd lad wounded and cut off in the wilds of Athole from the main body.

Constant sentinels watched the land from the fort of Dunchuach, that dominates every pass into our country, and outer guards took day and night about on the remoter alleys of Aora and Shira Glens. South, east, and west, we had friendly frontiers ; only to the north were menace and danger, and from the north came our scaith—the savage north and jealous.

These considerations seemed, on the surface, little to affect Inneraora and its adjacent parts. We slept soundly at night, knowing the warders were alert ; the women with absent husbands tempered their anxiety with the philosophy that comes to a race ever bound to defend its own doors.

The common folks had *ceilidhs* at night, gossip parties in each other's houses, and in our own hall the herds and shepherds often convocate to change stories, the tales of the Fingalians, Ossian and the Finne. The burgh was a great place for suppers too, and never *ceilidh* nor supper went I to, but the daughter of Provost Brown was there before me. She took a dislike to me, I guessed at last, perhaps thinking I appeared too often, and I was never fully convinced of this till I met her once with some companions walking in the garden of the castle, that always stood open for respectable visitors.

I was passing up the Dame's Pad, as it was called, a little turfed road, overhung by walnut trees brought by the old Earl from England. I had on a Lowland costume with a velvet coat and buckled shoes, and one or two vanities a young fellow would naturally be set up about, and the consciousness of my trim clothing put me in a very complacent mood as I stopped and spoke with the damsels.

They were pretty girls all, and I remember particularly that Betty had a spray of bog-myrtle and heather fastened at a brooch at her neck.

She was the only one who received me coldly, seemed indeed impatient to be off, leaving the conversation to her friends while she toyed with a few late flowers on the bushes beside her.

"You should never put heather and gall together," I said to her rallyingly.

"Indeed!" she said, flushing. "Here's one who wears what she chooses, regardless of custom or freit."

"But you know," I said, "the badge of the Campbell goes badly with that of so bitter a foe as the MacDonald. You might as well add the oat-stalk of Montrose, and make the emblem tell the story of those troubles."

It was meant in good humour, but for some reason it seemed to sting her to the quick. I could see it in the flash of her eyes and the renewed flush at her temples.

There was a little mischievous girl in the company, who giggled and said, "Betty's in a bad key to-day; her sweetheart has vexed her surely."

It was a trivial remark, but I went off with it in my mind.

A strange interest in the moods of this old school-friend had begun to stir me. Meeting her on my daily walks to town by the back way through the new avenue, I found her seemingly anxious to avoid me, and difficult to warm to any interest but in the most remote and abstract affairs. Herself she would never speak of, her plans, cares, ambitions, preferences, or aversions; she seemed dour set on aloofness. And though she appeared to listen to my modestly phrased exploits with attention and respect, and some trepidation at the dangerous portions, she had notably more interest in my talk of others. Ours was the only big house in the glen she never came calling to, though her father was an attentive visitor and supped his curds-and-cream of a Saturday with friendly gusto, apologising for her finding something to amuse and detain her at Roderick's over the way, or the widow's at Gearran Bridge.

I would go out on these occasions and walk in the open air with a heart uneasy.

And now it was I came to conclude, after all, that much as a man may learn of many women studied indifferently, there is something magical about his personal regard for one, that sets up a barrier of mystery between them. So long as I in former years went on the gay assumption that every girl's character was on the surface, and I made no effort to probe deeper, I was the confident, the friend, of many a fine woman. They all smiled at my douce sobriety, but in the end they preferred it to the gaudy recklessness of more handsome men.

But here was the conclusion of my complacent belief in my knowledge of the sex. The oftener I met her the worse my friendship progressed. She became a problem behind a pretty mask, and I would sit down, as it were, dumb before it and guess at the real woman within. Her step on the road as we would come to an unexpected meeting, her handling of a flower I might give her in a courtesy, her most indifferent word as we met or parted, became a precious clue I must ponder on for hours. And the more I weighed these things, the more confused thereafter I became in her presence. "If I were in love with the girl," I had to say to myself at last, "I could not be more engrossed in her mind."

The hill itself, with days of eager hunting after the red-deer, brought not enough distraction, and to stand by the mountain tarns and fish the dark trout was to hold a lonely carnival with discontent.

It happened sometimes that on the street of Inneraora I would meet Betty convoying her cousin young MacLachlan to his wherry (he now took care to leave for home betimes), or with his sister going about the shops. It would be but a bow in the bye-going, she passing on with equanimity, and I with a maddening sense of awkwardness, that was not much bettered by the tattle of the plainstanes, where merchant lads and others made audible comment on the cousinly ardour of young Lachie.

On Sundays, perhaps worst of all, I found my mind's torment. Our kirk to-day is a building of substantiality and even grace; then it was a somewhat squalid place of worship, in whose rafters the pigeons trespassed and the swallow built her home. We sat in torturous high-backed benches so narrow that our knees rasped the boards before us, and sleep in Master Gordon's most dreary discourse was impossible. Each good family in the neighbourhood had its own pew, and Elrigmore's, as it is to this day, lay well in the rear among the shadows of the loft, while the Provost's was a little to the left and at right angles, so that its occupants and ours were in a manner face to face.

Old Gordon would be into many deeps of doctrine no doubt while I was in the deeper depths of speculation upon my lady's mind. I think I found no great edification from the worship of those days—shame to tell it!—for the psalms we chanted had inevitably some relevance to an earthly affection, and my eyes were forever roaming from the book or from the preacher's sombre face.

They might rove far and long, but the end of each journey round that dull interior was ever in the Provost's pew, and, as if by some hint of the spirit, though Betty might be gazing steadfastly where she ought, I knew that she knew I was looking on her. It needed but my glance to bring a flush to her averted face. Was it the flush of annoyance or of the conscious heart? I asked myself, and remembering her coldness elsewhere, I was fain to think my interest was considered an impertinence. And there I would be in a cold perspiration of sorry apprehension.

(*To be continued.*)

THE BOOKMAN'S LETTER-BOX.

The holiday season has left us in a benignant mood; so that just for once we are going to let our correspondents have a little more space than usual in which to air their grievances and bewilder our minds.

I.

A lady in Alton, Illinois, who signs herself L. E. C., says some amiable things about the Letter-Box, and then propounds three searching questions. They are these:

"1. Why are editorial departments almost always conducted by unsigned talent?"

Partly because of long-established custom, and partly because of the well-known editorial modesty.

"2. Why do the critics speak with such unstinted praise of the writings of Henry James? His latter-day novels are to the average novel reader more stupid than a five-barrelled sermon."

Exactly; and so the average novel reader goes off and reads Marie Corelli for a change. But if one is a novel reader above the average, he is fascinated by Mr. James's subtlety, his psychology, and his delicate yet searching style.

"3. Why do the realistic writers persist in reproducing the commonplace types? . . . Surely it is time for an idealised realism. Not what we and our commonplace neighbours *are*, but what we *would* and *could* be."

Yes; but what you *are* is real, and realism deals with realities. What you *would* be is perhaps ideal; but—well, you surely see the point. Please don't make us write an essay.

II.

A gentleman in Middletown, Connecticut, writes:

"I grieve to learn from your editorial note on page 182 of the November BOOKMAN that Mr. Crawford has been 'broken' by his visits to America. Do you mean financially, or in health? Your sentence reads: '—— where (*i.e.*, in Sorrento) he has lived ever since, broken only by his visits to America.'"

The gentleman in Middletown, Connecticut, has scored.

III.

A correspondent who lives on Ellis Avenue, Chicago, writes us a letter. We don't know what on earth he is driving at, but we print his remarks, and will give a prize for their satisfactory elucidation if sent in before the expiration of thirty (30) days.

"DEAR EDITORS: Your common-sense defence of your Letter-Box in the November number encourages me in asking you a question or two.

"Has a speaker ever given you a gentle thought in one sentence? What do you think of the following: 'The birds rest at night'?

"In reading Ian Maclaren's *Beside the Bonnie Brier Bush*, have you noticed the power with which he uses the word 'when'? For example: 'When George came home for the last time.' How soothing the introductory word! How it shines after a thousand tortures!

"What do you think of the following:

"'O Star! Who knowest what thou art?
Who can on earth thy secret steal?
What matchless worth, what utter dross
Thy light conceals!'"

IV.

A lady of a very literal turn of mind, writing from the editorial rooms of the *Advance* (Chicago), asks this severely critical question:

"DEAR SIRS: Will you please inform a benighted reader how inserting *u* in such words as 'honor,' 'splendor,' 'valor,' etc., gives 'sonorousness' to them? (See November BOOKMAN, p. 201.)

"Please tell me what is really the difference of sound between 'honor' and 'honour.'"

Of course there is no difference in the actual sound as pronounced; but the eye, if accustomed to the fuller, more dignified, and more stately forms "honour," "valour," "splendour," recalls it to the ear when the words are spoken, thus translating terms of sight into terms of sound. We are all continually doing this sort of thing in ordinary life and speech, one sense mysteriously affecting or instructing another. Thus we heard a gentleman say the other day, after trying a foreign dish, "Well, it tastes exactly like old boots!" Now, it is not to be supposed that this gentleman had ever eaten any old boots, or even that he had ever gingerly nibbled at an old boot; but his sense of smell told him, by an interchange of sense-perceptions, just how an old boot must actually taste.

V.

C. H. D. of this city wants to get way down deep into a valuable secret. He asks:

"Is book-writing really as unprofitable as is often said?"

It all depends upon the book.

VI.

A Philadelphian who signs himself (or herself) "An Anxious Reader," writes this letter:

"Editors of THE BOOKMAN:

"The Letter Box of the November BOOKMAN in answer to a correspondent contains the following: 'We hold that a writer who has but one style at his disposal is in the same case as a man who has only one suit of clothes in his wardrobe.'

"1. Now we want to know if a man would be justified in keeping his only suit of clothes in his wardrobe?

"2. If 'he feels rather awkward when he has to wear it on the golf links or at a bicycle breakfast,' how must he feel on other occasions?"

Oh, come now!

VII.

A nice girl in Scranton, Pennsylvania, who signs herself "A Clear White Soul," writes us four pages that are most amusing. But we detect between the lines a lurking desire to have a little fun at our expense, under a show of meekness; so we shall not print the communication, because it is not written in good faith. But we salute her amicably; for, as we said before, she is undoubtedly a nice girl,—if she isn't a man.

VIII.

The lady in Sierra Madre, California, who writes a beautiful English hand, and who was asked by us in these columns to let us know her name for our personal information, has courteously complied with our request. We, in our turn, desire to express our thanks for this mark of her confidence and good will.

IX.

E B. S B. earnestly inquires:

"Do you think it possible to read THE BOOKMAN in its present style of binding without suffering from temporary cross-eyedness?"

Yes. Why not?

X.

A reader sends us a newspaper clipping of a column and a half in length and headed "From Writing Books to Killing Hogs." Then he asks:

"Will you please publish your opinion of the enclosed article?"

The clipping gives an account of a young man who began a literary career by writing a book of travel, and then suddenly decided to take up the business of pork-packing as being more profitable. Well, our opinion is at any one's disposal. We read the young man's book of travel last year when it appeared, and from its general style and merit, we think that it is most sensible and commendable of him to give up literature and take to pork.

XI.

Immediately after we put forth our last observation on "To-morrow *is*," Miss Carolyn Wells returned to the fray with an argumentative letter. We intended to publish it in the present Letter-Box, but cannot do so now, partly because we have temporarily mislaid it, and partly because other persons have also been taking a hand at the same question. So we shall wait until all the arguments are in before having a grand philological and polemical round-up, so to speak.

XII.

A number of readers have inquired why there was no Letter-Box in the Christmas number. We answer that the Letter-Box appears only when there are letters to answer. We do not promise to have one every month. Here is a chance for certain readers to write and say they are glad to hear it. But we know these persons. They are correspondents who have at sundry times sent us complicated questions, thinking to rattle us, but who didn't.

Judging, however, from the number of letters that are still on our files waiting for an answer, we should say that the Letter-Box will have to be kept going right through the rest of the epistolary season.

PHILOMEL TO CORYDON.

Shepherd, wilt thou take counsel of the bird,
  That oft hath hearken'd, from this leafy lair,
To love's entreaty, and the parting word?—
  Sue not so humbly to the haughty fair.
Pipe, in her praise, upon thine oaten straw;
  And pipe the louder when she says thee nay:
Swear that her lightest wish to thee is law;
  But break the law, twice twenty times a day.
Trust not to argument, or thou'rt undone;
  But calmly, gently, when she doth protest
  Her course is East, impel her to the West;
Approve her way, but lead her in thine own.
  For learn, fond youth, would'st thou escape disaster
  That woman likes a slave—but loves a master.

William Young.

NEW BOOKS.

THE HOUSE OF BLACKWOOD.*

We desire to give the most cordial welcome possible to these admirable and most interesting volumes. They are so interesting that the present reviewer sat up half a night to finish them. Mrs. Oliphant did her work so admirably that we do not hesitate to say that this, her last book, will outlive all the rest. She had a subject which she thoroughly knew, and into the treatment of which she could put all her great powers. Too often she wrote about things of which she knew just enough to make fireworks of them. Here she is throughout perfectly at home, and this consciousness of knowledge and of power gives a calmness and a geniality to her accomplished style which we miss in many of her books. Few can adequately appreciate the enormous difficulty of her labour. She was overwhelmed with materials. To examine conscientiously huge boxes of faded letters, to select the best, and to weave them into a narrative which carries the reader irresistibly on, to avoid mistakes of taste and temper in describing so many of the irritable race, to write the history of fiery controversies not even yet dead with a serene impartiality, is what very few could have done, and we believe no one so well as Mrs. Oliphant, unless possibly Mr. Andrew Lang, who has gone over part of the same ground, and acquitted himself no less triumphantly. The peculiar charm of this book lies in the fact that it is not merely a notable contribution to literary history—though it is certainly that—but also that in telling the story of the Blackwoods it has all the interest of a novel bringing us into contact with real and powerful personalities. In fact, the book has all the charm of the magazine itself. It has all its force, brilliancy, and occasional hardihood, and is altogether free from the occasional coarseness and ferocity which every one will admit characterised the early days of *Maga*. Mrs. Oliphant found a worthy and congenial task in writing the history of the great publishing house, and she did it as it ought to have been done. There could not be higher praise. These volumes are an addition to the standard literature of our day.

The difficulty which must embarrass every reviewer is the embarrassment of riches. Our copy of the book is turned down at almost every page. It is quite impossible even to touch one tenth of the subjects thus suggested, and all we can pretend to give is a few notes. It ought to be said that although the ground and much of the first volume is familiar, Mrs. Oliphant touches no subject without throwing fresh and welcome light on it. We vehemently disagree with an able critic who complains that there are not more extracts from *Blackwood's Magazine*. The very distinction of this book is that it is all original. As for *Blackwood's Magazine*, those who are worthy to criticise this book ought to have a set and to know the best part of it. If we have occasion to remark on any omission this is not to be taken as a complaint. Mrs. Oliphant was compelled to make a thousand omissions by the very nature of the case, and for our part we should have been glad if the work had run in the good old fashion to twenty volumes.

On the whole, perhaps, the most interesting and living figure in these volumes is that of William Blackwood himself, the founder of the firm and magazine. He appears in these pages as a strong, sturdy, shrewd Scot, as a man with a talent for business, and a perception for literary excellence which amounted to nothing less than genius. But we have more of him than this, much more. We see him in the intimacy of his private life, in the tenderness of his affections, in his profound and for the most part unexpressed piety. The most beautiful thing we have read for a long time is the letter he wrote to his son in India when that son announced his intention of getting married. The publisher, not old, but worn with the stress of life, was very near the end ; and the combination of solicitude, of love, of self-sacrifice, devotion, and chivalry, must leave a strong impression on the mind of every reader. The let-

* William Blackwood and His Sons : their Magazines and Friends. By Mrs. Oliphant. 2 vols. New York : Charles Scribner's Sons. $10.50.

ter, indeed, is one of the very best in the language, and there has been nothing to touch it in any recent biography, not even in Tennyson's. Every writer on the *Blackwood's* is confronted by the question, How did such a man as Blackwood permit the personalities which appeared in the early years of his magazine? We do not think it is very difficult to answer. For one thing, Mr. Blackwood saw with perfect clearness that there must be life in his magazine if it was to live. The *Edinburgh Review* had at any rate taught him as much as that—if, indeed, he needed the teaching. He perceived also that his chance was to get new writers, young men of vigorous and aggressive personality. He found them with a vengeance in Lockhart and in Christopher North. Having such allies, it was impossible he could altogether repress them. He controlled them to a large extent, but often he gave them their heads. Nor will it be denied that he had a certain secret sympathy with their rashness, and was willing to take his chance. Through all the clamour he was firm as a rock, meeting the abuse and threats that came from every quarter with supreme courage and firmness, and yet all the while prudent in his counsels and seriously anxious to do for his business what he could by enlisting the strongest recruits. In the second place, the manners of the time were rough, and but few writers could be acquitted of odious personalities. To our mind Hazlitt was a very much greater writer than either Lockhart or Wilson, but who does not hang his head when he reads Hazlitt's essay on Coleridge? In the third place, both Lockhart and Wilson, and especially the former, were masters of satire. It is a little difficult for us now to enjoy the articles which made in their day so great a sensation. To tell the truth, some of them remind one of Tom Paine and his description of Abraham as "the principal ruffian of a restless gang." Many of the jokes inevitably appear clumsy and floundering; and besides, the people attacked, though no doubt they were once real live monsters, whom it was thought creditable to kill, have now faded from memory. On the whole, we have come to sounder ideas about severe criticisms. Such there must always be, but we think it is now generally felt that they ought not to be anonymous. In fact, it is beginning to be accepted as a sound principle that no man should write any criticism to which he would be ashamed to affix his name. All that can be said is that much of the writing complained of was done under violent excitement, and may as well be forgotten. We wish we could say that either Wilson or Lockhart belonged to that small, strange and heroic class of writers referred to by Fitzjames Stephen, who, being men of great ability, have a genuine intellectual sympathy with the losing side. Lockhart and Wilson both loved to be in the majority, and their arguments suited the majority, for most certainly they were never fine spun or cloisterlike.

As to Lockhart, he appears in a less favourable light here than in the biography of Mr. Lang. His was a personality which is emphatically not to be described in a single phrase, or even in a few phrases. If we have any complaint against Mrs. Oliphant, it is that so far as we can see she entirely ignores what was at once the best and the worst thing Lockhart ever did in connection with *Blackwood*. She must have been aware of the extraordinary attack on Professor Playfair. Playfair began his career as a parish minister, and ended as a professor in the University of Edinburgh. He was a great mathematician, and a very amiable man. It is worth saying that his style was singularly beautiful and lucid, even when he was dealing with the most difficult subjects, and that his *Edinburgh Review* articles are always easily recognised. Perhaps it has not been said before that Brewster modelled his style on Playfair, though never successfully, for he attempted too much, and he had not a particle of imagination. Lockhart attacked Playfair as an apostate allied with a band of men like those whom St. Augustine calls "the corruptors." No more severe and unjustified attack was ever written, and there does not seem to have been the very slightest foundation for it. Playfair was no doubt a Moderate, both when he was a minister, and also when he was a professor. That he altered his convictions in the smallest degree there is no evidence, or rather what evidence there is points directly the other way. Lockhart had much more to justify him when he attacked the religion of the *Edinburgh Review*, and in the whole range of his writings there is nothing so calm, and yet so stinging and so crushing, as his dissection of Sydney Smith and his hatred of the awful mysteries of the soul. Lockhart, with all his aberrations, was a true son of the manse. None knew better that there are two great types of religion—the feeling of awe and responsibility, and the feeling of personal affection for the object of worship. In the *Edinburgh Review* he recognised neither type, and there was much to support his contention. He himself, though reticently, no doubt, adhered to the latter view, in this a singular contrast to his great father-in-law, Sir Walter Scott, who in the direst extremities of his life never seems once to have offered up a prayer. To Wilson justice is done. His daughter, Mrs. Gordon, in the silly and misleading biography which has hitherto been almost the only authorised source of information, makes out that her father had little part in the excesses of *Blackwood*. As it happened, he was far more guilty than Lockhart. It is shown in this biography that Wilson seemed sometimes to be possessed with an evil spirit. He could not refrain from lampooning Wordsworth, although he had accepted Wordsworth's hospitality, and had professed the warmest admiration for his poetry. It was Sir Walter Scott who practically won for him his professorship, and yet he wrote malignantly about his benefactor. When he was likely to be found out he wrote letters which one is humiliated to read, imploring Blackwood to keep him concealed. Mrs. Oliphant says well about one of these epistles : "It is a tragedy indeed, and shows an almost despairing collapse of every faculty." As might have been expected, Wilson was a most troublesome contributor, nearly always late with his copy ; yet with all his drawbacks he did much for the magazine, and the Blackwoods knew it, and most cordially recognised it. Ordinarily his writing was free from all qualms and refinement. His style was sturdy and full-bodied, and his attacks on books and authors were in the good old hang-him by-the-neck-till-he-is-dead style. Yet Wilson's real power lay in this, that he illustrated the vein of poetry and romance which runs through every part of the Scottish character, though it is so hard for observers to discern and understand it. Like Lockhart, he is practically forgotten, so far as his work goes, but like him, too, he will always be remembered for the great place he filled in the literature of the nineteenth century.

When William Blackwood died the business fell mainly into the hands of his very able and accomplished son John Blackwood. The worst thing that can ever be said of him is that he admired Warren's ridiculous "Lily and the Bee," of which it was said that as there was no reason in it there ought to have been some rhyme. Mr. Blackwood, however, was a critic of the first mark, and steadily carried forward the various enterprises of the house. His great discovery was George Eliot, whose *Scenes of Clerical Life* was published in the magazine. Looking over the old volumes recently, we were amazed to think that there should have ever been the smallest hesitation about the new writer's genius. In numbers that contained much excellent matter, she shines out so brightly as to put all the rest into dimness. In fact, it may be doubted whether she ever wrote anything so good on the whole as these *Scenes*, yet there was great hesitation about that even at the time. George Eliot rather encouraged the belief that she was a clergyman, and the *Saturday* reviewer had no doubts. Mrs. Oliphant does not mention that the *Guardian*, which at that time, as now, had good and careful reviews, criticised the book in a passage worth quoting as a contribution to the curiosities of criticism. Here is the whole notice :

> "*Scenes of Clerical Life*, by George Elliot (*sic*) (Blackwood), are a republication of some stories from *Blackwood's Magazine*. They were sufficient for their original purpose, but they did not deserve the honour of a more permanent shape There is some cleverness, mingled with a good deal of affectation, in the style, and there is incident enough to carry you through a few chapters at a time with interest. But the stories have no probability, and the characters no truthfulness. It is all melodramatic and unreal. And the name itself is partly resented as a deception. When you discover that the *Scenes* are supposed to be enacted some fifty years ago, it practically amounts to a confession that the author knows little of contemporary clerical life."

As usual the great soul of the world was just and pronounced its verdict unmistakably. We are told quite frankly that there was coldness at times between

George Eliot and her publisher. She received £800 for *Adam Bede* over and above the sum originally agreed upon, and haughtily declined to have her next story published in the magazine. Happily, however, the connection lasted to the end, and was in the highest degree honourable to both parties.

It was about this period that Lord Lytton took his new departure in fiction by writing *The Caxtons*, and the other volumes of the series. The late Mr. Hutton, always Lytton's stern antagonist, would not admit that even in this line Lytton had made a success. He allowed that the books were lively, but complained that they were deformed by direct and poor imitations of Sterne, for which Lord Lytton had not the requisite humour, and that they rarely rose above the ordinary novelist's work. He admitted, however, great merit in the figure of Jasper Losely, the modern bandit, and beyond that he would not go. Many criticisms can be made of Lord Lytton, and there is a great deal to be said for the thesis that he was merely a clever man, of varied knowledge, of vast ambition and industry, but without genius. The question is still undecided. We do not think Mrs. Oliphant has mentioned that in *Blackwood* the first sketch of *A Strange Story* appeared. Perhaps Lytton's claims to genius might be hazarded on that impressive and weird story. Lytton, though apparently blamable in his private life, had many things to recommend him. He had a genuine love for literature, and a feeling of genuine brotherhood for literary men. His tastes were unusually broad and catholic, and at the back of his mind there was a prevailing sense of justice. There are many of us still who rank *The Caxtons* very much higher than Mr. Hutton ranked it, although by no means blind to its faults.

Our space is exhausted, and we cannot dwell as we should like to have done on Maginn, the two Moirs, Thomas Aird, James Hogg, and many others. Neither can we say what we should like to have said of Major Blackwood and his letters. The great surprise of the book to students of literary history will be that so little is made of Aytoun. However, these subjects must be let alone. We have had a book which cannot be criticised, a book which we can only give thanks for, a book of books. If the next volume is half as well done there will be no reason for complaint. It is matter of great satisfaction to think that this great and honourable history is not in sight of the end. The present eminent head of the house has maintained its traditions nobly. The magazine was never better than it is, and there was never more enterprise shown in the publication of books. The Blackwoods have never been afraid, and they are not afraid now, to give their impression to whatever is worthy in the works of young writers; and some of the most prominent among recent English and Scottish writers, like Miss Beatrice Harraden, Mr. Meldrum, Mr. Neil Munro, and many others, promise to maintain the great traditions of which we are all thinking to-day.

W. Robertson Nicoll.

FRANCE UNDER LOUIS XV.*

"He who considers that the face of the monarch causes the felicity of the courtier, whose life is occupied with the desire of seeing him and being seen by him, may understand how the sight of God suffices for the glory and the bliss of the saints." This naïve sentence of La Bruyère's, quoted by Mr. Perkins in his *France under Louis XV.*, gives us a glimpse of the eighteenth century Frenchman's conception of heaven. It was a heaven of fine clothes, gold snuff-boxes, and punctilio, of *grandes* and *petites entrées*, of paint and powder and periwigs, and the god of it all was the poor, dull, insignificant little Louis, who had just intelligence enough to be bored by it, but not sufficient wit or force of mind to rise above it. The gossipy style of the author of these volumes and his free use of contemporary memoirs give a vivid impression of this fool's paradise. The scandals and extravagances of the court, the silly intrigues of the officers of the buttery and the ladies of the queen's chamber, the wrangles of the nobles as to who should have the privilege of handing the Dauphin a glass of water, and of the clergy

* France under Louis XV. By James Breck Perkins. Boston: Houghton, Mifflin & Co. 2 vols. $4.00.

as to the right of saying grace before him—these and all the other minutiæ in the tiresome ritualism of court etiquette are strung together and illustrated with anecdotes. It is the usual small beer chronicle, and would be as dull as it is familiar, if the author had not an unusual gift for description. As it is, he makes the matter interesting. His style is such that one reads fast and yet retains distinct impressions. In other words, he has the knack of the populariser. Neither in this nor in his previous work on *France under the Regency* is there evidence of great originality. He is concrete, definite, lucid, rather than profound, and gives you clean-cut, neat little pictures of people and things instead of large notions about the movement of history. After all, the lessons to be drawn from the times he is writing of are so obvious, that perhaps it is only courteous that he should leave you to do your own moralising. He is an agreeable, easy, well-bred guide, and neither a pedagogue nor a philosopher. He busies himself about the doings and misdoings of court and favourites, the amount of game the king bagged in a day, the perquisites of the queen's ladies, the sums lost at play by the duke of this and the marquis of that, and a hundred other details of this sort. How he can have the patience to narrate so many of them is surprising, for although they have value in their cumulative effect, one would think he would take refuge in an occasional generalisation. But his province is detail, and he is to be judged by what he does in it rather than by his essays in other fields. To be sure, there are chapters on the international relations of France, on wars and their effects, on social and intellectual progress, economic changes, and all the other topics that we should look for in a history of pre-revolutionary France, but in treating them he does little more than reinforce commonly accepted views by a pleasing narrative and pertinent illustrations. He is novel only in his choice of instances.

If any one is piqued by curiosity in regard to any point in the life of Louis XV., here is the chance of gratifying it. After reading these two volumes he will feel himself on terms of yawning intimacy with the monarch. He will understand just why a people that went wild for joy at the recovery of their "well-beloved" from a brief illness, that delighted in seeing his would-be assassins tortured with such barbarous cruelty, "as no tribe of Iroquois would have manifested in torturing a hostile chief," should have passed through the successive stages of disgust, hatred, and contempt till they greeted the death of their king with jocular epigrams and fired indecent jests at his passing cortége. A few of the clergy remained faithful. Bishops had crowded the salon of Madame du Barry, which no woman of rank could be induced to enter, and a bishop on the king's death fervently remarked: "I will not talk of the great achievements of this mighty king, his successes, his victories. A prince so dear to human hearts must have been according to God's heart."

Quite a little pathos is thrown into the account of the clever but mischievous Pompadour. "If the king found some one else with whom he could talk about his hunting and affairs, at the end of three days he would not know the difference if I were gone," she said. Hence a constant strain to amuse his sluggish mind and keep a little warmth in his battered old heart. "This frivolous woman led as anxious and agitated an existence as Richelieu or Mazarin." In practice she apparently regarded statecraft as merely the filling of offices with her friends, but oddly enough she secretly longed to be looked upon as a second Agnes Sorel, and grieved deeply when she found that foolish measures did not bring great results. If one wants to hear things that really concern the future of France, he will not listen long in the council chamber of the Pompadour, but rather hang about the *entresôl* where Quesnay is making physiocratic proselytes in the intervals of his duties as court physician.

Apropos of Quesnay and the physiocrats, the author gives us a bit of economic history which, though interesting, is somewhat superficial. "Political economy as a science," says he, "may be said to have begun its existence in the last century; . . . that a bag full of gold pieces stowed away in a garret added to the national wealth, and that a well-cultivated field, a house stored with articles of luxury and comfort, a warehouse filled with stout boots and warm clothes, were no part of the national wealth would have been disputed by few in the seventeenth century." This is forcible, but, like a good many forcible remarks, conveys only a half truth, for there was some intelligence even among the much-abused mercantilists of the seventeenth century. No doubt they laid too much emphasis on a favourable balance of specie, and deserved the rebukes of Adam Smith and his physiocratic teachers; but economic truths are relative, and the mercantilist policy, as Roscher shows, had a sound basis in existing facts. It is absurd to condemn a statesman for not applying nineteenth-century principles to seventeenth-century conditions. But the author does not fall into this error often. His account of Law's Mississippi Scheme in the earlier volume on *France under the Regency* is as fair as it is well written, and shows the grains of truth and common sense in some of Law's projects. Still in both works it is clear that Mr. Perkins is not at his best in tracing historical causes or analysing the intellectual life of the times. He is rather a historical photographer, and what fix themselves in our minds are such matters as the whirl and scramble of the Rue Quincampoix, the king's clandestine visits to the *parc aux cerfs*, the trial of Beaumarchais, and the scandals, cynicisms, and epigrams of a decadent society—the phosphorescence of social decomposition.

A reviewer innocently says of this book that it could not fail to be interesting on account of the subject with which it deals. Little does he realise the fatal facility of dulness or the variety of paths open to the tedious narrator. It would be easy to name a dozen very respectable scholars who would not have the slightest difficulty in making the subject tiresome. A lively, natural, simple style is not such a common possession that we can afford to belittle it. There is hardly a dull page in Mr. Perkins's two volumes, nor is there an obscure one. He is wholly without tricks or mannerisms or rhetorical flourishes. He is the ideal narrator—clear, compact, and impersonal, reaching his end so quickly and skilfully that you are unconscious of the means employed. In his own particular province as a populariser he is delightful, and we should be thankful that he generally stays in it. If he philosophises, he will be lost; for, like the messenger in the play, he will mar a curious tale in the telling, but can deliver a plain message bluntly.

Frank Moore Colby.

DOWDEN'S "FRENCH LITERATURE."*

In his review of Mr. Stopford Brooke's admirable *Primer of English Literature*, Matthew Arnold declared that the author of a guide-book which should show us in clear view the growth of a literature, its series of productions and their relative value, must needs have certain special qualifications. "He ought to be clear. He ought to be brief—as brief as is consistent with not being dry. For dry he must not be; but we should be made to feel, in listening to him, as much as possible of the power and charm of the literature to which he introduces us. His discourse, finally, ought to observe strict proportion and to observe strict sobriety. He should have one scale and should keep to it. And he should severely eschew all violence and exaggeration; he should avoid in his judgments even the least appearance of what is arbitrary, personal, fantastic."

Brevity, clearness, proportion, sobriety—these are the needful qualifications; and of the possession of these Professor Dowden gives proof in the pages of this history of French literature. He is brief, for in less than four hundred and fifty pages he carries the long record of French authors down to the middle of this century. He is clear; and he shows adroitly the successive movements of the French mind as each of these has produced its impression on literature. He keeps to his scale, and he is very tactful in the assignment of space to the great authors and in the due subordination of those of minor importance. And he is sober throughout; his judgments represent the consensus of the best criticism; nowhere in these pages is there any freakish obtrusion of personal preferences. Indeed, the one fault of this history is that it lacks individuality a little; that it is rather a summary and a redaction

* A History of French Literature. By Edward Dowden, Professor of English Literature in the University of Dublin. New York: D. Appleton & Co. $1 50.

than the chastened opinion of an expert who had thought out things for himself and had yet arrived at the same conclusions as the best of his predecessors. And here it is that Professor Dowden's book is less interesting than Mr. Stopford Brooke's *Primer of English Literature* and than Professor Jebb's *Primer of Greek Literature*—the two best brief histories of literature in our language, having both of them the elementary virtues Matthew Arnold insisted upon, and having each of them also a delightful savour of individuality.

But it is with original writers like Mr. Brooke and Professor Jebb that Professor Dowden is to be compared, and not with the day-labourers of the text-book, such as Professor George Saintsbury, for example. His fitness for the task he has undertaken is shown especially by his refusal to be tempted into digression, or trivial anecdote, or mere biography. He has given us a real history of French literature, not a collection of the lives of French authors. The biographical details are kept subordinate to the narration of the broader literary development.

The phrasing of the criticism upon many of the leading authors is as felicitous as the opinion expressed is just. Excellent is the characterisation of Villon (pp. 63–65). Villon, he says, "is modern in his passion for the real, and in those gleams of ideal light which are suddenly dashed across the vulgar surroundings of his sorry existence. . . . The ideas which he expresses are few and simple—ideas common to all men; but they take a special colour from his own feelings and experiences, and he renders them with a poignancy which is his own, with a melancholy gaiety and a desperate imaginative sincerity." Excellent also is the criticism of Rabelais (pp. 87–90): "Below his laughter lay wisdom; below his orgy of grossness lay a noble ideality; below the extravagances of his imagination lay the equilibrium of a spirit sane and strong." And it is absolutely accurate, although not at all obvious to say of Corneille (p. 169) that his drama "deals with what is extraordinary, but in what is extraordinary it seeks for truth. He finds the marvellous in the triumphs of the human will." This about Victor Hugo is also admirable in its understanding of the real position of the French poet in the history of literature: "To say that Hugo was the greatest lyric poet of France is to say too little; the claim that he was the greatest lyric poet of all literature might be urged. The power and magnitude of his song result from the fact that in it what is personal and what is impersonal are fused in one" (pp. 377, 378).

Where Professor Dowden is weakest is where English-speaking critics nearly always are weak—in the treatment of the dramatists. It is as men of letters that he considers them, and not primarily as play-makers. He has not firmly grasped the essential truth that in the dramatic literature which is really of value the drama preceded the literature. In his remarks about the comedies of Larivey, Professor Dowden almost enunciates this truth, but elsewhere he fails to act on it. He tells us, for instance (p. 206) that "as a writer Molière is not free from faults; but his defects of style are like the accidents that happen within the bounds of a wide empire." Now, this is wholly beside the mark. Molière's style is oral, and no oral style was ever better adapted to its purpose than his. Molière wrote to reach his audience through the mouths of actors on the stage, and not through the eyes of readers in the library.

Thus it is that there is a certain inadequacy in Professor Dowden's pages on Racine also and on Beaumarchais. He fails to bring out the weight of the influence upon Molière of the contemporary Italian *commedie dell' arte*, and he fails also to set forth the effect on Molière's choice of subjects exerted by the fact that Molière was a comedian himself and also the manager of a company of comedians. In general Professor Dowden has followed M. Lanson's invaluable work, but, oddly enough, he has not profited by what is perhaps the French critic's single original contribution to the history of French literature. M. Lanson makes clear (by an explanation of the simultaneous scenery of the French mysteries) how it was that the French welcomed the alleged unities as a simplification of an existing complexity, although the unities were rejected emphatically in England and in Spain. In Professor Dowden's book this difficulty is not faced.

It will be remembered by all who relish plain speaking and vigorous writing that Professor Dowden's style in his biography of Shelley was derisively analysed by Mark Twain, a critic of literature whose judgments are sometimes somewhat over-emphatic, but whose discrimination is remarkably keen. Mr. Clemens declared that the Shelley biography was "a literary cake-walk. . . . All the pages, all the paragraphs walk by sedately, elegantly, not to say mincingly, in their Sunday best, shiny and sleek, perfumed, and with *boutonnières* in their buttonholes; it is rare to find even a chance sentence that has forgotten to dress." From this reproach the present book is free; now and then the reader may find a sentence or even a paragraph open to Mark Twain's corrosive criticism; but in the main Professor Dowden has managed to get along here with an every-day vocabulary. It is pleasant to see that he is careful to follow the example of Macaulay, and to write "the Duke of Orleans," etc., and not "the Duc d'Orléans." Once (p. 148) he allows "Savoie" to retain the French form, although he prints it later (p. 355) in the English form, "Savoy." He is guilty once of the Gallo-Briticism of "costumier" for "costumer," and more than once of another Gallo-Briticism for which there is really no excuse, "Mdlle." for "Mlle.," although he is careful always to write "Mme." and never "Mdme," as the British pervert it. He makes the mistake also of quoting occasionally in French; and a book like this is necessarily addressed chiefly to those who do not read French. If a student has mastered the language sufficiently to understand these quotations of Professor Dowden's, he does not need Professor Dowden's volume, for there is M. Lanson's.

Brander Matthews.

KOREA AND HER NEIGHBOURS.*

Thirty years ago the Pacific Mail Steamship Company opened its Trans-Pacific line, making Yokohama a port of call on the voyage to Hong Kong and of divergence for the branch line to Shanghai. No steamers thought of stopping at any of the ports of Korea, a country then called "The Hermit Nation," "The Land of the Morning Calm," to indicate that which is no part of the great community of nations. To-day that land *is* a part of Us; it has opened its doors (just a little, to be sure) to Western influences, the palace of the king is lighted by electric lamps, railways have been staked out and are rapidly being built, its finances are being adjusted upon a firm basis, its commerce is reckoned as something to be considered, and what may be its ultimate fate is a matter of interest to diplomats, to merchants, to missionaries, and to the world at large.

A most valuable contribution to our literature on Korea is Mrs. Bishop's book, *Korea and Her Neighbours.* She is an old hand at Eastern travel, knows how to touch details and to dwell upon important matters, and we therefore expect to find much of value and interest in her book, and that expectation is fully realised. From first to last attention is held by her narrative of personal experiences or by her observations upon social matters and political developments. She frequently draws comparison between the characteristics of the Chinese and Japanese settlements at the places where they stand side by side, and always, and justly, to the advantage of the latter; for, say what we will of the conceit of the Japanese, their notions of sanitation are far ahead of the Chinese, even if they do fall behind our own highest ideal. It is not a matter of serious regret that Seoul's orientalism, attractive as it may have been, with its concomitant of "self-asserting dirt," is being fast improved off the face of the earth, for it was too much Chinese orientalism.

So well told are Mrs. Bishop's bits of curious manners and customs that it is difficult to refrain from commenting on all of them; but one must be contented with a few. The seclusion of Korean women of the better classes is more rigid than of the Japanese, of course, or even than of the Chinese, yet the feminine fondness for visiting and for gossip is recognised; and that it may be gratified without scandal, Mrs. Bishop tells us that:

"In the capital a very curious arrangement prevailed. About eight o'clock [P.M.] the great

* Korea and Her Neighbours. A Narrative of Travel, with an Account of the Recent Vicissitudes and Present Position of the Country. By Isabella Bird Bishop, F.R.G.S. Fleming H. Revell Co. $2.00.

bell tolled a sign for men to retire into their houses, and for women to come out and amuse themselves and visit their friends. The rule which clears the streets of men occasionally lapses, and then some incident occurs which causes it to be rigorously enforced. So it was at the time of my arrival, and the pitch-dark streets presented the singular spectacle of being tenanted solely by bodies of women, with servants carrying lanterns. . . . At twelve the bell again boomed, women retired, and men were at liberty to go abroad. A lady of high position told me that she had never seen the streets of Seoul by daylight."

It is extremely fortunate for us that Mrs. Bishop happened to be in Korea on what was probably the last time that the Kur-dong was celebrated in its fullest splendour. This "was a visit of the king in state to sacrifice in one of the ancestral temples of his dynasty." Her description (the only satisfactory one extant in the writer's knowledge) is too long to be given here, and no condensation would be satisfactory.

In telling of the marriage customs, the present of two pieces of silk which are sent to the bride for her outer wedding garments is mentioned, and we are told:

"A number of men carrying gay silk lanterns bear this present to the bride, and on the way are met by a party of men from her father's house bearing torches, and a fight ensues, which is often more than a make-believe one. . . . If the bridegroom's party is worsted in the *mêlée* it is a sign that he will have bad luck; if the bride's, that she will have misfortunes."

In either case, unless the fight be "drawn," there would seem to be unhappiness in store!

The success of the Korean peasants who have crossed the boundary into Siberia and have been encouraged and helped by the Russian authorities, indicates that they have a capacity for farming and stock-raising which needs only relief from the exactions of their own officials to develop them into a thrifty class, and the efforts which are now being made to correct the old, iniquitous methods of taxing and "squeezing" ought to produce that same thrift at home. There is no other country—perhaps some of those we call barbarous excepted—where prosperity is shunned by the middle and lower classes as it is in Korea. Success which brings a little accumulation marks the successful man as the prey of officials who extort from him his little hoard by forced "loans" never repaid!

Throughout the book there are many exquisite descriptions of scenery. One only is quoted, while all are commended.

"The beauty of the Han [river] culminates at To-tam in the finest river view I had then ever seen, a broad stretch, with a deep bay and lofty limestone cliffs, between which, on a green slope, the picturesque, deep-eaved, brown-roofed houses of the village are built. The gray cliff is crowned with a goodly group of umbrella pines, in Korea called 'parasol pines,' because they resemble in shape those carried before the king. Guarding the entrance of the bay are three picturesque, jagged, pyramidal rocks much covered with the *Ampelopsis veitchiana*, and, of course, sacred to dæmon worship. These sentinels are from 40 to 83 feet high. To the southwest the Han, dark and deep, rolls out of sight round a pine-clad bluff, among the magnificent ranges of the Sol-rak-San Mountains, masses of partially pine-clothed peaks and pinnacles of naked rocks. To the northeast the river makes an abrupt bend below superb limestone cliffs, and disappears at the foot of Sölmi-San, a triplet of lofty peaks."

The chapters on superstitions, Buddhist monasteries, and those containing accounts of special trips—*e.g.*, to Mukden, Vladivostock, etc.—are not only most interesting, but remarkably exact, showing an immense amount of care in procuring facts; while those which tell of political events must be read entire to be properly appreciated.

We must still turn to Griffis and to Lowell for the picturesqueness of old Korea, but for the practical side of Korea to-day, for a carefully written narrative of the transition from the hermit state to one of active modern life, Mrs. Bishop's book is to be highly praised.

J. King Goodrich.

EXPERIMENTAL SOCIOLOGY.*

The difference between the science of Plato's day and that of our own time, is that the one reasoned how things ought to be, the other tries to find out how they are. So the great disciple of Socrates erected for us a very magnificent ideal republic, in which there are many things hard to be understood, and many others which, if put into operation, would act in a manner precisely opposite to the design of the philosopher. Our own time, on the contrary, though it also has not failed to produce

* The Workers: An Experiment in Reality—The East. By Walter A. Wyckoff. New York: Charles Scribner's Sons. $1.25.

imaginary republics, has given us the College Settlement, and the work of Mr. Alvan Sanborn and Mr. Walter A. Wyckoff. It is with the last named that we are now concerned; the mention of the others is sufficient to show that we consider them to be working along the same lines and toward the same end.

To say that a young college graduate gave up, temporarily, a luxurious home, and for two years earned his bread as an unskilled labourer, seems at first glance sufficiently simple; so very simple, indeed, that, as one critic has already remarked, we are tempted to ask, "Is the man a fool?" But the sanity of the book is perfectly evident; its value, therefore, as a sociological investigation would seem to depend upon the equipment, mental, moral, and physical, of the investigator, and to be most readily tested through the following questions: With what motive, or motives, was it undertaken? With what degree of success was it carried out? What elements of danger or of weakness does it exhibit, for the warning of any future investigators along the same line?

Mr. Wyckoff states that he entered upon this experiment as a new and practically untried field of investigation, inspired by the "vital knowledge of men and things," and the "catholic sympathy with human nature," of the friend to whom the book is dedicated. We are thus enabled to classify his motives as scientific curiosity and altruism, both of which are not only lawful, but also expedient and commendable. And we may say just here that there is no trace in his record that he was swayed by any other or meaner motives than those referred to.

The success of the investigation depended upon Mr. Wyckoff's power of becoming an integral part of his new life; of getting out of his own skin and into that of an unskilled day labourer, and thus of appreciating the full power or value of every new factor of an environment hitherto untried. To do this absolutely without limitation would be manifestly impossible. Mr. Wyckoff, by divesting himself at the outset of money and of all personal belongings except strict necessities; by eating, sleeping, washing, and combing precisely on the same terms and with the same materials as his fellow-workmen, seems to have done all that a man could do in this direction. He tells us that on one occasion, failing to find work, he went without food for twenty-four hours, sleeping most of that time in a haystack; yet even thus, it seems to the present writer, the fact that this hunger was his own choice, was an important psychological difference between himself and his co-workers. On the other hand, details which to them were mere matters of course probably caused our author greater discomfort than he cares to describe.

But these divergencies are subjective; objectively, Mr. Wyckoff lived the life of the men around him, as an employé of a contractor for the removal of an old academic building at West Point, as a hotel porter, a farm hand, a hired man at an asylum, and in a logging camp; and he tells us about it in a delightfully easy and picturesque manner, with an admirable choice of material and a careful perspective. The value of his observations will probably be found to vary considerably for different readers; to one, each word or phrase will be pregnant with meaning, tingling with life, illuminative, inspiring; to another it will be "Words, words, words;" he will wonder why the man put himself out to that degree, and may conclude that he really likes to live with that sort of people.

Certain of his results, however, seem to have a very definite importance, as his record of the craving for stimulant, produced by his work at West Point; of the deadening of the mental and spiritual powers by excessive physical toil; of what seems the incompatibility between the unskilled labourer and religion, the "social cleavage which yawned to my vision from the new point of view." His observation of the status, moral and especially physical, of unskilled labour in a hotel; his personal preference for domestic service over out-of-door or factory work; his reasons for the preference, as also his explanation of the popular feeling upon the subject, have a special value as authoritatively confirming a great deal that has already been said in discussing the much-argued question of our American tendency to avoid household employment. It is also remarkable that he has but few remedies to propose even when conditions appear to him most unfortunate; we remember only two suggestions in this line—education and organisation. Upon these he dwells with the fervour of absolute assurance; but he writes not for the purpose of amending, but of observing; which scientific temper should give additional weight to every word that he permits himself.

There remains now the question of possible dangers to Mr. Wyckoff's successors and imitators in this field of research. Fortunately it is not likely to attract very many, for our author's experience has made it perfectly clear that unskilled labour finds strange bed-fellows. The physical dangers of work so violent and unwonted, and of food, which when one is "on a job" is coarse but abundant, and at other times is conspicuous by its absence, hardly require to be pointed out; there seems little peril otherwise, except the peril of failure. But our author writes with such straightforward simplicity, such apparent unconsciousness, that he has done anything at all remarkable except for its novelty, that he almost succeeds in blinding the reader to the very remarkable personality that made his experiment possible. He went among the poor not as a superior, nor even as an investigator, in the coldly scientific sense; in the words of an old-fashioned writer, "He made himself of no reputation, and took upon him the form of a servant." And, as we read, the conviction deepens within us, that on no other terms could the experiment have been brought to a conclusion in any degree successful.

August Max.

SOME QUESTIONS OF GOOD ENGLISH.*

Dr. Fitzedward Hall, the reader inexpert in erudite linguistic literature must be informed, is a distinguished American scholar, the classmate at Harvard of Professor Norton and the late Professor Child. Chance led him in early life to India, where he became master of much Eastern learning, and circumstances or preference have made him for many years a resident of England. He is the author of several volumes, as well as numerous articles and notes, dealing with present English usage, and is perhaps best known to Americans through a series of contributions to the New York *Nation*, signed "F. H.," which have been continued irregularly for some twenty years. The general trend of Dr. Hall's doctrine with regard to English usage has been, on the whole, radical. Again and again, in the English press, he has broken a lance with an opinionated adversary who had incautiously dubbed some chance phrase an Americanism. Again and again, in both countries, he has thrown a flood of light on the discussion of a puzzling idiom by bringing forward, from the same inexhaustible hoard by which Dr. Murray's dictionary has so often profited, a mass of pertinent information, gathered from every nook and corner of English literature. In almost all his writings he has ranged himself on the side of fact as opposed to that of theory, of the actual usage of the language as opposed to the dogmas of the formal rhetoricians, the conventional grammarians, and the schoolmarms.

With all these virtues, which should have made him a really great popular leader in all matters of diction, Dr. Hall has faults that have alienated from him much of the esteem which is rightfully due him. First, he has the infirmity of being unable to express his ideas without a considerable show of dogmatism, which often grows acrid in debate. Second, his English is, rhetorically speaking, atrocious. Accurate to an extraordinary degree in even the subtlest points of syntax and idiom, he writes our native language as a Chinaman might, without taste or elegance, building sentences that weigh like nightmares on the mind, and piling up learned words in ways that sometimes render his meaning obscure to those unfortunate persons who do not know the dictionary by heart. Third, he has lived so long in England, and stuck so close to his rigid theory of using only locutions for which precise precedents have been sanctioned in late British literature, that he has become extraordinarily touchy on the irritating question of American English. "Though I have lived away from America," he avows,

* Some Questions of Good English Examined in Controversies with Dr. Fitzedward Hall By Ralph Olmsted Williams. New York: Henry Holt & Co.

"upwards of forty-six years, I feel, to this hour, in writing English, that I am writing a foreign language, and that, if not incessantly on my guard, I am in peril of stumbling," a really pitiful confession for a great philologian, and one beautifully illustrative of the harm that comes from regarding with such solemn seriousness the trivial details of style.

Mr. Williams, the other speaker in this interesting dialogue, must now be introduced as a younger American scholar of Dr. Hall's own sort, who has had much experience in dictionary-making. He has evidently been irritated, as many of us have, by the dogmatic character of the elder sage's dicta and by his frequent strictures, especially of recent years, on the American "dialect," as Dr. Hall, with opprobious intent, is fond of styling our current use of the mother-tongue. As a champion of those who had been too long silent, Mr. Williams printed, in various numbers of the *Dial* and *Modern Language Notes*, a series of papers which had the avowed purpose of breaking down Dr. Hall's almost unchallenged reputation for impeccability. These papers, with Dr. Hall's rejoinders and his own final comments, Mr. Williams now publishes in book form—whether or not with his adversary's consent is not apparent.

Mr. Williams's task is an ungracious one. His opponent is an old man and a distinguished scholar. The charges are all matters of detail. The deliberateness of the attack, the persistency with which the author returns to it, are both unpleasing. Why, one feels, need just this method have been followed? Why should there be such grave insistence on slight imperfections in so honourable a service as that of Dr. Hall's, in a field of thought so antiquarian?

But if the animus is obvious, the dispute is interesting. Dr. Hall had condemned *known to*, in a remark of Marsh's that a certain word "had none of the meanings known to it," on the somewhat hypercritical ground that a word could not appropriately be said to "know" anything of the sort. Mr. Williams brings forward a whole batch of quotations—scarcely parallel, however—of analogous uses of the same phrase. Dr. Hall retorts that the quotations are not apposite, and Mr. Williams reaffirms his former statement. So far the victory is with the elder scholar. But Dr. Hall has meanwhile brought up a galaxy of similar alleged misuses of *to* by Lowell, Holmes, and other American writers, and here he does not escape so easily. Then comes up the propriety of the nominative in "none but *they*," the grave question whether Cardinal Newman was by any possibility addicted to verb-phrases of the *is-being-built* order, the distinction between *each* and *every*, the use of *only* in the sense of *but*, of *till* in the sense of *before*, and similar weighty matters, all so elaborately debated that one stops his ears in despair.

The real interest of the volume, however, lies in the discussion of the broader question as to the purity of our American speech. Dr. Hall says that it is a dialect, that the "phraseology of nearly all our recent popular authors is tarnished with vulgarisms, imported and indigenous, at which a cultivated taste cannot but revolt." He further asserts that the written style of the great body of our fellow-countrymen is conspicuous almost in like degree "for slovenliness, want of lucidity, breach of established idiom, faulty grammar, and needless Americanism, general or sectional." This charge he seemingly substantiates by liberal citations from a badly written American text-book by an author of some reputation. Mr. Williams appropriately retorts by showing that most of the locutions mentioned are frequent also in British writers. The matter resolves itself, therefore, so far as this discussion goes, into a mere question of taste. Dr. Hall, in spite of his latent radicalism, takes the position of the purist. Mr. Williams is strong only in so far as he takes the more catholic point of view—to wit, that there are often parallel locutions in English between which it is hard or impossible to choose. To take a typical instance, the use of *only* in the sense of *but* is certainly current, intelligible, and without a taint of illiteracy or vulgarity. It is, therefore, a sanctioned locution. We may in most instances prefer *but*, for one reason or another, but no one can fairly say that *only* is "wrong." Indeed, the less that is publicly said in condemnation of any usage that has once become really current among all kinds of people, the better for all concerned. Let it live its life; whether that will be long or short only time and chance can determine.

The astonishing point about the purist's position, however, is that it is adhered to not only by gentlemen of taste and belated scholars who have been brought up in the school of the Scotch rhetoricians, and pretend to hold the keys of authority, but by a large part of the people themselves. One can scarcely open a newspaper without stumbling on a heated discussion of *in our midst*, the crime of ending sentences with prepositions, or some similar nonsense. Certain dictionaries and textbooks on rhetoric, trading on their knowledge of that form of human frailty, proclaim widely that they and they alone have determined and codified the right and wrong in such matters. Scholars know, of course, that English usage is often floating, double, indecisive, sanctioning a host of variants. The mass of the people knows it also, dimly realising that it is the master, and that what it long continues to stamp with approval in speech and writing cannot be flouted out of the language. But there is a middle class that still likes to dally with these petty questions of taste in usage, and my only fear is that such a book as this, valuable mainly to antiquarians and rhetoricians, will encourage it in its endless and aimless discussions.

George Rice Carpenter.

ESSAYS OLD AND NEW.*

Somebody has said that with the development of critical genius in general literature the creative faculty has always seemed to decline. This need not restrain us from a few remarks based on Miss Repplier's *Varia* and the *Ars Recte Vivendi* of the late George William Curtis.

From Boston, the home of the New England school, comes Miss Repplier's volume, redolent, like all its successful predecessors, of as little of the commonly accepted New England spirit as any work that ever crossed the Mason and Dixon line. And the *Ars Recte Vivendi*, a series of stately essays from the "Easy Chair" of *Harper's Monthly*, comes forth in that *cosmopolis*—and, to believe some of our "patriots," un-American—New York, and is found to be imbued with a feeling that is almost provincial even if it be national. Has, then, the birthplace of a book ceased to be of any importance in a first estimate of it? Formerly it could not have been so. One knew what to expect from the far-removed presses of Philadelphia and Boston, Richmond and New York; the output of each bore the face-mark of its origin and reflected the influences at work in its respective community.

To take Miss Repplier's *Varia* into account from the home, we have been told, of Puritanism, rigidity, frigidity, and self-content. And what is her volume found to contain? A series of essays the most important of which are concerned with "Guides," "The Fête de Gayant," and "Cakes and Ale," reminiscences of foreign travel and reading afar from the beaten track of New England's educational establishments. This is a peculiarity pointed out long ago, it is true, in Miss Repplier's methods, and, moreover, it may be said that it is the environment of the author that is of account and not—in these days of reduced postage on manuscript—the abiding-place of the publisher.

But the case does not hinge entirely on Miss Repplier; a glance at the publishing lists of other publishing houses of Boston will tell a similar tale to one conversant with the character of their listed publications. For while it is true that the environment of the author is a great factor in a just estimation of his productions, it is nevertheless the publisher's environment that dominates; his tendencies decide the acceptance of a manuscript, and in that occult branch of divination, the discovery of the desires of his public, he is wiser than the serpent. Moreover, "temerarious if," we leave Boston and journey afar to Philadelphia, shall we not find represented at *Lippincott's* the newest and strongest influences abroad in the City of Brotherly Love? And in Chicago, at the sign of the *Chap-Book*, the high-water mark of the literary metropolis of the West? They represent, if even in a cosmopolitan way, their place of residence.

The old spirit that reigned in former times seems to have left Boston; but it has found a temporary housing in New York, and is the animating undertone of *Ars Recte Vivendi*. The author of *The Potiphar Papers* is an American of Amer-

* Varia. By Agnes Repplier. Boston: Houghton, Mifflin & Co. $1.25.
Ars Recte Vivendi. By George William Curtis. New York: Harper & Bros. $1.25.

icans in the strict New England sense of the word. Not his is the method of Miss Repplier and the growing school of her *confrères*, whose Americanism is that of the North and South, the East and West combined. Yet Mr. Curtis's Americanism is of the kind most generally accepted as characteristic of the nation. The readers of *Harper's Monthly* and of the essays comprising *Ars Recte Vivendi* know that his is the introspective method; in every page is shown the strict sense of duty and utility, and concern for the youth of the land as the promise of the nation to be. We are a people unique in our rapid development and conditions. What use, then, of foreign models on which to form ourselves to greatness? Let ours be a self-cultivation from taking thought unto ourselves; let us be more or less self-sufficient for our personal and national development. In one essay Mr. Curtis deals with "Extravagance at College," deplores the vulgarity of the new-rich (*prodigus æris*). "Secret Societies," "Theatre Manners," and "Duelling" are other topics; "The Soul of a Gentleman" shows a fine concern for the true norm of gentility, and in "Brains and Brawn" we learn that the athlete of old days received the same disproportionate meed of praise over the intellectual hero that he does to-day.

How different all this from the literary *insouciance* of Miss Repplier's *Varia!* She and her literary brothers (and sisters) fare afar in a sort of modern knight-errantry. From the four quarters—or, as a decadent suggests, the five quarters—of the globe she has gathered her goodly store of pleasing fact and illustration. She ventures into that "undiscovered country," womankind, and comes forth with some delicious trophies. "France"—Miss Repplier quotes Gouverneur Morris and her quotations are generally delightful—"is a woman's country;" and registers the good old American's opinion of political women, and Madame de Staël in particular. "She is a devilish creature." Clarissa Harlowe's uncle must have entertained somewhat similar opinions when he informs his niece, "I have always found a most horrid romantic perverseness in your sex. To do and to love what you should not is meat, drink, and vesture to you all." This has been improved on by a more modern student of the question, for George Meredith holds that "woman will be the last thing civilised by man."

Miss Repplier's guide through the Castle of St. Angelo deserves additional reputation.

"He was a bulky, dirty man, and understood no language but his own. It was impossible to misapprehend him. If he wished to show us the papal bed-chamber, he retired into one corner and snored loudly on an imaginary couch. When he came to the dining-room he made a feint of eating a hearty meal. With amazing agility he illustrated the manner of Benvenuto Cellini's escape, and the breaking of his ankles in the fall. He decapitated himself without a sword as Beatrice Cenci, and racked himself without a rack, as another unhappy prisoner. He lowered himself as a drawbridge, and even tried to explode himself as a cannon, in his efforts to make us better acquainted with the artillery."

In "Little Pharisees in Fiction" Miss Repplier's strictures on the "Fairchild Family" and the "Elsie" books for children are certainly amusing, however serious may be the character of their literature. Since the appearance of those classics for infants, the "Early Piety" Series, *Spiritual Milk for Boston Babes*, and *The Conversion and Exemplary Lives of Several Young Children*, this branch of literature has been without its proper censors. It will, therefore, be with astonishment that most readers will learn that the character of many of these children's series are of a morbid character, particularly unhealthy for the unformed minds that peruse them. Betty Sewell, as an instance, an innocent child of nine, "burst into an amazing cry after reading a page or two of Cotton Mather," and said "she was afraid she should goe to hell, her sins were not pardoned." A favourite illustration is Cotton Mather's infant son, who "made a most edifying end in praise and prayer" at the age of two and one half years. At the age of nine Lucy Fairchild comes to the conclusion "that a great part of the human race will be finally lost," and commits to memory the following prayer: "My heart is so exceedingly wicked, so vile, so full of sin, that even when I appear to be tolerably good, even then I am sinning. When I speak I sin; when I am silent I sin."

In the "Elsie" books Mr. Dinsmore, a harmless if foolish person, is taken ill, and the little heroine at the age of eight prays "in agonising supplication that her dear, dear papa might be spared—

at least until he was fit to go to heaven." In Elsie's more buoyant moments a tear merely "trickles down her cheek," and on comparatively cheerful nights she is content to shed "a few quiet tears upon her pillow."

This is enough poaching on Miss Repplier's preserves to show the character of her new volume, and enough, perhaps, to illustrate that latest phase of the cosmopolitan tendency in American letters of which there was mention made above. Whatever be the reader's views, he will do well not to neglect these two instructive and amusing volumes, *Varia* and *Ars Recte Vivendi*.

Thomas Walsh.

BODLEY HEAD POETS.*

Mr. Watson's new volume is a little one, and it should have been less. "The Lost Eden," "The Hope of the World," "The Unknown God" would have made five-and-twenty small pages, which might have been fairly increased to thirty by including the "Ode in May"—if only for the sake of the magnificent lines,

> "Magnificent out of the dust we came
> And abject from the spheres"—

and of these thirty we would not willingly have missed one. The increase to eighty-three is all pure loss. The complimentary verses have most indiscreetly strayed into good company; the love-songs are feeble, pointless things, with only weight enough to strain at Mr. Watson's reputation for judgment; and the "light verse" is apt, with elephantine step, to become the comic. The lady to whom they were addressed must sorely wish for the omission of such lines as

> "You are palpably *de trop*
> In the glades of Fontainebleau."

In the thirty-page remnant, the finest thing is undoubtedly a short poem, "The Lost Eden," where a worthy idea is finely treated; one of the greatest of the human tragedies is greatly divined. The lost Eden is man's lost belief of himself as the first of creatures, fashioned for eternity. It was Eve gave him the fatal knowledge.

> "Eve, the adventurous soul within his soul!
> The sleepless, the unslaked! she showed him where
> Amidst his pleasaunce hung the bough whose fruit
> Is disenchantment and the perishing of many glorious errors.
> * * * * *
> And the gold gates of Eden clanged behind.
> Never shall he return; for he hath sent
> His spirit abroad among the infinitudes,
> And may no more to the ancient pales recall
> The travelled feet. But oftentimes he feels
> The intolerable vastness bow him down,
> The awful, homeless spaces scare his soul;
> And half-regretful he remembers then
> His Eden lost, as some gray mariner
> May think of the far fields where he was bred,
> And woody ways unbreathed on by the sea,
> Though more familiar now the ocean-paths
> Gleam, and the stars his fathers never knew."

Here Mr. Watson has risen to the level of his master Arnold. The temper of the best poems is that of Arnold—a desire to hope, but a determination not to flatter Desire by giving it the name of Truth. This is the theme of the title poem, a noble, simple composition, with gleams of rare poetic beauty in it.

> "And though within me here
> Hope lingers unsubdued,
> 'Tis because airiest cheer
> Suffices for her food!
> As some adventurous flower,
> On savage crag-side grown,
> Seems nourished hour by hour
> From its wild self alone,
> So lives inveterate hope, on her own hardihood."

Mr. Watson's thought has not always been quite good enough for his clear, collected style. But the fearless, honest facing of facts making against old illusions and all the pretty sentiment of the comfortable world, gives promise of a wisdom that may one day probe deeper into the truth of things. In "The Unknown God," this complement to Kipling's warning may not tell Mr. Watson's final resting-place, but it is a wholesome sign of the pain amid which thought is born.

> "Best by remembering God, say some,
> We keep our high imperial lot.

* The Hope of the World, and Other Poems. By William Watson. New York: John Lane. $1.25.
The Fairy Changeling, and Other Poems By Dora Sigerson (Mrs. Clement Shorter). New York: John Lane. $1.25.
The Earth Breath, and Other Poems. By A. E. New York: John Lane. $1.25.

Fortune, I fear, hath oftenest come
When we forgot—when we forgot!
A lovelier faith their happier crown,
But history laughs and weeps it down!"

There follows a hint of an incitement to virtue that Fortune cannot rival.

Mrs. Shorter touches two strings of the Celtic lyre—pity and fear. The Celt loves the supernatural because he dreads it; is even familiar with it to jesting point because it has the fascination of fear. The eerie and the strange are in Mrs. Shorter's work like the cry of the Banshee at midnight. On these wild strings she plays wild music. She is a good ballad-writer, and her feeling for the supernatural stands her in good stead. Ballads which are on the lines of the old immortal ones that grew out of the very hearts of the people, on the lines of these, yet no whit imitative, are rare enough. The poets of our day who have excelled in the form have written something widely different from the old ballads. Rossetti, Kipling, Davidson, to mention three, have stamped their own individuality upon their work. Theirs are not the least bit in the world in the line of descent from those ancient ballads, the making of which extended over centuries, yet are so harmonious that they might be the work of one master-hand. Mrs. Shorter is simple, direct, dramatic, and passionate. Her thoughts are not in the least obvious, and the end of the poem comes often as a dramatic surprise. For instance, the "Ballad of Marjorie." Her lover has been brought up from the sea in a fisher's net, and the dead man spoke:

"'What said he that you seem so sad,
O fisher of the sea?'
(Alack I know it was my love
That fain would speak with me.)

"He said, 'Beware a woman's mouth,
A rose that bears a thorn.'
Ah me, these lips shall smile no more
That gave my lover scorn.

"He said, 'Beware a woman's eyes,
They pierce you with their death.'
Then falling tears shall make them blind.
That robbed my dear of breath.

"He said, 'Beware a woman's hair—
A serpent's coil of gold.'
Then will I shear the cruel locks
That crushed him in their fold.

"He said, 'Beware a woman's heart,
As you would shun the reef.'
So let it break within my breast
And perish of my grief.

"He raised his hands; a woman's name
Thrice, bitterly, he cried.
My net had parted with the strain—
He vanished in the tide.

"'A woman's name! What name but mine,
O fisher of the sea?'
'A woman's name'—but not your name,
Poor maiden Marjorie!"

Although Mrs. Shorter excels less in the lyric than in the ballad form, she has written some fresh and charming songs. She has the freshness of imagination of her country, with something individual added; something of thought and tenderness for all created things that makes her book a winning one. She has gained much in skill and restraint since her first volume. A few of the poems are hardly worthy of the rest. "A Suicide," for example; but there is nothing that is not individual and more or less radiant with the glamour of poetry.

"Homeward I go not yet," says A. E. in the dedicatory verses to Mr. W. B. Yeats, and the words point to two landmarks in the evolution of a very individual poet. The little volume of two or three years ago, *Homeward: Songs by the Way*, was a manifesto of the one reality, the Spirit Life, a finger-post to the one journey worth making, backward to the Infinite from which we wayfarers have strayed. Very simple, very sincere of utterance, were the songs, very austere of intent.

"Oh, be not led away,
Lured by the colour of the sun-rich day.
The gay romance of song
Unto the spirit life doth not belong.
* * * * * *
be it thine to win
Rare vistas of white light,
Half-parted lips through which the Infinite
Murmurs her ancient story."

Human ambitions died in this air; human energies were subdued to the tyrannous will of the spirit. Will and thought and hope and love were drowned in their own sources—

"What of all the soul to think?
Some one offered it a cup
Filled with a diviner drink,
And the flame has burned it up."

To this most fervent, simple-minded mystic common hopes and ambitions have not in the interval since he gave us *Homeward* gained in permanent value. Yet the "Earth Breath" is stronger in his words, and the essential meaning of the second book is a humble and loving alliance with his brethren. There was aloofness without scorn in his former attitude ; to let his soul dwell on veils and symbols seemed idolatry. Now the symbols have asserted their warm life, and some sacredness of beauty.

> " To-day a nearer love I choose,
> And seek no distant sphere ;
> For aureoled by faëry dews
> The dear brown breasts appear."

This is the extremest expression of the change, more aptly uttered perhaps in "The Garden of God" and in "Love"—

> " Ere I loose myself in the vastness and drowse myself with the peace,
> While I gaze in the light and the beauty afar from the dim homes of men,
> May I still feel the heart-pang and pity, love-ties that I would not release ;
> May the voices of sorrow appealing call me back to their succour again."

Mystic and philanthropist ; the alliance is at a crude stage ; but it is loyal and it is possible, as some saints have shown. A. E. will hardly grow into the poet of common joys, the praiser of the actual. But the resolve to take the longer human route homeward that he may be good comrade by the way, will give his voice a farther reach in its heartening call downward to the loiterers in the plain.

MRS. TRASK'S "JOHN LEIGHTON, JR."*

If the book, *John Leighton, Jr.*, is like its hero it will be able to make its way in the world and make it strongly, honestly, without any professional petting or friendly flattery. And this, I think, it surely will do.

The general assumption is that the poor and struggling author finds it harder to make his way and to make an impression on the world by his work than the writer who has ample means and a recognised position in business, or the professions, or society. But the truth is quite the converse of this supposition. The poor and struggling and at first unknown author has nearly everything in his favour except money. He is quite free from all the complications and heavy responsibilities of wealth and position ; and his opportunities for observing and experiencing life in many phases are far greater, more varied and untrammelled. Instead of being saddled with a conventional, artificial identity at the start—a superficial but fixed identity which may be entirely out of keeping with his real identity, yet is the one by which the hasty but dull world insists upon knowing and trying to judge him—he is able to form and establish and compel the world to recognise his own genuine identity as a mind and a soul. It is therefore doubly and trebly to the credit of an author when he or she produces fine and vital artistic work in spite of rich and beautiful yet conventional barriers with which circumstances have surrounded him or her.

Mrs. Katrina Trask is a woman of wealth and of high social position, but she has steadily, for a number of years now, devoted the highest and most intellectual portion of her powers to the production of strong and ennobling literature, in the form of poems and stories. These productions have become well known and have made a deep impression through their appearance in the best magazines and in book form. Her three idylls of the post-Arthurian period, entirely original and not in the least imitative of Tennyson or of any one else, but very sincere and beautiful in her own distinctive way, gathered under the title of *Under King Constantine*, have spoken for themselves, and have been received with such emphatic approval by competent critics that, when I merely mention them, I am giving the key or the pass word of her undemonstrative yet vigorous, charming, and uplifting quality as an authoress. When one can use conscientiously and with earnestness these three adjectives as truly describing an author's work, one has the privilege of saying what it is a rare pleasure to be able to say. Mrs. Trask's short stories in the magazines draw forth the same organ-stops of harmony : they are vigorous, charming, and uplifting.

John Leighton, Jr., is her first novel, and it fully confirms and carries out these characteristics of the writer. It is very strong and very simple, and absolutely without pretence of any kind. It comes to us straight from a serene and clear-seeing mind, which has studied life at first hand, and carries the resultant messages and lessons straight to

* John Leighton, Jr. A Novel. By Katrina Trask, author of "Under King Constantine." New York : Harper & Bros. $1.25.

our hearts. Leighton is a hero—a hero in the romantic sense, in that he lives, suffers, endures in the great, simple way of all great natures, however feverish and distracting their inner woe and the chafing of circumstances may be. He is a romantic hero in his sincerity, the directness of his character and his strength, and in his wholesome desire to know the truth of human life and then live that truth. Yet he is prosaic and commonplace, too, in a way; for he is not sentimental, he never for a moment imagines that he is a hero—would probably laugh at the idea that he was one—and I fancy that the author perhaps chose his not very striking name precisely with the idea of emphasising (for emphasis may often be produced by non-assertion or by a neutral tint or word) this fact that he is what we call a common man, merely a man. We are not generally alive to the truth that what we call a common or ordinary man is—when he embodies all the traits of real manhood—a very *un*common man. Katrina Trask, in her young John Leighton, teaches this not only to those who have never guessed it, but to those who have apprehended it and thought they "knew it all." None of us know it or can know it all, until we see it repeatedly shown in life, or, better still, in fiction; for in fiction we get the portrait of character isolated and have time to concentrate our thoughts upon it, and really *learn*.

Leighton is the son of a narrow, Calvinistic father, who is methodical and successful, rich in the world's goods, and admirable in his way, but limited, uncharitable, harsh. The young man breaks with him utterly, or rather the old man breaks with him; and John, Jr., goes out into the world to make his own way, penniless. He makes it. He has a most interesting and wonderful experience of false love and true love and of the tests of character, and he comes out whole and pure and full of innate power and energy, to which he has not been false, although at the end he is left before us in the attitude of bearing the greatest possible sorrow and loss that could have befallen him. Yet we are made to feel that he is, even then, going forth into the world with his old bright, indomitable force, and going to be a beneficent, strong man there. To feel this, and to know John Leighton the younger—is not this enough to lead others to read the novel?

George Parsons Lathrop.

MARCHESI AND MUSIC.*

Certain persons are interesting on account of their achievements, others for their personality, and still others because they have crossed the orbits of great and famous men and women. Mme. Mathilde Marchesi is interesting for all three of these reasons, and therefore one turns the leaves of her autobiography with many expectations, knowing what a rich store of material the author has to draw upon. The book is, however, somewhat disappointing if one desires to have the promise of the title fulfilled. It is not *Marchesi and Music;* it is rather *Marchesi and her Music-School.* Nothing is said or described that does not lead to or shed a glow upon the central figure—Marchesi.

Her pride in her own success is justifiable, for her life has realised her motto —"Faith, Labour, and Perseverance"—which she chose for a guiding principle. The battle was a hard and long one: she has fought it valiantly, and her fame has been carried abroad by such gifted pupils as Gerster, Ilma di Murska, Melba, Calvé, Emma Eames, Sybil Sanderson, Nevada, and others, who have passed directly from the *École Marchesi* to the lyric stage. With the exception of Garcia, Lamperti, and Liszt, no one has directed the talent of so many illustrious artists as Marchesi.

Her own career as a singer was brief, but successful. The daughter of a wealthy merchant of Frankfort, it was only when adversity overtook her family that Fräulein Graumann was permitted to indulge her artistic desire for a public life. She studied with Garcia, gained some celebrity in concerts, and in 1852 was married to Salvatore de Castrone, an Italian singer whose stage-name was Marchesi. She sang with him in concerts and taught in Vienna for twenty years, also in Cologne, and finally, in 1881, removed to Paris.

* Marchesi and Music: Passages from the Life of a Famous Singing-Teacher. By Mathilde Marchesi, with an Introduction by Massenet. New York: Harper & Bros. $2.50.

In the course of her half-century of artistic life, it is only natural that Marchesi should have known all the famous musicians of the century. We wish that she had contributed more detailed descriptions of these men who have now passed away. To begin with, she knew Mendelssohn in Frankfort, and we should like to hear more about the excursions made in the summer of 1845 with Mendelssohn and his family, when he would stroll into a village church and play the organ, or would rest with his friends under the shade of the oak-trees in the woods and sing the bass or tenor in his beautiful vocal quartettes, then in manuscript. We should like to hear more about the ever-witty Rossini, who relates the story of the first performance of his *Barbiere di Seviglia* to Marchesi, in whose album he writes a most ingenious canon for four voices with absurd words parodying the modern style of singing ; and more about Liszt, Rubinstein, Verdi, and Wagner. Of the latter she says :

> "This great man visited us in Vienna, where I had a long discussion with him on matters relating to singing, but there was one point on which we did not agree. He was of opinion that every voice should be at the composer's command. I, on the contrary, held that the composer must take into consideration the compass of the different voices, by which interpretation, pronunciation, and declamation must naturally benefit. Wagner remained true to his principle, and so, alas! many voices have been ruined through his music, and many talented singers, both male and female, have been lost to art."

This opinion gains in authority when we read her following criticism :

> "As a musician, my admiration is great for Wagner's bold innovations, but I consider that in trying to blend the three essential elements of melodrama—music, words, and action—he has only made them change places by giving predominance to the orchestra. After having heard one of his operas I am filled with sadness, for in following out his system, which counts numerous adepts among young composers, the art of singing is doomed to disappear. Formerly the melody and the words took first place ; now it is the orchestra which does so. The singer, having to dominate the loud strains of the orchestra, is forced to make superhuman efforts, as the composer, whose one idea is *symphonic* effects, treats the voice merely as an additional wind instrument. Rossini was right when he said that singing nowadays was like storming a barricade."

We wish that Marchesi had given us more criticisms of music. Her taste and judgment are very just when she does speak of a new work. For example, of *Hänsel and Gretel* she says :

> "The music forms a striking contrast to the exaggerated compositions which are now so much the fashion. A richness of melody that never becomes commonplace, a judicious and harmonious instrumentation, with every part admirably suited for the voice, such is Humperdinck's work, which was at once accepted throughout Germany, and will not be long in making, if it has not already made, the round of the civilised world. . . . Although an admirer of Wagner, Humperdinck has followed his own inspirations, and, without setting aside ancient traditions, has adopted all that is best in the modern declamatory school."

Of Verdi's *Falstaff* she writes :

> "Its rich and sparkling music, the astounding freshness and originality of the melodies, these and other things revealed the sprightly, humorous side, hitherto concealed, of this inexhaustible genius of more than fourscore years. The orchestral score is carefully worked up, and yet seems to flow spontaneously, demonstrating afresh that every possible concession may be made to the modern system of modulation without taking away from the clearness of the melody, which is, after all, the soul and chief aim in music."

Marchesi has very little to say with regard to the art of singing, but we agree with her when she says that it "has fallen a victim to empiricism," and that "this art, which was formerly a subject of unceasing care and attention, and was only imparted to students by competent teachers, has now become common property. Every musician—amateur or instrumental professor—fancies himself capable of undertaking the production of the voice and competent to teach singing. . . . It is only after years of patient study that a voice can be considered formed as regards compass, flexibility, evenness, and durability, so as to satisfy all the requirements of art." The sensational and vulgar journalistic headings with their meaningless capitals very seriously mar the book, and, as this is an autobiography, they strike a loud and discordant note. Here are a few of them : "Cutting Beans and Making Jam ;" "Our Heroine's Arrival in Milan ;" "Great Demand for the Artiste in Concerts ;" "She Makes the Acquaintance of Pauline Viardot, the Great Garcia's Daughter ;" "A Tenor of Handsome Face ;" "Earns a Very Small Salary ;" "No Court Patronage Shown to Art ;" "More Sorrows for Madame Marchesi," etc. We also wonder how such a mistake passed the musical editor as that on page 284, where the composer *Bemberg* appears as *Benberg*. Such an error is inexcusable.

Esther Singleton.

IMPRESSIONS OF SOUTH AFRICA.*

Passages of Mr. Bryce's American book have frequently been quoted against the author's own views as a politician. His *Impressions of South Africa* will supply scarcely any material to the Parliamentary controversialist. No expression of opinion on current controversies has been allowed to mar the historian's or the traveller's impartiality. Mr. Bryce refers to Mr. Rhodes as a "strong and strenuous man;" he describes President Kruger as shrewd, cool, dogged, wary, courageous, "adding to his trust in Providence no small measure of worldly craft." Nothing in the author's tour, which he made in the autumn of 1895, impressed him more than the fact, so vividly brought out by Olive Schreiner, that much of South Africa is a desert. The effect of its silence, its loneliness, its drear solemnity, has been specially marked on the Boers, whose resistance to the British has sprung largely from their wish to be left alone. That the English-speaking element in the Transvaal will, if the mining industry continues to thrive, become politically supreme is, in Mr. Bryce's opinion, inevitable. He thinks even that the Free State and the Transvaal may enter a Confederation, with the British monarchy as the protecting suzerain. Troubles may arise in the far future from the preponderance of the blacks, but meantime there is no serious friction, and so far as the Dutch at the Cape are concerned, we need have no reason for uneasiness if only we treat their kinsfolk with tact. On the whole, Mr. Bryce's book is reassuring. His allusions to literary matters are brief though not without interest. He points out that the Dutch language, while holding its ground in South Africa, has become so vulgarised into a dialect that many of the Boers can hardly understand a Dutch newspaper. "This defect," he says, "might give English a great advantage if the Boers wished to express abstract ideas. But they have not this wish, for they have no abstract ideas to express." Few books are composed or published in South Africa, and so far as Mr. Bryce knows, only three writers there have caught the ear of the European public. One of these was Robert Pringle, a Scotchman, whose poems, written sixty or seventy years ago, "possess considerable merit, and one of which, beginning with the line,

"'Alone in the desert I love to ride,'

remains the most striking picture of South African nature" in its early days. With regard to the author of *The Story of an African Farm*, Mr. Bryce merely mentions that she has "attained deserved fame." The third writer in his list is Mr. Scully, who is less known here, but whose little volume of *Kaffir Tales* is "marked by much graphic power, and shows insight into native character." In course of time, Mr. Bryce thinks the Europeans of South Africa will emulate their kinsfolk at home or in North America in literary and artistic fertility. The book, which has occupied him for nearly two years, is written in an easy, though sometimes loose, style; it is full of information and thoroughly readable. It is dedicated "To the companion of my journey." The author's companion was Mrs. Bryce.

* Impressions of South Africa. By James Bryce. New York: The Century Co. $4.50.

NOVEL NOTES.

A FOREST ORCHID. By Ella Higginson. New York: The Macmillan Co. $1.50.

The Flower that Bloomed in the Sand was such fresh work and so far above the average in several respects, that it has been interesting to look for the author's development. It is therefore somewhat disappointing to find no marked advance in this new group of tales. The scenes and the subjects are the same. It would seem, indeed, as if the author looked too close at the soil and the water of Puget Sound. For this, or for some other reason, one misses the feeling of the universal, the appreciation of the extraordinary that gave unusual breadth and beauty to her earlier work. A touch of the last gives charm to the first story, but most of those that follow are rather commonplace, and the apparent fidelity with which they are set down only increases this sense of loss. These small, hard, sharp photographs of "Belinda's One Beau," "Mandy's Organ," "The Arnspiker Chickens," and "Mis' Bunnel's Funeral" may be true to the local life, but they are certainly out of harmony with the width, the big breeziness of the author's *milieu*. Moreover, they seem imitative, as though the author had turned to New England, not only for her models, but for her methods, a mistake of judgment that can hardly be pardoned in one who has hitherto used rarer models and finer methods of her own. And yet, with this fault to find, there is much to praise in the new work. It realises now and then with clutching force. What heart has not ached to the appeal of "toil-knotted hands idle for the first time in death. No more floors to scrub or bread to bake or butter to churn! No more threshers to cook for in the burning summer noons! No more money to beg with hesitating lips and hopeless eyes"? Who has not wished in a way, as another starved soul in the story wishes that she "could fly clear off some'ers, where they ain't any cows to milk an' calves to wean. Jest flowers to lay down in an' smell of, and little cricks to hear go a-babblin' by"? The wavering balance between pathos and humour is also noticeable in this as in all the author's works, and the constructive quality is rather more firm than in the earlier stories; so that, after all, the main complaint is that the new tales seem cast in narrow, old fields rather than in *The Land of the Snow Pearls*.

THE KING'S HIGHWAY. By Amelia E. Barr. New York: Dodd, Mead & Co. $1.25.

Mrs. Barr's admirable work is so well known that it has long since ceased to be necessary to speak of its quality. All that her large audience need know is that she has written a new novel, and all that it cares to be told is the subject of the story. *The King's Highway* differs from the mass of the author's work in that it deals with modern American society. It touches indeed upon the burning question of international marriages, especially as regards the American estimate of the commercial value of a title. It is not, however, the heroine's mother who considers this, as is the case in most American novels, and seems to be the case in American real life. It is the grim, shrewd, money-making father who offers the price for the title, and who tries "preaching down a daughter's heart." For there is, of course, an humble lover belonging to no other than nature's nobility. These two young people are assumably the central characters, but they are not in reality the most interesting. It is a melancholy fact that unadulterated goodness rarely is so interesting as a spice of waywardness either in fiction or in life; and the other girl of the story and her vagabond sweetheart have just enough perversity to give them charm at the outset. Later the girl's waywardness begins to take on a less charming aspect, as is usual in such cases, both real and fictitious. Yet she holds a certain degree of sympathy throughout. Certainly it seems natural, if not inevitable, that an ambitious poor girl's head should be a little turned when she finds that the handsome, cultured Bohemian whom she has loved and married against her judgment is in reality a millionaire's son. Then it is thoughtlessness rather than lack of feeling that makes her stay on at the watering-place when she is needed at home. And so it happens in the story, as often in life, that it is Jessie the fallible rather than Alice the faultless who captures one's fancy.

THE SON OF A PEASANT. By Edward McNulty. New York: Edward Arnold. $1.50.

Mr. McNulty's novel is a readable addition to the group of Irish stories which have been multiplying and gaining popularity of late. It might, however, be more accurately described as a romance, and, indeed, the genuine Irish tale, with its inseparable atmosphere of superstition, could scarcely be anything else. In this one a changeling holds the central place, with an environment of fairies, magic, evil eye, and the death-tick. Yet the author has succeeded in blending these weird forces of Irish life with shrewdness and humour and tragedy, as they are blended in the Irish character. The Flanagans are alive, and even larger than life. The rhythmatical Mrs. Flanagan's attitude toward the conciliatory Mr. Flanagan is typical of the Matrimonial State rather than of the County Cork. Most of the characters are of humble station, but Sir Herbert O'Hara, the bankrupt landlord, is a conspicuous figure, and among the most representative, perhaps, of the whole story. Essie, his daughter, although the heroine, is much less distinct. Her unhappy experience, and, in fact, the general outline of the story, recalls distantly and faintly *Ten Thousand a Year*. She is, however, so far luckier than the luckless gentlewoman in that great tale, that the impostor dies before the contemplated marriage. The conclusion is most horrible, and the story ends with the wild keening of women across the frozen bog. And yet with all these elements of strength, the work lacks art so far that it misses success.

BYE-WAYS. By Robert Hichens. New York: Dodd, Mead & Co. $1.25.

The first thing that strikes the reader is the amazing cleverness of these stories. Mr. Robert Hichens's first book, *The Green Carnation*, was merely smart, and the success that attended it was something of a *succès de scandale*. But in *Flames*, and more especially in this new collection of short stories, Mr. Hichens shows himself to be much more than a brilliant caricaturist of the foibles of the younger generation. He now claims consideration as a very promising writer of what may be termed serious fiction.

The stories contained in *Bye-ways*— why *Bye-ways?*—were evidently written when Mr. Hichens was under the spell of the occult spiritualism that finds expression in the central idea of *Flames*. As studies in the weird, the fantastic, the terrible, they are successful in no ordinary degree. The first story, the tragedy of a woman with the nature of a snake, makes the flesh creep and haunts one like the remembrance of a nightmare. "The Tribute of Souls" is the story of Faust brought into touch with the nineteenth century. You shudder as you read of the tribute of three souls that Alistair Ralston brought to the "grey traveller" in payment for his new life. And the monk that haunted Hubert Blair through all his wild excesses is something more than the wild hallucination of a distraught brain; the "silent guardian" that watched over Mrs. Breene is something more than a marble statue. That Mr. Hichens can make the impossible seem possible, the unreal real, is a proof that he can write as few men can. And yet we are inclined to think he will do well to confine himself to the more prosaic but equally terrible, equally inexplicable realities of modern existence. "The Man Who Intervened" and "After To-morrow" are ample proof that his power is not dependent on the unseen and fantastic. We shall await Mr. Hichens's new novel with impatience. The author will, if we are not much mistaken, write a book that will last.

WHAT MAISIE KNEW. By Henry James. Chicago: H. S. Stone & Co. $1.50.

"I cannot say that I have ever received from him any supreme enlightenment as to the workings of that complex organ, the human heart, but I understand quite definitely that Mr. James knows all about it, and could show many things if he were only interested enough to make an effort. He is the apostle of a well-bred boredom." This is the most superficial judgment in all Mr. Christie Murray's recent criticism of his contemporaries. It would be easy to refute it out of Mr. James's past. But it is a busy age, and Mr. Murray's only chance of reparation is now and in the future. Let him take it by reading *What Maisie Knew*. It is all about the human heart, especially about a very human little heart indeed, and it is full to overflowing of eager, tender interest in it. Whoever can look back to a sensitive childhood that was shadowed by strange grown-up troubles, however much more respectable these may have been than were those out of which Maisie's knowledge grew, will corroborate every step in the wonderful dramatic analysis of this marvellous book. The child is tugged at, hugged, and made use of by each of a group of selfish, disreputable relatives and connections. There is no chance of ignorance of sin, and a regular world of order and good example is unknown to her. Sin is not sin to her, but it has no attractions; it is only an uncomfortable accident of other people which she cannot evade. Her growth into a quick-thinking, keen-guessing, fearfully precocious, most loyal little mortal, loyal to the good-hearted ones and the bad—for she has early learned the complexity of duty—is a sight pitiable and beautiful. Daudet would have made the story lachrymose without making it more terrible. Mr. James keeps his sense of fun, for he knows his little heroine, intelligent, uncorrupted, valiant, eager for life, will come through with an unbroken and gentle spirit.

BUBBLES. By Fannie E. Newberry. Boston: A. I. Bradley & Co.

It appears from a list on the title-page that this is the author's fifth novel. Without such indisputable evidence there would scarcely have been a doubt that it was the first work of a writer who could do better—given practice and experience. As the matter stands, it is hard to know what to say of such confirmed immaturity, if the effect produced by the story may be described in that way. It is crude in conception, it abounds in grammatical eccentricities, as when things are "made to look beautifully," to say nothing of split infinitives, and the whole feeling of the work is essentially inexperienced. Certainly only a very young person seems likely to have approached so unhesitatingly certain theses that the profoundest experience falters before. Most of us have doubtless wondered at times whether the woman of the world, skating successfully over thin ice, would have any better chance of acquittal than has her less lucky sister who goes down, but we do not recall any definite decision. Surely it is many a moon—more than we should like to confess—since we would have dared go on record as affirming that "many a poor girl who has flung honour and chastity at the feet of the man she worshipped must have been less guilty in the eyes of a just, discerning God than she." There is no more shading of character than qualification of statement. Everybody in the story is either wholly good or wholly bad—for the time; and the suddenness and completeness of the reformation in the worldly woman is among the most unreal features of the work. And yet it should be said in justice that the character drawing of the story, as a whole, is curiously distinct. The people seem to be sketches from life, but drawn at a distance and with a very imperfect comprehension on the part of the artist of what she has reproduced. Neither the characters nor the incidents are especially interesting or new. The angelic maiden aunt, the prodigal nephew, his worldly wife, her saintly sister and scheming mother, have all made many appearances in national fiction, but they all jog along together in an atmosphere of afternoon tea, more often found in English than in American novels.

LOCHINVAR. By S. R. Crockett. New York: Harper & Brothers. $1.50.

There never was a hero so harried and worried before. We knew from the ballad of a long wooing and a suit denied, but the smoothly successful abduction of the lady, while the "poor craven bridegroom said never a word," had not prepared us for the gallant's early history so very full of vicissitudes, now revealed by Mr. Crockett. The double outlawry, the hopeless courtship, the fightings, imprisonments, escapes, the homeless wanderings on sand-dunes, on the high seas, and in barren isles, would have worn out the constitution of any ordinary hero of romance. But his buffetings are so various and original in kind that we drown our sympathy in a demoralised enjoyment of them. Only one source of ill-usage do we resent. The lady he abducted so cleverly on her wedding day was not worth his long service. A woman that believes ill of her lover on the bare word of another, and refuses to hear an explanation; that pouts, and sulks, and taunts when he is down on his luck, even if she softens when his back is turned, is of a poor, ungenerous nature, a soil in which nothing very worthy can grow. We deeply regret Wat's innocent flirtation with Marie did not end in marriage. But then the story must have ended, too; for the wicked Barra's vengeance would presumably have ceased, and his wedding with Kate been a quite humdrum affair. Since we are bound fast to the facts of the ballad, we should have liked a nobler Kate.

Lochinvar is a vivacious story of adventure; you can hardly breathe between the quick changes of scene and incident. Yet it is in Mr. Crockett's second-best manner. There are interesting glimpses of William of Orange and Claverhouse, but the main personages do not breathe with a very real life. Barra is an inartistic villain, and the highlanders are caricatures. The rest are hardly realised. If, however, the hero and Scarlett are puppets, they are pulled and tugged through their lively parts by a vigorous and capable hand.

THRO' LATTICE WINDOWS. By W. J. Dawson. New York: Doubleday & McClure Company. $1.25.

The author of *London Idylls* has sought in village Nonconformity the inspiration for his latest book. It is difficult to say which of these idylls bears most distinctly the mark of genius. Nearly all are beautiful, and the fragrance of the country breathes from every page. Perhaps the best chapters are those which tell the story of Dexter and of Solomon Gill. Dexter, the gravedigger, who gets drunk every day, and sings wild songs even from the pit of death, has this soft spot in his heart, that he loves his two motherless children, and contrives to make them the cleanest and happiest boy and girl in the village. It is unkind of Mr. Dawson to rob him of his cherished Johnny. The idyll called "The Extravagance of Solomon Gill" seems to us the finest piece of work which the author has yet produced. Taken with the two chapters which complete the story of Solomon Gill, it proves that in Mr. Dawson English Dissent has at last found a worthy interpreter. There is humour as well as pathos in these idylls, but it is humour of a genial and kindly sort, with no trace of the sarcasm which was so marked a feature of *London Idylls*. The eyes that look through the lattice windows have a twinkle of old-world merriment; the talk of the Barford rustics is as quaintly original as that of the Dewy family in "Under the Greenwood Tree." "The Man from London" is the best of the humorous chapters. Mumsley, the grocer, who drives to meet the man from London, wearing black kid gloves in honour of the occasion; Mumsley, who is so poor as a preacher, so brilliantly successful as the chapel's auctioneer, is a creation of whom any novelist might be proud. Mr. Dawson's book is thoroughly fresh and wholesome. Every one who cares to know the inner life of rural Nonconformity should hasten to procure it.

A DAUGHTER OF STRIFE. By Jane Helen Findlater. New York: Dodd, Mead & Co. $1.25.

We were much too interested in the story to stop and count and scan the words here, but Miss Findlater's work leaves us with the impression that nowhere is there an adjective too much. It is written in the dry, clear style that demands skill and vigour, and skill and vigour are unmistakable gifts of this talented writer. Her first book, *The Green Graves of Balgowrie*, had a Scottish subject. The scenes here pass in London and the South of England, but the temper is still Lowland Scots. Dialect is but a poor key to the birthplace of a style. In the shrewdness, the good sense, the reticence of sentiment, the capable handling of a subject thoroughly understood before it is tackled, she suggests what one only knows by vague reputation, the good talkers of the Edinburgh of an earlier generation. Were she inclined more to laughter she might be a Miss Ferrier. Her temper is not modern—eighteenth century, rather, like her style, which seems to be adapted from that clear and strong if rather shortsighted age.

But the dry manner does not hinder the story from being a romance. It is a romance springing out of a grim tragedy. Yet it is pure and joyous romance. The loves of Philip and Caroline are more fresh and real and charming than any sentimentalist could have made them. The glimpses of their childhood are masterly. One thing only strikes us as somewhat incredible—that the good-hearted Sebastian's opposition to the marriage should have been so persistent. For the sake of his beloved daughter would he not have swallowed his pain; and if Philip was the son of his bitter foe, was he not likewise the son of the woman who had been the light of his eyes? But Miss Findlater holds to the hard possibilities of the case. In the hardest of all we must acquiesce. It is a strong scene where the villain is murdered, and thinking the murderer is his own son calls out with his last breath a warning to him to escape. From such excellent work we have a right to expect great things from Miss Findlater in the future.

BABOO JABBERJEE, B.A. By F. Anstey. Illustrated by B. Partridge. New York: D. Appleton & Co. $1.50.

Jabberjee the golden-mouthed can only be described worthily by quotation. One may pick at random: his eloquence never disappoints. His views on the Laureateship, for instance, are given in true characteristic style. The Prime Minister had an opportunity to throw the office open to competition, "instead of arbitrarily decorating some already notorious bard with this *cordon bleu* and thus gilding the lily." He, Jabberjee, would have been in the running. Alas, this chance of "throwing soup to Cerberus, and exhibiting colour-blindness, has been given the slip, though the door is perhaps still open . . . for retracing the false step and web of Penelope." The intelligent, shifty Hindoo, *exalté* by his Western education and ambitions, legal, literary, and romantic, is a most amusing rascal. Of the lower characteristics of the race, as spoilt by contact with our civilisation, he is a masterly study, even allowing for caricature.

UNKIST, UNKIND! By Violet Hunt. New York: Harper Bros. $1.25.

Miss Hunt has journeyed a long way from the air of *A Hard Woman* and *The Way of Marriage*. Frankly, we hope she has only gone for a holiday outing, to refresh herself after the company of the highly sophisticated modern women she was born to analyse and depict. All is old world here, and uncanny, and, we must add, theatrical. There are too many skulls and skeletons about. There is good material for a dark romantic story, but the shadows are too black, and the colours too lurid. The background is the wild heath country of

Northumberland, but we seem to see it by limelights. Sibella, the learned young secretary of Sir Anthony, despising all that is vain and worldly and modern, spending her days gladly among the dead, and most humanly in love with her master, should be a pathetic figure. But she is merely a child solemnly playing with chartularies and poisons and daggers instead of dolls. We cannot take her seriously while she insists so much on her picturesque witch properties. There is a great deal of good writing in *Unkist, Unkind!* but it would have been a cleverer book if it had ended in a farce instead of a murder.

AN AFRICAN MILLIONAIRE. Episodes in the Life of the Illustrious Colonel Clay. By Grant Allen. New York: Edward Arnold. $1.50.

Mr. Grant Allen continues to be a dangerous man. Under the guise of what we believe is looked on at this moment as the most desirable kind of family reading—the narrative of crime and its pursuit—under this innocent and beneficent guise he insinuates opinions subversive of the most sacred rights and customs of finance. He presents to us a millionaire, a man whose touch produces gold and diamonds, and a sharper who boasts of putting down the said millionaire in his income-tax paper as worth five thousand a year to him. With impious audacity he steals our sympathy from its legitimate owner, and bestows it on the clever swindler, the gay Robin Hood, the natural outlaw from a society largely plutocratic. More than that, he writes down the millionaire as an ass on every occasion. This is too much. Were it probable, it would bear consolation to a good many of us; but surely to deny his craft is to deny his millions. However, apart from the improbability of the tales and their dangerous effect, namely, every reader's lusty prayer that Colonel Clay may be released to vex yet again the soul and the purse of the millionaire, the episodes are excellent reading. No brighter and more varied detective stories have appeared for many a day.

A SPANISH MAID. By I. Quiller-Couch. New York: Dodd, Mead & Co. $1.25.

The evil genius of the story, the Spanish gipsy maid saved on the Cornish coast and kindly treated by the simple villagers, is a trifle stagy, but her staginess is very picturesque and effective, and we can hardly wish it away. Her benefactors and their friends in Landecarrock are, on the other hand, perfectly natural and lifelike, and draw our affections to them inevitably. Young squire, parson, fisherman, servant maid, all are made real and companionable people, for whose sake we hate the handsome invader, and refuse altogether to succumb to her charms. The end might be improved dramatically, but as it makes Landecarrock comfortable again, we do not quarrel with it. Miss Quiller-Couch's talent is undoubted, and it is maturing fast.

THE MONKEY THAT WOULD NOT KILL. Stories by Henry Drummond. With 16 full-page illustrations by Louis Wain. New York: Dodd, Mead & Co. $1.00.

Professor Drummond was once left in charge of a children's magazine, and a contributor of fiction failing, he found it necessary to take his place. He did it with very happy results, writing stories for his young readers as if to the manner born. "The Monkey that would not Kill," under the different names of Tricky and Gum, is the most spirited of heroes, a player of many parts both valiant and funny. His conduct during the burglarious assault on his master was a noble climax to a career that showed amazing and amusing impudence in its beginning, and astonishing vitality throughout.

THE BOOKMAN'S TABLE.

AT THE GATES OF SONG. Sonnets. By Lloyd Mifflin. Boston: Estes & Lauriat. $1.50.

With perfect propriety Mr. Mifflin might have named his volume *At the Flood-Gates of Song*, for its one hundred and fifty sonnets were selected from three hundred or more—the fruitage of twenty years of labour—and several other volumes of poetry are herewith advertised as "now in course of publication." Now that he has begun to publish, no pains are spared to place him and his purpose before the public in a true and convincing light. Besides the neat portrait of the author, there are attractive illustrations—somehow illustrated sonnetry strikes us as a startling innovation—from original drawings by Mr. Thomas Moran. And the author explains by preface and postlude what he has undertaken to do. He is "proud in the consciousness that, if he has added nothing to the lustre of that narrow and intricate domain of literature, at least he has not tarnished it with anything indecorous and unseemly." That he takes himself modestly as well as seriously may perhaps not unjustly be inferred from the lines:

> "Why do we sing? Alas! because we must."
>
> * * * * * * * *
>
> "Scorn for myself I feel, who being free,
> Held but my farthing candle to the sun."

Irreproachable as is Mr. Mifflin's technique, his thought-material is for the most part conventional and commonplace, yet, if rarely suggestive or exhilarating, uniformly seemly and decorous.

In essaying the warmer Rossettian hues of feeling and passion, the author is less successful.

> "The dazzle of her beauty's miracle
> Smote me as with a gleaming scymetar,"

is as unconvincing as "sweet neck" and "luscious of limb" are common. Some one has well said that the physical beauty of woman is the last thing in the world that can bear the touch of slovenly fingers. When the author approaches nature one misses, too, a certain sense of reality, as in the lines:

> "While on the darkening mirror of the stream
> Falls the effulgence of the evening star."

Here, as in the sonnets with a religious undercurrent, one imagines that one detects the influence of Cowper, and wishes that the author would lay to heart the words of Blake, that to particularise is the great distinction of merit. Mr. Mifflin is overfond of alliteration, and does not sufficiently avoid such unpoetic words as "decimation," "exterminate," "scum." Yet his diction is generally pure and fluent; and one must remember that if the glory is great the strife is hard. That Capri "dimly vague and blue" and "fair Frascati at the close of day" should cause his heart to leap westward o'er the rolling brine

> "To bask once more upon the purple hills—
> The Appalachian ridges"

round his Pennsylvanian home is, we suppose, a freakish display of the patriotism which inspires the words

> "America is for the Americans."

Nevertheless, the bathos suggests the remark of Mr. James's patriotic youngster in Rome, that "father's not here; he is in a better place"—meaning Schenectady, N. Y.

LIVES OF SEVENTY OF THE MOST EMINENT PAINTERS, SCULPTORS, AND ARCHITECTS. By Giorgio Vasari. Edited and annotated in the light of recent discoveries. By E. H. and E. W. Blashfield and A. A. Hopkins. 4 vols. Illustrated. New York: Charles Scribner's Sons. $8.00.

The excellent work in this new edition we owe to American critics and students. They have made us an admirable book, the special virtues of which only those who have toiled in the difficult field of modern art criticism and art history are worthy to know and value. The mass of technical literature respecting the authorship of pictures to be read and digested nowadays, before one has the right to hold opinions, is enormous; to be an authority concerning works scattered through the whole of Europe, means years of hard labour; even to repeat correctly what other authorities have decided is no light task. These editors have spared themselves no trouble. Their notes summing up the results of all the best research will bear the test of the most rigid examination, and are themselves as good as a guide to the literature of Italian art in its great days. The illustrations are well selected and mostly well reproduced, though there are unhappy exceptions; the Pesaro Madonna of Titian, for instance, seems not suitable for reproduction on a small scale.

It is not a perfect edition. We do not agree with the editors about there being no need for a new translation. Mrs. Foster's, which we have known all our reading lives, has great merits, but we should have one that does not need so much correction in the footnotes. And at all events, whether hers was used or not, we should have had a complete Vasari. The editors have certainly made a good selection of the lives; but no selection from a much-loved book leaves a reader satisfied. And the notice of Vasari himself is rather frothy, we think. No, the edition is not perfect; but it is so very much better than anything we have had in English before; so much superior, so far as editing goes, to any edition save the revised Milanese one, that we make our few criticisms with a full sense of what we owe both to editors and publishers for this issue of one of the most permanently interesting and delightful books in the world. We have said we should have a complete Vasari. Let us give another suggestion more easily carried out. We want a good small selection at a popular price. A year or so ago something of the kind was attempted in a very unsatisfactory fashion. It was not annotated, so far as we remember, and the Introduction, a miserable affair, was written by one who owned Italian art appealed very little to him! That he knew nothing about it was very evident. Will not the editors and publishers of this fine edition think of the gap in the libraries of poor art students?

THE GOD-IDEA OF THE ANCIENTS; Or Sex in Religion. By Eliza Burt Gamble. New York: G. P. Putnam's Sons.

The object of this book is to show that many different tendencies which are seen in the history of religion are in reality to be traced to the influence of sex; that in the earlier days of humanity women exercised more power upon thought and faith than did men; and that in consequence the earlier forms of religion are marked by the altruism which the author ascribes to her own sex. Later, when men began to attain their present importance in the world, religion began "to reflect the egoistic qualities acquired by the male." The book is really a very interesting one, written, in the main, very clearly and dispassionately, and with a citation of authorities that shows wide reading and a good grasp upon the central purpose of the author's thesis. Whatever one may think of the conclusions, any thoughtful person may read the chapters with curiosity and some degree of profit. It is obvious, however, that Mrs. Gamble is not discriminating in her reliance upon authorities; and as she gets nearly everything at second or even third hand, this is a fatal defect from a scientific point of view. The frequent references to Richard Payne Knight and Godfrey Higgins, the erudition gleaned from Spanish writers through Prescott, and the unqualified reliance upon various obscure theorists of a century or more ago, make it clear that to Mrs. Gamble a book is a book, and that any one who ever printed anything is about as good as any one else for her purpose. We note the frequent reference to the Greek divinities by the Roman names of Juno, Mars, Mercury, and so forth. We regret also the appearance in her pages of such expressions as "the Romish Church" and "Romish papists;" for these terms alone would of themselves lead one to view the whole treatise with suspicion.

VICTORIAN LITERATURE. Sixty Years of Books and Bookmen. By Clement K. Shorter. New York: Dodd, Mead & Co. $1.50.

We have had manuals of Victorian literature before now, but nobody has made one on Mr. Shorter's plan. Whether the compilers have been big writers or little writers, they have one and all essayed to be very solemn critics; to weigh this man and that, to cast this out and set the other on a pedestal. Mr. Shorter is much less solemn and a great deal more practical. We do not mean that he has given a place to all and sundry bookmakers of the period.

But his purpose has not been to play the judge of what will become immortal—a very premature thing to do—but to set down brief, concise accounts of the books and their makers that during the last sixty years have influenced thought and action, that have made a name in large circles or small, for investigation, inspiration, scholarship, judgment, imagination, or style, or simply because they happily hit the needs of the hour. Some of them may be out of date already, but they did their work, and earned a place in history if not in literature. Mr. Shorter has found an excellent motto for his purpose in Whitman's lines:

"Births have brought us richness and variety,
And other births will bring us richness and variety;
I do not call one greater and one smaller;
That which fills its period and place is equal to any."

We have a hundred essays on Tennyson, and shall have a hundred more, but of books that deign to notice all the good workers in any field of literature, whether of immortal destiny or not, we have hardly one. We must turn, in our need, to odd volumes of "Men of the Time" and such like, and there miss, what Mr. Shorter contrives to show, the trend of the age, the impulses and reactions, and the force contributed by each writer to the many-sided result. The book is nearly, not quite, up to date. It was probably wise not to include the newest reputations.

The very index, since it is classified, is of much service. Criticism is subservient to the purpose of information; but it is not absent. If we sometimes disagree with his frank and fearless judgments—as when he says "Sydney Smith left nothing that we can read to-day"—we must own that in the main they are able, commonsensible, and show a fine sense of rank and proportion.

JOURNEYS THROUGH FRANCE. By H. Taine. New York: Henry Holt & Co. $2.50.

Taine's *Carnets de Voyage* surpass all but the best of their kind—an unsatisfactory kind; for there is not one person in a thousand that cares to hear what another said and felt at dawn on the shores of Madagascar or by night on the Adriatic; and there is not one person in ten thousand who can express his feelings, if he happened to have any, and his vision, in such a way as to make it a reproach to all the indifferent rest not to listen. The *impression de voyage* habit is a modern method of boring, rather surprising in a business-like age. But Taine had eyes and a delightful style. These little descriptive accounts of what remained in his memory of the various provincial towns which he visited as examiner for admission to the Military School of St. Cyr, have a double force, that of the man who could read social life like a book, and that of the artist who had seen too much to pose, and seen enough not to rave indiscriminately. Charming to read for their unaffectedness, their grace, their brevity, they are also true. Test them by the bit of France you know best, be it Nancy, or Marseilles, or Carnac, they are incomplete, but you will know he has been there. There are a few telling phrases, such as "The Middle Age was an attic of the Muses," but in general no strain after effect. And there are a few scraps of personal opinion, and personal melancholy, and personal prejudices that are more interesting than the subject of his papers. As this: "I find myself coming back again and again to the idea that France is a democracy of peasants and workingmen, under a motherly administration, with a restricted town population which lives cheaply and grows rusty, and with needy officials who are on the lookout for promotion, and never take root." But yet he likes the Latins best. In pleasure, the others are "mere brutes or merely virtuous."

THE WATER OF THE WONDROUS ISLES. By William Morris. New York: Longmans, Green & Co. $2.50.

If we are to have nothing more from his pen, William Morris's last gift is a very gracious farewell. Since *The Earthly Paradise* he has written nothing so evenly charming. Birdalone is one of his most delightful heroines. She lives in the land of tapestry, of course; but we draw her down from among the foliage on the wall, and she smiles humanly, and we feel her sweet breath on us for a moment or two. When she has faded back to the wall again, we are not soon tired of looking at her and her companions.

It is a book that stands so many tests. Each time you take it up you feel the spell of its rhythm and the dignity of its wording. It is eminently quotable. Its archaisms are not cheap and flimsy. Why is it not a great book, then? Why does it leave only a dreamlike memory? Why is it that no one will read it through from cover to cover at a sitting, or be angry at the disturbance which should prevent this?

To read a portion is to read something remarkably like the good fairy tales that enchanted our youth, and that we return to with respect and wonder for the effective vigour of their simple art. To read the whole is to have a quite other impression. Perhaps part of the answer lies in the fact that Morris was saturated with the spirit of decorative art. Not life, but its symbols became his material. Date, climate, modifying circumstance, were merged by him in general truth and beauty. You may apply this method to literature, in a ballad like "The Blue Closet," or as the fairy-tale makers did; but only briefly, with the brevity of a gaze at a picture, or of the glance that takes in the design of a panel. Morris forgot that and kept us in the company of symbols and generalised human beings for hundreds of pages. It is not that his prose romances are too long, but that length disagrees with their model. Yet, read *The Water of the Wondrous Isles* leisurely and brokenly, and it is like rays of sunlight on old tapestry.

BOOKMAN BREVITIES.

We have before us a sort of bibliographical mystery in the shape of a copy of *Uncle Tom's Cabin*, described on the cover as being a "memorial edition." We have searched carefully through its pages without finding any indication as to who its publisher is or as to the place of its publication, or as to the price at which it is sold. The book is one of some six hundred and eighty large and handsomely printed pages, profusely and adequately illus-

5. In Kedar's Tents. By Merriman. $1.25. (Dodd, Mead & Co.)
6. The Story of Jesus Cnrist. By Phelps. $2.00. (Houghton, Mifflin & Co)

CLEVELAND, O.

1. Quo Vadis. By Sienkiewicz. $2.00. (Little, Brown & Co.)
2. The Choir Invisible. By Allen. $1.50. (Macmillan.)
3. The Honourable Peter Stirling. By Ford. $1.50 (Holt.)
4. Hugh Wynne. By Mitchell. $2.00. (Century Co.)
5. The Christian. By Caine. $1.50. (Appleton.)
6. Lochinvar. By Crockett. $1.50. (Harper.)

DETROIT, MICH.

1. Hugh Wynne. By Mitchell. $2.00. (Century Co.)
2. Captains Courageous. By Kipling. $1.50. (Century Co.)
3. Story of an Untold Love. By Ford. $1.25. (Houghton, Mifflin & Co.)
4. The Christian. By Caine. $1.50. (Appleton.)
5. Quo Vadis. By Sienkiewicz. $2.00. (Little, Brown & Co.)
6. Alfred, Lord Tennyson. By His Son. $10.00. (Macmillan.)

KANSAS CITY, MO.

1. Quo Vadis. By Sienkiewicz. $1.00, $1.60. (Little, Brown & Co.)
2. The Choir Invisible. By Allen. $1.50. (Macmillan.)
3. The Christian. By Caine. $1.50. (Appleton.)
4. Lullaby Land. By Field. $1.50. (Scribner.)
5. In Kedar's Tents. By Merriman. $1.25. (Dodd, Mead & Co.)
6. Soldiers of Fortune. By Davis. $1.50. (Scribner.)

LOS ANGELES, CAL.

1. Quo Vadis. By Sienkiewicz. New ed., $1.00. (Little, Brown & Co.)
2. In Kedar's Tents. By Merriman. $1.25. (Dodd, Mead & Co.)
3. St. Ives. By Stevenson. $1.50. (Scribner.)
4. Hugh Wynne. By Mitchell. $2.00. (Century Co.)
5. Story of an Untold Love. By Ford. $1.25. (Houghton, Mifflin & Co.)
6. Dariel. By Blackmore. $1.75. (Dodd, Mead & Co.)

LOUISVILLE, KY.

1. Story of an Untold Love. By Ford. $1.25. (Houghton, Mifflin & Co.)
2. The Kentuckians. By Fox. $1.25. (Harper.)
3. Potter's Wheel. Ian Maclaren. $1.25. (Dodd, Mead & Co.)
4. Quo Vadis. By Sienkiewicz. $1.00 ed. (Little, Brown & Co.)
5. Hugh Wynne. By Mitchell. $2.00. (Century Co.)
6. The Christian. By Caine. $1.50. (Appleton.)

NEW HAVEN, CONN.

1. Letters of Elizabeth Barrett Browning. Edited by Kenyon. $4.00. (Macmillan.)
2. Alfred, Lord Tennyson. By His Son. $10.00 net. (Macmillan.)
3. Hugh Wynne. By Mitchell. $2.00. (Century Co.)
4. The First Christmas Tree. By van Dyke. $1.50. (Scribner.)
5. Captains Courageous. By Kipling. $1.50. (Century Co.)
6. The Three Margarets. By Richards. $1.25. (Estes & L.)

NEW ORLEANS, LA.

1. Hugh Wynne. By Mitchell. $2.00. (Century.)
2. Dariel. By Blackmore. $1.75. (Dodd, Mead & Co.)
3. Story of an Untold Love. By Ford. $1.25. (Houghton, Mifflin & Co.)
4. Diana Victrix. By Converse. $1.25. (Houghton, Mifflin & Co.)
5. The Federal Judge. By Lush. $1.25. (Houghton, Mifflin & Co.)
6. The Choir Invisible. By Allen. $1.50. (Macmillan.)

PHILADELPHIA, PA.

1. Hugh Wynne. By Mitchell. $2.00. (Century Co.)
2. Quo Vadis. By Sienkiewicz. 55 cts. net. (Little, Brown & Co.)
3. Lochinvar. By Crockett. $1.50. (Harper.)
4. Old Virginia. By Fiske. $4.00. (Houghton, Mifflin & Co.)
5. Corleone. By Crawford. $2.00. (Macmillan)
6. Equality. By Bellamy. $1.25. (Appleton.)

PITTSBURG, PA.

1. Quo Vadis. By Sienkiewicz. $2.00, $6.00, and $12.00. (Little, Brown & Co.)
2. Farthest North. By Nansen. $10.00. (Harper.)
3. Hugh Wynne. By Mitchell. $2.00. (Century Co.)
4. The Latimers. By McCook. $1.50. (Jacobs.)
5. Soldiers of Fortune. By Davis. $1.50. (Scribner.)
6. The Choir Invisible. By Allen. $1.50. (Macmillan.)

PORTLAND, ME.

1. Quo Vadis. By Sienkiewicz. $1.00. (Little, Brown & Co.)
2. Hugh Wynne. By Mitchell. $2.00. (Century Co.)
3. Captains Courageous. By Kipling. $1.50. (Century Co.)
4. The Choir Invisible. By Allen. $1.50. (Macmillan.)
5. London. By Gibson. $5.00. (Scribner.)
6. Alaska, the New Eldorado. By Wells. 50 cts. (The J. K. Gill Co.)

PROVIDENCE, R. I.

1. Quo Vadis. By Sienkiewicz. $1.00. (Little, Brown & Co.)
2. Captains Courageous. By Kipling. $1.50. (Century Co.)
3. Hugh Wynne. By Mitchell. $2.00. (Century Co.)
4. First Christmas Tree. By van Dyke. $1.50. (Scribner.)
5. Story of Jesus Christ. By Phelps. $2.00. (Houghton.)
6. Gondola Days. By Smith. $1.50. (Houghton.)

ROCHESTER, N. Y.

1. Quo Vadis. By Sienkiewicz. $1.00. (Little, Brown & Co.)
2. Hugh Wynne. By Mitchell. $2.00. (Century Co.)
3. Captains Courageous. By Kipling. $1.50. (Century Co.)
4. The Choir Invisible. By Allen. $1.50. (Macmillan.)
5. The Christian. By Caine. $1.50. (Appleton)
6. Gondola Days. By Smith. $1.50. (Houghton, Mifflin & Co.)

SALT LAKE CITY, UTAH.

1. Quo Vadis. By Sienkiewicz. $2.00. (Little, Brown & Co.)
2. The Choir Invisible. By Allen. $1.50. (Macmillan)
3. The Christian. By Caine. $1.50. (Appleton.)
4. Hugh Wynne. By Mitchell. $2.00. (Century Co.)
5. Pursuit of the House-Boat. Bangs. $1.25. (Harper.)
6. Hon. Peter Stirling. By Ford. $1.50. (Holt.)

SAN FRANCISCO, CAL.

1. Wild Flowers of California. By Parsons and Buck. $2.00. (Doxey.)
2. Idle Hours in a Library. By Hudson. $1.25. (Doxey.)
3. The Lark. Books 1 and 2. $3.00 each. (Doxey.)
4. Quo Vadis. By Sienkiewicz. $2.00. (Little, Brown & Co.)
5. London as Seen by C. D. Gibson. $5.00. (Scribner.)
6. Drawings. By Remington. $5 00. (Russell.)

ST. LOUIS, MO.

1. Quo Vadis. By Sienkiewicz. $6.00. (Little, Brown & Co.)
2. Captains Courageous. By Kipling. $1.50. (Century Co.)
3. The Choir Invisible. By Allen. $1.50. (Macmillan.)
4. In Kedar's Tents. By Merriman. $1.25. (Dodd, Mead & Co.)
5. His Grace of Osmonde. By Burnett. $1.50. (Scribner.)
6. Threads of Life. By Rollins. $1.00. (Lamson, Wolffe & Co.)

ST. PAUL, MINN.

1. Quo Vadis. By Sienkiewicz. $2.00. (Little, Brown & Co.)
2. The Choir Invisible. By Allen. $1.50. (Macmillan.)
3. Year from a Reporter's Note-Book. Davis. $1.50. (Harper.)
4. Soldiers of Fortune. By Davis. $1.50. (Harper.)
5. The Christian. By Caine. $1.50. (Appleton.)
6. The Old Santa Fé Trail. Inman. $3.50. (Macmillan.)

TOLEDO, O.

1. Quo Vadis. By Sienkiewicz. $2.00. (Little, Brown & Co.)
2. Hugh Wynne. By Mitchell. $2.00. (Century Co)
3. The Christian. By Caine. $1.50. (Appleton.)
4. Jerome. By Wilkins. $1.50. (Harper.)
5. The Choir Invisible. By Allen. $1.50. (Macmillan.)
6. Story of Jesus Christ. Phelps. $2.00. (Houghton, Mifflin & Co.)

TORONTO, CANADA.

1. Spanish John. By McLennan. Paper, 75 cts. ; cloth, $1.25. (The Copp-Clark Co., Limited.)
2. His Grace of Osmonde. By Burnett. Paper, 75 cts. ; cloth, $1.25. (The Copp-Clark Co., Limited.)
3. Prisoners of the Sea. By Kingsley. Paper, 75 cts. ; cloth, $1.25. (The Copp-Clark Co., Limited.)
4. St. Ives. By Stevenson. Paper, 75 cts. ; cloth, $1.25. (The Copp-Clark Co., Limited.)
5. Dariel. By Blackmore. Paper, 75 cts. ; cloth, $1.25. (The Copp-Clark Co., Limited.)
6. The School for Saints. By Hobbes. Paper, 75 cts. ; cloth, $1.25. (The Copp-Clark Co., Limited.)

WORCESTER, MASS.

1. Quo Vadis. By Sienkiewicz. 2 vols., $6.00; 1 vol., $2.00 and $1.00. (Little, Brown & Co.)
2. Romance and Reality of Puritan Coast. By Garrett. $2.00. (Little, Brown & Co.)
3. Florence By Yriarte. $3.00. (Coates & Co.)
4. Lullaby-Land. By Field. $1.50. (Scribner.)
5. Rome. By Wey. $3.00. (Coates & Co.)
6. Hugh Wynne. By Mitchell. $2.00. (Century Co.)

THE BEST SELLING BOOKS.

According to the foregoing lists, the six books which have sold best in order of demand during the month are—

1. Quo Vadis. By Sienkiewicz.
2. Hugh Wynne. By Mitchell.
3. The Choir Invisible. By Allen.
4. The Christian. By Caine.
5. Captains Courageous. By Kipling.
6. In Kedar's Tents. By Merriman.

BOOKS RECEIVED.

AMERICAN BAPTIST PUBLICATION SOCIETY, Philadelphia.

Romans and I. and II. Corinthians, A People's Commentary, by George W. Clark, D.D.

D. APPLETON & Co., New York.

Memory and its Cultivation, by F. W. Edridge-Green, M.D., F.R.C.S.
New Letters of Napoleon I., from the French by Lady Mary Loyd.
Sweethearts and Friends, by Maxwell Gray.

EDWARD ARNOLD, New York.

Paul Mercer, by James Adderley.
Benin, the City of Blood, by R. H. Bacon.

RICHARD G. BADGER & Co., Boston.

The Children of the Night, by Edwin Arlington Robinson.

A. S BARNES & Co., New York.

Interpretations of Life and Religion, by Walton W. Battershall.

R. Baur & Son, Wilkesbarre, Pa.

Daniel North of Wyoming Valley, by S. R. Smith.

John C. Bauer, Chicago.

Songs and Stories from Tennessee, by John (Trotwood) Moore.

Bedford Publishing Co., Mt. Kisco, N. Y.

A Prince of the Blood, by Julius A. Lewis.

Benziger Brothers, New York.

Life of St. Aloysius Gonzaga.

Calvert Co., Seattle, Wash.

Sealth, by Elisabeth H. Calvert.

Century Co., New York.

Rubáiyát of Doc Sifers, by James Whitcomb Riley.

St. Nicholas, an Illustrated Magazine for Young Folks, by Mary Mapes Dodge. 1897. Vol. I. and II.

The Century Magazine, May–October, 1897.

Commonwealth Co., New York.

Henry Cadavere, A Study of Life and Work, by H. W. Bellsmith.

W. B. Conkey & Co., Chicago.

Three Women, by Ella Wheeler Wilcox.

T. Y. Crowell & Co., Boston.

In Tune with the Infinite, by Ralph Waldo Trine.

DeWolfe, Fiske & Co., Boston.

For Pity's Sake, by Sarah Nelson Carter.

Dodd, Mead & Co., New York.

The Ideal Life, by Henry Drummond.

The Monkey that Would Not Kill, by Henry Drummond.

Bye-Ways, by Robert S. Hichens.

Holy Bible, Polychrome Edition, The Book of Judges.

Doubleday & McClure Co., New York.

Prayers Ancient and Modern.

Hymns that have Helped, edited with the assistance of numerous helpers by W. T. Stead.

Drexel Biddle, Philadelphia.

Shantytown Sketches, by Anthony J. Drexel Biddle.

The Flowers of Life, by Anthony J. Drexel Biddle.

The Second Froggy Fairy Book, by Anthony J. Drexel Biddle.

E. P. Dutton & Co., New York.

My Father as I Recall Him, by Mamie Dickens.

Eaton & Mains, New York.

A Harmony of Samuel, Kings, and Chronicles, by William Day Crockett.

Editor Publishing Co., Cincinnati.

The Secret of Hamlet, by South G. Preston.

Forest & Stream Publishing Co., New York.

Trail and Camp-Fire, editors George Bird Grinnell, Theodore Roosevelt.

Fowler & Wells Co., New York.

The King's Daughter and the King's Son, A Fairy Tale of To day, written by a King's Daughter.

Not in It, by Anna Olcott Commelin.

Funk & Wagnalls, New York.

Hawaii Our New Possessions, by John R. Musick.

Ginn & Co., Boston.

Specimens of the Pre-Shakespearian Drama, with an Introduction, Notes, and a Glossary, by John Matthews Manly. Vol. II.

Studies and Notes in Philology and Literature. Vol. V., Child Memorial Volume.

Government Printing Office, Washington.

Report of the Commissioner of Education for the Year 1895–96. Vol. II.

Harper & Brothers, New York.

The Wooing of Malatoon: Commodus, by Lew Wallace, illustrations by Du Mond and Weguelin.

A Year from a Reporter's Note-Book, by Richard Harding Davis.

Lin McLean, by Owen Wister.

Harper's Round Table, 1897.

Picturesque Sicily, by William Agnew Paton.

Jimty, and Others, by Margaret Sutton Briscoe.

Spanish John, by William McLennan.

Secretary to Bayne, M.P., by W. Pett Ridge.

The Rock of the Lion, by Molly Elliot Seawell.

Hayworth Publishing, Washington, D. C.

The Trumpeters, and Other Poems, by Andrew Downing.

B. Herder, St. Louis.

The Dream of Bonaparte, by William Poland, S.J.

Autobiography of Madame Guyon, translated in full by Thomas Taylor Allen. Vol. II.

E. R. Herrick & Co., New York.

A Mince Pie Dream, and Other Verses, by Emily D. Elton.

Daily Souvenirs, an Olio of Treasure Thoughts, selected by Rose Porter.

For My Lady's Desk, A Writing-Desk Book for Every Day, by Rose Porter.

Henry Holt & Co., New York.

Selections from the Prose Writings of Matthew Arnold, edited with notes and an introduction by Lewis E. Gates.

A Book of Verses for Children, compiled by Verrall Lucas.

Literary Pamphlets, Vol. I. and II., by Ernest Rhys.

Political Pamphlets, selected and arranged by A. F. Pollard.

International Book Co., Chicago.

Truth and Poetry, by R. P. Brorup.

Lamson, Wolffe & Co., Boston.

Vivian of Virginia, by Hulbert Fuller, illustrated by Frank T. Merrill.

Mademoiselle de Berny, A Story of Valley Forge, by Pauline Bradford Mackie, illustrated by Frank T. Merrill.

The Levytype Co., Philadelphia.

The New Man, by E. P. Oberholtzer.

ROBERT LEWIS WEED CO., New York.

The Blue Ridge Mystery, by Caroline Martin.

J. B. LIPPINCOTT CO., Philadelphia.

Curiosities of Popular Customs, by William S. Walsh.

Men, Women and Manners in Colonial Times, by Sydney George Fisher. 2 vols.

A Son of Israel, an Original Story, by "Rachel Penn."

LITTLE, BROWN & CO., Boston.

Hania, by Henryk Sienkiewicz.

The Interest of America in Sea Power, Present and Future, by Captain A. T. Mahan.

Monsieur de Chauvelin's Will, by Alexander Dumas (New Series).

The Horoscope, a Romance of the Reign of François II., by Alexander Dumas.

LONGMANS, GREEN & CO., New York.

Harold, the Last of the Saxon Kings, by Lord Lytton, edited with Introduction and Notes by George Laurence Gomme.

The Camp of Refuge, by Charles MacFarlane, edited with Introduction and Notes by George Laurence Gomme.

The Sentimental Journey, by Laurence Sterne.

Masters of Medicine, John Hunter, Man of Science and Surgeon, by Stephen Paget, M.A., F.R.C.S.

Masters of Medicine, William Harvey, by D'Arcy Power, F.S.A., F.R.C.S.

THE MACMILLAN CO., New York

A Genealogy of Morals, by Friedrich Nietzsche.

Cambridge Described as Illustrated, by Thomas Dinham Atkinson.

The Story of a Red Deer, by the Hon. J. W. Fortescue.

M. F. MANSFIELD, New York.

Manners for Women, by Mrs. Humphry.

"And Shall Trelawney Die?" by Joseph Hocking.

NEW AMSTERDAM BOOK CO., New York.

Rienzi, by Edward Bulwer Lytton.

The Caxtons, by Edward Bulwer Lytton.

The Last of the Barons, by Edward Bulwer Lytton. 2 vols.

The Copy-Maker, by William Farquhar Payson.

THE OPEN COURT PUBLISHING CO., Chicago.

Buddhism and its Christian Critics, by Dr. Paul Carus.

Nirvâna, a Story of Buddhist Philosophy, by Paul Carus.

THE PHILOSOPHICAL PUBLISHING CO., Boston.

All's Right with the World, by Charles B. Newcomb.

THE PILGRIM PRESS, Boston.

Children's Day, by James Gardiner Vose, D.D.

Real Preaching, by Nehemiah Boynton, D.D.

JAMES POTT & CO., New York.

The Legend of the Thorn Road, by Evelyn Nichols Kerr.

THEODORE PRESSER, Philadelphia.

Pianoforte Study, by Alexander McArthur.

G. P. PUTNAM'S SONS, New York.

Vanity Fair, by W. M. Thackeray.

Rob Roy, by Sir Walter Scott.

Social Facts and Forces, by Washington Gladden.

A Note-Book in Northern Spain, by Archer M. Huntington.

RAND, MCNALLY & CO., Chicago.

Hernani the Jew, by A. N. Homer.

A. D. F. RANDOLPH CO., New York.

With the Seasons, by Mary Augusta Mason.

THE ANNA C. REIFSNIDER BOOK CO., St. Louis.

Gilgal, by Mrs. Calvin Kryder Reifsnider.

FLEMING H. REVELL CO., New York.

A Life for Africa, by E. C. Parsons.

Korea and Her Neighbours, by Isabella Bird Bishop, F.R.G.S.

R. H. RUSSELL, New York.

Going to War in Greece, by Frederick Palmer.

CHARLES SCRIBNER'S SONS, New York.

The Works of Rudyard Kipling, Verses XI.

Audubon and His Journals, 2 vols., by M. R. Audubon.

SILVER, BURDETT & CO., New York.

The World and its People, Book VIII., by Eva M. C. Kellogg, edited by Larkin Dunton, LL D.

STANDARD PRINTING CO., Hannibal, Mo.

The Voice of Christianity, by Frederick B. Newberry.

F. TENNYSON NEELY, New York.

Warrior Gap, by Captain Charles King.

The Shackles of Fate, by Max Nordau.

The Devil Worshippers, by Robert Montfort Lucky.

Squire John, by Sir George Rathbone.

My Illegal Wife, by Count Len Zolkoff.

A Bachelor's Box, by T. C. De Leon.

Just a Summer Affair, by Mary Adelaide Keeler.

Petronilla the Sister, by Emma Homan Thayer.

TRUSLOVE & COMBA, New York.

The Training of a Craftsman, by Fred Miller.

By Stroke of Sword, rendered into modern English by Andrew Balfour.

Italian Pronunciation, by T. E. Comba.

T. FISHER UNWIN, London.

Good Reading about Many Books Selected by Their Authors.

WAY & WILLIAMS, Chicago.

Afloat on the Ohio, by Reuben Goldthwaites.

The Choir Visible, by Mary M. Adams.

A Man and a Woman, by Stanley Waterloo.

THOMAS WHITTAKER, New York.

Hymns and Verses, by Louis F. Benson.

What Can I Do for Brady? and Other Verse, by Charles F. Johnson.

MERIT is the **HEAVY ARTILLERY** by which we are constantly winning victories.

BRENTANO'S

French Department

BRENTANO'S desire to draw the attention of readers of French literature to the very complete assortment of sets of Standard French Authors in fine bindings shown upon their shelves. Given below is a small list of authors carried in bindings, which, although not complete, will serve to give some idea of the complete stock.

D'Abrantés, Balzac, Bourget, Chateaubriand, Coppée, Corneille, Daudet, Dumas, Gautier, Guizot, Hugo, Labiche, Lamartine, Leconte de Lisle, Loti, Martin, Maupassant, Molière, Montaigne, de Musset, Racine, Saint Amand, Saint Simon, Sand, Shakespeare, Sue, Taine, Thiers, Voltaire, Zola.

Prices are Reasonable **Bindings are the Best**

BRENTANO'S

31 UNION SQUARE, NEW YORK

CHICAGO WASHINGTON PARIS

An Illustrated Catalogue

Containing miniature reproductions will be sent free post paid on receipt of one 2 ct. stamp, by George H. Daniels, Gen'l. Pass'r. Agt. Grand Central Station, New York.

VOL. VI. No. 6.

THE BOOKMAN.

AN ILLUSTRATED LITERARY JOURNAL.

CONTENTS FOR FEBRUARY.

Entered at the Post-Office, New York, N. Y., as Second-class Mail Matter.

LIVING POLITICAL ORATORS

which will present vivid pictures of the greatest living masters of eloquence in Italy, Germany, France, England, and the United States. Their oratorical styles will be analysed and characterised by writers of distinction who are intimately familiar with both the political and rhetorical attributes of the orator in question.

NEW WRITERS

THE BOOKMAN notes the rise of new authors and furnishes biographical facts of interest concerning them and their work, accompanied with portraits when these are accessible.

REVIEWS OF NEW BOOKS
NOVEL NOTES
BOOKMAN'S TABLE

Under this survey of the month's publications the more important and prominent books are reviewed at length over the names of competent critics, carefully chosen with a view to securing a just and sympathetic criticism of the subject.

NOVEL NOTES is especially intended as a judicious guide to readers through the mass of fiction that is daily issuing from the press, much of it being of ephemeral interest only, much of it also varying in character and appealing to as many various classes of readers.

THE BOOKMAN'S TABLE together with BOOKMAN BREVITIES gives in the same way succinct notices of many books of minor importance that are nevertheless well worthy of attention.

Of all the periodicals that criticise new books THE BOOKMAN has gained the reputation of printing the earliest reviews. Promptness, efficiency, and trustworthiness have characterised its work in this department since the start.

To the reader who is anxious to come in contact with our current literature, yet who in the absorption of a busy life cannot possibly read and choose for himself, this department is at once invaluable and indispensable.

THE BOOK MART

Among the original features of THE BOOKMAN which have stamped its pages with distinction and individuality was "The Book Mart." The interest taken in this department has steadily increased until it is now distinguished as one of the most remarkable features in the magazine literature of to-day. This department, which presents facts of an interesting and novel nature alike to Book Readers, Bookbuyers, and Booksellers, consists of an Eastern Letter, a Western Letter, and an English Letter from three great trading centres, giving reports of the conditions prevailing each month in the book market; over thirty lists of the best six selling books of the month supplied by reliable leading booksellers throughout the country, with a summary of the best selling books based on these reports, and, finally, a list of Books Received.

AMONG THE LIBRARIES

Mr. George H. Baker, Chief Librarian of Columbia University, conducts this department, in which especial attention is devoted to Library Economy and accurate news from the great libraries of the world.

CONTINENTAL AND EDUCATIONAL SURVEY

THE BOOKMAN surveys periodically the field of Continental literature and the latest educational publications.

LONDON AND PARIS LETTERS

THE BOOKMAN contains a monthly London Letter by W. Robertson Nicoll, M.A., LL.D., editor of the English BOOKMAN. Dr. Nicoll is one of the most vivacious and brilliant writers in the journalism of to-day, and his *causeries* are unique in their knowledge and observation of literary life in London, and in their delightful gossip and comment anent the latest happenings in the book world. A letter from Paris which appears each month covers the same general ground in its treatise of the current literary news of France.

A LITERARY DIRECTORY

Authors' Agency. SEVENTH YEAR. **Criticism, Advice, Revision, Copying, Disposal.** Thorough, careful attention to MSS. of all kinds.
References: Noah Brooks, Mrs. Deland, Mrs. Burton Harrison, Mrs. Julia Ward Howe, W. D. Howells, Mrs. Moulton, Charles Dudley Warner, Mary E. Wilkins, and others. For rates, references, notices, send stamp to

WILLIAM A. DRESSER, Director,
78 Pierce Building, Copley Square, Boston, Mass.
Mention The Bookman. (Opp. Public Library)

BOOKSELLERS

If you want **FRENCH BOOKS,** *or books of any description—School Books, Standard Books, Novels, etc.—send to* **WILLIAM R. JENKINS,** *Publisher and Importer,* **851** *and* **853 SIXTH AVENUE (48th Street), NEW YORK.** *Catalogue on application.*
Importations promptly made.

Established in 1857.

J. W. BOUTON, RARE and STANDARD BOOKS

Books on the Fine Arts, including . . **Architecture, Decoration, etc.**

English and French Illustrated Books, Illuminated MSS., Early Printed Books, First Editions, Fine Bindings, Books on Ancient Religions, Symbolism, etc.

New Publications in English and French.
English and French Novels.

10 W. 28th St. (Bet. 5th Ave. and Broadway) **New York**

Libraries Purchased for Cash.

SOMETHING GOOD FOR EVERYBODY.

I refer to my recent Catalogue No. 45, the best collection of second-hand "out-of-print" books I have ever offered to the confiding public.

A. S. CLARK, 174 Fulton St., (opposite St. Paul's), **New York City.**

Old Books

SEND STAMP FOR LIST. Address **A. J. CRAWFORD, 312 N. 7th Street, St. Louis, Mo.**

LIBRARIES

We solicit correspondence with book buyers for private and other **Libraries** and desire to submit figures on proposed lists. Our topically arranged **Library List** (mailed gratis on application) will be found useful by those selecting titles.

THE BAKER & TAYLOR CO.,
WHOLESALE BOOKS,
5 & 7 East Sixteenth St., New York.

BOOKSELLERS

New York, 150 Fifth Ave. **Established 1880**

E. Miriam Coyriere, Teachers' Agency

Colleges, schools, and families supplied. Teachers placed. Schools conscientiously recommended to parents. Musical Department. School property rented and sold.

MAGAZINES, ETC., ETC.

BACK NUMBERS OF *BOOKMAN*, AND ALL Periodicals, Bought, Sold, or Exchanged.

American Magazine Exchange
Emilie Building, **St. Louis, Mo.**

OUT-OF-PRINT MAGAZINES.
ALSO AUTOGRAPHS. **Send for my Bulletins.**
H. WILLIAMS, 25 EAST 10TH ST., NEW YORK.

JUST OUT. 1. Interesting Catalogue of Choice English and American Books, in Fine Bindings, quoting extremely low, tempting prices. 2. London Weekly Circular of Rare Books. Bookman readers should send for both!

H. W. HAGEMAN, Importer, 160 Fifth Ave., New York.

Write for Catalogue Just Published.

Sign of the Ark. **NOAH FARNHAM MORRISON**

Rare, Old and Curious BOOKS Americana, Genealogies and General Literature

No. 877 Broad St., Newark, N. J.

Libraries and small collections of books purchased from executors and others.

OLD AND RARE BOOKS

First Editions, etc., etc., for sale. AN ILLUSTRATED CATALOGUE OF PART 2, with seventy-one reproductions of title pages, plates, etc., etc. Works relating to the Civil War and Cromwell, Coaching, Cookery, Costume, Queen Elizabeth, Freemasonry, Gardening. Books, chiefly first editions, by Charles Cotton, Abraham Cowley, William Cowper, Daniel Defoe, Charles Dickens, Dr. John Donne, Michael Drayton, John Dryden, Thomas Durfey, John Evelyn, Henry Fielding. First Editions of books illustrated by George and Robert Cruikshank, Richard Doyle, and Harry Furniss; and a large collection of curious Facetiæ. Part 2, 8vo, 74 pages, post free, 1s.

PICKERING & CHATTO, 66 Haymarket, London, S. W.

IN JANUARY

We will issue a special catalogue of Standard, Rare and Curious Books at Clearance Prices. If you are not on the list send for it and we will mail it free to you. When you can't find what you want, try us.

GEO. H. RICHMOND & CO.,
12 E. 15th St., N. Y.
Successors to S. B. LYSTER and D. G. FRANCIS.

IMPORTANT RELIGIOUS WORKS

The Potter's Wheel

By Rev. JOHN WATSON (Ian Maclaren). 12mo, cloth, $1.25.

The Mind of the Master

By Rev. JOHN WATSON (Ian Maclaren). 12mo, cloth, $1.50.

The Cure of Souls

By Rev. JOHN WATSON (Ian Maclaren). 12mo, cloth, $1.50.

The Old Testament

And Modern Life. By the Rev. STOPFORD A. BROOKE. Crown 8vo, $1.50.

Modern Methods in Church Work

The Gospel Renaissance. By Rev. GEORGE WHITEFIELD MEAD. With an introduction by Charles L. Thompson, D.D., President of the Open and Institutional Church League, United States of America. 12mo, cloth, $1.50.

Chief Contents: The Sunday-Evening Service—Men's Clubs—Athletics—Church Libraries—Women's Work—The Social Problem of the Church—Lectures to Boys Only—The Boys' Club—Church Architecture—Mobilizing the Work—Results of the New Methods.

The Gospel of the Divine

Sacrifice. A Study in Evangelical Belief, with Some Conclusions Touching Life. By CHARLES CUTHBERT HALL, D.D. 16mo, cloth, gilt tops, $1.25.

The Return to the Cross

By the Rev. W. ROBERTSON NICOLL, LL.D., editor of *The Expositor*. 12mo, cloth, $1.50.

The Clerical Life

A Series of Letters to Ministers. By JOHN WATSON, D.D.; Prof. MARCUS DODS, D.D.; Prin. T. C. EDWARDS, D.D.; Prof. JAMES DENNEY, D.D.; T. H. BARLOW, M.A.; T. G. SELBY; W. ROBERTSON NICOLL, LL.D.; J. T. STODDART. 12mo, cloth, $1.25.

The Teaching of Jesus

By Rev. ROBERT F. HORTON, author of "Inspiration of the Bible," etc. Third edition. 12mo, cloth, $1.50.

Biblical Study

By Rev. A. S. PEAKE, M.A. With an Introduction by A. M. Fairbairn, D.D., Principal of Mansfield College, Oxford. 12mo, cloth, $1.50.

The Incarnation

A Study of Philippians II. 5–11. By E. H. GIFFORD, D.D., formerly Archdeacon of London, and Canon of St. Paul's. 12mo, cloth, $1.75.

The Lady Ecclesia

An Autobiography. By GEORGE MATHESON, D.D., F.R.S.E., Minister of the Parish of St. Bernard's, Edinburgh. 12mo, cloth, $1.75.

Side-Lights from Patmos

By GEORGE MATHESON, D.D., author of "Voices of the Spirit," "The Lady Ecclesia," etc. 12mo, cloth, $1.75.

The Silence of God

By ROBERT ANDERSON, C.B., LL.D. 12mo, cloth, $1.75.

DODD, MEAD & COMPANY, Publishers

149 FIFTH AVENUE, NEW YORK CITY

The International Cyclopaedia

A New Edition, January 1898

We have just Completed

at a large expense

A Careful Revision of this

Standard Work of Reference

Making it the latest, most accurate, and best cyclopaedia on the market.

Our new illustrated sample pages free on application.

Sold on easy payments.

Chicago **DODD, MEAD & COMPANY** New York

Important Notice

TO ALL BOOKSELLERS

On March 1st I shall publish at Florence, New Mexico,

Alamo and Other Verses

Cloth, 12mo, gilt top, rough edges.

The proceeds of the sale of this volume are to be applied to the purchase of books for Free Public Libraries in this and other similarly isolated districts. All booksellers who feel in sympathy with my aims and are disposed to further them are invited to apply to me for circulars and specimen copies, which will be supplied free of charge. Liberal terms.

E. McQUEEN GRAY,

Croftonhill Ranch, near Florence, New Mexico.

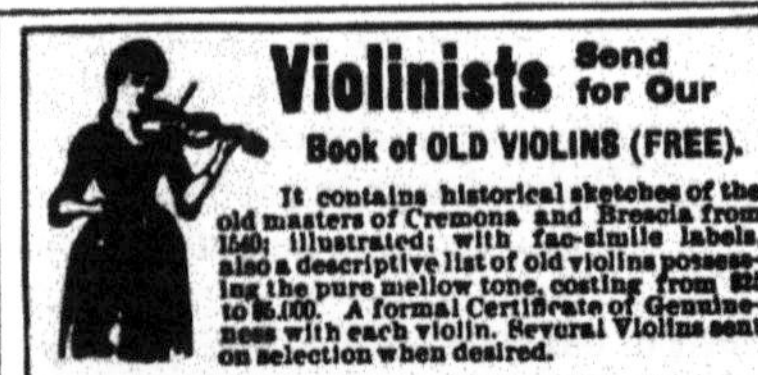

MASSACHUSETTS, Greenfield.

Prospect Hill School for Girls.

A thorough education with good home influence.

Established 1869. Miss IDA F. FOSTER, } Principals.
Illustrated circular. Miss CAROLINE R. CLARK,

Lightning Source UK Ltd.
Milton Keynes UK
UKHW021327100219
336936UK00006B/528/P

9 780428 935221